Hardcore
Visual
Basic®

SECOND EDITION

Bruce McKinney

PUBLISHED BY
Microsoft Press
A Division of Microsoft Corporation
One Microsoft Way
Redmond, Washington 98052-6399

Library of Congress Cataloging-in-Publication Data
McKinney, Bruce, 1953–
    Hardcore Visual Basic / Bruce McKinney. -- 2nd ed.
       p.   cm.
    Includes index.
    ISBN 1-57231-422-2
      1. Microsoft Visual Basic.   2. BASIC (Computer program language)
    I. Title.
    QA76.73.B3M398 1997
    005.26'8--dc21   97-15486
                                           CIP

Printed and bound in the United States of America.

2 3 4 5 6 7 8 9 MLML 2 1 0 9 8

Distributed to the book trade in Canada by Macmillan of Canada, a division of Canada
Publishing Corporation.

A CIP catalogue record for this book is available from the British Library.

Microsoft Press books are available through booksellers and distributors worldwide. For
further information about international editions, contact your local Microsoft Corporation
office. Or contact Microsoft Press International directly at fax (206) 936-7329.

MacBASIC is a registered trademark of Azonix Corporation. Cliffs Notes is a registered
trademark of Cliffs Notes, Inc. Pentium is a registered trademark of Intel Corporation.
IBM is a registered trademark of International Business Machines Corporation. Lotus and
1-2-3 are registered trademarks of Lotus Development Corporation. Microsoft, Microsoft
Press, Microsoft QuickBasic, MS-DOS, Visual Basic, Visual C++, Win32, Windows, and
Windows NT are registered trademarks and ActiveX and Developer Studio are trademarks
of Microsoft Corporation. Java is a trademark of Sun Microsystems, Inc. True BASIC is a
trademark of True BASIC, Inc. Visio is a registered trademark of Visio Corporation.

Acquisitions Editor: Eric Stroo
Project Editor: Patricia N. Wagner
Technical Editor: Marc Young

To J. Laufer, whoever he or she is.

The first manual I ever wrote for Microsoft (Macro Assembler 3.1416, if you must know) went out with a postage-paid feedback card requesting a rating for the manual's usability, completeness, and readability. On the overall scale of 5 for excellent and 1 for poor, Laufer checked all the 1 boxes and drew an arrow to the bottom of the page, where the following words (toned down a little) were scrawled in unmistakable outrage: "Examples!!!!! Damn it."

OK, J. Laufer. You got 'em.

CONTENTS

ACKNOWLEDGMENTS

I feel like an Oscar winner. This is my chance to drop a few names, make a political statement, credit my kids and pets, and reminisce about old times. So let's start at the top.

Hi, Mom. Hi, Dad. Hi, Chuck and Kandace.

To the people who put up with me when I was writing this book, or when I was learning how to write it: Thanks, Rhonda. Thanks, Sarah. Thanks, Sam. Thanks, Leslie. Thanks, Peggy.

I've had some writing mentors. Thanks to Linda Jaech and Stewart Konzen for hiring me when I had little or no qualifications—at least not on paper. Thanks to Bill Johnston for making me a journalist, albeit a bad one. And thanks to Strunk and White.

As for programming mentors, I'd have to go back to Cleon White, the best teacher I ever had. Mr. White crammed as much math as possible into my stubborn head until my junior year in high school, when I decided to become a famous writer instead of an engineer. I'm sorry, Mr. White; every day, I'm sorry.

Then there's Rich Gillman, who believed I was a programmer when hardly anyone else did, and Gene Apperson, who actually uttered the words falsely attributed later in this book to Joe Hacker: "It doesn't matter how fast your code is if it doesn't work." Thanks to José Oglesby who kept pushing me when I wanted to give up on FORTRAN. On second thought…No, let it stand.

I'd like to recognize the remarkable John Kemeny, who died in 1992 after a long career as administrator, mathemetician, computer language inventor, and most important (to him) teacher. Read the tribute at http://math.dartmouth.edu/general/TBasic.html. Thanks also to Basic coinventor Thomas Kurtz. I also give credit to Alan Cooper, sometimes known as the "Father of Visual Basic," although the language actually had (and has) many parents—perhaps too many. In any case, the current parents should be required to read Cooper's *About Face: The Essentials of User Interface Design* (IDG Books 1995).

I want to especially thank two people who saved this second edition from bugs and inaccuracies too horrible to imagine. Marc Young was more than a technical editor; he was an accomplice. He didn't just find and fix bugs. He cleaned up some of my sloppy first drafts of code, and wrote new code to implement ideas I didn't have time for (such as changing an Outline to a TreeView in WinWatch). If there is ever a third edition, Marc should be qualified to write it (and he'll have to because I've had enough).

Glenn Hackney served as official devil's advocate in opposition to this book. Glenn is the author of all the hardcore stuff in the Visual Basic documentation (especially the Component Tools Guide). We had some arguments that would make your ears burn—mostly good natured, but sometimes pushing the bounds of civilized interpersonal communications. He defended the indefensible with brilliant logic and moderated or killed some of my worst flames. He found some howling mistakes that would have left me standing before you naked. Thanks, Glenn, and good luck in your return to real life without computers.

I want to dedicate the Basic part of this book (all the rest of it) to everyone on a certain e-mail alias whose name I've been asked not to mention. Microsoft maintains this internal alias for discussion of Visual Basic issues. Most people on the alias are Microsoft employees, many of them working on Microsoft internal tools. Some work for other companies but are on Microsoft e-mail because of contract work or other connections. On this alias, questions come from everyone, but answers tend to come from the same people. Some of the regulars are experts because they wrote parts of Visual Basic or its manuals. Others became experts in the same way you will be an expert if you get the spirit of this book—because they wouldn't take no for an answer.

To name a few, and mention some of their contributions: Adam Braden, Anthony Evans, Bruce Prang, Bruce Ramsey, Bryce Ferguson, Curtis Patrick Koppang, Daniel Rairdan, Dave Thompson, Doug Stewart, Ed Staffin (sub-classing guru and author of Message Blaster), Geoff White, Jack Bell, Joe Robison, Jon Brichoux, John Walker, Ken Bergmann, Kevin Nixon, Keith Pleas (lots of cool tricks including error message lookup), Kenneth Lassesen (lots of ideas and a few good arguments), Malcom Stewart (interface casting, console, and more), Mike Blaszczak (for stirring up my thinking on errors), Nick Malik (powers of two table), Paresh Joshi, Peter Wheat, Randy Russell (system color control), Scott Mason (threads), Simon Bernstein (mci), Troy Cambra, Victor Arteaga, and Zack Stonich (Wiper). This list is specific to the second edition, but many other contributions acknowledged in the first edition survived into the second.

On the Visual Basic team, several people put up with my "negative attitude" and helped me understand the strengths and limitations of object-oriented program-ming in Basic. Thanks especially to Craig Symonds of the Visual Basic for Applications team. Matt Curland, graphics and COM wizard extraordinaire, is responsible for many of the hardest of the hardcore techniques in this book. Thanks also to Alan Carter (type library syntax), Betty Chin (configuration expert), Brian Lewis (p-code and memory allocation), Drew Fletcher, Doug

Franklin (type libraries), Jim Cash (Resize, SetParent, and attitude adjustment), John Norwood, John Burke, Mark Chase, Mike Garlick, Peter Loforte, Rob Copeland, Scott Wiltamuth, Tom Campbell, Steven Lees, Stephen Weatherford, Tim McBride (collections), Tim Patterson, Todd Apley, and Yann Christensen (palettes and compilation).

My folder of e-mail from readers of the first edition contains more than 600 messages. I can only mention a few of those who sent me suggestions, bug reports, new code, arguments, or compliments: Adam Tompkins, Andrea Wyss, Bert Sirkin, Bob O'Brien aka Bob O'Bob, Brad Riegel, Carlos de Miranda, Carlos Alberto Silva, Charles F. Randall, David Wilner, Elliott Whitticar, Eric Smith, Gary Beene, Greg Glass, Holland G.W. Rhodes, Jeff Kilbride, Jim Albea, Larry Linson, Magnus Brorsson, Mark Schlageter, Michael Rickard, Mike McGoodwin, Owen Graupman, Ralf Kretzschmar, Ramon Guerrero, Randy Giese, Richard Clark, Rob Babcock, Robert Mowery, Ron Stewart, Ron Weaver, Ronald R. Martinsen, Scott D. Killen, Sergei Dumnov, Silvio Lupo, Simon Carter, Stuart Rackham, Tibor Polgar, Tim Pearson, Timothy Koors, Todd A. Canniff, and Vadim Katsman.

At Microsoft Press, thanks to my editor, Pat Wagner, for polishing my prose, pushing me to abandon hopeless ideas so I could finish, and protecting me from my own exaggerations and the PC police. Thanks to all my bosses and bosses' bosses during this project for leaving me alone: Peggy McCauley, Sally Brunsman, and Kim Field. Thanks to my acquisitions editor, Eric Stroo. Thank you, Jim Fuchs, for setup and for being around to chat about techie stuff even though it seldom had anything do with Basic. Thanks to artist Michael Victor for Joe Hacker, the author caricature, and lots more. Joel Panchot also helped with artwork. And thanks to many others: proofreaders Patty Masserman, Devon Musgrave, Richard Carey, Teri Kieffer, Jocelyn Markey, Dan Robb, Roger LeBlanc, Cheryl Penner, Pamela Buitrago, Pat Forgette, and Paula Thurman; typesetting and production experts Peggy Herman, Barb Runyan, Barbara Remmele, Steven Hopster, Anne Kim, Sue Prettyman, Linda Robinson, Paul Vautier, and Dick Carter; and indexer Lynn Armstrong.

Thanks to the translators who converted the first edition into German, French, Spanish, Italian, Russian, Traditional Chinese, and perhaps other languages I haven't seen yet. This can't be an easy job. Good luck with the second edition.

And thanks to all you imaginary end-users in Swinen and Cathistan for the opportunity to serve you, however indirectly.

Bruce McKinney

INTRODUCTION

If you study your ten favorite Windows-based applications as models for your own programs, you'll probably come up with a wish list: "I want one of those. That's nice, but I want mine to be a little different. What if I combined one of these and one of those and then added something else?" But when you try to figure out how to implement these features with Visual Basic, you sometimes come up short.

Microsoft Visual Basic makes it easy to write 95 percent of your application, but when you reach that last 5 percent (down 5 percent from the last edition of this book), it seems to be fighting you every step of the way. There's no way to do a seemingly simple task like modifying the Control menu. The language provides little support for sorting, searching, or parsing. You can use Visual Basic's Collections, but writing your own is a different matter.

Let's face it. Visual Basic is a language with limits. Eventually you'll want to do something that Visual Basic won't do, or you'll want to do something fast that Visual Basic does slowly. You can understand why a language this easy has to make some compromises in flexibility and power—but you don't want to accept it. There must be a way.

Visual Basic Without Limits

Hardcore Visual Basic, Second Edition is a book for people who like Visual Basic but don't like limits. It's for people who won't take no for an answer. If you're willing to go the extra mile for better performance and more functionality, you'll have fun with this book.

Beyond the Windows API Limits

Back in the old days before Microsoft Windows, there was MS-DOS. It was easy to start programming under MS-DOS, especially with Basic. You could go a long way without really understanding what you were doing. But if you wanted to program without limits, you had to learn about low memory, ports, and MS-DOS and BIOS interrupts. Visual Basic is the same way, but more so. If you're serious, you have to get under the hood.

In Windows programming, getting under the hood means learning about messages, windows, processes, and all the other elements of the Windows application programming interface (API). Unfortunately for Visual Basic programmers, you have to learn most of this stuff in another language—C. Just a few years ago, the idea of doing all your API work in Visual Basic seemed foolish. Sure, you could write Declare statements, even in version 1, but often it was easier to write or buy a DLL written in another language.

That was the official line anyway, but lots of hardcore programmers never bought it. *Hardcore Visual Basic, Second Edition* tries to prove that you can indeed break through any API barrier if you have the right attitude and enough time for research and experimentation. You can judge for yourself, but I think I did prove it, even in some cases where the time spent could hardly justify the benefits gained. But if you buy this book, you get the benefit of my experiments without expending the time and brain cells.

Beyond the Performance Limits

Previous versions of Visual Basic generated an intermediate code form called p-code. Code in this format had its advantages, but it couldn't match the native code performance of true compiled languages such as C. This version of Visual Basic finally offers a compiler, promising to break the Visual Basic speed limits.

How well does compiled Visual Basic meet that promise? We'll be examining the sometimes surprising answer to that question in this book. In the past, there were certain things that you did in Visual Basic. There were certain other things that you didn't even attempt. Why bother doing processor-intensive programming in p-code?

In the previous version of this book, I said that if you were willing to use two langauges, you could get the best of both worlds. Use Visual Basic for what it does best—creating user interfaces quickly with the most efficient development and debugging environment available. Use C++ (or Pascal or whatever) for the meat of your program, the parts where no sacrifice of performance or functionality is acceptable, no matter what the cost. I hinted that my next book would tell you how to write C++ objects for Visual Basic. And I did attempt to write that book, but unforseen circumstances prevented me from finishing it.

Along the way, however, a surprising thing happened whenever I mentioned in mail or in conversation that I was writing a book on C++ for Visual Basic programmers. People didn't want it. In fact, some of them seemed to feel betrayed that I would even consider such a thing. Even in the version 4 time frame it was common knowledge that the next version of Visual Basic would have a compiler. Why would anybody want to write code in C++ if they could write the same code more easily in Visual Basic and then watch it run almost as fast—and with fewer bugs?

Why indeed? Is the two-language solution finally dead? Can you write fast, small programs with sophisticated user interfaces—and do it fast—in just one language? We'll find out. This book is all Visual Basic. You decide for yourself whether it's fast enough.

Beyond the Object Limits

Visual Basic is now an object-oriented language. Nobody quite understood what that meant with Visual Basic version 4. Now we do.

The class model of version 4 was fundamentally flawed. Many object-oriented features were missing, and it was a struggle, requiring ugly hacks and tedious workarounds, to write class-based programs in Visual Basic. Still, the improvement was so great from version 3 to version 4 that most people were willing to give Visual Basic the benefit of the doubt. It wasn't perfect, but we didn't necessarily know enough to understand where the object limits really were anyway.

But with version 5, I for one am not letting Visual Basic get away with anything. We're not pioneers any more. This is the second object-oriented version, and it should allow us to do the things that other object-oriented languages allow. Visual Basic shouldn't be like C++ or SmallTalk or Delphi or any other language, but it should allow us to do what needs to be done. We should be able to work with the language, not around it, to write efficient object-oriented code.

So how does Visual Basic version 5 measure up? Again, we'll find out. I won't be doing a feature by feature comparison with any other language, but neither will I shy away from criticism if Visual Basic fails to make object-oriented programming easy.

Free at Last

The previous edition of this book contained a solemn oath that I would never again write a book that had the *S* word in the index. If you don't know what the 16-bit *S* word is, consider yourself lucky. If you do, just try to find it in the index of this book. For that matter, just try finding anything specific about 16-bit programming (except in a historical context). I can't tell you how happy I am to live in a world where memory stretches on and on and 64 is just another number.

Visual Basic has forced this change on us by providing version 5 as a 32-bit-only product. Only time will tell whether the majority of customers will come along for the ride. No doubt there will be some programmers who just can't abandon Windows 3.1 customers. If you're one of these, I understand your pain, but I don't feel it. If you must continue to support 16-bit programs, don't waste your money on this book. I'm sorry to gloat, but after many years of supporting multiple code bases and trying to hack 32-bit code into 16-bit operating systems, I'm not looking back. This is a 32-bit-only book for a 32-bit language.

What This Book Is About

Hardcore Visual Basic, Second Edition is targeted at intermediate and advanced programmers who use Visual Basic Professional Edition version 5 to develop applications for Microsoft Windows 95 and Microsoft Windows NT (but not Windows 3.1). That's the short mission. In fact, the book might prove useful to others as well.

Visual Basic version 5 is actually several languages. Most of it is Visual Basic for Applications, a language introduced in 1993 in Microsoft Excel and Microsoft Project. It is currently available in all other Microsoft Office applications, and is being licensed to other software publishers. Visual Basic is now just another client of Visual Basic for Applications (a very important one) in the same way that Microsoft Excel and Microsoft Word are clients. The language engine is technically separate from the environment. You can see this in the separate VB and VBA entries in the Object Browser.

What does this difference mean to you? It means that if you know Visual Basic, you know Visual Basic for Applications and, to a lesser extent, vice versa. The version number and exact features of Visual Basic for Applications can vary depending on the release date of the application in which it resides, but many of the programming techniques shown in this book will be portable to all VBA-enabled Applications. The line between Visual Basic and Visual Basic for Applications is sometimes fuzzy. You're on your own in figuring out the differences.

Although I've written *Hardcore Visual Basic, Second Edition* primarily for users of Visual Basic Professional Edition, owners of two other Visual Basic products can also use the book. Visual Basic Learning Edition is designed for beginners and has less Windows API documentation and fewer controls. I didn't test using the Learning Edition, so you'll have to work out any problems for yourself if you're one of the few Learning Edition owners who purchases an advanced programming book. Visual Basic Enterprise Edition is a more expensive client/server superset of Visual Basic. Everything I say about Professional Edition also applies to this product, but the enterprise edition has many additional features that I don't discuss.

You'll need access to current Windows API documentation to take full advantage of this book. That's no problem for most readers because the Microsoft Developers Network CD comes with both Professional and Enterprise editions. If you have the Learning Edition or if you're using Visual Basic for Applications, you'll need to find separate Windows API documentation. Microsoft's Windows API documentation, whether in help files or in books (and now on www.microsoft.com/msdn/sdk), is oriented toward the C language. Figuring out how to use C documentation for Visual Basic programming is one of the topics of this book, but you might want additional help. I'm a great admirer of *Dan Appleman's Visual Basic 5.0 Programmer's Guide to the Win32 API* (Ziff-Davis Press, 1997). This book presents Windows API documentation in Visual Basic format. Appleman covers some of the same material I cover, but with a different slant. I don't think of his book as a competitor. If you have room on your bookshelf for two advanced Visual Basic books (and if the shelf won't break under the weight of 1584 pages), Appleman's book should be the second one.

I wrote *Hardcore Visual Basic, Second Edition* using two different operating environments—Windows 95 and Windows NT version 4.0. Many of the techniques would work in Windows NT version 3.51, but I had already moved to version 4.0 beta by the time I started writing and so nothing has been tested in the older version. I present many techniques for manipulating the new Windows interface, and you'll need version 4.0 to test these under Windows NT. Using multiple environments is a difficult business, and if there are bugs in my code (incredible as it might seem), that's the area where I'd expect to find them.

One more point: this book assumes knowledge of Visual Basic 5 features— classes, collections, properties, optional arguments, OLE servers, add-ins...the list goes on. Version 5 is a major update, and you'll see a lot of new features. I'm going to be talking about these features as if you already know the basics. There will be no hand-holding or introduction to new features. I try to make my book an additon to the documentation, not a replacement.

What This Book Is Not About

What is this book *not* about? Hard to say, exactly. It's about advanced programming techniques, but some advanced topics aren't covered. It's about professional programming, but again, that's a wide topic whose surface I'll barely scratch. It's about taking advantage of new features in Visual Basic version 5, but some of the code would work in version 1.

Here are some topics that *Hardcore Visual Basic, Second Edition* doesn't cover:

- Database programming. Programming databases is a very hot topic, and somebody should definitely write a book about it. Some people already have but I'm not one of them. A chapter or two on databases wouldn't be enough, and besides, who would want to read anything about databases by the only Visual Basic programmer in the world who has never used the Data control?

- MDI forms and menus. I must confess to an irrational dislike of the MDI interface. I like my programs to be single document with lots of buttons and no menus. I don't defend this prejudice, but neither do I think that MDI and menus are really advanced topics that should be included here. The documentation has them covered.

- Help authoring and the Setup Toolkit. These are worthy topics, and, in some cases, advanced topics—but for the most part they are not programming topics and therefore are not in this book.

- APIs to the max. I'd love to spend a few months writing code for MAPI or WINSOCK or multimedia. Networks and telephony sound interesting, and I wish that I had time for enhanced graphics APIs such as OpenGL or DirectX. New acronymns such as ASP, MTS, IIS, and CSP keep rolling out faster than I can count them. I'm sure these are all great topics—for other books.

- The Internet. That's my obligatory mention of the word that has sold a million books. If you see advertising copy for this book saying "Contains the word Internet," you can assume it's referring to this paragraph. Many of the techniques described here can apply to Internet programming, but I have rejected pressure to turn this into an Internet book.

- Visual Basic, Scripting Edition. Sorry, but that's a different language. In any case, VBScript should be easy. The language will sink like a stone (and rightly so) if programming it turns out to be a hardcore task.

- Project management, interface design, team programming, testing, feedback evaluation, system analysis, caffeine procurement, sponge basketball, and most of the other elements that make up successful software development. This book is about code only. My user interfaces are nothing to write home about. My programs are small and manageable. I wrote and designed them myself without having to coordinate with others. They didn't go through the exhaustive testing you'd expect in code for end users. In other words, my job as a software developer isn't quite as real as yours. (My other job as an author is just as real as anybody's, with its own version of deadline hell.) Nevertheless, I did have time to explore some programming problems that you might have put off until "real soon now." Being a hardcore code jockey isn't all there is to software development, but it is worth something.

The Companion CD-ROM

The code you see in this book is the tip of an iceberg. For every line shown, probably 10 more appear on the companion CD. It's true that some of the code on the companion CD isn't very interesting. You already know how to fill list boxes, open files, and respond to button clicks. But you'll also find a lot of hardcore code. Some of this code is described but not shown in the book. Some of it you'll have to find by exploring on your own. Most programmers will find something of value to use with their own programs, but code you can use is only one benefit. A more important goal is to show by example that you can do anything you want with Visual Basic.

Source Code and Components

When you pick up a copy of *Hardcore Visual Basic, Second Edition* you probably think of it as a book with an accompanying CD that contains code samples.

I suppose this traditional view is technically correct, but I think of *Hardcore Visual Basic, Second Edition* as some components with source code and an accompanying book. This is a significant difference from most computer books and a big change from the first edition. It means that you can use the book in several ways:

■ Take the companion CD out of the back and throw the remaining block of paper in the recycle bin. Run the setup program, but then save yourself a lot of disk space by deleting all the sample programs and the component source code. You'll be left with a type library and several ActiveX controls and other components. Use the Object Browser to figure out the methods and properties of these components so that you can use them in your programs. You'll get your money's worth of new functions, classes, interfaces, and controls, but you'll have trouble figuring them out because they're not documented at the level you would expect if you bought a standalone component.

■ If the preceding suggestion seems too radical, you could go the other way. Read the book. When you see code that interests you, find it on the companion CD and paste it into your programs. You can paste code from the components or from the samples that use the components. Many of the procedures in the book have dependencies on other procedures in other modules, so you might end up doing a lot of pasting from different places to get things working. As a slightly less extreme option, use the modules from the components, but not the compiled components themselves.

■ You've probably guessed that my recommendation lies somewhere between these two extremes. Read the book for explanations of what the components do, how they work, and why they're needed. Look at the sample programs as examples of how to use the components. Look at the component source code to see exactly how the component works. Decide on a case-by-case basis whether you want to use the whole component, use component modules, or paste specific bits of code. Chapter 5 will give you more information on how to make the choice.

Before I summarize the components provided with *Hardcore Visual Basic, Second Edition* I want to introduce an idea that will be explained in detail in Chapter 5. When you purchase this book you buy the text of the book and all the source code on the companion CD. You can use that source code any way you see fit (except distribute it to others as your own work). You also buy the compiled programs and components on the companion CD. The components are not licensed and can be distributed to customers with your applications. You bought it. It's yours.

What you didn't buy is the right to modify those components. I own the components. You own only the right to use them. ActiveX components come with a contract designed to solve the multiversion compatibility problems common with system DLLs. If everyone who finds a bug in a component fixes the bug, recompiles the component, and ships a slightly different version with the bug fix, incompatible versions will proliferate until the earth explodes in a great ball of fire. Fortunately, most component developers don't ship source code with their components. Those of us who do have to request your cooperation in maintaining the integrity of our components. Of course there aren't any bugs in my components, but if you find one anyway, here are the rules.

Send me a bug report and eventually I'll post an updated component. If you can't wait for that, you can combine modules from my components into your own component. Just don't give it the same name or GUIDs as mine. Although you can do this as an out, don't do it lightly. If your customer purchases another product that uses one of my components, you might end up duplicating code that the customer already has.

The Windows API Type Library

The Windows API type library supplied with this book eliminates the need to write Declare statements—almost. Chapter 2 explains why my code uses only a handful of Declare statements in very limited circumstances. All the other declares, types, and constants for Windows API functions come from my type library. Once you install this type library, the Windows API becomes just another part of Visual Basic. For many programmers, the type library can save more than enough time to justify the cost of this book. This version is much more comprehensive and powerful than the one provided with the first edition. Visual Basic version 5 does a better job of supporting type libraries so I was able to add more types and change many constants to Enums. I also added two features that you can't get through Declare statements: interfaces and Unicode function definitions.

The source code for the type library is provided on the companion CD as an example of type library syntax, but as with my components, I request that you send bug reports to me rather than fix any problems you find in my library. Writing a comprehensive type library would be a full-time job since Microsoft seems to release a new API or system interface every day. If you don't find support for your favorite API, you can use my source as a template for extending the library. If you want to win fame and the gratitude of other hardcore programmers (but no fortune), send me your source and I'll integrate it (with credit) into the official library.

The CommonConst module of the type library needs a little more explanation. It contains constants I use frequently plus some of the constants that Visual Basic won't let you define. You'll see these constants throughout the book. Visual Basic offers equivalents for some, but not all, of my constants. The most useful constant, for example, is a carriage return/linefeed combination. I call it *sCrLf*; Visual Basic calls it *vbCrLf*. I call my version of a null pointer *sNullStr*; they call theirs *vbNullString*. My version of an empty string is called *sEmpty*; theirs is called "". In other words, they don't have one. The origin of this discrepancy goes back to the beta period of Visual Basic version 4 when I donated my type library source for common constants to Visual Basic, and then enhanced my version after theirs had been cast in stone.

ActiveX Components

Most of this book is about one big component called VBCore. You can think of VBCore.DLL as an extension of the Visual Basic library. It extends and wraps the Windows API. It adds useful functions not provided by Visual Basic. It encapsulates common functionality in classes and global objects. Most of the sample programs don't do real work themselves; they just provide a user interface to illustrate features of VBCore.

At last count, VBCore consisted of 42 classes, 30 global classes, 8 interfaces, 9 standard modules, and 1 resource file, but by the time you read this it will probably have learned to reproduce itself without human intervention. A few of the areas covered include file system control; registry management; API wrappers for windows, processes, and device contexts; data structure encapsulation; bit and byte manipulation; error handling; sorting; random number generation; and animation. I can't believe I wrote the whole thing. Chapter 5 describes some of the architectural issues that went into the design of VBCore.

Although VBCore is the heart of the book, I provide several other ActiveX DLL and EXE components:

Component	Description
VisualCore.DLL	Contains the following public classes that wrap forms: CColorPicker, CAbout, and COpenPictureFile. These classes were originally in VBCore, but when I changed VBCore to work for Unattended Execution, I had to move all classes with a user interface into a separate DLL. VisualCore depends on VBCore, but not vice versa. Chapter 11 tells why I made this choice.
SubTimer.DLL	Contains the CTimer class (designed to replace the Timer control) and has an ISubclass interface and global functions that simplify subclassing windows. I moved the code out of VBCore into a separate component to avoid debugging problems that occur with uncompiled subclassing and timer code. Also, some programmers might find the code useful without the additional overhead of VBCore. Chapter 6 describes these issues. VBCore uses SubTimer, but SubTimer can also stand alone.
Notify.EXE	Encapsulates file system notification through the CNotify class and the IFileNotifier interface. The class resides in an EXE server so that its operation won't interfere with or affect the performance of clients.

Table A. *Hardcore DLL and EXE components.*

This isn't a book about control development. In fact, you'll see frequent complaints about controls that I don't think should be controls. But if you really need a visual component, a control is the best way to provide it. I provide the following controls:

Control	Description
XEditor	Turns a rich text box into a real editor. You provide the user interface. XEditor provides the editing features.
XListBoxPlus	My idea of what a ListBox ought to be. It sorts every which way, gives you collection-like features, and does command completion.
XDropStack	Provides a visual list of most recently used items—like the drop-down list in Visual Basic's Find dialog box.
XPictureGlass	Provides a transparent PictureBox control with only 4 lines of new code.
XColorPicker	Gives your applications a color palette like the one that drops down in the Visual Basic Properties window.

Table B. *Hardcore controls.*

Wizards and Helpers

Most of the samples illustrate points made in this book, and a few manage to do something useful in the process. Here are a few programs that you might find useful even if you don't care about how their code works:

Program	Description
Debug Wizard	Maintains temporary assert and profile procedures.
Global Wizard	Converts public classes and global classes to private classes and standard modules, and vice versa.
Collection Wizard	Creates collection classes.
Address-O-Matic	Generates random base addresses for your controls and DLL components.
RegTlb	Registers type libraries.
ErrMsg	Translates API error numbers into messages.
WinWatch	Tells you everything you ever wanted to know about windows, processes, and resources.
TimeIt	Tests various performance problems throughout the book. You can add your own problems.

Table C. *Hardcore wizard and utility programs.*

Using Sample Programs

The setup program on the companion CD sets up the sample source code to make it as easy as possible to use. All the components are installed and registered in the proper places automatically. Compiled versions of utility programs are installed on your disk for easy use, but simple test programs exist only in source format (to save disk space). The EXEs for all programs are on the companion CD, and you can run them from there.

When you finish the setup, you'll end up with a new directory called by default HardCore2. (You can override it.) This directory will contain Visual Basic Project (VBP) and Visual Basic Project Group (VBG) files for all the samples and components. If you want to step through the sample client program, load the VBP file. You'll see client source, but use the compiled version of VBCore and any other components. If you load the VBG file, you'll have access to the complete source for both the client and the components. Chapter 5 explains how this system works.

A Short Jeremiad

This book has been an endless project, following the Visual Basic beta cycle through many unexpected turns and switchbacks. Hard disks have crashed. Deadlines have been missed. Operating systems have appeared. Lies have been told. Files have been trashed. Love has been lost. Mail has flamed. Sources have been unsafe. Networks have crawled. Midnight oil has burned. Hair has fallen out or turned gray. Managers have departed. Bugs have entered bug-free programs with absolutely no programmer assistance.

But that's nothing new. I'm sure similar things (or worse) happen during your projects.

There is one thing about this edition that's a little different. I think readers of the first edition will detect a change in attitude.

I might as well come out and say it rather than letting you guess. I don't like some of the directions Visual Basic has taken in version 5. I think the product moved on to new features without consolidating the ones added in version 4. Don't get me wrong. I like the compiler and ActiveX control creation, and I'm willing to cut them some slack on the first versions of these features. But I'm not giving any slack on limited features introduced in version 4 but not improved in version 5. Visual Basic version 1 set a standard for easy programming, and I expect every new version to live up to that standard.

Unfortunately, Visual Basic version 5, has quite a few features that don't meet my expectations for a high-level user-oriented language. Beginners might not see these weak points, but if you push the limits of the language like I do, you'll hit them every day. You'll see what I mean (whether you agree or not) if you get to the end of this book.

Here are some specific wrong turns that I think Visual Basic has made:

- Too many pointers. You can now do any pointer operation you could do in C, except harder. Visual Basic isn't supposed to be a pointer language, much less a really bad one. I use pointers to the max, but under protest.

- Not enough bits. You might say Visual Basic is a 30-bit or 31-bit language. The really cool 32-bit stuff hasn't come through yet.

- Too many wizards. Visual Basic used to be the only language that didn't need them, but now it's well on the way to becomming just another wizard language.

- Not enough class. Encapsulation isn't bad and polymorphism is coming along, but delegation is too hard and inheritance is nowhere.

You'll find these points expanded between the lines throughout the book. Fortunately, there's still time to turn back to the origins and purpose of Basic. I wouldn't be so upset with Visual Basic limitations if I didn't genuinely like the language and have high hopes for it to emerge as a general purpose programming language rather than a thin wrapper for user interfaces and data access.

So with the negative stuff out of the way, let me get back to the reason I chose Visual Basic in the first place. It's still the fastest way to get an interesting idea up and running. No other language gives the same instant gratification. Basic has always been fun, and this version offers a lot of new toys. I don't mean to sound ungrateful. I did have some fun writing this book. I did work my way through some pretty difficult problems so that you won't have to. I hope you'll find the result entertaining and enlightening.

1

The Spirit of Basic

Every computer language has its own feel, its own atmosphere, its own spirit. You can't really define this spirit, but you know what it is when you see it. I think of Basic as the antithesis of a statement attributed to Albert Einstein:

> Make things as simple as possible—but no simpler.

Had that quote been written by the original designers of Basic, John Kemeny and Thomas Kurtz, it would have been simplified further:

> Make things simpler than possible.

That is the contradiction hardcore Visual Basic programmers live with. We want things to be simple, elegant, and intuitive—but they aren't. We want our programs to model reality—but they don't. We want our language to work the way we think, not the way computers or operating systems want us to think—but we're not willing to pay the price.

The nebulous Spirit of Basic exists only in our minds. Real implementations of Basic, including Microsoft Visual Basic, have to compromise. Sacrilege keeps creeping in. There's an inherent conflict between the desire to keep it simple and the desire to do what needs to be done, whatever the cost. I use the term *un-Basic* to describe these compromises, whether they are built into the language or built into our code.

This book tries to maintain the Spirit of Basic, against all odds. Sometimes it's tough. First, the book deals at length with the Microsoft Windows Application Program Interface (API), which was written in C and is permeated with the Spirit of C. Second, the book's philosophy is to accept no limits, although Visual Basic has built-in limits that can be overcome only with great effort. Third, Basic is slowly becoming an object-oriented language, but it remains to be seen how well objects can be realized in the Spirit of Basic. Version 4 made a good opening argument. I've been disappointed by the slow progress in version 5. Maybe next time....

Despite the inclusion of techniques that can only be described as un-Basic, this book is not about how to write C in Basic. I'll try to keep things Basic and to wrap un-Basic code in wrapper routines so that you can use it without constantly thinking about the heresies involved.

Language Purification

Basic is an old language—developed in 1964—and it still carries a lot of baggage from the past. During its 30 years, Basic picked up a lot of bad habits, which it has only recently begun to shed. Over the years, Microsoft has played a large role in both the good and the bad developments in Basic.

If you'd like to know the history of the language you're programming in, try to find a copy of the book *Back to BASIC: The History, Corruption, and Future of the Language* (Addison-Wesley, 1985), by Basic inventors Kemeny and Kurtz. The book is largely a diatribe against unnamed "Street Basics" that poisoned the language with line numbers, unnecessary data types, and Gotos. The book mentions no names, but anyone who programmed in the 1980s knows that Microsoft's GW-BASIC and IBM's version of the same program, called BASICA, are the worst of the Street Basics under attack. As a self-taught programmer who wrote his first programs with GW-BASIC, I can confirm that these were indeed wretched languages, richly deserving all the opprobrium piled on them by defenders of the true faith.

Back to BASIC was also propaganda for True BASIC, a compiler designed to restore Basic as a structured language. By the time it hit the streets, however, True BASIC was too late. QuickBasic from Microsoft and Turbo BASIC from Borland were already attempting to undo the damage caused by GW-BASIC. In fact, Microsoft had started the atonement earlier with both interpreted and compiled versions of MacBASIC. True BASIC was destined to lose the battle, but in a larger sense it won the war. Visual Basic has become almost as structured as C, almost as flexible as Pascal, almost as good for scientific work as FORTRAN, better for business work than COBOL, more powerful for manipulating data than Xbase, and, in a few more iterations, it might even become as object-oriented as Smalltalk and as good at list processing as LISP.

Because Visual Basic ran in the Microsoft Windows environment and had a completely new programming model, it didn't need to be compatible with earlier Basics. It was a time for purification. For example, you won't find the following abominations in the Visual Basic documentation: PEEK, POKE, DEF SEG, CALL ABSOLUTE, DEF FN, BLOAD, BSAVE, FRE, SADD, VARPTR, and VARSEG—not to mention debugging statements such as the infamous TRON (which inspired a movie) and TROFF. Nevertheless, some language purists are still not satisfied.

Here is my personal list of features that you should cross out of your Basic language reference. If Microsoft won't clean up the language, you should do it on your own. You don't have to agree with my version of Basic (although you'll need to get used to it for the duration of this book), but I hope that it will get you started defining your own subset of the language.

While/Wend

There's nothing terribly wrong with the While/Wend looping structure of Basic, other than the ugliness of the pseudoword Wend. Some people on the Visual Basic team suggested changing Wend to the more consistent End While for version 5. This is the wrong idea. Instead, they should have just ripped the whole While/Wend looping structure out of the documentation but kept it in the language for compatibility.

Why waste your coding energy on a vague feature when Basic offers a clear, concise one? The Do Loop control structure of Basic is a thing of elegance compared with the crude looping of C and Pascal. You can test at the beginning or at the end for true or false conditions in a natural, English-like way. Perpetual loops can be coded clearly instead of requiring an ugly hack such as Pascal's *While (True)* or C's *for (;;)*. The Exit Loop statement allows you to escape a loop cleanly. I hate to see beautiful code ruined with While/Wend, even though I admit that this is an aesthetic preference with no connection to efficiency or correctness.

Gosub/Return

Gosub was useful in the bad old days when all variables were global and Select Case didn't exist. But why Gosub, Return, and On Gosub remain in Visual Basic is beyond me. Perhaps they were left in for compatibility of some kind, although I find it hard to imagine a procedure using these statements that one could port from an earlier Basic.

I've heard it argued that it's more efficient to use Gosub and Return than to use subs and functions. Well, yes, but technically you could write all your code using only If, Then, and Goto—that would be more efficient still, if you ever got it debugged. If Gosub is what it takes to write efficient code in Basic, I'll take C. Fortunately, it's not.

Goto

You're probably expecting an anti-Goto diatribe, but I don't mind Goto at all. It has its uses, primarily with error traps. Because error handling is inherently unstructured, an unstructured feature like Goto fits right in. If you use Goto for any other purpose, however, chances are you're writing bad code. The C version of Goto actually makes some code easier to read as well as more efficient, but that's because C's switch statement is less powerful than Basic's Select Case.

Old versions of Pascal needed Goto because they lacked Basic's complete syntax for early exit from loops and procedures. Basic provides the tools for structured programming.

Nevertheless, a procedure containing Goto is hidden in at least one example in this book. I'm so ashamed of myself for not devising a clearer way to write this code that I'm not going to point it out. A free bucket of bits to the first person who finds it and tells me how I should have written the procedure.

FLAME　One minor hole in the Visual Basic looping structure is the lack of a Continue statement. Other languages offer a way to jump from the middle of a loop to continue with the next iteration. Basic only lets you jump completely out of the loop. You can work around this annoying limitation with Goto, but you shouldn't have to.

Exiting from Procedures

One of the rules of structured programming is: a procedure should have one and only one exit. Some members of the coding police criticized the code in the first edition of *Hardcore Visual Basic* for violating this rule. I plead guilty.

I respect this rule. I honor the intention of encouraging disciplined code with carefully structured exits. I admire programmers who follow the rule without twisting code into contortions. But after careful thought, I have chosen not to follow it myself. If you make a different choice, that's fine with me.

My justification, pitiful as it might seem to purists, is that multiple exits can make code shorter and, to my eye, more natural. You can always get just one exit, but you might have to introduce Gotos or extra levels of indentation to do it. Exit Sub and Exit Function work for me. Take the Among function, which gives Visual Basic something comparable to one of my favorite Pascal features, the *in* operator. Here's how I wrote it:

```
' Pascal:    if ch in ['a', 'f', 'g'] then
' Basic:     If Among(ch, "a", "f", "g") Then
Function Among(vTarget As Variant, _
               ParamArray a() As Variant) As Boolean
    Among = True          ' Assume found
    Dim v As Variant
    For Each v In a()
        If v = vTarget Then Exit Function
    Next
    Among = False
End Function
```

This code can exit from the middle of the loop if a match is found or from the end of the function if a match is not found. Is that really less structured, more prone to errors, or less readable than this kosher version?

```
Function Among(vTarget As Variant, _
               ParamArray a() As Variant) As Boolean
    ' Among = False        ' Assume not found
    Dim v As Variant
    For Each v In a()
        If v = vTarget Then
            Among = True
            Exit For
        End If
    Next
End Function
```

Decide for yourself how strictly you want to follow this rule, but get off my case.

Let

According to Kemeny and Kurtz, omitting Let on any assignment is a sign of bad programming practice, and only Street Basics allow such horrible habits. The reason: Let distinguishes use of the equal sign (=) for assignment from its use for tests of equality. It's true that Basic is the only popular modern language that overloads the equal sign to mean both assignment and equality. C uses = for assignment and == for equality. Pascal uses the symbol := for assignment and = for equality. In FORTRAN, = means assignment, and .EQ. means equality.

If you think about it, *Let a = 1* is technically accurate. It also lets compilers optimize more efficiently. In other words, this pedantic nonsense makes perfect sense. Fortunately, Microsoft didn't buy this argument, and neither should you.

Rem

I used to think that no one had actually used Rem for comments since 1985. Recently, however, I encountered a long piece of complex Basic code that looked strangely like an MS-DOS batch file. All the comments were preceded by Rem. Please don't do this. Basic is probably the only computer language ever invented that has a keyword to initiate comments. In the last version of this book, I suggested that if everyone would pretend that Rem doesn't exist, maybe Microsoft would remove it in the next version. Not only did they not remove it, they carried the wretched thing over to Visual Basic, Scripting Edition. Yuck!

Option Base and Zero-Based Arrays

Programmers start counting at 0. The rest of the world starts counting at 1. Kemeny and Kurtz tell the story of how they dealt with this difference of opinion. Originally, the first dimension of a Basic array was 1 because that's how normal people count and Basic was designed for normal people. But Basic also needed to work for mathematicians, who usually think of matrices as starting at 0, so Basic changed to start the first element at 0.

This wasn't so great either. Common sense tells you that in the statement *Dim ai(10)*, the array *ai* contains 10 elements—but in fact it contains 11. That might be OK in C, where common sense is not a high priority, but it rubs Basic programmers the wrong way. So the Option Base statement was added, which lets you specify whether you want your arrays to make sense (start at 1) or be mathematically correct (start at 0).

Of course, as Pascal programmers knew all along, 1 and 0 aren't the only places you might want to start counting. Kemeny and Kurtz finally figured this out and changed Basic to let you specify the starting and ending points of arrays:

```
Dim ai(1 To 10) As Integer
Dim ad(0 To 49) As Double
Dim av(-10 To 10) As Variant
```

Kemeny and Kurtz didn't add this modification to Basic until 1979. ANSI Basic didn't get it until 1983. Microsoft Basic got it several years later. And I didn't figure it out until I wrote the first edition of this book. But now I'm a convert. I always use To when declaring arrays. There's nothing wrong with zero-based arrays, but you should declare the starting point specifically:

```
Dim asTitle(0 To 29) As String
```

Consider the extra five keystrokes cheap insurance against off-by-one errors.

Of course, that technique doesn't save you from needing to know that the default starting point is 0 in Basic-created arrays such as the controls array.

WARNING If you buy my argument about always using To in array definitions, you must also stop making assumptions about the use of array elements. In other words, you can't assume that *aBears(0)* is the first bear in the array. An alternative rule used by many programmers is to completely avoid both To and Option Base 1. That's OK with me (although you won't see it in this book). Just be sure that you don't mix the two approaches.

For Next Loops

Basic lets you do the following:

```
For x = 1 To 10
    For y = 1 To 10
        For z = 1 To 10
            ' Do something
Next z, y, x
```

Don't do it. Type out each Next at the appropriate indent level. Some programmers always put the variable name after Next. In fact, many programmers do this with comments even in languages that don't support it, and they do it for all ending statements, not only Next. For example:

```
End Function ' GetStuff
End Sub ' DoStuff
End Select ' iChoice
Loop ' Do While x
End If ' i < 10
End With ' oftFirst
```

I salute this careful coding style, and I wish that I had the self-discipline to follow it myself.

Data Types

Basic started as a language with only two data types: numbers and strings. It might seem as though the language has come a long way to user-defined types, forms, and classes in the current version, but you could make a case that Basic has actually gone the other way, becoming a language with only one type—which essentially means a typeless language. To state it more accurately, Basic has become a language with two modes: typed and typeless.

As you'll see in Chapter 4, typeless mode (using Variant for all variables) is increasingly important. Features such as parameter arrays and collections work only in typeless mode. On the other hand, optional arguments, which used to work only for variants, now work for any type. That throws some confusion into what I'm about to propose. Nevertheless, full steam ahead.

Visual Basic allows a variety of programming styles for handling variable declarations (or the lack of same). No other language offers such flexibility. In Pascal or C, you declare the type of each variable at the top of the procedure, and that's that. In Basic, you don't need to declare any variables except arrays, but if you choose, you can make Basic as strict about variable declarations as Pascal. Let's look back at the history of Basic to understand where this confusion came from.

For Ever

Everyone knows how a For loop works. Well, maybe. Consider this loop:

```
For i = 1 To Len(s)
    ' Do something with characters of string s
Next
```

This For loop is a shortcut for a Do loop like the following:

```
i = 1
Do While i <= Len(s)
    ' Do something with characters of string s
    i = i + 1
Loop
```

The comparison is not exact, however. What if the statements in the loop change the length of the string *s* by deleting or adding characters? In fact, something very different is happening. In the Do loop, the length of the string is checked every time through; in the For loop, it's checked only once. So the Do loop equivalent of the For loop is actually this:

```
i = 1
iTemp = Len(s)
Do While i <= iTemp
    ' Do something with characters of string s
    i = i + 1
Loop
```

There are two morals to this story:

■ To write efficient Do loops, try to keep While and Until tests simple. Don't test the length of a string every time through the loop if you know that the length won't change. Consider reorganizing simple Do loops into For loops.

■ If you're changing what's being tested inside the loop, consider changing a For loop to a Do loop. Another trick that sometimes works is to process a For loop backward, changing only items that have already been counted. The following loop, which removes selected items from a list box, works as written, but it would fail if you counted forward, because deleting items changes the list count and the current item:

```
For i = lstData.ListCount - 1 To 0 Step -1
    If lstData.Selected(i) Then lstData.RemoveItem i
Next
```

A Short History of Basic Types

Kemeny and Kurtz designed Basic with numbers and strings as its two data types. A variable was always a number unless it ended with a dollar sign, in which case it was a string. A number was actually a floating-point number, although users didn't need to know this. There was no such thing as an integer. Kemeny and Kurtz claimed that this was a feature. For example, in comparing Basic to Pascal, their book *Back to BASIC* had this to say:

> Incidentally, Pascal requires that the user know about two kinds of numbers—integer and real. Reals are used for general computation, while integers must be used in for-loops and as array subscripts. Pascal thus permanently burdens the user with matters that are temporary peculiarities of the ways computers do arithmetic. (page 96)

Is the difference between integers and floating-point numbers simply a relic of computer technology? I think not. In any case, performance was obviously not a priority. Developers of Basic compilers and interpreters never bought this line. The compilers and particularly the interpreters castigated by Kemeny and Kurtz as "Street Basic" added types for integers, long integers, and various sizes of real numbers. User-defined types and fixed-length strings crept into the language. Basic acquired the types of Pascal without the discipline of enforced data declarations. You could simply add a type-declaration character ($, &, %, !, #, or @) to a variable to specify its type. Or you could use the Def statement (borrowed from a similar feature in FORTRAN) to specify that variables with a certain initial character would have a particular type.

Then Microsoft shook things up again, returning to the roots of Basic with the introduction of the Variant type, which can contain any native type. You need only this one type; the computer, not the programmer, chooses which type goes into a Variant. You pay a price for this convenience (refer to the "Performance" sidebar on page 34), but in many cases it's worth the cost. Variants contain not only the variable data but also information about the variable. This enables Basic to do automatic type conversion and lets you do your own type checking. Variants can also include special values such as Null, Nothing, Empty, and Error. I'll be talking about variants and the trade-offs involved in using them throughout this book.

The introduction of Option Explicit in Visual Basic version 2 was another milestone in the history of Basic data types. By setting Option Explicit, you force yourself to declare every variable, just as you do in Pascal. This feature prevents one of the most common and annoying Basic bugs, the misspelling error. If you misspell the name of a variable, Basic creates a new variable with the new spelling and the default data type (formerly Single, now Variant). You think that you're assigning a value to or calculating with the original variable, but you're actually using the new one. You don't need to hit this bug very often to decide that declaring every variable is not too high a price to pay to avoid it.

Dollar Signs in Basic Functions

Visual Basic is moving away from type-declaration characters. Version 4 offered three new simple types—Date, Byte, and Boolean. But Basic does not provide a type-declaration character for any of these types. Nor does it provide type-declaration characters for complex types such as Object, Form, Control, and Variant. There just aren't enough unused punctuation characters to go around.

Despite this trend, the dollar-sign character for strings still rules in one important context. Basic functions that return strings come in two styles: naked and dressed to kill. The naked version of Mid takes a variant argument and returns a variant. The dressed-up version (Mid$) takes a string argument and returns a string. Basic manuals no longer note this difference, but it exists just the same. (The Time It program described later in this chapter demonstrates the difference between calling Mid and Mid$ in different contexts.)

I really don't like the looks of those dollar signs. I'd much rather use the naked version. But I'm not willing to take a noticeable speed hit for cosmetic reasons. Therefore, you'll see the dressed-up version in samples that use strings (common) and the naked version in samples that use variants (rare).

Choosing a Data Style

In deciding your personal style for handling variables, you need to consider several factors:

- Do you want to declare a specific type for every variable? Or do you want to use default types?

- Do you want the convenience (and the risk) of automatic variable allocations? Or are you willing to declare every variable in order to make your code more reliable?

- How do you feel about Basic shortcuts such as the DefInt statement or the type-declaration characters?

Let's look at several popular data declaration styles.

Joseph

He's been programming in Basic since the first IBM PC rolled off the assembly line. Back in the days of BASICA, he learned to start all programs with *DefInt A-Z*. He still does. Most of his variables are integers, and he can simply make them up and use them on the fly. Same with strings and real numbers, except that he has to add $, !, and other type-declaration characters. Joseph never declares simple variables before use. He thinks that Dim is for arrays. It annoys him to have to use Dim for user-defined types, but he's gotten used to that as just one more Basic anomaly. He finds it particularly useful to make up variables in the Debug window.

Joseph is a disciplined coder with a complicated naming convention for variables. He doesn't run into the misspelled-variable problem very often, and when he does, he has enough experience to track down the problem quickly. Joseph writes so much good code so quickly that many of the younger programmers try to imitate his style. Somehow it doesn't work as well for them. They spend a lot of time debugging.

Susan

She came to Visual Basic from C. She thought that Basic was a toy language, and she wasn't happy about being assigned to work with it. She still makes disparaging comments about Basic's lack of pointers and its other limitations. Nevertheless, although she hates to admit it, she's hooked. She gets more work done in Visual Basic than she ever imagined doing in C. But old habits die hard.

She programs in Basic as if it were C. She always uses Option Explicit and declares every variable with an explicit data type. She never uses Variant. Susan thinks that type-declaration characters are an abomination and uses them only when absolutely necessary in constants. She doesn't even know that DefInt is a legal statement.

Karin

She got hooked on programming while writing Lotus 1-2-3 macros. Later she added WordBasic macros to her repertoire. From there it was an easy step to Visual Basic for Applications in the latest version of Microsoft Excel. Recently someone told her that if she knew Visual Basic for Applications, she automatically knew Visual Basic. She tried it; she likes it.

Karin is writing a front-end application that puts a friendly interface on Microsoft Word for Windows, Microsoft Excel, and Visio. Most of the Excel samples use Variant, so she acquired that habit. She declares every variable with Dim, but she doesn't give a data type, relying on the default Variant type instead. Last week she spent two late nights debugging a program that was getting random values in one of the variables. As it turned out, she had misspelled a variable name. Karin was surprised that Basic would let her do that. One of her colleagues explained Option Explicit. The whole idea sounded kind of weird, but she hasn't had any trouble since she started using it.

Her colleague is trying to persuade her to use integers rather than variants as loop counters. She understands the concept, but it seems like a lot of trouble, and she doubts it would make a noticeable difference in her programs.

Bruce

He's writing a book about Visual Basic. He wants to use a consistent coding style throughout the book and to recommend this style to others without being dogmatic. He's written code in Basic, FORTRAN, Pascal, C, and C++. He liked them all (except FORTRAN) and wishes he had a language that combined the best of each.

One of his first programs with the old GW-BASIC was an accounting program. After several weeks of work and hundreds of lines of code, the accounts didn't balance because he had created all the variables with the default Single data type instead of Integer. In the spirit of Kemeny and Kurtz, he hadn't known the difference. He's been leery of default data types ever since.

He uses Option Explicit religiously and declares every variable with Dim and an explicit data type. He likes variants and uses them for variables that will need a lot of data conversions. But he has a great deal of experience with coding in assembly language, and he hates to write code that is less than optimally efficient, even when he knows the extra efficiency isn't critical. Therefore, he uses specific simple data types whenever he can.

From Pascal and C programming, Bruce learned the habit of declaring all variables at the top of the block. But when he discovered that C++ allows you to declare variables wherever you first need them, he was an instant convert and adapted his Basic style accordingly. Unlike most Basic coders, he puts Dim statements next to the first use and when possible initializes the variable on the next line. One of his pet peeves about Basic is that it doesn't allow him to combine the Dim and the initialization statements, but he fakes it the best he can.

Bruce is tempted by the convenience of type-declaration characters, but he's decided not to use them because they're available only for some types but not for others. Besides, they're ugly. He thinks that the Def*type* statement is a ridiculous feature that should be chopped out of the language.

Visibility and Lifetime of Variables

Every language has rules for defining the visibility and the lifetime of variables and procedures. Basic is no exception, although unfortunately the rules seem to change with each version. Throughout the twisted history of the language, attempts to add new features without breaking old ones have created a mess. The Basic landscape is dotted with abandoned scope and visibility modifiers such as Shared, Common, and now Global. In the current version, even the best intentions have not made matters any clearer. Consider the following.

The Dim keyword (the least mnemonic name in the language) creates a variable with local visibility and temporary lifetime when used within a procedure (except that lifetime is permanent if the procedure is declared to be static), but when used outside a procedure, Dim creates a variable with private visibility and permanent lifetime (despite the fact that lifetime is meaningless in a standard module, although it is important in a class or form module). Private and Public are declarators for variables, but they are modifiers for constants, declarations, types, and procedures.

If you can understand that and if you always use Dim correctly, you don't need this book. For the rest of us, it might help to create a myth and pretend to believe it. Here are the "commandments" that are embodied in my Basic data myth:

- The word *Dim* actually means *Local* in the native tongue of the Basic ethnic group of northeastern Cathistan. Therefore, you should use Dim only for local variables. Basic might pretend to let you use Dim in other contexts, but your code will be haunted by evil spirits.

- Use Static for local variables with permanent lifetime. Never declare procedures static, because doing so changes the meaning of Dim and causes warts.

- Use Private for variables with module visibility. Resist the temptation to use Dim in this context even though it might seem to work for a time.

- Use Public for variables with global visibility. In the distant past (two versions ago, according to some sources), Global meant public. Some corrupters of the true faith claim that it still works as a form of homage to the evil god Compatibility. Ignore this rumor.

- Always declare dynamic (resizable) arrays with empty parentheses and the proper variable keyword. (See the four previous commandments.) The claim that Redim can be used on local variables without a prior declaration leads to madness.

- Always specify Public or Private for user-defined types and Declare statements. Basic will enforce this for class and form modules, but it provides a default for standard modules, although you will never remember it. Some experts believe that you should also follow this rule for constants and procedures, although I have used the defaults and lived to tell the tale.

For those literal-minded readers who want facts rather than opinions, Table 1-1 lists the public, private, and default visibility for the various elements you can declare in your programs.

	Standard Module	Form and Class Modules
Constants	Default private	Default private
	Private OK	Private OK
	Public OK	Public illegal
User-defined types	Default public	Default illegal
	Private OK	Private required
	Public OK	Public illegal
Declare statements	Default public	Default illegal
	Private OK	Private required
	Public OK	Public illegal
Variables	Default private*	Default private*
	Private OK	Private OK
	Public OK	Public creates property
Functions and subs	Default public	Default creates method
	Private OK	Private OK
	Public OK	Public creates method
Properties	Default public	Default public
	Private OK	Private OK
	Public OK	Public OK

* Default means declaring with Dim rather than with Public or Private.

Table 1-1. *Public, private, and default visibility of module elements.*

Watch Your Types

One of the most dangerous errors in Visual Basic occurs when you try to put several declarations on one line. For example:

```
Dim c, i, h As Long
```

You believe that you've defined three Longs, but you haven't. Instead, you have two variants (the default type for the first two) and one specifically declared Long. Here's another variation:

```
Dim c As Long, i, h
```

Pascal programmers might be more likely to write the first line, whereas C programmers might tend to write the second. In either case, the problem is particularly dangerous because the code will work correctly 90 percent of the time, although perhaps not efficiently.

Naming Conventions

The most important thing about a naming convention is that you should have one. If you name each variable according to the whim of the moment, you'll not only end up with strange names that you won't remember later but you'll also spend your mental energy dreaming up clever variable names instead of clever algorithms. A naming convention should be automatic. Two people using the same convention should come up with the same variable names a high percentage of the time. That might be unrealistic in practice, but it's a worthy goal.

In reading working code and programming books over the years, I've seen a lot of styles, many of them well thought out and helpful to the development process. I've also seen bad variable names make some good code hard to read. Frequently, however, wretched naming conventions go hand in hand with wretched code. And one of the most wretched conventions is offered to you free by the Visual Basic environment.

When the environment offers default names such as Form1, Control2, and Text3, just say no! I first encountered this bizarre behavior when I was invited to participate in a usability test of Visual Basic version 1 several months before its release. For my first button, Visual Basic helpfully provided the caption Command1 and the variable name *Command1*. I didn't understand the difference. How could anyone imagine that I would ever want a button with the caption Command1? And the idea that I would want a variable named *Command1* seemed only slightly less ridiculous.

I still find the default variable names mildly annoying and wish that Visual Basic had options to always leave the Caption, Text, and Name properties blank. You

---

I've made a similar error in Declare statements, thinking that, because I put ByVal with the first parameter, I didn't need it with the second:

```
Declare Sub Line Lib "MyDll" (ByVal x As Integer, y As Integer)
```

Some programmers avoid this problem by declaring every variable on a separate line:

```
Dim c As Integer
Dim i As Integer
Dim h As Long
```

That's a bit too extreme for me. I salute the intention, but I'm satisfied with this:

```
Dim c As Integer, i As Integer, h As Long
```

won't see this terrible convention in the controls I create later in the book. I strongly recommend that you do the same in your own controls. When I insert one of Visual Basic's controls, I immediately set the Caption (or Text) property and then give the control a reasonable name. It's tempting to leave the default name on static labels that will never be accessed by name, but I resist even that. Instead, I put my static labels in a control array. This saves a little memory, and if I copy and paste an existing label, Visual Basic automatically names it and adds it to the array.

FLAME In writing this book, I read a lot of Basic code from many programmers. I'm tempted to publicly curse all those who post code (including large programs) to the public domain using the write-only naming convention provided by Visual Basic. Folks, it is *very* difficult to interpret your code. But I suspect that my curse is unnecessary. If you haven't already paid the price, you will when you try to go back and modify your own code a year from now. The convenience of whipping out code this way is not worth the pain of trying to maintain it.

Basic Hungarian

Hungarian works for me. No doubt you've seen this convention used sometimes, sort of, in some code contained in Visual Basic samples and documentation. I don't claim that this convention is better than other naming conventions or that it doesn't have problems. But I've used Hungarian in various languages (including, believe it or not, FORTRAN), and it applies well to Visual Basic.

I'm not trying to evangelize Hungarian. Everyone I know who uses it (including me) hated it at first. It just grows on you. Maybe it will grow on you enough to make you a convert during the course of this book—or maybe it won't. In any case, being able to read Hungarian is a skill you won't regret acquiring. If you haven't really understood the point of the snippets of Hungarian code you have seen in various Microsoft manuals, here's a brief introduction that will make reading the sample code easier.

Long-time Microsoft developer Charles Simonyi, who happens to be Hungarian by birth, developed the convention. That—along with the fact that C code written in this style looks like foreign gibberish to the uninitiated—prompted the name. The idea (simplified to a point that would probably horrify Simonyi) is that variables should consist of two parts: a lowercase base type indicating the kind of variable and an initial-cap qualifier that distinguishes this variable from others of the same kind.

For example, an integer that keeps track of the file position would have the base type *i* for index and the qualifier *Pos* to form the variable *iPos*. If you must keep track of both a file position and a line position in the same context, you need to qualify further: *iFilePos* and *iLinePos*. If you were creating a Project Save As dialog box, you might call it FProjectSaveAs and fill it with controls such as cboFiles, cboDirs, lstFileTypes, lstDrives, cmdOk, cmdCancel, and cmdNetwork. If you had an array of buttons to activate different windows, the base type *cmd* wouldn't be enough, so you could modify it with the array prefix *a*, as in *acmd-Window*. To access this array, you might need a count variable showing the number of windows, *cWindow*, and an index to the current window, *iWindow-Cur*. In a small function using only one local index variable, you don't need a qualifier—just call it *i*.

This doesn't begin to touch on the complexity of the original Hungarian convention. In addition, the whole idea has been bastardized. At least three incompatible official dialects of Hungarian are used by C programmers at Microsoft, and now the Visual Basic documentation group has introduced their own variation of Hungarian. Unfortunately, the crudest of these variations is the one used in the Windows Software Development Kit (SDK), and it is now spreading confusion to the world. In a few short years, the Hungarian coding convention has evolved as much as natural languages evolve in a thousand years.

Compare, for example, the naming convention in the Windows SDK Help file with the one in the Visual Basic API Help file shipped with Visual Basic version 3. (If you don't remember version 3, never mind.) Both files are aimed at C programmers—the first at those writing Windows-based programs in C, and the second at those writing VBX controls in C. You'd expect both files to use the same convention, but the names for similar variables are in fact very different, although both systems are vaguely recognizable as Hungarian.

In the SDK, for example, a Boolean variable has the prefix *b* for Boolean. In the Visual Basic API, a Boolean variable has the prefix *f* for flag. In the SDK, a variable used as a bit flag has the prefix *w* or *dw* for Word or DWord, indicating its type—or at least the Windows include file version of its type. In the Visual Basic API, a similar variable has the prefix *fs* or *fl* for flag of short or flag of long, respectively, indicating both its use and its type. This goes on. Windows SDK names sometimes indicate the use of the variable, but more often they simply indicate the data type, and even then in an artificial form that has no relation to Basic (or to C, for that matter).

Alas, the version of Hungarian used in the Visual Basic documentation is a cousin of the Windows version. It uses prefixes based on the types (*lng* for Long, *str* for String, *sng* for Single, and so on). Worse, it uses generic prefixes for different kinds of multimember types rather than specific prefixes for each type. For example, you'll see *frm* for all forms, *cls* for all classes, and *udt* for all user-defined types. I invented my version of Hungarian before all the others, so don't ask me to copy them.

Variable prefixes

Much of the confusion in current Hungarian variations comes from trying to make the prefix do too many conflicting things. At various times, I've seen the prefix used to indicate several different concepts. Even if you don't buy into Hungarian, any naming convention must deal with some of the following elements:

- **The purpose of the variable.** Is the variable used as a handle, a Boolean flag, a bit flag (an array of bits), an index, a count, an ordinal, a string, or an ID? Generally, this is the most useful piece of information you can provide, and it's language independent. A handle is a handle, regardless of the language.

- **The data type of the variable.** This information is usually irrelevant because the data type is implied by the purpose. Furthermore, the data type is language specific. If you design your naming convention for a language that supports signed and unsigned types (C and most variations of Pascal), the convention becomes irrelevant for languages that have only signed integers (Basic and FORTRAN). And if you use specific features of your language (such as C's type-def) to rename standard types, those names will be irrelevant in languages that don't let you rename types (most languages). If you're familiar with the Windows API, you're sensing that I don't think much of its naming conventions. Right you are. A good deal of Chapter 2 will be spent telling you how to translate these names into something intelligible to Basic. The naming conventions proposed here ignore the data type.

- **The context of the variable.** Generally, this means using a modifier indicating that the variable is in an array or a collection. Languages that support pointers require a modifier to distinguish a pointer to a variable from the variable itself. You can use a count modifier to indicate a count of variables. For example, if the modifier h is for a handle, a is for an array, p is for a pointer, and c is for a count, then you could have an ah (an array of handles), a ph (a pointer to a handle), or a ch (a count of handles).

- **The scope of the variable.** Some conventions clearly distinguish variables that are local, global, or somewhere in between (module-level in Visual Basic). Usually, local is assumed to be the default, requiring no modifier, and g is used as a prefix modifier for globals. You could use m as a prefix modifier for module-level variables (as the Visual Basic convention does). This isn't a bad idea in principle, but in practice I don't find it very useful. I don't use globals often, and the distinction between local and module-level variables is usually clear from the context. Also, it would be easy to get carried away with distinguishing between static and normal locals or between fixed and dynamic arrays. You could go further and add prefix letters to distingish between ByVal and ByRef, to indicate the subtypes within variants, and to show whether the moon was full when the code was written.

- **The modifiability of the variable.** Many conventions distinguish constants from variables, usually by making constants all uppercase. I don't find this distinction very useful. A constant can be identified when necessary by its name and the context. If *clr* is the prefix for a color, it's pretty clear that *clrTitle* is a variable and *clrRed* is a constant. In addition, if you want to make the title red by assigning *clrRed* to *clrTitle*, it doesn't make much difference whether *clrRed* is a variable or a constant.

What I'm creating here is a more portable Hungarian that works for Basic. I often don't care what type a variable has when I use it; I'm much more interested in whether a handle is a handle to a window, a file, or a GDI object than in what data type it is. I use integers for different purposes: counts, indexes, handles, ordinals, and bit fields. Whether they are Longs or Integers usually doesn't matter after the declaration. If I need to know, I can always go back to the declaration and check.

The point of Hungarian is not to be an absolute standard for everyone but to be standard across a given department, project, program, or, in this case, book. I've used the conventions defined in Table 1-2 throughout (consistently, I hope).

Some prefixes modify other prefixes. For example, *acmd* is an array of buttons, *ccmd* is a count of buttons, and *ncmd* is a collection of buttons. Strict Hungarian always uses *c* as a modifier. You could use *ciWindow* as a count of indexes to windows or *chWindow* as a count of handles to windows, but I often find that I can make the meaning clearer by omitting the second part of the prefix. If I'm counting windows, *cWindow* is sufficient.

I'll introduce and explain some additional conventions later in the book. In particular, some of the new object-oriented features of Visual Basic require further discussion and variations.

Prefix	Variable or Object
i	integer index (type Integer or Long)
h	handle
ord	ordinal (a numeric identification code used when the specific value is unimportant except to distinguish the variable from others)
x, y	*x* and *y* coordinates of points
dx, dy	delta (or distance) in terms of *x* and *y* coordinates (*dx* is width, *dy* is height)
f	Boolean
af	bit flag (an array of Booleans represented by bits)
r	real number (either Single or Double)
b	Byte
v	Variant
cur	Currency
time	time
date	Date
dt	Date and time combined
s	String
p	pointer (Long variable from or for an API function)
cmd	button
chk	check box
txt	text box
pb	picture box
pic	picture
lst	list box
cbo	combo box
lbl	label
mnu	menu
tmr	timer
opt	option button (radio button)
c	count
a	array
n	collection

Table 1-2. *Hardcore Hungarian for variables.*

Class prefixes

Variable naming conventions are one thing; type naming conventions are another. You can define several kinds of types in Basic, including forms, classes, controls, global modules, enums, and user-defined types. Like other types, they are essentially templates that define the features of the type. I start my type names with an uppercase letter. Table 1-3 shows the different kinds of types and my prefixes for them. I end up with type names like these: CDrive, FGetColor, and ESortType.

Prefix	Type
C	Class
F	Form
T	User-defined type
X	ActiveX control
D	ActiveX document
P	Property page
E	Enum
I	Interface class for Implements
G	Global object class module
M	Standard module

Table 1-3. *Hardcore Hungarian for types.*

FLAME User-defined type must be the worst name ever given to a major language feature. Why couldn't the QuickBasic developers who added this feature have given it a one-word name? If you borrow features from other languages, why not borrow the names (*structure* or *record*) of those features? Language is a living thing that doesn't accept bad terminology without a fight. On the Visual Basic programming team, user-defined types have become known as UDTs. Think of them as Unified Data Templates or whatever seems to fit the acronym. In any case, this book calls them UDTs from here on out.

I borrowed the one-character type prefix from similar conventions in C++. It avoids one of my pet peeves—naming conventions that make it difficult to distinguish between types and variables. Some conventions use a lowercase prefix to indicate different kinds of types and the same prefix for variables of that type. Such a convention might use clsDrive for a drive class or udtPoint for a point type. When the same kind of prefix is used for variables as for types, you might end up with statements like this:

```
Dim clsAnimal As clsAnimal
```

But of course that's illegal, so you end up modifying it like this:

```
Dim clsAnimalVar As clsAnimal
```

Another common problem is to not use a naming convention for classes. Instead, give the class the obvious name (Animal). But then you end up with the same problem:

```
Dim Animal As Animal
```

You're using up the best name for the class, but you'd be better off saving it for the variable. This confusion comes from an ambiguity in human language. Nouns indicating a type of thing (animal) are often identical to the noun for a particular object of that type (animal). It's as if our brains were automatically parsing the following statement:

```
Dim animal As Animal
```

That works for humans, and it even works for some case-sensitive computer languages, but it's not specific enough for Visual Basic. That's why I prefer a different kind of prefix for types than for variables. You can use more natural statements like this:

```
Dim animal As CAnimal
```

Some conventions use a single prefix to represent all variables of a particular type. For example, *udt* represents all user-defined types and *cls* represents all classes. The original Hungarian required a separate variable prefix for every type defined by the user—class, form, control, enum, or UDT. I prefer this because prefixes like *cls* and *udt* tell me nothing useful about the variables or object variables that use them. Sometimes the variable prefix for new classes just jumps out at me. For instance, *drive* and *drives* were the obvious choices for CDrive and CDrives, discussed in Chapter 4. These might be long prefixes, but generally you'll have only one variable of each type, so it works out. The main point is to choose prefixes you can remember. In some cases, I use the first letter of each uppercase letter of the type to form the prefix. For example, my prefix for the enum ESortType is *est*.

The latest trend is to apply Hungarian to filenames as well as to variables and types. You end up with filenames like clsAnimal.Cls and frmOpen.Frm. This convention was unintelligible in 16-bit operating systems with uppercase eight-character names. Mixed-case long filenames make it more readable but no less redundant under Microsoft Windows 95 and Microsoft Windows NT. At any rate, you won't see it in this book. If I have a CAnimal class and an FOpen form, the filenames are ANIMAL.CLS and OPEN.FRM.

Stir It Up

The trouble with naming conventions is that you'll have a hard time sticking to just one. Let's say that you buy my arguments and adopt my Basic dialect of Hungarian. But you also use a lot of Windows API calls, so you need to be familiar with Windows Hungarian as used in the Windows SDK. In addition, you read a lot of sample code from the Basic manuals, which use a different version of Hungarian. The code you paste from Visual Basic Help usually doesn't use Hungarian. Visual Basic for Applications is gradually developing its own conventions for dealing with Visual Basic components. And of course you probably have several other third-party books in your Basic library, each with a different convention. Some of them might even use the dreaded Command1 default convention.

And that's just Basic. If you write the occasional components or DLL in C++, you'll have to deal with conflicting conventions from Windows, the Microsoft Foundation Class Library (MFC), and the Component Object Model (COM).

It's a hard life. All you can do is choose the naming convention that makes the most sense to you and then stick with it, no matter what other folks (me included) might say.

Efficient Code

When Visual Basic version 4 was compared with Borland's Delphi versions 1 or 2, the conversation tended to go like this:

Delphite: Your pitiful language generates p-code. Our language generates native code. Our programs run circles around yours.

VBer: Native code won't make your hard disk faster. Our data access application runs just as fast with p-code as yours does with native code. And we developed it faster. We don't have to compile our program before running it, and edit-and-continue lets us fix bugs in the environment while the program is running.

Delphite: Nonsense. We have the fastest compiler around, and our debugger is easy to use. Besides, we're serving customers, not ourselves. The bottom line is program speed. Don't tell me you don't have bottleneck sections in your code.

VBer: Well, there are a few places…. But we write C++ DLLs or controls to get around them. Besides, p-code is smaller. Your language creates giant EXE files.

Delphite: Well, at least we can generate stand-alone EXE files. You have to ship megabytes of support DLLs to make even your tiniest program run. And by the way, if we need a DLL, we can write it in Delphi, not C++.

VBer: Well, we can create DLLs too.

Delphite: Yeah, p-code DLLs. Forget it.

VBer: This is all irrelevant. The bottom line is that our language is Basic. It's the easiest, most popular language in the world. Pascal is dead.

Delphite: Basic? Pascal is a much easier language than Basic.

VBer: Basic!

Delphite: Pascal!

Joe Hacker (breaking in): A pox on both of you. I don't want to choose between native code and p-code. I want both: p-code for the user interface and data access, native code for bottlenecks. I don't want a fast compiler. I want an interpreter. I don't want my language to choose whether I get a little EXE with big DLLs or a big EXE. I want to choose. And I don't care about language wars. I'll find a way to make any language do what I want. Just wait for Visual Basic version 5. Then we'll be able to match languages feature for feature.

Well, Visual Basic version 5 is here. Let's see how it measures up against Joe Hacker's wish list.

Compiled Code—Not a Panacea

P-code is good. Native code is good. Visual Basic has them both. That doesn't mean you can mix and match at will (although Chapter 5 will suggest a strategy for doing just that). Sometimes you have to make trade-offs. So let's take a closer look at some of the basic facts of life for program size and speed.

First, program speed is important—it's just not equally important everywhere. To listen to certain marketing material for previous versions of Visual Basic, you might think speed didn't really matter. In fact, I could paraphrase what has been said by certain people at Microsoft (who will remain nameless) who thought of a compiler as more of a marketing bullet than a real feature: "Visual Basic programmers (in their ignorance) think they want a compiler, so we'll give it to them. But they're going to be disappointed when their forms don't load any faster with native code than with p-code."

Well, that's true. If forms load faster in version 5 (and I'm told that they do), it's not because of the compiler. The Form Show method isn't now, and never was, written in p-code. Neither are the Data Access Objects (DAOs) or the Remote Data Objects (RDOs). What's different about the speed of native code is not that it makes what you used to do faster. The difference is that it makes new things possible. For example, nobody in their right mind tried to write action video games with Visual Basic version 4. I'm not saying it would be easy now, but you could at least consider it.

Between writing the first and second editions of this book, I planned to write a book on C++ for Visual Basic. I ran out of time before I could finish it, but part of that book is available as a series of articles on Microsoft Developer Network (MSDN) and on the companion CD for this book. When I told readers of the first edition of *Hardcore Visual Basic* that I was working on a C++ book, a frequent reaction was surprise and even anger—as if I were betraying Visual Basic by writing about C++. A typical comment: "The next version of Visual Basic is going to have a compiler, so why would you ever want to use C++ for anything?" Good question. This book will attempt to answer it, but I'm sorry to say that there are still some important and useful tasks that require C++ or some other low-level language.

Some of them include:

- You can't write Declare statements for some API functions, and you don't want to write them for others. For example, Visual Basic doesn't do Unicode Declare statements. If you really want to prove a point, there's not much you can't do one way or another with a Declare statement, but it's easier and more efficient to use a type library written in Interface Description Language (IDL). This book won't tell you how to write type libraries, but you will get the Windows API type library for free (described in Chapter 2). Furthermore, the companion CD contains the source code and an article describing how I wrote it.

- Visual Basic can't use most standard COM interfaces that are implemented by Windows. Just try using IShellLink to create shortcuts. Or beat your head against a wall trying to use IStorage. There is a way to get past the limitations, but it requires mucking around with type libraries. We'll do it in Chapter 10.

- Visual Basic can't implement standard COM interfaces. The one you probably need the most is IEnumVARIANT. You can fake it in some cases by delegating from the Collection class, but in other cases your best option is C++. This book will provide a death-defying hack to enumerate variants, but it's not something you'll want to show your mother.

- Visual Basic can't create a self-contained executable file. If you really can't fit a setup program on a floppy disk or if you aren't willing to require your web customers to download the Visual Basic run-time DLL over the Internet, you'll need to develop programs and components in another language.

- Some things are easier to do in other languages. For the most part, Visual Basic's lack of pointers is an advantage, but sometimes you really need them. Visual Basic also lacks some fundamental language features that are common in other languages, such as compile-time initialization of variables, procedures parameters, and easy bit manipulation. You can hack around these limitations in Visual Basic, or you can just write the code without hacks in another language. We'll be hitting some of these walls in the rest of the book. Sometimes we'll go over them. Sometimes we'll go around.

I have been a tireless proponent (some Visual Basic developers and designers will say an obnoxious pest) of fixing these limitations so that Visual Basic really could do anything any other language could do (and I think it could be done without pointers). But alas, not this time. The compiler opens a lot of new doors, but I'm afraid that when Visual Basic programmers pass through those doors, they'll find some language limits that never bothered them before.

According to my friend Joe Hacker, it takes at least one version after a major new feature is added before anybody (language user or language designer) fully understands the implications. So that means the next version of Visual Basic had better be a full-featured compiled language with no compromises (or at least not major ones). Unfortunately, that's what I said last time.

P-Code Versus Native Code

When you write a line of code in the IDE, Visual Basic breaks it down into expressions and encodes the expressions into a preliminary format called opcodes. In other words, each line is partially precompiled as it is written. Some lines contain shared information that cannot be precompiled independently (mainly Dim statements and procedure definitions). This is why you have to restart if you change certain lines in break mode. The opcodes are compiled into p-code instructions when you compile (in the background if you have the Compile On Demand and Background Compile options set).

At run time, the p-code interpreter works through the program, decoding and executing p-code instructions. These p-code instructions are smaller than equivalent native code instructions, thus dramatically reducing the size of the executable program. But the system must load the p-code interpreter into memory in addition to the code, and it must decode each instruction.

It's a different story with native code. You start with the same opcodes, but instead of translating to p-code instructions, the compiler translates to native instructions. Because you're not going to be expecting an instant response while stepping through native code instructions in the IDE, the compiler can look at code from a greater distance; it can analyze blocks of code and find ways to eliminate inefficiency and duplication. The compiler philosophy is that, since you compile only once, you can take as long as you want to analyze as much code as necessary to generate the best results possible.

These two approaches create a disjunction. How can you guarantee that such different ways of analyzing code will generate the same results? Well, you can't. In fact, if you look at the Advanced Optimizations dialog box (available from the Compile tab of the Project Properties dialog box) you'll see a warning: "Enabling the following optimizations might prevent correct execution of your program." This might sound like an admission of failure, but welcome to the real world of compilers. Users of other compiled languages understand that optimization is a bonus. If it works, great. If not, turn it off.

On the other hand, very few developers are going to be used to the idea of working in an interpreter during development but releasing compiled code. Most compilers have a debug mode for fast compiles and a release mode for fast code. Visual Basic doesn't worry about fast compiles because it has a no-compile mode that is faster than the fastest compiler. You get the best of both worlds, but it's going to take a little while for people to really trust the compiler to generate code that they can't easily see and debug.

> **NOTE** Even with a compiler, Basic code might be slower than the compiled code of some other languages. That's because Basic always does run-time error checking. You can't expect a language that validates every statement to offer the same performance as a language that leaves you at the mercy of your own error checking. Of course, if you were to write a C program that does all the run-time error checking Basic does, you not only would pay the same performance penalty but also would have to write the error handlers.

Static Versus Dynamic-Link Libraries

Programmers coming from other compiled languages are in for one more surprise. Often people associate compiled code with static libraries and self-contained EXE files, but if you think about it, there's no particular requirement that a compiled language support static linking. Visual Basic version 5 is the proof. It doesn't support static linking, and that means you can't create one big EXE file containing everything in your whole program. If you thought compiled Visual Basic was going to take you back to the old MS-DOS days when you could just compile a program and hand off the EXE to customers without a setup program or support DLLs, think again. Visual Basic supports only the DLL model, and you'll still need a setup program for your compiled programs.

There's a trade-off between using dynamic-link libraries and static libraries. If you use dynamic-link libraries, all your customers' programs share the same copy of the code. If you use static libraries, all your customers' programs duplicate the same code. For example, there's only one copy of the Windows API wsprintf function in USER32.DLL, but try to imagine how many copies of the binary code for the C printf function you might have duplicated in all the statically linked C programs on your disk. If your customers have lots of programs developed with the same language, it definitely pays to use DLLs. But if a customer has only one small program developed with the language, the customer ends up with a lot of wasted code in support DLLs. In some cases, you really want a single executable file even if it's big and potentially redundant.

I could go on with more advantages and disadvantages. The point is that with many languages, you choose the trade-offs for a particular program. With Visual Basic, you don't choose; it chooses. There's no such thing as a stand-alone EXE. If you want to share your own code between programs, you can write an ActiveX DLL. There's no option to put that code in a static library and share it at link time. I suspect that this limitation will prove unpopular and that some future version of Visual Basic will give you more choices.

What You Don't Know Hurts You

Whether you use native code or p-code, you probably want your code to be as fast as possible. You wouldn't have picked this book otherwise. Of course, it doesn't make sense to optimize every statement. If you have a trade-off between speed and size, or between speed and reliability, or between speed and some other factor, you might not always choose speed. But you always want to understand the trade-offs, and you don't want to write code that is unnecessarily slow when there is no trade-off.

But what's faster? You can guess how Basic works and try to think through which techniques might be faster, but how can you know for sure? There's only one answer. You have to time it. But timing code in a multitasking operating system is difficult and inconsistent. Let's summarize what you don't know about Visual Basic timing:

- Code in Windows DLLs is written in C or assembler and is thus native code, but you don't know exactly when you're running Windows code and when you're running Basic code. Performance loss from p-code isn't going to make much difference in code where Windows does most of the work.

- Code for Basic statements and functions is also native code—in the Basic run-time library. Disk access in particular is so much slower than native code or p-code that the difference between the two won't be significant.

- A good algorithm in p-code usually beats a bad algorithm in native code. So get your algorithms right before you worry about anything else.

- In virtual memory operating systems such as Windows, smaller code often means less disk swapping. Any speed increase you get from native code is going to be washed out instantly if you have to hit the disk to swap your fast code into memory.

- Windows NT and Windows 95 are preemptive operating systems, which means that other programs can interrupt your code at any time. If you test a piece of code several times, you will get different results each time.

- Anything you do to time your code will itself take time, thus changing your results. You need to time the code while timing it and then time it while not timing it, and compare the results to see how timing it affects the timing. But you can't.

A lot of variables come into play, but one thing is clear: to find the most efficient way of performing an operation, you need to test it multiple times.

Examining Code

Before we get to my recommended way of testing performance (writing performance tests), let's examine ways to look at your code and see exactly what goes on under the hood. It turns out that this is a little different depending on whether you use p-code or native code.

If you're the adventurous type who isn't afraid of disassembled machine code, you can examine Basic p-code. The key to breaking into Visual Basic code is the DebugBreak API routine. (It's in the Windows API type library described in Chapter 2.) In case you're curious, its assembly language implementation looks like this:

```
DebugBreak PROC
    int 3
    ret
DebugBreak ENDP
```

The INT 3 instruction signals any active debugger to break out of execution. That's how debuggers work—by temporarily putting an INT 3 wherever they want a breakpoint.

Put a DebugBreak statement in your Basic source just before the line you want to examine. You should start with something simple but recognizable:

```
DebugBreak
i = &HABCD
```

Now run your program in the Visual Basic environment. When you hit the breakpoint, an application error box will appear, telling you that you've hit a breakpoint. It gives you a choice of terminating Visual Basic or debugging the application. If you're running under Windows 95, click Debug; if you're running under Windows NT, click Cancel. You'll pop up in your system debugger. (Mine is Microsoft Visual C++, but yours might be different.) You'll see the INT 3 instruction, followed by a RET instruction. Step through them. When you step past RET, you'll be in the code that calls API functions like DebugBreak. If you keep stepping through a lot of confusing code to get to the next Basic statement, eventually you'll find yourself in the strange world of p-code.

Let's just say that this code doesn't look like any C or assembler code I've disassembled before. If you want to know more, there are articles describing the p-code concept in MSDN and in the Visual C++ manuals. The main point is how many instructions it takes to do a simple task. In disassembled C code, the example statement would translate into something like this:

```
mov WORD PTR i, 0ABCDh
```

It is sobering to see how many instructions it takes to do the same thing in p-code.

The story is different for compiled code. All you have to do is compile with debugging information. Choose the Create Symbolic Debug Info check box and the No Optimization radio button on the Compile tab of the Project Properties dialog box. (If you don't turn off optimizations, the compiler might rearrange code in ways that are difficult to trace through.) After compiling, you can load the executable file into a source debugger. I use the Microsoft Developer Studio (MSDEV.EXE), but any debugger that understands Microsoft's debug format will work. For example, load from an MS-DOS session with this command line:

```
start msdev timeit.exe
```

You'll pop up in the assembly language decode window at some undetermined point, but it is possible to debug with source code. Use the File Open command to load the startup module (or any module you're interested in). Put a breakpoint somewhere in the code, and press F5 or the Go button. You'll stop at your breakpoint, and you can start tracing. You might find a few surprises. The Microsoft Developer Studio isn't designed for debugging Visual Basic code and doesn't have a Basic expression evaluator. You might not be able to evaluate expressions the way you expect in the Watch window. If these limits seem annoying, try debugging p-code again; you'll appreciate the native code.

The Time It Application

The Time It program is designed to answer performance questions. Its interface is simple, as you can see in Figure 1-1. You select a performance problem from a list box. Time It displays a description of the problem and the default number of iterations needed to run the test. You can modify the number of iterations. Click the Time It button (or double-click the list box item) to run the test. Nothing fancy. The goal of the Time It design is simply to make it easy to add new problems to the list box. (That turns out to be unexpectedly difficult in Visual Basic, but for now let's look only at the mechanics of timing operations in Visual Basic and Windows.)

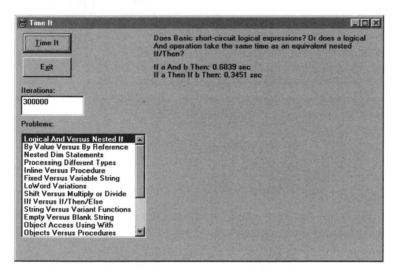

Figure 1-1. *The Time It application.*

Timing in Basic

Timing should be easy in Visual Basic. You get the start time from the Timer function, carry out the operation, and get the ending time. Subtract the start time from the end time, and you have the operation time. But in what units of time?

According to the Visual Basic documentation, Timer returns the number of seconds since midnight. You'd need a lot of iterations to get meaningful timing results if Timer actually returned whole seconds, but fortunately it returns seconds as a real number, nominally accurate to hundredths of a second. Actually, the Timer function is much less accurate—in fact, too inaccurate to be of much use. The sidebar "Better Basic Through Subclassing" tells how to replace the Timer function with your own better version.

Instead of Timer, I use a set of profile procedures, keeping them in DEBUG.BAS along with my debug procedures. As I do with the debug procedures, I use conditional compilation and various other debugging techniques so that the profile procedures can disappear in the release version of my program. ("Assert Yourself," page 35, discusses issues of writing debugging code in more detail.) The design of the procedures is simple and not very interesting, so I'll concentrate on how to use them.

Before timing an operation, you need to declare two Currency variables to contain the result:

```
Dim sec As Currency, secOut As Currency
```

"Large Integers and Currency," page 62, tells how this works and explains the somewhat surrealistic practice of measuring seconds in Currency. You pass one of these variables to ProfileStart:

```
ProfileStart sec
```

ProfileStart gets the start time from the system and stores it in the argument variable. You do the operation and then pass the start time to ProfileStop, which calculates the duration and returns it in the second variable:

```
ProfileStop sec, secOut
```

You can use the result—*secOut*, in this case—in an expression or wherever you happen to need it.

You're probably thinking that it would be more convenient to have ProfileStart and ProfileStop as functions rather than returning values through reference parameters. Maybe so, but I specifically designed them as subs to discourage calling them in expressions where they might cause side effects. "An Assertion Implementation," page 37, describes another reason for writing debug procedures as subs.

Short-Circuiting Logical Expressions: A Timing Example

As an example, consider the problem of short-circuiting logical expressions. Assume the following code:

```
If i <= 20 And i >= 10 Then i = i + 1
```

Looking at this logically, you can see that if *i* is greater than 20, it's pointless to check whether it's also less than 10. Some compilers and interpreters know this and skip the second condition (*short-circuiting* is the technical term) if the first condition settles the matter. But is Visual Basic among them? Consider an alternative but equivalent statement:

```
If i <= 20 Then If i >= 10 Then i = i + 1
```

In this case, I'm not trusting Visual Basic to optimize. I tell it to always check the first condition and to check the second only if the first is true. If Visual Basic can optimize the first example, these two pieces of code should run at about the same speed. There's only one way to find out:

```
Function LogicalAndVsNestedIf(cIter As Long) As String
    Dim sec As Currency, secOut As Currency
    Dim sMsg As String, i As Integer, iIter As Long

    i = 21
    ProfileStart sec
    For iIter = 1 To cIter
        If i <= 20 And i >= 10 Then i = i + 1
    Next
    ProfileStop sec, secOut
    sMsg = sMsg & "If a And b Then: " & secOut & " sec" & sCrLf

    i = 21
    ProfileStart sec
    For iIter = 1 To cIter
        If i <= 20 Then If i >= 10 Then i = i + 1
    Next
    ProfileStop sec, secOut
    sMsg = sMsg & "If a Then If b Then: " & secOut & " sec" & sCrLf

    LogicalAndVsNestedIf = sMsg

End Function
```

The results will vary, depending on the computer and operating system used, on what other programs are running at the same time, whether the code is compiled or not, and on whether the moon is full. I ran all the timing tests in this book on a 90-MHz Pentium-based computer running Windows 95. The "Performance" sidebar on page 34 indicates the results. Although the timings are significantly different for native code versus p-code, you can reach a reasonable conclusion: no short-circuit.

Just so you don't think that Visual Basic is unsophisticated and unnecessarily inefficient, it has its reasons. In Visual Basic, the And and Or operators double as logical operators and bitwise operators. You would have a different situation with the following line:

```
If a Or b Or c = &HEACC Then Exit Sub
```

In this case, you're combining the bits of *a*, *b*, and *c* and then testing to see whether the result has a specific value. A short-circuit would be inappropriate.

But for Basic to know that, it would need to look at the entire expression and make some assumptions (possibly erroneous) about your intentions. For example, Basic could assume that an expression with an equal sign is always bitwise but that an expression without an equal sign is always logical. That's an iffy assumption, and Visual Basic doesn't make it.

WARNING Visual Basic's failure to short-circuit logical expressions can cause problems other than poor performance. Consider the following expression:

```
If (iStart > 1) And Mid$(s, iStart - 1, 1) = " " Then
```

The first condition attempts to protect against an illegal condition in the second. If *iStart* is 1, the second argument of Mid$ is 0, which causes an illegal function call. You might hope that since the first condition is false, the second illegal statement won't be executed and you won't get that obnoxious error. Wrong!

PERFORMANCE

Problem: Does Visual Basic short-circuit logical expressions? Or does a logical And operation take the same time as an equivalent nested If/Then?

Problem	Native Code	P-Code
If a And b Then	.0215 sec	.5307sec
If a Then If b Then	.0220 sec	.3518 sec

Conclusion: This is the first of many timing notes. Don't take the numbers too seriously; they're for rough comparison only. For real results, run the Time It program yourself on machines like the ones you expect your customers to use. In this case, however, the difference in p-code is dramatic enough to justify a conclusion: Visual Basic does not short-circuit logical expressions. But you can also see that for compiled code there is virtually no difference. The numbers above actually show an insignificant edge for the logical expression. But remember, this result is for a very trivial example in my TimeIt test. You wouldn't get the same result if the right side of the expression were actually an expensive function call.

Assert Yourself

Basic programmers have been too long deprived of one of the common tools of debugging—the assertion procedure. Assertion deals with the concept of proof. If you write a piece of code, how can you prove that it works? If it crashes, you've proved that it doesn't work. But if it runs successfully, you've proved only that it ran successfully this time, not that it will run next time, with different input.

The way to approach proof in programming is to rule out all invalid inputs, call the procedure, and then verify that its output is valid. Although you can't always determine which inputs are invalid and you can't always figure out a way to validate output, it's nevertheless worth trying. You can often rule out many invalid inputs and at least partially validate output by using assertion procedures. An assertion procedure simply evaluates an expression, terminating the program with an appropriate message if the asserted expression is false.

For example, the following sub insists that users call it according to internal rules not enforced by the language:

```
Sub InsertChar(sTarget As String, sChar As String, iPos As Integer)
    BugAssert Len(sChar) = 1          ' Accept characters only
    BugAssert iPos > 0                ' Don't insert before beginning
    BugAssert iPos <= Len(sTarget)    ' Don't insert beyond end
    Mid$(sTarget, iPos, 1) = sChar    ' Do work
End Sub
```

The secret of successful assertion is to assert every possible condition that might go wrong. Of course, you won't feel comfortable asserting aggressively if you know that each assertion increases the size and decreases the speed of your finished application. For that reason, assertion procedures are traditionally coded conditionally so that they exist during a debugging phase but disappear when the finished product is shipped.

Since Visual Basic's conditional compilation features are significantly less powerful than those of most languages, version 5 tries to solve the assert problem by adding a built-in Assert method for the Debug object. Unfortunately, Debug.Assert doesn't measure up to the needs of professional programmers. We'll discuss it briefly but then move on to a real asserting and logging system based on conditional compilation.

Assert the Basic Way

If you assert a lie (for instance, that 2 and 2 is 5) in an MS-DOS C program, your program will terminate and you'll see output such as this on the command line:

```
Assertion failed: 2 + 2 == 5, file c:\lies.c, line 6
```

It would be nice to get similar output from Visual Basic. If you had an assert system like this, your test team could run compiled versions of programs through test suites and get useful error reports when programs failed. You could send compiled programs with asserts to your beta customers. If they exercised code paths not hit by your testers (customers do the darnedest things), you could get useful reports back from them. If you've ever been on a beta program for Visual Basic or any other professional program, you know what I'm talking about.

Unfortunately, Debug.Assert won't help you do this. If the Debug object were based on a CDebug class written in Basic, Assert would look something like this:

```
' CDebug.Cls
Public Sub Assert(fExpression As Boolean)
    If fExpression = False Then Stop
End Sub
```

Of course, that's not exactly what Debug.Assert does, because the Debug object disappears in compiled programs. It exists only in the Visual Basic Integrated Development Environment (IDE), which most of your beta customers won't have. If you wrote your own Assert that looked like the one above, the Stop statement would terminate an EXE program. But since Assert is a method of Debug and Debug doesn't exist in an EXE or in a DLL or in an OCX, your program won't stop anywhere except in the debugger.

I hate to say it, but I don't think Debug.Assert is worth the trouble. Professional programmers need a better system, but when you try to implement one, you'll run into some of the problems that probably prevented the Visual Basic team from providing a more useful Assert. The problem is that at run time, Visual Basic doesn't know the text of the expression that failed, and it doesn't know the filename and line number, either. The C compiler knows this information through the wonders of a feature called a preprocessor. I'm not going to get into a sticky debate about the value of preprocessors as a language feature. Let's just say that most languages don't have one, or at least not a sophisticated one like C's. Pascal, Java, and Visual Basic are some of the languages that can't use a preprocessor to do assertions.

Of course Visual Basic does parse the assertion at compile time, and it could theoretically store the expression text, filename, and line at that time for use at run time. Some languages that don't have preprocessors still manage to provide assertions or equivalent language features. I suspect that one reason Visual Basic doesn't do so is that it has always been an expression-oriented language. P-code is evaluated as expressions without any reference to line numbers. Most native code compilers report compile errors by line and file number. Maybe there's a connection. Maybe not. In any case, if you want assertions any place other than the IDE, you'll have to do them yourself. In other words, write your own preprocessor. That's what I did.

An Assertion Implementation

Here's one way to code an assertion procedure in Visual Basic:

```
Sub BugAssert(ByVal fExpression As Boolean, _
              Optional sExpression As String = sEmpty)
#If afDebug Then
    If fExpression Then Exit Sub
    BugMessage "BugAssert failed: " & sExpression
    Stop
#End If
End Sub
```

This short assertion procedure packs in some interesting twists. First is the optional argument. The intention is to fill the argument with a string containing the same information you would get from the C compiler. You could fill in both arguments yourself when writing code, but normally you would just use the simple version at design time:

```
BugAssert 2 + 2 = 5
```

Later you use a text-processing program that scans through source code and automatically fills in the second argument:

```
BugAssert 2 + 2 = 5, "2 + 2 = 5, file LIES.BAS, line 325"
```

Visual Basic might not know the expression, file, and line, but it's easy enough to write a program that does. Microsoft refers to programs that modify source code as *wizards,* and Visual Basic includes several of them. The Debug Wizard (BUGWIZ.EXE) shown in Figure 1-2 is the first of several wizards used in this book. For now, we're interested only in the program; we'll return to the code in Chapter 3.

The line number displayed in asserts was of limited use in previous versions of Visual Basic, but finally, in version 5, you can actually see a status display that tells what line and column the cursor is on. Unlike all the other programmer's editors I've seen, the Visual Basic editor doesn't have a Goto command to move to a specified line. But first things first. At least we get the current line displayed on the toolbar (even though it took five versions).

The next interesting thing about the code is the Exit Sub statement in the first unconditional line. For readability of structured code, I would normally use an If/End If block around the rest of the code rather than an Exit Sub. In this case, however, the important thing is not readability but that the Stop statement be the last executable statement of the procedure. This makes it more convenient to step back through the assertion procedure and come out in the calling procedure ready to debug.

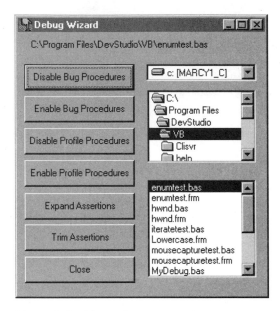

Figure 1-2. *The Debug Wizard.*

Speaking of the Stop statement, this is a wonder that C compilers and preprocessors can't match. It puts you in a perfect position to step into the code that caused the bug and fix it on the spot, assuming that you're working in the IDE. Of course it doesn't help if your program is an EXE or DLL, but in that case you just want to terminate with a message anyway. BugMessage will display the message, and then Stop will terminate.

You might wonder why I call the procedure BugAssert instead of Assert. I put all my debug procedures in the DEBUG.BAS module and start each name with *Bug*. Then I can easily search for all words that start with *Bug* and replace them with '*Bug*, thus commenting out all debug calls before I ship my program. Debug Wizard performs this operation automatically. (Incidentally, that's another reason all my Bug routines are subs, not functions. You can't comment out functions in expressions mechanically.)

You might also wonder why you can't use conditional compilation to automatically comment out unnecessary code. Well, you can if you have a preprocessor that supports macros. In C, assert is a macro that, when debugging is on, converts the statement

```
assert(2 + 2 == 5)
```

to a statement roughly equivalent to this:

```
if !(2 + 2 == 5)
    printf("Assertion failed: %s, file %s, line %d\n",
            "2 + 2 == 5", "lies.c", "6");
```

Conditional Compilation for Blockheads

Conditional compilation is a familiar feature in many languages, but it might be new to Basic programmers (although old-timers might remember metacommands from MS-DOS and Macintosh Basic compilers). Basic conditional statements (like their metacommand ancestors) give instructions to the compiler (or interpreter) about how to create the program. The results of the commands live on at run time, but the commands themselves are long gone.

Another way to think of this is that conditional compilation is an easy way of commenting out blocks of code. Let's say you want to try out different destroy algorithms. In previous versions of Visual Basic (or perhaps using the Comment Block and Uncomment Block buttons on the Edit toolbar in this version), you might have written this:

```
SafeSlowDestroy earth
'FastRiskyDestroy earth
```

After running the safe, slow version a few times to ensure that it works, you would have commented out the first line and removed the comment from the second to test it. Of course, in reality, each block would probably have more than one line, and affected code might be scattered in several places. Changing these calls by hand is a major inconvenience with great potential for bugs. Conditional compilation makes it easy to switch back and forth:

```
#Const fSafeSlow = 1
#If fSafeSlow Then
    SafeSlowDestroy earth
#Else
    FastRiskyDestroy earth
#End If
```

To try the fast, risky version, simply change the definition of the *fSafeSlow* constant to 0. Notice that the syntax for compile-time tests and constants is exactly the same as for run-time tests and constants except that the compile-time lines start with a pound sign (#). If you don't define an *fSafeSlow* constant in this example, it is assumed to be 0. This default enables you to fake the C language #ifdef and #ifndef statements even though Visual Basic doesn't directly support them.

In Visual Basic, there's no relation or communication between compile-time and run-time statements. You can't use a constant created with #Const in an If statement, and you can't use a constant created with Const in an #If statement. Despite syntax similarities, compile-time Visual Basic and run-time Visual Basic are different languages handled by different language interpreters at different times.

If debugging is off, the preprocessor will produce a blank—absolutely no code. If you look back at BugAssert, you'll see that if debugging is off, it will produce something—an empty procedure.

Imagine calling an empty procedure hundreds of times in the code you ship to customers. Imagine doing it in p-code. In native code, an empty procedure is just one instruction, but you still have all the code to evaluate the expression and push arguments onto the stack. An empty procedure might be comparatively cheap, but the motto of the defensive programmer is "When in doubt, assert." Personally, I can't follow this advice comfortably if I know that every assertion costs a call, a return, and many worthless bytes of code. I wrote Debug Wizard to eliminate all that code. I need to run it only occasionally during the life of a project.

Other Debug Messages

Assertions aren't the only kind of debug message you might want to see. In a previous life, I worked on a FORTRAN run-time library containing an extremely complex system of debug outputs. By setting various command line options during a library build, you could dump different parts of the library entrails for easy run-time divination. Nothing (except good sense) prevents you from enhancing my debug code to something just as complex.

That's up to you. I'm simply going to show you BugMessage. You can call it directly to display messages about your status and location, or you can write procedures that call it the way BugAssert does. My debug module (DEBUG.BAS) also contains a BugProfileStop sub that calls BugMessage to write profile information to the output destination.

BugMessage uses the following compile-time constants:

```
#Const afLogfile = 1
#Const afMsgBox = 2
#Const afDebugWin = 4
#Const afAppLog = 8
```

These identify the output destination for the message. Because your program is running under Windows, you have no command line to write to. You must send the message somewhere that won't interfere with your program screen.

You can write to a dialog box, although dialog debug messages can get annoying. If you're running in the Visual Basic IDE, you can write to the Immediate window. You also can write debugging output to a log file for later inspection. Finally, you can write messages to Visual Basic's log system, which is controlled by properties and methods of the App object.

The problem with using the new logging system for debug messages is that it's designed for a different purpose—logging events in unattended applications.

If you're using the built-in logging system for its intended purpose, you might want to use a different BugMessage setting so that debug messages don't get mixed in with other logged events. If you do decide to use the App object log features, you can control whether events are written to a log file or, under Windows NT, to the Application Event Log. The official logging system unfortunately doesn't work at all in the IDE (a fatal flaw in my opinion). My logging system doesn't attempt to call the StartLogging method or set the LogMode or the LogPath properties. It simply writes messages with the LogEvent method. If you use this option, you'll need to initialize the logging system yourself.

FLAME The new Debug.Assert method only works in the IDE, not in executables. The new log methods and properties of the App object work only in executables, not in the IDE. It's a conspiracy. Sometimes a flawed feature is better than no feature, but in this case neither feature is good enough to be used for real debugging scenarios.

A log file often works best in addition to (not instead of) one of the other output destinations. In theory you could set all four BugMessage bits at once, but in reality you'll usually pick one of the first three and then consider adding the log file as a secondary destination.

Here's the code to handle different output destinations:

```
Sub BugMessage(sMsg As String)
#If afDebug And afLogfile Then
    If iLogFile = 0 Then
        iLogFile = FreeFile
        ' Warning: multiple instances can overwrite log file
        Open App.EXEName & ".DBG" For Output Shared As iLogFile
        ' Challenge: Rewrite to give each instance its own log file
    End If
    Print #iLogFile, sMsg
#End If
#If afDebug And afMsgBox Then
    MsgBox sMsg
#End If
#If afDebug And afDebugWin Then
    Debug.Print sMsg
#End If
#If afDebug And afAppLog Then
    App.LogEvent sMsg
#End If
End Sub
```

If you open a log file for debug information, who's going to close it? Well, DEBUG.BAS contains a BugTerm sub that you can call in the Unload event of your main form to close the file. If you don't bother, however, you'll probably still be OK because Visual Basic closes all open files when it terminates. Notice that log files have the project executable name and the extension DBG. You might want to clean up once in a while so that your disk doesn't fill up with obsolete DBG files.

CHALLENGE The traditional Windows output destination is a debugging terminal. You hook up a dumb terminal to your serial port and send debugging output to the port. Assertions and other debug messages scroll past on this Neanderthal device without interfering with the operation of your program. The Windows API provides the OutputDebugString function to send output to a debugging terminal, but I was never able to get this to work satisfactorily under 32-bit Windows. You could enhance the BugMessage sub by adding an option that opens a COM port and then writes output to it.

Setting Debug Constants

BugAssert and other debug procedures expect a constant named *afDebug* to indicate not only whether debugging is on but also where to send debug output. You can set the constant in several ways.

The easiest way to set *afDebug* is to ignore it, which has the effect of setting it to 0 (False). Your code will work, but your assertions won't. This is a good setting for your release builds.

You can also set the constant in the DEBUG.BAS source module. You might think that it would be handy to set the *afDebug* constant in each source file so that you could debug some modules and not others. Unfortunately, that doesn't work. Constants defined in source modules are module-level variables. BugAssert and other routines that test the *afDebug* constant are located in DEBUG.BAS. They don't know or care about constants defined in other modules. Since you'll use the DEBUG.BAS module in various projects, you don't want the value of the *afDebug* constant to change every time you modify it in the source file. Instead, you want a projectwide way of setting the constant.

You can set project constants on the Make tab of the Project Properties dialog box (as shown in Figure 1-3), or you can set them on the VB5.EXE command line. If you spend all of your time working on one project, the command line method might work for you. I switch projects constantly, so I find the Project Properties dialog box more convenient. This puts the constant entry into the project, as you can see by examining the VBP file.

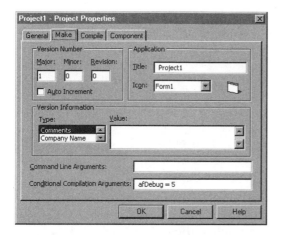

Figure 1-3. *The Make tab of the Project Properties dialog box.*

The Project Properties dialog box and the command line don't know Basic. You can't enter True or False, constants that are defined in the source file, hexadecimal numbers, or Basic operators. If you need to combine bit constants, you can't use an expression such as *afDebugWin And afLogFile*. Instead, you have to figure out that this means *&H1 And &H4*, calculate, convert to decimal, and enter *afDebug = 5* in the Conditional Compilation Arguments field.

Because my standard configuration is to send debugging output to the Immediate window and create a log file (*afDebug* = 5), I make it a standard setting in my default project and in my templates.

> **NOTE** Visual Basic now provides two ways to customize your startup projects. You can define a default startup project by creating a project with all your favorite settings and naming it AUTO-LOAD.VBP. You can also define templates for common project types by creating skeleton projects and placing them in the Visual Basic template directory. Both techniques are handy, but the documentation for templates is thin and the documentation for AUTOLOAD.VBP is nonexistent. You'll have to experiment.

What to Assert

Asserting is an art form. Languages have been specifically designed—Eiffel comes to mind—to encourage it. Books have been written about it. Steve Maguire's *Writing Solid Code* (Microsoft Press, 1993) is an excellent book on asserting and other debugging topics, although you'll have to translate from C to Basic as you read it. I can only touch on the subject here, but you'll see examples throughout the sample code.

The most important thing to know about debugging code is when to assert and when to validate. Validating means checking the input at run time and taking appropriate action. If you ask the user for a number between 1 and 10, you have to recognize when the user enters 11 and ask again politely (or handle 11 anyway, or round down to 10, or delete everything on the idiot's hard disk, or whatever). But you can't assert.

Here's an example. Lots of Windows API functions return error values, but errors don't always mean the same thing. A common Windows sequence (as you'll see in future chapters) is to create, use, and delete. It works like this:

```
hSomething = CreateSomething(x, y, clr, AND_SO_ON)
' Do something with hSomething
f = DeleteSomething(hSomething)
```

In this case, CreateSomething either returns a handle to a Something or returns a 0 handle (the constant *hNull*) indicating failure. DeleteSomething returns True or False, depending on whether you can delete the object.

If you get *hNull* back from CreateSomething, it's not your fault. There's probably not enough memory, or Windows has used up all the Somethings. It's your responsibility to politely tell the user to choose some other action. If DeleteSomething fails, however, it probably *is* your fault. You passed *hSomething* to the wrong procedure, or you traded an *hSomething* for an *hAnything* and forgot to swap it back. For whatever reason, the *hSomething* variable no longer contains a Something handle. There's no point telling the user. What could you say? You must do some soul-searching to fix the bug. But an assertion such as this one catches the mistake:

```
hSomething = CreateSomething(x, y, clr, AND_SO_ON)
If hSomething = hNull Then
    BackWayOut
    Exit Sub
End If
' Do something with Something
f = DeleteSomething(hSomething)
BugAssert f
```

WARNING Resist the temptation to combine assertions with other statements. The line

```
BugAssert DeleteSomething(hSomething)
```

seems to work, but if you replace *BugAssert* with ' *BugAssert*, you'll get an unpleasant surprise when DeleteSomething disappears along with the assertion.

Incidentally, if you notice more assertions in the examples in early chapters of this book than in late ones, well…that's no excuse for you. Never let tight deadlines compromise your efforts to write correct code. It takes longer to debug than to write it right the first time.

2

The Second Level of Basic Enlightenment

Visual Basic doesn't do pointers. Windows does. That's the contradiction you must resolve in order to achieve the second level of enlightenment.

You've already mastered the first level—designing forms and using Basic statements. The second level—calling the Windows API—requires a different kind of understanding. Even if you have experienced moments of clarity and truth with previous versions of Visual Basic, you must now learn again as a little child, because the gods have changed the rules.

Although on the surface this chapter appears to be about how to write Declare statements for Windows API functions, it is actually a meditation on the mysteries of pointers. Although it takes you step by step through the syntax of passing integers, user-defined types, arrays, and strings to DLL functions, below the surface its theme is addresses and how to become one with them. Lest you feel that your growing enlightenment comes from your own efforts, the chapter starts off with a type library that makes much of what you'll learn irrelevant.

So let's start at the beginning—with *addresses,* locations in memory that contain data or instructions. Everything a running program does consists of manipulating addresses and their contents. As designed by Kemeny and Kurtz, however, Basic shielded you from addresses. You could have programmed for years without knowing that memory even existed, much less that locations within it were called addresses.

Meanwhile, Brian Kernighan and Dennis Ritchie designed C, a language that not only allowed you to get addresses but also let you put them in variables called pointers, manipulate those variables to point at different addresses, and do almost anything that you could previously do only in assembly language. The C philosophy is pretty much the opposite of the Basic philosophy in every way. And C is the language in which—and seemingly for which—Microsoft wrote Windows.

Basic is abstract; C is specific. Basic is high-level; C is low-level. Basic is protective; C is undisciplined. Basic is basic; C is un-Basic. A good C programmer can write a Basic interpreter. A good Basic programmer can write a C pretty printer while the C programmer is still declaring variables.

Fortunately, you don't have to learn C to be a Windows programmer. But you do need to know some of the things C programmers know—things that Basic programmers aren't supposed to worry their pretty little heads with. Nevertheless, this chapter won't wander too far from the Basic Way. It will show you some tricks for keeping your un-Basic excursions short and for wrapping up the results so that they look Basic.

Never Write Another Damn Declare Statement

Sounds too good to be true, doesn't it? Well, this time it's not. You can use the Windows API type library to replace all your Windows Declare, Const, and Type statements. Load WIN.TLB (or its Unicode cousin WINU.TLB) in the References dialog box. Suddenly the whole Windows API becomes just another part of Visual Basic. You can examine the types, constants, and procedures in the Object Browser, and use the ones you need in your program without any extra work or resource cost.

The version of the Windows API type library provided with the first edition of this book was much less powerful and comprehensive than the one provided here. Visual Basic version 4 had significant limitations in its ability to use type libraries. With that version, you could get rid of most of your Declare statements, but not all by a long shot. Now you can. Almost. There's still one obscure situation that requires Declare statements, and I'll discuss it in "System Specific API Functions" in Chapter 6. There are also a few differences in the way you use type library functions and Declare functions, but they're minor and I'll deal with them as they come up in the rest of the chapter.

Just because you don't need to write Declare statements for the API functions in my type library doesn't mean you can't or that you would never need to. My type library contains most of what you need, but if you run into a function that isn't in the type library, it might be easier to write a few Declare statements than to modify the type library or create your own. Besides, Declare statements are a good teaching tool. If you understand how to declare a function, you'll certainly have no trouble calling it. Therefore, this chapter takes a "back-to-basics" approach. It explains how Declare statements work even though you probably won't need them very often.

Before I start talking about specific API functions, we need to take a brief look at what type libraries are.

What Is a Type Library?

A type library is a binary file containing all the type information you need to use procedures or classes in DLLs. Forget about classes for the moment; in this chapter, we're interested only in procedures and any constants and types those procedures use.

You get lots of type libraries with Visual Basic. You can examine the standard ones by clicking the Object Browser toolbar button or by pressing F2. If you click the Libraries drop-down list box of the Object Browser, you'll see short names for these standard libraries: stdole, VB, VBA, and VBRUN. If you select one of these libraries, you'll see its full name displayed in the bottom pane. You'll also see the type libraries for your current application and for any additional controls or components used by your project.

If you open any of the sample projects provided with this book, you'll also see a type library with the short name Win and the full name *Windows API (ANSI)*. The Classes pane on the left will show the function groups, types, and enums of the library. The Members pane on the right shows the members of the element chosen on the left, as shown in Figure 2-1. What's it for? In short, using this type library is equivalent to including WIN32API.TXT in your project—with one big difference. You don't pay a resource penalty for any type library elements you don't use.

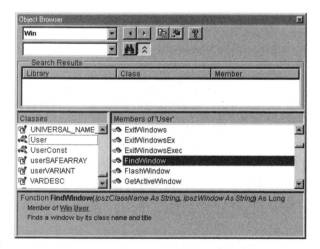

Figure 2-1. *Browsing in the Windows API type library.*

For example, WIN32API.TXT contains about 1500 Declare statements, most of which you would never use from Visual Basic even in your wildest dreams. The hardest of hardcore Basic programmers would be lucky to use 100 in a single project. If you were foolish enough to load WIN32API.TXT into a project, you would pay a memory penalty of about 20 bytes minimum for each Declare in the file—and that's not even counting the constants. So nobody actually loads all of WIN32API.TXT directly into their programs. Instead, they cut and paste the parts they need for each project. But no more.

WIN.TLB isn't as comprehensive as WIN32API.TXT. It contains over 700 function entries focused specifically on those functions Visual Basic programmers are most likely to need—as chosen and implemented by yours truly. In contrast, WIN32API.TXT was implemented by a program that converted C include files to Declare statements in a somewhat mechanical and sometimes inaccurate way. So whom do you trust? Me? Or a machine? Unfortunately, WIN32API.TXT has a well-earned reputation for being full of errors. The first version of my type library also had a few troublesome errors, and I doubt that this version will be without sin. That's one reason this chapter tells you how to roll your own. But the biggest difference between WIN.TLB and WIN32API.TXT is that if you use only three functions, you pay for only three functions. In this sense, a type library is more like a C++ header file or a Pascal unit than like a Basic module.

To include the type library in every project you create from now on, simply load it into AUTOLOAD.VBP and into your favorite project templates. You might also want to load it into existing projects to replace Declare and Const statements. Figure 2-2 shows the References dialog box, where you load type libraries. The checked references are the type libraries used by your current project. The unchecked references are others that have been registered in the Windows Registry.

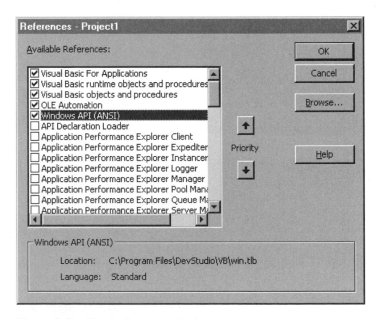

Figure 2-2. *The References dialog box.*

If a type library has already been registered, you'll see it in the References dialog box. The long and short of it is that if you ran the setup program provided on the companion CD, the Windows API type library is already registered on your machine. That's because setup runs a program called REGTLB to register the type libraries. You can run this program yourself if you ever have any problem registering a type library. (Run it once without arguments to get a syntax screen.) I'll talk about the code for this program later in this chapter. You can also register a type library by clicking the Browse button in the References dialog box.

Your customers don't need the Windows API type library to run programs that you develop using the type library. The exception to this rule is if you sell programming tools containing Visual Basic source code that uses the type library. (In that case, your customers should also buy this book.) You can build a setup that copies the type library files to the customer's disk and calls REGTLB to register them (as the setup program on the companion CD does).

Normally, you'll want to use WIN.TLB, the ANSI version of the library that works on Microsoft Windows 95 and Microsoft Windows NT. But if you're targeting Windows NT, you can use the Unicode version WINU.TLB. It is faster and more efficient, but it doesn't work on Windows 95.

Rolling Your Own

The source code for the Windows API type library is provided on the CD for this book, but I'm not going to describe it. This is a Basic book, but type libraries aren't written in Basic. They're written in Interface Description Language (IDL), which is similar to the subset of C used for writing function prototypes, structures, and constants. You can use a program called MIDL to compile IDL source code into type libraries. If you thought type libraries were written in Object Description Language (ODL) and compiled with MKTYPLIB, get with the program. That was last year.

Unfortunately, MIDL isn't provided with Visual Basic. Instead, the Visual Basic CD provides MKTYPLIB in the Tools\Unsupprt\Typlib directory. I don't know why they chose to provide the ancient MKTYPLIB instead of the newer MIDL. Either tool can be used not only for creating API type libraries but also for creating interface type libraries. Perhaps MKTYPLIB works better for interfaces, but MIDL is by far the better program for creating API type libraries. In any case, all my type library source code uses IDL rather than ODL, and I advise you to get your hands on MIDL version 3 or higher (it comes with newer versions of Visual C++) if you ever want to write type library entries for the API functions I don't handle. That's all I'm going to say on the subject. The IDL source code is on the CD that accompanies this book if you want to know more. Most people don't need to write API type libraries anyway because I've already done it.

So now that I've explained why you never need to write Declare statements again, let's move on to the rest of the chapter where I'll talk about how to write Declare statements. That might sound like a contradiction, but no matter. To master the Windows API, you still need to understand what's going on behind the scenes, and Declare statements are the most Basic way to learn that. You won't regret anything you learn here even if you never use it.

You might be tempted to skip this chapter because you already have both WIN.TLB and WIN32API.TXT as alternate sources of API declarations, but before you do, listen to this little story of heartbreak, despair, and wasted effort.

WritePrivateProfileString used to be one of the most popular functions in the Windows API because it allowed you to save data between sessions—functionality that Basic should have provided long ago but didn't until version 4. Everyone wanted to use this function. Everyone pasted the declaration from the API declare file. Everyone had trouble using it. Everyone then called Microsoft Product Support or, if they worked at Microsoft, sent e-mail to the internal Visual Basic programming alias. I used to see at least one such query a month about WritePrivateProfileString.

The problem was that the declaration shipped with Visual Basic was, to put it charitably, strange. It wasn't wrong. In fact, a note in the text file (which no one

PERFORMANCE

Problem: Compare counting with various Basic types: Integer, Long, Single, Double, Currency, and Variant.

Problem	Native Code	P-Code
Integer	0.0153 sec	0.4012 sec
Long	0.0224 sec	0.4250 sec
Single	0.1124 sec	0.5248 sec
Double	0.1402 sec	0.5185 sec
Currency	0.3232 sec	0.6179 sec
Variant	0.6578 sec	1.0241 sec

Conclusion: Notice how the compiler gives huge speedups for simple types, but as the types get larger and more complex, the margin narrows. For example, most of the work for handling Variants is done by the Automation system, so native code isn't going to make much difference.

seemed to read) explained how to use the declaration. I would say, however, that of the four or five alternatives for writing this declaration, the one chosen was the worst and the most likely to cause problems. Fortunately, the GetSetting, SaveSetting, DeleteSetting, and GetAllSettings functions make this problem irrelevant.

The point is, don't trust anyone's declarations—especially not mine. If you roll your own (or at least know how), you won't suffer because of someone else's bad choices. You have a lot of options, many of which I'll show you later in this chapter.

Calling the Windows API from Basic

The vague concept we usually call the Windows API is, in practical terms, a growing collection of dynamic-link libraries. Basic programmers can simply think of DLLs as libraries of procedures. You don't really need to know that DLLs are loaded at run time, that multiple programs can use the same DLL at the same time, or that the procedures in DLLs must be carefully written to allow this to happen safely.

As a Basic programmer, the key fact you need to know about system DLLs is that they are written in another language—it doesn't matter that it's usually C. That other language has a different idea than Basic does about the best way to use addresses. This difference extends to all the fundamental questions of life:

- What is a string?

- What is an array?

- How big is an integer?

- What is an argument, and how should it be passed?

- What is a type, and how can it be ignored?

- What can a procedure return, and how?

These are closed questions with simple answers in Basic, but when you start calling DLLs, everything you know is, if not wrong, at least incomplete. To reach a deeper understanding of DLL functions, you have to go to that mysterious place where Basic parameters and variables meet C pointers and references: the stack.

Anatomy of a Basic Procedure Call

To pass by value or not by value: that is the question. To answer it, you need to go farther down than Basic programmers normally go. Programming languages from Basic to C use the stack to pass arguments from caller code to a callee procedure. I'll first examine how this works for calls to Basic procedures and later expand our knowledge to cover calls to API procedures.

Basic programmers can afford to have a simplified view of the stack as an area of memory used for temporary one-way communication. The caller puts arguments on the stack and then calls a procedure. The callee can examine or modify the information. As soon as the callee returns, the portion of the stack used by the callee disappears. (Actually, it is reused.) In other words, the stack is write-only to the caller and effectively read-only to the callee (because no one will be around to see the results of stack writes). The purpose of this mechanism is protection: caller and callee can't access each other's data without permission.

There are as many ways to pass data on a stack as there are languages and data types. When a caller in one language (say, Basic) tries to pass data to another (say, C), the connection works only if both languages agree on a convention. The caller must put the data on the stack in the exact place and format expected by the receiver. For now, we're concerned with only one aspect of calling conventions: whether the caller and the receiver agree to pass by value or by reference. Left to their own devices, Basic will pass by reference, and C will receive by value.

As an example, take the ZapemByRef and ZapemByVal procedures defined in the ZAPI library. This new dynamic-link library (ZAPI.DLL) makes it easy for Windows-based programs to zap space aliens in a consistent and portable manner, regardless of what Zap hardware and Zap device driver happen to be attached to the computer. If the ZapemByRef procedure were written in Basic, it might look something like this:

```
Sub ZapemByRef(ordAlien As Integer)
    If ordAlien = ordMartian Then
        ' Do whatever it takes; then set 0 for successful zap
        ordAlien = 0
    End If
    ' Handle other aliens
End Sub
```

Now assume that this procedure is called with the following lines:

```
Const ordMartian = 7
⋮
Dim ordCur As Integer
ordCur = ordMartian
ZapemByRef ordCur
If ordCur = 0 Then BuryEm
```

Figure 2-3 shows what the stack looks like to the caller and to the callee. The caller passes its argument using the default Basic convention of calling by reference. It puts the address of the variable being passed on the stack.

Caller's View

```
ordCur = ordMartian   ' 7
ZapemByRef ordCur
If ordCur = 0 Then
   ⋮
```

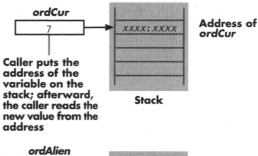

Callee's View

```
Sub ZapemByRef(ordAlien As Integer)
    If ordAlien = ordMartian Then   ' Read
    ⋮
        ordAlien = 0                ' Write
    ⋮
```

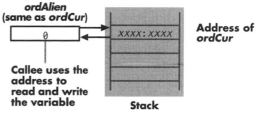

Figure 2-3. *Passing by reference.*

Giving another procedure an address is an act of trust. You've given away the key to modifying whatever is located at that address (and, incidentally, any adjacent addresses). In this case, the ZapemByRef procedure can read or write the parameter (which it calls *ordAlien*, even though the address is actually the same as *ordCur*). Technically, reads and writes are done indirectly through a pointer, an operation that takes a little more processing than modifying a variable directly. Basic hides this, however, and makes writing to a by-reference parameter look the same as writing to any other variable.

ZapemByRef is a textbook example of bad design. To mention only one of its problems: what if a user passed the *ordMartian* constant directly instead of assigning it to a variable? Would the caller really pass the address of a constant? How constant would that constant be if you were passing its address around? What if the user passed the number 7 instead of *ordMartian*? It turns out that passing a constant by reference is perfectly legal, but Basic implements this feature by creating a temporary variable and passing the address of that variable. ZapemByRef could then write to that variable (using the *ordAlien* alias), but the caller wouldn't be able to check the results because it wouldn't have a name for the temporary variable.

PERFORMANCE

Problem: How does the timing of arguments passed by value compare to the timing of arguments passed by reference (the default)?

Problem	Native Code	P-Code
Integer by value	0.0063 sec	0.2508 sec
Integer by reference	0.0069 sec	0.2518 sec
Long by value	0.0073 sec	0.2563 sec
Long by reference	0.0072 sec	0.2553 sec
Single by value	0.0072 sec	0.2521 sec
Single by reference	0.0073 sec	0.2585 sec
Double by value	0.0078 sec	0.2579 sec
Double by reference	0.0073 sec	0.2599 sec
Variant by value	0.1585 sec	0.5561 sec
Variant by reference	0.0602 sec	0.4222 sec
String by value	0.3388 sec	0.8279 sec
String by reference	0.1669 sec	0.5901 sec

Conclusion: For intrinsic numeric types, there isn't enough difference to spit at. Notice what happens as the variables get larger. A reference variable is always four bytes, but if you have to push all eight bytes of a Double or all 16 bytes of a Variant onto the stack, it's going to cost you. I threw strings into the table for comparison, but in fact they work a little differently. You're not really saving the whole string on the stack when you pass a string by value. You are making an extra copy though—through a mechanism that we won't worry about in this chapter. Just take a look at the extra cost, and then make the obvious decision: always pass strings by reference in your Basic code. Calling API functions is a different matter.

Let's move on to ZapemByVal. This procedure is a function that returns a Boolean value to indicate success or failure:

```
Function ZapemByVal(ByVal ordAlien As Integer) As Boolean
    If ordAlien = ordMartian Then
        ' Do whatever it takes; then set True for successful zap
        ZapemByVal = True
```

```
      Exit Function
   End If
   ' Handle other aliens
End Function
```

Now assume that this function is called with the following lines:

```
Const ordMartian = 7
⋮
If ZapemByVal(ordMartian) Then DoWhatNeedsToBeDone
```

This looks better. The call takes fewer lines of code because the constant is passed directly. Success or failure comes back through the return value.

Under the hood, caller and callee treat the argument in completely different ways. Instead of copying the address of the argument onto the stack, the caller copies the value. Figure 2-4 shows the stack from the viewpoint of both caller and callee. If ZapemByVal were to modify the *ordAlien* variable, the stack value would change, but this value will disappear into the sunset as soon as ZapemByVal returns. So if the function happens to need a scratch variable, there's no technical reason not to use *ordAlien* for this purpose after it has been read. (In practice, however, using a variable for anything other than what its name implies is a good way to write unmaintainable code.)

Which parameter passing method should you choose? Since passing by reference is the default, the temptation is to accept it without thinking for Basic

Caller's View

```
If ZapemByVal(ordMartian) Then
⋮
```

Callee's View

```
Function ZapemByVal(ByVal ordAlien As Integer) _
   As Boolean
   If ordAlien = ordMartian Then      ' Read
⋮                                      ' Don't write
End Function
```

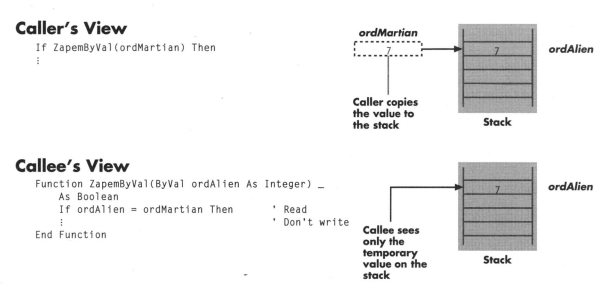

Figure 2-4. *Passing by value.*

procedures. And if you compare the timing of the two methods, as I did in the "Performance" sidebar on page 54, you'll see that this isn't a bad strategy. Results vary depending on the arguments, but the difference isn't great enough to justify changing code. Other factors, many of which I will discuss later, are more important. When you are dealing with Windows API calls, however, the primary factor is what Windows tells you to do. Why Windows chooses one method or another in different circumstances should tell you something about choices in your Basic code.

Anatomy of a DLL Procedure Call

We've been pretending that the ZAPI functions are written in Basic to be called by Basic, but in reality they are written as a C DLL to be called from C, Pascal, Logo, Scheme, and the current language of the month. The ZAPI library couldn't be a Visual Basic DLL because it needs to support all languages directly, not through COM Automation. Also, many callers won't have the Visual Basic run-time DLL on their disks. The last thing the author of ZAPI had in mind was making it easy to call API functions from Basic. Internally, ZAPI uses whatever conventions are most efficient (usually taken from C, but sometimes from Pascal).

In order to call a procedure in a DLL, you need either a type library entry or a Declare statement for it. Since Declare statements are written in Basic, I'll concentrate on them. The Zapem API function, shown in Figure 2-5, serves as a preliminary model for writing and using Declare statements.

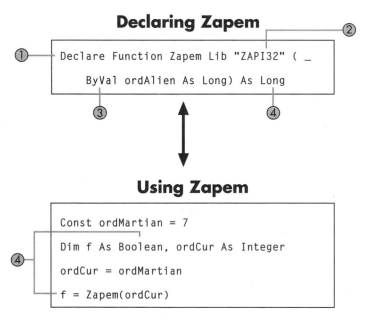

Figure 2-5. *Declaring and using a DLL function.*

A lot is packed into this short bit of code. Take a look at the labeled sections in Figure 2-5, which correspond to the numbered sections here:

1. A Declare statement looks sort of like the first line of a procedure definition except that it starts with the Declare keyword. You specify whether the procedure is a Sub or a Function and then give the name of the procedure followed by the argument list and, for Functions, the return value.

2. You must include the name of the DLL containing the procedure in a Lib clause. If you're calling your own DLL, you probably know the name. If you're calling the Windows API, you sometimes have to guess. C programmers don't need to put the DLL name in their declarations, and since most API documentation is designed for C programmers, you might have trouble figuring it out. Microsoft Visual C++ comes with a file named WIN32API.CSV that tells all for Win32. Another technique is to use the /DUMP option of the LINK program provided with Visual Basic. The command *LINK /DUMP /EXPORTS ODBC32.DLL*, for example, will show all the functions provided by the ODBC32 DLL. If that doesn't help, use the trial-and-error method, starting with the DLLs shown in Table 2-1.

Services	DLL
Common controls	COMCTL32
Common dialogs	COMDLG32
Drag and drop, icon extraction, Windows 95 shell	SHELL32
Graphics Device Interface	GDI32
Graphics (3-D lines and surfaces)	OPENGL32 (NT only)
Graphics (games and animation)	WING32
Memory, disks, processes, resources, tasks, modules	KERNEL32
Multimedia, sound, MIDI, joysticks, timing	WINMM
Networks (WNet)	MPR
Networks (LanMan)	NETAPI32
NT Security, Registry, and other advanced services	ADVAPI32
Component Object Model (COM)	OLE32
Automation and type conversion	OLEAUT32
Version checking	VERSION
Windows, menus, strings, messages	USER32

Table 2-1. *Windows system DLLs.*

3. The big question is whether to pass by value or by reference. Most arguments should be passed by value, but you'll hear a lot about the exceptions later in this chapter.

4. The original Basic version of Zapem returned a Boolean value, but the Windows BOOL type isn't the same as a Basic Boolean. A BOOL is actually an int, which is 32 bits wide. To C programmers, a Boolean is actually a typedef called VARIANT_BOOL that evaluates to a C short (16 bits). In other words, a Boolean is the same size as a Basic Integer. Although you should declare what Windows calls BOOL as Long, you can assign the result to a Boolean. Basic automatically performs the type conversion from Long to Boolean on return values.

That's the quick introduction to API calls. When you get down to actual coding, though, things get complicated. Every type of argument has its own quirks and patterns, and you must look at each type specifically. Fortunately, the Windows API never uses the Variant, Currency, Single, or Double type. The remaining types fall into patterns that I can discuss one by one.

> **NOTE** The COM Automation API uses Variant and other Visual Basic data types. Theoretically, you could use them in declarations for the COM Automation system DLLs or for COM Automation–compatible DLLs that you write. You can even use the Optional and ParamArray attributes in Declare statements. This chapter, however, concentrates on the integer and string types used by the Windows API.

The API Contract

You can think of the interface between Basic and the Windows API as a legal contract. On the one side, Basic wishes to acquire certain services and resources. On the other side, the Windows API is in the business of providing those services and resources. However, since each party is providing information that could be dangerous to the other, and since the parties don't speak the same language, both feel the need for a legal contract spelling out the terms and limits of the transaction.

The Windows API provides its side of the contract as part of the specifications of its DLLs. These are spelled out in the API documentation and are partially enforced by the actual DLL interfaces. Visual Basic submits a legal request in the form of a Declare statement. It checks the declaration against the DLL interface and rejects anything incompatible.

As any lawyer can tell you, it's impossible to fully specify the terms of a transaction in a legal contract. You try to define everything you can think of and handle the rest on an ad hoc basis. If something goes wrong, you can sue after the fact. Unfortunately, "lawsuits" in the Windows world often end up as unhandled exceptions, general protection faults, unrecoverable application errors, and cold boots. The next sections explain how far the API contract goes and how to avoid conflicts in areas the law doesn't cover.

Integer Parameters

Most parameters in the Windows API are integers of one kind or another. C makes a distinction between signed and unsigned integers, but to Basic they're all signed. You can assign all integers—signed and unsigned—to Integers and Longs. "Hammering Bits," page 271, discusses some of the problems you might have dealing with integers when you think they are unsigned but Basic thinks they are signed.

In the Windows API, you usually pass integers by value using the ByVal attribute. Table 2-2 lists the kinds of integers you'll see in the API documentation and shows how to handle them in Declare statements.

Windows API	Basic
int, INT	ByVal Long
UINT	ByVal Long
BOOL	ByVal Long
WORD	ByVal Integer
DWORD	ByVal Long
WPARAM	ByVal Long
LPARAM, LRESULT	ByVal Long
COLORREF	ByVal Long
ATOM	ByVal Integer
HANDLE and friends	ByVal Long
BYTE	ByVal Byte
char	ByVal Byte

Table 2-2. *Integers in the Windows API.*

For passing integers, the API contract is simple. Basic agrees to put integer values on the stack and never see them again. Windows can do whatever it wants with those values. All that can go wrong here is that you could pass an integer too large for an Integer type or a Long type. Basic will catch this error before it gets anywhere near Windows. Of course, you could always pass a value that a particular API function doesn't understand, but Windows promises to fail politely and return an error code in these cases.

Here's a simple integer example. The Win32 documentation shows FloodFill as follows:

```
BOOL FloodFill(
    HDC hdc,            // Handle of device context
    int nXStart,        // X-coordinate of starting position
    int nYStart,        // Y-coordinate of starting position
    COLORREF crFill     // Color of fill boundary
);
```

You declare it this way in Basic:

```
Declare Function FloodFill Lib "GDI32" (ByVal hdc As Long, _
    ByVal nXStart As Long, ByVal nYStart As Long, _
    ByVal crFill As Long) As Long
```

You don't have much choice about how to declare this function, but you can choose how to declare any variables you plan to pass to it. Because you're passing by value, Visual Basic can do type conversion on any variables you pass. For example, the X- and Y-coordinate variables could be stored in Integers. You'd need an awfully big monitor to be higher than 32,767 or lower than −32,768 if you're measuring in pixels. I hope to have such a monitor on my desk someday, but for now I consider it fairly safe to use Integer variables. Basic will convert them to Longs before passing them to FloodFill.

> **NOTE** I use the Windows version of Hungarian in sample declarations, although I don't like it. "Basic Hungarian," page 16, explains what I don't like and how my version of Hungarian differs. Apologies for any confusion this causes. The parameter names in declarations are ignored anyway, and I thought it would be better for my declarations to match the API documentation. Besides, I created a lot of my Declare statements by cutting, pasting, and modifying C prototypes, and I was too lazy to change the names.

Pointers to Integers

Basic programmers can pass by reference without really knowing how or why, but C programmers don't have this luxury. The C language doesn't have an automatic way to specify that a variable should be passed by reference instead of by value (although C++ and Pascal do). Instead, C programmers pass by reference by explicitly passing a pointer to the variable. In other words, C programmers do on purpose what Basic programmers do by accident. But when you mix the two approaches by accessing the Windows API, Basic must defer to C.

The only reason the Windows API uses pointers to integers is to return them. You can put only one value in the function return, so if you need to return more than one value, you have to use by-reference parameters. For a few procedures, you put a meaningful value into the variable before passing it and then get a modified version back. More commonly, you simply pass an empty variable; the return is all that matters.

Windows API documentation usually shows pointers with defined pointer types such as LPDWORD and LPHWND. (See Table 2-3.) These are actually aliases (called typedefs in C) for DWORD * and HWND *. The LP in the type names (and lp as a Hungarian prefix for parameter names) apparently meant long pointer, which is what everyone in the world except the author of this strange convention called far pointers. Almost all pointers were far, even in the 16-bit world, so there was never any need to qualify them, but we're probably stuck with the notation forever. You might also occasionally see FAR * in the API documentation, but you should ignore the FAR. It's just an alias for nothing, retained for theoretical compatibility with mythical ancient operating systems.

Windows API	32-Bit Basic
LPINT, int *	Long
LPUINT, UINT *	Long
LPBOOL, BOOL *	Long
LPBYTE, BYTE *	Byte
LPWORD, WORD *	Integer
LPDWORD, DWORD *	Long
LPHANDLE, HANDLE *, and friends	Long

Table 2-3. *Pointers to integers in the Windows API.*

The GetScrollRange function illustrates how and why to pass integers by reference. It needs to return two Longs—the top and bottom of the scroll range—so it uses pointers to Longs to return them. The Windows API documentation shows this:

```
BOOL GetScrollRange(
    HWND hwnd,          // Handle of window with scroll bar
    int nBar,           // Scroll bar flags
    LPINT lpMinPos,     // Receives minimum position
    LPINT lpMaxPos      // Receives maximum position
);
```

The Basic declaration looks like this:

```
Declare Function GetScrollRange Lib "User32" ( _
    ByVal hWnd As Long, ByVal nBar As Long, _
    lpMinPos As Long, lpMaxPos As Long) As Long
```

Calling the function is simple:

```
Dim iMin As Long, iMax As Long
f = GetScrollRange(txtTest.hWnd, SB_HORZ, iMin, iMax)
```

Of course, there's no reason to ever declare the variables any differently than this (although there was a very good reason back in the 16-bit days). But for the sake of argument, let's say you declared those variables as integers.

```
Dim iMin As Integer, iMax As Integer
```

After all, any number you would use as a scroll range would easily fit in an Integer. But if you do this, you'll see the message *ByRef argument type mismatch*. To understand why this error occurs, consider what would happen if Basic allowed you to pass Integer variables to GetScrollRange. Once Basic passes the address of the variable to Windows, it has no control over what Windows does to that variable. For example, Windows might decide to write 1 into *iMin* and 100 into *iMax*. But it will write that 1 as a Long. If *iMin* is an Integer variable, Windows will write zero (the high word) into *iMin* and 1 (the low word) into the next word in memory, which happens to be *iMax*. When it tries to write 100 into *iMax*, it will actually write a Long 100 into the two words of memory beginning at *iMax*. The results of this operation might actually be a little different because the order in which GetScrollRange decides to fill the values is undefined. In any case, the results are unlikely to be pleasant. To prevent random behavior, the API contract insists that all arguments passed by reference must be the exact size specified in the declaration. In fact, the rule goes beyond the API contract and applies to procedures written in Basic, for the same reasons. Basic is very picky about by-reference arguments because it has to be. If you want type conversion of input-only parameters, declare them ByVal.

Large Integers and Currency

Windows and COM sometimes use 64-bit integers, but unfortunately, standard C++ doesn't support integers of this size. Nevertheless, there are ways to get around the limitations of C++, just as there are ways to get around the limitations of Visual Basic. In C++, the most convenient workaround is to use a vendor-specific type such as the __int64 type supported by Visual C++. A more portable solution is to use the LARGE_INTEGER type, which looks something like this:

```
typedef union _LARGE_INTEGER {
    struct {
        DWORD LowPart;
        LONG  HighPart;
    };
    LONGLONG QuadPart;     // In Visual C++, a typedef to __int64
} LARGE_INTEGER;
```

This union allows C++ programmers to use the structure part if their compiler doesn't support 64-bit integers, or to use the LONGLONG part if it does. There are no unions in Basic, so the closest you can get is the following type:

```
Type LARGE_INTEGER
    LowPart As Long
    HighPart As Long
End Type
```

The Win32 API even provides functions (such as Int32x32To64) to manipulate the high and low parts of a 64-bit integer, but I wouldn't touch them with a pole because Visual Basic actually provides a 64-bit integer type called Currency.

But, you say, Currency isn't an integer type, it's a fixed-point type. Well, yes, but the bits are the same. It's just that behind the scenes, COM Automation is moving a decimal point four places to the left on all currency integers. All you have to do to display a Currency value as a true integer is multiply by 10,000 (or use the CURRENCY-MULTIPLIER type library constant).

One of the best places to use Currency is with the QueryPerformanceCounter API function and its friend, QueryPerformanceFrequency. The C version looks like this:

```
BOOL QueryPerformanceCounter(LARGE_INTEGER *lpPerformanceCount);
```

The Basic version looks like this:

```
Declare Function QueryPerformanceCounter Lib "KERNEL32" ( _
    lpPerformanceCount As Currency) As Long
```

The function gives a high accuracy timing count that can be used in place of less accurate timing counts from API functions such as timeGetTime or GetTickCount. You can see it in action in the Profile functions in DEBUG.BAS.

```
Sub ProfileStart(secStart As Currency)
    If secFreq = 0 Then QueryPerformanceFrequency secFreq
    QueryPerformanceCounter secStart
End Sub

Sub ProfileStop(secStart As Currency, secTiming As Currency)
    QueryPerformanceCounter secTiming
    If secFreq = 0 Then
        secTiming = 0 ' Handle no high-resolution timer
    Else
        secTiming = (secTiming - secStart) / secFreq
    End If
End Sub
```

QueryPerformanceCounter returns a counter too accurate to fit in a Long. You can turn this timer number (which might vary in accuracy depending on your hardware) into a recognizable number by dividing by the number of counts per second, as returned by QueryPerformanceFrequency. Normally, you'll be subtracting a beginning count from an ending count and then dividing by the frequency to get a duration. The result comes out nicely as a fixed-point Currency number representing seconds. Multiply by 1000 to convert to microseconds.

There are other places you could use Currency. For example, Win32 stores file time values as 64-bit integers in a FILETIME structure that looks a lot like a LARGE_INTEGER structure. Windows won't know or care whether the bits you pass on the stack are Currency, FILETIME, or LARGE_INTEGER. Chapter 11 explains why I use Currency rather than FILETIME.

Another place you could use the Currency type is for API functions that deal with file sizes. Under Win32, a file size is a 64-bit integer, and so file sizes are usually returned in a low part and a high part. I personally have never seen a file larger than four gigabytes, and don't expect to soon. In most applications, it's safe (and simple) to assume that the high part of the file length is zero, but if you really need to handle all possible cases, you could receive the file size in a Currency variable and multiply the result by 10,000 rather than getting the high and low parts separately. Unfortunately, some Win32 structures store the high part first, making this trick impossible. It's more useful for disk sizes anyway. Use it with GetDiskFreeSpaceEx.

User-Defined Types

In Basic, you pass UDTs (*structures* in C) to Windows API functions by reference for three possible reasons. The first is the same reason you pass integers by reference—so that you can get something back. The second is that most UDT variables are too large to pass efficiently by value. The third and deciding reason is that Basic won't let you pass them by value even if you want to. You'll see an example in Chapter 6 ("Window position and size," page 312) in which the first two reasons don't apply and you have to jump through hoops to get around the third.

The window placement functions illustrate UDT parameter passing. The GetWindowPlacement function returns window position values through a WINDOWPLACEMENT type, and the SetWindowPlacement function saves values in the same structure. As with most examples in this chapter, it's not important what these functions do; we're concerned only with the syntax and what is passed at the lowest level.

The C documentation for the placement functions looks like this:

```
BOOL GetWindowPlacement(
    HWND hWnd,                          // Handle of window
    WINDOWPLACEMENT * lpwndpl           // Address for position data
);

BOOL SetWindowPlacement(
    HWND hWnd,                          // Handle of window
    CONST WINDOWPLACEMENT * lpwndpl // Address for position data
);
```

The only difference between the two functions, other than the name, is that SetWindowPlacement has *CONST* in the WINDOWPLACEMENT type. I'll explain that difference shortly.

The Basic user-defined type looks like this:

```
Type WINDOWPLACEMENT
    length As Long
    Flags As Long
    showCmd As Long
    ptMinPosition As POINTL
    ptMaxPosition As POINTL
    rcNormalPosition As RECT
End Type
```

The Basic Declare statements look like this:

```
Declare Function SetWindowPlacement Lib "USER32" ( _
    ByVal hWnd As Long, lpwndpl As WINDOWPLACEMENT) As Long
Declare Function GetWindowPlacement Lib "USER32" ( _
    ByVal hWnd As Long, lpwndpl As WINDOWPLACEMENT) As Long
```

In the last edition of this book, I made the mistake of changing the names of Windows API structures. I renamed WINDOW-PLACEMENT to TWindowPlacement. Of course, none of the software parties to API transactions care what you name a structure as long as it's the right size. But the human parties find it confusing if you change the names of standard operating system features. It's not really a good idea, even if the official names are great big, ugly, all-uppercase names that conflict with your naming conventions. People don't want better standards, they want standard standards. I apologize for any inconvenience caused by my original misnaming or my belated correction. There is still one big exception to the rule. Unfortunately, the very common POINT structure conflicts with the rare Visual Basic Point method, so I had to use the equivalent POINTL structure for all cases where API functions take POINT structures.

You simply pass GetWindowPlacement an empty WINDOWPLACEMENT variable and read the result out of the variable afterward:

```
Dim wp As WINDOWPLACEMENT
' First set type length for Windows
wp.length = Len(wp)
' Get coordinates and other data about the window
f = GetWindowPlacement(hWnd, wp)
' Read and use the data
sValue = wp.showCmd & ","
sValue = sValue & wp.Flags & ","
```

Notice how the length field is set to the length of the structure before the call. This is called planning ahead. If Microsoft designs a new version of Windows that has more fields in the WINDOWPLACEMENT type, your old code won't necessarily be broken. Windows will be able to tell from the length field whether you have the new and improved structure or the old standby. You'll see length fields in a few of the original Windows structures—and a lot more of them in new Win32 structures.

WARNING While writing this book, I forgot to set the length field and wasted several hours in fruitless debugging so that you won't have to. Don't let my suffering be in vain.

The SetWindowPlacement function looks almost the same, but it works in the opposite way. You put values into the variable first and then call the function to pass them to the system:

```
' Remember to set length
wp.length = Len(wp)
' Send all your settings to the system
f = SetWindowPlacement(hWnd, wp)
```

If you look back at the declarations, you can see that the WINDOWPLACEMENT variable is passed by reference in both the Set and Get functions. In the Get function, it must be passed by reference so that Windows can fill in the new value. In the Set function, it's passed by reference only to avoid wasting stack space. That's where the CONST keyword in the C parameter definition comes in.

C allows you to specify that a variable is being passed by reference for convenience, not for modification. When you pass the address of a variable, you give the receiver the right to modify it. The CONST keyword revokes that right. It would be nice if this protection were written into the Basic side of the API contract. Just imagine being able to put a ReadOnly attribute on Visual Basic by-reference parameters so that an error is generated if the callee changes the value. Fortunately, it's unnecessary for the Basic-to-Windows interface because Windows enforces the CONST attribute. You can rest assured that if the documentation for an API parameter says that it's CONST, anything passed to it will come back untouched.

Arrays

Like UDTs, arrays must be passed by reference, and for the same reasons. The big difference is that Windows knows the size of a UDT used by an API function, but it doesn't know how many elements an array contains. In fact, that's usually the reason you pass arrays to Windows—so that you can give varying numbers of elements. This means, however, that the API function needs to ask for the length in a separate parameter.

This requirement highlights another difference between C and Basic. Basic always knows how many elements an array contains (just as it knows the size of a string). C doesn't, forcing the C programmer to keep track. Windows, in the C tradition, has the same requirement. This isn't true of COM Automation, however. From the interface, you might almost think that COM Automation was written in Basic. It wasn't, but Visual Basic types had a strong influence on the design. COM Automation supports a type called the *safe array* that just happens to have exactly the same format as a Basic array. Or perhaps it's the other way around. In any case, arrays passed to COM Automation functions are more intuitive than those passed to Windows API functions.

For example, the Polygon API function (discussed in Chapter 7) passes an array of POINT variables (which we must call POINTL variables, as noted on page 66) along with the number of points in the array. Polygon connects the dots.

The function looks like this on the C side:

```
BOOL Polygon(
    HDC hdc,                     // Handle of device context
    CONST POINT * lpPoints,      // Address of polygon's vertices
    int nCount                   // Count of polygon's vertices
);
```

The Basic UDT and declaration look like this:

```
Type POINTL
    x As Long
    y As Long

End Type


Declare Function Polygon Lib "GDI32" (ByVal hdc As Long, _
    lpPoints As POINTL, ByVal nCount As Long) As Long
```

Notice that the *lpPoints* parameter is passed by reference. You might think this is because POINTL is a user-defined type and UDTs are always passed by reference. Not so. The reason *lpPoints* is passed by reference is that in C an array is actually the address of the first element. If you pass a variable by reference, you're actually passing its address, which is just what C (and Windows) thinks an array is. Another way to see this is to think of a variable as an array with one element. That's why the Polygon declaration looks exactly as it would if the function took one by-reference POINTL variable instead of an array of them.

To pass an array, you pass the first element. Here's an example:

```
Dim ptPoly(1 To 5) As POINTL
For i = 1 To 5
    ' Calculate each point
    ⋮
Next
Call Polygon(hdc, ptPoly(1), 5)
```

This gives you lots of rope—enough to hang yourself. For example, you don't have to pass the start of the array or all the elements in it. The call

```
Call Polygon(hdc, ptPoly(2), 3)
```

passes the second through fourth elements of the array.

If you look at arrays in legal terms, the contract isn't worth the polish on the shoes of the lawyer who wrote it. Windows wants an array, but Basic can't be sure that's what you're giving. Windows wants the number of elements in the array, but Basic isn't going to count them. It's up to you to tell the truth. If you claim that the array contains 10 elements when it really has 5, Windows will happily use those last 5 elements whether they exist or not. Your machine might head south in a hurry.

When you look up the syntax for declarations, you'll see that it's possible to put empty parentheses on a parameter to indicate that you're passing an array. Don't try it with API functions. This feature is used for calling COM DLLs that know about Basic-style safe arrays with an encoded size. If COM had a GDI library, the ComPolygon function might look like this:

```
Declare Function ComPolygon Lib "COMGDI" (ByVal hdc As Long, _
    lpPoints() As POINTL) As Boolean
  ⋮
Call ComPolygon(hdc, ptPoly)
```

You'll get errors if you try to pass an entire array to a C-style procedure that expects the first element of an array, or if you try to pass the first element of an array to a COM-style function that expects the entire array.

Typeless Variables

The Windows API frequently requires typeless parameters. The idea is to pass different types of data to the same function. For example, the GetObject function handles pens, brushes, fonts, bitmaps, and palettes through the same parameter. This works fine in weakly typed languages such as C. It doesn't work so well in Basic, a schizophrenic language that can't make up its mind whether to be strongly typed or weakly typed. The Declare statement, at any rate, is strongly typed, most of the time. (Basic is also a typeless language, through its Variant type; but just as Basic doesn't do pointers, Windows doesn't do Variants.)

Every variable has a type, explicit or assumed, regardless of the host language. When you pass a variable to a function, that function must figure out the type so that it knows what to do with the variable. The type can be embedded in the data (as in Basic Variants), or it can be supplied as a separate parameter to the function. That's the easy part. The tricky part is getting Basic to turn off its data typing so that you can pass different kinds of data. The Alias attribute of the Declare statement and the Any parameter type enable you to lie, cheat, steal, and have your way with data.

The GetObject API function illustrates several points about untyped parameters. The C version looks like this:

```
int GetObject(
    HGDIOBJ hgdiobj,    // Handle of graphics object
    int cbBuffer,       // Size of buffer for object information
    LPVOID lpvObject    // Pointer to buffer for object information
);
```

To use GetObject, you pass it the handle of a logical pen, a brush, a font, a bitmap, or a palette. You pass the length of the data you want to get back and the address of the variable where you want the data placed. This variable will have type LOGPEN, LOGBRUSH, LOGFONT, BITMAP, or int, depending on the data. Windows will use the handle to find the data and will then copy it to the variable.

The Basic prototype presents several problems. First, GetObject is the name of a Visual Basic function. In old versions of Visual Basic, you got an error if you tried to declare a function with an existing function name, but the current version (and version 4) offers no objections if you redefine GetObject with either a Declare statement or a Basic function. Nevertheless, don't do it. You should rename this function. I call mine VBGetObject.

NOTE You can redefine a function to replace the built-in version with a new version. For example, you could write your own version of InStr. Any code you wrote earlier that uses the built-in InStr will work with your new version. This is how you use the renaming feature. You abuse it by giving your function the same name as the built-in version but different behavior. See the sidebar "Better Basic Through Subclassing," page 240, for a more complete discussion of this feature.

You'll encounter the name problem in several cases in the Windows API, and it's likely to come up anytime you try to use a DLL written for another language. For example, the Windows API includes the _lopen, _lread, _lwrite, and _lclose functions, but you can't write declarations for them because a Basic name can't start with an underscore. (My type library calls them lopen, lread, lwrite, and lclose.) Basic provides the Alias attribute to let you specify that a name recognized in one way by the DLL can have a different Basic name.

The second problem is to turn off Basic's type checking. In other words, you need a type that corresponds to a C void pointer. The Any type passed by reference is a rough equivalent. When you declare a parameter with As Any, you cancel the contract. Basic no longer promises the Windows API anything in particular. Windows promises to write no more than the specified number of bytes to the specified variable, whether they fit or not. It's up to you to pass a variable that can accept the data. If you're the kind of programmer who doesn't mind working without a net, you might be getting bright ideas about using As Any in your own Basic procedures. Forget it. Basic accepts As Any only in Declare statements. Use Variant, not As Any, to write typeless functions in Basic.

The declaration for VBGetObject looks like this:

```
Declare Function VBGetObject Lib "GDI32" Alias "GetObjectA" ( _
    ByVal hObject As Long, ByVal cbBuffer As Long, _
    lpvObject As Any) As Long
```

Notice that the real name of the function is GetObjectA, not GetObject. I'll explain why in the next section.

The Basic version of C's BITMAP type looks like this:

```
Type BITMAP
    bmType As Long
    bmWidth As Long
    bmHeight As Long
    bmWidthBytes As Long
    bmPlanes As Integer
    bmBitsPixel As Integer
    bmBits As Long
End Type
```

You can pass a BITMAP variable to VBGetObject:

```
Dim bmp As BITMAP
⋮
c = VBGetObject(pbBitmap.Picture, Len(bmp), bmp)
```

That's easy enough if you happen to know that the Picture property of a picture box containing a bitmap is actually a bitmap handle. (Chapter 6 explains this and related issues.) But you'd better be sure that whatever gets passed to the function is what you say it is. If you pass a bitmap handle in parameter 1, the length of a LOGPEN in parameter 2, and a LOGBRUSH variable in parameter 3, you won't like the results.

If you ignore the safety net that Basic offers, you must be ready to accept the consequences. Or, better yet, use the safety net. You can alias as many functions as you want to the same API function, so why not do a type-safe version for each data type?

```
Declare Function GetObjectBrush Lib "GDI32" Alias "GetObjectA" ( _
    ByVal hBrush As Long, ByVal cbBuffer As Long, _
    lpBrush As LOGBRUSH) As Long
Declare Function GetObjectBitmap Lib "GDI32" Alias "GetObjectA" ( _
    ByVal hBitmap As Long, ByVal cbBuffer As Long, _
    lpBitmap As BITMAP) As Long
```

The Windows API type library provides these functions and several other GetObject variations, but don't let the increased safety make you overconfident. If you pass a LOGPEN variable to GetObjectBrush, you get the error *ByRef argument type mismatch*. But if you pass a Pen handle to GetObjectBrush, neither Basic nor Windows complains. Windows gets the data type and the data from the handle, but it can't tell whether you passed the matching length and destination variable.

Visual Basic 4 didn't support a type library equivalent to the As Any syntax, and it didn't support structures in type libraries. Therefore, VBGetObject had to be implemented with the Declare statement. Those limitations are gone. You'll find VBGetObject and all its aliases in the current Windows API type library.

Dealing with Strings

An integer is an integer is an integer in any language, but every language has its own ideas about strings. In Basic, a string is supposed to be a black box. You put data in through Basic statements; the system allocates, moves, and resizes the data without your knowledge or interference; you get data back in the expected format. In C, in contrast, you must understand exactly how strings are stored in memory to process them correctly and efficiently. Nothing is allocated, moved, or resized unless you do it.

This fundamental difference between C strings and Basic strings is probably the biggest problem you face in dealing with the Windows API. Essentially, you have to get un-Basic with strings—you have to know what Basic programmers aren't supposed to know.

Strings Inside Out

The C string format, known in API jargon as LPSTR, is a sequence of characters terminated by the null character (ASCII value 0), as shown in Figure 2-6 on the facing page. The LPWSTR format is the same except that it uses 16-bit Unicode characters. Notice that the length of the string isn't stored. C programmers must either keep track of the length themselves or call a function that calculates the length by looping through each character until it finds a terminating null.

Supposedly, the implementation of Basic strings isn't documented because it might change in a later version of Basic. In fact, the format of Basic strings is well known and changed little from QuickBasic to Visual Basic 3. These strings were at least partially documented in the VBX custom control documentation, where they went by the name HLSTR (high-level string). Figure 2-6 illustrates the format.

However, if you ignored Microsoft's advice and wrote C DLLs that took advantage of your knowledge of Basic strings, Visual Basic version 4 sent you officially up the creek, and version 5 leaves you there. Basic now uses the BSTR format, described in the COM Automation documentation. Figure 2-6 points out the difference. BSTRs are better than HLSTRs for two reasons. First, they have one less pointer. Second, they are already null terminated, so Basic doesn't have to null-terminate before passing them on to C.

LPSTR (What Windows 95 Requires and Windows NT Accepts)

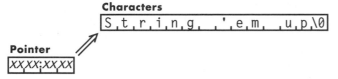

LPWSTR (What Windows NT Prefers)

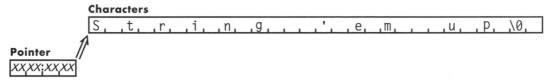

HLSTR (What Visual Basic 3 Had)

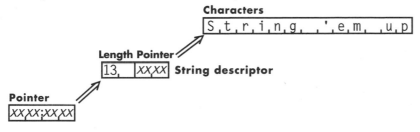

BSTR (What Visual Basic Has)

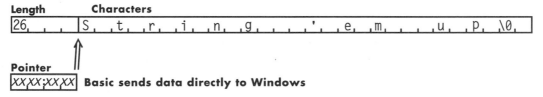

Figure 2-6. *Four kinds of strings.*

As a Basic programmer, you must make an unnatural distinction when passing strings to the Windows API: you have to separate input strings from output strings and handle each case in a completely different fashion. This takes some getting used to.

Sending Strings to the Windows API

Sending input strings to the Windows API is simple and direct. Your API calls look pretty much the same as calls to Basic procedures. The trick is in defining the declarations.

The designers of Visual Basic enabled Basic-to-C conversion by overloading the ByVal attribute to mean something other than what its name implies—that is, they lied. Passing a string by value doesn't actually pass it by value. Doing so would imply that all the bytes of the string are placed on the stack. Instead, Basic simply passes by value a pointer to the string. In Visual Basic 3, Basic also needed to ensure that the HLSTR was null terminated, which sometimes meant that the string had to be copied to a temporary string for processing by Windows and then copied back to the real Basic version afterward in case Windows modified the string copy. Those days are over because BSTRs are already null terminated. Now Basic makes a temporary copy for a completely different reason. But I'll get to Unicode conversion later.

In the Windows API documentation, C string parameters have the type LPCTSTR if the string is to be used only as input. (The C in the name indicates constant.) Parameters have the type LPTSTR if the string is to be used as an output buffer filled by the function. The T in the names indicates that the string could be either ANSI (LPCSTR or LPSTR) or Unicode (LPWCSTR or LPWSTR), depending on constants passed to the C compiler at compile time. I'll examine this issue in more detail later on.

For example, the FindWindow documentation looks like this:

```
HWND FindWindow(
    LPCTSTR lpszClassName,    // Address of class-name string
    LPCTSTR lpszWindow        // Address of window-name string
);
```

You can declare the function as follows:

```
Declare Function FindWindow Lib "USER32" Alias "FindWindowA" ( _
    ByVal lpszClassName As String, ByVal lpszWindow As String) As Long
```

First notice the alias to FindWindowA. It turns out that USER32.DLL contains two different FindWindow functions, neither of which is named FindWindow. FindWindowW handles 16-bit Unicode strings. FindWindowA handles the 8-bit ANSI character strings that most programmers are used to. For now, all you need to know is that every Win32 function that deals with strings requires similar aliases. You will probably want to use the ANSI version in most cases because it works for both Windows 95 and Windows NT, but you'll get slightly better performance in Windows NT–only programs if you use the Unicode version. If you use Declare statements, you have no choice: you must use the ANSI alias because the Declare statement is still crippled and unable to deal with Unicode directly. You have to use a type library (like the one supplied with this book) to use the Unicode versions.

Now assume that you want to call FindWindow to find the window handle of a running instance of the Calculator program. You could write the following code:

```
hWnd = FindWindow("SciCalc", "Calculator")
```

SciCalc is the class name of the Calculator window, and *Calculator* is the name shown in the window title bar. (Chapter 6 explains window classes and titles; for now, we're concerned only with the syntax.)

What's really going on here? The string *SciCalc* appears to be 7 characters long, but because it includes a terminating null character—Chr$(0)—the real length is 8 characters. Internally, the string also includes a preceding Long that contains the length of the string. Therefore, the string uses 12 bytes of memory, although the stored length is 7, which is what Basic would expect. Basic needs to know the length of the string at all times. The Basic Len function grabs the length out of the preceding length placeholder (using the SysStringLen function) without checking the characters. When you pass the string to the Windows API, however, the length is lost. Because it's written in C, Windows doesn't know or care how long a string is.

If you look at this exchange as a contract, Basic promises that when it passes a string with the ByVal attribute, the string will be null terminated and the address of the first character will be passed on the stack. The Windows API promises that if the string is constant (LPCTSTR), it will not modify the string or assume anything about the characters after the terminating null.

But this contract is less than bulletproof. Windows expects that the string will contain only one null character, the last. Basic makes no such promise. A passed string could have multiple null characters, which are perfectly legal in a Basic string. You as the programmer must ensure that the strings you pass don't have inappropriate embedded nulls. As a practical matter, however, this usually isn't a problem because few Basic programmers embed nulls in strings intended for Windows functions.

Passing Null Pointers

If C were a type-safe language like Basic, passing input strings to the Windows API would always be simple, but many Windows API functions accept a null pointer for string parameters. When you pass a normal string, you are actually passing a pointer to the characters of the string—in other words, the address of the first character. But the C language and the Windows API recognize one special pointer that represents no address. The value of this pointer is 0, but it doesn't represent address 0 even if that address is valid in the current environment. The null pointer is used as a signal to ignore a given parameter.

Passing a null pointer to a string procedure was a major hassle in previous versions of Visual Basic. A null pointer was a Long constant zero (0&), which you couldn't pass to a String parameter. You had to write special versions of Declare statements to accommodate parameters that might take null pointers, using one of the choices described earlier (see "Typeless Variables," page 69). You could either throw away type safety with As Any, or you could write multiple aliases to accommodate all the possible combinations of strings and null pointers. In today's modern Basic, those hacks are just a bad memory—like those throwaway pop-can tabs that used to litter highways before many readers of this book were born. Now you can simply pass the predefined constant *vbNullString* as a string argument.

The previous section assumed that you pass the FindWindow API function a window title and a window class, but in reality you can pass a string for one of these and pass a null pointer in the other to signal that you don't care about it. For example, assume that you know the title of the window but not the class. You might think that you could pass an empty string for the class:

```
hWnd = FindWindow("", "Calculator")
```

This searches for the window with title *Calculator* and class nothing—but you're unlikely to find a window without a class. To search by title only, you must pass a null pointer rather than an empty string. If you skipped from version 3 to version 5, you might try the following:

```
hWnd = FindWindow(0&, "Calculator")
```

Because Basic sees that FindWindow wants a string, it politely converts 0& to "0". You don't get an error (as you would have in Visual Basic version 3), but neither do you find the window unless you happen to have a window with class 0. ("Evil Type Conversion," page 280, discusses other side effects of Basic's new ability to convert integers to strings and vice versa.)

Here's the correct way to solve this problem in Basic:

```
hWnd = FindWindow(vbNullString, "Calculator")
hWnd = FindWindow("SciCalc", vbNullString)
hWnd = FindWindow("SciCalc", "Calculator")
```

This might seem obvious, but it looks like a miracle to old hands who remember the hacks of yesteryear.

Null and Empty

Don't let the various definitions of *null* and *empty* confuse you:

- The *null character* is ASCII character 0. You can represent this string as Chr$(0), but it's more efficient to use the constant *vbNullChar* or the VBCore version, *sNullChr*.

- The term *null string* is commonly used to describe what this book calls an *empty string,* that is, a string with no characters. You can represent this string with empty quotes (""), but it's more efficient to use the constant *sEmpty*. The Basic keyword Empty is a Variant constant representing an empty string for string Variants or 0 for numeric Variants. You can use it anywhere you use *sEmpty*, but it's significantly less efficient for string operations.

- A *null pointer* is a 32-bit integer with value 0 representing address 0. You will normally pass a null pointer to a string parameter with the constant *vbNullString* (or its equivalent in my type library, *sNullStr*). In a few Windows API situations, you might need to pass a null pointer to a numeric parameter. You can use the constant *pNull* for these cases. Incidentally, the *vbNullString* constant also works as an empty string, although you can't use *sEmpty* as a null pointer.

- Another null you'll run into frequently is a *null handle*. You can use the constant *hNull*.

- The Null keyword represents a Variant that contains no valid data. It is commonly used for databases and gives an error if used in a string context.

- The Nothing keyword also has nothing to do with strings, but I include it here for completeness. It represents an object variable that hasn't yet been set to an object. (See Chapter 3.)

The constants *sEmpty*, *pNull*, and *hNull* are not part of Basic, but they are provided as part of the Windows API type library. The constant *sNullChr* can't be defined in my type library because of a bug in the MIDL compiler, but for compatibility with the first edition, I provide it in UTILITY.BAS and the VBCore component.

Use constants whenever you can. If you use empty quotes ("") in your program 5000 times, you'll end up with 5000 empty strings, each taking up at least 5 bytes. If you use *sEmpty* 5000 times, you'll get one empty string.

Wrapping String Functions

Although passing vbNullString as a string argument is a vast improvement, it's still un-Basic. The Basic Way to signal that a string should be ignored is to use optional parameters. Before Visual Basic version 4, you couldn't define your own optional parameters, although you could fake them by using an empty string as a signal to ignore the argument. For example, you could write a wrapper function that worked as follows:

```
hWnd = VB3FindWindow("", "Calculator")
hWnd = VB3FindWindow("SciCalc", "")
hWnd = VB3FindWindow("SciCalc", "Calculator")
```

Visual Basic version 5 not only allows optional parameters but also lets you assign them by name. You can write a function that can be called as shown here:

```
hWnd = VBFindWindow(, "Calculator")
hWnd = VBFindWindow("SciCalc")
hWnd = VBFindWindow("SciCalc", "Calculator")
hWnd = VBFindWindow(Title:="Calculator")
hWnd = VBFindWindow(Class:="SciCalc")
```

The code for this function is simple:

```
Function VBFindWindow(Optional Class As String, _
                      Optional Title As String) As Long
    VBFindWindow = FindWindow(Class, Title)
End Function
```

This version uses the new typed optional argument syntax available in Visual Basic version 5. Version 4 supported optional arguments only for Variants. The syntax was more complicated and the performance worse because of Variant conversions. Normally, I would initialize the default arguments for clarity:

```
Optional Class As String = vbNullString
```

Unfortunately, Visual Basic won't let you do that for strings. It appears to work during debugging, but fails when you try to build a compatible ActiveX component. Fortunately, *vbNullString* is the default value for strings, so leaving it out does no harm except to readability. You could achieve the same effect by using optional arguments in a Declare statement:

```
Declare Function FindWindow Lib "USER32" Alias "FindWindowA" ( _
    Optional ByVal Class As String, _
    Optional ByVal Title As String) As Long
```

However, you can't write an equivalent type library entry, so VBFindWindow is the only way to provide a standard version so that you don't have to insert the Declare statement in every project.

I don't use my normal Hungarian naming convention for optional arguments. Since optional arguments can be omitted or given out-of-order by name, they are part of the public interface. It's rude to impose your private naming convention on parameter names or properties that might be used by other programmers who don't share your conventions.

Getting Strings from the Windows API

Now let's look at the other reason for passing strings—to get a string back from Windows. In Basic, if you want a procedure to return a string, you can simply make the procedure a function with a String return type. This doesn't work well in C and many other languages, for reasons I won't examine. Suffice it to say that you could never get two language designers to agree on a format for string returns.

The safe, portable way to get a string back from a procedure is to pass the address where the string is to be placed along with the maximum length of the string. Figure 2-7 on the following page shows an abbreviated version of how this works when using normal ANSI Declare statements. You might need to study "Unicode Versus Basic," page 83, to fully understand the Unicode part of the transaction.

Let's step through the parts in more detail. The C version of the GetWindowText function looks like this:

```
int GetWindowText(
    HWND hWnd,        // Handle of window
    LPTSTR lpString,  // Address of buffer for text
    int nMaxCount     // Maximum number of characters to copy
);
```

The Basic version looks like this:

```
Declare Function GetWindowText Lib "USER32" Alias "GetWindowTextA" ( _
    ByVal hWnd As Long, ByVal lpString As String, _
    ByVal nMaxCount As Long) As Long
```

The following fragment uses this function the long way. (We'll consider short-cuts later.)

```
Dim sTemp As String, sTitle As String, c As Integer
sTemp = String$(255, 0)
c = GetWindowText(hProject, sTemp, 256)
sTitle = Left$(sTemp, c)
```

Let's look carefully again at this call as a contract. Basic promises that it will null-terminate a string and pass its address (although null-terminating the string is wasted in this case because Windows doesn't care about nulls in output strings). Windows promises that it will not write more than the maximum character count

1. Empty string is null pointer (vbNullString).

```
Dim c As Long, s As String
```

2. Initialize string and variable.

```
c = 8
s = String$(c, "*")
```

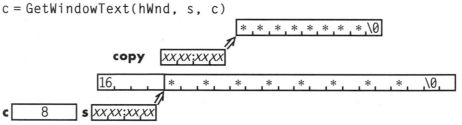

3. Basic passes ANSI copy to function GetWindowTextA.

```
c = GetWindowText(hWnd, s, c)
```

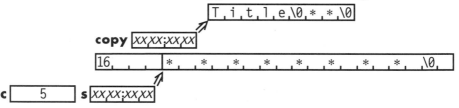

4. Windows writes to the ANSI copy and returns real length.

5. Basic converts ANSI copy to Unicode and throws away copy.

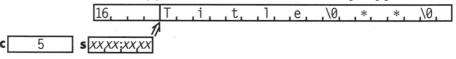

6. You must resize string.

```
s = Left$(s, c)
```

Figure 2-7. *Life as a string.*

passed to it into the address it receives, that it will append a null to whatever it writes (the null is included in the maximum number written), and that it will return the actual number of non-null characters written in the return value.

Neither side promises enough room in memory for the characters to be written. That part is up to you. If you pass a 10-byte string but claim that the size is 255, Windows might cheerfully write 245 bytes of data into whatever resides in memory next to your string. You will be in for a rude surprise, possibly much later in your program, when you try to use whatever used to be in that memory before Windows overwrote it.

The example ensures that the string is long enough by changing *sTemp* to a string of 255 null characters, using the String$ function. (You actually get 256 nulls because Basic always appends a null.) You can use the Space$ function to create a space-padded string in the same way. Another way to ensure that you never overwrite anything useful is to pass the actual length of the string as the maximum:

```
c = GetWindowText(hProject, sTemp, Len(sTemp) + 1)
```

If you do this when the actual length of *sTemp* is 0, you won't overwrite anything but you will get a truncated version of the window title that might give the mistaken impression that the window has no title when in fact you simply didn't allow space for the title.

Let's assume that you provide a 255-character string and that the title of the window is *Hello*. You get back from the function the 5 characters of the string, followed by a null, followed by 249 nulls. GetWindowText returns 5. When a C program sees this string, it assumes from the placement of the first null character that the string is 5 characters long. Basic doesn't care about embedded nulls and assumes that the string is 255 characters long. If you really want a Basic string of 5 characters, you must assign it. The return value gives you the information you need to do this politely with the Left$ function. Incidentally, you could use just one string for both the temporary and the permanent versions:

```
sTitle = String$(255, 0)
c = GetWindowText(hProject, sTitle, 256)
sTitle = Left$(sTitle, c)
```

You might expect that it would be more efficient to pass a fixed-length string than to use the String$ function to pad a string. Well, that might be true in some situations for stand-alone fixed-length strings. I don't know because I never use fixed-length strings anywhere other than in UDTs. The problem is that fixed-length strings are incompatible with many COM features. You can't use them in methods and properties of public classes. They make a lot more sense in UDTs where you want all your data, including strings, to be in a fixed-size chunk. The TimeIt program has a test that compares variable- and fixed-length strings for various operations. Results are mixed, and they might be different with different tests, but generally I found fixed-length strings to be inefficient for the most common operations.

You can avoid padding a string every time you need to pass one to Windows. Define the string at the module level, and pad it out only once—in Form_Initialize or Class_Initialize. Just make sure that this string is really temporary and large enough for any API call. Never change its size, don't use it for anything except API calls, and always copy the relevant portion to a permanent string immediately after use. That way, later calls won't overwrite useful data.

Wrap It Up

Face it. Passing empty string buffers with lengths is un-Basic; the Basic Way is to simply return the string. You can choose to put up with the C style of strings every time you call GetWindowText or a similar function, or you can deal with it once by wrapping the Windows API function in a Basic function. Here's how to do this for GetWindowText:

```
Function WindowTextFromWnd(ByVal hWnd As Long) As String
    Dim c As Integer, s As String
    c = GetWindowTextLength(hWnd)
    If c <= 0 Then Exit Function
    s = String$(c, 0)
    c = GetWindowText(hWnd, s, c + 1)
    WindowTextFromWnd = s
End Function
```

The trick in this type of function is to decide the length of the string to allocate. GetWindowTextLength and GetWindowText are the only function pair in the Windows API in which one returns the length expected by the other. Even in this case, it might be more efficient to assume that no window title will be larger than 255 bytes and to allocate that size without checking the actual size. The string will just be thrown away when the function returns, so no harm is done if you allocate too much space. Worst case is that someone will use a window title 300 bytes long and that you'll truncate it to 255. Serves them right.

The Windows API offers many variations on this theme. When the string is informational, the function usually truncates if you don't provide a large enough buffer. If the string is a filename, the function copies nothing but returns the actual size of the data (a truncated filename would be worse than no name at all). If you get back more than you put in, you need to allocate a bigger string and call again. Sometimes, the Windows API documentation clearly states the maximum size you need to pass in; other times, you can guess. For example, if a function returns a full file specification, you can safely pass the maximum Win32 path size—260 characters.

Unicode Versus Basic

Stringwise, we are cursed to live in interesting times. The world according to Microsoft (and many other international companies) is moving from ANSI to Unicode characters, but the transition isn't exactly a smooth one.

Most of the Unicode confusion comes from the fact that we are in the midst of a comprehensive change in the way characters are represented. The old way uses the ANSI character set for the first 256 bytes but reserves some characters as double byte character prefixes so that non-ANSI character sets can be represented. This is very efficient for the cultural imperialists who got there first with Latin characters, but it's inefficient for those who use larger character sets such as Chinese ideograms and Sumerian hieroglyphics. Unicode represents all characters in two bytes. This is inefficient for the cultural imperialists (although they still get the honor of claiming most of the first 128 characters with zero in the upper byte), but it's more efficient (and more fair) for the rest of the world. Instead of having 256 unique characters, you can have 65,535—enough to handle all the characters of almost all the world's languages.

Eventually, everybody will use Unicode, but different systems have chosen different ways of dealing with the transition.

- **Windows 3.x.** Doesn't know a Unicode from a dress code and never will.

- **16-bit COM.** Ditto.

- **Windows NT.** Was written from the ground up—first to do the right thing (Unicode) and second to be compatible (ANSI). All strings are Unicode internally, but Windows NT also completely supports ANSI by translating internal Unicode strings to ANSI strings at runtime. Obviously, Windows NT programs that use Unicode strings directly can be more efficient by avoiding frequent string translations, although just as obviously, Unicode strings take about twice as much data space.

- **Windows 95.** Is based largely on Windows 3.x code and therefore uses ANSI strings internally. Furthermore, it doesn't support Unicode strings even indirectly in most contexts—with one big exception.

- **32-bit Component Object Module.** Was written from the ground up to do the right thing (Unicode) and to hell with compatibility. COM doesn't do ANSI. The COM string types—OLESTR and BSTR—are Unicode all the way. Any 32-bit operating system that wants to do COM must have at least partial support for Unicode. Windows 95 has just enough Unicode support to make COM work.

- **Visual Basic.** The Basic designers had to make some tough decisions about how they would represent strings internally. They might have chosen ANSI because it's the common subset of Windows 95 and Windows NT, and converted to Unicode whenever they needed to deal with COM. But since Visual Basic version 5 is COM inside and out (as Chapters 3 and 10 will pound into your head), they chose Unicode as the internal format, despite potential incompatibilities with Windows 95. The Unicode choice caused many problems and inefficiencies both for the developers of Visual Basic and for Visual Basic developers—but the alternative would have been worse.

- **The Real World.** Most existing data files use ANSI. The WKS, DOC, BAS, TXT, and most other standard file formats use ANSI. If a system uses Unicode internally but needs to read from or write to common data formats, it must do Unicode to ANSI conversion. Someday there will be Unicode data file formats, but it might not happen in your lifetime.

What does this mean for you? Trouble.

What Is Unicode?

We've been skipping lightly over some of the implications of Unicode, but it's time to get our hands dirty.

If you think about Unicode, it seems like a whole lot of zeros going nowhere. All the text characters employed by those of us who use English fit in the first 128 Unicode bytes, meaning that half of each 16-bit Unicode character is 0. If you do a hex dump of a 32-bit Visual Basic program (English and most European versions), you'll see all those zeros lined up in neat little columns in the part of the file where string constants are stored. Every 0 must be filtered out when you send a string to an ANSI API function and then reinserted when you get the string back. But the Unicode conversion is more than just converting to and from zeros. Try the following code to find out which characters use more than 8 bits:

```
For i = 0 To 255
    Debug.Print Hex$(AscW(Chr$(i)))
Next
```

For those of you too lazy to try this, I'll tell you the result. Every character has zeros in the high byte except characters 145–156 and character 159. Weird, huh?

For the most part, you don't need to worry about Unicode conversion. Once you've set up your Declare statements (or loaded the Windows API type library), everything happens automatically. But just when you think you've got Unicode under control, something turns up that doesn't work quite the way you expected.

For example, Win32 supports both Unicode and ANSI versions of all functions, but 32-bit COM supports only Unicode. If you want to call 32-bit COM functions from Visual Basic, you'll have to pass Unicode strings (even in Windows 95, which doesn't support Unicode in any other context). Normally, you don't call COM functions, because Basic does it for you, but I'll show you some exceptions in the next section.

When Basic sees that you want to pass a string to an outside function, it conveniently squishes the internal Unicode strings into ANSI strings. But if the function expects Unicode, you must find a way to make Basic leave your 16-bit characters alone. The new Byte type was added specifically for those cases in which you don't want the languages messing with data behind your back. I'll show you more examples of this in "Reading and Writing Blobs," page 277. For now, let's look at some Unicode basics that will set the stage for calling Unicode API functions.

Basic allows you to assign strings to byte arrays and byte arrays to strings:

```
Dim ab() As Byte, s As String
s = "ABCD"
ab = s
s = ab
```

What would you expect these statements to do? If you guessed that the first byte of *ab* will contain the ASCII code for "A", the second the code for "B", and so on, you guessed wrong. Check it out in the Locals window. The *ab* array contains 65, 0, 66, 0, 67, 0, 68, and 0. Although Visual Basic will now show the contents of a Byte array (unlike version 4), I find it easier to compare Strings and Byte arrays by calling my HexDump functions (in UTILITY.BAS). HexDump works on Byte arrays, and HexDumpS works on strings. HexDumpB, too, works on strings, but it dumps them as bytes rather than as characters. Here's what you get if you dump the variables shown earlier in the Immediate window:

```
? HexDump(ab)
41 00 42 00 43 00 44 00    A.B.C.D.
? HexDumpB(s)
41 00 42 00 43 00 44 00    A.B.C.D.
? HexDumpS(s)
41 42 43 44                ABCD
```

But what if you want to put the 8-bit ANSI characters of a string into a byte array without the zeros? Basic lets you force Unicode conversion by using the StrConv function:

```
ab = StrConv(s, vbFromUnicode)
```

A hex dump shows the bytes without zeros:

```
? HexDump(ab)
41 42 43 44                 ABCD
```

Now let's assign the byte array back to the string:

```
s = ab
```

If you look at *s* in the Immediate window at this point, you might be surprised to see the string "??". What is this? Well, what you have in the first 16-bit character is "AB" (&H4241). The Unicode character &H4241 represents the *sacatai* hieroglyphic in the Basic dialect of northeastern Cathistan. In the second character, you have another, the *boganit* hieroglyphic. Visual Basic doesn't know anything about *sacatai* or *boganit* or any other Unicode characters above 255, so it just displays them as question marks.

To convert the byte array back to a recognizable string, undo the previous StrConv function:

```
s = StrConv(ab, vbUnicode)
```

The string now looks "right" in the debugger and "wrong" in the byte hex dump.

Unicode API Functions

I've been assuming that you want to use only the ANSI versions of API functions, but if all your customers are running Windows NT, you can increase the efficiency of your programs by using Unicode functions. There are several ways to do this. One hard way is to fake Unicode strings by using byte arrays in Declare statements. The other hard way is to use a real pointer to the internal Unicode data. The easy way is to use a type library. Try the hard ways first so that you'll appreciate the easy way.

There's another reason to use Unicode functions. All COM API functions are Unicode by definition. You must define these as Unicode even if you're dealing with Windows 95. Let's take an example. REGTLB is a command-line program that can register type libraries. It calls the LoadTypeLib and RegisterTypeLib functions, which are COM functions in OLEAUT32.DLL. Both these functions are defined as Unicode functions in the Windows API type library. You can simply call them from Visual Basic and they'll do the right thing. Of course, one of the type libraries you might want to register is WIN.TLB. Catch 22: you can't register a type library using functions that are defined in that type library.

So let's take a look at two ways of defining LoadTypeLib (RegisterTypeLib is similar). After cleanup of extraneous macros, the C definitions of LoadTypeLib and RegisterTypeLib look like this:

```
HRESULT LoadTypeLib(LPCWSTR szFile, ITypeLib ** pptlib);
HRESULT RegisterTypeLib(ITypeLib * ptlib, LPWSTR szFullPath, _
                    LPWSTR szHelpDir);
```

An HRESULT is a COM error type that is closely related to Visual Basic's Err object. Any function that returns an HRESULT will recognize Basic-style error traps with On Error. In other words, to Visual Basic, HRESULT isn't really a return value and LoadTypeLib and RegisterTypeLib aren't really functions. It's as if they were defined like this:

```
Sub LoadTypeLib(szFile As String, pptlib As ITypeLib)
Sub RegisterTypeLib(ByVal ptlib As ITypeLib, szFullPath As String, _
                    szHelpDir As String)
```

ITypeLib is a standard COM type. I'll use Object instead. You get late binding instead of early binding, but that's OK in this example. More on that later.

If you define these functions with Declare statements, you have to fake two things. First, you can't define the HRESULT type. Bitwise, an HRESULT is a Long, and you'll have to receive it as a Long and handle errors yourself rather than letting Basic do it for you. Second, you'll have to come up with some way to pass Unicode strings. Here are two versions of the Declare statements:

```
#If ordUnicode = ordRawBytes Then
' Receive string arguments as Byte arrays
Private Declare Function LoadTypeLib Lib "oleaut32.dll" ( _
    pFileName As Byte, pptlib As Object) As Long
Private Declare Function RegisterTypeLib Lib "oleaut32.dll" ( _
    ByVal ptlib As Object, szFullPath As Byte, _
    szHelpFile As Byte) As Long
#ElseIf ordUnicode = ordStrPtr Then
' Receive string arguments as pointers
Private Declare Function LoadTypeLib Lib "oleaut32.dll" ( _
    ByVal pFileName As Long, pptlib As Object) As Long
Private Declare Function RegisterTypeLib Lib "oleaut32.dll" ( _
    ByVal ptlib As Object, ByVal szFullPath As Long, _
    ByVal szHelpFile As Long) As Long
#ElseIf ordUnicode = ordTypeLib Then
    ' No Declare needed!
#End If
```

Page 88 has some conditional code that uses the Declare or the type library entry depending on how you set the constant *ordUnicode*.

```
Function RegTypelib(sLib As String) As Long
#If ordUnicode = ordRawBytes Then
    Dim suLib() As Byte, errOK As Long, tlb As Object
    ' Basic automatically translates strings to Unicode Byte arrays
    ' but doesn't null-terminate, so you must do it yourself
    suLib = sLib & vbNullChar
    ' Pass first byte of array
    errOK = LoadTypeLib(suLib(0), tlb)
    If errOK = 0 Then errOK = RegisterTypeLib(tlb, suLib(0), 0)
    RegTypelib = errOK
#ElseIf ordUnicode = ordStrPtr Then
    Dim errOK As Long, tlb As Object
    ' Pass pointer to real (Unicode) string
    errOK = LoadTypeLib(StrPtr(sLib), tlb)
    If errOK = 0 Then errOK = RegisterTypeLib(tlb, StrPtr(sLib), 0)
    RegTypelib = errOK
#ElseIf ordUnicode = ordTypeLib Then
    Dim tlb As ITypeLib
    On Error GoTo FailRegTypeLib
    ' Real HRESULT and real Unicode strings from type library
    LoadTypeLib sLib, tlb
    RegisterTypeLib tlb, sLib, sNullStr
    Exit Function
FailRegTypeLib:
    MsgBox Err & ": " & Err.Description
    RegTypelib = Err
#End If
End Function
```

Notice that in the first two versions you have to treat the procedures as functions
and handle the return value. The version that uses the type library is processed
like a sub. You use error trapping to deal with the hidden HRESULT. The StrPtr
function used in the second version gets a pointer to the real Unicode string and
passes the pointer directly. I'll have more to say about StrPtr in the next section.

Dealing with Pointers

Some Windows API functions return pointers. Sometimes the pointer comes back
in the return value, sometimes in a reference argument. And sometimes it comes
back in a field of a UDT. Regardless of how you get it, you can do only one
thing with a pointer: pass it on. In Basic, you should treat pointers the same way
you treat handles. A handle is a sacred object passed to you for safekeeping,
and modifying it will incur the wrath of the gods. As far as Basic is concerned,
pointers should be treated with the same reverence.

You'll see pointers in the Windows API documentation as either a type followed by * (often void *) or a defined type starting with LP (such as LPVOID). The LP in LPVOID stands for long pointer, which is what everyone except the designers of Windows called a far pointer. Nowadays a pointer is a pointer—no near or far or huge about it. In C, when you declare a pointer, you must specify what it points to. You can't do that in Basic. In fact, you have to lie to force Basic to accept pointers at all. You claim that the pointer is a Long. Once you get the pointer, you never do anything with it except pass it to another Windows API.

Bring Your Hatchet

Dealing with pointers in Basic is kind of like getting in a hatchet fight without a hatchet. If you're going to hack into places where you're not supposed to go, you'd better arm yourself appropriately. The weapons of the well-equipped Basic pointer hacker are these: CopyMemory, VarPtr, StrPtr, and ObjPtr.

Of these, CopyMemory is the weapon of choice when you want to chop through Basic type limitations. The sidebar on the following page tells the bizarre history of CopyMemory, which isn't really named CopyMemory. Here, we're more interested in what it can do. For example, if you've ever tried manipulating bit fields in Visual Basic, you know that Basic's lack of unsigned types and strong typing can make simple operations difficult. Here's how you have to write a simple function that extracts the low Integer of a Long:

```
Function LoWord(ByVal dw As Long) As Integer
    If dw And &H8000& Then
        LoWord = dw Or &HFFFF0000
    Else
        LoWord = dw And &HFFFF&
    End If
End Function
```

It's not particularly readable, but as we'll see in Chapter 5, it is efficient. We can make this code simpler with CopyMemory. Ignore Basic's picky requirements and simply blast the bits you want to wherever you want them:

```
Function LoWord(ByVal dw As Long) As Integer
    CopyMemory LoWord, dw, 2
End Function
```

To see exactly how this works, let's pretend for a moment that CopyMemory is written in a dialect of Basic that doesn't yet exist. It looks something like this:

```
Sub CopyMemory(anyDestination As Any, anySource As Any, _
            ByVal c As Long)
```

Of course there's not really an Any type in Basic, and most of the time you wouldn't want a feature so dangerous—although it's nice to have it as an out in API functions. The first parameter of CopyMemory is a ByRef parameter (the address) of a variable of any type that you'll write some bytes to. The second parameter is the ByRef variable you'll copy from. The third parameter is the number of bytes to copy. If your finger slips and you type 20 instead of 2 in your CopyMemory call, nobody will complain until crash time.

What good is a LoWord function without a HiWord function? But this one gets a little more complicated.

CopyMemory: A Strange and Terrible Saga

Here's the long, strange story of how the Win32 function for copying raw memory came to be called CopyMemory, even though there's no such function in Visual Basic or in the Windows API.

It started when I first began searching for the Win32 equivalent of the Win16 hmemcpy function for use in Visual Basic version 4. No such thing—not even a note that the function might be obsolete. But...

The closest I could come up with was the CopyMemory function, which has exactly the same arguments and is documented the same as the old hmemcpy. Unfortunately, despite what you might read in Win32 documentation, there is no such thing as CopyMemory. You can search all the 32-bit DLLs with the DumpBin utility, but you won't find any DLL containing CopyMemory. But...

If you search carefully through the Win32 C include files, you'll turn up the following in WINBASE.H:

```
#define CopyMemory RtlCopyMemory
#define MoveMemory RtlMoveMemory
#define ZeroMemory RtlZeroMemory
```

This C equivalent of an alias indicates that CopyMemory is another name for a function called RtlCopyMemory. Don't ask why; just check for RtlCopyMemory in KERNEL32.DLL. Again, nothing. More sleuthing in the Win32 include files reveals the reason. WINNT.H contains something like this:

```
#define RtlCopyMemory(dst, src, len) memcpy(dst, src, len)
```

In other words, RtlCopyMemory is an alias for the C memcpy function, but you can't use memcpy or any other C library function from Basic. The documenta-

```
Function HiWord(ByVal dw As Long) As Integer
    CopyMemory HiWord, ByVal VarPtr(dw) + 2, 2
End Function
```

The destination and the size part work the same as in LoWord, but the source must be the upper two bytes of a Long, and there's no way to specify part of a variable by reference. You have to calculate the address of that variable just like you would in assembly language. First you get the start of the variable with VarPtr, then you skip over two bytes to the middle of the variable, and finally you override CopyMemory's normal ByRef parameter passing with ByVal.

tion is simply lying when it claims that CopyMemory is a Windows function rather than a C function. If it's not exported from a DLL, you can't call it. But... KERNEL32.DLL does contain an entry for RtlMoveMemory. If you check the Win32 documentation, you'll see that MoveMemory does the same thing as CopyMemory except that it handles overlapped memory in a different fashion. I can't imagine a situation in which a Basic programmer would be copying overlapped memory. No reason not to use MoveMemory instead. The name CopyMemory seemed more intelligible than hmemcpy or MoveMemory, so I used this alias for both 16-bit and 32-bit versions:

```
#If Win32 Then
Declare Sub CopyMemory Lib "KERNEL32" Alias "RtlMoveMemory" ( _
    lpvDest As Any, lpvSource As Any, ByVal cbCopy As Long)
#Else
Declare Sub CopyMemory Lib "KERNEL" Alias "hmemcpy" ( _
    lpvDest As Any, lpvSource As Any, ByVal cbCopy As Long)
#End If
```

The Windows API type library has an equivalent (or almost equivalent) CopyMemory function.

That explains why I used CopyMemory, but why does everybody else use it? Because I sent a copy of my sidebar to an internal alias at Microsoft, and someone who read it decided it would make a good Knowledge Base article. I agreed to let them use it if they mentioned it was an excerpt from my book. Good advertising, I thought. Ever since then I've read articles and heard speakers at the VBITS conference talking about CopyMemory as if it really existed. And none of them mention my book as the source. So don't be fooled by false advertising. If they talk about RtlMoveMemory, they figured it out on their own. If they talk about CopyMemory, they got it (perhaps without knowing) from me.

If you remember VarPtr, you're a real Basic old-timer. VarPtr was a function in QuickBasic, Basic Professional Development System, Macintosh Basic, GW-BASIC, and BASICA. You pass VarPtr a variable; it returns a pointer to that variable. Street Basic squared. Obviously, Visual Basic can have no trace of this abomination. Or can it? In previous versions of Visual Basic, VarPtr was a secret known only to the most hardcore of programmers (including readers of the first edition of this book). You had to figure out its secret DLL location and write a Declare statement for it. Well, now VarPtr has come halfway out of the closet. It's part of Visual Basic, and you don't need a Declare statement to use it. But you won't find any official documentation on it. If you call product support to complain about bugs in code that uses it, I expect that they will deny all knowledge.

They'll probably also deny knowledge of VarPtr's cousins, StrPtr and ObjPtr. VarPtr doesn't work on Strings because the pointer you would get back would be the pointer to the ANSI buffer that Visual Basic creates when calling API functions. StrPtr returns a pointer to the real Unicode string value. ObjPtr returns a pointer to an object. It makes me dizzy to even think about what hardcore programmers might think of to do with object pointers. I won't talk about them in this chapter.

Fixed-Length Strings in UDTs

A few Windows functions use structures (UDTs to Basic programmers) containing strings. This creates a problem because a Basic string in a Basic UDT differs somewhat from a C string in a C structure. I once made the foolish mistake of asserting on a Microsoft e-mail alias where Visual Basic is discussed that Basic programmers cannot use Windows structures containing strings. Take my word for it: don't try to tell hardcore programmers what they can and cannot do. This was back in the old days when dealing with strings in the HLSTR format was more difficult, but even then the real hackers found a way.

In C, as in Basic, a structure can contain two types of strings. In Basic, the first type is called a fixed-length string; in C, it is called an array of characters. The WIN32_FIND_DATA type (used with FindFirstFile and friends) illustrates. It looks like this in C:

```
typedef struct _WIN32_FIND_DATA {
    DWORD    dwFileAttributes;
    FILETIME ftCreationTime;
    FILETIME ftLastAccessTime;
    FILETIME ftLastWriteTime;
    DWORD    nFileSizeHigh;
    DWORD    nFileSizeLow;
    DWORD    dwReserved0;
    DWORD    dwReserved1;
    TCHAR    cFileName[ MAX_PATH ]; // 260
    TCHAR    cAlternateFileName[ 14 ];
} WIN32_FIND_DATA;
```

In Basic, it looks like this:

```
Public Type WIN32_FIND_DATA
    dwFileAttributes As Long
    ftCreationTime As FILETIME
    ftLastAccessTime As FILETIME
    ftLastWriteTime As FILETIME
    nFileSizeHigh As Long
    nFileSizeLow As Long
    dwReserved0 As Long
    dwReserved1 As Long
    cFileName As String * 260
    cAlternateFileName As String * 14
End Type
```

No problem. The *cFileName* and *cAlternateFileName* fields work the same in both C and Basic. You can use them just the way you would expect:

```
Dim fnd As WIN32_FIND_DATA
hFind = FindFirstFile("*.*", fnd)
Debug.Print fnd.cFileName
```

Of course, some additional work goes on in the background. Basic fixed-length strings are stored as Unicode, but they must be converted to ANSI when passed to API functions.

Unfortunately, the type library version of the WIN32_FIND_DATA works a little bit differently. Language-independent type libraries don't know anything about Basic fixed-length strings. You have to define this structure to store the strings in byte arrays. You can check WINBASE.IDL on the companion CD to see how this is done in a type library. Here's what it would look like if you coded the same type in Basic:

```
Public Type WIN32_FIND_DATA
    dwFileAttributes As Long
⋮
#If Unicode Then
    cFileName(0 To 519) As Byte
    cAlternateFileName(0 To 27) As Byte
#Else
    cFileName(0 To 259) As Byte
    cAlternateFileName(0 To 13) As Byte
#End If
End Type
```

In reality, you couldn't use the Unicode version of such a type because you can't write Unicode Declare statements (except with the hacks described in "Unicode API Functions," page 86). But if you could (or if you used the type library version), using the data would look like this:

```
Dim fnd As WIN32_FIND_DATA
hFind = FindFirstFile("*.*", fnd)
If UnicodeTypeLib Then
    Debug.Print fnd.cFileName
Else
    Debug.Print StrConv(fnd.cFileName, vbUnicode)
End If
```

The UnicodeTypeLib constant is defined with a value of zero in the ANSI version of the Windows API type library (WIN.TLB). It's defined to nonzero in the Unicode version (WINU.TLB). Notice that the Unicode test is done at runtime. You could also define a Unicode constant in the IDE and test with #If rather than If. Although compile-time testing is faster, it wouldn't work with the VBCore component that we'll examine in Chapter 5. Having tests for the Unicode type library scattered throughout code would be ugly and difficult to maintain. Therefore, I hide the test in the BytesToStr wrapper function:

```
Function BytesToStr(ab() As Byte) As String
    If UnicodeTypeLib Then
        BytesToStr = ab
    Else
        BytesToStr = StrConv(ab, vbUnicode)
    End If
End Function
```

This lets me shorten the calling code:

```
hFind = FindFirstFile("*.*", fnd)
Debug.Print BytesToStr(fnd.cFileName)
```

The difference between fixed-length strings in type libraries and in Basic UDTs is annoying. Fortunately, Windows rarely uses fixed-length strings in structures. One solution is to write Declare statements and UDTs rather than the type library. Although easier and more familiar, this strategy works only for ANSI functions because Visual Basic doesn't directly support Unicode Declare statements. For most users, this probably won't be an issue, but in the long run I think Windows NT will be an important platform and Unicode will be the best way to target it. I use the type library solution consistently because it works for both kinds of strings.

Variable-Length Strings in UDTs

The other type of string is relatively rare in Windows API functions, although it shows up all the time in the common dialog functions in COMDLG32.DLL. It appears, for example, in the OPENFILENAME structure used by the GetOpenFileName function:

```
typedef struct tagOFN {
    DWORD       lStructSize;
    HWND        hwndOwner;
    HINSTANCE   hInstance;
    LPCTSTR     lpstrFilter;
    ⋮
} OPENFILENAME;
```

In this structure, *lpstrFilter* is not a string but a pointer to a string whose data is located somewhere else. What a coincidence. A Basic string in the BSTR format is also a pointer to a string located somewhere else. You code this type in Basic in the obvious way:

```
Private Type OPENFILENAME
    lStructSize As Long
    hwndOwner As Long
    hInstance As Long
    lpstrFilter As String
    ⋮
End Type
```

With your type defined this way, you can simply assign the string:

```
opendlg.lpstrFilter = sFilter
```

Although this might seem obvious to new Basic programmers, it would seem like a minor miracle to any Visual Basic programmer who happened to be trapped in a time capsule during the version 4 era. Refer back to Figure 2-6, page 73, to see why this technique would never have worked in version 3. The old HLSTR format was a pointer to a pointer to characters, but the new BSTR format is a direct pointer to characters. The only difference between an LPWSTR and a BSTR is that the BSTR has a prefix. In other words, the BSTR type is a superset of the LPWSTR type, and the common subset is the only thing Windows cares about.

Don't forget that a string used as an input buffer must be large enough to receive the data. Using strings in UDTs looks so simple and natural that it's easy to forget that you're dealing with an unforgiving API. Frequently, structures that have buffers to receive strings have an accompanying field containing the maximum length. Be sure to set the maximum-length field and pad your strings before assigning them to the string field. In some cases, the API will return the actual length through a field of the UDT, and you can use this to truncate the string with the Left$ function. If the length isn't returned, you can truncate after the first null with the StrZToStr function from UTILITY.BAS. If you need to assign a null pointer to a string field, use vbNullString or sNullStr.

Unfortunately, you can't define fields of type String in a type library. Common dialog structures such OPENFILENAME, CHOOSEFONT, and PRINTDLG must be implemented as Visual Basic UDTs. This means that the associated Declare statements must also be written in Visual Basic. And if you've gone that far, you might as well put the constants in the same file. The MCommonDialog module wraps the common dialog API functions in Basic-friendly procedures based on optional arguments. The dirty work of using API declarations is hidden so that once you figure out the wrappers, you never need the API functions and you don't miss not having them in a type library. "Common Dialog Extensions" in Chapter 9 discusses this code in detail.

Other Pointers in UDTs

Once in a while, you might need to load a pointer to something other than a string into a UDT field. For example, the CHOOSEFONT structure used by the ChooseFont function has a field for a pointer to a LOGFONT structure. This is an obscure problem, and the sample that illustrates it is obsolete, so I'll be brief here.

Notice that the ChooseFont function and the CHOOSEFONT structure have the same name except for case. That works for C, and apparently the designer of this Windows function didn't recognize that not all languages are case sensitive. You have to work around this by changing the name of the Basic UDT to TCHOOSEFONT. It looks like this:

```
Private Type TCHOOSEFONT
    lStructSize As Long         ' Filled with UDT size
    hwndOwner As Long           ' Caller's window handle
    hDC As Long                 ' Printer DC/IC or NULL
    lpLogFont As Long           ' Pointer to LOGFONT
    :
```

You need to fill the *lpLogFont* field with a LOGFONT pointer, but how? Assume that you have the following:

```
Dim cfnt As TCHOOSEFONT, lfnt As LOGFONT
```

Here's how to make the assignment:

```
cfnt.lpLogFont = VarPtr(lfnt)
```

See "Bring Your Hatchet," page 89, for more information on VarPtr.

One other problem. When you pass a UDT variable directly to an API function, Basic knows what you've done and will convert any fixed-length strings in the UDT to ANSI. But when you assign a pointer to a LOGFONT variable to the *lpLogFont* field of a TCHOOSEFONT variable, Basic has no idea what the pointer points to and it will do no conversion on the UDT field. Normally, LOGFONT could used fixed-length strings in a UDT, such as the following field to hold the font name:

```
lfFaceName As String * 32
```

But in this case you have to define *lfFaceName* as an array of bytes:

```
lfFaceName(0 To 31) As Byte
```

Of course, you'd have to do this anyway if you were using a type library. You must handle Unicode conversion yourself, using the BytesToStr and StrToBytes functions described in "Reading and Writing Blobs," page 277. You can check out the details in COMDLG.BAS.

Typeless Strings

Now that you understand Unicode and pointers, you have the knowledge to understand how to hack strings and string pointers with CopyMemory. This is a little bit tricky because the type library version of CopyMemory doesn't work exactly the same as the Declare version. At first I thought this was a bug or at least a limitation of type libraries. After studying the issue, I'm inclined to consider it a bug or at least a mistake in how the Declare statement handles As Any.

Let's assume that we define an aliased version of CopyMemory with the following Declare statement:

```
Declare Sub CopyMemoryD Lib "KERNEL32" Alias "RtlMoveMemory" ( _
    lpvDest As Any, lpvSource As Any, ByVal cbCopy As Long)
```

We'll further assume that the type library defines the same thing with its own peculiar syntax but calls its version CopyMemoryT. You can look in WINBASE.IDL on the companion CD if you're interested in the syntax.

```
sSrc = "This is text"
sDstD = "************"
sDstT = "************"
CopyMemoryD ByVal sDstD, ByVal sSrc, Len(sSrc)
CopyMemoryT ByVal sDstT, ByVal sSrc, Len(sSrc)
Debug.Print sDstD
Debug.Print sDstT
```

The output looks like this:

```
This is text
This i******
```

What happened here is that the Declare version, because it is written in Basic, noticed that the arguments being passed to it were Strings. It did the normal Unicode conversion, creating two temporary ANSI buffers. It copied the ANSI source to the ANSI destination, which was then converted back to Unicode. The type library version, because it is written in the language-independent IDL language, had no idea of the type being passed to it. Instead of creating ANSI buffers, it just copied the internal Unicode source to the Unicode destination. But the string length passed to it was the character count, not the byte count. Only half the characters got copied. The solution is to use LenB rather than Len so that you'll pass a byte count.

```
CopyMemoryT ByVal sDstT, ByVal sSrc, LenB(sSrc)
```

So far, so good. But one of the reasons to use a CopyMemory with As Any parameters is so that you can also pass pointers. Let's say some API function (GetEnvironmentStrings, to name one) returns a pointer as a Long. You might want to call CopyMemory like this:

```
CopyMemoryD ByVal sDstD, ByVal pSrc, Len(sDstD)
CopyMemoryT ByVal sDstT, ByVal pSrc, LenB(sDstT)
```

What's going to happen here depends on whether *pSrc* is a pointer to a Unicode string or an ANSI string. Let's assume that it's a pointer to ANSI characters that you got from an ANSI API function. In the Declare version, you'll copy from the ANSI pointer to the temporary ANSI buffer, and all will be fine when Visual Basic converts that temporary buffer back to Unicode. In the type library version, you'll copy from the ANSI pointer to the Unicode string. The result will be a string of question marks that you'll have to convert with StrConv.

If, on the other hand, *pSrc* points to a Unicode string (from a Unicode or COM API function or from StrPtr), the Declare version CopyMemoryD will copy both the characters and the zero bytes of the Unicode string into the temporary ANSI buffer, which will then be converted back to an unintelligible Basic string. The type library CopyMemoryT will copy from Unicode to Unicode with no conversion.

If that description leaves you scratching your head, don't worry about it. You can bypass all this trouble by using the CopyMemory aliases in the type library: Copy-MemoryStr, CopyMemoryToStr, and CopyMemoryStrToStr. Call them like this:

```
CopyMemory ByVal pDst, ByVal pSrc, cDst
CopyMemoryStr ByVal pDst, sSrc, cDst
CopyMemoryToStr sDst, ByVal pSrc, cDst
CopyMemoryStrToStr sDst, sSrc, cDst
```

These will do the right thing whether you're using WIN.TLB or WINU.TLB.

The Ultimate Hack: Procedure Pointers

The last edition of this book contained a sidebar entitled "No Pointers in Basic." I promised that the next version of Visual Basic would not support pointers. But here they are.

The AddressOf operator gives Basic programmers a feature they've long requested, but in a format so crude and fraught with danger that the inventor of Basic, the late John Kemeny, would be shocked. Although something is better than nothing, I can't say I approve of this un-Basic throwback to the bad old days of PEEK, POKE, SADDR, and VARPTR. I lobbied for high-level type-safe procedure variables usable in Basic—similar to the feature enjoyed by programmers in Pascal, C, and even the wretched FORTRAN.

But enough groaning and complaining. Let's make do with what they gave us. Procedure pointers will put your hacking skills to the ultimate test.

Limits of Procedure Pointers

First, let me make one thing clear. The new AddressOf operator affects only calls to Windows API functions and other DLL calls. It has nothing to do with solving the problems that procedure parameters solve in other languages. Those problems are solved by other hacks in Visual Basic, as described in "Sorting, Shuffling, and Searching," page 282. What AddressOf does do is eliminate the need for message tools such as Message Blaster and callback tools such as the Callback Server—both provided with the first edition of my book.

Message Blaster remains the easiest, most reliable method for softcore programmers to handle messages. The Callback Server still exists, and it will work fine in Visual Basic version 5. You don't have to change anything. I personally prefer to use AddressOf for most simple callback tasks because I don't like to add an extra component to my programs, but there are a few major caveats to keep in mind when using AddressOf:

- There is no type safety. You're dealing with pure, raw pointers, and you must live with the consequences.

- AddressOf doesn't work with objects. You can get the address of a procedure in a standard module, but you can't get the address of a method on an object. AddressOf is not hard to use, but very difficult to encapsulate, even though it's the kind of ugly, low-level stuff that you most want to encapsulate. Despite the difficulties, we'll encapsulate it in Chapter 6.

■ Callback procedures don't know Basic. In particular, they don't know about Basic strings. It takes a whole different level of hacking to deal with strings passed as parameters to callback procedures.

So. Before us we see a freshly chopped hole in the frozen lake. Let's take our clothes off and jump in.

Enumerating Stuff

The most common, and often easiest, functions that take callbacks are the enumeration functions. You can enumerate windows, fonts, resources, GDI objects, and all sorts of other stuff. The test program TestEnum (TENUM.VBP) shown in Figure 2-8 enumerates some Windows things. Let's start with the easiest things: windows.

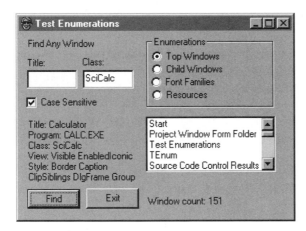

Figure 2-8. *Enumerating.*

The EnumWindows function will enumerate all the top-level windows and, for each window, do whatever you tell it to do. The C prototype looks like this:

```
BOOL EnumWindows(
    WNDENUMPROC lpEnumFunc,      // Pointer to callback function
    LPARAM lParam);              // Application-defined value
```

WNDENUMPROC is an unintelligible typedef that looks something like a spilled bucket of worms:

```
typedef BOOL (CALLBACK* WNDENUMPROC)(HWND, LPARAM);
```

To summarize, this is what C calls a function pointer type. It means that the EnumWindows function expects the address of a function that returns BOOL and has two parameters—an HWND and an LPARAM. The C compiler will not accept anything else—it will fail, for example, if it gets the address of a function that takes three arguments or returns a double type. When Windows receives a call to EnumWindows, it will iterate through its internal window list and call the given function pointer with the appropriate arguments for each window. It will accept a BOOL return that indicates whether to keep iterating. You define the function and pass its address.

Of course, under the surface, a pointer is a pointer. If you could get past C's type protection, you could pass EnumWindows the address of a function with ten arguments, or the address of an array of Variants, or the address of a String of graffiti. EnumWindows would pass control to whatever junk happened to be at the address you passed it, and after doing a few random things, it would crash. But of course a thing like that couldn't happen in Basic because Basic is a type-safe language. Or at least it used to be.

In this case, Visual Basic is a lot less type-safe than C or C++. The Declare for EnumWindows looks like this:

```
Public Declare Function EnumWindows Lib "USER32" ( _
    ByVal lpEnumFunc As Long, lParam As Any) As Long
```

Notice that all that wimpy nonsense about return values and parameter types is gone. The address of *lpEnumFunc* is a Long containing a pointer—just like in assembly language. The *lParam* is an LPARAM in C, which is just a typedef for Long, but that's OK because C allows us to typecast that Long to an address, a string, or whatever other data we want. The Basic equivalent is to use As Any by reference so that you can pass anything. The Windows API type library defines LPARAM as LPVOID—the type library equivalent of As Any (see "Type Variables," page 69).

Now all you need is a function to pass and a way to get its address. Here's the function:

```
Public lstEnumRef As ListBox

Function EnumWndProc(ByVal hWnd As Long, lParam As Long) As Long
    ' Increment count
    lParam = lParam + 1
    ' Get window title and insert into ListBox
    Dim s As String
    s = WindowTextFromWnd(hWnd)
    If s <> sEmpty Then
        lstEnumRef.AddItem s
```

(continued)

```
        lstEnumRef.ItemData(lstEnumRef.NewIndex) = hWnd
    End If
    ' Return True to keep enumerating
    EnumWndProc = True
End Function
```

And here's how you tell Windows to call the function:

```
f = EnumWindows(AddressOf EnumWndProc, c)
lblResult = "Window count: " & c
```

The *c* variable passed to EnumWindows is the *lParam* argument received by the EnumWndProc procedure. The variable is passed by reference so that the same variable (not a fresh copy) will be passed each time. In the example, it's a count of the number of times EnumWndProc is called, but you could pass any data that you want to be read or modified for each window.

The *hWnd* parameter of EnumWndProc is passed by Windows itself as it iterates through the available windows. EnumWndProc uses the *hWnd* parameter to get some text from the window and write that text to a ListBox. In this case, the data is written to a global ListBox reference variable, which was set to a real ListBox in Form_Load of the form that owns the ListBox. Finally EnumWndProc returns True. If you wanted to iterate through all the windows until you found one that met certain conditions, you could return False at the chosen window to stop the iteration. I'll do this in a few pages.

Crash Testing

There is no type safety when you call EnumWindows. You can pass anything you want in the first parameter as long as it's a Long. This sounds dangerous, but it's not quite as bad as you might expect. Let's try some of the more obvious mistakes you might make and see whether we can bring the system to its knees. Save your data before continuing.

First, let's try passing the address of a variable instead of a function:

```
f = EnumWindows(AddressOf c, c)
```

No way. Visual Basic gives a compiler error: *Expected Sub, Function, or Property.* You might think from its name that AddressOf would give you the address of anything, but actually it works only with procedures.

To continue our quest for a spectacular crash, we might try this:

```
f = EnumWindows(AddressOf Form_Load, c)
```

Form_Load doesn't have any arguments, so it's bound to crash. Nope. The compiler error is: *Invalid use of AddressOf operator.* This cryptic error message points out a problem I mentioned earlier. What it means is that you're using AddressOf with a procedure in a form or class module. Visual Basic won't let you do that. The EnumWndProc function must be located in a standard module (BAS file).

This unintuitive limitation has to with a big difference between standard modules and class modules that you ordinarily don't have to worry about. A method in a form or class has an address, doesn't it? Why can't you pass that address to EnumWindow? Because a procedure in a standard module is just a procedure, but a method is a procedure associated with a specific instance of an object variable. Visual Basic would have to jump through some hoops to find the object and then find the address of a particular method. It doesn't jump through those hoops, so you must jump through them instead. You must exchange global data between the form or class module where you're using the callback and the standard module where you had to put the callback function. This is why the test form has to Set a public copy of the ListBox object variable in the standard module.

Let's continue our quest for the perfect crash. I'll add an invalid function (one that doesn't pass two Longs as expected) to the standard module:

```
Function CrashMe() As Long
    CrashMe = 1
End Function
```

Try calling it like this:

```
f = EnumWindows(AddressOf CrashMe, c)
```

At this point, you'll get undefined behavior. On my test machine, it runs with no error or warning. Who knows what it will do on your machine. But what about this one?

```
Function CrashMe(hWnd As Long) As Long
    Debug.Print hWnd
    CrashMe = 1
End Function
```

Here you have one parameter when you're supposed to have two, and that one parameter is by reference when it's supposed to be by value. You'll get a good crash this time.

Here's another way to crash. Visual Basic won't let you use AddressOf to get the address of a variable, but it won't prevent you from getting one with VarPtr:

```
f = EnumWindows(VarPtr(c), c)
```

It's not difficult to make callbacks crash. I've done it not only on purpose in tests, but by accident in real programs. At least Visual Basic prevents some of the most obvious mistakes, but it will also prevent one thing (using a method) that doesn't seem like a mistake.

Putting Procedure Pointers in Variables

Sometimes you need to put the address of a callback procedure into a variable. No problem. You should be able to say this:

```
Dim procWindow As Long
procWindow = AddressOf EnumWndProc
```

That might seem obvious to you, but it isn't obvious to Visual Basic, which recognizes AddressOf only in procedure arguments. The code above just gives a syntax error. You have to jump through more hoops to get this one to work. First write the following function:

```
Function GetProc(proc As Long) As Long
    GetProc = proc
End Function
```

Then call it like this:

```
procWindow = GetProc(AddressOf EnumWndProc)
```

That's kind of a roundabout way to do it, but I suppose it's easier for thousands of users to write a one-line function and put it in UTILITY.BAS than for Visual Basic to make the AddressOf operator work in data assignments. You'll occasionally have to use the GetProc function in UDTs. For example, the MSGBOX-PARAMS UDT used by MessageBoxIndirect has a MSGBOXCALLBACK field called *lpfnMsgBoxCallback*. You can fill it like this:

```
Dim msgpars As MSGBOXPARAMS
msgpars.lpfnMsgBoxCallback = GetProc(AddressOf MyMsgBoxProc)
```

I had to search to find this example. It's not a problem you'll run into every day.

Strings in Callback Procedures

Enumeration of windows and fonts is a relatively simple matter, but enumeration of resources brings us to another level. I won't get to what resources are or what you can do with them until later. The important thing here is that the callback procedures for the resource functions take string arguments.

Here's what EnumResourceTypes looks like in C:

```
BOOL EnumResourceTypes(
    HMODULE hModule,              // Resource-module handle
    ENUMRESTYPEPROC lpEnumFunc,   // Pointer to callback function
    LONG lParam                   // Application-defined parameter
    );
```

The ENUMRESTYPEPROC parameter requires a procedure that looks like this:

```
BOOL CALLBACK EnumResTypeProc(
    HANDLE hModule,              // Resource-module handle
    LPTSTR lpszType,            // Pointer to resource type
    LONG lParam                 // Application-defined parameter
    );
```

The question is, how will you write an EnumResTypeProc that takes an LPTSTR parameter in Basic? Your first try might look something like this:

```
Function EnumResTypeProc(ByVal hModule As Long, _
                        ByVal lpszType As String, _
                        lParam As Long) As Long
```

That's how you would write the parameters if you were writing a Declare statement for a function to be called from Basic. You'd use a String type for *lpszType*, knowing that Basic would automatically translate to Unicode. But you're not writing a Declare statement; you're writing a function. And it won't be called by Basic; it will be called by Windows. And Windows hasn't a clue about the String type. The only way Windows is going to understand what to do is if you write the function like this:

```
Function EnumResTypeProc(ByVal hModule As Long, _
                        ByVal lpszType As Long, _
                        lParam As Long) As Long
```

Windows will pass you a pointer to the string, but then what will you do with it in Basic? By now you should have figured out what you can do when the API passes a pointer: pass it on. The hack to convert an API pointer requires several API calls, so I wrap it in a function called PointerToString:

```
Function PointerToString(p As Long) As String
    Dim c As Long
    c = lstrlenPtr(p)
    PointerToString = String$(c, 0)
    If UnicodeTypeLib Then
        CopyMemoryToStr PointerToString, ByVal p, c * 2
    Else
        CopyMemoryToStr PointerToString, ByVal p, c
    End If
End Function
```

This looks simple, but if measured in the hours it took me to figure it out, PointerToString would be a pretty long function. First you get the length of the string. The normal version of the lstrlen function takes a string argument, but in this case we have a pointer, not a string, so you must use the lstrlenPtr alias. Keep in mind that lstrlenPtr might actually be lstrlenA or lstrlenW, depending on whether the API type library you have loaded is WIN.TLB or WINU.TLB. In either case, it returns the internal string length so that you can create a Basic string to hold it.

The length is returned in characters, but CopyMemory expects bytes. The Unicode version (as indicated by the test of UnicodeTypeLib) must double the character count. The ANSI version will actually be working on a temporary ANSI copy of the string created for the Unicode conversion. "Dealing with Strings," page 72, describes what goes on behind the scenes in more detail. Given PointerToString, you can define the contents of the EnumResTypeProc:

```
Function EnumResTypeProc(ByVal hModule As Long, ByVal lpszType As Long, _
                          lParam As Long) As Long
    If lpszType < 65535 Then
        ' Enumerate resources by ID
        Call EnumResourceNamesID(hNull, lpszType, _
                                  AddressOf EnumResNameProc, lParam)
    Else
        ' Enumerate resources by string name
        Call EnumResourceNamesStr(hNull, PointerToString(lpszType), _
                                  AddressOf EnumResNameProc, lParam)
    End If
    EnumResTypeProc = True
End Function
```

Uh-oh. You can see how PointerToString is used to convert *lpszType* to a string, but the rest of the code raises more questions than it answers. What does it mean to pass a resource ID, and why would the value of the *lpszType* pointer be relevant? Those questions have more to do with resources than callbacks, so I'll defer them until later.

FindAnyWindow

Lest you think enumerating things has little practical use, I'm going to respond to a challenge I posed in the first edition of this book. I asked readers to send me a FindAnyWindow function that would allow me to use the same wildcard characters recognized by the Like operator. If I wanted to find the first window with the word *Fool* in the title, I could search like this:

```
hWnd = FindAnyWindow("*Fool*")
```

Of course, this function would also need to be able to search by class name (we'll see what a class name is in Chapter 6), and it should have an option to search case-insensitive.

```
Function FindAnyWindow(Optional Title As String = sNullStr, _
                       Optional Class As String = sNullStr, _
                       Optional CaseSense As Boolean = True) As Long

    ' Pass Title, Class, or both, but not neither
    BugAssert Title <> sEmpty Or Class <> sEmpty
    ' Store parameters in UDT
    Dim find As TFindAny, f As Long
    find.fCase = CaseSense
    find.sClass = IIf(find.fCase, Class, UCase(Class))
    find.sTitle = IIf(find.fCase, Title, UCase(Title))
    ' Ask FindHelper to check each window
    f = EnumChildWindows(GetDesktopWindow, AddressOf FindHelper, find)
    FindAnyWindow = find.hWndTarget

End Function
```

I'm still ticked off that no one answered my challenge in the first edition, so I'm going to make you look up the private FindHelper function yourself. It simply gets the class and title variables from the window handle (using techniques described in Chapter 6) and compares them, using the Like operator, to the stored parameters in the *find* UDT variable. Your challenge for this version is to write a FindAnyWindows function that stores all matching windows, not just the first one, in a collection.

There's a lot more to say about callback functions, and some of the most important things have to do with receiving window messages. I'll say some of those things later in "Sending and Receiving Messages" in Chapter 6.

3

An Object Way of Basic

On the Microsoft campus, you sometimes see employees sporting T-shirts that advertise a mythical product called Object Basic. Not every Microsoft product that reaches the T-shirt stage reaches the product stage, at least not under the same name; just ask a Microsoft old-timer about Cirrus or Opus or Cashmere. In a larger sense, however, Visual Basic has become Object Basic, regardless of the name the marketing department puts on the box.

Object Basic has been on the horizon for a long time, and it still has a way to go. But, starting in version 4, objects became more than an afterthought, and they continued their march toward objectness in version 5—although not at a fast enough pace to suit me. Form modules provide a way to create visual objects with properties and methods, and class modules provide a way to create your own nonvisual objects. Controls, forms, classes, the Data Access Object—all can be created with Dim, assigned with Set, manipulated with properties and methods, and grouped in collections.

Objects are more than a new feature; they're a way of thinking. Objects can help you make your code more modular, and you can make your objects available to any program that understands COM Automation. In other words, your objects can be used by programs written in Visual Basic, by programs written in most versions of C and C++, and by macros in many applications, including Microsoft Word, Microsoft Excel, and the Visual Basic environment itself.

This chapter (and the rest of the book) preaches the object religion. From here on out, we'll be talking about Object Basic not as a product but as an attitude, a state of mind. By the time you finish, you'll be telling your children to change their methods and properties or face Punishment events. You'll go into a restaurant and ask your waitperson to create a Hamburger object and set its Tomato and Onion properties to True but set its Mustard property to False. You'll write your representatives letters demanding fewer Tax events and more Service methods. For Each friend in your Friends collection, the friend will call the Wish method with the named argument *NeverSeenThisBook:=True*.

The Three Pillars

Visual Basic has its own style for doing object-oriented programming, just as it has its own style for doing most everything else. Let's look briefly at how Visual Basic both resembles and differs from other object-oriented languages.

Purists will no doubt argue that Visual Basic isn't an object-oriented language at all because it doesn't fully support the three pillars of object-oriented languages—encapsulation, reusability, and polymorphism. (Most books describe the second pillar as inheritance rather than reusability, but bear with me.) In the first edition of this book, I just eyeballed the language and said it supported one and a half out of three pillars of object-oriented programming. In retrospect, this was an extremely generous rating. If I rated version 4 according to the rigorous scientific test I'm about to apply to version 5, it would come out at about 1.2 (.6 for encapsulation, .2 for reusability, and .4 for polymorphism).

So here's a complete scoresheet supporting my current rating of 1.9 (with an error factor of .2) for Visual Basic version 5 as an object-oriented language.

WARNING One of the early reviewers of this manuscript accused me of arrogance for claiming the ability to scientifically rate a language with an error factor of .2. Well, for those with a sense of humor slightly different than mine, let me point out the bulge in the side of my face (tongue in cheek). The reviewer in question, whose opinions I value, used a method at least as scientific as mine to give Visual Basic an OOP rating of 2.95. I considered his rating ridiculous. He considered mine ridiculous. But you, dear reader, have the only scientific rating system that matters.

Encapsulation

Encapsulation means bringing data to life. Instead of you, the outsider, manipulating data by calling functions that act on it, you create objects that take on lives of their own, calling each other's methods, setting each other's properties, sending messages to each other, and generally interacting in ways that more closely model the way objects interact in real life. Early versions of Visual Basic allowed you to use objects that were created in other languages; version 4 allowed you to create your own objects, although there were significant holes in the encapsulation model.

Visual Basic version 5 has got most of encapsulation right on the second try. Big problems with public constants have been fixed by the Enum statement. You can now set a default property or method (although it's unnecessarily difficult), and you can create collections (but that's even harder). Property procedures give Visual Basic an edge over C++ and many other object-oriented languages in the way they allow you to access data with a natural syntax—and without exposing internal data to unauthorized changes.

Visual Basic still lags behind other object-oriented languages in the way it allows data sharing between classes and between instances of the same class. The new Friend modifier allows you to share data between classes, but the design is debatable. On the one hand, it allows you to specify exactly what you want to share with other classes (unlike some languages that say if you share any private part of a class you share all of it). On the other hand, the Friend modifier doesn't allow you to specify with whom you're sharing data within a project (unlike other languages that allow you to specify who your friends are).

Visual Basic provides no language feature for sharing data between instances of an object (static variables in C++), but you can fake it with public variables in what Visual Basic still quaintly calls "standard" modules ("irregular" modules would be a better term). This hack exposes your data not only to multiple instances of an object, but to any other module that wants to see it. When you create a public class or control, friend members and public variables in standard modules within the project become invisible to clients outside the component, so there is some protection. But it's a kind of accidental feature that isn't up to the carefully designed protection schemes of C++ or Java, which provide protection for all classes, not just those in components. The protection mechanism isn't the most important feature of a language, but I still have to deduct points for an inferior design.

The biggest problem in Visual Basic encapsulation is its inability to initialize an object in its declaration. Unless your object can be successfully initialized with default properties, it will be invalid from the time it is created until the time you initialize the key data properties. This isn't a big problem with controls, which have property pages as their initialization mechanism. It is a big problem for most other objects, which must be initialized through some convention defined by the class designer. Convention is not a reliable way to create rock-solid objects. Despite the seriousness of this limitation (which you'll hear a lot more about), I don't deduct much for it because lack of initialization syntax is a fault of the language, not just of classes. You can't initialize an Integer any more than you can initialize a CMyClass object. If I were going to rate Visual Basic as a general language, I'd list this as its most serious limitation.

Rating for encapsulation: .8

Reusability

This pillar of object-oriented programming is usually called inheritance, but inheritance is actually one of several techniques for achieving the broader goal of reusability. Reusability means being able to create a new class that uses the features of an existing class without recoding those features. There are actually several ways to achieve reusability in object-oriented programming.

Inheritance means reusing code in a hierarchical structure. For instance, a BasicProgrammer is a Programmer is a Worker is a Person is an Animal. All Animals have heads, and therefore the Head property of a BasicProgrammer should inherit all the general features of Animal heads plus all the features of Person heads plus all the features of Worker heads plus all the features of Programmer heads. When creating a Head property for a BasicProgrammer object, you should need to write only the head code unique to BasicProgrammers. There's a lot of debate in the object-oriented community about the value of deep levels of inheritance such as the one described above, but there's no doubt that inheritance can be a useful way to achieve reusability. And Visual Basic doesn't have it.

The way to get reusability in Visual Basic is through a process called *delegation* (also called *containment*). For example, you put an Animal object inside your Person class. You write code to expose the appropriate Animal methods and properties as Person methods and properties. Then you put a Person object in your Programmer class and expose its methods and properties, and so on.

Many object-oriented design books talk about two kinds of reuse relationships. In the *is-a* relationship, one class is an enhanced version of another class. A Person, for example, is an Animal with additional features. Normally, these relationships are defined with inheritance. In the *has-a* relationship, one class has features of another class. Normally, these relationships are defined with delegation. For example, an Animal class might delegate blood circulation to a Heart class and digestion to a Stomach class. Since Visual Basic doesn't support inheritance, it forces you to define both kinds of relationships with delegation. If you could achieve the same results with delegation, this would be a problem only for object-oriented design purists. Unfortunately, inheritance is automatic while delegation is usually manual (although nothing stops a language designer from making it automatic). When using inheritance to model *is-a* relationships, you have to write code for the new features only. When using delegation for *is-a* relationships, you delegate everything, even the methods and properties that don't change. This mechanical process ought to be automated, and in fact, Visual Basic does automate it, but it works only for controls, not for classes. Furthermore, automatic control delegation is not a language feature. It's a wizard program that writes the code it thinks you want. The pitfalls and limitations of wizards are a subject I won't get into here.

The Component Object Model (COM) supports a third reuse technique called *aggregation*. Aggregation means combining several inner objects so that they appear to be part of an outer object. This is a collective organization rather than a hierarchical organization. If you tried to combine a BasicProgrammer, a Programmer, a Person, and an Animal using this method, you'd end up with a lot of duplication and confusion. Clients would have to decide whether to use the Person.Head or the Programmer.Head, so instead you would use an organization that adds features rather than extends them. If you started with an Animal class, you might then add person features, such as Reasoning and Emotions. Later you add programmer features, such as Coding and Debugging. Finally you add Visual Basic programmer features, such as IterateWithForEach and HandleEvents. Although Visual Basic doesn't directly support this feature, you can get some of the advantages of it with the new Implements statement.

The bottom line: reuse is unnecessarily painful and inconvenient in Visual Basic—a language that is supposed to make things easy.

Rating for reusability: .4.

Polymorphism

Polymorphism means that any object will be able to do the right thing if you send it a message it understands. If I call the Hack method of a Programmer object, a Woodcutter object, and a Butcher object, each object should be able to Hack in its own special way without knowing who sent the message.

Visual Basic supports polymorphism in two ways. First, you can achieve polymorphism by using the Object type. Any Hack method works on an Object as long as the caller uses compatible arguments and return types. This dumb form of polymorphism was available in version 4 and remains in version 5, but you should avoid it because it is terribly slow and has no type protection. On the other hand, there are times when excessive type protection gets in the way and speed isn't critical. If you want your polymorphism dumb (that is, you don't know the type until run time), use Object.

Most of the time it's better to use interfaces through the new Implements statement to get fast, safe polymorphism. Visual Basic's syntax for Implements makes it work kind of like events. I find this syntax awkward and confusing, but perhaps it's a matter of taste. The mechanism would be more comfortable if you could typecast to interfaces to avoid creating extra object variables. But once you get used to it, Implements enables a lot of cool new techniques. Furthermore, Implements is almost a direct implementation of the powerful COM concept of interfaces. Unfortunately, some of the advantages of using COM interfaces get washed out because Visual Basic doesn't support the types used in most standard COM interfaces.

That's an important part of the polymorphism story, but only part. In most object-oriented languages, polymorphism goes hand-in-hand with inheritance. If Woodcutter and Butcher both inherit from Cutter, but Programmer inherits from Thinker, then Programmer.Hack will fail in contexts that expect Cutter.Hack. There are lots of techniques you can use in languages that have both inheritance and polymorphism that you can't do easily in Visual Basic. Java, for example, gives you the choice of polymorphism straight or with a side of inheritance, so I have to deduct for Visual Basic's one-track polymorphism.

Rating for polymorphism: .7

Object-Oriented Anyway

So Visual Basic comes out with a rating of 1.9 as an object-oriented language. I'd set a higher cutoff level for what can be considered a "real" object-oriented language—maybe about 2.5. Languages like C++, Delphi, Java, and SmallTalk rate above that line, although they, too, have their faults. But object-orientation isn't the only basis for rating a language. Visual Basic has many advantages those other languages lack.

Regardless of limitations, you can certainly write object-oriented programs with Visual Basic. In fact, all my programs are object-oriented. I try not to use "irregular" modules any more than necessary, although avoiding them turns out to be harder than you might expect or hope it to be. Let's take a closer look at some of the things that make object-oriented programming object-oriented.

Object-Oriented Programming, Visual Basic Style

You don't have to know exactly what an object is in order to use one, but it helps. The following section might look like an academic essay about types, and at some point you might be tempted to skip to the part where we start playing with objects. And perhaps that will be OK for those of you who started object-oriented programming with Visual Basic. Perhaps the Basic Way of objects seems natural to you and you don't need my feature-by-feature comparison with UDTs and intrinsic types. It might be easier to just start out thinking of objects as being completely different from the other types and leave it at that.

But I started my object-oriented career with C++. When the light finally dawned and I understood how Visual Basic objects worked, it seemed like a revelation worth sharing. Unfortunately, some of those revelations came after I wrote the first edition of this book and I'm afraid I passed on some misinformation. I hope you'll at least attempt to wade through this, not only so I can atone for past sins, but also so you can avoid some of my mistakes.

Types

A type is a template that describes the kind of data that variables of that type can contain and how variables of that type should behave. Visual Basic supports three kinds: intrinsic types, user-defined types, and classes. Types can be used to define variables and objects that hold data. Types also define the operations that variables or objects can perform. Before we look at how the three kinds of types manage this, let's define some terms for this discussion. These aren't necessarily standard terms, but they help me describe my mental model of how types work.

- *Type* is the specification of the data.

■ *Instance* is a particular location of memory containing data that meets the type specification.

■ *Variable* is the name of the memory location where an instance is stored.

Now let's look at how these terms apply to different types.

Intrinsic types

Of course, you already understand intrinsic types such as Long, Double, and String. They contain data of the size specified by the type, and they contain built-in methods. Methods? On intrinsic types? Yes, they're called operators. You probably don't think of operators as methods—unless you've programmed in C++ or some other language that lets you redefine operators. But think about it for a minute. An operator is just a symbol that defines some standard operation for a type. Consider this statement:

```
iSum = iPart + 6
```

It's as if the Integer type had a Plus method:

```
iSum = iPart.Plus(6)
```

In fact, in C++, an operator can use a function syntax:

```
iSum = iPart.operator+(6)
```

Operators are even polymorphic. The String, Integer, and Double types all have + operators that look the same and work in a way that intuitively looks the same, although what happens on the chip is very different for each type.

Operations on Integer and other intrinsic types are predefined. The only way to add new operations is to write procedures that have parameters of the given type. This is called functional programming, and it looks like this:

```
Sub SquareInteger(i As Integer)
    i = i * i
End Sub
```

The point I want to make about intrinsic types is that the variable contains the instance data. After the expression *i = 6*, the variable *i* refers to an instance containing 6. Technically, you can make a distinction between the variable *i* and the instance containing 6 that *i* names. But nobody except me even uses the term instance when talking about intrinsic types, and I wouldn't either if I weren't leading up to an explanation of classes.

User-defined types

User-defined types are aggregates of other types. Here's a type:

```
Type TChunk
    Title As String
    Count As Integer
End Type
```

And here's a variable that uses it:

```
Dim chunk As TChunk
chunk.Title = "Thick and Chunky"
chunk.Count = 6
```

As with the Integer variable, the UDT variable contains the instance. The name *chunk* refers to an instance containing the String *Thick and Chunky* and the Integer *6*. (The string characters aren't really an instance, but don't confuse me with facts.) Unlike intrinsic types, UDTs have only two standard operations: assignment and member access.

Assignment works only on UDTs of the same type:

```
anotherchunk = chunk
```

Member access lets you do additional operations on the fields of a UDT variable:

```
c = chunk.Count
```

The other operations allowed on the fields are those supported by the field type. For example, Integer type supports assignment, so *chunk.Count* supports assignment. You can't give a TChunk any additional operators or methods any more than you can give an Integer more operations. The only way to operate on a UDT is the functional way:

```
Sub SquareTChunk(chunk As TChunk)
    chunk.Count = chunk.Count * chunk.Count
End Sub
```

I'm stating the obvious limitations of types here so that I can contrast them to the real subject of this section—classes.

Classes—types that act

On the surface, a class has some things in common with other types. Often you can use a class type with a syntax similar to that of user-defined types, but don't let these similarities lull you into ignoring fundamental differences.

Like a UDT, a class aggregates data members, but the syntax is very different. It might be handy to define certain classes in the same way that you define UDTs, as follows:

```
Class CThing
    Title As String
    Count As Integer
End Class
```

That looks like Visual Basic, but it isn't. Many languages define classes with a similar syntax, but in Visual Basic, classes are more like forms. One form, one file; one class, one file. A CThing class definition might actually look more like this:

```
Public Title As String

Private c As Integer
Property Get Count() As Integer
    Count = c
End Property
Property Let Count(cA As Integer)
    iCount = IIf(cA > 0, cA, 0)
End Property

Sub Square()
    c = c * c
End Sub
```

The difference between the CThing class and the TChunk type is obvious. CThing does things. It squares itself. TChunk just sits there waiting for some outsider to square it.

You might say that a class is a type that acts. I'll go into a lot more detail about what it means to be a type that does things, but first let's take a closer look at how to create and use class instances.

Declaring Class Instances

Class instances are usually called objects, but let's keep calling them instances for a little while longer. Creating them works like this:

```
Dim thing As CThing
Set thing = New CThing
thing.Title = "Things Fall Apart"
thing.Count = 6
```

You can't just declare a variable and start partying on it. You have to create a New one first (often with Set). Bear with me if you think you already know why.

The reason you have to use New is because with class instances, the variable isn't the same as the instance. Figure 3-1 shows the difference. The variable is your only means of communicating with the instance, but it's not the same thing.

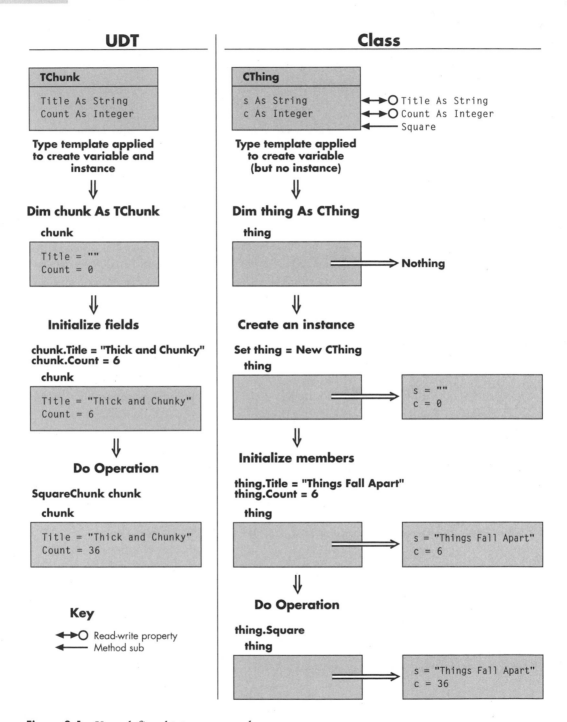

Figure 3-1. *User-defined types versus classes.*

Let's look at an example that illustrates the difference:

```
Dim chunkJoe As TChunk, chunkSue As TChunk
Dim thingJoe As CThing, thingSue As CThing
```

Like all Visual Basic variables, these are automatically initialized. The TChunk variables have their strings initialized to vbNullString and their integers to 0. The CThing variable doesn't have an instance yet, so the instance can't be initialized, but the variable is initialized to Nothing. To make them do something useful, you can assign properties as follows:

```
chunkJoe.Title = "Call me Joe"
chunkSue = chunkJoe
Set thingJoe = New CThing
thingJoe.Title = "Call me Joe"
Set thingSue = thingJoe
```

It might seem that you've created four objects and set them all to the same value. If you test in the Immediate window, the results indicate that everything is the same:

```
? chunkJoe.Title, chunkSue.Title
Call me Joe     Call me Joe
? thingJoe.Title, thingSue.Title
Call me Joe     Call me Joe
```

This is an illusion, as you can see if you change Title:

```
chunkSue.Title = "My name is Sue"
thingSue.Title = "My name is Sue"
```

Print out the values:

```
? chunkJoe.Title, chunkSue.Title
Call me Joe     My name is Sue
? thingJoe.Title, thingSue.Title
My name is Sue  My name is Sue
```

Each TChunk variable contains its instances, so changing *chunkSue* doesn't affect *chunkJoe*. But the *thingJoe* and *thingSue* variables both reference the same instance. Changing one changes the other because there isn't any other. If you want another, you have to create it with the New operator:

```
Set thingJoe = New CThing
thingJoe.Title = "Call me Joe"
Set thingSue = New CThing
thingSue.Title = "Call me Sue"
```

This difference between instances of classes and the instances of other types is so fundamental that we generally use different names. With classes, variables are called object variables and instances are called objects. With other types, the term variable usually refers both to the variable and the instance, because they are the same. I'll switch to this more standard terminology from here on out.

This certainly isn't the only way a language can declare, create, initialize, and use objects. But it is the most efficient way for a language to manage objects if you don't have pointers, which is why Java looks to me more like Visual Basic than like C++.

Initializing Objects

The CThing object might be complete as soon as it's created, but in real life most objects aren't meaningful at the instant of creation. Visual Basic allows you to initialize a class or a form with the Initialize event and clean it up with the Terminate event, but that's rarely enough information to construct a working object; most objects need more information from the user before their state is complete. This isn't a problem with controls and forms because their initial state can be set with properties at design time. But classes can be initialized only in code.

What you need (and what most object-oriented languages have) is a means to specify initialization data as part of the New syntax. If Visual Basic had constructors like other object-oriented languages, the syntax might look like this:

```
Set thing = New CThing(1, "Object") ' You can't do that
```

Instead, if you want to pass initialization data to a class, you must do so by convention and hope that your users will follow the rules. A traditional name I use for initialization methods is Create:

```
thing.Create 1, "Object"              ' Initialize with Create method
```

Another convention I use with objects that have one primary property is to make that one property the default:

```
Dim shsTitle As CSharedString
Set shsTitle = New CSharedString
shsTitle = "Share and share alike"  ' Initialize with default property
```

In Visual Basic, most objects of substantial size and complexity will be invalid between the time you create them with New and the time you initialize them with a Create method (or whatever other technique you choose). You also have to worry about what to do if the user fails to follow your initialization convention—assert, raise an error, or let it be.

The lack of initialization—both of variables and of objects—is, in my opinion, the greatest flaw of the Visual Basic language. No other major high-level language shares this flaw. You'll hear a lot more about initialization problems in this book. If I start to sound like a broken record, it's because the language feels like a broken record.

Declarations with New

The New statement is often used in object declarations. This gives the declaration a syntax so similar to an intrinsic variable declaration that you might be tempted to think they work the same way. You understand how this works:

```
Dim chunk As TChunk
chunk.Title = "Chunk-a-lunk"
```

Surely this must be the object equivalent:

```
Dim thing As New CThing
thing.Title = "Thing-a-ling"
thing.Square
```

Those statements seem simpler and shorter than these:

```
Dim thing As CThing
Set thing = New CThing
thing.Title = "Thing-a-ling"
thing.Square
```

You might be tempted to fall into the old C trap of assuming that the more expressions you can cram into each line of code, the faster your program will run. It just isn't so. Whether you use Set to create the object in a separate step or whether you use New in the declaration, you're going to end up with the same thing—an object variable that references a separate object. You can get a clue about what's happening by stepping over these statements in the debugger. In neither case will you step on the Dim line. You can't set a breakpoint on it, either. That's because it's not executed at run time. The statement reserves space for the object variable at compile time, but it doesn't create the object.

Visual Basic intrinsic variables are always initialized to something—usually zero or empty. Object variables are initialized to Nothing. So whichever version you use, you still end up with Nothing. The difference occurs when you execute the next statement. If you declared the variable with New, Visual Basic automatically creates a CThing object for you the first time you use it. It's as if you wrote the following code:

```
Dim thing As CThing
If thing Is Nothing Then Set thing = New CThing
thing.Title = "Thing-a-ling"
If thing Is Nothing Then Set thing = New CThing
thing.Square
If thing Is Nothing Then Set thing = New CThing
' Continue like this for all properties and methods
```

You don't have to write all that extra code to check for Nothing; Visual Basic writes it for you. But you do have to execute it. Why can't the compiler see that you've already created the object variable after the first statement and quit checking? Because it's a compiler. Consider this statement:

```
Dim thing as New CThing
If fHellFrozenOver Then thing.Title = "The latest thing"
```

The compiler can't tell at compile time whether hell is frozen over. That won't be known until run time. Thus it won't know whether to create a new CThing object without checking. Theoretically, you could write an optimizing compiler that would analyze conditionals and eliminate redundant checks in cases where there was only one possible code path. But that compiler couldn't work on p-code, where every statement has to stand on its own. You're better off just using the Set statement to create the objects yourself.

Now, before you throw New out of your declarations toolbox, take a look at the results of the Performance sidebar on page 133. The real-world penalty for using New in declarations for compiled code just isn't worth worrying about. It's all but free.

Furthermore, using New in declarations can be a powerful way of managing memory allocation, especially with global or form-level variables. Let's say you declare this variable at the form level:

```
Private thing As New CThing
```

The *thing* variable is set to Nothing and no memory is allocated for the CThing object. If you follow a code path that never uses the *thing* variable, it never gets created. You pay no penalty (except for one object variable) for the unused object. But let's say you do use the *thing* variable at some point. It is automatically created and you can use it up. Once you've milked it dry, you might want to throw the worthless thing away. Since it's declared at the form level, *thing* isn't going to automatically go out of scope and destroy itself until the form is destroyed, but you can free that unused memory specifically like this:

```
Set thing = Nothing
```

As long as no other object variable has a reference to the same object, it will go away and its memory will become available for other uses. But if you later decide you need that object again, just reference it again and it will spring to life again (but without any previous state values).

This form of automatic memory management is often used with form objects, including the automatic ones used for startup forms. They're also used in global classes, as you'll see later.

Procedures Versus Methods

Object-oriented programming turns traditional functional programming on its ear. In functional programming, you call a procedure indicating what you want to do and then pass arguments specifying what to do it to, and how to do it:

```
DoThis ToThat, WithThese
```

In object-oriented programming, you indicate what you want to work on and then specify methods to indicate what you want to do:

```
ToThis.DoThat WithThese
```

In traditional functional programming, you can pass two kinds of arguments: one indicates what you want to work on, and the other provides additional information about how to do the work. In object-oriented programming, you sometimes don't need to indicate what you want to work on, because a default object is understood. In Visual Basic terms, the statement

```
DoThis WithThese
```

might mean

```
Me.DoThis WithThese
```

At other times, you don't need to specify how to work on something because you have only one possibility:

```
DoThis    ' WithDefaultThese
```

Internally, the processor doesn't know anything about object-oriented programming; assembly language is always functional. Object-oriented languages fake object-oriented programming internally by passing a hidden argument. When you write the code

```
ToThis.DoThat WithThese
```

in Visual Basic (or any object-oriented language), what the processor really sees, in simplified terms, is this:

```
DoThat ToThis, WithThese
```

To attach the DoThat method to the *ToThis* object in Visual Basic, you create a class for CThis objects, of which *ToThis* will be an instance. Within the class, you create a public DoThat sub and give it a *WithThese* parameter. When you create a new *ToThis* instance of the CThis class, you can call DoThat using object-oriented syntax:

```
Dim ToThis As New CThis
ToThis.DoThat WithThese
```

Of course, you can still use the functional style on objects. You must be able to do this so that one object can work on another. Only one object can be the base object, so if there are two objects involved, one has to be passed as a method parameter.

Creating a functional version of a method is easy. Assume you have the following object method:

```
Private iCount As Integer
    :
Sub Square()
    iCount = iCount * iCount
End Sub
```

It's easy to create a functional version that uses it:

```
Sub SquareThing(ByVal thing As CThing)
    thing.Square
End Sub
```

This procedure can be either a Sub in a standard module, or a method in another class module.

More About Properties

Let's talk about properties. The syntax for using properties looks exactly the same as the syntax for using member fields of a UDT. But in fact, a property is very different from a UDT field.

Essentially, a property looks like a procedure to the implementor, but works like a variable to the user. The purpose of using property procedures rather than just giving the world access to internal variables is two-fold. You can validate the input data you receive from users, and qualify or process output data before giving it out to users. Another advantage is that procedures abstract data so that you can change the implementation without breaking client code.

Every object-oriented language has this problem, but most of them have a less elegant solution. C++ and Java, for example, depend on conventions such as always using Get and Set in the names of access methods.

```
c = thing.GetCount();    // C++ or Java access internal data
thing.SetCount(c + 6);
```

But in the Basic philosophy, the details of data protection should not affect clients. They shouldn't have to use an unnatural syntax in order to be protected.

Instead, Visual Basic allows you to protect internal data with property procedures—Let, Get, and Set. The classic Get/Let property pair looks like this:

```
Private sStuff As String
  :
Property Get Stuff() As String
    ' Qualify or process data output here
    Stuff = sStuff
End Property
Property Let Stuff(sStuffA As String)
    ' Validate data input here
    sStuff = sStuffA
End Property
```

There are lots of ways to validate data. But what if you have data that just doesn't need validation? This often happens with Boolean properties. How are you going to come up with invalid input for a Boolean? By definition, everything is either True or False. Sometimes strings are the same way; if empty and null strings are valid for your property, then there probably isn't any need to validate them. Visual Basic provides a shortcut for defining properties that can't go wrong:

```
Public Stuff As String
```

This syntax makes Stuff appear to be a data member of the class in the same way that a field is a data member of a UDT. This is an illusion. Don't expect to get any noticeable speedup from using a Public property instead of a property procedure. What the syntax means is that Visual Basic will generate the property procedures for you behind the scenes. In the COM standard on which Visual Basic is based, all access to objects is through procedures.

Technically, property procedures are also an illusion. What you really get with a property procedure is something that would look more like this if you could write it in Visual Basic:

```
Private sStuff As String
  :
Function GetStuff(sStuffRet As String) As HResult
    sStuffRet = sStuff
    GetStuff = 0    ' Always return error code or 0 for success
End Function
Function LetStuff(sStuffA As String) As HResult
    sStuff = sStuffA
    LetStuff = 0    ' Always return error code or 0 for success
End Function
```

Visual Basic with Curly Braces

If Visual Basic is your mother tongue or if you have real work to do, you can skip this sidebar. On the other hand, if you enjoy seeing people make fools of themselves in public, you might want to watch me try to prove that Java and Visual Basic are twins, separated at birth, while C++ isn't even the same species.

To make this difficult argument, I'll ask you to put aside the issues that language aficionados normally argue about. I don't care whether the type or the variable comes first. Perhaps Dim is the worst keyword name ever; maybe it's typedef. Should blocks be enclosed in curly braces or terminated with an End statement? Who cares? Are free-format languages better than line-oriented languages? Leave it to the lawyers.

What really matters is how memory is allocated and used. For example, here's how you declare object variables in Visual Basic:

```
Dim thing As CThing          ' VB declare object variable
```

This is similar to a C++ pointer variable, which you create like this:

```
CThing * pthing;             // C++ declare object pointer variable
```

Java, like Visual Basic, has no pointers. Object variables are created like this:

```
CThing thing;                // Java declare object variable
```

Java and C++ might look similar, but that asterisk in the C++ declaration makes a world of difference. In what really counts, Visual Basic and Java are the same.

All of these statements create a reference to a theoretical object, but none of them actually creates a CThing object. The Visual Basic statement creates a variable initialized to Nothing. The Java statement does something equivalent. The C++ statement creates an uninitialized variable. The big difference is that accessing *thing* in Visual Basic or in Java results in a polite, predictable error, while accessing an uninitialized C++ pointer variable fails rudely and unpredictably.

You can't create an object directly in Visual Basic or Java, but you can in C++:

```
CThing thing;                // C++ declare object
```

This C++ statement creates a CThing object in memory. Notice that it looks the same as the Java statement shown earlier, but it means something quite different. It works more like a Visual Basic UDT, except that it can have methods as well as data members. You can start calling its methods immediately after you declare it. Some of you (such as those who read the mistaken claims in the last edition of this book) might say that the following Visual Basic variable is equivalent:

```
Dim thing As New CThing
```

Not at all. This is just a shortcut that creates an object variable, but delays automatic creation of it to a later time. If you want to create an object from an object variable, you do it like this in Visual Basic:

```
Set thing = New CThing          ' VB creates object
```

Set creates a CThing object and connects it to the *thing* variable, and disconnects the *thing* variable from the object it was previously connected to.

The equivalent Java statement is similar, except that there's no Set:

```
thing = new CThing();           // Java create object
```

The nearest equivalent in C++ is this:

```
pthing = new CThing;            // C++ create object and point to it
```

The C++ new operator allocates storage for a class in much the same way that New does in Visual Basic or new does in Java. The difference is that you have to use the delete operator to get rid of that storage in C++. Visual Basic and Java do the cleanup (sometimes called garbage collection) for you.

At this point you can use the *thing* variable as if it were a CThing object. You can call the CThing object's methods and use its properties:

```
thing.Square()
```

That's the Visual Basic version (the parentheses are optional). The Java version is the same except it needs a closing semicolon. But C++ can create either a *pthing* pointer variable or a *thing* variable. These two versions need a different syntax to distinguish them.

```
thing.Square();        // C++ variable containing an object
pthing->Square();      // C++ variable pointing to an object
```

And that's not even mentioning a third possibility, a C++ reference variable which looks like an object and works like a pointer to an object. But we won't get into that.

I could continue with this comparison, but it would come to more of the same. Java looks like C++, but acts like Visual Basic. There are two kinds of languages, and the thing that separates them is their attitude toward pointers. C++ embraces and honors them. Java refuses to recognize their existence. Visual Basic—well, pointers seem to have squeezed a foot in the door, but only in relation to the Windows API. In the difference that matters most, Visual Basic and Java are on the same side.

Behind the scenes, property access would actually look something like this:

```
On e <> 0 Goto EHandler
' iLine = txtNote.Line
e = txtNote.GetLine(iLine)
' txtNote.Line = iLine + 1
e = txtNote.LetLine(iLine + 1)
    ⋮
EHandler:
    HandleError e
```

Fortunately, Visual Basic handles these bookkeeping details so that you don't have to worry about them.

Where Do Objects Come From?

Visual Basic provides numerous ways to create an object and Set it to an object variable. We're going to look at several of them, but first there's one important truth that you should keep in mind at all times when dealing with objects: Visual Basic objects and classes, be they public or private, are all handled through the Component Object Model (COM).

Even in early versions before COM, Visual Basic had controls and forms that were like objects; however, the current implementation uses COM below the surface for everything. (Microsoft was just kidding when it told you not so long ago that you should call COM by the nonsense acronym OLE.)

Objects from CreateObject

Let's start with the granddaddy of object creation statements, CreateObject.

In the old days, the only way to define a class was to write it as a COM Automation component in another language (usually C++). You might not think of a COM Automation-enabled application such as Excel or Visio ShapeWorks as a group of classes, but to a Visual Basic program, that's pretty much what it is.

So let's say you have the COM Automation-enabled StoryTeller application and you want to create a CStory object in your Visual Basic program. To do this, you'll call some methods and properties to manipulate stories. (StoryTeller was one of the first COM Automation applications and the first version came out long before type libraries even existed. Stories, Inc., sent you a type library for the old version last year, but you thought it was marketing junk and threw the disk away.) To use a CStory class, you need to declare an object variable:

```
Dim objStory As Object
```

You might prefer to declare this object with type CStory or something more specific than Object, but you can't because you don't know the name of the class, and even if you did, you can't use it in Visual Basic at design time without a type library, and you don't yet know there is such a thing. You have to connect to the class at run time using CreateObject. In order to use CreateObject, you must learn the programmatic ID ProgID string of the class either from documentation or from samples provided by the vendor. By convention, the ProgID string consists of the name of the server application followed by a dot, followed by the name of the class. Nothing enforces this convention except the desire of vendors to meet the expectations of users. Fortunately, the StoryTeller documentation tells the ProgID and even gives an example of how to use it:

```
Set objStory = CreateObject("StoryTeller.CStory")
objStory.Declaim 9, "Easy"
⋮
```

Now let's look at what happens behind the scenes. The CreateObject function looks in the system registry (in HKEY_CLASSES_ROOT) to find the key called *StoryTeller.CStory*. Under this entry, it finds the CLSID for the CStory class. The CLSID is a 128-bit Globally Unique ID (GUID). (I'll tell you more about GUIDs in Chapter 10.) CreateObject looks up this number in a table of GUIDs under the CLSID key and learns (among other things) the full path of the StoryTeller program, C:\STELLER\STELLER.EXE. Next it checks to see if STELLER.EXE is already running and, if not, runs it. Finally COM binds the CStory class to the *objStory* variable.

Binding means that the *objStory* variable is assigned the base address of the code for CStory objects within the running STELLER.EXE program. Whenever your program uses a CStory property or method, COM will look up the pointer for that property or method code as an offset from the base address of the object. You got all that? Well, never mind. We'll be getting into more COM details in Chapter 10.

For now, the important point is that the variable is bound to the class, and it's bound late. You'll hear a lot about early binding and late binding in the rest of this book. Late binding means that the variable is connected to the class at run time. This is evil. If you learn only one thing from this book, it should be how to avoid late binding. Early binding means that the variable is connected to the class at compile time. This is good. You should always try to achieve early binding. Alas, there was no such thing back in the old days when the story server was written.

When you call the Declaim method of the CStory object, Visual Basic has to look up the method by name in the class data table to determine where the Declaim code is located. It has to pass arguments in Variants (whether the parameters are Variant or not) and do various other time-consuming things to get everything set up. It uses a COM interface called IDispatch (which I'm not going to explain) to do all this messy stuff. The important thing is that late binding always goes hand in hand with IDispatch calling. Like late binding, IDispatch calling is—well, perhaps evil is too strong a word—but it's definitely in bad taste. We want to avoid late binding and IDispatch whenever possible.

Although Visual Basic programmers should avoid CreateObject if at all possible, a similar convention is still commonly used in a related language, VBScript. Objects are created through their CLSIDs (not their ProgIDs) in VBScript, and all object references are late-bound. But that's another book.

New Objects from Type Libraries

Let's fast forward. Stories, Inc., has updated its StoryTeller program by providing a type library. You download the type library STORIES.TLB from www.stories.com. Then you load it in the Visual Basic References dialog box. You open the Object Browser and find the class you want. Then you declare a variable for it:

```
Dim story As CStory
Set story = New CStory
story.Declaim 9, "Easy"
⋮
```

This time, something very different happens. When your source file is compiled, Visual Basic looks in its type libraries and finds the CStory class. The class is essentially a data table with offsets to the address of each property and method. These offsets are bound to each property access and method call in your program when the program is compiled. All you need to execute those properties and methods is the base address of the CStory object they are part of. When the Set statement is executed at run time, Visual Basic gets all the information it needs to create a CStory object from the type library instead of from the system registry. This speeds things up a little, but the big savings comes from having looked up all the method and property offsets at compile time.

ActiveX Control Objects

Let's look at some other ways of getting objects. Here's the most common. Stories, Inc., decides that the StoryTeller application is overkill for many users. What users want is a fast DLL version of StoryTeller's components. This version should have a visual interface for initializing property values, and it should be able to respond to story events, such as audience laughter or boredom. In other words, it should be an ActiveX control. So they write STORYSPINNER.OCX in a language that they won't specify and that is none of your business anyway (but that might be Visual Basic). You click the Toolbox to put this control onto a form. Visual Basic automatically provides hidden code that does the following:

```
Set spinner = New CStorySpinner
```

You don't have to Set this variable. It's pre-Set. You also don't have to initialize its properties with code (although you can) because you probably already set them at design time in the property page.

Form Objects

Another way to create COM objects is with forms. You insert a new form into your project and Visual Basic automatically generates something equivalent to the following:

```
Dim Form1 As New Form1
```

Like any competent programmer, the first thing you do is go to the Name field of the property page and change the Name property from Form1 to a real name such as FStoryDialog. Visual Basic automatically changes the hidden statement to the following:

```
Dim FStoryDialog As New FStoryDialog
```

If you follow my advice, you won't use this weirdly named object variable. Instead, you'll define your own sensible name like this:

```
Dim dlgStory As FStoryDialog
Set dlgStory = New FStoryDialog
dlgStory.TaleLength = "Tall"
dlgStory.Show vbModal
```

This way, you specifically control form creation rather than having it done behind your back by hidden statements. But what happens to that FStoryDialog object variable created by Visual Basic? Check the last section where we discussed how New in declarations works. The FStoryDialog object variable is set to Nothing, but if you never use it, no form object is ever created for it.

Class Objects

Finally, we're ready to create COM classes with Visual Basic. Perhaps you don't care for the Stories, Inc., approach, or maybe it's just overkill for your project. To create the CYarn class, insert a class module into your project and name it CYarn. Add the methods and properties you need and use it the obvious way:

```
Dim yarn As CYarn
Set yarn = New CYarn
yarn.Spin "That wanders away from the truth"
```

You can use CYarn as a local class inside the same project, or turn it into an EXE or DLL server. If you like, you can wrap the whole package up as an ActiveX control with property pages and a Toolbox button. These are all manifestations of the same concept: an object whose properties and methods are referenced through an object variable.

Dual Interfaces and IDispatch

When you call a method or property, it will work in different ways, depending on a factor that is mostly beyond your control. Some OLE classes have IDispatch interfaces, some have COM (sometimes called vtable) interfaces, and some have both (dual interfaces). From Visual Basic's viewpoint, IDispatch represents evil and COM represents virtue. Dual interfaces represent a pact with the devil to make do in a world of sin, but you should never need the darker IDispatch side.

This doesn't mean IDispatch is evil in general. You still need it for VBScript and other environments that always do late binding. Some authorities will claim that there are realistic situations where you don't know a server's name until run time and therefore you will need late binding. For example, you might have two polymorphic servers that provide the exact same services in two different ways. You have to ask your user (or perhaps ask an external database or a Web site) whether to use the UglyFast server or the PrettySlow server. These might be completely different servers running on different remote machines. You could write code like this:

```
If fFastAtAnyPrice Then
    Set obj = CreateObject("UglyFast.CJumpInTheLake")
Else
    Set obj = CreateObject("PrettySlow.CPlungeIntoThePool")
End If
```

I have yet to see a practical example of this situation under Visual Basic, but I'm told that there are some. Even in cases where you need CreateObject, it might still be possible to get early binding with the new Implements statement.

The IDispatch interface was designed for late-bound objects. It works (and works much faster) with early-bound objects, but it's less flexible. It still filters all arguments through Variants and it still does a certain amount of parsing and general thrashing to find the addresses and specify the arguments of methods and properties. Some of the information it finds is already known by the type library.

The COM interface, by contrast, is simple and direct. It consists of a simple table of addresses for each of the methods and properties. When you call a method, Visual Basic looks up its address and calls it. There are only two steps, and they translate into very few assembly language instructions. The table that makes this possible is called a *vtable,* and it has the exact same format as the vtable that makes virtual functions possible in C++. The tradeoff is information. If you have information, you construct a vtable and make fast calls through it. If you don't

PERFORMANCE

Problem: If you choose a class solution over an equivalent functional solution, what performance penalty, if any, must you accept? There's no easy one-to-one comparison, but the following information might give you a clue about the relative performance of methods, procedures, properties, and variables. As a bonus, you get a comparison of creating objects with New in the declaration versus using Set with New.

Problem	P-Code	Native Code
Call method function on object	0.0476 sec	0.0090 sec
Call method function on New object	0.0466 sec	0.0096 sec
Call method function on late-bound object	1.0185 sec	0.7828 sec
Call private function	0.0438 sec	0.0071 sec
Pass variable to method sub on object	0.0268 sec	0.0055 sec
Pass variable to method sub on New object	0.0287 sec	0.0071 sec
Pass variable to method sub on late-bound object	0.8585 sec	0.6980 sec
Pass variable to private sub	0.0384 sec	0.0088 sec
Assign through Property Let on object	0.0232 sec	0.0094 sec
Assign through Property Let on New object	0.0252 sec	0.0057 sec
Assign through Property Let on late-bound object	0.7661 sec	0.6229 sec
Assign through private Property Let	0.0176 sec	0.0014 sec
Assign from Property Get on object	0.0327 sec	0.0069 sec
Assign from Property Get on New object	0.0301 sec	0.0068 sec
Assign from Property Get on late-bound object	0.8045 sec	0.6790 sec
Assign from private Property Get	0.0172 sec	0.0005 sec
Assign to public property on object	0.0068 sec	0.0020 sec
Assign to public property on New object	0.0058 sec	0.0019 sec
Assign to public property on late-bound object	0.8582 sec	0.7918 sec
Assign to private variable	0.0032 sec	0.0003 sec
Assign from public property on object	0.0079 sec	0.0018 sec
Assign from public property on New object	0.0090 sec	0.0016 sec
Assign from public property on late-bound object	0.9445 sec	0.8459 sec
Assign from private variable	0.0035 sec	0.0004 sec

Conclusion: Hard to say. Using classes and objects definitely has a performance cost. Classes that wrap very simple operations might cost more than they are worth, but for most classes, the overhead is tiny compared to the total cost of what the class actually does.

have information, you look up that information the hard way and make slower calls. If you have the information but don't use it, you're wasting your time.

So if COM servers with dual interfaces are better than those with IDispatch interfaces, where do you find dual interfaces? The answer is: almost everywhere. For example, you'll always get them from Visual Basic. In fact, there are only two development tools I know of that create dispatch-only ActiveX components. Unfortunately, one of them is probably the most common tool for creating components: the Microsoft Foundation Class (MFC) library. The other is the Delphi programming environment (version 2). Both Microsoft and Borland are moving to new tools that create dual interfaces.

Lest you think that MFC creates slow, fat COM objects, let me clarify one thing. What has the greatest effect on the speed of any component is its slowest part. If COM calls through IDispatch are the slowest part of a component's operation, then you can blame the provider of that component. Generally, the bottleneck for controls is window creation and management. The bottleneck for COM EXE servers is transfer across process boundaries through a process called marshaling. You'll see performance examples demonstrating this in Chapter 10. The Performance sidebar in Chapter 10 illustrates that a Visual Basic DLL component compiled to native code is significantly faster than an equivalent C++ MFC component. Dual interfaces, not the programming language or the compiler, make the difference.

First Class: CDrive

Visual Basic doesn't provide much help in the simple task of analyzing the disk drives in the system, but fortunately, the Windows API does have some functions. GetDriveType, GetDiskFreeSpace, and GetVolumeInformation provide the information but, like most Win32 functions, they're oriented toward C programmers, not Visual Basic programmers.

Let's turn those Win32 functions into a Visual Basic-friendly class. Our drive objects won't simply *get* information about drives—they will *be* drives, telling the user everything about the physical drives the objects represent.

Drive Design

When I write a new class, I start by using it before I create it. I write some code using the class as if it existed, and then I declare a few object variables. If the class has a Create method, I call it in different ways to create different objects. Next, I set some object variables to refer to existing objects. I pass objects as arguments to subs and functions. I assign values to or read values from the properties of the objects. Finally, I call the methods.

It's easy and it's fun. I never get design-time or run-time errors. Imaginary objects of imaginary classes can acquire new methods and properties as fast as I can think them up.

But we all know that air code doesn't work. Once I start implementing methods and properties, some of them turn out to be more difficult than I expected. Sometimes I have to cut features or change the design. When I change the implementation, I change the test code to match.

When the implementation gets to a certain point, I start using it, one feature at a time. I comment out most of the client code, and implement some key properties and methods in the server code. Gradually, I uncomment more and more of the client code until everything works. Design is an iterative process. When you actually try to use your implementation, you might find that it's clumsy. Or you might find that your client code wants to do something that can't be done. Often, the process of implementing might give you new ideas for features that users would appreciate.

On major projects, you don't always have the luxury of designing by trial and error. A designer might write a specification describing all the interface elements in detail. The spec is then handed to an implementor, who makes it happen. Interface changes can have major repercussions for everyone involved. Even in this situation, however, the designer follows the same process, if only in his or her imagination. Any design-implementation process that depends on the infallibility of the designer is bound to fall short. I've seen language specs aplenty with sample code that never worked and never could have worked— or, worse yet, specs with no sample code. If you find features that don't quite seem to be designed for programmers on this planet, you can guess that the designer never actually tried out the feature—either in a virtual or a real sense. Unfortunately, we'll soon have to deal with some Visual Basic features that match this description.

We'll follow a use-first-implement-later strategy with the CDrive class, and you'll see a lot more of it throughout the book. Of course, I get to cheat; you won't see all my stupid ideas that got weeded out during implementation.

Test Drive

When I write a new class, I start by creating a test form that exercises the class. I put a command button and either a large label or a TextBox control on the form. Before I start writing the class itself, I declare an object of the proposed class in the command button's Click event procedure and write some code that uses the properties and methods of the class, outputting any status information to the label or the text box. Normally, I name the test program using the name preceded by a *T*, for example, TDRIVE.FRM to test the CDrive class in DRIVE.CLS. In this case, however, I combined drive testing with testing of other information classes and forms, including an About form. The actual name of the test project is ALLABOUT.FRM in ALLABOUT.VBG. You can see it, with output from CDrive, in Figure 3-2.

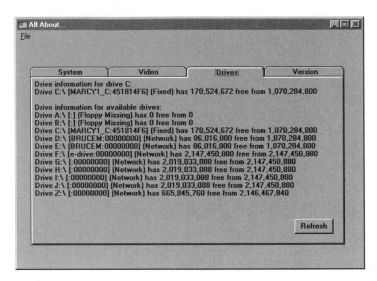

Figure 3-2. *The Drives tab of the All About program.*

To examine the class, let's start by declaring three CDrive object variables:

```
Dim driveDat As New CDrive
Dim driveCur As New CDrive
Dim driveNet As New CDrive
```

At this point, the drive objects have no meaning; they aren't yet connected with any physical disk drive. You must somehow connect each Basic drive object to a real-world drive object.

The modern way of specifying a drive is with a root path—the standard system introduced by the Win32 API. Lettered drives have root paths in the form *D:*, and network drives that are not associated with letters have root paths in the form *\\server\share*. Notice that root paths always end in a backslash. Our CDrive class will have a Root property as the means of specifying a drive:

```
driveDat.Root = "a:\"           ' Set to lettered drive
driveCur.Root = sEmpty          ' Set to current drive
driveNet.Root = "\\brucem1\root\" ' Set to network drive
```

Back in the ancient days of MS-DOS, drives were sometimes represented by the numbers 0 through 26 (with 0 representing the current drive) and sometimes by the numbers 0 through 25 (with 0 representing drive A). You needed to read the documentation carefully to see which system to use for any MS-DOS function call. One of the reasons for using a class is to eliminate such inconsistencies. The CDrive class recognizes numeric Root property values, with the number 0 representing the current drive and the numbers 1 through 26 representing local drives.

You can initialize a drive as follows:

```
driveDat.Root = 1                     ' Set to A:
driveCur.Root = 0                     ' Set to current drive
```

Of course, in Basic a class can have a default property, and the obvious one for the CDrive class is Root:

```
driveDat = 1                          ' Set to A:
driveCur = 0                          ' Set to current drive
driveDat = "a:\"                      ' Set to lettered drive
driveCur = sEmpty                     ' Set to current drive
driveNet = "\\brucem1\root\"          ' Set to network drive
```

If you don't like any of those, you don't have to set anything. By default, the Root property will be *sEmpty* and you'll get the default drive.

Once the drive is initialized, you can read its Root property (which has been converted to the root path format) or its Number property. The Number property is 0 for network drives:

```
' Assume that current drive is C:
Debug.Print driveDat.Number           ' Prints 1
Debug.Print driveCur.Number           ' Prints 3
Debug.Print driveNet.Number           ' Prints 0
Debug.Print driveDat.Root             ' Prints "A:\"
Debug.Print driveCur.Root             ' Prints "C:\"
Debug.Print driveNet.Root             ' Prints "\\BRUCEM1\ROOT\"
```

Of course, what you really want is the drive data in the form of read-only properties FreeBytes, TotalBytes, Label, Serial, and KindStr. You can use them this way:

```
    Const sBFormat = "#,###,###,##0"
    With driveCur
        s = s & "Drive " & .Root & " [" & .Label & ":" & _
                .Serial & "] (" & .KindStr & ") has " & _
                Format$(.FreeBytes, sBFormat) & " free from " & _
                Format$(.TotalBytes, sBFormat) & sCrLf
    End With
```

This code displays information in the following format:

```
Drive C:\ [BRUCEM1:1F81754F](Fixed) has 3 bytes free from 1,058,767,000
```

The CDrive class is designed with the assumption that drive objects don't change their properties. In real life, of course, drives sometimes do change. You might remove a 14.4 megabyte disk from your *A* drive and insert a 7.2 megabyte disk.

You might disconnect a large network drive from your *O* drive and connect a small one. CD-ROM technology might change while your program is running. You can make sure that a drive object reinitializes its state from the drive it represents by setting the object variable to a new drive object or by assigning the Root property (even if you reassign the current value).

Class Diagrams

This is a good time to introduce the class notation that I'll use throughout the rest of this book. Class notations are a dime a dozen in object-oriented programming books, and I don't claim that my notation has any special advantages. It does address the specific features of Visual Basic classes in a way that can either show off the methods and properties of a specific class or, at a higher level, indicate relationships between classes. Figure 3-3 shows the diagram for the CDrive class.

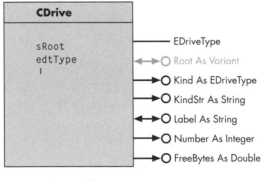

Key

――――― Type
――▶O Read-only property
◀―▶O Read-write property
(Default item shown in gray)

Figure 3-3. *The CDrive class.*

Types are shown for methods and properties in this example, but they might be omitted in later examples. If it's useful to show private members of a class, they'll go inside the object box. (This is seldom necessary, however; normally, the public interface is all that matters.)

Implementing CDrive

Now that you know exactly what you want, you can start to create the CDrive class. You can declare a class to be either private or public. I provide a public version in the VBCore DLL project. (VBCore is discussed in more detail later.) CDrive can just as easily be private. I provide a separate, private copy of the CDrive class in a file called PDRIVE.CLS. If you want to use the private version, put PDRIVE.CLS into your project rather than DRIVE.CLS.

NOTE   Unfortunately, you can't use the same class file for a private class in one project and a public class in another. I provide separate but otherwise identical private copies of all my public classes. The private module names are the same as the public names with *P_* as a prefix letter. They can be created by using the Save As command and then changing the Instancing property to Private. The Global Wizard described in Chapter 5 can translate private classes into public classes and vice versa automatically. This is an annoyance for maintenance, but you have to live with some similar scheme if you want to use the same class in different contexts.

There are two ways to define a property. The first way looks like a variable declaration:

```
Public Root As String
```

But if you define the Root property this way, you lose all control of it. The user can set or read it at any time without your knowledge. In CDrive, you need to do a lot of work whenever anyone sets the Root property. First you must confirm that the user has passed an actual root path. Next you calculate and store permanent data about the drive as soon as it is initialized. Then, when the user asks for the information later, you return the pre-calculated values.

The mechanism that makes this possible is the property procedure. Property Get, Property Let, and Property Set enable you to write procedures that look like public variables.

There are generally two strategies for defining properties, and CDrive follows them both. For properties that don't change dynamically, it does all the initialization and calculation up front. In other words, the Property Let procedures do all the work and the Property Get procedures simply return pre-calculated internal data. But some data about a drive might change from moment to moment (for example, the number of free bytes). You want to recalculate these dynamic properties each time their Property Get is called. In other words, the Property Get procedure does all the real calculation and validation, while the Property Let does the least work it can get away with.

Initializing CDrive data

First let's look at the private variables that CDrive will have to fill:

```
Private sRoot As String
Private edtType As EDriveType
Private iTotalClusters As Long
Private iFreeClusters As Long
Private iSectors As Long
Private iBytes As Long
Private sLabel As String
Private iSerial As Long
Private fDriveMissing As Boolean
```

The key property for users is Root because it is the default property. Users will normally set it before they set anything else. The Property Let looks like this:

```
Public Property Let Root(vRootA As Variant)
    ' Some properties won't work for \\server\share\ drives on Windows 95
    sRoot = UCase(vRootA)  ' Convert to string
    InitAll
End Property
```

Clearly, the key procedure from the programmer's standpoint is InitAll. This function gets called when a CDrive object is created (in Class_Initialize) and each time the user sets the Root property. InitAll looks like this:

```
Private Sub InitAll()
    sLabel = sEmpty: iSerial = 0
    iSectors = 0: iBytes = 0: iFreeClusters = 0: iTotalClusters = 0
    fDriveMissing = False
    ' Empty means get current drive
    If sRoot = sEmpty Then sRoot = Left$(CurDir$, 3)
    ' Get drive type ordinal
    edtType = GetDriveType(sRoot)
    ' If invalid root string, try it with terminating backslash
    If edtType = edtNoRoot Then edtType = GetDriveType(sRoot & "\")
    Select Case edtType
    Case edtUnknown, edtNoRoot
        Dim iDrive As String
        iDrive = Val(sRoot)
        If iDrive >= 1 And iDrive <= 26 Then
            sRoot = Chr$(iDrive + Asc("A") - 1) & ":\"
        Else
            sRoot = sEmpty
        End If
        ' Start over
        InitAll
```

```
      Case edtRemovable, edtFixed, edtRemote, edtCDROM, edtRAMDisk
         ' If you got here, drive is valid, but root might not be
         If Right$(sRoot, 1) <> "\" Then sRoot = sRoot & "\"
         GetLabelSerial
      Case Else ' Shouldn't happen
         BugAssert True
      End Select
End Sub
```

That might look like a lot of work, but essentially this procedure is the CDrive class. It calculates almost everything necessary to allow the Property Get procedures simply to read internal variables.

Notice the recursive call to InitAll when the drive type is unknown or invalid. This happens if the user sets the Root property to a bogus value, such as an empty string. In other words, you have an error. Or have you?

There are many ways to handle errors in classes, but one choice is to refuse them. If you accept any input (including no input), there can't be any user error. If something goes wrong, it's the programmer's fault. The CDrive class attempts to follow this strategy. For example, if you enter the string *invalid drive* as the Root property, CDrive will first interpret it as a root drive string. If that fails (and it will), CDrive will interpret it as a drive number. If that fails (and it will), CDrive will interpret it as the current drive, and there's always a current drive. We'll look at other error strategies later.

Reading CDrive data
The Kind, Number, and Root Property Get procedures can return pre-calculated data:

```
Public Property Get Kind() As EDriveType
    Kind = edtType
End Property

Public Property Get Number() As Integer
    Number = Asc(sRoot) - Asc("A") + 1
    ' Network drives are zero
    If Number > 26 Then Number = 0
End Property

Public Property Get Root() As Variant
    Root = sRoot
End Property
```

The remaining properties can change dynamically, and shouldn't be pre-calculated. Instead, the calculations are done in the Property Get procedures:

```
Public Property Get FreeBytes() As Double
    ' Always refresh size since free bytes might change
    GetSize
    If Not fDriveMissing Then
        FreeBytes = CDbl(iFreeClusters) * iSectors * iBytes
    End If
End Property

Public Property Get TotalBytes() As Double
    ' Get size info only on first access
    If iTotalClusters = 0 And Not fDriveMissing Then GetSize
    If Not fDriveMissing Then
        TotalBytes = CDbl(iTotalClusters) * iSectors * iBytes
    End If
End Property

Public Property Get Label() As String
    If Not fDriveMissing Then Label = sLabel
End Property

Public Property Get Serial() As String
    If Not fDriveMissing Then Serial = MUtility.FmtHex(iSerial, 8)
End Property

Public Property Get KindStr() As String
    KindStr = Choose(edtType + 1, "Unknown", "Invalid", "Floppy", _
                                  "Fixed", "Network", "CD-ROM", "RAM")
    If fDriveMissing Then KindStr = KindStr & " Missing"
End Property
```

The FreeBytes and TotalBytes property procedures depend on GetSize, which calls the Win32 GetDiskFreeSpace Function and sets the *fDriveMissing* flag:

```
Private Sub GetSize()
    Call GetDiskFreeSpace(sRoot, iSectors, iBytes, _
                          iFreeClusters, iTotalClusters)
    fDriveMissing = (Err.LastDllError = 15)
End Sub
```

Notice that TotalBytes and FreeBytes return Double rather than Long (as I originally coded them). When I wrote the original CDrive for the first edition of this book, disks larger than 2 gigabytes didn't exist and I didn't encounter one until I tested CDrive with a network server. Now 2 gigabyte drives are common.

The Label, Serial, and KindStr property procedures call GetLabelSerial to retrieve the appropriate disk information and to determine whether the disk is present. GetLabelSerial is a wrapper for the GetVolumeInformation API function:

```
Private Sub GetLabelSerial()
    sLabel = String$(cMaxPath, 0)
    Dim afFlags As Long, iMaxComp As Long
    Call GetVolumeInformation(sRoot, sLabel, cMaxPath, iSerial, _
                              iMaxComp, afFlags, sNullStr, 0)
    If Err.LastDllError = 21 Then   ' The device is not ready
        fDriveMissing = True
    Else
        fDriveMissing = False
        sLabel = MUtility.StrZToStr(sLabel)
    End If
End Sub
```

TotalBytes, FreeBytes, Serial, Kind, and KindStr have no Property Let statements because you can't directly change the size or type of a disk. To make a property read-only, you define the Property Get procedure but not the Property Let. You can change the Label, and CDrive provides a Property Let to do so:

```
Public Property Let Label(sLabelA As String)
    If SetVolumeLabel(sRoot, sLabelA) Then sLabel = sLabelA
End Property
```

Drive methods
A method is simply a public sub or function inside a class (or form) module. CDrive has no methods, only properties. But it's easy enough to add one:

```
Public Sub Format()
    Shell Environ$("COMMSPEC") & " /c FORMAT "  sRoot, vbHide
End Sub
```

No! Wait! It's a joke. It's not in the sample program. Look, it has a syntax error; it won't work even if you type it in yourself. I'm not trying to reformat your hard disk.

Default members
Visual Basic's support of default members is one of the features that distinguishes it from other languages. Historically, Visual Basic supported default members on controls back in version 1—long before the Component Object Model borrowed the feature. Unfortunately, although Visual Basic recognized default members in controls or classes written in other languages, it didn't support creating your own default members until version 5. And it still doesn't support default members directly through the language.

The only way to set the default member for your class is through a dialog box that seems to have been carefully designed for the sole purpose of violating as many user-interface principles as possible. Visual Basic calls the dialog box shown in Figure 3-4 the Procedure Attributes dialog box. I call it the DBFH

(Dialog Box From Hell). It's kind of embarrassing even to describe this feature, and an advanced programming book shouldn't have to explain specific fields of a dialog box. But there's no getting around it.

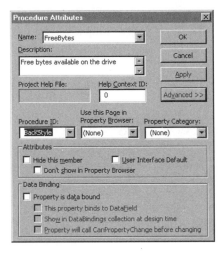

Figure 3-4. *The Procedure Attributes dialog box (a.k.a., the Dialog Box From Hell).*

The first step in setting the default property is to choose the best one. It's not always obvious. If no member waves its hand and hollers "pick me," you might be better off skipping the default member rather than picking one at random. That's not the case with the CDrive class; the Root property is clearly the right choice. You can initialize the object by setting it, or you can read it to get the most important element of the object:

```
driveCur = "c:\"              ' Initialize a drive
Debug.Print driveCur          ' Print the drive name
```

NOTE The default member is normally a property, but it's also possible to define a method function as the default. There's not much difference semantically between a method function and a property get procedure. In fact, if you want a read-only member, the only reason to implement it as a property get rather than as a method is that the property will generate a better error message if a user tries to assign to it.

Having chosen the Root property as the default, you might expect to be able to set the default property with a Default keyword or some other language feature. Nope. You have to do it with the dialog box that sets all the attributes of your methods and properties. The key attribute that you ought to provide for every single member of public classes is the description. The description will appear in the Object Browser, and your customers will consider you rude if you don't provide it. The previous version of Visual Basic had a way to set the description through the Object Browser, but it was so obscure and unintuitive that many users never figured it out. It's a little easier in version 5. You should get in the habit of providing descriptions even if you don't set default properties. Do as I say, not as I do.

Since you're going to be using this dialog box for every single member, let's start it off right. Put the cursor on the chosen property and press the accelerator key…oops. Now why would there not be an accelerator key or toolbar button for a dialog box you were going to call continually? Well, at least you can customize the toolbar and context menus to make access easier.

OK, so you choose Procedure Attributes from the Tools menu. The top half of the dialog box in Figure 3-4 appears. At this point, you can enter the description. In real life, you would also enter the Help Context ID. There's also a field for the project help file, but you must enter the help file elsewhere—in the Project Properties dialog box.

There's no visible place to specify that this is the default property. You must click the Advanced button to set a default member. Is setting a default member an advanced operation? Apparently someone thinks so.

When you click the Advanced button, the other half of the dialog box appears and you see several fields that have absolutely nothing to do with what we're doing. It turns out that this dialog box was designed for creators of controls, and since we're creating a class, not a control, most of the fields are irrelevant. Of course, Visual Basic knows whether we're creating a control or a class, so you might expect it to disable the extraneous fields. Nope. The dialog box lets you set a class property to be data bound or to have a property category even though these features have absolutely no effect on classes.

You might notice a checkbox that says User Interface Default. Perhaps checking this will make the current property the default. Don't even think it. This checkbox, too, is for control developers and will have no effect, although you can set it to your heart's content. Can you guess which of the gadgets in the dialog box actually sets the default property? OK, I'll give you a hint. Internally, in a way that is completely hidden from and irrelevant to Visual Basic programmers, the Component Object Model decides which class member is the default by looking at a variable that assembly language programmers would call an ID (even C++ programmers don't have to know this). Yes, you guessed it. The Procedure ID combo box is where you set the default property.

When you click the down arrow of the combo box, you'll see a list of random words. The first two, *None* and *Default*, are in parentheses for reasons that I couldn't even guess. The obvious choice is to select *Default*, and in fact that happens to be correct. But just out of curiosity, let's take a look at some of the other choices. What do you think it would mean to set the Root property of the CDrive class to *BackColor* or *hWnd*? If you guessed that it would have no effect whatsoever, you win a trip to Disneyland and the honorary title of Visual Basic Dialog Box Designer for a Day.

Naming Private Data

No matter what object-oriented language you use, you will probably run into a common naming problem. Often, you must assign different names to variables that represent the same value. For example, assume that you are defining a FileName property. The program using the property might have a variable containing a filename that it wants to assign to the FileName property. A user following the Hungarian naming convention described in Chapter 1 ("Basic Hungarian," page 16) might name the variable *sFileName*. When a user assigns that value to the property, the value is actually passed as an argument to the Property Let procedure. You need a name for the filename parameter; *sFileName* springs to mind. Now you need to store the same value internally. Again, *sFileName* is the obvious choice for the name of the internal version. And what about the property name itself? From the outside, the property looks like a variable, smells like a variable, and tastes like a variable. Why shouldn't it have a variable name? How about *sFileName*?

In practical terms, using the same name for the external and internal variables is not a problem. The external variable has a different scope than all the others and might be written by a different programmer years later; therefore, similar names are OK.

Nevertheless, following the Hungarian naming convention for properties is usually a bad idea. Your code ends up as gobbledygook: *thgMyThing.nMyCollection.iProperty*. Besides, your code will then be using a convention very different from the one used in controls, forms, and other predefined objects. Generally, it's bad manners to impose your own naming conventions on the outside world.

A conflict still exists between the parameter name in the Property Let procedure and the name in the internal version. You must arbitrarily make these different, even though they represent the same thing. You can mangle the internal version in one of two ways. The MFC class library for Visual C++, for instance, always prefixes the internal member variables in a similar situation with *m_* (as in *m_sFileName*). But I have an irrational prejudice against underscores in variable names, particularly in front of Hungarian prefixes; I'd much rather use a postfix. I considered using *I* (for internal) for all my internal variables, but I eventually switched to using *A* (for argument) with all parameter variables in Property Let statements. That way, the modified name doesn't affect Property Get procedures.

Of course, if you find anything about this dialog box confusing, no problem. Just click the Help button. Or click the What's This icon. Oops! There is none. At least you can press F1 to get help that will attempt to explain the mess. But you haven't seen anything yet. Just wait until we talk about creating collections in Chapter 4.

Other Class Features

The CDrive class doesn't exercise all the features of classes. I'll give a preview of some other features that we'll be covering as I get to them.

Static Members

In most object-oriented languages, an object can share data with other objects of the same class. For example, each object might need a count of how many other objects of the same type exist. An object might behave differently if it is the last object, or it might refuse to be created if there are too many objects. Visual Basic does not provide a direct means of sharing data between instances, but you can fake it using Public variables in a standard module. There is only one instance of a Public (global) variable, and all instances of a class can access it. But so can any other module in your project. In other words, this system violates all standards of encapsulation decency. It works, but only if everyone behaves themselves.

Do you trust other people to always behave? Do you trust yourself? Neither do I.

Now, in defense of using Public variables in standard modules to communicate between instances, keep in mind that these variables are visible only inside a component. If you behave yourself inside your component, users of the component won't be able to get inside and find those Public variables that aren't supposed to be public. Of course, if you're using a bunch of private classes inside an EXE, you are the component and everything is visible. You just have to remember that Public isn't supposed to mean public.

The other disadvantage is that you end up with a lot of dummy standard modules that serve no purpose other than to get around limitations of the encapsulation model. You'll be seeing a lot of this in coming sections.

Friend Members

Often, the best way to implement an object-oriented algorithm is with two or more cooperating classes. These classes need to share data with each other, but not with other classes. Many object-oriented languages provide a Friend modifier to allow classes to share data with each other and Visual Basic is no exception.

Unfortunately, Visual Basic's interpretation of friends is pretty loose. Most languages that support the Friend concept allow you to say who your friends are.

Visual Basic only allows you to say that you have friends. If anybody is your friend, then everybody is your friend. Or, more specifically, everyone in your component is your friend and everybody else doesn't know you. Again, this works fine if everybody in your component behaves. But the implicit assumption is that you won't put totally unrelated classes in the same component. Well, guess what the VBCore component does?

We'll be using the Friend keyword to share data between classes when we get to the CRegNode and CRegItem classes in Chapter 10. The Friend keyword can also be used to make class data available to standard modules and forms within the component. You can see this in the CTimer class (TIMER.CLS).

Events

Visual Basic now allows you to declare events in your server with the Event statement and raise them with the RaiseEvent statement. Your client programs can receive events from a server using the WithEvents statement. That's the easy way.

You can also create events by defining an interface in the server and having the client implement the interface. The client must also pass a reference from the implementing object to the server so that the server can call the client, thus creating the events. That's the efficient way.

Either way, events are an important new class feature, but we'll temporarily skip them.

The Form Class

Forms are just classes with windows. Think of it this way: somewhere in the heart of the source code for the Basic language lives a module named FORM.CLS.

You didn't know that Visual Basic is written in Visual Basic? Well, I have inside information (incorrect, like most inside information) that Visual Basic is actually written in Visual Basic. The FORM.CLS module contains Property Let and Property Get statements for AutoRedraw, BackColor, BorderStyle, Caption, and all the other properties you see in the Properties window. It has public subs for the Circle and Line methods and public functions for the Point method. It defines events with the Event statement. All forms automatically contain a hidden WithEvents statement for their own events and one for each control on the form.

The FORM.CLS module didn't change much in Visual Basic versions 1 through 3—a few new properties here, a few new methods there. But for version 4, somebody got the bright idea that if a form is just a class, users should be able to add their own properties and methods. By customizing a form with properties and methods, you make it modular. It's easy to define your own standard forms that can be called from any project.

Get With It

The With statement—stolen from Pascal and modified to fit Basic—is a fancy form of Set. The primary purpose is to make it easier and more efficient to access nested objects. For example, consider this With block:

```
With Country.State.City.Street.Houses("My")
    .Siding = ordAluminum
    .Paint clrHotPink
    .LawnOrnament = "Flamingo"
End With
```

This is equivalent to the following:

```
Dim house As CHouse
Set house = Country.State.City.Street.Houses("My")
house.Siding = ordAluminum
house.Paint clrHotPink
house.LawnOrnament = "Flamingo"
```

The With version is more readable, and you don't have to declare the reference variable. Instead, a hidden one is created for you. Of course, you don't absolutely need With or Set. You can do the same thing this way:

```
Country.State.City.Street.Houses("My").Siding = ordAluminum
Country.State.City.Street.Houses("My").Paint clrHotPink
Country.State.City.Street.Houses("My").LawnOrnament = "Flamingo"
```

This code is not only harder to read but is also much less efficient. Internally, Basic must look up every nested object for every access.

When you're not using nested objects (and we're not, in this chapter), the With statement is mostly syntactical sugar. It might save you some line wrapping, particularly if you need to access an object more than once in a line:

```
With lstHouses
    .ItemData(.ListIndex) = Len(.Text)
End With
```

You might find that more readable than this:

```
lstHouses.ItemData(lstHouses.ListIndex) = _
    Len(lstHouses.Text)
```

But you won't see a large difference in performance. In fact, the With statement can actually slow you down in some cases, although usually not enough to change my code style.

The only problem with custom forms is that they can't be public. You can't expose your standard forms in components. This turns out to be an advantage. Forms have all sorts of properties and methods that you don't want clients messing with. If anybody can do anything with your standard form, it's not standard. The way you expose standard forms in components is to wrap them in a class. The class initializes and controls the form by manipulating the appropriate methods properties, but it blocks clients from doing so except through properties and methods you control. We'll get to an example of this with a standard About form in Chapter 11.

Polymorphism and Interfaces

Interfaces are the hottest concept in language design. It's not as if they're new. COM has had interfaces all along, and Visual Basic version 4 had them behind the scenes. They're very similar to what C++ calls abstract base classes. But things really started popping when Java incorporated interfaces as a language feature. In fact, the Java literature claims that interfaces are a better replacement for the much maligned concept of multiple inheritance.

Who am I to say that Visual Basic copied Java interfaces? But the new Implements keyword provides essentially the same feature. (Coincidentally, a very similar feature appears in the latest version of Delphi.) Visual Basic's Implements keyword has a very different syntax than Java's interface and implements keywords. The Visual Basic version looks a lot like the event syntax, and requires setting extra object variables in situations where Java gets by with type casting.

It's ironic that Visual Basic gets a feature designed to replace multiple inheritance before it even gets single inheritance. Of course, if avoidance of irony were our chief goal, we wouldn't choose programming as a profession. In any case, the purpose of Implements is not multiple inheritance, but polymorphism.

Visual Basic version 4 had polymorphism, but the price was exorbitantly high. In order to use polymorphism, clients of polymorphic classes had to receive them as Objects. This worked, but it always resulted in minimal type protection, late binding, and slow operations. I described this crude version of polymorphism in the first edition of this book, but warned against using it for operations that required high performance. The new Implements keyword gives you safe, fast polymorphism. Let's check it out.

Interfaces

Interfaces are one of the most important foundations of the Component Object Model. You can't read more than a page or so of COM documentation without running into IReadThisBook, IDontUnderstand, or some other interface. By convention, interface names always start with the capital letter *I* followed by initial-cap words that describe the interface.

Actually, interfaces exist whether you use this convention or not. In fact, every Visual Basic class or form you create has a hidden interface that directly violates the standard. For example, if you create a class called CCallMeIshmael, Visual Basic will create an interface for it called _CCallMeIshmael.

I won't go into all the details of how interfaces work, but I can recommend a good tool for exploring them on your own. The OleView program provided in the \TOOLS\OLETOOLS directory of the Visual Basic CD-ROM will tell you all you ever wanted to know about classes (coclasses to COM) and interfaces. It's interesting to see the COM view of classes that you're familiar with. For example, load OleView, click the View TypeLib button, and open VBCORE.DLL. Expand the CoClasses list and then expand the CDrive coclass.

The resulting information is a little overwhelming, but you can see that the C-Drive coclass has a _CDrive interface. The _CDrive interface shows the names, parameter types, and return type of methods and properties, but it doesn't give any hints about the implementation. You can change the implementation of a class and clients won't care in the least as long as you don't change its interface. In fact, you can have several different classes with completely different implementations, but as long as they have the same interface, you can use them interchangeably. That's polymorphism.

Polymorphic Filters

Interfaces are the COM way (and the Visual Basic way) of providing polymorphism. Let's define an interface for polymorphic filter classes. Filters are the class equivalent of MS-DOS filters such as SORT or MORE. The role of a filter is to convert data from one form to another by applying a set of rules.

The filter we'll define consists of two parts. It must iterate through lines of text, reading them from a source and writing them to a target. This code works the same regardless of what the filter does. The filter must also apply the transformation to each line. This code is different for every kind of filter. It's a familiar problem. One part of the code is generic; one part is specific. You want to reuse the generic part but provide different implementations of the specific part. So you write an interface for the generic part and you write classes that implement the interface for the specific part. The generic code uses the objects with specific implementations without knowing or caring what those objects do or how they do it. All that matters is that the objects match the interface.

This technique turns object-oriented programming on its head, as shown in Figure 3-5 on page 152. The primary purpose of the CDrive class discussed earlier was encapsulation. All implementation details of a particular operation are hidden within the class, and many different users call the same class in different ways to get different results. With polymorphism, you implement multiple versions of a class with the same interface. One user calls the standard interface of any of the class implementations to get different results.

Encapsulation

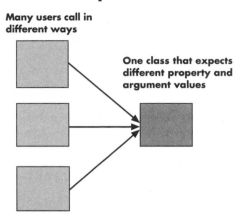

Polymorphism

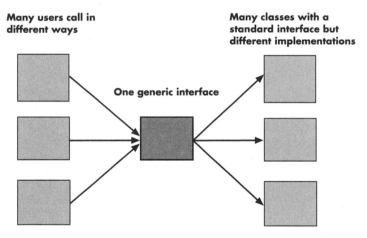

Figure 3-5. *Encapsulation and polymorphism.*

Another way to look at interfaces is that they provide one more level of abstraction. Interfaces encapsulate classes in the same way that classes encapsulate members and methods. Just as a class hides the internal state of its objects, an interface hides the implementation of its classes. If that leaves you more confused than before, well, let's get to the examples.

I use filter classes to implement wizard programs. For example, the Bug Wizard program uses the CBugFilter class to transform assertion and profile statements. The Global Wizard program uses several different classes to transform global classes into standard modules and vice versa. All these classes implement the IFilter interface.

In the filter problem, the generic part is the FilterTextFile or the FilterText procedure (in FILTER.BAS). FilterTextFile applies a filter to a text file specified by name in the Source and Target properties of the filter. FilterText works similarly except that the actual text to be transformed (rather than the name of a file containing the text) is passed in the Source and Target properties. Both of these procedures work the same no matter what the filter does. The specific part is the filter class (CBugFilter, one of the global filter classes, or your own favorite filter class). The filter class implements the generic IFilter interface with class-specific code that analyzes each line of text and modifies it according to its own rules.

In languages with inheritance, the generic part of the algorithm (the FilterTextFile or FilterText procedure) might be provided as a non-virtual method in a base class that also contains virtual methods for the specific part. Filter classes would inherit the FilterTextFile or FilterText method from the base class and use it without change, but would implement the virtual methods. You use a different strategy in Visual Basic, mixing functional and object-oriented techniques. The generic FilterTextFile and FilterText procedures go in a standard module. They take IFilter parameters to receive the object that provides the application-specific part of the algorithm. There are many other ways to use polymorphism, and we'll see some of them in later chapters.

Interfaces in Visual Basic

To create an interface in Visual Basic, you simply create a class module with empty methods and properties. Here's an IFilter interface (in IFILTER.CLS) that defines the standard members of a filter. IFilter has Source and Target properties to specify the data to be processed. It has a Translate member to do the work. And, in this case, there's an EChunkAction Enum type that indicates the results of the Translate method:

```
Enum EChunkAction
    ecaAbort
    ecaSkip
    ecaTranslate
End Enum

Property Get Source() As String
End Property
Property Let Source(sSourceA As String)
End Property

Property Get Target() As String
End Property
Property Let Target(sTargetA As String)
End Property

Function Translate(sChunkA As String, ByVal iChunkA As Long) As EChunkAction
End Function
```

Nothing to it. Literally. An interface has no code because it doesn't do anything. You have to create at least one separate class that implements the interface. The interface itself doesn't care how the members work, or even whether they work.

Since IFilter is an interface class, I use the convention of starting the names of such classes with an uppercase *I*. IFilter is what you would call an abstract base class in many object-oriented languages. Its purpose is to provide a type that your program can bind to at compile time, even though you won't know the actual object type until run time.

Using an interface class

Now let's look at the generic FilterTextFile procedure (in FILTER.BAS). Notice that it takes an IFilter parameter:

```
Sub FilterTextFile(filter As IFilter)

    BugAssert filter.Source <> sEmpty
    ' Target can be another file or replacement of current file
    Dim sTarget As String, fReplace As Boolean
    sTarget = filter.Target
    If sTarget = sEmpty Or sTarget = filter.Source Then
        sTarget = MUtility.GetTempFile("FLT", ".")
        fReplace = True
    End If

    ' Open input file
    On Error GoTo FilterTextError1
    Dim nIn As Integer, nOut As Integer
    nIn = FreeFile
    Open filter.Source For Input Access Read Lock Write As #nIn

    ' Open target output file
    On Error GoTo FilterTextError2
    nOut = FreeFile
    Open sTarget For Output Access Write Lock Read Write As #nOut

    ' Filter each line
    On Error GoTo FilterTextError3
    Dim sLine As String, iLine As Long, eca As EChunkAction
    Do Until EOF(nIn)
        Line Input #nIn, sLine
        iLine = iLine + 1
        eca = filter.Translate(sLine, iLine)
        Select Case eca
        Case ecaAbort
            GoTo FilterTextError3   ' Stop processing
        Case ecaTranslate
```

```
        Print #nOut, sLine      ' Write modified line to output
    Case ecaSkip
                                ' Ignore
    Case Else
        BugAssert True          ' Should never happen
    End Select
Loop

' Close files
On Error GoTo FilterTextError1
Close nIn
Close nOut
If fReplace Then
    ' Destroy old file and replace it with new one
    Kill filter.Source
    On Error Resume Next    ' No more errors allowed
    Name sTarget As filter.Source
    ' If this fails, you're in trouble
    BugAssert Err = 0
End If
Exit Sub

FilterTextError3:
    Close nOut
FilterTextError2:
    Close nIn
FilterTextError1:
    MErrors.ErrRaise Err
End Sub
```

If you study the code carefully, you can see that it does not depend in any way on what the filter actually does. FilterTextFile just loops through each line of Source, calling the Translate method on each line and writing the result to Target. It doesn't matter what file names Source or Target contain or what Translate does to the text.

If you have read the previous edition of this book, you might remember that the old version of FilterTextFile took an Object parameter rather than an IFilter parameter. The description of the old FilterTextFile was largely a diatribe on what real object-oriented languages did and how that compared to Visual Basic's pitiful version of polymorphism. Well, that flame is gone. Visual Basic's version of polymorphism didn't come out the way I expected. But, the functionality is there, and…well, judge for yourself.

Now that FilterTextFile takes an IFilter, you can't just pass a form or a ListBox or some other random object. Any object you pass must have a class that implements IFilter. Passing an inappropriate object causes a polite error at compile time rather than a rude one at run time. More importantly, Visual Basic can bind the IFilter calls at compile time, making polymorphic classes almost as fast as non-polymorphic ones. That's a big turnaround from version 4 where polymorphic algorithms were often as much as 10 times slower than comparable non-polymorphic algorithms.

I've shown FilterTextFile here because it's more interesting, but I'll be using FilterText in some of the examples. FilterText does a similar operation, but it assumes that Source and Target contain a text string with each line of text separated by a carriage return/line feed combination. The code just grabs lines of text from Source, filters them, and writes the result to Target. The Bug Wizard uses FilterTextFile and the Global Wizard uses FilterText for reasons that need not concern us. There's nothing sacred about Source and Target. You could write filter procedures that assume Source and Target are URLs or database record identifiers.

> **NOTE** The error trap in FilterTextFile doesn't have anything to do with polymorphic classes, but it does illustrate a stair-stepped error trap. Often, when something goes wrong while you're building something with a series of Basic statements, you need to unbuild it in the opposite order, undoing only the parts you have finished. A carefully designed series of error traps can take you back to the initial state.

Implementing an interface

Let's begin the process with a simple implementation of the filter class in Bug Wizard, CBugFilter. The key statement in an interface implementation is the Implements statement. At first glance, there's not much to it:

```
' CBugFilter implements IFilter
Implements IFilter
```

The interesting thing about this statement is not what it looks like, but what it does to the code window containing it. The object dropdown gets a new entry for IFilter. If you select IFilter, the procedure dropdown shows the event procedures that you must implement. When you select the Source property get procedure, the IDE automatically puts the cursor on the property method, if one exists, or creates a Source property get procedure if one doesn't exist. The IDE creates the following procedure and puts the cursor on the blank line in the middle, ready for you to type in the implementation code:

```
Private Property Get IFilter_Source() As String

End Property
```

Interface procedures look like event procedures because, like event procedures, you can't change their names. But unlike event procedures, you can't ignore them. You must implement each and every member defined by the interface. By using the Implements keyword, you are signing a contract. You agree to implement all members exactly as they are defined in the interface. Try violating the contract. Change IFilter_Target to IFilter_Targot, or change the return type of IFilter_Translate to Integer. When you try to compile, Visual Basic will inform you in no uncertain terms that you are a cad and a deceiver and that you must fulfill your obligations if you wish to continue.

Here's the interface part of the implementation I gave my CBugFilter class:

```
' Implementation of IFilter interface
Private sSource As String, sTarget As String

Private Property Get IFilter_Source() As String
    IFilter_Source = sSource
End Property
Private Property Let IFilter_Source(sSourceA As String)
    sSource = sSourceA
End Property

Private Property Get IFilter_Target() As String
    IFilter_Target = sTarget
End Property
Private Property Let IFilter_Target(sTargetA As String)
    sTarget = sTargetA
End Property

Private Function IFilter_Translate(sLine As String, _
                                   ByVal iLine As Long) As EChunkAction
    IFilter_Translate = ecaTranslate   ' Always translate with this filter

    Select Case eftFilterType
    Case eftDisableBug
        CommentOut sLine, sBug
    Case eftEnableBug
        CommentIn sLine, sBug
    Case eftDisableProfile
        CommentOut sLine, sProfile
    Case eftEnableProfile
        CommentIn sLine, sProfile
    Case eftExpandAsserts
        ExpandAsserts sLine, iLine
    Case eftTrimAsserts
        TrimAsserts sLine
    End Select
End Function
```

Source and Target are unvalidated properties that you would normally implement with a Public member rather than with separate property procedures. The Implements statement won't let you take that shortcut. If you look back at the IFilter class, you'll notice that it also doesn't take the Public member shortcut, although it could. You might want to experiment with Public members in interface classes, but don't be surprised if Visual Basic makes choices about parameter names and ByVal attributes that you wouldn't make yourself. By defining the Property Get and Let procedures yourself, you get better control over the code that will be used in the implemented class.

There's no room for creativity in how you declare interface members in the implementing class. The creativity comes in the implementation of members such as the Translate function. Notice how the *sLine* parameter is passed by reference so that the modified version will be returned to the caller, but *iLine* is passed by value so that the caller's copy can't be changed.

As for what Translate actually does, it calls other procedures that do the actual work. If you reread the description of the Bug Wizard program, you can probably guess most of what these procedures are actually doing. The decision of which procedure to use is based on another property that is part of CBugFilter but not part of IFilter:

```
Property Get FilterType() As EFilterType
    FilterType = eftFilterType
End Property

Property Let FilterType(eftFilterTypeA As EFilterType)
    If eftFilterTypeA >= eftMinFilter And _
        eftFilterTypeA <= eftMaxFilter Then
        eftFilterType = eftFilterTypeA
    Else
        eftFilterType = eftMaxFilter
    End If
End Property
```

This property uses an EFilterType Enum and an eftFilterType member variable (not shown). Next we'll see how a client can use both the IFilter properties and the CBugFilter properties.

Using an interface

We have an interface. We have a class that implements it. Now for the tricky part: the code that actually uses the filter object. The Bug Wizard program has a control array of command buttons whose indexes correspond to the filter types in the EFilterType enum. The code to perform the appropriate filter action on a text file looks like this:

```
Private Sub cmdBug_Click(Index As Integer)
    HourGlass Me
    ' CBugFilter part of object
    Dim bug As CBugFilter
    Set bug = New CBugFilter
    ' IFilter part of object
    Dim filter As IFilter
    Set filter = bug
    ' Set FilterType property on bug variable
    bug.FilterType = Index
    ' Set Source property on filter variable
    filter.Source = sFileCur
    ' Pass either variable to FilterTextFile
#If fOddDayOfTheMonth Then
    FilterTextFile bug
#Else
    FilterTextFile filter
#End If
    HourGlass Me
End Sub
```

NOTE The HourGlass sub is a useful little procedure that displays an hourglass cursor during an operation and then removes it. Check it out in UTILITY.BAS. Always use a pair of HourGlass procedures—the first to display the hourglass cursor and the second to remove it.

If you're like me, you might have to study this code for a few minutes before you get it. Notice that there's only one object (because there's only one New statement), but there are two object variables that refer to that object—and each object variable has a different type. You set the *filter* variable to the *bug* variable. This works because a CBugFilter is an IFilter (because it implements IFilter).

Next we set the properties. We set the FilterType of the *bug* object. We set the Source of the *filter* object. It wouldn't work the other way around because a CBugFilter doesn't have a Source, and an IFilter doesn't have a FilterType. Notice that we use *filter* as if it had both public Source and Target properties, even though we know the real properties in CBugFilter are private and that their names are IFilter_Source and IFilter_Target.

When you get ready to pass the object to the FilterTextFile function, however, it doesn't matter which object variable you pass because the FilterTextFile function is defined to take an IFilter parameter. You can pass the *filter* object variable because it has the same type as the parameter. But you can also pass the *bug* object variable because it is also an IFilter (because CBugFilter implements IFilter). It doesn't work the other way around. An IFilter is not a CBugFilter. It's the object itself, not the object variable, that has type CBugFilter. This is an interesting concept—an object with a different type than the object variable that references it.

I can't say that I find this intuitive. The virtual method syntax used in most other object-oriented languages seems more intuitive. But the syntax grows on you the more you use it.

I do have one complaint. Visual Basic lacks class type casting. Most object-oriented languages allow you to cast the outer type to the inner type. Instead of creating a separate *filter* variable, you could cast the *bug* variable to an IFilter like this:

```
' Set Source property on filter part
IFilter(bug).Source = sFileCur
```

Chapter 10 will tell how to fake this syntax.

Implementing another interface

To get another view on this strange phenomenon, let's look at another implementation of IFilter. Like Bug Wizard, Global Wizard does several conversion operations. But unlike Bug Wizard, it handles each operation with a separate IFilter class rather than a Select Case block.

We'll look at a typical global conversion class, CModGlobDelFilter. The Source and Target properties are implemented exactly the same as for CBugFilter, so we'll skip to Translate:

```
' Great big, long, complex state machine all in one ugly chunk
Private Function IFilter_Translate(sLine As String, _
                                   ByVal iLine As Long) As EChunkAction
⋮
```

That comment looks so intimidating that we'll just skip over what a global class is and how you might convert one until Chapter 5. The important point is that IFilter_Translate will convert each line of one, count the line numbers, and return an indicator of what it did.

CModGlobDelFilter, like all of the other Global Wizard filter classes, has a Name property, which I won't show because it's simply the classic Get/Let property procedure pair wrapping an *sName* variable. The Name property is a property of the class, not of the IFilter interface. But its internal *sName* variable is visible inside the class to the implementation of the interface Translate method.

Hmmm. These conversion classes are all polymorphic through the IFilter class. But they also all have a Name property with the same String type. That's dumb polymorphism. Why would anybody want to do that?

Using another interface

The Global Wizard program picks which conversion it wants to perform through some logic that we don't care about, and sends the results to the following function:

```
Sub UpdateTargetFileDisplay()
    HourGlass Me

    ' Select the appropriate filter and assign to any old object
    Dim filterobj As Object
    Select Case emtCur
    Case emtStandard
        If chkDelegate Then
            ' Translates standard module to global class with delegation
            Set filterobj = New CModGlobDelFilter
        Else
            ' Translates standard module to global class w/o delegation
            Set filterobj = New CModGlobFilter
        End If
    Case emtClassPublic
        ' Translates public class to private class
        Set filterobj = New CPubPrivFilter
    Case emtClassGlobal
        ' Translates global class to standard module
        Set filterobj = New CGlobModFilter
    Case emtClassPrivate
        ' Translates private class to public class
        Set filterobj = New CPrivPubFilter
    Case Else
        txtDst = ""
        Exit Sub
    End Select
    ' Setting name isn't performance sensitive, so do it late bound
    filterobj.Name = txtDstModName

    ' Use early-bound variable for performance sensitive filter
    Dim filter As IFilter
    Set filter = filterobj
    filter.Source = txtSrc
    FilterText filter
    txtDst = filter.Target
    HourGlass Me
End Sub
```

You might recall my saying at the start of this chapter that the Object type and late binding are evil, and yet look at the type of the *filterobj* variable at the top of this procedure. Call me a liar. Call me a realist. All these filter classes have a

Name property, but it's set only once. No one will be able to tell the difference if the class-specific objects are bound late rather than early. On the other hand, the properties and methods of the IFilter variable passed to FilterText will be called over and over. You'd notice the difference on large conversion operations if you passed a variable with Object type rather than IFilter type.

Variations on Implements and Polymorphism

Methods and properties of Visual Basic interfaces are similar to what C++ and many other object-oriented languages call virtual functions. As with virtual functions, many syntactical variations are available, but not all of them make practical sense. And sometimes polymorphism needs a little help from other techniques—especially delegation. Let's check out some simple scenarios.

Implementing multiple interfaces

The CBugFilter class presented earlier implemented the IFilter interface. You could access the IFilter interface or the default _CBugFilter interface through separate object variables. Think about this for a moment. If you can get two interfaces through polymorphism, why not three interfaces? Why not 12? Why not 137 interfaces?

No problem.

Consider the CJumpHop class. It implements two interfaces: IHop and IJump. Here's IHop:

```
' IHop interface
Function Hop() As String
End Function
```

You can probably guess the IJump interface:

```
' IJump interface
Function Jump() As String
End Function
```

The CJumpHop class implements both of these interfaces:

```
' CJumpHop class
Implements IJump
Implements IHop

Private Function IHop_Hop() As String
    IHop_Hop = "Hop"
End Function

Private Function IJump_Jump() As String
    IJump_Jump = "Jump"
End Function
```

You can access the implementation of either interface through an appropriate object variable:

```
Dim h As IHop, j As IJump
Set h = New CJumpHop
Debug.Print h.Hop
Set j = h
Debug.Print j.Jump
```

You can access the Hop method polymorphically through the *h* object variable or you can access the Jump method polymorphically through the *j* object variable. Notice also that you can get at the IJump interface through an IHop object variable (*Set j = h*).

You could extend the CJumpHop class to have members of its own:

```
' Additional methods belonging to CJumpHop
Function Skip() As String
    Skip = "Skip"
End Function

Function Hop() As String
    Hop = IHop_Hop
End Function

Function Jump() As String
    Jump = IJump_Jump
End Function
```

These methods aren't polymorphic. They belong directly to the class and can be used like this:

```
Dim j As New CJumpHop
    Debug.Print jh.Skip
    Debug.Print jh.Hop
    Debug.Print jh.Jump
```

Notice that the Hop and Jump methods simply delegate to the polymorphic versions so that the CJumpHop class can have non-polymorphic versions without doing any work. The Hop method and the IHop_Hop method are separate methods accessible through different parts of the object, but they share the same implementation code.

This probably looks like a whole lot of nothing, and with interfaces this simple, it is. But imagine that you have a collection of graphical objects—stars, polyhedrons, ovals, and so on. There's a separate class for each kind of object, but the classes all implement the same interfaces. The IDrawable interface has methods and properties for setting the position and color of the shape object, and for drawing it. The IScaleable interface has methods and properties for scaling the objects to different sizes. The IMangleable interface has methods and properties for twisting and skewing the object. Now let's say you have a collection of these objects, and you want to draw the ones that are scaleable. You might do it something like this:

```
Dim scaleable As IScaleable, drawable As IDrawable, shape As CShape
    On Error Resume Next
For Each shape In shapes
    Set scaleable = shape
    ' An error indicates that the shape isn't scaleable
    If Err = 0 Then
        scaleable.Scale Rnd
        Set drawable = shape
        drawable.Color = QBColor(GetRandom(1, 15))
        drawable.X = GetRandom(0, pbShapes.Width)
        drawable.Y = GetRandom(0, pbShapes.Height)
        drawable.Draw pbShapes
    End If
Next
    On Error Goto 0
```

Like most air code, this snippet is probably full of bugs and errors, but I'm sure you could make it work. In fact, there's an example that does something very similar with multiple interfaces on the Visual Basic CD.

Enhancing public classes

When you create a public COM class or control, you are signing a contract never to change that component in any way that would break existing clients. I'll talk more about this in Chapter 10. In real life, things change, contract or no contract. The convention for creating a new class that is a superset of an existing class is to give it the same class name, but to append a digit. For example, if your main client, Big Brother And Company, complains that your CMotivate class just isn't doing the job, it might be a good idea to enhance it by creating the CMotivate2 class.

First, let's check CMotivate:

```
' CMotivate
Function Cheer() As String
    Cheer = "Rah, rah!"
End Function
```

That's OK, but maybe Big Brother wants to try some different incentives. Since you don't want to rewrite the whole class from scratch, you can use delegation to reuse the existing part of the class and add new features in CMotivate2:

```
' CMotivate2
Private motivate As New CMotivate

Function Cheer() As String
    Cheer = motivate.Cheer & " Rah!"
End Function

Function Threaten() As String
    Threaten = "Shape up!"
End Function
```

This class contains a CMotivate object, which it uses to provide the existing functionality. It enhances the existing Cheer method and adds a Threaten method. The technique of including an object in a class and using that object's features to enhance the new object is called containment—your outer object contains an inner object to which the outer object delegates part of the work. We'll be seeing a lot more delegation in this book—too much, in fact. We'll have to use delegation for tasks that would be done with inheritance in other object-oriented languages.

The CMotivate2 class does everything CMotivate does and more, but it doesn't do that work in the same contexts. For example, Big Brother might want to pass a CMotivate2 object to their Motivator function. Motivator was written by Big Brother and we have no control over it. They are perfectly satisfied with Motivator and have no intention of changing it. But they want the other benefits of the CMotivate2 class. Motivator looks like this:

```
Function Motivator(motivate As CMotivate) As String
    Motivator = motivate.Cheer
End Function
```

The client wants to use it like this:

```
Dim motivate2 As New CMotivate2
Debug.Print motivate2.Cheer
Debug.Print motivate2.Threaten
Debug.Print Motivator(motivate2)
'Error! Fail because motivate2 is not a CMotivate.
```

You receive a nasty note from Big Brother telling you that if they're going to have to rewrite all their programs, they might as well rewrite them with classes from some other vendor. You assure them that the CMotivate2 error was a fluke and that the CMotivate3 class will not only be compatible with CMotivate, but will also add more new features. In real life, CMotivate3 would have to be compatible with both CMotivate and CMotivate2, but to keep things simple, we'll pretend CMotivate2 was a beta version that was never deployed and that Big Brother doesn't need compatibility with it.

To be truly compatible, the CMotivate3 class needs to use the Implements statement to make the new class polymorphic with CMotivate. The methods and properties of the interfaces we've implemented so far have been empty, but that's not a requirement. In fact, every class you define has an interface, and in a sense, is an interface. IFilter is an interface by convention. Technically, it's an ordinary class that happens to have empty members and a name that follows the interface convention. Under the hood, IFilter has a real COM interface called _IFilter, but the Visual Basic Implements statement lets you use the class name to access the interface. It doesn't matter whether the implemented methods have their own implementation.

In object-oriented languages with inheritance, virtual functions are frequently given base functionality in the base class. Other classes inherit the base functionality and extend it. Since the functions are virtual, the extended class can work polymorphically. You'll find it difficult to do this with Visual Basic because it lacks inheritance, protected members, and other common features of object-oriented languages. Instead, you must use delegation to fake inheritance. Here's how the CMotivate3 class does it:

```
' CMotivate3
Implements CMotivate
Private motivate As New CMotivate

'Delegate to internal CMotivate object
Private Function CMotivate_Cheer() As String
    CMotivate_Cheer = motivate.Cheer & " Rah!"
End Function

'Reuse inner implementation for outer method
Function Cheer() As String
    Cheer = CMotivate_Cheer
End Function

Function Threaten() As String
    Threaten = "Shape up or ship out!"
End Function

Function Bribe() As String
    Bribe = "Cash under the table!"
End Function
```

By implementing the CMotivate_Cheer method with delegation, CMotivate3 provides an enhanced version of the Cheer method for CMotivate clients. It must provide a separate Public Cheer method for CMotivate3 clients, but it can delegate the work to CMotivate_Cheer.

Implementing windows and COM classes

Interfaces are a very important part of COM, and they're also the latest fad in API design. Many of the coolest new features of both COM and Windows aren't provided through traditional Windows API functions. Instead, they're provided by interfaces.

There are two kinds of standard interfaces. Some are implemented by the system so that you can call them. Examples include IShellLink (shortcuts) and IStorage (a new model for file I/O). You create the objects that implement these interfaces through API calls or through coclasses in type libraries. It's a case-by-case deal. We'll examine some specific examples later.

Other interfaces are implemented by you so that the system can call your objects. For example, if you implement IContextMenu, Windows can call your implementation to handle context menus associated with your documents. Techniques for registering or installing these interfaces vary on a case-by-case basis.

It's unfortunate that most of the standard interfaces you might want to use have Visual Basic–hostile definitions. Here are some of the common problems with interfaces:

- The designers of most standard interfaces don't provide type libraries for their interfaces. Imagine how C programmers would feel about the designer of an API system DLL who failed to provide C include files: "Real programmers can figure out the interface by hex-dumping the DLL files."

- Most standard interfaces use unsigned integer types even though Visual Basic only recognizes signed integer types.

- Most standard interfaces use LPSTR or LPWSTR type instead of the BSTR type used by Visual Basic.

- Many standard interfaces use structures (UDTs in Visual Basic) even though these are not legal types for public classes.

- Some standard interfaces return [out] parameters. This is a type library problem with a type library solution that you don't really want to know about.

- A few standard interfaces (including the important IEnumVARIANT) return positive HRESULT types, which Visual Basic can't handle. You don't really want to understand this one either.

In short, most standard interfaces are designed for C++ and other low-level languages. High-level languages like Visual Basic and FORTRAN are out of luck. Fortunately, Visual Basic programmers who buy my book have a workaround.

They can use the Windows API type library. It contains most of the standard interfaces you might want to use, but the names have been changed to protect the innocent. (The flame below takes care of the guilty.)

FLAME The Visual Basic people and the Windows and COM people don't seem to be talking to each other. New Windows and COM interfaces keep coming out, but they're language-specific and have no type libraries. So whose fault is it? Should the Windows and COM developers start writing Basic-friendly interfaces and type libraries? Or should the Visual Basic designers add features that allow Basic to use interfaces the way they are? Both. The origin of this problem is the split between COM Automation and the rest of COM. Automation is handled by the Visual Basic group and is mostly language-independent. The rest of COM is handled by different groups that until recently didn't seem to realize that non-C-based languages even existed. In fact, some Windows development is done by masochists who actually do COM development in C rather than C++ (check out the samples for new Windows 95 interfaces). I see some evidence that both sides are beginning to recognize that they have a problem, but in the meantime, Visual Basic programmers are the losers.

So how do my interface definitions get around the problems discussed above? Well, I lie. I claim that unsigned integers are signed. I change the definitions so that Visual Basic understands them. My type library uses a specific type library technique to make interfaces private to the applications that use them so that they won't overwrite the official interfaces used by other programs on your machine. Comments in the type library source files and in other documents on the CD describe the process in general. It's a type library problem, so I won't explain the details in this Visual Basic book.

As a Visual Basic programmer, you need to know only that the interfaces exist in the type library and that they follow a specific naming convention. I add the letters *VB* after the *I* in the interface name. So my version of IShellLink is IVBShellLink. My IEnumVARIANT is IVBEnumVARIANT. In theory, you can simply use the Implements statement on standard interfaces in the type library the same way you implement Visual Basic interfaces. In practice, many interfaces require workarounds and hacks. We'll be looking at some examples in later chapters.

4

Collecting Objects

"Visual Basic isn't a real language because it doesn't have pointers, and without pointers you can't do data structures."

Ever heard that one? You might even believe it if you've ever taken a computer science course on data structures. People devote entire careers to figuring out new ways of writing linked lists, trees, hash tables, stacks, queues, and other abstract data types—all of which are implemented with pointers. Meanwhile, until recently, Visual Basic was stuck with only one data structure—the humble array—all because, as I noted before, Visual Basic doesn't do pointers.

There have always been workarounds. In ancient versions of Basic, linked lists and other abstract data structures were sometimes implemented using parallel arrays of data and indexes, with the indexes used to fake pointers. It's not a pretty sight, and, fortunately, it's no longer necessary. In modern Visual Basic, there are a lot more options. You can create your own data structures, you can use the predefined ones (arrays and the Collection class), or, as the rest of this chapter explains, you can wrap those predefined data structures in classes that make them behave like more sophisticated data structures.

Visual Basic supports two built-in data structures: arrays and the Collection (with an uppercase *C*) class. This chapter will describe how to create classes that encapsulate other data structures. These data structure classes—sometimes called collection (with a lowercase *c*) classes—come in two forms.

Generic collection classes abstract a particular data structure for storing user variables and objects. The point is the organization of the data and the standard operations for using it. You can store any kind of data you want (as long as it fits in a Variant) in these collection classes. Visual Basic's Collection class serves as a rough model for some of the generic classes I'll create. These include CList, CVector, and CStack classes. The difference between them is how they handle common operations such as adding, removing, searching, indexing, and iterating.

In addition, you can create *specific collection classes* that provide controlled access to specific types of variables or objects. Visual Basic comes with several such collections: Forms, Printers, and Controls. Some controls provide specific collection classes: Nodes in TreeView, ListImages in ImageList, ListItems in ListView, and so on. Specific collection classes are also common in object models exposed by applications such as Excel. I'll create a CDrives class that contains a CDrive object for each drive in the system. These classes are carefully designed to control addition and deletion of items so that the collection never contains incompatible items.

One warning before we get started—you'll find some pretty dense code and text in parts of this chapter. Don't get discouraged if you have trouble following it the first time. You don't have to understand every detail of a linked list or iteration class to use one. Some early parts of the chapter are setting the stage for concepts introduced in the last part. It's OK to skim and come back later.

A List of Link Objects

Although Visual Basic doesn't do pointers, it does do objects. It is possible to use objects to create data structures in the same way that other languages use pointers to create data structures. Let's take a brief look at a linked list class and see if you agree with my conclusion—which is that you should think twice before using this technique in real life.

To create a linked list, you need something to link and something to link it with. Object-oriented linked lists are usually written with two classes—a link class representing the items in the list, and a list class that manages the links. Often there's a third class—an iterator class—that walks through the list. Users interact with the list and the iterator classes; the link class is private. We will follow this pattern. You can follow the code by loading the Test Collections project (TCOLLECT.VBG).

A Link Class

The CLink class looks like this:

```
' CLink class
Public Item As Variant  ' Default member
Public NextLink As CLink
```

This is that rarest of beasts—a no-code class. The data is stored in Item. Because Item is a Variant, different links can contain different kinds of data. Other languages use untyped pointers to hold any kind of data, but the Variant solution is more convenient. You could, of course, make Item a specific type if you wanted a linked list of Strings or Doubles. Such a class would be more efficient, but less flexible. Visual Basic uses the Variant strategy—there's only one Collection class, no LongCollection or StringCollection.

Item is the default property, so you can actually use the object name to refer to the Item property. Get used to it. In this book, any property or method named Item is likely to be the default. The Collection class sets a standard, and I'm following it. Incidentally, when you look at the CLink class, it's easy to think of Item and NextLink as fields of a UDT. Don't be deceived. They are properties, and you'll get a procedure call every time you use one.

The NextLink property has the same type (CLink) as the current link. This link might contain another link, which might contain another link, and so on. Actually, it's more accurate to think of the first object as pointing to the second object. The objects in the list are separate and independent of each other. Internal pointers give them the illusion of containing other objects.

Using a List Class

The real work of managing the links is done by the CList class. As I mentioned earlier, users never access the CLink class directly. But before we examine how CList works, let's see how it's used:

```
' Insert item into list
Dim list As New CList
list.Add "Bear"
list.Add "Tiger"
list.Add "Lion"
list.Add "Elephant"
list.Add "Horse"
list.Add "Dog"
```

This code adds some entries to the list. If you look at the *list* variable in the Locals window at this point, you'll be impressed and perhaps a little surprised. The list object has a Head member that shows the first item in the list. You can expand it and expand its NextLink, and expand the NextLink of that, and so on to the end of the list. For this short list, there's room in the Locals window to confirm that all the items are really there but not necessarily in the order you'd expect. The last item added appears at the head of the list.

Because clients don't have access to the Locals window, they might want some methods and properties to get at the entries:

```
s = s & "Count: " & list.Count & sCrLf
s = s & "Head: " & list & sCrLf
s = s & "Item 2: " & list(2) & sCrLf
s = s & "Item Tiger: " & list("Tiger") & sCrLf
```

Here's the output from these statements:

```
Count: 6
Head: Dog
Item 2: Horse
Item Tiger: Tiger
```

The string index doesn't make much sense for this list of strings; it just returns what you already know. But it might be useful for a list of class objects:

```
Debug.Print list("Tiger").Fierceness
```

In this case, you are asking for the object whose default property has the value *Tiger*. You can also use the string index to replace an item, as follows:

```
s = s & "Replace Elephant with Pig" & sCrLf
list("Elephant") = "Pig"
```

The list also has a Remove method that removes either the first item (by default) or another item (specified by a string or an index) as shown below:

```
s = s & "Remove head: " & list & sCrLf
list.Remove
s = s & "Remove Bear" & sCrLf
list.Remove "Bear"
s = s & "Remove 3: " & list(3) & sCrLf
list.Remove 3
```

This is all fine as far as it goes, but it's hard to tell whether the list works because there's no way to iterate through it to see all the entries.

One way or another, you need to be able to iterate through the list. So why not just add a NextItem method to the CList class so that you can iterate through the items? Well, you could, and I did in an early implementation of CList. Originally, I based my linked list class on a C++ list in *The C++ Programming Language* (Addison-Wesley, 1986) by C++ creator Bjarne Stroustrup. His list had a separate iterator class, but I thought this was an unnecessary complication that I didn't need to follow. Well, as the design progressed I began to realize why he's a language designer and I'm a mere book author. So I'm going to start things off right with a separate CListWalker class. I think this will make sense by the time I finish, even if it doesn't now.

Using a List Iterator Class

If you write a separate iterator class that walks through the items in the list, you'll be able to create multiple iterator objects. Each one will be able to walk through the list separately. Who would want a road with only one car permanently attached? It's much better to make the road and the car separate objects and allow multiple cars at different places on the same road. If you're not convinced by this analogy, hold your piece. There are other reasons for separate iterators.

Here's an example of how to use an iterator:

```
Dim walker As New CListWalker
walker.Attach list
Do While walker.More
    s = s & Space$(4) & walker & sCrLf
Loop
```

First you have to tell the iterator object which list to iterate by passing a list object to the Attach method. Then you loop through the items in the list. The Item property is the default member, so you can omit the method name. The CLink, CList, and CListWalker classes all have default Item properties. Don't confuse them.

Since CListWalker is a separate class, two objects can iterate separately without interfering with each other. For example, here's a nested iterator. The outside iterator walks partway, then the inside iterator walks the entire list, and finally the outside iterator regains control and continues where it left off:

```
Dim walker2 As New CListWalker
s = s & "Nesting iterate:" & sCrLf
walker.Attach list
Do While walker.More
    s = s & Space$(4) & walker & sCrLf
    If walker = "Pig" Then
        walker2.Attach list
        s = s & Space$(4) & "Nested iterate:" & sCrLf
        Do While walker2.More
            s = s & Space$(8) & walker2 & sCrLf
        Loop
    End If
Loop
```

Stop! You probably think I'm missing the obvious. You don't want to iterate with Do Loop. You want to iterate with For Each. It should be simple:

```
s = s & "Iterate with For Each:" & sCrLf
Dim v As Variant
For Each v In list
    s = s & Space$(4) & "V: " & v & sCrLf
Next
```

That does, in fact, work, but I'm not going to tell you why until the end of the chapter. For now, all I can say is that classes that work with For Each work because they have an iterator class just as CList has a CListWalker.

Implementing a List Class

There are many ways to implement linked lists, but I chose one of the most simple. Don't assume, however, that the list will be obvious. The simple class you see before you went through a lot of iterations and a lot of testing to reach its current state.

The CList class has the following private members:

```
Private lnkHead As CLink
Private c As Long
```

The *lnkHead* member is what makes the list work. The *c* member is just for counting the members for the Count property. The *lnkHead* member is the only access to the list; in addition, all new members must be added here. It's also the only access the CLinkWalker will have. The following Friend property makes the Head available to cooperating classes:

```
' Make data structure available to cooperating classes
Friend Property Get Head() As CLink
    Set Head = lnkHead
End Property
```

The Add method should give you a feel for the implementation:

```
' Insert at head of list
Sub Add(vItem As Variant)
    ' Create temporary link with new value
    Dim lnkTmp As CLink
    Set lnkTmp = New CLink
    If IsObject(vItem) Then
        Set lnkTmp.Item = vItem
    Else
        lnkTmp.Item = vItem
    End If
    ' Point it where previous head pointed
    Set lnkTmp.NextLink = lnkHead
    ' Attach it to front
    Set lnkHead = lnkTmp
    ' lnkTmp temporary goes out of scope and disappears
    c = c + 1
End Sub
```

If this code seems confusing, try stepping through it in the TCOLLECT.VBG project. Put watches on the *lnkTmp* and *lnkHead* object variables. Watch as the first item is added to the list, and keep watching as more items are added.

I could show you more methods and properties, but they wouldn't make sense until you understand the CListWalker class.

Implementing a List Iterator

Although I'm going to show you a specific iterator class, you should be thinking of iterators as a general concept. Any collection of data might need an iterator class, regardless of its organization. In fact, the interface of all iterator classes ought to look the same, no matter what objects they iterate.

CListWalker has the following internal variables to keep track of its state:

```
' Connect back to parent collection
Private connect As CList
' Current link
Private lnkCur As CLink
```

This is typical. Any iterator has these two requirements: a reference (*connect*) to the collection it will iterate through and at least one state variable to keep track of its current position (*lnkCur*).

First let's look at an example of how an iterator connects to its collection. CListWalker does this with the Attach method:

```
' Attach a list to iterator
Sub Attach(connectA As CList)
    ' Initialize position in collection
    Set connect = connectA
End Sub
```

If you look at the real code in LISTWALK.CLS, you'll see that it is actually a little more complicated, but the other parts don't matter at this point.

Clients must call Attach before doing anything else with the class. In fact, it would be part of the constructor in languages that support object initialization at creation. The connection between CList and CListWalker is two-way. CList provides a Head friend property for CListWalker, and CListWalker provides a CurLink friend property for CList:

```
' Expose current link to friends
Friend Property Get CurLink() As CLink
    Set CurLink = lnkCur
End Property
Friend Property Set CurLink(lnkCurA As CLink)
    Set lnkCur = lnkCurA
End Property
```

CListWalker also provides access to the current data through its Item property:

```
' Default member
Property Get Item() As Variant
    If IsObject(lnkCur.Item) Then
        Set Item = lnkCur.Item
    Else
        Item = lnkCur.Item
    End If
End Property
```

Here's another default Item. The *lnkCur* member is of type CLink, and CLink also has a default Item member. So, in theory, you could omit Item from *lnkCur*. But what would the following statement mean?

```
Set Item = lnkCur
```

Would you be setting the Item property to the link or to the default member of the link? Do you want to find out, or do you want your customers to find out? This is why Joe Hacker claims that default properties are an invention of the devil. Personally, I kind of like them, but I don't deny that they can be confusing and dangerous.

You might as well get used to this little block of code. Any container class based on variants needs to check for objects before any assignment is made. Someday you're going to forget to do this. Let's hope you find the bug easier to identify and fix than I did.

The real work of the iterator is done by the More method. It figures out whether there is more data in the list and, if so, advances to the next member. I wanted to name the More method Next, because this is a common name for the equivalent method in other languages. Visual Basic already uses Next as a keyword, so I had to choose another name:

```
' Report whether there are more links to iterate
Function More() As Boolean
    If lnkCur Is Nothing Then
        ' Don't skip the first time through
        Set lnkCur = connect.Head
    Else
        ' Skip to the next item
        Set lnkCur = lnkCur.NextLink
    End If
    ' When the next link is nothing, we're done (handles empty list)
    If Not lnkCur Is Nothing Then More = True
End Function
```

Often, a More method has to take a different action the first time through the list than on subsequent passes. You'll see more Mores with different organizations before the end of this chapter.

Back to CList for Iterators

I skipped some of the most important methods of the CList class with no explanation. For example, you might have wondered why I didn't explain the Item method. Or you might have cheated and looked ahead. If so, you realized that Item finds a specified entry the same way you would find it from outside the class; it creates a local iterator and uses it to search through the list.

This is another reason to make CListWalker a separate class. Although this code is long and messy, it would be even more so if iteration weren't abstracted in a separate class.

Here's the code for the Property Get. The Property Let and Property Set procedures use a similar technique. Although it takes a lot of code to find the appropriate item, returning it in the Get procedure or modifying it in the Set or Let procedures is a simple operation.

```
' Default property
Property Get Item(Optional vIndex As Variant = 1) As Variant
    If lnkHead Is Nothing Then Exit Property
    ' Walk through to find the item
    Dim walker As New CListWalker, v As Variant
    Dim i As Long, iIndex As Long, sIndex As String

    ' Find the matching link
    walker.Attach Me
    If VarType(vIndex) = vbString Then
        ' Search by string key
        sIndex = vIndex
        ' Ignore error for entries that can't be string compared
        On Error Resume Next
        Do While walker.More
            With walker.CurLink
                If .Item = sIndex Then
                    If IsObject(.Item) Then
                        Set Item = .Item
                    Else
                        Item = .Item
                    End If
                    Exit Property
                End If
            End With
        Loop
```

(continued)

```
    Else
        ' Search by numeric index
        iIndex = vIndex
        Do While walker.More
            i = i + 1
            With walker.CurLink
                If iIndex = i Then
                    If IsObject(.Item) Then
                        Set Item = .Item
                    Else
                        Item = .Item
                    End If
                    Exit Property
                End If
            End With
        Loop
    End If
    ' Item = Empty
End Property
```

The Remove member works essentially the same way. It creates an iterator and walks through the list until it finds the item to be removed.

If you study this code carefully, you'll begin to see why a linked list has limited utility. If you have 100 entries in the list and you want entry 99, you have to iterate through 99 entries to get there.

The advantage of a linked list is that it can grow or shrink, and it contains exactly the number of entries you put in. It's easy to get at the first entry, and it's easy to iterate from the front to the back. Accessing entries in the middle is not a strong point of lists. If these features meet your needs, fine. If not, you might prefer a doubly linked list—one with references to both the previous and the next links. The iterator for such a list should be able to move either forward or backward. The trade-off is more data for each link and more code for managing both links.

Perhaps you're starting to get the idea that no data structure can be ideal for every kind of data. There's always a trade-off. That's why programmers in low-level languages like to have lots of data structures; you can pick the one that best fits your needs. Visual Basic programmers now have greater flexibility (and confusion) in choosing among multiple data structures.

CHALLENGE   Although the CList class proves that lists based on objects are possible, these lists have more overhead and are bound to be slower than comparable lists based on pointers. If you really want an efficient linked list class, consider implementing it as an ActiveX component in C++ rather than in Visual Basic. This leads to my main point: the component industry has let us down.

By now, we Visual Basic programmers ought to have a lot of fast, efficient collection components, giving us a wide choice of how we want to organize our data. Sure, we ought to be able to create collections in Visual Basic, and, as you'll see later in this chapter, it is possible, although Visual Basic won't help much. But I would use Visual Basic mainly for creating specific collections such as disks, drives, Registry nodes, and so on. I don't think Visual Basic is the best language for creating generic container classes such as stacks, queues, dictionaries, lists, sparse arrays, etc. That's what C++ is for. I want better collection classes, and I don't think it's Microsoft's responsibility to provide them. If someone wants to step up and provide these tools, I'll be first in line with cold cash. Otherwise, I might have to take on the job myself.

Vectors as Resizeable Arrays

When Visual Basic version 4 was released, many programmers saw the new Collection class as an improved version of arrays. They started automatically replacing their arrays with Collections. Then they discovered the high performance cost and started changing Collections back to arrays.

This is the wrong way to look at it. Collections don't replace arrays; both are useful data structures with advantages and disadvantages. Choose the one that best fits the need.

The advantage of arrays is their fixed size and structure. If you put an element in a certain position in an array, you can be sure that it will be there when you come back. You can access an element easily and efficiently as long as you remember its location.

The disadvantage of arrays is their fixed size and structure. If you don't know how many items you have, you don't know how big to make the array. If you remove or add items, you have to jump through hoops to keep track of where everything is.

Often, Collections are overkill if a variable number of elements is all you need to handle. If string indexing and other Collection features don't do anything for you, perhaps you need a simpler, faster data structure known as a resizeable array, or vector.

Using Vectors

Before Collections, Visual Basic programmers used to get around the array size problem by resizing arrays in chunks. My CVector class uses the chunk technique but hides the ugly details.

As usual, I'll show you what you can do with a CVector before I show you how it works. Here's a typical initialization loop:

```
Dim vector As New CVector, i As Long, s As String
s = "Insert numbers in vector: " & sCrLf
For i = 1 To 15
    vector(i) = i * i
    s = s & Space$(4) & i * i & ": vector(" & i & ")" & sCrLf
Next
```

Vectors can grow to whatever size you want. Just keep adding more elements, and the vector automatically adjusts.

Notice that the vectors are one-based. That's a design choice. I could have started them at 0 or −1 or 5. In an early implementation, I started them at 0 but often used them as if they started at 1. Since vectors always waste space, I felt wasting that extra 0 element wasn't a big deal. But with use, I discovered that ignoring that extra element wasn't such a good idea. If you like negative vectors, go ahead, but you'll end up with a different class with different implementation problems.

Don't worry about inserting elements far beyond the end of the array. That works. You can even initialize from the top down:

```
For i = 100 To 1 Step -1
    vv(i) = i * i
Next
```

Normally, you'll want to read only the elements that have been initialized:

```
s = s & "Read numbers from vector: " & sCrLf
For i = 1 To vector.Last
    s = s & Space$(4) & "vector(" & i & ") = " & vector(i) & sCrLf
Next
```

The vector keeps track of the last element to be initialized and reports it through the Last property.

CVector addresses the problem of growing arrays, but what about shrinking arrays? Well, it is possible to shrink the vector by setting the Last property:

```
s = s & "Shrink vector to 5 and read numbers: " & sCrLf
vector.Last = 5
For i = 1 To vector.Last
    s = s & Space$(4) & "vector(" & i & ") = " & vector(i) & sCrLf
Next

s = s & "Read numbers with For Each: " & sCrLf
Dim v As Variant
For Each v In vector
    s = s & Space$(4) & "v = " & v & sCrLf
Next
```

If you shrink the vector, all the elements beyond the new Last get thrown into the bit bucket. Expanding the vector to the original size won't bring them back, and there's no way to delete entries in the middle of the vector. As with arrays, entries stay exactly where you put them unless you move them.

If this looks too good to be true, well, there is a cost—and it's one that experienced programmers know well. You spend data space to get better performance.

CVector Implementation

The CVector class is essentially a wrapper around an array. Here's the internal data that makes it work:

```
Private av() As Variant
Private iLast As Long
Private cChunk As Long

Private Sub Class_Initialize()
    cChunk = 10      ' Default size can be overridden
    ReDim Preserve av(1 To cChunk) As Variant
    iLast = 1
End Sub
```

Most of the implementation is in the Item property. Because CVector is a variant container class and because you don't know whether the variants in the internal array will be objects or variables, you must implement all three property procedures—Get, Let, and Set. Here's the code:

```
' Item is the default property
Property Get Item(ByVal i As Long) As Variant
    BugAssert i > 0
    ' If index is out-of-range, return default (Empty)
    On Error Resume Next
    If IsObject(av(i)) Then
        Set Item = av(i)
```

(continued)

```
        Else
            Item = av(i)
        End If
End Property

Property Let Item(ByVal i As Long, ByVal vItemA As Variant)
    BugAssert i > 0
    On Error GoTo FailLetItem
    av(i) = vItemA
    If i > iLast Then iLast = i
    Exit Property
FailLetItem:
    If i > UBound(av) Then
        ReDim Preserve av(1 To i + cChunk) As Variant
        Resume        ' Try again
    End If
    ErrRaise Err.Number      ' Other VB error for client
End Property

Property Set Item(ByVal i As Long, ByVal vItemA As Variant)
    BugAssert i > 0
    On Error GoTo FailSetItem
    Set av(i) = vItemA
    If i > iLast Then iLast = i
    Exit Property
FailSetItem:
    If i > UBound(av) Then
        ReDim Preserve av(1 To i + cChunk) As Variant
        Resume        ' Try again
    End If
    ErrRaise Err.Number       ' Other VB error for client
```

As I stated earlier, CVector is the *av* Variant array in a thin class wrapper. The Item property accesses elements of the array, but because it is marked as the default property, clients don't have to give the Item method name. Access to the indexed Item property looks like access to an array. The sidebar on page 184 gives more details on how property procedures can be used to simulate array indexes.

The main complication in the Property Get is that you have to check to see whether the variant being accessed is a variable or an object so that you can use Set to assign objects. My implementation turns off error checking and lets invalid data requests return Empty. I could have chosen to raise an out-of-range error, and that might be more appropriate in vectors of integers or other types that don't have an equivalent of Empty.

The Let and Set property procedures use error trapping to identify when you try to insert beyond the end of the array. The array is then resized. The size of the *cChunk* variable determines the efficiency of the vector. A larger chunk size means faster element writes because the expensive redimensioning is less frequent, but it also means more wasted data space.

The CVector class has a couple of other properties. The Chunk property just gets or (more likely) sets the size of the data chunks. The default size (10) is a good compromise for most vectors, but you can fine-tune it if you like. The Last property returns or sets the last element in the array:

```
Property Get Last() As Long
    Last = iLast
End Property
Property Let Last(iLastA As Long)
    BugAssert iLastA > 0
    ReDim Preserve av(1 To iLastA) As Variant
    iLast = iLastA
End Property
```

Notice that setting Last specifically resizes the array. Usually it is used to shrink a vector when you know you'll no longer need data beyond a certain point. You can also use it to expand an array specifically rather than automatically.

What's the cost? Well, in the Item Property Get, you pay for accessing the array through a procedure call rather than inline code. You also pay for checking to see if the entry is an object, but that's not really the vector's fault; you'd have to do the same thing with an array of variants. In the Item Property Let and Property Set, you also pay for the procedure call. In addition, there's an extra expense for an error trap, even when you don't hit it. And when you do hit the error trap, you pay an even bigger penalty for resizing the array.

What does this add up to? It depends on what you're comparing it to. Check the Performance sidebar on page 191. You could get the same benefits at less cost by hard-coding similar error traps into each program that needs an expandable array. But since CVector exists as compiled native code in the VBCore DLL, the cost usually isn't worth worrying about.

If you want even greater efficiency, use the typed versions in VBCore. I started with the general CVector class for variants, and then I did a Save As to create the CVectorInt class. Next I did a global search and replace to change Variant to Integer, and then I cut out the variant-specific features. From there it was easy to create CVectorInt, CVectorLng, CVectorBool, CVectorStr, CVectorSng, and CVectorDbl.

Of these, the most interesting is CVectorBool. A Visual Basic Boolean is a 16-bit value (the same as an Integer). This is kind of a strange choice, but don't blame Visual Basic; COM Automation defines the size. Many languages make Boolean types 8-bit to save data space in arrays. Windows makes its BOOL type the system integer size (Long in 32-bit) for greater efficiency. But all it really takes to store a Boolean is one bit. That's how many bits CVectorBool uses for each element. It actually stores its elements as Longs and crams 32 Boolean values into each of them, using logical operators to insert and extract the bits. All this happens behind the scenes. The Item property returns the bits as Boolean, just as you would expect. The CVectorBool class is 16 times more data efficient than an array of Booleans, and the performance cost for this savings is small. Check it out in VECTORBOOL.CLS.

Property Arrays

Visual Basic is the only language I know that uses parentheses for array subscripts. (Most languages use square brackets.) This practice leads to ambiguity in the language. Does

```
i = Zap(4)
```

assign element 4 of the *Zap* array to *i*, or does it call the Zap function with argument 4 and assign the result to *i*? I used to think this was a flaw in the language, but it's handy when you create properties that look and act like arrays.

For example, assume that you are creating a CParanoia class, whose objects have an EnemyList property. You want to use it as follows:

```
scared.EnemyList(i) = "Jones"
Calumniate scared.EnemyList(i)
```

EnemyList looks like an array and acts like an array, but you must implement it as a property, and properties can't be arrays. You might expect that if you declare a public array in a form or a class, it would become a property array:

```
Public EnemyList(1 To 10) As String
```

Visual Basic throws this statement out at compile time with a message telling you that arrays can't be public. You can usually create more reliable properties with Property Get and Property Let anyway, but it's not immediately clear how to do this. The answer is that you fake subscripts with property parameters.

Behind your properties, you must have a private array or a collection. Let's use an array here:

CHALLENGE You can have lots of fun enhancing my CVector class. Start with multiple dimensions. How about a CMatrix class? Maybe you could write some functions that do math on vectors or matrices. FORTRAN can do addition, subtraction, multiplication, division, and even exponentiation on arrays. Why can't Visual Basic? You can also do comparisons and logical operations. Without operator overloading, Visual Basic might not be able to make array expressions as natural as they are in some languages, but with care, you can probably come up with a fairly clean syntax. With native code, the operations themselves can be as fast in Visual Basic as they are in other languages.

```
Private asEnemies(1 To 10) As String
```

Property Get procedures normally don't have parameters, but when faking subscripts, you need one argument for every array dimension. Since you're faking a one-dimensional array, you need only one argument:

```
Property Get EnemyList(i As Integer) As String
    If i >= 1 And i <= 10 Then EnemyList = asEnemies(i)
End Property
```

Normally, Property Let procedures have one argument, but you'll need an extra argument for each array dimension. The assignment parameter must be the last parameter:

```
Property Let EnemyList(i As Integer, sEnemyA As String)
    If i >= 1 And i <= 10 Then asEnemies(i) = sEnemyA
End Property
```

Expanding on this technique, you can easily design properties that represent multidimensional arrays:

```
iHiCard = deck.Cards(iClubs, iJack)
```

You can even have array properties with string or real number indexes:

```
iHiCard = deck.Cards("Clubs", "Jack")
Print patient.Temperature(98.6)
```

Obviously, this syntax would be impossible with real arrays. You decide how your parameters relate to the data hidden in your class.

Stacking Objects

A stack is a data structure in which you can add items only to the top and remove them only from the top. The technical term is *LIFO* (last in, first out), but anyone who has ever stacked plates or books knows the concept. You might find it convenient for storing forms, controls, or files. The idea is that you can't get anything out of a stack in the wrong order because the stack allows only one order. The traditional terminology for stack operations is that you "push" things onto a stack and "pop" them off.

There are many different ways to implement a stack. To illustrate this point, I'm going to start with a stack interface rather than a stack class. (See "Polymorphism and Interfaces" in Chapter 3 for an introduction to interfaces.) I'll implement three different versions of the stack and test them to see which is the fastest. Here's the IStack interface:

```
' IStack interface class
Public Sub Push(vArg As Variant)
End Sub

Public Function Pop() As Variant
End Function

Property Get Count() As Long
End Property
```

The CStackLst class is based on the linked list technique and the CStackVec class is based on the vector technique described earlier in this chapter. The CStackCol class is based on Visual Basic's Collection class. Because all three stacks implement the same interface, the client program can use any of them with exactly the same code.

As a practical matter, the interface approach doesn't make much sense. There's no reason to keep three different implementations of the stack around—you want only the fastest one. So once we figure out which one that is, we'll use Save As to create the one and only CStack class for the VBCore component.

Using a Stack

Before we get into implementation details, here's how you use the interface and the classes that implement it:

```
txtOut.Text = s
txtOut.Refresh
Dim beasts As IStack
Select Case GetOption(optStack)
Case 0
```

```
        Set beasts = New CStackLst
Case 1
        Set beasts = New CStackVec
Case 2
        Set beasts = New CStackCol
End Select
s = s & Space$(4) & "Push Lion" & sCrLf
beasts.Push "Lion"
s = s & Space$(4) & "Push Tiger" & sCrLf
beasts.Push "Tiger"
s = s & Space$(4) & "Push Bear" & sCrLf
beasts.Push "Bear"
s = s & Space$(4) & "Push Shrew" & sCrLf
beasts.Push "Shrew"
s = s & Space$(4) & "Push Weasel" & sCrLf
beasts.Push "Weasel"
s = s & Space$(4) & "Push Yetti" & sCrLf
beasts.Push "Yetti"

s = s & "Pop animals off stack: " & sCrLf
Do While beasts.Count
    s = s & Space$(4) & "Pop " & beasts.Pop & sCrLf
Loop
```

In the example, an array of option buttons determines which class will be instantiated with the IStack object variable. (The sidebar on the following page demonstrates the GetOption function.) The output looks like this:

```
Push animals onto stack:
    Push Lion
    Push Tiger
    Push Bear
    Push Shrew
    Push Weasel
    Push Yetti
Pop animals off stack:
    Pop Yetti
    Pop Weasel
    Pop Shrew
    Pop Bear
    Pop Tiger
    Pop Lion
```

In addition, the sample starts timing, pushes the number of integers specified by the Count text box onto a stack, pops them off, and then stops the timing. You can check the source in TCOLLECT.FRM. I'll tell you the timing results later.

A Control Array Is Not an Array

One of the least understood data structures in Visual Basic is the control array. You won't find it in the object browser and the documentation on it is…well, it exists, but not necessarily where you expect to find it.

The most important feature of a control array is that it isn't an array. It's more like a collection, complete with properties and an iterator. Here's a summary of what I've been able to figure out.

First, a control array has LBound and UBound *properties*. Don't confuse these with the LBound and UBound *functions,* which take a real array (but not a control array) as a parameter. A control array also has a Count property, but the count isn't necessarily the same as the number of places in the array (UBound - LBound + 1) because a control array can have unused entries. The best way to handle a control array is to ignore the properties and iterate with For Each. That way you skip any empty entries.

Here's an example that solves the annoying problem of trying to figure out which option button is selected in a control array of option buttons:

```
' Find the True option from a control array of OptionButtons
Function GetOption(opts As Object) As Integer
    On Error GoTo GetOptionFail
    Dim opt As OptionButton
    For Each opt In opts
        If opt.Value Then
            GetOption = opt.Index
            Exit Function
        End If
    Next
    On Error GoTo 0
    ErrRaise eeNoTrueOption
    Exit Function
GetOptionFail:
    ErrRaise eeNotOptionArray
End Function
```

The error handling technique used here is explained in Chapter 5.

Implementing a Stack

The easiest way to implement a stack is to use an internal Collection. You simply add new members to the end of the Collection in the Push method and take them off the end in the Pop method:

```
' CStackCol implements IStack
Implements IStack
Private stack As Collection

Private Sub Class_Initialize()
    Set stack = New Collection
End Sub

Private Sub IStack_Push(vArg As Variant)
    stack.Add vArg
End Sub

Private Function IStack_Pop() As Variant
    If stack.Count Then
        If IsObject(stack(stack.Count)) Then
            Set IStack_Pop = stack(stack.Count)
        Else
            IStack_Pop = stack(stack.Count)
        End If
        stack.Remove stack.Count
    End If
End Function

Private Property Get IStack_Count() As Long
    IStack_Count = stack.Count
End Property
```

The Collection version is easy to implement, and its performance isn't bad—for a small stack. The problem with the Collection-based stack is that it slows way down if you push too many things onto it. This isn't really surprising. Implementing IStack with a Collection is like shooting ducks with a grenade launcher.

A linked list might be more appropriate. I won't show the implementation because it looks a lot like a simplified version of the CList code you've already seen. Check it out for yourself in STACKLST.CLS.

The list version is a little slow for small stacks, but its speed is constant. In fact, it turns out to be a lot faster than the Collection version for large stacks. Also, it doesn't waste data space like this vector version:

```
Private av() As Variant
Private Const cChunk = 10
Private iLast As Long, iCur As Long
```

(continued)

```
Private Sub IStack_Push(vArg As Variant)
    iCur = iCur + 1
    On Error GoTo FailPush
    If IsObject(vArg) Then
        Set av(iCur) = vArg
    Else
        av(iCur) = vArg
    End If
    Exit Sub
FailPush:
    iLast = iLast + cChunk   ' Grow
    ReDim Preserve av(1 To iLast) As Variant
    Resume                       ' Try again
End Sub

Private Function IStack_Pop() As Variant
    If iCur Then
        If IsObject(av(iCur)) Then
            Set IStack_Pop = av(iCur)
        Else
            IStack_Pop = av(iCur)
        End If
        iCur = iCur - 1
        If iCur < (iLast - cChunk) Then
            iLast = iLast - cChunk        ' Shrink
            ReDim Preserve av(1 To iLast) As Variant
        End If
    End If
End Function

Private Property Get IStack_Count() As Long
    IStack_Count = iCur
End Property
```

The vector version is the most complicated and has the most lines of code, but don't let that fool you. It's far and away the fastest, as the Performance sidebar on the facing page shows. It does waste a little data space, but you can adjust that by changing the *cChunk* constant. In fact, if you set *cChunk* to 1, you won't waste any data space and you'll still be faster than the other versions—even though you'll be resizing the array for every push and pop.

Problem: Compare the speed of stacks based on Collections, linked lists, and vectors.

Problem	P-Code	Native Code
Use Collection stack of 500 numbers	0.1161 sec	0.0853 sec
Use Collection stack of 5000 numbers	10.0181 sec	9.3406 sec
Use linked list stack of 500 numbers	0.1357 sec	0.0972 sec
Use linked list stack of 5000 numbers	1.3360 sec	1.0265 sec
Use vector stack of 500 numbers	0.0294 sec	0.0162 sec
Use vector stack of 5000 numbers	0.2929 sec	0.1597 sec

Conclusion: Not even close. Vectors win by several laps. The CStack class in VBCore is a noninterface version of CStackVec.

The Collection Class

You've probably used Visual Basic's Collection class, but you might not understand exactly what it is. Let's take a look behind the curtain.

To put it simply, the Collection class is a souped-up C++ version of the CList class described in "A List of Link Objects," page 170. In fact, if you enhance CList to be a doubly linked list and give it a few more features (and perhaps use a hash table to look up string keys), you'll have a collection class much like the one provided with Visual Basic. You could even add the code required to make it iterate with For Each.

But before we get to the part about writing your own enumeration classes, let's review some of the tried and true features of the Collection class.

Collections 101—Data Storage

A Collection is what some computer science books refer to as a *dictionary,* that is, a table of items in which you can look up an entry by using a key. Collections start out simple, but they can easily become complicated. Let's briefly run through the features of Collections by looking at a simple one:

```
Dim animals As New Collection
```

Here's the code to load a Collection with strings—which are actually converted to Variants because that's the only data type Collections recognize:

```
' Create collection
animals.Add "Lion"
animals.Add "Tiger"
animals.Add "Bear"
animals.Add "Shrew", , 1
animals.Add "Weasel", , , 1
```

The first three Add methods put *Lion*, *Tiger*, and *Bear* in the Collection in that order, as items 1, 2, and 3. The Collection class is one-based, and new items go at the end unless you specify otherwise. The fourth Add method uses the third parameter to specify that the new item will precede existing item 1. The last Add method uses the fourth parameter to specify that the new item will follow existing item 1.

Once you have a Collection, you'll want to access its members. You can use indexes, just as you do for an array:

```
Debug.Print animals(3) & " " & animals.Item(3)
```

Notice that *animals(3)* is a shortcut for *animals.Item(3)*. Item is the default member and can be omitted.

You might also want to replace one item of a Collection with another.

```
animals(2) = "Wolverine"
```

If you think this should work with a simple assignment, think again. Visual Basic could have made this work. (It was requested.) Look back at the implementation of Item in the CVector or CList class to see how easy it would have been to add assignment to the Collection class. All you have to do is implement the Item property with Get, Let, and Set procedures. Instead, they implemented Item as a function, and of course you can't Let or Set a function. As a result, the only way to replace an item is to delete the old item and insert a new one in its place:

```
animals.Add "Wolverine", , 2
animals.Remove 3
```

Here's the standard way to iterate through a Collection:

```
Dim vAnimal As Variant
For Each vAnimal In animals
    s = s & Space$(4) & vAnimal & sCrLf
    Debug.Print vAnimal
Next
```

NOTE In the previous edition of this book, I suggested replacing items with the following code:

```
animals.Remove 2
animals.Add "Wolverine", , 2
```

Hardcore reader Ralf Kretzschmar pointed out that this syntax fails if you're trying to replace the last item. Here's a procedure that always gets the syntax right regardless of whether you specify the item to be replaced by index or by key:

```
Sub CollectionReplace(n As Collection, vIndex As Variant, _
                      vVal As Variant)
    If VarType(vIndex) = vbString Then
        n.Remove vIndex
        n.Add vVal, vIndex
    Else
        n.Add vVal, , vIndex
        n.Remove vIndex + 1
    End If
End Sub
```

Of course, you can still iterate through a Collection by index:

```
Dim i As Integer
For i = 1 To animals.Count
    s = s & Space$(4) & animals(i) & sCrLf
    Debug.Print animals(i)
Next
```

This technique is risky, however. It's easy to confuse the indexing system because the Collection class is one-based, while many of the predefined Visual Basic collections (Forms and Controls) are zero-based for compatibility with previous versions. Furthermore, as you might have discovered with ListBox controls, you can't delete members from or add members to a collection while iterating because this changes the index and the count, which often causes the loop to fail. Yet this is one of the most frequent reasons to iterate. You can sometimes get around the limitation by iterating backward, but For Each is a more reliable looping technique.

If you want to remove everything from a Collection, you have to do it in a loop:

```
Do While animals.Count
    animals.Remove 1
Loop
```

It would be handy if the Collection class had a Clear method like the CList class does, but no such luck. You can also clear a Collection by setting it to Nothing, but then you'll have to Set it to a New Collection before using it again.

Collections 201—Indexing

Simple Collections, like the one above, provide a handy storage place when you don't know how many data items you'll have. But as we saw with the CVector, CList, and CStack classes, there are other ways to store a variable number of items. The unique feature of Collections is that you can look up items with string keys.

To do this, you specify the key as the second argument of the Add method. Later you can use the key instead of an index to access the item. Technically, you can make any string the key. You can also assign a string key to each item in a Collection of integers. For example:

```
Do
    s = GetName          ' Gets name from dialog or file
    i = GetAge(s)        ' Gets age from dialog or file
    If s = sEmpty Then Exit Do
    people.Add i, s      ' Store data (age) first, then key (name)
Loop
```

Now you have the age of each person stored in the items of a Collection. Later you might need to get that data. You could access it like this:

```
iAge = people(7)
```

But the index merely reflects the order in which people were added and probably isn't a significant value. You're much more likely to know the person's name and use it when you need to look up the data:

```
iAge = people("George")
```

Figure 4-1 shows how the data is stored in this Collection. The name is the key. The age is the data. The Collection might have additional internal values (possibly to assist in hashing to look up values), but these are the obvious ones. Notice that the string data isn't actually stored in the Collection. The Collection contains a BSTR (see "Dealing with Strings" in Chapter 2), which is actually a pointer to string data. Usually, this is a detail we can ignore, but it will be relevant in the next example.

The age Collection isn't a very realistic example. You're not likely to use a Collection with a key just to store one piece of data. A much more likely scenario is that you'll put objects with several properties into a Collection. You'll put an identifying property (one that you can reconstruct from other sources) into the Collection as the key. Let's assume the following simple class:

```
' CPerson class
Public Age As Integer
Public Coolness As Double
Public Name As String
⋮
```

The Name property is the obvious choice for the key. You'll choose a particular property as the key because it represents a value unique to the object—a value that you'll know in circumstances when you don't know the object's position in the Collection.

Collection of Integers

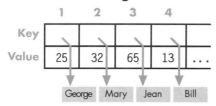

Collection of Strings

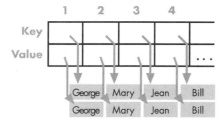

Collection of Objects

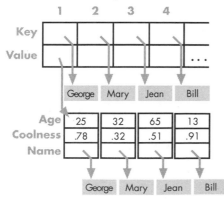

Figure 4-1. *How data is stored in Collections.*

Let's take a look at some code to add people objects to a Collection:

```
Dim person As CPerson, s As String
Do
    s = GetName
    If s = sEmpty Then Exit Do
    Set person = New CPerson
    person.Age = GetAge(s)
    person.Coolness = GetCoolness(s)
    person.Name = s
    ⋮
    people.Add person, person.Name
Loop
```

Later if someone asks you how cool George is, it's easy to find out:

```
Debug.Print "How cool is George? " & people("George").Coolness
```

But there is a problem. See if you can identify it in Figure 4.1. In the first example (see page 195), the age data is actually stored in the Variant item. In this example, the data is an object and an object won't fit in a 16-byte variant even if you want it to. An object in a Variant is actually a reference to an object outside the Variant. Strings in the object are actually BSTR pointers to data outside the object.

The problem is that the string data for the Name property exists in two different places. The key data copy is attached to the Collection, and a second copy is attached to the CPerson object. If you have a lot of people in your Collection, you might be wasting a lot of memory. A frequently requested Collection enhancement is to provide an Index property that returns the index of an item by its key, and a Key property that would return the key data by its index:

```
iIndex = people.Index("George")
sKey = people.Key(iIndex)
```

In some collections, these properties could save you from storing duplicate strings for the key. In other cases, the key is a calculated string that you wouldn't need to access anyway. These properties would give the Collection class flexibility similar to the associative arrays of the Perl language.

FLAME The Collection class provided with Visual Basic version 4 was a good 1 version. The Collection class provided with Visual Basic version 5 is not a good 2 version. Users offered many complaints and suggestions. None of them were implemented.

PERFORMANCE

Problem: What is a Collection? You know its user interface, but you don't really know what internal data structure makes it work. Normally, this isn't a concern. Who cares how it works as long as it works? But, on second thought, the internal implementation is bound to affect the efficiency of operations. If some operations are less efficient than others, it might be nice to avoid the slow ones. While writing the Collection sort procedures in Chapter 5, I began to suspect that inserting elements into the middle of a Collection might be an operation to avoid.

I theorized that it would be faster to insert elements at the end of a Collection than at the beginning or in the middle and that insertion would get slower as you added more elements. To test this idea, I tried inserting a lot of elements (8000) into different parts of a Collection. The results weren't quite what I expected.

Problem	P-Code	Native Code
Add first half to end of Collection	0.0635 sec	0.0509 sec
Add last half to end of Collection	0.0696 sec	0.0573 sec
Add first half to start of Collection	0.0965 sec	0.0735 sec
Add last half to start of Collection	0.0987 sec	0.0766 sec
Add first half to middle of Collection	1.2021 sec	1.1732 sec
Add last half to middle of Collection	4.0951 sec	3.8412 sec

Conclusion: What kind of data structure allows fast insertion at the beginning and at the end but not in the middle? This stumped me for a while, but here's a theory. If a Collection were implemented internally as a doubly linked list, insertion would always cost the same. But finding a particular position (with the *before* or *after* parameter of the Add method or the *index* parameter of the Remove method) would involve iterating from the start or the end until you reached the given point. To find a position near the middle, you'd have to start at the beginning or the end, whichever was closest, and iterate almost halfway through. The more elements in the list, the farther you'd have to go. This would explain the results shown. And, as a matter of fact, I have been told by Visual Basic developers that Collections are doubly linked lists (with additional features to support indexing).

Of course, anything you think you know about the implementation of a Collection might be wrong for this version and probably will be wrong for the next version. Still, you might want to think carefully about whether you really need to insert elements in the middle of a large Collection.

What Makes a Collection Walk?

The For Each syntax provides a natural way to iterate through a collection. You don't have to worry about how the collection is organized or what it does. For each trip through the loop, you just go to the next item. The designer of the collection determines what that means.

There's nothing sacred about the way Visual Basic's Collection class works. If you want to design your collection to iterate backward or to generate a random number for every iteration, that's up to you. The problem is, Visual Basic doesn't provide an easy way to make your collection work with For Each. But if you understand how collection iterations work, you can do the impossible (or at least the impractical). You just have to understand a few facts about the IEnumVARIANT interface.

The Component Object Model defines IEnumVARIANT as the standard way to iterate through data structures. Any collection class that wants to allow clients to walk through variant data should provide an iterator that implements IEnum-VARIANT. Any client program that wants to iterate through variant data classes that follow the standard can do so by calling the IEnumVARIANT methods.

That's how Visual Basic's For Each syntax works. When you write a For Each code block, Visual Basic calls the Next method of IEnumVARIANT for each iteration. The Collection class works with For Each because it provides an iterator class that implements the methods of IEnumVARIANT.

So how do you implement IEnumVARIANT? With great difficulty.

Delegating a Collection

The Collection class creates a helper class that implements the IEnumVARIANT interface. To create your own collection, put the data into a real Collection inside your class and make it available to the world as if it were yours. This technique was available in Visual Basic version 4, but only in an indirect, unsafe way that threw encapsulation to the winds. Version 5 fixes those problems, but it does so in a way that...well, judge for yourself.

The CDrives collection, version 1

You can use the CDrive class from Chapter 3 to create a CDrives collection class. Notice the naming convention: collectionlike classes should always be plural. Figure 4-2 shows the CDrives collection and its relationship to the CDrive class. But before we get to the real CDrives class, let's look at my first implementation, which I saved under the name CDrivesO.

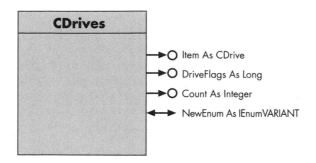

Key

→O Read-only property
←→ Method function

Figure 4-2. *The CDrives class.*

The following code (from TCOLLECT.FRM) shows that CDrives and CDrivesO are mostly polymorphic classes that can be called using the same code:

```
s = s & "Drive information for available drives:" & sCrLf
Dim drives As Object, drive As CDrive
If chkOld Then
    Set drives = New CDrivesO
Else
    Set drives = New CDrives
End If
For Each drive In drives
    With drive
        s = s & "Drive " & .Root & " [" & .Label & ":" & _
                .Serial & "] (" & .KindStr & ") has " & _
                Format$(.FreeBytes, sBFormat) & " free from " & _
                Format$(.TotalBytes, sBFormat) & sCrLf
    End With
Next
```

Most of the work in a class representing an internal Collection is done in the Class_Initialize event procedure. Here's how it works in CDrivesO:

```
Private drives As New Collection

Private Sub Class_Initialize()
    Refresh
End Sub
```

(continued)

```
' Argument handy for refreshing local and/or remote, but not floppies
Public Sub Refresh(Optional iFirst As Integer = 1)
    Dim i As Integer, af As Long, sRoot As String
    Dim drive As CDrive
    ' Remove old ones
    Do While drives.Count > iFirst
        drives.Remove iFirst
    Loop
    ' Insert new
    af = GetLogicalDrives()
    For i = iFirst To 26
        If RShiftDWord(af, i - 1) And 1 Then
            Set drive = New CDrive
            drive.Root = i
            drives.Add drive, drive.Root
        End If
    Next
End Sub
```

The Class_Initialize Sub simply calls Refresh to do the real work. Calling a public initialization method from the initialization event is a common technique in classes that sometimes need to override automatic initialization. Refresh uses the Win32 GetLogicalDrives function and the RShiftDWord function (described in Chapter 5) to calculate which drives actually exist in the system. The drives are then initialized and added to the internal Collection. The Refresh method is important and useful for the old version, but you'll soon see that it's now history in the real CDrives class, which calculates drives as they are needed.

With the internal Collection in place, it's easy to implement the standard properties and methods of a collection. You expose the Count and Item properties by passing through the Count and Item of the internal Collection as follows:

```
Public Property Get Count() As Integer
    Count = drives.Count
End Property

' Default property
Public Property Get Item(v As Variant) As CDrive
    ' Return default (Nothing) if error
    On Error Resume Next
    Set Item = drives(v)
End Property
```

Embedding a Collection object in the class and passing its members through with similar external members is another example of delegation. In a classic object-oriented language, you would use inheritance for the same purpose. Specifically, you would derive the CDrivesO class from the Collection class. You wouldn't have to write any code to get the Count and Item properties. You would have to write code for any additional members you wanted (such as Refresh), and you'd disable or enhance any members you wanted to eliminate or change (such as Add and Remove).

At first glance, you might think it impossible to implement the Add and Remove properties. If you could add a new drive to your system just by calling the Add method, you'd never run out of disk space, but even the Plug and Play standard can't promise that. On the other hand, it's easy enough to use Add to connect to a network drive and Remove to disconnect one. Check out the WNetAddConnection2 and WNetCancelConnection2 API functions. I'll leave it to you to enhance the CDrives collection to make it fully network-aware.

Delegating the iterator

There's just one more step to make CDrivesO a real collection—a step so bizarre that I'm embarrassed to describe it. But I'm going to put the literary equivalent of a bag over my head and forge ahead.

If you write a collection in another language, you have to create a method named _NewEnum. When a programmer codes a For Each block using your collection class, Visual Basic calls the _NewEnum method to create a hidden iterator object that implements the IEnumVARIANT interface. This object is essentially an iterator like the ones we created earlier with the CListWalker class. For each time through the loop, the Next method of the iterator object gets the next item in the collection.

In order for you to get Visual Basic to use your collection with For Each, you have to give your collection a _NewEnum that will delegate its creation of the enumeration object to the internal Collection. This is easier said than done, and easier shown than explained:

```
' NewEnum must have the procedure ID -4 in Procedure Attributes dialog
Public Function NewEnum() As IEnumVARIANT
    Set NewEnum = drives.[_NewEnum]
End Function
```

The first peculiarity about this method is that it's named NewEnum rather than _NewEnum; this is because underscores are illegal as the first character of Visual Basic symbol names. The second peculiarity is that, legal or not, the Collection class has a _NewEnum method, and you'll have to delegate whatever it does to your NewEnum property. One of the more obscure features of Visual Basic is that you can access illegal names by putting them in square brackets. The third peculiarity is that NewEnum returns an IEnumVARIANT type. This is the type of the iterator in the Collection class. (Some samples in other books use IUnknown as the return type, but it comes to the same thing.)

The last and most outstanding peculiarity is how you tell Visual Basic that your NewEnum method is really the _NewEnum method. It's a simple recipe. You mix together eye of newt, toe of frog, wool of bat, and tongue of dog…. No, wait. That's a different kind of magic. In this case, you assign a magic number to the procedure ID in the Dialog Box From Hell (DBFH). Figure 4-3 shows you how.

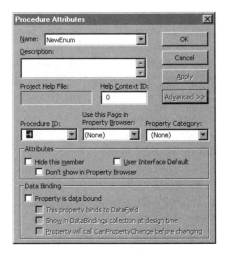

Figure 4-3. *Assigning the magic ID to NewEnum.*

As you might remember, the Procedure ID combo box in the DBFH has several entries, including (None), (Default), AboutBox, and a bunch of other irrelevant nonsense. But it doesn't have an entry for NewEnum, _NewEnum, or any other name that matches what you want. Fortunately, the Procedure ID value is set with an ordinary combo box that allows you to either select one of the suggested entries or type in your own. That's what you do: you type in the magic ID number, which is—drumroll please—negative four.

FLAME

This magic works, even though it violates all standards of Basic decency. This is formula stuff. There's no room for creativity. Computers are better than humans at following formulas. Visual Basic is supposed to make things easy. You ought to be able to simply click a check box to indicate that you want this class to be a collection. You could then select which internal Collection variable you wanted to delegate to (in the unlikely event there was more than one internal Collection). Visual Basic would automatically create the NewEnum property. It wouldn't be as easy as inheritance, but at least it wouldn't be an object of ridicule.

Creating a Collection

Can you spot the fundamental problem with the CDrivesO collection as shown previously?

You might start with the performance question. Because a Collection of items operates significantly more slowly than an array of the same items, and because you don't need most of the features of a Collection, it might seem much more efficient to save the items (such as drives) in an array rather than in a Collection. That would indeed be faster, and that's exactly how programmers often create a collection in other languages. But you can't do that in Visual Basic because arrays don't have a _NewEnum method—or at least not one that you can get at. Actually, Visual Basic does create an IEnumVARIANT object for arrays when you iterate through them with For Each. But the Performance sidebar on page 218 gives you a good idea of what that does to performance.

In any case, arrays versus Collections really isn't the problem. With either method, you have to calculate all the available items before you can return any of them. With the CDrivesO collection, that's only 26 items. But some of those items take a long time to come through. The floppy drives at the start of the list are the slowest, and sometimes network drives are slow, too. When iterating through a drives collection, it might be nicer to display the drives one at a time as they are calculated rather than waiting until they've all been counted.

And of course, drives aren't the only things you might put in a collection. Imagine a collection that includes all the files in your Windows System directory. On my system, that's over a thousand files (most of them unknown). I wouldn't want to process all of them before displaying the first one. In fact, that's how the IEnumVARIANT interface is supposed to work. You're supposed to count one at a time or, if that's too slow, in small chunks for greater efficiency. Creating such a collection is a fundamental feature of COM, and using it is a fundamental feature of Visual Basic. So why can't you create it in Visual Basic?

Well, you can. And we're about to do so using a hack so gross and dangerous that I won't even put the source code in this book. I never thought I'd encounter a trick that was actually too hardcore for *Hardcore Visual Basic,* but this is it. I got the technique from COM guru Matt Curland. Essentially, it consists of writing C++ in Visual Basic. In fact, some parts of it are even lower-level—more like writing a C++ compiler in Visual Basic. I'm in awe of Matt's audacity in even thinking it would be possible to take over a COM object by copying function pointers into its vtable.

But ultimately we're not concerned with amazing code tricks. We want to do something very simple and intuitive. We want to enumerate variants.

Variant Iterators

Before I get into the details, I want to connect the For Each syntax with the concept of iterators introduced in "Using A List Iterator Class," page 172. You'll remember that CList had a CListWalker class that could iterate through the items in a list. To prove it worked, I demonstrated a nested loop. (See page 173.) The outer loop created an iterator object and used it to walk through the list, but in the middle of the walk, the outer iterator suspended operation and created an inner iterator object. When the inner iterator finished walking, it returned control to the outer iterator, which remembered its position and kept walking. The outer and inner iterators were separate objects, each with its own state variables.

The For Each syntax works the same way. If you're like me, you might program for several years without ever using a nested For Each loop on the same collection. But they do work, as this example illustrates:

```
s = s & sCrLf & "Nested iteration loops with For Each: " & sCrLf
Dim vAnimal2 As Variant
For Each vAnimal In animals
    s = s & Space$(4) & vAnimal & sCrLf
    If vAnimal = "Lion" Then
        For Each vAnimal2 In animals
            s = s & Space$(8) & vAnimal2 & sCrLf
        Next
    End If
Next
```

The output looks like this:

```
Shrew
Wolverine
Lion
    Shrew
    Wolverine
    Lion
    Tiger
    Bear
Tiger
Bear
```

Here's how it works. Each time your code hits a For Each block, Visual Basic creates a new iterator object. The iterator object's class must implement the IEnumVARIANT interface, and Visual Basic knows that such an object will have a Next method (like the More method of CListWalker). So each time through the loop, Visual Basic calls the Next method and uses the result as the current variant entry.

To enumerate variants, we'll have to implement IEnumVARIANT in an iterator class. Our collection class will have to create iterator objects of type IEnum-VARIANT. The collection object will have to somehow let Visual Basic know about these iterator objects. Unfortunately, we can't do any of this stuff directly.

Enumerating Variants

There's a lot going on here, and we're going to explain away part of it as magic. Instead of implementing the IEnumVARIANT interface and doing filthy hacks to make it work, we'll implement the IVariantWalker interface. This is cheating. We'll have to implement IEnumVARIANT behind the scenes, but the details are so ugly that we'll hide them inside a class named CEnumVariant. Our iterator classes will delegate to a private instance of CEnumVariant.

I won't say that the resulting collection and iterator classes will be simple. But they will be possible, and I'll provide a wizard to generate them quickly. To illustrate the concept, I'll redesign the CDrivesO class. Instead of precalculating all the drives and hiding them in an internal collection, I'll calculate each drive as it is needed.

The CDrives class, version 2

The CDrives class has no special relationship with the CDrive class. It uses CDrive objects as needed, but it knows only the public methods of CDrive—something any other class could know. But the CDrives class does have a close and intimate relationship with the CDriveWalker class. CDriveWalker must know what CDrives knows so that it will be able to walk the collection. The CDrives class must make this information available by providing a friend property:

```
' Private version of data structure
Private af As Long

Private Sub Class_Initialize()
    ' Initialize internal data
    af = GetLogicalDrives()
End Sub

' Friend properties to make data accessible to data walker class
Friend Property Get DriveFlags() As Long
    DriveFlags = af
End Property
```

The only thing you need to determine all the drives in the system is a bit flag variable (an array of bits) returned by the GetLogicalDrives API function. The CDrives class uses this variable to calculate the number of drives in the collection:

```
Public Property Get Count() As Integer
    Dim c As Long, i As Long
    For i = 0 To 25
        If MBytes.RShiftDWord(af, i) And &H1 Then c = c + 1
    Next
    Count = c
End Property
```

The CDriveWalker class will also need this variable, but it must get it indirectly through the DriveFlags friend property. Unfortunately, this makes the DriveFlags property available to every other class, form, and standard module in the project. Because the project is the VBCore component, that's a whole lot of chances to make a mistake. Of course, you and I would never use a friend property in a class that wasn't designed to be a friend, but for those less careful coders who need more than convention to make them behave, it might be nice if the language let us specify who our friends are.

CDrives is an unusual collection class in that it can share all its internal data in one bitflag variable. A more common scenario is that the collection class wraps some other kind of data structure such as an array, a vector, or a linked-list. In that case, the collection must share whatever internal variable makes the data structure work. For example, it might share an array through an indexed property (as described in "Property Arrays," page 184).

The property that makes CDrives a collection is the NewEnum method. We've already seen one NewEnum method on page 205, but that one is simply delegated to the _NewEnum method of the Collection class. We didn't know or care how the Collection class created its iterator. But this time we'll need to create our own iterator in the NewEnum method. This is where the real magic begins:

```
' NewEnum must have the procedure ID -4 in Procedure Attributes dialog
' Create a new data walker object and connect to it
Public Function NewEnum() As IEnumVARIANT
    ' Create a new iterator object
    Dim drivewalker As CDriveWalker
    Set drivewalker = New CDriveWalker
    ' Connect it with collection data
    drivewalker.Attach Me
    ' Return it
    Set NewEnum = drivewalker.NewEnum
End Function
```

The first requirement is described in the comment. You must give this procedure the ID -4 in the Procedure Attributes dialog box so that Visual Basic will know that it's a collection. Otherwise, the first time you try to iterate through the collection with For Each, you'll get a cryptic error at run time telling you that the object doesn't support this property or method. What it means is that when you write *For Each thing In things*, Visual Basic looks for a property or a function with ID -4 on the *things* collection. We name this function NewEnum out of tradition, but the -4 is what really matters.

NewEnum creates a CDriveWalker object. This object will need to use the DriveFlags property of CDrives, but you can't use a property unless you have a reference to the object that owns that property. The Friend keyword gives you permission, but it doesn't automatically give you the connection. In this case, we're going to make a connection by passing a copy of ourselves (Me represents CDrives) to the Attach method of the CDriveWalker object. We'll see the other side of this connection in a moment.

Finally, the NewEnum method must return a reference to an IEnumVARIANT interface. When you iterate through your collection using For Each, Visual Basic calls methods on this interface—specifically the Next and Skip methods. If NewEnum doesn't return an IEnumVARIANT, you'll see the error message *Object not a collection*. CDrives' NewEnum returns the IEnumVARIANT interface it gets from CDriveWalker's NewEnum property. Now we're ready for even more magic in CDriveWalker.

The CDriveWalker class

You don't have to go far to figure out that the CDriveWalker class is a little unusual. Take a look at the first few lines of code:

```
' Implement Basic-friendly version of IEnumVARIANT
Implements IVariantWalker
' Delegate to class that implements real IEnumVARIANT
Private vars As CEnumVariant
' Connect back to parent collection
Private connect As CDrives
```

We're going to implement a nice, friendly Basic-style interface (IVariantWalker) that does all the stuff the For Each syntax expects us to do. But because the real IEnumVARIANT is so Basic-hostile that we can't afford to deal with its horrors every time we want to write a collection, we'll delegate to a CEnumVariant object, which will actually implement IEnumVARIANT. When your client code hits a For Each block, Visual Basic will think CEnumVariant is an IEnumVARIANT (if you implement it, you are it) and will call its methods. Those methods will, in turn, through a process too horrible to describe, call the IVariantWalker methods, which will iterate through the collection. Figure 4-4 on the following page tries to make sense of the whole iteration mess.

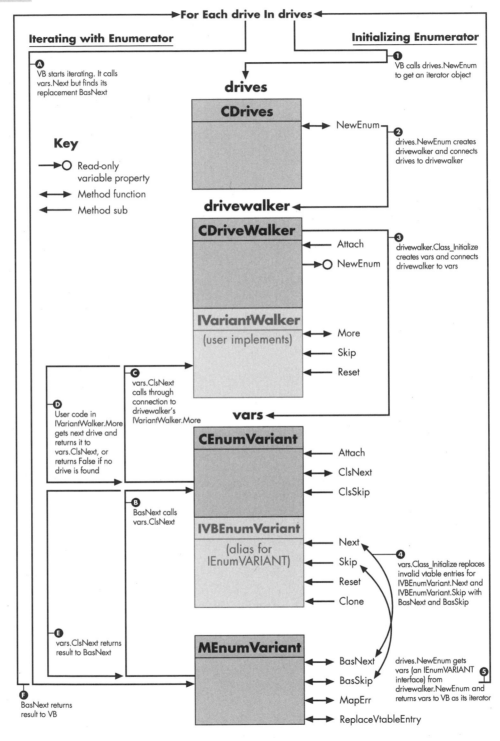

For Each drive In drives

Iterating with Enumerator

Initializing Enumerator

Ⓐ
VB starts iterating. It calls vars.Next but finds its replacement BasNext

❶
VB calls drives.NewEnum to get an iterator object

drives

CDrives

Key

→O Read-only variable property

↔ Method function

← Method sub

← NewEnum

❷
drives.NewEnum creates drivewalker and connects drives to drivewalker

drivewalker

CDriveWalker

← Attach

→O NewEnum

❸
drivewalker.Class_Initialize creates vars and connects drivewalker to vars

IVariantWalker
(user implements)

← More

← Skip

← Reset

Ⓒ
vars.ClsNext calls through connection to drivewalker's IVariantWalker.More

Ⓓ
User code in IVariantWalker.More gets next drive and returns it to vars.ClsNext, or returns False if no drive is found

vars

CEnumVariant

← Attach

↔ ClsNext

← ClsSkip

Ⓑ
BasNext calls vars.ClsNext

IVBEnumVariant
(alias for IEnumVARIANT)

← Next

← Skip

← Reset

← Clone

❹
vars.Class_Initialize replaces invalid vtable entries for IVBEnumVariant.Next and IVBEnumVariant.Skip with BasNext and BasSkip

Ⓔ
vars.ClsNext returns result to BasNext

MEnumVariant

↔ BasNext

↔ BasSkip

↔ MapErr

↔ ReplaceVtableEntry

❺
drives.NewEnum gets vars (an IEnumVARIANT interface) from drivewalker.NewEnum and returns vars to VB as its iterator

Ⓕ
BasNext returns result to VB

Figure 4-4. *The whole iteration mess.*

In real life, you can ignore most of the details; just implement IVariantWalker and delegate it to CEnumVariant. Here's the internal data the CDriveWalker class uses to maintain its position and connections:

```
' Private state data
Private i As Long

Private Sub Class_Initialize()
    ' Initialize position in collection
    i = 1
    ' Connect walker to CEnumVariant so it can call methods
    Set vars = New CEnumVariant
    vars.Attach Me
End Sub
```

CDriveWalker also needs methods and properties to receive a connection from the CDrives collection and to pass a connection back from the CEnumVariant object (*vars*) to the CDrives collection (which will pass it back to the client program).

```
' Receive connection from CDrives
Sub Attach(connectA As CDrives)
    Set connect = connectA
End Sub

' Return IEnumVARIANT (indirectly) to client collection
Friend Property Get NewEnum() As IEnumVARIANT
    Set NewEnum = vars
End Property
```

Finally, with all this paperwork out of the way, you can actually write the code to move to the next item, skip some items, and reset the iteration.

```
Private Function IVariantWalker_More(v As Variant) As Boolean
    ' Find the next drive and return it through reference
    Do While i <= 26
        ' Check flags to see if next drive exists
        If MBytes.RShiftDWord(connect.DriveFlags, i - 1) And 1 Then
            Dim drive As CDrive
            Set drive = New CDrive
            drive.Root = i
            Set v = drive
            IVariantWalker_More = True
            i = i + 1
            Exit Function
        End If
```

(continued)

```
        i = i + 1
    Loop
End Function

Private Sub IVariantWalker_Skip(c As Long)
    ' Skip ahead in the iteration
    i = i + c
End Sub

Private Sub IVariantWalker_Reset()
    ' Reset the iteration
    i = 1
End Sub
```

The More method (which would be named Next if Visual Basic allowed it) is the most important method and the only one called by For Each. Notice how it returns a Boolean indicating whether there are more items and also returns the next item through a reference parameter.

The Skip and Reset methods are not called by For Each, but they are called by the Locals window in the IDE. If it looks like a miracle that Visual Basic can display all the items in a collection before you've even iterated through them, well, it's not—although it is remarkable. The Locals window is iterating, skipping, and resetting behind the scenes to display the parts of the collection you request. If you have enough patience and memory, you can verify that the Locals window actually has limits—it won't display more than 256 items in a collection.

If all this sounds complicated, you ain't seen nothin' yet. And you don't need to see nothin'. The Collection Wizard can write all the repetitive hack code, leaving you to worry only about how your collection works. We'll take a look in a few pages.

Stupid code tricks

As I said earlier, the implementation of CEnumVariant is too hardcore to show in this book. The code is thoroughly commented, but slogging through it is no picnic. And you don't really need to understand this code; it's a gross hack that shouldn't be necessary. Because you can create collections without understanding the details, why not skip to the next section? If you wanted to understand how vtables work, you wouldn't have chosen Visual Basic. On the other hand, if you weren't curious about what's going on under the surface, you wouldn't have picked this book.

So I'll compromise. I'll tell you a little bit about MEnumVariant (ENUMVAR.BAS) and its partner, CEnumVariant (ENUMVAR.CLS), without showing the source code. You can also check Figure 4-4 for a high-level view.

Chapter 3 explained some of the problems of implementing standard interfaces in Visual Basic. The IEnumVARIANT interface has all these problems and more. (The Next method has the name of a Visual Basic reserved word.) The CEnum-Variant class can't really implement IEnumVARIANT. Instead, it implements IVBEnumVARIANT. At the binary level, these two interfaces are the same; it's just that IVBEnumVARIANT describes the bytes in a little different way for Visual Basic's sake. It claims that unsigned integers are signed and tells a few other little white lies. The Windows API type library defines the IVBEnumVARIANT interface, and you can look it up in the object browser.

The IEnumVARIANT interface defines four methods—Next, Skip, Reset, and Clone. The IVariantWalker interface defines three methods—More, Skip, and Reset. What happened to Clone? The Clone method creates a duplicate iterator object with the same state as the current iterator object. You could be iterating through a collection and at some point decide you might want to come back to exactly the same point and try again. You could ask the iterator object to clone itself, and when you're ready to start over, you could use the duplicate iterator. This would be a very fine thing for clients that want it, but Visual Basic isn't such a client. It never clones iterators as part of the For Each syntax, and it doesn't use them when filling the Locals window. Of course, nothing prevents you from using collections created in Visual Basic in client languages that do call the Clone method. In fact, nothing prevents you from writing your own client code in Visual Basic that uses the IEnumVARIANT or IVariantWalker interfaces in more sophisticated ways. But if you think Clone is a really useful feature, you'll have to implement it yourself. The version in the CEnumVariant class simply raises a "Not implemented" error.

When you hit a For Each block in Visual Basic code, the first thing that happens is that an iterator is created for the collection. Visual Basic calls your collection's NewEnum function, which creates your iterator (walker) class, which implements IVariantWalker and delegates to a private CEnumVariant object, which implements IVBEnumVARIANT and does some magic to replace the invalid Next and Skip methods with fake methods in the standard module MEnumVariant. The right side of Figure 4-4 shows this part of the transaction. The bottom line is that Visual Basic now has an IEnumVARIANT interface. Fortunately, it has no idea how this baby was made.

Every time through the For Each loop, Visual Basic calls the Next method of its IEnumVARIANT interface, which is actually the BasNext function in MEnum-Variant, which calls the ClsNext method of the CEnumVariant object, which calls the More method of the IVariantWalker interface, which is implemented by your walker class, which returns the next Variant in the collection (if any). The left side of Figure 4-4 shows this part of the transaction. In other words, the CEnum-Variant object creates events in your iterator class. In an early version of

CEnumVariant, I used the Event syntax to communicate between CEnumVariant and the collection iterator object. I created Next, Skip, and Reset events in CEnumVariant, raised them with RaiseEvent in the appropriate CEnumVariant methods, and received them with WithEvents in the collection iterator class. The resulting code was a little cleaner and easier to understand, but it was also about 15 percent slower. Events are great for things that happen occasionally, but you'll get better performance with Implements if your callbacks are going to be called frequently. I'll be talking more about events in later chapters.

I suppose the less said about replacing methods in an object vtable the better. This probably isn't what Visual Basic designers had in mind when they added the AddressOf operator to the language, but there it is. I expect that a few intrepid souls will try even slimier hacks with AddressOf, VarPtr, and CopyMemory. The CEnumVariant class replaces only the vtable entries of the Next and Skip methods because they are the ones whose official definition is incompatible with normal Visual Basic techniques. These two methods must be in a separate standard module (ENUMVAR.BAS) so that they can be used with the AddressOf operator. Check the source file to see how the first parameter of the methods (the *this* pointer to C++ programmers) actually contains the object pointer of the CEnumVariant object. The Reset and Clone methods are implemented with no tricks in CEnumVariant (ENUMVAR.CLS).

FLAME No need. CEnumVariant is self-flaming code.

Collection Wizard to the Rescue

If you're feeling dazed and confused, the Collection Wizard can make everything simple again. Let's take it for a trial run.

Creating the CThings collection

Suppose you want to create a collection of things and that the things happen to be integers corresponding to the numbers 1 through 10. It might seem like overkill to create a collection to iterate through ten numbers, but it certainly makes for a simple example.

Figure 4-5 shows the Collection Wizard at work on a things collection. The Base Name field at the top of the form is where you enter the name of a single item. In this case, type in *thing* and click View Class. (When you click View Class, its caption changes to Clear All.) The wizard automatically picks some class names, variable names, and filenames for you and displays the result. If you don't like its choices, change them and the wizard updates automatically. Since I designed the wizard, it's no big surprise that I do like its choices. You have the source code if you get tired of overwriting defaults you don't like.

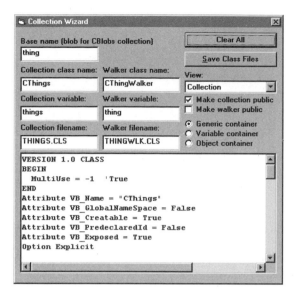

Figure 4-5. *The Collection Wizard.*

You can also choose whether you want to make the collection public. For this throwaway sample, we don't want a public collection. If you plan to put your collection in a component, you should make it public. There's no need to make the iterator class public unless you plan to use it directly rather than providing it only for use with the For Each syntax. If you do specify a public iterator class, then public More, Skip, and Reset methods (that delegate to the IVariantWalker methods) will be created for you.

Finally, you can choose whether your collection will be able to hold objects, variables, or both. For example, the CDrives class is an object container and the CList class is a generic container. Our CThings class will handle only variables. A generic container is the most flexible choice, but if you specify an object or variable container, the wizard can code the Item method more efficiently.

You can see either of the proposed files by selecting the appropriate file from the View combo box, and you can write the files out to disk by clicking the Save Class Files button. The wizard specifically marks the spots where you must modify code. Search for the comment character followed by an exclamation point ('!) to find places where you must fill in the blanks. The dummy classes generated by the wizard actually compile and run if you put them in a project as is, although you'll end up with an iterator object that walks through your empty collection.

The first thing you'll do is define the collection data, initialize it, and share it with the iterator class. Normally, you would replace what the wizard gives you, but the following code leaves the wizard's original comments for comparison.

```
' Private data structure
'!Private data() As DataType
Private ai(1 To 10) As Integer

Private Sub Class_Initialize()
    ' Initialize private data
    '!data = initval
    Dim i As Integer
    For i = 1 To 10
        ai(i) = i
    Next
End Sub

' Friend properties to make data structure accessible to walker
'!Friend Property Get Things(i As Long) '! As DataType
'!    Things = data(i)
'!End Property
Friend Property Get Things(i As Long) As Integer
    Things = ai(i)
End Property
```

These are obvious fill-in-the-blank changes. The wizard gives hints, but you define the data.

There's no need to mess with the wizard's implementation of NewEnum, but you have to do your own Count and Item members:

```
Public Property Get Count() As Integer
    '!Count = curcount
    Count = 10
End Property

' Default property
'!Public Property Get Item(vIndex As Variant) '! As DataType
Public Property Get Item(iIndex As Integer) As Integer
    '!Item = data(vIndex)
    If iIndex >= 1 And iIndex <= 10 Then Item = ai(iIndex)
End Property
```

The wizard makes some general suggestions, but it doesn't know whether to calculate your Count at run time or save it from an internal member (although you can bet it won't often be hardcoded to a constant, as in this sample). The wizard knows even less about the Item property. It doesn't know whether you want to support indexing by string, integer, or both. It can't help with index validation or string lookup, but it can set the behind-the-scenes ID number that makes Item the default property. As for Add and Remove properties, the wizard doesn't even try to guess whether you want them, much less how they should be coded.

Walking the CThings collection

The wizard does an even better job on the CThingWalker class. You can simply go through and eliminate the search-and-replace comment markers, accepting all the wizard's suggestions. The wizard's suggestions are optimized for array-based collections; often you can use them with little or no change. Without showing all the code, I'll just accept the suggestion to name the state variable *iCur* and initialize it to 0.

Wait a minute. If the array had the values 1 through 10, why would I initialize *iCur* to 0? Let's take a look at IVariantWalker_More to see why:

```
' Implement IVariantWalker methods
Private Function IVariantWalker_More(v As Variant) As Boolean
    ' Move to next element
    iCur = iCur + 1
    ' If more data, return True and update data
    If iCur <= connect.Count Then
        IVariantWalker_More = True
        v = connect.Things(iCur)
    End If
End Function
```

The More method advances to the next element and returns that element. You need to start *iCur* at 0 so that when you advance the first time through, you end up pointing at the first element. This works with an array-based collection, but sometimes you'll need to check a flag or other condition to identify the first element and handle it differently. In this array-based collection, you can use the Count property to identify the last element, but other types of collections will find the end with other techniques.

The Reset and Skip methods reinitialize the state variable and advance it the given number of places, respectively:

```
Private Sub IVariantWalker_Reset()
    ' Move to first element
    iCur = 0
End Sub

Private Sub IVariantWalker_Skip(c As Long)
    ' Skip a given number of elements
    iCur = iCur + c
End Sub
```

The CThings collection is too good to be true. Let's revisit some familiar collections—CList and CVector—to see more realistic implementations.

Walking the CVector collection

The CVector class doesn't need to work with For Each. It's more efficient to iterate with an index anyway, as you can see from the Performance sidebar on page 218. But Visual Basic has an internal iterator class for arrays, so why shouldn't CVector have an iterator class? If nothing else, it will show you how Visual Basic makes For Each work with arrays.

The CVectorWalker class has the standard code for implementing IVariantWalker and delegating CEnumVariant, so let's ignore that and concentrate on its state variable. All it needs is an *iCur* variable initialized to 0.

```
' Private state data
Private iCur As Long

Private Sub Class_Initialize()
    ' Initialize position in collection
    iCur = 0
    ⋮
```

You've already seen the code for the CVector class, but I had to go back and add one detail. You might remember that CVector is actually based on an array variable named *av*. I had to add a friend property that shared that array through an indexed property named Vector.

As usual with iterator classes, the More method is the most interesting part of the implementation:

```
Private Function IVariantWalker_More(v As Variant) As Boolean
    ' Move to next element
    iCur = iCur + 1
    ' Return False if no more data
    If iCur > connect.Last Then Exit Function
    ' Return element through reference
    If IsObject(connect.Vector(iCur)) Then
        Set v = connect.Vector(iCur)
    Else
        v = connect.Vector(iCur)
    End If
    IVariantWalker_More = True
End Function
```

More simply moves on to the next item until it passes the last item, as indicated by the Last property. Since CVector is a generic container, it has to check for objects and handle them differently.

Walking the CList collection

The CList collection class already has an iterator class, and it already attaches itself to that iterator. You got a sanitized preview of the Attach method on page 175.

Here's the real code:

```
' Attach a list to iterator
Sub Attach(connectA As CList, Optional fEnumerate As Boolean = False)
    ' Initialize position in collection
    Set connect = connectA
    If fEnumerate Then
        ' Connect walker to CEnumVariant so it can call methods
        Set vars = New CEnumVariant
        vars.Attach Me
    End If
End Sub
```

If you create the iterator object yourself (as we did in earlier examples), it doesn't need a connection with CEnumVariant and any implementation of the IVariantWalker interface should be ignored. The *fEnumerate* flag should be true only when Attach is called by the NewEnum method of CList.

But we do want CList to work with For Each, and since the iteration mechanism is already in place, it's extremely easy for the IVariantWalker members to take advantage of the existing public More method through delegation. You might remember that the original CListWalker class had a More method that returned True or False to indicate whether there were more items. It returned the actual data through a separate Item property. Here's how IVariantWalker_More takes advantage of those methods.

```
Private Function IVariantWalker_More(v As Variant) As Boolean
    ' Move to next element
    IVariantWalker_More = More
    If IVariantWalker_More = False Then Exit Function
    ' Return element through reference
    If IsObject(lnkCur.Item) Then
        Set v = lnkCur.Item
    Else
        v = lnkCur.Item
    End If
End Function
```

The implementation of Skip does something even more interesting. It delegates its work to IVariantWalker_More in a loop:

```
Private Sub IVariantWalker_Skip(c As Long)
    ' Skip a given number of elements
    Dim i As Long, v As Variant
    For i = 1 To c
        If IVariantWalker_More(v) = False Then Exit For
    Next
End Sub
```

PERFORMANCE

Problem: Compare iterating through various data structures, and for each data structure, compare iterating with For Each to iterating with For and an index variable.

Problem	P-Code	Native Code
For I on Variant Integer array	0.0005 sec	0.0002 sec
For Each on Variant Integer array	0.0009 sec	0.0006 sec
For I on Integer array	0.0004 sec	0.0001 sec
For Each on Integer array	0.0008 sec	0.0004 sec
For I on Integer collection	0.0125 sec	0.0082 sec
For Each on Integer collection	0.0013 sec	0.0011 sec
For I on Variant Integer vector	0.0038 sec	0.0033 sec
For Each on Variant Integer vector	0.0231 sec	0.0228 sec
For I on Integer vector	0.0017 sec	0.0013 sec
For Each on Integer vector	0.0183 sec	0.0196 sec
For I on Integer list	0.9113 sec	0.8657 sec
For Each on Integer list	0.0184 sec	0.0195 sec
For I on Variant object array	0.0570 sec	0.0567 sec
For Each on Variant object array	0.0615 sec	0.0607 sec
For I on object array	0.0008 sec	0.0004 sec
For Each on object array	0.0597 sec	0.0625 sec
For I on object collection	0.0834 sec	0.0862 sec

You might want to keep this technique in mind. Usually, you can optimize the Skip method by changing the state variable, but in some kinds of collections (such as lists), the only way to get ahead is to keep iterating.

The original list iterator didn't have the equivalent of a Reset method (you could restart with the Attach method), so IVariantWalker_Reset has to be implemented from scratch by resetting the Head friend property.

```
Private Sub IVariantWalker_Reset()
    ' Move to first element
    If connect.Count Then Set lnkCur = connect.Head
End Sub
```

Problem	P-Code	Native Code
For Each on object collection	0.0035 sec	0.0036 sec
For I on object vector	0.0750 sec	0.0745 sec
For Each on object vector	0.0258 sec	0.0241 sec
For I on object list	0.9805 sec	0.9887 sec
For Each on object list	0.0234 sec	0.2240 sec

Conclusion: The results speak for themselves, but let me highlight a few points. I provide two array tests. One is a Variant array, because it's only fair to compare Variant arrays to Variant collections, vectors, and lists. But if you're doing real work with integers, you don't care what's fair—you just want speed. The difference between using Variant arrays and type-specific arrays is a minor one for Integers but a major one for objects.

Nothing beats an array for raw speed, but vectors do get decent performance. You can't necessarily see it from the data here, but if you actually run the TimeIt application with different numbers in the Iterations field (iterations here is actually the number of items in the data structure), you'll see that collections and lists get much slower as you add more data, while arrays and vectors slow at a constant rate. Lists are shown for comparison, but they come in last in every category and you probably don't want to use them for this kind of operation.

When comparing For Each to For with an index variable, arrays and vectors are far faster with an index variable. Collections and lists are faster with For Each; if you study the implementation of the CVector and CList classes, you can get a good idea why. The internal iterators for Collections and arrays are probably implemented much like the ones for CList and CVector, respectively.

The iterator for the CList class is crucial to its performance. You don't even want to think about iterating with indexes, because they depend on the iterator anyway. It might look from the outside as if you're walking through one item at a time, but you're actually using the internal iterator to walk all the way from the start of the list to the current index. The Performance sidebar above shows the heavy toll this takes.

5

Functional Programming's Last Gasp

One of the first readers of the first edition of *Hardcore Visual Basic* sent me a program he was working on. When I opened the project, something very strange jumped out at me. No standard modules. Just forms and classes.

Wait a minute! You can't do that with Visual Basic. But hardcore programmer Peter Wheat did, and the program worked just fine.

The object-oriented only approach is a lot easier with version 5. Many of the object-oriented holes in Visual Basic have been plugged.

Still, we're not quite ready to give up on functional programming. Visual Basic doesn't. Imagine if it did. You'd have methods and properties on the String type:

```
Dim s As String, c As Long, i As Long
s.Text = "Stuff"              ' Or use Text default: s = "Stuff"
c = s.Len                     ' Not c = Len(s)
i = s.In("f")                 ' Not i = InStr(s, "f")
Print s.Mid(2, 4)             ' Not Print Mid$(s, 2, 4)
```

Why not? That's how most object-oriented languages handle strings. Theoretically, you shouldn't have anything left in the globals section of the VBA library. But how far are you willing to go? Take a look at the following examples before you decide:

```
Dim r As Double, i As Long
r.Value = 5.2                 ' Or use Value default: r = 5.2
r.Plus(1)                     ' Not r = r + 1
i = r.CInt                    ' Not i = CInt(r)
Me.Print r.Cos                ' Not Print Cos(r)
```

Some of these examples might be getting a little marginal. Even completely object-oriented languages support operators and passing objects as parameters. I think there's still a place for a tight library of procedures that aren't methods of anything.

This chapter will explain an efficient way to create such a library. Then it will discuss some of the general purpose tools you might still want to put in such a library. Even though the focus of this chapter is functional, we won't escape objects. COM depends on object-oriented programming, and Visual Basic depends on COM, and we depend on Visual Basic, so objects will keep popping up.

Functional DLLs

The DLLs in Visual Basic version 4 were a useful feature, but some programmers wanted more. They wanted to put functions in DLLs, just as you can do with most other languages that support DLLs. Visual Basic seemed to be split into two different worlds. In programs, object-oriented programming was voluntary. In DLLs, it was mandatory. If you wanted to put ordinary procedures in a DLL, well, you could write that DLL in some other language.

If you looked in the Object Browser, you could see that Visual Basic itself wasn't playing by the same rules. It had the Visual Basic Objects and Procedures library and the Visual Basic for Applications library. Somebody was writing DLLs containing both procedures and classes in some language. Why couldn't that language be Visual Basic? This is a familiar story. Visual Basic used optional arguments, controls, properties on forms, and who knows what else before it let us use them. But eventually it lets us play ball.

Visual Basic version 5 lets you put procedures in DLLs, but the feature isn't as simple as you might hope. Something strange is going on behind the scenes. You can see it in the Object Browser. Sure, it looks like FileLen is a function in the Visual Basic for Applications library. You can use FileLen as if it were a function. But it's not. It's a method of the VBA object. Anytime you want to use FileLen, you have a choice. You can say this:

```
cFile = VBA.FileLen(sFile)
```

Or you can say this:

```
cFile = FileLen(sFile)
```

It's a pretty obvious choice in most cases, although the sidebar "Better Basic Through Subclassing" describes a situation where you want to qualify library procedures. The VBA object is kind of a default object—comparable to a default property. You can leave off the object name just as you can leave off the property name of a default property. Visual Basic instantiates the VBA object for you, and you can pretend it doesn't exist.

The secret to putting procedures in a DLL is that you write them as methods of what Visual Basic calls a global object. We're now ready to write a library called VBCore, based on global objects.

The VBCore Component

In the previous edition of this book, I provided a DLL written in C and a bunch of Visual Basic modules. Even if you never read the book, you could use any of the modules or the DLL in your own projects. But providing source code isn't exactly code reuse in the classic sense. And providing a DLL written in another language doesn't give you too many customization options if you don't know the other language. So this time I'm doing it differently.

First, everything is in Basic. All the procedures provided in the C DLL last time have been rewritten in Visual Basic. You might lose a few microseconds on some of these procedures because C can be a faster language than Basic. But if you compile to native code, I don't think you'll notice. And normally you will use the native code version because all the general-use procedures and classes that were provided as separate modules in the first edition are now provided in a component called VBCore.

The programming model used throughout most of this book is that your programming tools go in the component—in most cases VBCore, but sometimes in other components. The components are compiled to native code with as much optimization as their features will stand. The VBCore component is kind of big—about 580 KB—and you do have to ship it to customers. But if you put all your speed-critical code in the core, you can use p-code in the main program and get smaller programs. Or you can compile the main program too, if you prefer.

Using a component instead of modules has its pluses and minuses, but I'd say the positive side of the scale outweighs the negative. For example, I frequently encountered a problem that must have driven users of my book crazy. Let's say I'm writing a program that needs to work on Widgets. Widgets.Bas has the very function I need, but when I add it to my project, it turns out that the module uses Sockets.Bas. And Sockets.Bas requires Clamps.Bas, which requires some other module. That problem disappears with VBCore. You get everything you need from one component. Sure, it's larger than the individual modules. You might end up with some stuff you don't need, but that's only on the disk. The modules in the component don't get into memory unless a program uses them. Furthermore, many programs can share the same component.

There is a downside. If your customer has only one program that uses the component, code sharing is wasted. Furthermore, although you have access to the source code for the component, you can't just go changing it willy-nilly. This is a published COM component after all, and the whole idea of COM starts to fall apart if everyone feels free to modify other people's components. In fact, if I find people modifying my code and sending it to customers with the name

VBCore, I'm going to be more than a little peeved. What happens if Hardcore programmer A modifies VBCore and sends it to a customer, but that customer also buys a product from Hardcore programmer B who has also modified VBCore—and then I sell that customer another program that uses the original VBCore? Sending out the source code to a component (as I'm doing with this book) is a pretty dangerous thing. Don't try this at home.

But you do have an out. You don't have to use the component. You can use each of the modules in the source files directly in your program without the component. You can cut out any of my code and paste it into your code. You can create your own new component that uses my modules, but you must rename any public modules. In other words, you bought the code with the book. It's yours. (Curses on anyone who uses my code without buying my book!) But the component is mine. You bought the right to use it, but you have no right to change it. If you find that one (and only one) bug that I put in VBCore to keep you on your toes, send me a bug report. I'll fix VBCore and post a new version on my Web site (with credit to you, of course).

VBCore consists of three things: classes, global procedures, and global objects. There's not much to say about adding classes to a component, but adding global procedures and global objects can be difficult. We'll look at them next.

Creating Global Procedures

On the surface, it's a simple matter to convert standard modules containing utility functions into global class modules that can be used in a component. Let's do it. We'll create the VBCore component, step by step—including a few false steps.

The AllAbout program is a good starting point. It uses many of the procedures, classes, and objects of the VBCore component. In the old version, AllAbout consisted of an FAllAbout form with the real functionality of the program and a bunch of support modules, classes, and forms that might be used in any program. The goal was to move all those functions from the AllAbout project to the VBCore project and make AllAbout use VBCore.

You can see the final results of the whole operation in the files ALLABOUT.VBP and VBCORE.VBP. I also provide a project named LOTABOUT.VBP, which is essentially the AllAbout project before I converted it to use VBCore. You could re-create AllAbout from LotAbout using steps similar to those I'm about to describe (although changes to AllAbout in the course of writing this book would make the steps slightly different). If you want to experiment with this, do it in a separate directory so that you won't overwrite existing files.

I started by adding a new project to the AllAbout project by selecting the Add Project item from the File menu. I made it an ActiveX DLL project and named it VBCORE.VBP. This created a new project group, which I named ALLABOUT-.VBG. In VBCore, I added a reference to the Windows API type library, and then I started moving the general-purpose modules from AllAbout to VBCore. I planned to eventually compile the component into a native-code DLL, but at first I just used the uncompiled component project. AllAbout or any other program that uses VBCore must select it in the References dialog box so that Visual Basic will know to use the component.

You might expect that I would start with the module used by almost every other module—DEBUG.BAS. But stop. This isn't such a great idea. DEBUG.BAS makes extensive use of conditional compilation. The key routines, BugAssert and BugMessage, disappear if you turn off the debug constant. The disappearing act happens at compile time. When all the bugs are gone and clients start using the compiled component, there won't be any debug routines. So I left DEBUG.BAS in AllAbout but added a separate copy to VBCore. Every project that uses debug procedures needs DEBUG.BAS. That causes a little bit of duplication but not enough to worry about since the debugging procedures will disappear in the long run in both the component and in the client.

The next module I selected was BYTES.BAS, but I couldn't just move the standard module to VBCore because the only thing you can make public in a component is a class. That hasn't changed in version 5. The solution was to create a new class module named BYTES.CLS in VBCORE.VBP. I copied all the code from BYTES.BAS, pasted it into a new class, named the new class GBytes, and set its Instancing property to GlobalMultiUse. Notice that I didn't name the class CBytes because, although it is a class, it will look like a standard module to clients. I didn't call it MBytes because it won't be a standard module no matter how much it looks like one (and it won't even look like one to other classes).

The resulting class module had all the functionality of BYTES.BAS, and to a user of VBCore, it worked like BYTES.BAS. How could this be? Normally, a class without an object is like a bicycle without a fish, but in this case, we want clients to call the class as if it had no object. This is an illusion caused by setting the Instancing property to GlobalMultiUse (which might better be called Looks-LikeAModuleWorksLikeAClass). There's actually a kind of default object behind the scenes. I'll get to the unexpected complications caused by this hidden object shortly.

With BYTES.CLS in place, I no longer needed BYTES.BAS, so I deleted it from ALLABOUT.VBP. I tried to run ALLABOUT again but encountered a predictable problem. BYTES.BAS uses UTILITY.BAS, so BYTES.CLS must use UTILITY.CLS. I created UTILITY.CLS using the same technique. I got a "Sub or Function not defined" compiler error from StrToBytes in the following statement:

```
If IsArrayEmpty(ab) Then
```

Next I right-clicked IsArrayEmpty and selected Definition from the context menu. The IDE reported *Identifier under cursor is not recognized*. Notice that it said the identifier was not recognized, not that it didn't exist. In fact, it did exist right there in UTILITY.CLS.

What's going on here? Why can't code in BYTES.CLS recognize public procedures in UTILITY.CLS? To make a long story short, the modules in the AllAbout project can see procedures in UTILITY.CLS with no problem, but the modules in VBCore can't. When Visual Basic says that modules with global instancing are public, it means exactly what it says, not what any sane programmer would expect. To most of us, public includes private, but global classes are actually public only to outside projects; they're invisible to other modules in the same component.

I'll tell you what I think of this feature shortly, but for now I'll just say that there are two workarounds. Actually, there are more than two workarounds, but the others are terrible, whereas the ones I'm going to explain are merely bad. I know this because I tried all the terrible ones before I figured out the bad ones. For example, one terrible solution is to create a separate component for every module—UTILITY.DLL, ERRORS.DLL, BYTES.DLL, and so on. But then UTILITY-.DLL won't work unless ERRORS.DLL is loaded….Let's not even think about it. Another terrible solution is to throw all those standard modules into a single global class—KITCHENSINK.CLS. Not only is this idea terrible, it doesn't work because non-global classes such as CDrive and CVersion will also be part of VBCore, and they'll need to use the invisible procedures in KITCHENSINK.CLS.

Let's just skip the how and why. In the long run, I used one or the other of the bad techniques to convert all the standard modules used by AllAbout to global class modules in VBCore. The new AllAbout consisted of only two modules— ALLABOUT.FRM and DEBUG.BAS. Everything else was in VBCore. The AllAbout project ran in the IDE. Furthermore, I could compile the component to native code. To switch from the source version to the compiled version, I had to make sure VBCore rather than AllAbout was selected in the Project Explorer window. Then I chose Make VBCore.dll from the File menu to compile the DLL. The section "Developing for the Real World" later in this chapter will explain how to switch easily between the version of the client that uses the compiled component and the version that uses component source files.

Using internal objects to access global classes

The preferred technique for making global classes visible to other classes in a component is to qualify every reference with the name of a global object. To call a method of the GUtility class from the GBytes class, you'll need to create an object of type GUtility and use it to qualify any references to methods of GUtility. For example, you can declare the following object in a standard module:

```
Public MUtility As New GUtility
```

Then GBytes could access methods in GUtility like this:

```
If MUtility.IsArrayEmpty(ab) Then
```

I could give the object any name I want, but you'll see shortly why I want to use the name of the corresponding standard module. Because the *MUtility* object is defined with the New statement, it won't be created until some other module in VBCore calls a GUtility method. If no other module ever uses GUtility, the *MUtility* object won't be created. You might want to review the discussion of the New statement in Chapter 3 for more details on how this works.

Now let's look at the difference between outside clients and internal modules that might call the IsArrayEmpty function. Somewhere internally in some secret standard module, Visual Basic has the following declaration:

```
Public outsideutility As New GUtility
```

When the first external client calls a GUtility method, an *outsideutility* object will be created and used to access it like this:

```
outsideutility.IsArrayEmpty(ab)
```

Fortunately, Visual Basic doesn't make you reference the hidden *outsideutility* object. You can just say:

```
IsArrayEmpty(ab)
```

So if Visual Basic can create and then hide the outside object, why can't it do the same with the inside object? I don't know. Good question.

If inside and outside clients call GUtility methods, you'll have two different objects. And that's just the start. The client program might use an ActiveX control that uses VBCore, and that DLL (actually called an OCX) would get its own *outsideutility* object and its own *MUtility* object.

So all you have to do to make inter-module calls work throughout VBCore is define one of these global variables for each global class. I put all these declarations in the standard module OBJECTS.BAS. The reason I give all the objects the same name as the corresponding standard module is that it allows me to call procedures with exactly the same code in both standard and global versions of the module. Some clients will use the GUtility global class module (UTILITY.CLS) and its corresponding object in OBJECTS.BAS. Some will use the MUtility standard module (UTILITY.BAS). The following line works for either, although something very different happens in each case:

```
If MUtility.IsArrayEmpty(ab) Then
```

It's usually redundant to qualify a public procedure in a standard module, but it doesn't do any harm.

The process of converting a standard module to a global class module or vice versa is so mechanical that it can be done by a wizard (as we'll see shortly). But don't be lulled into thinking that if you call a rose a violet, the thorns will disappear. A global class module is a class with all the limitations of a class no matter what you do to pretend otherwise.

FLAME This sucks! There's no nice way to put it. All I want to do is write functions in a DLL. Other languages don't tell me I can't call DLL functions from within the DLL. Don't give me the technical reasons. It's not my problem—or shouldn't be. Global classes are good enough for trivial uses but not good enough for serious component libraries (and we've just started on the problems). Sure, you can hack around the limitations by explicitly stating the connections, but you're not supposed to have to hack to use standard features. Eliminating visible connections between modules is one of the main reasons to use a component rather than individual modules in the first place. It's another case where the Visual Basic implementation takes the easy way, forcing you to take the hard way. In other words, they shoved their implementation problems off on us. If this feature had been implemented in the original Spirit of Basic, global modules wouldn't even look like classes. You'd just set a Public property on a .BAS module, and all the details of making it into a class would be handled behind the scenes.

Instance data versus shared data

When you start to create DLLs, you're going to run smack into one of the standard problems that programmers in other languages have been dealing with all along. How do you distinguish instance data from shared data?

Imagine you have a program that uses the completed VBCore component. This program uses an ActiveX control that also uses VBCore. The program attaches to VBCore and calls the InstanceCount property in the GInstance global class module. InstanceCount looks like this:

```
' GInstance global class
Private c As Long
Property Get InstanceCount() As Long
    InstanceCount = c
    c = c + 1
End Property
```

The first time the program calls InstanceCount, it gets back 0. The second time it gets 1. At this point, the control calls InstanceCount. Will InstanceCount return 0 or 2? In other words, will both users be indirectly accessing the same copy of the private variable *c*? The answer is…no. The control will get 0 because it gets a completely separate MInstance object with its own copy of the InstanceCount property and the *c* variable.

But what if you want one count for all users? In other words, you want shared data rather than instance data. Most languages have a keyword (usually Static) specifying that data should exist in one and only one place. Visual Basic doesn't have this feature, but you can get it indirectly by putting the data in a standard module. A standard module always has one and only one instance, whereas class modules of any type (including forms) have a separate instance for each object.

It's easy enough to declare data in a standard module, but how are you going to make it public to users of your DLL? Standard modules can't be public, but you can create a global class that delegates to a standard module. To accomplish this, you're going to need cooperating module pairs. The GShared module looks like this:

```
' GShared global class module
Property Get SharedCount() As Long
    SharedCount = MShared.SharedCount
End Property
```

The MShared module looks like this:

```
' MShared standard module
Private c As Long
Property Get SharedCount() As Long
    SharedCount = c
    c = c + 1
End Property
```

Assume user one calls SharedCount twice. When user two calls SharedCount, it gets back 2, not 0. User two has its own separate copy of the GShared object, but that doesn't matter because the real work is being done in the MShared module, which has only one instance.

Before we get too carried away with the instance data problem, let's look at a different situation. Imagine we have two completely different programs that both use the VBCore DLL. Will they use the same copy of the SharedCount data? No, because separate programs are in separate processes, and in 32-bit Windows, separate processes are like separate galaxies. You'll need more than shared data in a DLL to communicate between processes. Chapter 6 will talk more about processes, and Chapter 11 will discuss inter-process communications.

The instance data versus shared data problem has many variations. It's not just concerned with data that is made directly available to the outside through properties. It applies to any module-level or static local data, even if that data is never directly exposed. For example, you often have to use Static variables in procedures to make sure that data is initialized properly. Chapter 8 will discuss many of the techniques required. But whenever you initialize Static data in a component, you should think carefully about whether you want that data to be initialized just once for the whole process or once for every user. If you need to initialize just once, you must use the delegation technique.

In fact, you might be tempted to use delegation as your default means of exposing global procedures in a component. It certainly has some attractions from a maintenance standpoint. For example, assume another module in the VBCore component, GMeToo, calls the SharedCount property. With the delegation technique, there's no need to qualify the call to SharedCount with a module name. Instead of

```
c = GShared.SharedCount
```

the other module can call directly:

```
c = SharedCount
```

If an outside user calls SharedCount, the SharedCount in the global class gets called and it calls the standard module version of SharedCount. If another global module calls SharedCount, it calls the standard module SharedCount directly.

If you delegate all your global procedures to standard modules, you'll only have to maintain the standard module because it does all the work. You have to add new delegation procedures to the global class every time you add a new procedure to the standard module. With the global object technique described earlier, you have to keep separate copies of the code in the standard and global modules. From a maintenance standpoint, the global object technique is a nightmare, while delegation is merely a bad dream. But from a correctness and efficiency standpoint, the global object technique is usually the right thing to do because most DLL data should be instance data rather than shared data.

To illustrate this point, consider the Rnd function from the VBA library. It uses private variables to create a random number sequence. If you call Rnd with the same seed from different users, it will return the same random number sequence for each user. Apparently, the VBA library uses instance data for the variables used to maintain the random number sequence. On the other hand, what about the Screen object? There's only one screen in the system (at least as far as Visual Basic is concerned), so the DLL could use shared data to maintain one and only one copy of the Screen object. In fact, I don't know if that's the case. Visual Basic might use only local data for the Screen object, and there might be multiple identical Screen objects for each client. I do know that the System object we'll be creating later in this chapter uses shared data to create one and only one instance.

There's one situation where you have no choice in the matter. Any procedure that uses the AddressOf operator to set up callbacks must delegate the procedure from a standard module. This limitation of the AddressOf operator applies to all classes, not just to global classes, but the difference might be less obvious when you're converting a standard module to a global class. Code that worked fine in the standard module starts giving errors when you put it in a global class. The fact that you can have one and only one copy of a callback procedure doesn't change the fact that you might have more than one user trying to use the callback at the same time. You have to consider this possibility and deal with it. The FindAnyWindow function deals with it by locking out any second client until the first client is finished. It's also possible to make the callback function figure out which object is using it and deal with that object only. We'll get to that technique later.

The Global Wizard

If it weren't for compatibility, programmers would live simpler, happier lives with only one annoying thorn in their sides—customers. In the case of the VBCore component, I'd have a lot less trouble if I simply made VBCore a requirement for all my samples. Instead of giving you the choice between UTILITY.BAS and the same procedures in VBCore, I would just make you use VBCore.

Perhaps that's not such a bad idea, and probably I would have done it had I understood how much trouble it would be to maintain two different versions of each procedure module. But I started to give you a choice, and here it is—complete with a wizard that helps with the tedious dirty work. Figure 5-1 shows the Global Wizard in action.

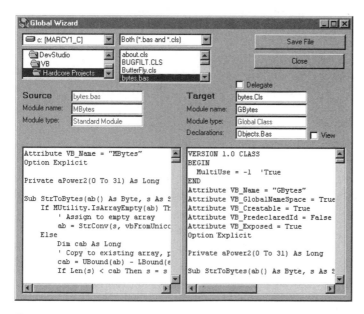

Figure 5-1. *The Global Wizard.*

The Global Wizard handles the following tasks:

- Translating a standard module into a global class containing exactly the same source code. This is very similar to creating an empty global class and pasting all the code from a standard module into it, but the wizard actually does a little more. It maintains the global object declarations for each module in a shared standard module. You can do this as a one-time conversion if you don't need to keep the standard module and global class in sync.

- Translate a global class into a standard module containing exactly the same source code. This is useful for keeping a global class in sync with a related standard module.

- Translate a standard module into a global class that delegates all its functionality back to the standard class. You can do this when your modules use the AddressOf operator or have a lot of shared data or when you are willing to trade off performance for the convenience of easier maintenance.

- Translate a public (non-global) class to a private class. If you want to use a class both within a component and in stand-alone programs, you'll need private and public versions. Since both classes are exactly the same except for the visibility, you'll need to keep them in different files. I add a P (for private) to the name of the private class.

- Translate a private class to a public (non-global) class. This helps you keep a private and public class in sync and depends on the same file naming convention.

Let's look at how I might use the wizard to convert the LotAbout program (the version that uses standard modules and private classes) to AllAbout (the version that uses VBCore). I'm going to use the global object technique for most of the modules in VBCore, but I'm going to use delegation for ERRORS.BAS (for reasons explained later) and for WINANY.BAS (because it uses AddressOf).

I start by running all the private classes and standard modules through the Global Wizard. The result is a matching global class for each module. But any of those global classes that call other global classes is going to fail because it doesn't qualify inter-module calls. Visual Basic will give me compile-time errors for those problems, and I'll be able to qualify them appropriately using the global objects created by the wizard in OBJECTS.BAS.

I'll probably run into a few other problems due to the differences between classes and standard modules described in the next few sections. Some of these differences must be handled with conditional compilation. I define the compile-time constant *fComponent* in the project properties for VBCore so that it will always be True in the global class version and always False in the standard module version. You should add the same constant to any component you create that uses my modules. After I add all the qualifying objects and fix other differences, my global modules will be out of sync with the standard modules. I'll have to run the Global Wizard again to convert the modified global classes back to standard modules.

You have to repeat this cycle every time you add add new procedures or modify the parameters of existing procedures.

<table>
<tr><td>FLAME</td><td>Visual Basic knows a lot about your compile-time environment. It knows, for example, whether you're in a component. It knows whether you're compiling for an executable or for the IDE. It knows whether a module is global, public, or private. Most language compilers and interpreters share this kind of information with programmers through predefined constants. Visual Basic version 4 provided Win32 and Win16 as compile-time constants, but now they're obsolete because everything is Win32 in version 5. It would be nice to get some useful predefined constants for information the compiler knows. Of course, you can define the appropriate constants yourself, but it's better to have standard information shared in a standard way by the system rather than having every programmer come up with a different convention.</td></tr>
</table>

Module initialization versus component initialization

Global classes have one feature that standard modules desperately need—an initialization event. Chapter 8 discusses some of the hacks required to initialize data in standard modules. Many of those problems disappear with global classes (although I'd trade initialization events for a variable initialization syntax in a minute). With components, you not only have the option of initializing data in Class_Initialize, you can also use the DLL initialization event—better known as Sub Main.

The choice is closely related to the one between instance data and shared data. If you want something to happen just once when the DLL is first loaded, you create a Sub Main in a standard module and do the work there. My convention is to put Sub Main in a shared data module (SHARED.BAS). This module is the place to put any shared variables used by the entire DLL but not tied to any particular module. I also provide a global class (SHARED.CLS) that uses delegation to expose the shared data for outside users. Real instance data should be placed in a separate module (INSTANCE.CLS).

Let's look at an example where initialization is a big winner. Many of the functions in BYTES.BAS work by calculating powers of two. We'll be looking at some more interesting functions later, but here's a simple example:

```
Function GetBit(ByVal iValue As Long, ByVal iBitPos As Integer) As Boolean
    BugAssert iBitPos >= 0 And iBitPos <= 31
    GetBit = iValue And (2 ^ iBitPos)
End Function
```

If you think about this for a minute (as did the source of this tip, Hardcore programmer Nick Malik), there's no reason to calculate 2 to the *nth* power every time you come into this function. We already know the powers of 2. They aren't going to change any time soon, so why not look them up in an array rather than calculate them?

```
Function GetBit(ByVal iValue As Long, ByVal iBitPos As Integer) As Boolean
    BugAssert iBitPos >= 0 And iBitPos <= 31
    GetBit = iValue And Power2(iBitPos)
End Function
```

Power2 is an indexed property that reads a private array containing powers of 2. Lookup functions are a common and easy technique in languages that support initialization of arrays, but it's annoyingly difficult to fill that array in Visual Basic—especially in a standard module. The MBytes module initializes differently, depending on the *fComponent* variable.

```
Private aPower2(0 To 31) As Long
⋮
Property Get Power2(ByVal i As Integer) As Long
    BugAssert i >= 0 And i <= 31
#If fComponent = 0 Then
    If aPower2(0) = 0 Then
        aPower2(0) = &H1&
        aPower2(1) = &H2&
        aPower2(2) = &H4&
        ⋮
        aPower2(31) = &H80000000
    End If
#End If
    Power2 = aPower2(i)
End Property

#If fComponent Then
Private Sub Class_Initialize()
    aPower2(0) = &H1&
    aPower2(1) = &H2&
    aPower2(2) = &H4&
    ⋮
```

```
aPower2(31) = &H80000000
End Sub
#End If
```

In the standard module, we initialize the first time a user calls the Power2 property. Testing for that first occurrence takes time, even after the first time when the test is always going to be false. In the global class, the initialization happens the first time anybody accesses anything in BYTES.CLS. There's no extra cost within Power2.

I could have made this code infinitesimally more efficient by initializing the array in Sub Main instead of in the Initialize event. That way, the initialization would be done once for the whole DLL rather than once for each user. After all, the powers of 2 are going to come out the same for all users. The cost of this optimization would be decreased modularity, leading to maintenance difficulties. You would have to put the initialization code in Sub Main rather than in the module where the array is used and exposed. That tradeoff may be worthwhile in some cases, but it doesn't make much difference here.

Class gotchas

The Global Wizard makes it so easy to convert a standard module to a global class that it's easy to forget that you've just created a completely different kind of module. But you'll soon get a rude reminder if your standard module procedures use incompatible types.

You can't have parameters that are UDTs or fixed-length strings in classes. There's no easy workaround, but since I generally avoid these types in components, the restriction doesn't bother me. Forms and Controls are a different matter. I have several functions that take Control parameters. Here's one from the MWinTool module:

```
#If fComponent Then
Function LookupItem(ctl As Object, sItem As String) As Long
#Else
Function LookupItem(ctl As Control, sItem As String) As Long
#End If
    LookupItem = SendMessageStr(ctl.hWnd, LB_FINDSTRING, -1&, sItem)
End Function
```

By using the Control type in the standard module version, this function forces at least minimal compile-time checking. It will fail if you pass a form instead of a control. That's better than nothing, but what you really want is not a Control type but an IListBox type. An IListBox would be an interface that included any kind of listbox control (such as the ComboBox control) but excluded any other control type such as EditBox or CommandButton. Unfortunately, IListBox doesn't exist, and the Control type is a private class that isn't recognized in public classes.

Therefore, you have to be satisfied with Object (and late binding) in the global class version of LookupItem.

Here's another little gotcha with global class modules. One of my favorite functions is GetRandom, which returns a random number within the range of two boundary numbers. The normal output of the Rnd function (a floating point number between 0.0 and 1.0) has little to do with my normal use of random numbers, so I used to use the following function instead:

```
Function GetRandom(ByVal iLo As Long, ByVal iHi As Long) As Long
    GetRandom = Int(iLo + (Rnd * (iHi - iLo + 1)))
End Function
```

But there's a problem with GetRandom. When a client program uses VBCore, there are two independent instances of the Visual Basic library. The client program uses one. The VBCore component uses another. If you use the Randomize statement in the client, it seeds the random number sequence for the client program, but it has no effect on the component's GetRandom function. During the development of VBCore, I used GetRandom for several weeks before I noticed that it was always generating exactly the same results no matter what parameters I gave to Randomize. I never had these problems with the standard module because GetRandom was in the client program.

I have three solutions. The first is to call Randomize in an initialization statement in the MUtility module.

```
#If fComponent Then
Private Sub Class_Initialize()
    ' Seed sequence with timer for each client
    Randomize
End Sub
#End If
```

The default behavior of Rnd is to always use a hard-coded seed number picked by Visual Basic. I always use a seed number picked by fate (in the form of the system timer). This initialization keeps me from forgetting and using the default sequence by mistake.

The second solution is to delegate the Randomize statement to a component version that the client can call to initialize the library.

```
' Seed the component's copy of the random number generator
Sub CoreRandomize(Optional Number As Long)
    Randomize Number
End Sub
```

Those who want to initialize their own random sequences for nefarious cheating schemes can use this version.

The third solution is to throw Visual Basic's random number functions in the trash and roll your own. The sidebar that follows tells how I did it.

Really Random

Random number generators are not all created equal. Chapters, if not books, have been written about random number generation. Although Visual Basic documentation doesn't completely describe its random number generator and the source code is not available, the new compiler makes it easily accessible to anyone with a debugger who can read assembly code. I looked at it and would describe it as a first-level generator—better than the one in Microsoft's C run-time library but probably not as good as the one I added to the FORTRAN run-time library back in another lifetime.

In those days (circa 1992), the FORTRAN group had a little argument with the C group. The C group provided the random number generator that we used in our random functions, but we wanted an improved version. The C group refused because they wanted compatibility with their existing algorithm. In theory (but rarely in practice), a program created with a new version of the language might need to get the same random number sequence from the same seed as it did in previous versions. The original C generator used a 16-bit algorithm with 16-bit limitations, but the C group didn't want to update the code for their 32-bit library because they feared breaking client code. When we lost the battle for a new algorithm, we abandoned the C run time and implemented our own improved algorithm, based on research of the extensive literature on random numbers.

The VBCore component provides that better algorithm as an alternative to the Randomize and Rnd procedures. I'm not saying this algorithm is better, just that it's different and that the pedigree for it is provided in the comments. This is still a first-level randomizer. It randomizes by using some carefully chosen constants to do some multiplication and subtraction operations on the last random number in the sequence. Second-level randomizers usually have a two-level system in which one random number is generated and then used to generate another.

You can check the code in RANDOM.CLS. The Seed sub starts the sequence (like Basic Randomize). The RandomReal function returns a floating-point number between 0 and 1 (like Basic Rnd). The Random function returns an integer within a given range (like GetRandom). Unlike Rnd, my algorithm uses the timer count as the seed by default so that you will come up with a different random sequence each session unless you specifically give a random seed. I use my own random module throughout the book instead of the Basic version.

Creating Global Objects

Have you ever wondered exactly what the App object is? Have you ever wanted to create something similar to the Screen object? With Visual Basic version 4, you could create a global instance of a class but you couldn't stop others from using the class to create additional objects at different scopes. This would defeat the purpose. You want one and only one System object because there's only one system.

With Visual Basic, you can create a System object in a component and be sure that there is one and only one instance of it for the outside world. The technique is Byzantine, to say the least, so we'll have to step through it slowly.

First we need a CSystem class. I have one, and many of its features will be described in Chapter 11. (Readers of the first edition are already familiar with my System object.) For now, it doesn't matter what the System object does, just that one and only one instance of it exists for clients of VBCore. To prevent outsiders from creating unauthorized instances of CSystem, we set its Instancing property to PublicNotCreatable. That means that we (the royal We who created VBCore) are the only ones who can create instances of the class, and if we create just one, that's the only one. Those who want to use CSystem as a private class outside VBCore are still stuck with nothing but the honor system to keep them from creating multiple System objects.

One way to make the System object available to the world is to make it a read-only property of a global module. We could define it like this in the instance data module, INSTANCE.CLS:

```
Private sys As New CSystem
    ⋮
Property Get System()
    Set System = sys
End Property
```

The problem with this is that each user of VBCore gets a separate copy of the System object. If you study the code of the CSystem class, you'll see that this probably wouldn't cause any problems. Each System object would be separate but identical. Nevertheless, it's more efficient and correct for the System object to be shared data. There's only one system, so there should be only one System object. When you create your own system-wide objects, think carefully about the clients. In some cases, instance data might be more appropriate.

To make the System object shared data, simply move the data declaration to the shared data module, SHARED.BAS. Of course, you'll still need to make the object public through a global class. You can do this with a property procedure in SHARED.CLS that delegates to the real object in SHARED.BAS:

```
Property Get System() As CSystem
    Set System = MShared.System
End Property
```

The System object and its cousin, the Video object, can be used by outside clients indirectly through global properties in SHARED.CLS. The objects are also used by one inside client. The CAbout class gets some of the information for its About dialog box from the System and the Video objects, but it accesses them directly through the properties in SHARED.BAS.

Developing for the Real World

Now that Visual Basic has a compiler, it needs tools to create debug and retail builds like other compilers. Alas, Visual Basic doesn't know any real-world development practices other than the ones you tell it about. So let's take a look at what we'd need to tell Visual Basic to get it to behave professionally.

An Imaginary Real Project

Many professional development projects address the needs of different kinds of users: developers, testers, beta sites, and end users. Each of these groups uses the product at different points (sometimes overlapping) during the life of the project. As an example, let's consider the Hexer program being developed by the Radices Unlimited Corporation. Hexer depends on a HexTool DLL component that provides much of the core functionality. HexTool is also used by several other Radices Unlimited products, including Octalizer and Decimator. Hexer also uses a HexIt control, which is used by various internal programs and which will be sold to developers. All the project files are kept under source control (although the issues would be the same even if the files were shared using a less formal system). Several developers work on different parts of the project.

Who does what

First there's the application developer, Adam App. Adam's responsibility is to write the Hexer application. He uses the HexTool DLL library and the HexIt control but doesn't have development responsibility for either of them. When he encounters a bug, he reports it to the library developer, Linda Library, or to the control developer, Connie Control.

The three developers are served by Barb Buildmaster, whose job is to coordinate regular builds of all the Radices Unlimited programs and components. She tries to make daily debug builds and weekly release builds. A debug build contains asserts and log messages that provide testers and developers with useful information when they encounter problems. Barb uses the debug system I described in "Examining Code" in Chapter 1. Release builds are pure code with no debugging information. Often, one part of the project has bugs that prevent its being built on schedule, so Barb tries to make each build independent of the others. That way, one bug won't necessarily bring down the whole project.

Tim Test is the tester for HexTool. Tom Test works on HexIt. Tadd Test works on Hexer. Tim and Tom have to write hundreds of test programs that validate HexTool.DLL and HexIt.OCX. They don't have access to the component source, working instead with the compiled debug components. Tadd never sees any source, just the completed debug version of Hexer.EXE. He tests it interactively, in batch mode, and with a scripting program that feeds in keystroke macros. The Test triplets also run test scripts on release builds to make sure debug code isn't masking bugs, and they sometimes use release builds for performance testing. When early beta versions start going out, beta customers will get debug builds. Late in the cycle, they'll switch to release builds. In the last few weeks before release, everybody uses the release versions to make sure they're seeing exactly what customers see.

How they do it

It's easy to work on a project that contains several ActiveX controls and DLL components—if you're the only person working on the project. Just use a project group (the VBG file) containing the program project and the component projects (the VBP files). When you want to build the program, select Make Project Group from the File menu. You'll end up with an EXE that uses each of the compiled components. The problem is, this ties all your components together. You'll end up rebuilding everything even if only one component is out of date. And if several client programs depend on the same components, you'll have to rebuild each component for each client project group.

Real-world development requires a more flexible system, and through trial and error, Radices Unlimited has come up with one. Figure 5-2 shows how the parts fit together.

Barb uses independent project files to build each part of the project. She also has responsibility for building all the other programs that depend on HexTool-.DLL and HexIt.OCX. Barb uses whatever project files she finds under source control without checking the files out. She has, however, laid down rules for checking in projects. Basically, no file is checked in unless it is complete and stable at the current level. In other words, the developers had better not break the build. Although Hexer might look messy to you, it's one of the simpler projects Barb works with. Octalizer, for example, consists of one application file, two ActiveX DLL components, one ActiveX EXE component, and four ActiveX controls. Many of the parts have dependencies on each other. Barb builds all the parts from the command line with a make program and a make file—just like in the old days when she built C projects under UNIX.

Barb's Project (build Hexer.EXE, HexTool.DLL, and HexIt.OCX)

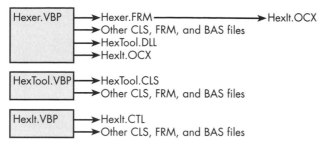

```
Hexer.VBP ──►Hexer.FRM──────────────►HexIt.OCX
          ──►Other CLS, FRM, and BAS files
          ──►HexTool.DLL
          ──►HexIt.OCX

HexTool.VBP──►HexTool.CLS
           ──►Other CLS, FRM, and BAS files

HexIt.VBP ──►HexIt.CTL
          ──►Other CLS, FRM, and BAS files
```

Adam's Project (develop and debug Hexer application)

```
Hexer.VBP ──►Hexer.FRM──────────────►HexIt.OCX
          ──►Other CLS, FRM, and BAS files
          ──►HexTool.DLL
          ──►HexIt.OCX
```

Linda's Project (develop and debug HexTool component)

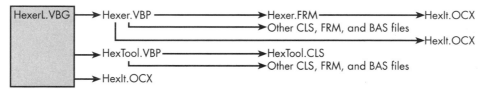

```
HexerL.VBG ──►Hexer.VBP ──────────────►Hexer.FRM ──────────────►HexIt.OCX
            └─────────────────────────►Other CLS, FRM, and BAS files
                                                              ──►HexIt.OCX
           ──►HexTool.VBP ──────────────►HexTool.CLS
            └─────────────────────────►Other CLS, FRM, and BAS files
           ──►HexIt.OCX
```

Connie's Project (develop and debug HexIt Control)

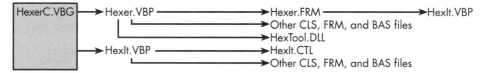

```
HexerC.VBG ──►Hexer.VBP ──────────────►Hexer.FRM ──────────────►HexIt.VBP
            └─────────────────────────►Other CLS, FRM, and BAS files
                                      ──►HexTool.DLL
           ──►HexIt.VBP ──────────────►HexIt.CTL
            └─────────────────────────►Other CLS, FRM, and BAS files
```

Figure 5-2. *Radices Unlimited Hexer Builds.*

Adam works in the IDE with the same Hexer.VBP file that Barb uses. Since Hexer is his responsibility, he owns Hexer.VBP and is the only one who has authority to modify the project file or the modules in it. Adam can look at the source for HexTool and HexIt, but he has no authority to check them out and modify them without express permission from their owners.

Linda does most of her HexTool development using her own HexTest application. She has a HexTest.VBG that points to HexTest.VBP and HexTool.VBP. HexTest is a private tool and no one else has access to it, although Linda sometimes informally shares test code with Tim, the library tester. Linda sometimes uses Hexer to track down bugs reported by Adam. In order to debug HexTool with Hexer, she has to have Hexer source code, but she doesn't normally check it out of source control. She just reports any bugs she encounters to Adam.

The official Hexer.VBP references HexTool.DLL, however, Linda needs to use HexTool.VBP. Fortunately, Linda can get Hexer.VBP to ignore its reference to HexTool.DLL and instead use HexTool.VBP. She does this by using a private project group, which we'll call HexerL.VBG (although Linda calls it Hexer.VBG). Linda's VBG references Hexer.VBP and HexTool.VBP but not HexIt.VBP because Linda always wants to use the OCX rather than the source.

FLAME	The VBG file controls whether a client project references the compiled component or the component source. When you compile a component for the first time from within a client VBG, Visual Basic will automatically switch the reference from the component VBP file to the compiled DLL or OCX file (assuming that Project or Binary compatibility is set on the component). You can confirm this by examining the client VBP file with a text editor. But as long as you use the component from a VBG, the References dialog box will show a connection to the component VBP. When you switch to the client VBP, the references will show the real reference to the compiled component. Don't look for an explanation of this in Visual Basic documentation. I discovered this feature by accident after many hours of trying to come up with a hack that would fake the same behavior. The person who wrote the documentation was as surprised as I was when I described it to him. So here's a gentle reminder from all of us hardcore technical writers to all you hardcore programmers. It doesn't matter how &%$#(*& clever your *%@&$ features are if you %*@#+^*& don't tell us about them, ^%~$*##!

Connie Control has a few extra maintenance problems. At one point, the HexIt control used a few functions from the HexTool library, but the problems of having Hexer and Hexit both depend on HexTool proved to be a nightmare. Fortunately, Connie (like all employees of Radices Unlimited) has a copy of *Hardcore Visual Basic*. She now uses the Global Wizard described earlier in this chapter to generate standard modules and private classes from the source modules in HexTool. It's not the preferred method of reuse, but it works despite some inconvenience. Besides, HexIt will eventually be released as an independent tool and customers won't want an extra DLL.

Like Linda, Connie uses a private test program, Hexercize, for most of her development. She also uses Hexer for real-world testing and when responding to bugs. She has a private project group (HexerC.VBG) that references Hexer.VBP and HexIt.VBP but not HexTool.VBP. Notice that Connie's situation is a little more complicated than Linda's because HexIt.OCX is referenced not only from Hexer.VBP but also from Hexer.FRM. Fortunately, Visual Basic knows that when a VBG is used, it should ignore all references to the compiled component and use the component VBP instead.

Developing Real Imaginary Projects

The sample projects provided with this book are real in the sense that they exist on your disk. But most of them aren't exactly typical real-world projects. Nevertheless, you might be interested in how I built them, and you certainly want to know how to use the resulting components.

The samples serve two purposes. Most of the client programs (with the exception of the wizards) aren't particularly useful except to illustrate the techniques discussed. You might be able to cut and paste a few bits of code, but most of the reusable stuff is in the components, not in the client programs. You might find it interesting to load some samples and step through parts of the code—especially the parts I didn't get around to explaining. But the components are the real point. I like to think of *Hardcore Visual Basic* as some components with an accompanying book, not the other way around.

In order to make the components more useful, I provide them in two forms: debug and release. If you write programs that use the components, you can use the debug versions during development. These versions will give you some output errors and asserts if you give parameters that are legal to Visual Basic but that violate the definition of the component. When you're ready to create your release candidate, you can build with the release versions.

You might want to step through code while reading about it in the book. You have two choices: you can debug the client programs with the compiled components, or you can debug the components through a test client. For example, to debug Edwina the Editor from Chapter 9 as a client program, load Edwina-.VBP. By default, Edwina.VBP will use the debug versions of VBCore.DLL and other components. To switch between debug and release components, you can run the batch files TODEBUG.BAT and TORELEASE.BAT. This will register the debug or release version of the component.

To debug the XEditor control, the XDropStack control, or the VBCore library through Edwina, load Edwina.VBG. This allows you to step into any component. This is a good time to repeat my earlier warning. It's tempting to just fix any bugs you might find in my code and rebuild my components. Please don't. The last thing I need is multiple versions of my components floating around. You can put any of my code (including whole classes and controls) in your own components as long as you change the names and the GUIDs.

Better Basic Through Subclassing

"If I had designed Visual Basic, I could have made that procedure better."

Well, quit complaining and do something about it. You don't have to accept the Visual Basic run-time library. You can replace procedures with your own versions, or you can enhance procedures by subclassing them. The BETTER.BAS module fixes some of the Visual Basic procedures I didn't like. For example, the Timer function isn't accurate enough for my taste, so I replaced it:

```
Function Timer() As Single
    Static secFreq As Currency, secStart As Currency
    If secFreq = 0 Then QueryPerformanceFrequency secFreq
    QueryPerformanceCounter secStart
    If secFreq Then Timer = secStart / secFreq
    ' Else Timer = 0 if no high resolution timer
End Function
```

The Basic version is apparently based on the system time and date features. It is nominally accurate to a hundredth of a second, but in practice it appears to be even less precise. The QueryPerformanceCounter API function gets whatever accuracy your machine is willing to return—normally better than a millisecond.

The problem with the better version of Timer is that it returns what most Basic programmers want (an accurate time count) rather than what the documentation says (seconds since midnight). Normally, you use Timer to measure the difference between two times. You don't care whether the unit of time returned is seconds since midnight, seconds since the last boot, or seconds since the first MITS Altair was switched on. If for some reason you really need to know the number of seconds since midnight, you can specify the original Timer:

What's Wrong with That?

It happens. Objects fall apart. You can't make a class hierarchy without breaking methods. Code isn't always a bowl of cherries.

When things go wrong, what can you do? Like other languages, Visual Basic offers many alternatives, most of them wrong. Let's look at some of the more common strategies, pick one to emphasize in this book, and explain some techniques for making it work.

Any discussion of error handling has to consider two sides. What should your components do with errors? And what should clients of those components do with whatever you do with errors? In this section, we'll be wearing the hat of the component creator, but of course, any civilized programmer has to consider the effect on the client side.

```
iSecondsToday = VBA.Timer
```

Does this give you an idea of how to enhance rather than replace library functions? Here's how I enhanced the Hex function to add leading zeros:

```
Function Hex(ByVal i As Long, Optional iWidth As Long = 0) As String
    If iWidth <= 0 Then
        Hex = VBA.Hex$(i)
    Else
        Hex = Right$(String$(iWidth, "0") & VBA.Hex$(i), iWidth)
    End If
End Function
```

You can see more of my improved procedures in BETTER.BAS. Most of them follow the same pattern. Use optional arguments to add new features to an existing procedure. If the user doesn't provide the argument, use the original procedure. Otherwise, call the original procedure for base functionality and add your own embellishments.

You can override library procedures because of Visual Basic's name space priority list. It starts with your project, goes on to the VB, VBA, and VBRUN libraries, and continues with other loaded controls and components. That's why I don't have a global class named BETTER.CLS in the VBCore component. The standard Visual Basic libraries would always override anything in the component. If you want better Basic procedures, you must include the standard module BETTER.BAS directly in your project.

Although replacing standard procedures is a cool trick, it's kind of a questionable programming practice and in real life I rarely use BETTER.BAS. Instead, I use FmtHex (in UTILITY.BAS) rather than the Hex function. I use ProfileStart and ProfileStep in DEBUG.BAS rather than the Timer function.

What Can You Do?

We're talking about errors here, not bugs. Errors are bad things that can happen. Bugs are bad things that should never happen. Use asserts to avoid bugs. It's not a bug if the user misspells a filename in a dialog box, but you do have to do something about it. Here are some of the error-handling strategies that Visual Basic programmers adopt:

Let 'er rip. Visual Basic has built-in error handling, so you don't have to do anything. If the user does something wrong, a nice, friendly error box will pop up with a clear, intuitive message, and your program will terminate. If your users complain, blame Visual Basic. If you think this is a good idea for clients, you deserve your horrible fate. But sometimes this terrible-sounding technique is actually the right strategy for components.

Forbid errors. Don't laugh. This is sometimes a viable option. If you consider all input to be valid, don't do anything that could fail and make sure all your output is valid. Then nothing can go wrong—except bugs. Be very careful about using this strategy with any user interface. Users do the darndest things!

Return an error code. This is a common strategy, but one with problems. First, everything becomes a function—no Subs allowed. On the other hand, you can say that everything becomes a Sub. No functions are allowed because you've already used up the return value. Any value that must be returned has to come back through a reference parameter.

The Component Object Model uses this system. All functions return an HRESULT, which is a 32-bit value containing status bits and a numeric code. Negative HRESULTs are errors. Positive HRESULTs are nonerror results. I've programmed these functions in C++, and it's not very natural or intuitive. Even property get functions have to return values through references. It's certainly a structured and consistent system, but for Basic…Well, I'd have to call it un-Basic.

There are some less drastic variations. If a function returns only positive values, you can return errors as negative values. Another variation is to reserve one special value as an error return. If you need more information about the error, use the system discussed in the next item. If the return value has a String or Variant type, return an empty string or the Empty value, respectively. If it's numeric, the special value might be 0, −1, or some other number that is out of range. The Win32 API uses this technique. It's an inconsistent system because you have to check the documentation of every function to see which values represent errors. Furthermore, the whole scheme depends on finding at least one value you can use to represent "invalid." If there isn't one, you're out of luck.

Provide an error function or property. The Win32 functions indicate in the return value whether an error has occurred, but you have to call GetLastError to see what the error was. You can't use this function from Visual Basic, but the Err object has a LastDllError property that returns the last error from an API call. You can follow a similar strategy. Define a global Error function that can be called from anywhere, or give your classes an Error property that reports more details about the last error.

This scheme creates a modal system where every procedure call sets a new error mode. As soon as you call another procedure, you move to its error mode and the error code for the last procedure is lost forever. Your implementation also has to set the internal error variable for every procedure—either to an error code or to a no-error code (usually zero).

Raise errors. This is how Visual Basic statements and procedures work, and it's how all but the rudest of controls work. It's also the method this book will use as its default. I might use some variations on the strategies discussed above, but mostly I'll be raising errors from inside methods, properties, and procedures.

This gives the client the most flexibility. They can ignore errors (God forbid) and let Visual Basic handle them. They can use *On Error Resume Next* to handle errors as if they were invalid function returns, or they can use *On Error Goto* to send errant behavior to error traps.

The following sections explain techniques for raising errors.

When to Raise Errors

There are four common situations in which your components might raise errors. Let's take a look:

- The good news is that most of the time you don't have to do anything. If the user passes an invalid argument or does some other bozo illegal thing when calling your component, you can ignore it. Visual Basic will automatically raise the appropriate error. Since you didn't handle the error, it will fall through to the client. It's the client's problem, not yours.

- Often the errors raised by illegal operations in your components won't make sense to clients. You might get the error "Object doesn't support this property" inside your component method, but you don't want to pass it back that way because you know from the context exactly which property is expected. You can create and raise a new error with a more specific message.

- Some errors you detect in your component might map to standard Visual Basic run-time errors. If you ask for a filename parameter and the user passes an invalid file, you can raise the standard "File not found" error rather than creating your own. This is a judgment call. Sometimes you might want to create your own more specific message.

- When you detect errors from API functions, you'll usually want to generate your own error messages, but you don't necessarily have to do it from scratch. Windows has an embedded string for every API error, and you can reuse those strings as your error descriptions.

How to Raise Errors

You probably already know the tedious techniques required to raise your own errors. It's covered in the manuals, so I'll be brief. Let's say we wanted to create and raise the bozo error from the GUtility module of the VBCore component. We might do it like this:

```
Err.Raise vbObjectError + 22000, "VBCore.Utility", "You are a bozo"
```

You're supposed to raise errors by adding the mysterious *vbObjectError* constant to your error number. But what exactly is *vbObjectError*? You can get a good idea by checking its hexadecimal value: &H80040000. To programmers who have worked with COM in other languages, this looks a lot like the status bits of an HRESULT. The 8 sets the severity bit, indicating that it is an error. The 4 sets the facility code to a standard value that C programmers know as FACI-LITY_ITF (ITF is an abbreviation for interface). There are other facility codes for errors from Windows, Win32, and some other sources, but since everything made public by Visual Basic is an interface, there's no need to get creative.

The key point is that you're combining the bits of your error code with the bits of a severity code and a facility code. Normally, you combine or test bits with logical operators, not arithmetic operators. That's why I think it's more accurate to code your errors like this:

```
Err.Raise 22000 Or vbObjectError, "VBCore.Utility", "You are a bozo"
```

> **NOTE**
>
> So what happens if, ignoring all warnings in the documentation, you simply raise your errors directly without vbObjectError?
>
> ```
> Err.Raise 22001, "MyProject.MyModule", "I am a bozo"
> ```
>
> Will your program suddenly disappear in a puff of smoke? Will the error police break down your door in the middle of the night? No, but behind your back Visual Basic will set the facility code of error to FACILITY_CONTROL. In other words, your code will actually do this:
>
> ```
> Err.Raise 22001 Or &H800A000,...
> ```
>
> COM documentation says that FACILITY_CONTROL errors should be raised for control-related errors. I'm not sure, but I think they mean the system code that creates controls rather than the code in controls. As always, ignore documented instructions at your own risk.

For clients, the only thing that matters about these bits is that you have to get rid of them to get an intelligible error message. You can do that easily by masking out the high bits (the bit flags) of the error, leaving only the low bits containing the code. I use the following functions for masking out the irrelevant bits or masking in the relevant ones:

```
Function BasicError(ByVal e As Long) As Long
    BasicError = e And &HFFFF&
End Function

Function COMError(e As Long) As Long
    COMError = e Or vbObjectError
End Function
```

So if you raise the bozo error shown earlier, the client can get back the error number you set (22000 in this case) like this:

```
e = VBError(Err.Number)
```

You're also supposed to raise errors with integer values greater than 512 in order to avoid conflicts with Visual Basic's errors. That leaves me and all other component developers the range of 512 to 32768. I hereby claim the number 13000 as my unlucky number and order other component developers to cease and desist from using this number as the base for their error numbers. In exchange, I promise not to use up any more precious numbers than I have to. OK? Well, I know it's a hopeless request. It's inevitable that component error numbers will overlap occasionally. If you use two components with the same numbers, you'll have to figure out who's who from the context.

Notice also that you're supposed to return the source in a *project.module* format. If you don't fill in this optional parameter, Visual Basic will provide the project but not the module.

If you don't provide an error message, one will be provided for you, but you probably won't like it. This is pretty mechanical stuff, and we ought to be able to automate at least part of it. The module ERRORS.CLS provides procedures that allow you to shorten error raising code to this:

```
ErrRaise eeBozo
```

My system depends on convention. Each module gets an Enum for all the error messages it can raise. Here's the one for UTILITY.CLS (and it's the same in UTILITY.BAS):

```
Public Enum EErrorUtility
    eeBaseUtility = 13000   ' Utility
    eeNoMousePointer       ' HourGlass: Object doesn't have mouse pointer
    eeNoTrueOption         ' GetOption: None of the options are True
    eeNotOptionArray       ' GetOption: Not control array of OptionButton
End Enum
```

Here's the procedure that makes it work in the ERRORS.CLS module of VBCore:

```
#If fComponent Then
Sub ErrRaise(e As Long)
    MErrors.ErrRaise e
End Sub
#End If
```

Wait a minute! The global class version of ErrRaise is just delegating to a standard module version using the technique described in "Creating Global Procedures." Delegation works better here because it avoids the requirement to qualify every single call with a global object. There's no instance data in the error functions, and they aren't called in situations where performance is critical. Most calls to ErrRaise will be from internal modules anyway. Therefore, the real work is done in the delegated standard module ERRORS.BAS:

```
#If fComponent Then
Sub ErrRaise(e As Long)
    Dim sText As String, sSource As String
    If e > 1000 Then
        sSource = App.ExeName & "." & LoadResString((e \ 10) * 10)
        sText = LoadResString(e)
        Err.Raise e, sSource, sText
    Else
        ' Raise standard Visual Basic error
        Err.Raise e, sSource
    End If
    ' Challenge: Enhance to use help files
End Sub
#End If
```

The component side of the code (where *fComponent* is True) loads error message strings out of the VBCore resource file. Here's part of the VBCORE.RC file from which VBCORE.RES is built:

```
// VBCore.RC - Resource script for VBCore

STRINGTABLE
BEGIN
#if !defined(idLang)
    13000    "Utility"
    13001    "HourGlass: Object doesn't have mouse pointer"
    13002    "GetOption: None of the options are True"
    13003    "GetOption: Not a control array of OptionButton"
    ⋮
// #elif idLang == idOtherLang
    // Add other languages here
#endif
END
```

Each module gets slots for ten strings. The first string is reserved for the name of the module, which will be returned as part of the source. If you really need more than nine errors per module (rare in my experience), you'll need to duplicate the module string for each error block.

All you have to do to make VBCore work in Bulgarian is translate the error messages to Bulgarian and add them to VBCORE.RES. I'll explain more about resources later.

One problem—I can't make the same ErrRaise procedure work when ERRORS-.BAS is used as a stand-alone module because I don't know how the client wants to handle error strings. If users of UTILITY.BAS and other standard modules want to use resource strings, that's up to them. They can write their own error resource files and their own ErrRaise function. The best I can do is provide private ErrRaise functions in the standard modules so that they'll at least work in English as the default. Here, for example, is the one from UTILITY.BAS:

```
#If fComponent = 0 Then
Private Sub ErrRaise(e As Long)
    Dim sText As String, sSource As String
    If e > 1000 Then
        sSource = App.EXEName & ".Utility"
        Select Case e
        Case eeBaseUtility
            sText = "Utility"
        Case eeNoMousePointer
            sText = "HourGlass: Object doesn't have mouse pointer"
        Case eeNoTrueOption
            sText = "GetOption: None of the options are True"
        Case eeNotOptionArray
            sText = "GetOption: Argument is not a control array" & _
                    "of OptionButtons"
        End Select
        Err.Raise COMError(e), sSource, sText
    Else
        ' Raise standard Visual Basic error
        Err.Raise e, sSource
    End If
End Sub
#End If
```

Maintaining the error Enums and error strings is a nuisance. You have to update each error in three different places—the error Enum, the standard module Select Case block, and the VBCore resource file. This kind of mechanical work is unfit for human beings. If you're going to use errors in this format frequently, consider writing a wizard to automate the process. I considered it, but unfortunately for you it never reached the top of my project stack.

Turning API Errors into Basic Errors

One of the more common tasks for the hardcore API programmer is to turn an error returned from an API function call into a Visual Basic error. For example, here's how you can call registry API functions (which always return 0 for success or an API error code):

```
ApiRaiseIf RegCloseKey(hKey)
```

If the return value from RegCloseKey (or any other registry API function) is 0, nothing happens. If it's an error code, ApiRaiseIf creates a new Visual Basic error containing the official Windows error string for the associated error.

Sometimes with Windows functions, the return value indicates whether an error occurred but the code is returned through GetLastError (which Basic sees as Err.LastDllError) rather than through the error code. In that case, you raise the appropriate error with the ApiRaise procedure:

```
c = GetTempPath(cMaxPath, sRet)
If c = 0 Then ApiRaise Err.LastDllError
```

And if for some reason you just want to display the official error message without raising an error for it, you can call the ApiError function like this:

```
Debug.Print ApiError(Err.LastDllError)
```

How does this magic work? Well, Windows maintains all those error messages as resources in KERNEL32.DLL. These messages are localized: Bulgarian Windows has Bulgarian messages. You can get the error messages out of the DLL with the FormatMessage API function, using code like this:

```
Function ApiError(ByVal e As Long) As String
    Dim s As String, c As Long
    s = String(256, 0)
    c = FormatMessage(FORMAT_MESSAGE_FROM_SYSTEM Or _
                    FORMAT_MESSAGE_IGNORE_INSERTS, _
                    pNull, e, 0&, s, Len(s), ByVal pNull)
    If c Then ApiError = Left$(s, c)
End Function
```

The FormatMessage function is overloaded to do many tasks. You pass constants in the first parameter to indicate which task you want. When retrieving error messages, most parameters are ignored. FormatMessage is an interesting function, but this is one of the few tasks it performs that makes sense in Visual Basic.

NOTE The Error Message program (ERRMSG.VBP) is the shortest useful utility provided with this book. It puts a simple user interface around the message lookup code from ApiError. Just type in an error number and it shows you the corresponding message. I keep a copy of it on my desktop.

As you can imagine, the ApiRaise function just calls ApiError:

```
Sub ApiRaise(ByVal e As Long)
    Err.Raise vbObjectError + 29000 + e, _
            App.ExeName & ".Windows", ApiError(e)
End Sub
```

Most common API errors fall in the range 1 through 999. I've randomly chosen 29000 as the base for API errors. So once again, let me raise a hopeless request that no one use error codes between 29001 and 29999 for anything other than creating fake API errors. I return the source as the project name combined with *Windows*. I'd prefer to give the specific system DLL that caused the error, but I couldn't figure out any way to get that information.

The ApiRaiseIf procedure just uses the ApiRaise procedure to make the error-raising syntax a little cleaner:

```
Sub ApiRaiseIf(ByVal e As Long)
    If e Then ApiRaise e
End Sub
```

Handling Errors in the Client

Wrong book. That's a user interface problem, not a programming problem. But I can give you a few quick suggestions. Put up a dialog box telling users they are filthy, unwashed idiots with ugly children. Tell them they have just committed error −2147211501 (&H80042713). Display the message "I am unworthy," and make them click OK. Then terminate the program, throwing all their wretched, unsaved work into the bit bin.

But I digress. What I meant to recommend is that you read Alan Cooper's book *About Face: The Essentials of User Interface Design* (IDG Books, 1995). His diatribe against bad error handling is more caustic than anything I could write, but he softens the blow by providing positive suggestions.

Code Review

In many programming departments, code review comes with the territory. The author of a piece of code offers it up for group consumption. Participants sit down together to read the code line by line, looking for inefficiencies, wrong assumptions, unchecked errors, and better algorithms.

In theory, code review takes place in a positive atmosphere of camaraderie, with the implicit assumption that no one writes perfect code every time. But you can surely imagine situations in which comments might get brutal. In practice, most programmers host code review with fear and loathing.

So let's do some code review. Let's pick an innocent, naive rookie and rip his pitiful efforts to shreds. Let's examine some code that has been seen by millions and see if it's really up to snuff. Let's review REMLINE, the program that wouldn't die. To introduce the code, I'll turn the floor over to the owner of the code, Bruce McKinney, circa 1987. The reviewers are Joe Hacker, Jane Sensible, and their manager, Mary Hardhead.

The Program That Wouldn't Die

Bruce: As you know, this is my first work as a professional programmer—although at this point I'm only a sample programmer. This is also my introduction to parsing. I was assigned to fix REMLINE.BAS as a sample program for QuickBasic.

Joe: What the heck is a sample programmer?

Bruce: Well, there are real programmers, and there are sample programmers. I'm just a sample.

Mary: Bruce has been hired by the documentation department as a programmer. In the past, all the sample programs in the manuals and on the disk have been just thrown together by whoever happened to have time. Coding style and quality varied a lot. Bruce's job is to make all the samples use a consistent style and have consistent quality.

Joe: Well, if he works for documentation, why don't the documenters review his code?

Mary: We thought it'd be good experience for him to have his code reviewed by programmers from Basic development. A sort of baptism by fire.

Jane: It might also be nice for C programmers writing the Basic language to see what it's like in the trenches. How long has it been since you tried to write serious code in Basic?

Joe: Serious code in Basic? Hmph! Can't be done.

Bruce: We'll see. Back to REMLINE. I didn't write it, and I don't know the original author. The version I got was lightly commented, had a clumsy user interface, didn't take full advantage of new Basic features, and had undocumented limitations that some people might call design bugs. My job was to clean up this private code for public consumption.

Joe: So this isn't even your code?

Bruce: Well, what we're going to talk about today is mine. I revised it heavily, and I take responsibility for it. Now, the purpose of REMLINE is to remove all unnecessary line numbers from GW-BASIC and BASICA programs so that they look semistructured. In theory, you can then go through and change the remaining line numbers to labels as a first step toward making the code readable by humans as well as by modern versions of Basic.

Joe: You're better off just throwing away your BASICA code and starting over from scratch.

Jane: Oh, sure! That's a good marketing line. Put that on the box. "QuickBasic: Now you can rewrite all your old code."

Bruce: When I started on REMLINE, I thought it was a pretty cool program, and I had all kinds of ideas for making it even cooler. Now I tend to agree with Joe. Dump your BASICA code in the trash. In any case, we're not reviewing REMLINE; we're reviewing the parsing code in it.

REMLINE is a very simple compiler that tokenizes a source file. It recognizes certain Basic keywords associated with line numbers—Goto, Gosub, Then, Else—and indexes each one with its target line number. When it's finished indexing, it strips out all the line numbers that haven't been targeted by a keyword. A good portion of the code deals with tokenizing keywords, variables, and line numbers. REMLINE does this with imitations of the C parsing functions strtok, strspn, and strcspn.

Joe: This is crazy. I don't have time to review sample code that no one will see. Even if you ship this crap, no one will pay any attention to it, and you won't bother to ship it with the next version.

Mary: You don't have to like this assignment, but you do have to do it. Try to have a positive attitude.

Archaeologist's Note: REMLINE *went on to become the most widely distributed source code in the history of the planet. It shipped not only with various versions of Microsoft Basic but also with MS-DOS 5, and it still ships with every copy of Windows NT version 4. For reasons unknown, the problems discovered in the code review described here were never fixed. Fortunately, most of the millions of people who saw this code didn't look at it.*

StrSpan and StrBreak

Bruce: In C, the basic building blocks of parsing are strspn and strcspn. My Basic names for them are StrSpan and StrBreak. To use StrSpan, you pass it the string you want to parse and a list of separator characters—space, tab, and comma—and line-break characters if the string can span multiple lines. StrSpan returns the position of the first character that is not a separator. You pass StrBreak the same arguments, and it returns the position of the first character that is a separator.

You can probably guess how to use these functions. Find the start of a token with StrSpan, find the end of the token with StrBreak, cut out the token, find the start of a token with StrSpan, find the end of the token with StrBreak...and so on to the end of the string. That's pretty much what GetToken does, but first let's take a look at StrSpan:

```
Function StrSpan1(sTarget As String, sSeps As String) As Integer

    Dim cTarget As Integer, iStart As Integer
    cTarget = Len(sTarget)
    iStart = 1
```

(continued)

```
    ' Look for start of token (character that isn't a separator)
    Do While InStr(sSeps, Mid$(sTarget, iStart, 1))
        If iStart > cTarget Then
            StrSpan1 = 0
            Exit Function
        Else
            iStart = iStart + 1
        End If
    Loop
    StrSpan1 = iStart

End Function
```

StrBreak is identical except that the loop test is reversed:

```
' Look for end of token (first character that is a separator)
Do While InStr(sSeps, Mid$(sTarget, iStart, 1)) = 0
```

Archaeologist's Note: Names of functions and variables have been changed to protect the guilty. Joe Hacker's diatribes against the stupid naming conventions of the original have been edited out of this text, along with other rude remarks deemed irrelevant. The code has been updated to reflect the Visual Basic language, ignoring QuickBasic syntax differences. Different versions of the procedures are numbered. Interested historians can find the original code in most versions of QuickBasic, the Basic Professional Development System, MS-DOS 5, and Windows NT.

Joe: If they're identical except for one line, why have two functions? Why not have one function—say, StrScan—with a flag argument that can be either Span or Break? Put the loop test in a conditional. That should save some code.

Jane: Yeah, but at what cost? You might loop through these functions hundreds of times if you're parsing a big file. Is the size cost of duplicating tiny functions worth the cost of adding an extra test in a loop that will be called in a loop? Besides, the interface feels better with separate functions.

Joe: I don't care what "feels" better, but I guess I'll buy your performance argument. Let's stick with two functions.

Mary: Any other comments?

Jane: The length *cTarget* is calculated just once, outside the loop. That's good. The body of the loop looks pretty clean. The loop test with Mid$ called inside InStr looks messy.

Joe: It's taking one character at a time off the test string and searching for it in the separator list. Kind of an unusual use of InStr. You don't care where you find the character, only *whether* you find it. I can't think of a better way to do it, short of rewriting it in a real language, like C.

Bruce: Well, if StrSpan is OK, StrBreak is also OK because it's the same except backward. Let's move on to GetToken.

GetToken

Bruce: The original GetToken in REMLINE worked exactly like the C strtok function. It follows a classic design for iteration functions that have to be called repeatedly until they report no more items to iterate. In this type of function, you call it with one set of arguments the first time, and then you call it with another set of arguments each subsequent time.

GetToken works the same way. The first time, you pass the string to be parsed; after that, you pass an empty string. It goes like this:

```
sSeparator = ", " & sTab & sCrLf
sToken = GetToken(sCommand, sSeparator)
Do While sToken <> sEmpty
    ' Do something with sToken
    sToken = GetToken(sEmpty, sSeparator)
Loop
```

That's the philosophy. Here's the code:

```
Function GetToken1(sTarget As String, sSeps As String) As String

    ' Note that sSave and iStart must be static from call to call
    ' If first call, make copy of string
    Static sSave As String, iStart As Integer
    If sTarget <> sEmpty Then
        iStart = 1
        sSave = sTarget
    End If

    ' Find start of next token
    Dim iNew As Integer
    iNew = StrSpan1(Mid$(sSave, iStart, Len(sSave)), sSeps)
    If iNew Then
        ' Set position to start of token
        iStart = iNew + iStart - 1
    Else
        ' If no new token, return empty string
        GetToken1 = sEmpty
        Exit Function
    End If

    ' Find end of token
    iNew = StrBreak1(Mid$(sSave, iStart, Len(sSave)), sSeps)
```

(continued)

```
If iNew Then
    ' Set position to end of token
    iNew = iStart + iNew - 1
Else
    ' If no end of token, set to end of string
    iNew = Len(sSave) + 1
End If
' Cut token out of sTarget string
GetToken1 = Mid$(sSave, iStart, iNew - iStart)
' Set new starting position
iStart = iNew

End Function
```

Trouble in Paradise

Bruce: This function always works on the same string. Notice how the first block of code saves the *sTarget* argument in the static *sSave* variable for later iterations. The rest of the code uses *sSave* and ignores *sTarget*. The next block of code uses StrSpan to get the start of the token, and then the next block uses StrBreak to get the end. Once you have the start and the end, you cut out the token and return it.

Joe: What the heck are you doing with that Mid$ in your StrSpan call? And there it is again in StrBreak. Why are you passing the string length?

Bruce: Well, the first argument is the string, the second argument is the starting position—it's a static that gets updated each time through—and the last argument is the string length....

Joe: And the string length never changes. You're calculating it again and again. Furthermore, it's wrong. If you're halfway through the string, you're giving the whole length of the string. I'm surprised this works at all.

Jane: It's legal. If you give a length that goes past the end of the string, it just takes the characters to the end. But it is kind of ugly. You can drop that whole argument:

```
iNew = StrSpan1(Mid$(sSave, iStart), sSeps)
```

Bruce: Will that make it any faster?

Joe: I don't remember the Mid$ code exactly, but I doubt that it will make much difference. The main point is that it will be right instead of working by accident.

Bruce: Embarrassing. I knew better than that.

Joe: You should be embarrassed.

Jane: Oh, come on. It's the kind of mistake anybody might make.

Joe: I wouldn't make it.

Mary: Joe, we don't need this kind of negative attitude.

Joe: All right. So maybe anybody could make a slip. But the real problem with this code is deeper. It comes from coding C in Basic.

Coding C in Basic

Bruce: What do you mean?

Joe: Look what you're doing every time you call StrSpan or StrBreak. You're cutting off the remaining part of the string and passing it as an argument. That would work fine in C because C just passes pointers to strings. The whole string stays put in memory, but you're pointing only to the tail end of it. But in Basic, when you pass the result of Mid$ to a function, you create a new temporary string. It's a separate string that has to be created for the function it's passed to and then destroyed when the function leaves. You don't want to create any more new strings than you need.

Bruce: Well, OK, but how do I keep from creating new strings?

Joe: You just pass one string—*sSave*—but you also pass the current position.

Jane: But that means changing the design of StrSpan and StrBreak.

Joe: Yeah. So the call changes from

```
iNew = StrSpan1(Mid$(sSave, iStart), sSeps)
```

to

```
iNew = StrSpan2(sSave, iStart, sSeps)
```

Then your StrSpan implementation changes to this:

```
Function StrSpan2(sTarget As String, ByVal iStart As Integer, _
                  sSeps As String) As Integer

    Dim cTarget As Integer
    cTarget = Len(sTarget)
    ' Look for start of token (character that isn't a separator)
    Do While InStr(sSeps, Mid$(sTarget, iStart, 1))
        If iStart > cTarget Then
            StrSpan2 = 0
            Exit Function
        Else
            iStart = iStart + 1
        End If
    Loop
    StrSpan2 = iStart

End Function
```

Jane: But you're making StrSpan and StrBreak harder to use. They get a confusing extra argument. I mean, who'd guess how to use these things from the arguments?

Joe: That's just how Basic works. Nothing but GetToken will call them anyway. If anybody else did use them, they'd have to deal with the same efficiency problem. If you don't like Basic, use C.

Mary: Joe, sometimes I wonder why a guy who hates Basic so much chooses to work on it. You just like to criticize, and Basic is an easy target.

Jane: He's not as tough as he acts. Actually, he has a soft spot for Basic.

Bruce: Instead of criticizing the language, you ought to fix it. Look how I have to use this stupid Mid$ function just to get a character out of a string:

```
Do While InStr(sSeps, Mid$(sTarget, iStart, 1))
```

In most languages, you access a character in a string the same way you access an element in an array of bytes—maybe something like this:

```
Do While InStr(sSeps, sTarget(iStart))
```

I hope that, internally, you're at least optimizing the special case of extracting a single character.

Joe: Well, I'm not sure....There might not be anything we could do. A one-character string is no different from any other string in Basic.

Mary: Maybe you should make sure. Check the code.

Archaeologist's Note: We have no record of whether the changes Joe suggested resulted in any performance benefit in the ancient Basic language of the day, but the same changes in modern Visual Basic provide a 19 percent performance improvement even after improving the error checking. However, you still have to use Mid$ to extract a single character.

Fastest Versus Safest

Bruce: OK, so we've optimized this code, and we're going to get a giant performance benefit. Anything else?

Jane: What happens if you pass GetToken an empty string?

Bruce: Why would you do that?

Joe: Maybe just out of orneriness.

Jane: Or maybe you're parsing a file a line at a time, and some lines are blank. I just want to know whether you're handling boundaries.

Bruce: I guess I'm not sure what would happen. I suppose a user might also pass an empty string for the separators. What else could go wrong?

Archaeologist's Note: An interminable discussion about error handling has been edited out. Here is the end of that discussion.

Bruce: OK, so we end up with this:

```
Function GetToken5(sTarget As String, sSeps As String) As String

    ' Note that sSave and iStart must be static from call to call
    ' If first call, make copy of string
    Static sSave As String, iStart As Integer, cSave As Integer

    ' Assume failure
    GetToken5 = sEmpty
    If sTarget <> sEmpty Then
        iStart = 1
        sSave = sTarget
        cSave = Len(sSave)
    Else
        If sSave = sEmpty Then Exit Function
    End If

    ' Find start of next token
    Dim iNew As Integer
    iNew = StrSpan2(sSave, iStart, sSeps)
    If iNew Then
        ' Set position to start of token
        iStart = iNew
    Else
        ' If no new token, return empty string
        sSave = sEmpty
        Exit Function
    End If

    ' Find end of token
    iNew = StrBreak2(sSave, iStart, sSeps)
    If iNew = 0 Then
        ' If no end of token, set to end of string
        iNew = cSave + 1
    End If

    ' Cut token out of sTarget string
    GetToken5 = Mid$(sSave, iStart, iNew - iStart)
    ' Set new starting position
    iStart = iNew

End Function
```

Bruce: But isn't this error-handling code going to slow us down?

Joe: So what?

Jane: I never thought I'd hear you say that.

Joe: Well, speed is important, but it isn't everything. If all I wanted was speed, I could write GetToken like this:

```
Function GetToken(sTarget As String, sSeps As String) As String
    GetToken = sEmpty
End Function
```

That would really be fast. I could parse huge files in no time at all.

Bruce: But it doesn't work.

Joe: It works as well as the original if you pass it invalid arguments—better, in some cases.

Mary: OK, OK. We get the point.

Joe: It doesn't matter how fast your code is if it doesn't work.

Archaeologist's Note: At this point, the code review broke down into arguments about language features and proposals for enhancements. Suffice it to say that the discussion resulted in at least one variation of GetToken, named GetQToken, which recognized each quoted string as a single token. Another version, named GetOptToken, was discussed but not implemented. It would have recognized command-line options initiated with the forward slash or the hyphen character, skipped the option characters, and returned the value of the argument. You can find modern translations of the parsing routines (including GetQToken) in PARSE.BAS. The global class PARSE.CLS in the VBCore component delegates its implementation to PARSE.BAS. The parsing functions are used in several samples, including GLOBWIZ.VBP.

Fixing the Windows API

At some point, you're bound to run into limitations that have no solution in Basic. If you need low-level information that Basic doesn't provide, you must go to the operating system.

Win32 has a ReadFile and a WriteFile, but these functions are normally worthless for Visual Basic programmers because the Basic Input and Print statements handle the same tasks in a friendlier manner. But Win32 also provides functions that Basic doesn't provide.

It's a common belief that you can speed up your Visual Basic I/O by using API calls such as ReadFile and WriteFile rather than Basic features such as binary I/O with Get and Put. I don't believe it. Any slight advantage you might get from the API will be washed out by the cost of disk access. Do you doubt it? Prove me wrong. I won't argue with facts. If anybody can show me code demonstrating that API calls are significantly faster than Basic I/O for comparable operations, I'll publicly grovel in abject humiliation. I've posted this challenge in several online forums, but so far nobody has made me bow. There are reasons to use API I/O calls (compatibility with other API calls), but I maintain that speed isn't one of them.

For example, the Windows API has GetDiskFreeSpace, which tells you the size of a disk and how much of it is used. Basic won't give you this information. If you want the disk size under 32-bit Visual Basic, you simply write a Declare statement for GetDiskFreeSpace and call it.

Unfortunately, some of the most useful API functions aren't Basic-friendly. They return pointers to string positions that do you no good in Visual Basic because of Unicode conversion problems. Others return usable data, but in a style unbefitting what Visual Basic programmers are accustomed to. The previous edition of this book provided a C DLL to supply a few key functions that Visual Basic allegedly couldn't handle. But we don't need no stinkin' DLL for this edition. If it's worth doing, it's worth doing in Basic.

NOTE Under Visual Basic version 3, many programmers discovered a secret tool for getting the free space on a disk. The following Declare statement gave you a function that returned the free bytes on the current drive:

```
Declare Function DiskSpaceFree _
    Lib "SETUPKIT.DLL" () As Long
```

This didn't work in version 4 because the function moved to STKIT432.DLL, and that didn't work in version 5 because the function moved toVB5STKIT.DLL. You could change the Declare statement for every version, but I suggest you pass. This function reports only the free disk space, not the total disk space. Furthermore, there's no guarantee that the DLL will remain on every user's disk after setup.

GetFullPathName

When you are given a filename or a relative path, you'll often need to convert it to a full pathname. You could write the code to find the pathname in Basic, but the operating system can provide the information more reliably. That way, your code will work even if the rules defining paths and filenames change (as they did for Windows NT and Windows 95). Win32 provides the GetFullPath-Name function.

Use GetFullPathName as shown here:

```
Dim sBase As String, pBase As Long
sFullName = String$(cMaxPath, 0)
c = GetFullPathName(sName, cMaxPath, sFullName, pBase)
sFullName = Left$(sFullName, c)
If c Then s = s & "Full name: " & sFullName & sCrLf
```

Notice the last argument passed to GetFullPathName. The function returns a pointer to the filename portion of the full pathname. That's handy in C, but it's not much use in Basic. The Basic Way is to return the 1-based position of the filename string within the full pathname string. Then you can use Mid$ to cut out the filename.

The only way to convert that filename pointer to a position index is to write a wrapper function in C that calculates the index by comparing the pointer to the start of the full pathname to the filename pointer. You can't do the pointer arithmetic in Basic because the *pBase* pointer returned by GetFullPathName is a pointer to the temporary ANSI string used during Unicode conversion. That temporary string is gone, so a pointer to it is meaningless.

But let's put that aside for the moment. Instead, let's take another look at GetFull-PathName. Do you notice anything missing? It returns only the pathname but no other useful information, such as the extension or the directory. Why not? Many languages provide a function to split a full pathname into its parts. For example, Microsoft Visual C++ provides _splitpath. A language that lacks this invaluable tool is unthinkable. One way or another we must add it to Visual Basic, and the Win32 GetFullPathName function provides part of the solution. But to make it fully functional, you need to parse the rest of the full pathname to provide the directory and extension parts. If you're going that far, it's easy enough to ignore the filename pointer provided by GetFullPathName and just parse for the basename position in Basic.

That's exactly what my GetFullPath function does. It returns indexes to the pathname parts through optional reference parameters, and it returns the full pathname in the return value. You can use the whole works like this:

```
s = s & sCrLf & "Test GetFullPath with all arguments" & sCrLf & sCrLf
sFullName = GetFullPath(sName, iBase, iExt, iDir)
If sFullName <> sEmpty Then
    s = s & "Relative file: " & sName & sCrLf
    s = s & "Full name: " & sFullName & sCrLf
    s = s & "File: " & Mid$(sFullName, iBase) & sCrLf
    s = s & "Extension: " & Mid$(sFullName, iExt) & sCrLf
    s = s & "Base name: " & Mid$(sFullName, iBase, _
                                iExt - iBase) & sCrLf
    s = s & "Drive: " & Left$(sFullName, iDir - 1) & sCrLf
    s = s & "Directory: " & Mid$(sFullName, iDir, _
                                iBase - iDir) & sCrLf
    s = s & "Path: " & Left$(sFullName, iBase - 1) & sCrLf
Else
    s = s & "Invalid name: " & sName
End If
```

It would be annoying to have to provide all those index arguments in cases where you didn't need them, but fortunately they're optional. The following list shows just about all the possible permutations, although some of these make more sense than others.

```
sFullName = GetFullPath(sName, iBase, iExt, iDir)
sFullName = GetFullPath(sName, iBase, iExt)
sFullName = GetFullPath(sName, iBase)
sFullName = GetFullPath(sName)
sFullName = GetFullPath(sName, , iExt)
sFullName = GetFullPath(sName, , iExt, iDir)
sFullName = GetFullPath(sName, , , iDir)
sFullName = GetFullPath(sName, iBase, , iDir)
```

Although these cover the bases, they're not particularly convenient, so UTIL-ITY.BAS (and UTILITY.CLS through delegation) also provides wrappers for some of the most common operations:

```
sName = "Hardcore.frm"
sPart = GetFullPath(sName)          ' C:\Hardcore\Hardcore.frm
sPart = GetFileBase(sName)          ' Hardcore
sPart = GetFileBaseExt(sName)       ' Hardcore.frm
sPart = GetFileExt(sName)           ' .frm
sPart = GetFileDir(sName)           ' C:\Hardcore\
```

Now that we've seen how GetFullPath works, let's take a look at how it's implemented in Basic, as shown on the following page.

```
Function GetFullPath(sFileName As String, _
                     Optional FilePart As Long, _
                     Optional ExtPart As Long, _
                     Optional DirPart As Long) As String

    Dim c As Long, p As Long, sRet As String
    If sFileName = sEmpty Then ApiRaise ERROR_INVALID_PARAMETER

    ' Get the path size, then create string of that size
    sRet = String(cMaxPath, 0)
    c = GetFullPathName(sFileName, cMaxPath, sRet, p)
    If c = 0 Then ApiRaise Err.LastDllError
    BugAssert c <= cMaxPath
    sRet = Left$(sRet, c)

    ' Get the directory, file, and extension positions
    GetDirExt sRet, FilePart, DirPart, ExtPart
    GetFullPath = sRet

End Function
```

Most of the function is straightforward API calling as discussed in Chapter 2. The error-handling functions ApiRaise and ApiRaiseIf were discussed in "What's Wrong with That?" earlier in this chapter. Actually, most of the code is hidden in the call to GetDirExt, which contains big, ugly chunks of inconsistent parsing code for finding the different file parts. I'll spare you the details of how I parse from the front to find the directory position and from the back to find the extension and base positions. The code (like that for all the procedures in this section) is in UTILITY.BAS.

SearchPath

Another common file task is to find out where a file is located, if anywhere, in a path list (usually the one in the PATH environment variable). Most language libraries provide a function for this purpose. Microsoft Visual C++, for example, has _searchenv. Visual Basic has zip. Actually, you could do this task in Basic. It's simply a matter of getting the directory list with Environ$, parsing off each directory, appending the filename, and checking to see whether the file exists. But that's a lot of work that the operating system already knows how to do.

Win32 provides the mother of all path-searching functions: SearchPath. Some of its many features, like those of GetFullPathName, don't work well for Basic. The previous edition of this book provided a SearchDirs function that attempted to solve these problems. It was modeled closely on the SearchPath function. You could call it like this:

```
sFullName = SearchDirs(sEmpty, "calc.exe", sEmpty, iDir, iBase, iExt)
```

The function would return the full path in the return value and the indexes of the directory, base file, and extension through reference variables. The first and third arguments were for the path to search and for the extension, but in most cases you would just pass an empty string (the sEmpty constant from my type library). You could use the returned indexes with the Mid$ function to extract the parts of the full path. This was nice, but you always had to declare and pass those index variables whether you wanted them or not, and you always had to pass empty variables for the path and extension.

The new SearchDirs function takes optional arguments for five of its six parameters. The original SearchDirs tried to maintain a parameter order similar to that of SearchPath, but SearchDirs orders the arguments logically in order to make it easier to leave off ones that usually aren't needed. Any of the following Basic statements are OK:

```
sFullName = SearchDirs("calc", ".exe", , iBase, iExt, iDir)
sFullName = SearchDirs("calc.exe", , , iBase, iExt)
sFullName = SearchDirs("calc", ".exe", Environ("PATH"), iBase)
sFullName = SearchDirs("calc.exe")
```

That's a lot of parameters, so let's step through them. The first parameter is the file to be found. The filename is first because it is required and is often the only argument needed. It can include the extension, or the extension can be given in the second parameter. The third parameter is the path to be searched. No argument signals a search of the default Windows search path. The remaining arguments hold the variables in which the function can return the name, extension, and directory positions—in the same order as GetFullPath.

If you leave the third argument blank (as you usually will), SearchDirs looks for files in the following order:

1. the executable directory

2. the current directory

3. the Windows system directory

4. the Windows directory

5. the directory list in the PATH environment variable

When using SearchDirs, consider this order carefully. You might not always find what you expect to find where you expect to find it.

SearchDirs has other uses. It can search a different path list in an environment variable:

```
sFullName = SearchDirs("WINDOWS.H", , Environ("INCLUDE"))
```

It can test for the existence of a file in the current directory:

```
sFullName = SearchDirs("DEBUG.BAS", , ".")
```

That statement looks a lot like this one:

```
sFullName = GetFullPath("DEBUG.BAS")
```

But there's a subtle difference. GetFullPath gives a valid filename whether or not the file exists. You can use it to get the full pathname of a file you're about to create. SearchDirs confirms that a file with that name already exists.

You can also use SearchDirs to search for a file when you're not sure of the extension:

```
sName = "EDIT"
Dim asExts(1 To 4) As String
asExts(1) = ".EXE": asExts(2) = ".COM"
asExts(3) = ".BAT": asExts(4) = ".PIF"
For i = 1 To 4
    sFullName = SearchDirs(sName, asExts(i))
    If sFullName <> sEmpty Then Exit For
Next
```

This is why SearchDirs (and SearchPath) has a separate parameter for the extension.

GetTempPath and GetTempFileName

Visual Basic doesn't give you much help with the common task of generating temporary files. The Windows API fixes the problem with the GetTempPath and GetTempFileName functions, but both suffer from C interfaces and need Basic wrappers. Here's the raw GetTempFileName:

```
sFullName = String$(cMaxPath, 0)
Call GetTempFileName(".", "HC", 0, sFullName)
sFullName = Left$(sFullName, InStr(sFullName, sNullChr) - 1)
```

The first argument is the directory for the temporary file, and the second is a prefix for this file. For the third argument, you can supply a number yourself, or you can use 0 as a signal to let Windows choose a random hexadecimal number for the last part of the filename. I can't think of a reason to pass anything other than 0. The final argument is the buffer to receive the name. You should pass a buffer with the maximum file length for your operating system; you have no protection if you pass one that is too short. The return value is the number used for the last part of the name. I can't imagine why you would need this. Unlike most API functions, this one doesn't return the length of the string, so you have to find the length yourself by searching for the terminating null.

In other words, this is an inconvenient and somewhat dangerous function that takes one useless argument and returns garbage. The Basic wrapper GetTemp-File cleans it up, as shown on the next page.

The Problem of Existence

Testing for the existence of a file ought to be easy (and is in most languages), but it turns out to be one of the most annoying problems in Visual Basic. Don't count on simple solutions like this:

```
fExist = (Dir$(sFullPath) <> sEmpty)
```

That statement works until you specify a file on an empty floppy or on a CD-ROM drive. Then you're stuck in a message box. Here's another common one:

```
fExist = FileLen(sFullPath)
```

It fails on 0-length files—uncommon but not unheard of. My theory is that the only reliable way to check for file existence in Basic (without benefit of API calls) is to use error trapping. I've challenged many Visual Basic programmers to give me an alternative, but so far no joy. Here's the shortest way I know:

```
Function ExistFile(sSpec As String) As Boolean
    On Error Resume Next
    Call FileLen(sSpec)
    ExistFile = (Err = 0)
End Function
```

This can't be very efficient. Error trapping is designed to be fast for the no fail case, but this function is as likely to hit errors as not. Perhaps you'll be the one to send me a Basic-only ExistFile function with no error trapping that I can't break. Until then, here's an API alternative:

```
Function ExistFileDir(sSpec As String) As Boolean
    Dim af As Long
    af = GetFileAttributes(sSpec)
    ExistFileDir = (af <> -1)
End Function
```

I didn't think there would be any way to break this one, but it turns out that certain filenames containing control characters are legal on Windows 95 but illegal on Windows NT. Or is it the other way around? Anyway, I have seen this function fail in situations too obscure to describe here.

I hate to waste brain cells on a function so trivial. But 99 percent effective existence tests aren't good enough on a disk containing thousands of files.

```
' Get temp file for current directory
sFullName = GetTempFile("VB", ".")
```

For the GetTempPath function, my GetTempDir wrapper simply returns the temporary directory. You can use it with GetTempFile:

```
' Get temp file for TEMP directory
sFullName = GetTempFile("VB", GetTempDir)
```

Of course, this is where you'll usually want to put temporary files, so GetTemp-File assumes just that if you omit the second optional argument

```
' Get temp file for TEMP directory default
sFullName = GetTempFile("VB")
```

you can omit the prefix, too, if you don't care what the file looks like:

```
' Get temp file for TEMP directory with no prefix
sFullName = GetTempFile
```

The calls to GetTempFile in the samples above generated *C:\CURDIR\VB4B-.TMP*, *C:\TEMP\VB4C.TMP*, *C:\TEMP\VB4D.TMP*, and *C:\TEMP\4E.TMP*. The filenames vary on different operating systems and different file systems. The only guarantee is that the generated file doesn't currently exist. Windows will keep incrementing the number and trying the file until it finds a unique name. It's up to you to open the file, process it, and—unless you want to be considered the crudest and most illiterate of programmers—delete it when you're done.

FLAME

This flame is directed at myself—in other words, it's an apology for a crime I hope you will never commit (and that I will never repeat). I changed the interface of GetFullPath, SearchDirs, and GetTempFile. These functions did not use optional parameters in the C DLL versions described in the first edition of this book. Later I wrote a series of articles published on the Internet and in MSDN (also provided on the CD of this book) that described a different C++ version of the VBUTIL DLL. In this version, the functions used optional parameters—and that changed the design. The original parameter order matched the order of the API functions—a design decision that showed a lack of imagination. I "fixed" the order problem in the second version. The second DLL version was targeted at Visual Basic 4, which supported optional parameters only through Variants. But when I rewrote the functions in Basic for this edition, I changed to typed optional parameters. The bottom line is that if you've been a faithful follower of my writing, your code has been broken twice by incompatible versions of my functions. Fortunately, the interfaces of the wrapper functions—GetFullPath, GetFileBase, GetFileBaseExt, GetFileExt, and GetFileDir—haven't changed, although their implementation has. The moral of the story is: get your design right the first time. This is a good rule for all code, and it's the law for ActiveX components. Since I've published VBCore as a component, I'd have to write new functions rather than change the old ones if I came up with more bright ideas.

Hammering Bits

Basic was never designed to mess with bits. Sure, it has Xor, And, Or, and Not operators. In fact, it even has Eqv and Imp logical operators that you won't find (or need) in most other languages. But it lacks unsigned integers, and its numeric type conversion facilities are extremely safe—excessively so for bit operations. As a result, the simplest operations turn out to be unexpectedly messy.

At the risk of boring some readers, let's review what a 16-bit integer is to a computer, what it is to Basic, and what it is to the Windows API. To a computer, a 16-bit integer is simply a stream of 16 bits of data. A computer language can look at this stream of bits as a signed integer with a value in the range −32768 through 32767, as an unsigned integer ranging from 0 through 65535, or as 16 independent bits. (In a signed integer, the high bit signals negative numbers; in an unsigned integer, the high bit is just more numeric data.)

The Basic language simplifies matters by recognizing integers only as signed integers and, to a certain extent, as bit flags. As long as you stick with 16 bits, this is sufficient. When you mix 16-bit and 32-bit numbers, however, you get into trouble. The problem: Basic claims that 32768 is always a 32-bit number, although any assembly language programmer will assure you that it's a perfectly valid 16-bit unsigned number. When you specify a number in hexadecimal (&HFFFF), as you tend to do when working with bits, it's easy to forget that the high bit (&H8000) represents the negative sign.

Visual Basic version 4 added one more spice to this stew. The Byte type is actually an unsigned type representing values from 0 through 255. You can't assign −25 to a Byte variable.

To clarify this discussion, we can use the low-level terminology of debuggers (which also happens to be the high-level terminology of Windows). An unsigned character is a Byte. An unsigned 2-byte integer is a Word. An unsigned 4-byte integer is a DWord.

The two most common bitwise operations are cramming Bytes into Words and Words into DWords, and ripping Bytes out of Words and Words out of Dwords. Let's have a look.

Five Low Words

Consider the simple LoWord function, which extracts the low word of a DWord. What could be simpler? Just mask out the high byte of the argument and return the result:

```
Function LoWord1(ByVal dw As Long) As Integer
    LoWord1 = dw And &HFFFF&
End Function
```

This works fine as long as the low word is less than or equal to 32767. But now try this:

```
w = LoWord1(32768)
```

You get an overflow because 32768 is out of the integer range (−32768 through 32767). If you're accustomed to another language, you might expect that you could use a conversion function to force the assignment to an integer. Basic conversion functions such as CInt, however, don't force anything. They request politely. If you change the guts of LoWord as shown here, you get the same overflow error:

```
LoWord1 = CInt(dw And &HFFFF&)
```

In most languages, type conversion or casting means "force by wrapping, truncation, or whatever it takes." In Basic, it means "Mother, may I?" And in this case, the answer is always "No." You might argue that any Long from −32768 through 65535 can legitimately be converted to an Integer, and I'll agree with you. But we lose.

In order to do the right thing for all integers, you must specifically check for the sign bit:

```
Function LoWord2(ByVal dw As Long) As Integer
    If dw And &H8000& Then
        LoWord2 = dw Or &HFFFF0000
    Else
        LoWord2 = dw And &HFFFF&
    End If
End Function
```

Checking for the sign bit takes time; this version of LoWord is a few ticks slower than the previous one. But remember Joe Hacker's motto: "It doesn't matter how fast your code is if it doesn't work."

There's more than one way to get a DWord in Basic. You could simply copy the bits of the low word to the result. Basic provides a roundabout method of doing this with the LSet statement. You have to set up two structures that split the data in different ways:

```
Private Type TLoHiLong
    lo As Integer
    hi As Integer
End Type

Private Type TAllLong
    all As Long
End Type
```

Then you write the data into one structure and read it out of the other:

```
Function LoWord3(ByVal dw As Long) As Integer
    Dim lohi As TLoHiLong
    Dim all  As TAllLong
    all.all = dw
    LSet lohi = all
    LoWord3 = lohi.lo
End Function
```

This code looks complicated, but internally it's not doing a lot. This version is slower than the LoWord2 version, but it has the advantage of always working at the same speed, regardless of the number passed to it.

There's another way to copy bits using the Windows API CopyMemory function. See the sidebar "CopyMemory: A Strange and Terrible Saga" in Chapter 2 for the bizarre story of what CopyMemory really is. Here's the code to simply copy the contents of the low word to a separate word-sized variable:

```
Function LoWord4(ByVal dw As Long) As Integer
    CopyMemory LoWord 4, dw 2
End function
```

I expected this code to beat the LSet version, but it usually came out a little slower. While LoWord is short and sweet, HiWord is a bit more difficult, as you will soon see.

Keep in mind that this version works only on Little Endian systems such as the Pentium. Visual Basic is now available on machines running Digital's Alpha chip, which is a Big Endian system. *Endian* refers to the order in which bytes are stored. The term is taken from a story in *Gulliver's Travels* by Jonathan Swift about wars fought between those who thought eggs should be cracked on the Big End and those who insisted on the Little End. With chips, as with eggs, it doesn't really matter as long as you know which end is up.

The Big Endian version of LoWord4 would probably look like the following code:

```
Function LoWord4(ByVal dw As Long) As Integer
    CopyMemory LoWord4, ByVal VarPtr(dw) + 2, 2
End Function
```

That's what HiWord looks like on Little Endian systems, so the Big Endian HiWord would probably look like the Little Endian LoWord. I didn't have an Alpha machine to test this on. I don't know if Alphas even have a CopyMemory equivalent. If you're fortunate enough to develop on an Alpha machine, you'll have to check carefully all the hacks I do with CopyMemory. If you have problems, it should be easy to fix them with conditional compilation.

Face it, Bit bashing isn't Basic's strong point. Here's what the same function looks like in C++:

```
WORD DLLAPI LoWord(DWORD dw)
{
    return (WORD) (dw & 0xFFFF);
}
```

The C++ version is simpler, but it turns out to be slightly slower (probably because of the cost of calling it through a DLL). But even if C++ bit bashing were faster, the difference wouldn't justify adding an extra DLL. The official LoWord in the VBCore component and in BYTES.BAS has the same code shown in LoWord2 above. It's fast enough.

PERFORMANCE

Problem: Compare several methods of stripping the low word of a DWord.

Problem	P-Code	Native Code
AND positive low word	.0191 sec	.0016 sec
AND negative low word	Overflow	Overflow
AND positive low word after sign check	.0226 sec	.0017 sec
OR negative low word after sign check	.0228 sec	.0016 sec
Copy low word with LSet	.0232 sec	.0033 sec
Copy low word with CopyMemory	.0259 sec	.0068 sec
AND low word in C++	.0084 sec	.0024 sec

Conclusion: It's a close race with p-code but no contest with native code. A compiler covers a multitude of sins. Realistically, of course, that extra speed isn't noticeable except in the most deeply nested of loops.

Not only is the C++ version easier to write, it's also faster. Realistically, of course, that extra speed is seldom noticeable except in the most deeply nested loops. It's certainly not worth adding a C++ DLL just for this function (or its relatives). In fact, if you check the performance sidebar, you can see that I have been cheating—comparing the p-code versions instead of the compiled versions. The version in the VBCore component (or BYTES.BAS) is actually the one that uses CopyMemory. It's fast enough.

Shifting Bits

Occasionally, you need to shift bits. This bit operation doesn't come up that often in Basic, but when you need to get a certain bit into a certain position, nothing else will do.

Shifting left 1 bit means multiplying by 2, shifting left 2 bits means multiplying by 4, and so on. Similarly, shifting right 1 bit means dividing by 2, and so on. In Basic terms, the operation starts out looking simple:

```
Function LShiftWord1(w As Integer, c As Integer) As Integer
    LShiftWord1 = w * (2 ^ c)
End Function

Function RShiftWord1(w As Integer, c As Integer) As Integer
    RShiftWord1 = w \ (2 ^ c)
End Function
```

These functions work as long as you feed them positive integers and the results come out as positive integers. Otherwise, things go wrong. Before we get to the real version, let's take a look at a C++ version:

```
// Shift bits of DWord right
DWORD DLLAPI RShiftDWord(DWORD dw, unsigned c)
{
    return dw >> c;
}
```

That's it. Even if you're not a C++ programmer, you can probably guess the code for LShiftDWord, RShiftWord, and LShiftWord. There's still a function call for shifting. What Visual Basic really needs are Shl and Shr operators as in most other languages. Then the work would be done automatically inline. Unfortunately, you have to do the messy job yourself if you're not willing to add a C++ DLL.

```
Function LShiftWord(ByVal w As Integer, ByVal c As Integer) As Integer
    BugAssert c >= 0 And c <= 15
    Dim dw As Long
    dw = w * Power2(c)
```

(continued)

```
    If dw And &H8000& Then
        LShiftWord = CInt(dw And &H7FFF&) Or &H8000
    Else
        LShiftWord = dw And &HFFFF&
    End If
End Function
```

Notice that this function uses the Power2 property to look up powers of 2 rather than calculating them. See "Module initialization versus component initialization" earlier in this chapter.

Since shifting is faster than the equivalent multiplication and division operations in assembly language, hardcore programmers in other languages often shift bits to optimize multiplication and division by multiples of 2. But you can see why the functions I just mentioned are useless for optimization: it doesn't do any good to fake division by shifting if your shift function fakes shifting by dividing.

The function works by doing the arithmetic on a temporary Long variable and then converting the result back to an Integer. But you can't do that for the LShiftDWord and RShiftDWord functions because there isn't a larger integer size to cast down from. The functions have to use error trapping to identify overflow, and they will fail on some input. It's the best I could do, and rarely will you ever hit the limits.

The Win32 GetLogicalDrives function returns a Long in which the corresponding bit is set for each existing drive. The easiest way to check those drives is to loop through all 26 bits, shifting them one at a time into the rightmost position and then testing them. Here's a function that translates bits into a more Basic-like string of pluses and minuses:

```
Function VBGetLogicalDrives() As String

    Dim f32 As Long, i As Integer, s As String
    f32 = GetLogicalDrives()
    For i = 0 To 25
        s = s & IIf(f32 And 1, "+", "-")
        f32 = RShiftDWord(f32, 1)
    Next
    VBGetLogicalDrives = s

End Function
```

The CDrives class described in Chapter 4 has a more realistic example of RShift-DWord and GetLogicalDrives.

Reading and Writing Blobs

One of the more tedious tasks in programming is reading arbitrary binary data from files. If you're lucky, the data is logically arranged as records and you can simply read it into UDTs. But sometimes you have to read the data blob from hell. For example, the ExeType function (EXETYPE.BAS) reads in a given executable file and determines what kind of program it is—MS-DOS, 16-bit Windows, OS/2, or Win32—by reading random binary data from magic locations. We're not going to look at this atrocity, but we will examine the blob-processing procedures that make it work.

When old-timers gather to tell tall tales around the campfire, some claim that there were once versions of Visual Basic that used only 16 bits. I know it sounds ridiculous. But they claim that in those versions you had to read and write binary data as strings—although we all know that Unicode characters would make such techniques unreliable. Nonetheless, it is rumored that these ancient dialects provided a complete set of string functions that neither knew nor cared whether the data fed to them was a string of characters or a sequence of binary bytes. Of course today we know that Byte arrays are the only way to store binary data in a stable format that won't be modified by Unicode conversion. You might want to review "Unicode Versus Basic" in Chapter 2, if you don't remember the problem.

Basic provides two versions of each string function. I'll refer to the Byte versions —MidB, InStrB, LeftB, and so on—as the B versions. The recommended way to handle binary data goes something like this:

```
sBinFile = Dir("*.*")
nBinFile = FreeFile
Open sBinFile For Binary Access Read Write Lock Write As #nBinFile
ReDim abBin(LOF(nBinFile))
Get #nBinFile, 1, abBin
sBin = abBin
' Process file with MidB$, InStrB$, LeftB$, and friends
abBin = sBin
Put #nBinFile, 1, abBin
Close #nBinFile
```

Notice that you copy the array of bytes into a string and work on that rather than on the original array. The B functions work on byte arrays, but they do so through type conversion—meaning that a temporary string is created for each string parameter that receives a byte array argument. It's much more efficient to create a single temporary string yourself than to let Basic create one for every call to a B function.

Although the technique shown above works, it's not very efficient or intuitive. We'd be a lot better off using procedures designed to work directly on byte arrays. No need to convert to and from strings. The rest of this section proposes a set of procedures that extract numbers or strings from various locations in a blob (byte array). It's not as easy as you might expect. You keep running smack into the nemesis of Basic data conversion: unsigned integers where Basic expects signed integers. Here's my first shot at a function to read a Word from a byte string:

```
Function WordFromStrB(sBuf As String, iOffset As Long) As Integer
    BugAssert (iOffset + 2) <= LenB(sBuf) - 1
    Dim dw As Long
    dw = AscB(MidB$(sBuf, iOffset + 2, 1)) * 256&
    dw = dw + AscB(MidB$(sBuf, iOffset + 1, 1))
    If dw And &H8000& Then
        WordFromStrB = dw Or &HFFFF000
    Else
        WordFromStrB = dw And &HFFFF&
    End If
End Function
```

First you must adjust the offset from a zero-based buffer offset to a one-based string offset. You also need to do significant work with AscB and MidB$ to extract the byte. Finally, you have to do data conversion tricks to turn the unsigned character into a signed Basic integer. If you think this looks ugly, try doing the same for a DWord.

The BYTES.BAS module uses a different strategy to convert bytes to numeric or string data. BytesToWord and BytesToDWord read numeric data from blobs. BytesFromWord and BytesFromDWord write numeric data. You could add similar functions to read and write Double, Single, and other types.

Let's start with BytesToWord, since it is equivalent to the WordFromStrB function shown earlier:

```
Function BytesToWord(abBuf() As Byte, iOffset As Long) As Integer
    BugAssert iOffset <= UBound(abBuf) - 1
    Dim w As Integer
    CopyMemory w, abBuf(iOffset), 2
    BytesToWord = w
End Function
```

That's one way to avoid data conversion problems—just blast the data directly into memory. BytesFromWord looks the same except that the first two arguments to CopyMemory are reversed. You can guess the implementation of BytesToDWord and BytesFromDWord.

Converting byte arrays to strings (and vice versa) is a different matter. The strings you extract from byte arrays must look like strings to the outside, which means that you must do Unicode conversion. Here's a function that converts a byte array to a string:

```
Function BytesToStr(ab() As Byte) As String
    If UnicodeTypeLib Then
        BytesToStr = ab
    Else
        BytesToStr = StrConv(ab(), vbUnicode)
    End If
End Function
```

This is just a wrapper function, and you can use StrConv directly if you're concerned about performance.

Generally, you won't be looking at a blob as one big string, but BytesToStr is useful for converting arrays of bytes in UDTs. Normally, you'll use fixed-length strings rather than byte arrays in UDTs, but BytesToStr comes in handy if you need to pass a UDT variable to a Unicode API function (such as an OLE function). "Unicode Versus Basic" and "Other Pointers in UDTs," in Chapter 2, discuss this issue. BytesToStr is also a handy way to watch a byte array that represents an ANSI string; simply type the expression *? BytesToStr(ab)* in the Immediate window.

StrToBytes goes the other way, but its implementation is very different. First, a function can't return an array of bytes directly, so you must modify the array by reference. Second, if the array already has a size, you might need to truncate or null-pad the string. Here's the code:

```
Sub StrToBytes(ab() As Byte, s As String)
    If MUtility.IsArrayEmpty(ab) Then
        ' Assign to empty array
        ab = StrConv(s, vbFromUnicode)
    Else
        Dim cab As Long
        ' Copy to existing array, padding or truncating if necessary
        cab = UBound(ab) - LBound(ab) + 1
        If Len(s) < cab Then s = s & String$(cab - Len(s), 0)
        CopyMemoryStr ab(LBound(ab)), s, cab
    End If
End Sub
```

The first part of the conditional handles unsized arrays like this one:

```
Dim ab() As Byte
```

Unfortunately, Basic provides no way to distinguish an empty array from a sized array, so I had to write the IsArrayEmpty function. The error trapping in this function is too obscene to show in this family-oriented book, but you can look it up in UTILITY.BAS.

Evil Type Conversion

Without fanfare, the Basic language made a major turn in Visual Basic version 4. In one sense, the change was subtle; if you never wrote code that contained a certain type of bug, you might never have noticed. But in another sense, it was a startling break with Basic tradition that provoked much lively debate among Basic language lawyers. In fact, the new feature came to be known on Visual Basic 4 beta forums, and subsequently, in online forums and magazine articles, as "Evil Type Conversion."

Imagine writing the following code:

```
Dim i As Integer, s As String
s = 3
i = "12345"
i = Mid$(i, s)
```

You know what this code will do—generate type errors. You can't assign an integer to a string, assign a string to an integer, pass an integer argument to a string parameter, pass a string argument to an integer parameter, or assign the result of a string function to an integer variable.

Oh, yes, you can. This code assigns the value 12345 to *i* without complaint. When you look at the variables in the Locals window, you'll notice that the integer 3 is converted to the string *3* and the string *12345* is converted to the integer 12345. Then they are converted back when passed as arguments, and the string result is converted to an integer. These types of conversions used to work with variants, but they never worked with strings and integers.

Let's take a more realistic example:

The second part of the conditional handles sized arrays. First, you calculate the target size and null-pad the source string if necessary, and then you blast the string into the array. The string that comes into this function is Unicode, but notice that there's no explicit Unicode conversion. It's not necessary because Basic does implicit Unicode conversion whenever you pass a string to an API function (such as CopyMemory).

I know I just said that you can't return a byte array from a function, but consistency isn't my strong point. Following is the code to do it indirectly through a variant:

```
Function StrToBytesV(s As String) As Variant
    ' Copy to array
    StrToBytesV = StrConv(s, vbFromUnicode)
End Function
```

```
i = 3
s = "12345"
s = Mid$(i, s)
```

I've assigned values to i and s, but imagine that these are actually calculated values—s, for example, is the first token in a file I'm parsing, and it happens to be numeric. I accidentally coded the Mid$ function with the arguments reversed. In previous versions of Basic, I'd get an error, immediately see what was wrong, and fix it. In the current version, I get garbage. There's nothing at position 12345 of the string 3, so the result is an empty string. If I parse a file that has a non-numeric string as its first token, I'll instantly get an invalid function call, but I might spend hours debugging before I figure this out.

Basic used to be a strongly typed language with an optional typeless mode through the Variant type. You could choose the better performance and better error facilities of strong type checking, or you could choose the greater flexibility of typelessness. (That's not to say Basic no longer has type checking. It still won't assign the value 60000 to an integer variable, no matter how much you might want it to.)

So why the change? Believe it or not, for compatibility. The Text property of TextBox controls used to be type Variant. You could assign an Integer to this property, which was both convenient and important. The developers of Visual Basic version 4 didn't want to break this feature, but they needed the better performance of a String variable. So they added type conversion of Integers to Strings. If you go that far, why not convert Strings to Integers?

I respect the motivation, but loss of type safety seems like a significant price to pay. I must admit, however, that I haven't been hitting as many debugging problems related to the change as I expected.

This version isn't as efficient because it has the overhead of converting the byte array to a variant. The caller then has to convert the variant back to a byte array. Also StrToBytesV works only with dynamic arrays. The following lines show equivalent calls with StrToBytesV and StrToBytes:

```
StrToBytes ab, "1234567890"
ab = StrToBytesV("1234567890")
```

StrToBytes and BytesToStr have a very specific use for converting complete arrays of bytes, but when working with blobs, you'll more often need to extract or insert fixed-length strings at an arbitrary location in memory. What you want is a Mid function and a Mid statement that both work directly on arrays of bytes. The techniques shown in BytesToStr can be enhanced slightly to create a MidBytes function that works directly on byte arrays. For example, here's how you extract a string from a 5-byte field:

```
sTest = MidBytes(abTest, 7, 5)
```

Unfortunately, you can't implement a similar MidBytes statement in Basic because the Mid$ statement isn't a procedure. Look closely at this code:

```
Mid$(sTest, 1, 5) = "NOWAY"
```

How would you write a function that takes an assignment on the right side of an expression? You can't. Basic cheats to do this. The Basic parser translates this code into a hidden internal call that probably looks like this:

```
Ins$ "NOWAY", sTest, 1, 5
```

You can do the same with an InsBytes function that inserts a string at an arbitrary location in a byte array:

```
InsBytes "WAYOUT", abTest, 0, 6
```

Note that both MidBytes and InsBytes take zero-based offsets rather than one-based offsets. I'll let you look up the implementation of MidBytes and InsBytes in BYTES.BAS. They're essentially BytesToStr and StrToBytes with optional arguments. You'll also find LeftBytes, RightBytes, and FillBytes. These compare roughly to Left$, Right$, and String$, but, like MidBytes and InsBytes, they have syntactical differences to accommodate the normal use of byte arrays.

For an example of blob processing in action, check out the ExeType function in EXETYPE.BAS.

Sorting, Shuffling, and Searching

Entire books have been written about the art of sorting. More specifically, sorting has been explored in the granddaddy of all Microsoft demo programs, SORTDEMO, which was written for QuickBasic by former Microsoft documentation author Michael Morrow. In a previous life as a sample programmer for the Microsoft languages department, I inherited the Basic version and presided over various enhancements and translations to C, Pascal, and FORTRAN. I later saw translations by others to COBOL (believe it or not) and to C++ with MFC.

If you own older versions of Microsoft C, FORTRAN, Pascal, Basic, or COBOL, you've probably seen this program. It randomizes colored bars on the screen and then presents a menu of sorting algorithms: bubble, shell, exchange, heap, and quick. You can see how the different algorithms compare elements and exchange them, and you can compare timings. More annoying, you can *hear* the difference, because each bar plays a different tone based on its length. I can still hear the difference between a QuickSort and a HeapSort.

Unfortunately, SORTDEMO has never been translated to Visual Basic. I was tempted, but this section is about sorting as a practical task, not sorting as a science. Therefore I'll present only the sorting algorithm that SORTDEMO shows to be the most efficient—QuickSort. Computer scientists might argue that Quick-Sort isn't always the fastest. The efficiency of sorting algorithms varies, depending on the number of elements, how random they are, how long it takes to compare elements, how long it takes to swap them, and so on. But QuickSort is more than adequate for the tasks in this book.

Recursive QuickSort

The following QuickSort algorithm for sorting arrays is taken directly from the SORTDEMO program, with only slight modifications to make it more modular and to accommodate differences between Visual Basic and QuickBasic:

```
' Recursive QuickSort algorithm
Sub SortArrayRec(aTarget() As Variant, _
                Optional vFirst As Variant, Optional vLast As Variant, _
                Optional helper As ISortHelper)
    Dim iFirst As Long, iLast As Long
    If IsMissing(vFirst) Then iFirst = LBound(aTarget) Else iFirst = vFirst
    If IsMissing(vLast) Then iLast = UBound(aTarget) Else iLast = vLast
    If helper Is Nothing Then Set helper = New CSortHelper

With helper
    If iFirst < iLast Then

        ' Only two elements in this subdivision; exchange if
        ' they are out of order, and end recursive calls
        If iLast - iFirst = 1 Then
            If .Compare(aTarget(iFirst), aTarget(iLast)) > 0 Then
                .Swap aTarget(iFirst), aTarget(iLast)
            End If
        Else

            Dim iLo As Long, iHi As Long
            ' Pick pivot element at random and move to end
            .Swap aTarget(iLast), aTarget(MRandom.Random(iFirst, iLast))
            iLo = iFirst: iHi = iLast
            Do

                ' Move in from both sides toward pivot element
                Do While (iLo < iHi) And _
                        .Compare(aTarget(iLo), aTarget(iLast)) <= 0
                    iLo = iLo + 1
                Loop
                Do While (iHi > iLo) And _
```

(continued)

283

```
                    .Compare(aTarget(iHi), aTarget(iLast)) >= 0
                iHi = iHi - 1
            Loop

            ' If you haven't reached pivot element, it means
            ' that two elements on either side are out of
            ' order, so swap them
            If iLo < iHi Then .Swap aTarget(iLo), aTarget(iHi)
            Loop While iLo < iHi

            ' Move pivot element back to its proper place
            .Swap aTarget(iLo), aTarget(iLast)

            ' Recursively call SortArrayRec (pass smaller
            ' subdivision first to use less stack space)
            If (iLo - iFirst) < (iLast - iLo) Then
                SortArrayRec aTarget(), iFirst, iLo - 1, helper
                SortArrayRec aTarget(), iLo + 1, iLast, helper
            Else
                SortArrayRec aTarget(), iLo + 1, iLast, helper
                SortArrayRec aTarget(), iFirst, iLo - 1, helper
            End If
        End If
    End If
End With
End Sub
```

For the moment, ignore the helper object parameter and concentrate on the algorithm. QuickSort works on the divide-and-conquer principle. It splits the array into two groups and then sorts both the top and the bottom. It does this by calling itself to sort each group. Recursion makes QuickSort intelligible but also subjects it to stack limitations. A recursive algorithm has the potential to run out of stack space as it pushes more arguments and local variables onto the stack each time it calls itself.

Iterative QuickSort

For every recursive algorithm, there is an iterative algorithm. In the first edition of this book, I challenged readers to write the iterative version of SortArray. Scott D. Killen answered the call with an implementation that used my CStack class to save sections of the array for later sorting. Scott credits the book *Practical Algorithms in C++* (John Wiley and Sons, Inc., 1995) by Bryan Flamig as his source. Here's the code:

```
' Iterative QuickSort algorithm
Sub SortArray(aTarget() As Variant, Optional vFirst As Variant, _
            Optional vLast As Variant, Optional helper As ISortHelper)
    Dim iFirst As Long, iLast As Long
    If IsMissing(vFirst) Then iFirst = LBound(aTarget) Else iFirst = vFirst
    If IsMissing(vLast) Then iLast = UBound(aTarget) Else iLast = vLast
    If helper Is Nothing Then Set helper = New CSortHelper

With helper
    Dim iLo As Long, iHi As Long, iRand As Long, stack As New CStack
    Do
        Do
            ' Swap from ends until first and last meet in the middle
            If iFirst < iLast Then
                ' If we're in the middle and out of order, swap
                If iLast - iFirst = 1 Then
                    If .Compare(aTarget(iFirst), aTarget(iLast)) > 0 Then
                        .Swap aTarget(iFirst), aTarget(iLast)
                    End If
                Else
                    ' Split at some random point
                    .Swap aTarget(iLast), _
                        aTarget(MRandom.Random(iFirst, iLast))
                    ' Swap high values below the split for low values above
                    iLo = iFirst: iHi = iLast
                    Do
                        ' Find any low value larger than split
                        Do While (iLo < iHi) And _
                                (.Compare(aTarget(iLo), aTarget(iLast)) <= 0)
                            iLo = iLo + 1
                        Loop
                        ' Find any high value smaller than split
                        Do While (iHi > iLo) And _
                                (.Compare(aTarget(iHi), aTarget(iLast)) >= 0)
                            iHi = iHi - 1
                        Loop
                        ' Swap too high low value for too low high value
                        If iLo < iHi Then .Swap aTarget(iLo), aTarget(iHi)
                    Loop While iLo < iHi
                    ' Current (iLo) is larger than split (iLast), so swap
                    .Swap aTarget(iLo), aTarget(iLast)
                    ' Push range markers of larger part for later sorting
                    If (iLo - iFirst) < (iLast - iLo) Then
                        stack.Push iLo + 1
                        stack.Push iLast
                        iLast = iLo - 1
```

(continued)

```
                Else
                    stack.Push iFirst
                    stack.Push iLo - 1
                    iFirst = iLo + 1
                End If
                ' Exit from inner loop to process smaller part
                Exit Do
            End If
        End If

        ' If stack empty, Exit outer loop
        If stack.Count = 0 Then Exit Sub
        ' Else pop first and last from last deferred section
        iLast = stack.Pop
        iFirst = stack.Pop
        Loop
    Loop
End With
End Sub
```

Scott's code proves two points. First, iterative algorithms aren't necessarily faster than recursive ones. If you check the two versions in the TimeIt application, you'll see that the recursive version wins by half a hair. But in a race that close you have to give the advantage to the code that uses the least resources. The iterative version gets the nod as the official SortArray procedure in the VBCore component because it can never run out of stack space.

The second point is that recursive algorithms can be a lot simpler than iterative ones. In fact, I think of the recursive version as documentation for the iterative version. You can read the recursive code and it makes sense. Not so the iterative code. I stepped through it and added comments that attempt to explain what's going on, but I still don't really understand the details. Mainly I just pray that it works.

Don't read too much into this particular result. You'll have to analyze your algorithms on a case-by-case basis. Think carefully before you start trying to reorganize natural recursive algorithms into twisted iterative ones. For algorithms that don't recurse deeply, saving stack space probably won't matter. In fact, 32-bit programs aren't nearly as likely to run out of stack space as were 16-bit programs. Sometimes iterative algorithms are clearer anyway. The iterative binary search algorithm at the end of this chapter could have been written recursively, but it wouldn't have been any clearer.

The SortArray sub is used to sort arrays containing strings and integers in the Test Sort program (TSORT.VBP), shown in Figure 5-3. This program sorts arrays and is used in the implementation of sorted collections and a sorted list box control. For now, we're interested only in arrays. (I've already discussed sorted collections and list boxes.) SortArray is also used to sort an array of playing cards in the Fun 'n Games program (FUNNGAME.VBP) described in Chapter 6.

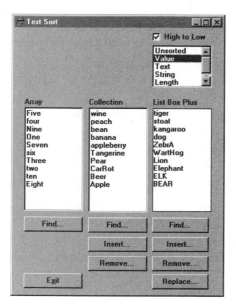

Figure 5-3. *The Test Sort program.*

I'm embarrassed to admit that the recursive version of this algorithm in the first edition contained an example of one of the oldest and most pervasive bugs you can write. It made several assignments inside a loop that could just as easily have been made outside the loop. As a result, the function was four to five times slower than necessary. Sharp-eyed reader David Wilmer identified the problem. To make matters worse, the same bug actually showed up in five different places on the CD. I reported the problem and provided a fix (with abject apologies) on the Internet site for the book, but some readers might have missed it. My only excuse (a weak one) is that it wasn't originally my bug. The code came from an old version of SORTDEMO, but I learned later that the bug and the fix were described years ago in the Knowledge Base for QuickBasic. I don't spend a lot of time wandering through bug reports in defunct products, so I missed it. Sorry about that.

Sorting Different Types

My version of SortArray sorts arrays of Variants. This is the most flexible way to define the procedure, but it won't help if you have an array of Integers or Strings to sort. You can pass an Integer argument to a Variant parameter, but you can't pass an array of Integers to a Variant array parameter. All those elements must be lined up in a row, and Basic must know the distance between them, which will be different for Integers than for Variants.

One solution is to put anything you want to sort in a Variant array. You can stuff the array with strings, integers, or real numbers, and SortArray will do the right thing with them. But it won't necessarily be fast. You probably won't see any difference if you're sorting 150 integers or 50 strings. But if you're doing the Mondo Double Sort From Down Under, you'll want to write a separate Sort-ArrayDouble for it. This process is so mechanical that you might be tempted to do it with conditional compilation:

```
# If SortArrayType = 0 Then
Sub SortArray(aTarget() As Variant, iFirst As Integer, __
            iLast As Integer, helper As ISortHelper)
    Dim vSplit As Variant
# ElseIf SortArrayType = 1 Then
Sub SortArray(aTarget() As Integer, iFirst As Integer, _
            iLast As Integer, helper As ISortHelper)
    Dim vSplit As Integer
# ElseIf SortArrayType = 2 Then
Sub SortArray(aTarget() As Long, iFirst As Integer, _
            iLast As Integer, helper As ISortHelper)
    Dim vSplit As Long
# ElseIf SortArrayType = 3 Then
Sub SortArray(aTarget() As String, iFirst As Integer, _
            iLast As Integer, helper As ISortHelper)
    Dim vSplit As String
# ElseIf SortArrayType = 4 Then
⋮
End Sub
```

This trick is so ugly and fraught with potential for error that I hesitate to include it. Still, it's interesting to see how you can change the internal operation of a procedure simply by changing parameter and variable types. Because the default value for a conditional constant is 0, you will get the Variant version of SortArray by doing nothing. You need to define a value for SortArrayType in the Make tab of the Project Properties dialog box to get any other type. One disadvantage of this hack is that you can have only one type of SortArray per project. That's one reason I recommend the cut-and-paste method of getting different SortArray routines over the conditional compilation method. C++

provides a feature called templates for getting around this kind of problem, but I don't expect to see anything like this in Visual Basic for a long time—if ever.

Comparing and Swapping

Sorting is a simple operation. You compare the elements and swap the ones that are out of order until all are in order. A QuickSort does this differently than a Heap sort or an Insertion sort does, but all that matters to the programmer using the procedure is how you compare and swap. Both these operations can vary greatly, depending on what you're sorting and how you want to sort it.

By changing the comparison routine, you can control whether data is sorted in ascending or descending order and other aspects of sorting. You can sort integers by value only, but you can sort strings by case-sensitive value, by case-insensitive value, by length, by the sums of the Roman numeral values of the characters, or by whatever you choose. To sort objects, you'll probably want to compare based on a property such as size, color, name, position, or type.

The sort algorithm always works the same no matter what you're sorting, but the compare operation varies. You need a way to combine a generic sort routine with a specific compare routine. The way to do this is to pass in a helper object that has Compare and Swap methods with the appropriate arguments (enforced through an interface). If you don't like my Compare and Swap methods, define your own helper class. We're going to get to helper classes in a moment. For now we're interested only in the methods. For example, here's a very simple Compare method that sorts numeric data in ascending order:

```
Private Function ISortHelper_Compare(v1 As Variant, _
                             v2 As Variant) As Integer

    If v1 < v2 Then
        ISortHelper_Compare = -1
    ElseIf v1 = v2 Then
        ISortHelper_Compare = 0
    Else
        ISortHelper_Compare = 1
    End If
End Function
```

You can compare numeric values (and non–case-sensitive strings) with relational operators. You return negative, zero, or positive (usually −1, 0, or 1), depending on whether the first value is less than, equal to, or greater than the second value. No matter how complex your comparison, only these three results are valid. (Ignore errors for now.) Incidentally, the Basic StrComp function works the same way, for the same reasons.

The SortArray sub uses Compare this way:

```
If .Compare(aTarget(iFirst), aTarget(iLast)) > 0 Then
    .Swap aTarget(iFirst), aTarget(iLast)
End If
```

Because this code simply checks to see whether the value is greater than 0, Compare could still work if it returned only 1 and 0. Comparison routines are also used by search routines (as you'll see in "Binary Search," page 295), and these routines must be able to distinguish all three results.

Here's a specific Compare function from the CSortHelper class (SORTHELP.CLS):

```
Private Function ISortHelper_Compare(v1 As Variant, _
                                     v2 As Variant) As Integer
    ' Use string comparisons only on strings
    If TypeName(v1) <> "String" Then esmMode = esmSortVal

    Dim i As Integer
    Select Case esmMode
    ' Sort by value (same as esmSortBin for strings)
    Case esmSortVal
        If v1 < v2 Then
            i = -1
        ElseIf v1 = v2 Then
            i = 0
        Else
            i = 1
        End If
    ' Sort case-insensitive
    Case esmSortText
        i = StrComp(v1, v2, 1)
    ' Sort case-sensitive
    Case esmSortbin
        i = StrComp(v1, v2, 0)
    ' Sort by string length
    Case esmSortLen
        If Len(v1) = Len(v2) Then
            If v1 = v2 Then
                i = 0
            ElseIf v1 < v2 Then
                i = -1
            Else
                i = 1
            End If
        ElseIf Len(v1) < Len(v2) Then
            i = -1
        Else
            i = 1
        End If
```

```
    End Select
    If fHiToLo Then i = -i
    ISortHelper_Compare = i
End Function
```

This code tests the private class variables *esmMode* (of Enum type ESortMode) and *fHiToLo*.

Swapping presents similar problems. To swap data, you simply assign the first element to a temporary variable, assign the second element to the first, and assign the temporary variable to the second. Here's the default swap routine for SortArray:

```
Private Sub ISortHelper_Swap(v1 As Variant, v2 As Variant)
    Dim vT As Variant
    vT = v1
    v1 = v2
    v2 = vT
End Sub
```

This works well for simple types, but if you're swapping objects, files, or some other data, you'll probably need a different swap routine. For example, if you were swapping files, you might want to simply swap the names rather than actually exchange all the data. Also, the sort, shuffle, and search procedures in this chapter will need a custom helper class to work with object variants. For one thing, you'll need to use the Set statement to make assignments in the swap routines. For another, you'll have to specify which properties to work on in the compare routines.

The Helper Class Hack

In most languages, you can implement user-defined compare and swap routines using a feature called *procedure variables* in Pascal, *function pointers* in C, or, more generically, *callbacks* in the Windows SDK documentation. A procedure variable contains the address of a procedure. You can change the procedure by changing the address value. You can call the procedure by calling the variable. You can pass a procedure variable to a second procedure, thereby specifying the procedure that the second procedure calls to do its job.

The Windows API uses this concept freely, and now Visual Basic lets you take advantage of it with the AddressOf operator. But that applies only to the API. You can't do the same with your Basic code.

If Basic supported procedure variables, the SortArray sub might look like this:

```
Sub SortArray(aTarget() As Variant, _
             Optional vFirst As Variant, Optional vLast As Variant, _
             procCompare As SortCompareProc, _
             procSwap As SortSwapProc)
    ⋮
    If procCompare(aTarget(iFirst), aTarget(iLast)) > 0 Then
        procSwap aTarget(iFirst), aTarget(iLast)
    End If
    ⋮
```

You might then call the routine with one of these statements:

```
SortArray aNames(), 20, 48, CompareCaseSensitive, SwapString
SortArray aThings(), 1, 100, CompareCaseInsensitive, SwapThings
SortArray aAliens(), 0, 32, CompareAliens, SwapAliens
```

But the gods of Basic haven't seen fit to give us this simple feature, which even the lowly FORTRAN peons take for granted. It's just one more feature that keeps Basic from playing with the big kids. I'm not even going to suggest that we might see procedure variables in the next version because I said that last time. Instead, we're stuck with another hack. But this hack is at least an elegant one—unlike the two filthy hacks described in the first edition of this book. Some might even call it a feature; its performance is certainly acceptable.

What we have to do is create a polymorphic helper class that provides the required Compare and Swap methods. This might sound familiar to readers of the first edition. I demonstrated the same technique there but advised against using it because the performance was abysmal. That's because helper objects had to be passed as type Object, thus forcing late binding. The new Implements statement allows us to use the same technique to get early binding and good performance. Polymorphism with Implements has already been described, so we needn't go into complete detail here.

The interface class that all sort helper classes must be compatible with looks like this:

```
' ISortHelper interface class

Function Compare(v1 As Variant, v2 As Variant) As Integer
End Function

Sub Swap(v1 As Variant, v2 As Variant)
End Sub

Sub CollectionSwap(n As Collection, _
                   i1 As Variant, _
                   i2 As Variant, _
```

```
        Optional key1 As Variant, _
        Optional key2 As Variant)
End Sub
```

Any class that implements this interface must provide all three of these members, although it can make some of them dummies. For example, a sort helper class that will never sort collections must still include CollectionSwap, but it need not provide any code for CollectionSwap. A sort helper class can also implement additional methods and properties beyond what the interface requires.

The ISortHelper interface (along with SORT.CLS) is located in the VBCore component. In addition, VBCore contains a default helper class named CSortHelper. If you look back at the sort procedures earlier in this chapter, you can see that if you don't pass a sort helper object through the final optional parameter of SortArray, one will be instantiated for you. Furthermore, the default helper object will be initialized to a state that makes sense for most sort tasks. You can often ignore the whole helper issue and call SortArray the way you expect:

```
SortArray aStuff()
```

But if that seems too simple, or if the data you're sorting is too complicated, you can use CSortHelper as a model. I've already shown the Compare and Swap methods on pages 289–291. As well, the class has a HiToLo Boolean property for setting whether to sort in ascending or descending order, and a SortMode property for indicating whether string values should be sorted by case-sensitive compares, case-insensitive compares, or by their lengths.

At this point, you might ask what all the fuss is about. This is a flexible system with good performance, so why am I moaning about the lack of procedure variables? Well, because this is bad design. Ask any object-oriented design guru. Object-oriented programming is supposed to model the world. You don't need a sort helper to sort in the real world. In fact, an object that has no data, just methods, isn't really an object. If there's no data, you should be able to skip the class and use the functions directly. You might point out that the CSortHelper does have data—the internal variables for the HiToLo and SortMode properties. But that's a side effect. Because we have to have a class, we might as well give it data. You could just as easily have one sort helper for case-sensitive compares and another for case-insensitive—except that the class syntax of Visual Basic makes this inconvenient. But if you could use procedure parameters, you would have different kinds of Compare procedures—not one Compare procedure that varies its behavior based on property values.

And if that's not enough, why are the Swap and Compare methods in the same class? Frequently, you use the same Swap method for many sorting problems that require a different Compare method. Why should you have to reimplement Swap when all you wanted was a new Compare? Well, they're tied together for no reason other than convenience—because adding separate ISortHelperSwap and ISortHelperCompare interfaces would lead to a brain overload of similar classes. Much easier to put all the Compare and Swap procedures you can think up in one standard module.

> **NOTE** The first edition of this book described another hack for faking procedure variables by taking advantage of quirks in the Visual Basic name space. I have abandoned this hack as too inflexible. The code is still used in a test in the TimeIt program. If you prefer to hard-code a sorting procedure for a particular application rather than using a flexible component procedure, the old method gives slightly better performance.

Shuffling

The opposite of sorting is shuffling, a common task in games. Shuffling means randomizing each element in an array. The trick is that each element must appear in the array once and only once, but in a random position. You can't go through the array randomizing wildly, because you would end up with duplicate elements.

ShuffleArray uses the same helper object as SortArray. It uses the Swap method but doesn't need the Compare method.

```
Sub ShuffleArray(av() As Variant, Optional helper As ISortHelper)
    Dim iFirst As Long, iLast As Long
    If helper Is Nothing Then Set helper = New CSortHelper

    iFirst = LBound(av): iLast = UBound(av)
    ' Randomize array
    Dim i As Long, v As Variant, iRnd As Long
    For i = iLast To iFirst + 1 Step -1
        ' Swap random element with last element
        iRnd = MRandom.Random(iFirst, i)
        helper.Swap av(i), av(iRnd)
    Next
End Sub
```

The algorithm works by choosing any random element between the first and last elements and exchanging it with the last element, which then is random. Next it finds a random element between the first and the next-to-last elements and exchanges it with the next-to-last element. This process continues until the shuffling is finished.

The Fun 'n Games program, which is discussed in Chapter 6, uses the Shuffle sub to shuffle a deck of cards.

Binary Search

Once you sort a list of items, you can search it quickly with a binary search. A binary search splits the list into two parts, determines which one contains the search item, and then searches only that part by splitting that list into two parts. It continues in this fashion until the item is found. You can also use a binary search to insert an item into a sorted list. Instead of inserting the item at the beginning or at the end and then re-sorting, you search the list for the appropriate place to insert the item.

The BSearchArray function uses the same helper object as SortArray and ShuffleArray. It uses the Compare method but doesn't need the Swap method.

```
Function BSearchArray(av() As Variant, ByVal vKey As Variant, _
                      iPos As Long, _
                      Optional helper As ISortHelper) As Boolean
    Dim iLo As Long, iHi As Long
    Dim iComp As Long, iMid As Long
    If helper Is Nothing Then Set helper = New CSortHelper

    iLo = LBound(av): iHi = UBound(av)
    Do
        iMid = iLo + ((iHi - iLo) \ 2)
        iComp = helper.Compare(av(iMid), vKey)
        Select Case iComp
        Case 0
            ' Item found
            iPos = iMid
            BSearchArray = True
            Exit Function
        Case Is > 0
            ' Item is in lower half
            iHi = iMid - 1
            If iLo = iHi Then Exit Do
        Case Is < 0
            ' Item is in upper half
            iLo = iMid + 1
            If iLo > iHi Then Exit Do
        End Select
    Loop
    ' Item not found, but return position to insert
    iPos = iMid - (iComp < 0)

End Function
```

For an interesting example of binary search, check out the sorted list box control discussed in Chapter 11. This control uses a binary search procedure to insert new list items at the correct location in a sorted list box.

In addition to procedures for sorting, shuffling, and searching arrays, SORT.BAS contains similar procedures for collections. Sorting arrays and sorting collections are different enough to require separate procedures but not different enough to justify separate discussions. Both versions depend on the Compare method, but swapping works differently in collections. I'll let you figure out the details from the source.

6

Taking Control of Windows

Visual Basic brings Windows programming to the masses by hiding and redefining the details. Most Visual Basic programmers are content to accept this new, simplified model because forms, controls, and events are easier to program than windows, dialog boxes, and messages. Why put up with the hassle of programming bare-bones Windows?

Well, some of us are just masochists. And even if you don't need to prove anything, Visual Basic provides plenty of good reasons to learn Windows inside and out. It seems that every Visual Basic program ever written needs just one feature that the designers of the language didn't anticipate. Furthermore, none of those missing features overlap. The Visual Basic bug database is crammed with great ideas, feature requests, and design improvements marked "Postponed." Many of those ideas are mine.

But I'm not waiting for my favorite features to appear in some future version of Visual Basic. I want them now, even if I have to cheat. Unfortunately, the solutions to my problems probably aren't the solutions to your problems. Chances are this chapter won't tell you directly how to implement that one little feature that's been driving you batty for the past few weeks. But perhaps I can help you figure it out on your own by telling you everything you never really wanted to know about processes, modules, instances, classes, messages, resources, and, of course, windows.

WinWatch

The WinWatch program monitors Windows in action. In essence, WinWatch is a teaching tool. It's not useful for much except borrowing resources, making screen shots, and learning about window titles and classes. Still, you can pick up ideas and information that you can use in more practical programs.

We'll first take the quick-and-dirty WinWatch tour and then come back for a more detailed look at the code that makes it work. You might want to load the WinWatch project now.

NOTE If you owned the first edition of *Hardcore Visual Basic*, you might remember that the 16-bit version was empowered and the 32-bit version was, uh, challenged. In this version, 16 bits is like the 13th floor of a high-rise—no such thing. The 32-bit WinWatch is empowered, but empowered somewhat differently than its predecessor.

Elements of WinWatch

WinWatch is a complicated program with lots of features, many of them marginal. Figure 6-1 shows WinWatch on a busy day.

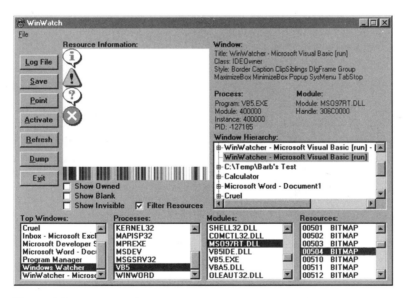

Figure 6-1. *WinWatch.*

Beginning with the list boxes at the bottom of the interface, let's examine the elements of WinWatch:

- The Top Windows list box displays the names of all the visible top windows of programs currently running in Windows. Selecting an item in this list box updates the next two list boxes to its right and the Window Hierarchy box; conversely, selecting an item in any one of those three boxes updates the Top Windows list box.

- The Processes list box shows all the processes that are currently running, including invisible ones. If you run two instances of a program, you'll see them both listed as separate entries. Each process is listed by its module name, which is the base name of the executable filename.

- The Modules list box shows all the executable files—both programs and DLLs—used by the currently selected process. In the 16-bit WinWatch provided with the first edition of this book, the module list showed all the modules being used by the system, but in 32-bit there is no global module list.

- The Resources list box indicates the resources of the program or DLL selected in the list boxes to its left. Chapter 8 covers resources in detail.

- The Windows, Process, and Module areas summarize what you know about the currently selected items. We'll see later how you get this information.

- The Window Hierarchy box shows all the windows in the system in outline form. You can expand a window to see its child windows. When you select a different window in this box, various screen elements (the lists of top windows, modules, and processes, as well as the Current Window Information area) change.

- The Resource Information picture box displays the currently selected resource, if one is selected. You'll see a graphical display for visual resources such as bitmaps and icons (see the bitmap in Figure 6-1); other resources are described with text. When you select a new module in the Modules list box, WinWatch finds any available version resources and displays them in the Resource Information area.

- Clicking the Log File button saves a log file named WINLIST.TXT, which contains the current window hierarchy. The log file is a text version of the information shown in the Window Hierarchy box.

- Clicking the Save button saves the current resource if it is a bitmap or an icon. You can copy pictures embedded in various programs to files. Chapter 8 explains how WinWatch steals pictures. Don't call me with hard-luck stories about lawsuits.

- Clicking the Point button puts WinWatch in point mode. When you point to a window, WinWatch selects it and updates the display appropriately.

- Clicking the Activate button activates the current program. (A double click in the Top Windows list box does the same thing.)

- Clicking the Refresh button forces WinWatch to refresh the list boxes and the window hierarchy outline. Use this button if you load new programs or activate new windows while WinWatch is running.

■ The three Show check boxes determine what windows will be displayed in the Top Windows and Window Hierarchy boxes. You'll probably find the display more attractive and less confusing with none of these boxes checked, but you might want to experiment with the complete list.

■ The Filter Resources check box filters out some resources that you usually won't need to see.

All About Windows

All you need to know to undermine Windows, generate chaos, and muck up the system is the handle of any window you want to trash. Normally, of course, you want to enhance Windows, not subvert it. You'll discover lots of legitimate uses for window handles inside and outside your program.

In the Windows environment, almost any distinct element that you see on the screen is a window. Visual Basic programmers might think of forms as windows, but in fact most controls—command buttons, list boxes, scroll bars, option buttons, and check boxes—are also windows. Any object that has an hWnd property is a window at heart. The hWnd property is the link between the Visual Basic world of forms and controls and the SDK world of windows, dialogs, and the pitiful version of controls known to C programmers.

WinWatch provides several features for exploring windows. At any point, the Window, Process, and Module areas tell you more than you need to know about the current window. You can change the current window by clicking an item in any of the list boxes except Resources, by navigating the window hierarchy outline, or by clicking the Point button and pointing to a window. This section looks at the code that makes these features work.

The Window Class

Imagine for a moment that Windows is written in Visual Basic and that every window you see on the screen is actually a window object of type CWindow. You might create a new window this way:

```
Dim wndMy As New CWindow
wndMy.Create("MyClass", "My Window", _
            afEnabled Or afVisible Or afOtherStyle, _
            x, y, dx, dy, hwndParent, hMenu, hInst, objOther)
```

After creating the window, you could access its properties as shown here:

```
With wndMy
    .Caption = "My New Window Title"
    afStyle = .Style
    x = .Point.x
End With
```

You could also call window methods such as these:

```
With wndMy
    .Move xNew, yNew
    If .Enabled Then .MakeActive
End With
```

Does this look at all familiar? Doesn't it look like initializing a form? In fact, this imaginary code is a very simplified view of what Visual Basic asks Windows to do when you ask Visual Basic to load a form. It's also what Visual Basic does when it loads most controls.

Inside CWindow

Let's take an inside look at CWindow. This class is undocumented, but it exists, and Windows explorers have mapped out its contents. In their flat-earth ignorance, these pioneers (of whom Matt Pietrek, author of *Windows 95 System Secrets,* is captain) believe that Windows was written in C, and so they call this hidden data the WND structure. Our more enlightened view is that this block of data is nothing less than the private variables of Visual Basic's CWindow class.

And now, revealed for the first time, the secret heart of every window:

```
Private hWndNext As Long            ' Next sibling window
Private hWndChild As Long           ' First child window
Private hWndParent As Long          ' Parent window
Private hWndOwner As Long           ' Owning window
Private rectWindow As RECT          ' Rectangle of entire window
Private rectClient As RECT          ' Rectangle of client area
Private hQueue As Integer           ' Application message queue
Private hrgnUpdate As Integer       ' Region needing update
Private wndClass As Integer         ' Window class
Private hInstance As Integer        ' Instance handle
Private lplfnWndProc As Long        ' Window procedure
Private afFlags As Long             ' Internal flags
Private afStyle As Long             ' Style flags
Private afStyleExt As Long          ' Extended style flags
Private afMoreFlags As Long         ' More internal flags
Private hMenu As Long               ' Menu used by window
Private hBuffer As Long             ' Buffer for title
Private scrollBar As Integer        ' Scroll bar word
Private hProperties As Integer      ' First window property
Private hWnd16 As Integer           ' The 16-bit window handle
Private pWndLastActive As Long      ' Last active popup window
Private hMenuSystem As Long         ' System menu
Private atomClass As Integer        ' Class name
Private pidAlternate As Long        ' Process ID
Private tidAlternate As Long        ' Thread ID
```

This is the Microsoft Windows 95 version; Microsoft Windows NT might vary slightly. What can you do with this information? As a practical matter, absolutely nothing. The only way you can change these private variables is through properties and methods of the public interface. In a more abstract sense, however, knowing what's inside helps you understand what the public methods and properties must work with and, thus, what they can and cannot do.

Although Windows is object-oriented in the philosophical sense of hiding data, inheriting attributes, and allowing polymorphic access to objects, its public interface is completely functional. Thus, instead of providing window objects with properties and methods, Windows provides functions that take a window handle argument.

You might like to do things the object-oriented way:

```
wndMy.Enabled = True
f = wndMy.Enabled
wndMy.Flash True
```

But in fact you have to call functions:

```
fOld = EnableWindow(hWnd, True)
f = IsWindowEnabled(hWnd)
FlashWindow hWnd, True
```

Of course, if you're dealing with Visual Basic windows, the Enable functions don't matter because the form or control representing the window has an Enabled property. If you want to flash the window, however, you'll have to do it the Windows Way because flashing a window is an obscure feature not deemed worthy of inclusion in Visual Basic. No problem. All you need is a declaration for FlashWindow so that you can call it like this:

```
FlashWindow Me.hWnd, True
```

A Basic CWindow class

WinWatch looks at windows from the outside and must do things the Windows Way, not the Basic Way. But this was a choice, not a requirement. It's not impossible to access window features in an object-oriented way; all you need is a CWindow class written in Visual Basic. I actually wrote this class, but WinWatch doesn't use it. Sometimes the functional philosophy is more convenient than the object religion.

You might find it amusing to check out CWindow on the companion CD, in the TWINDOW.VBP project. This class might even work for some of your projects. I'll describe the design, but frankly, I wrote CWindow more to show that it could be done than as a practical tool. It simply wraps the more common API functions related to windows in a thin layer.

CWindow has only one private member variable, *hWnd*. You initialize this internal variable using the Handle property, but you don't have to use the name *Handle* because it is the default property:

```
Dim wnd As New CWindow
wnd = Me.hWnd
```

You can also initialize the object with one of a variety of Create methods:

```
wnd.CreateFromPoint x, y              ' WindowFromPoint
wnd.CreateFromFind "MyClass", "My Title"    ' FindWindow
wnd.CreateFromActive                  ' GetActiveWindow
```

Once you initialize the object, you can get and read properties or call methods:

```
wnd.Caption = "My Title"              ' GetWindowText
wnd.Capture True                      ' SetCapture
wnd.Capture False                     ' ReleaseCapture
sClass = wnd.ClassName                ' GetClassName
```

Most of these methods and properties have one-line implementations. Here are a couple to give you the idea:

```
Private hWnd As Long
Public Property Get Handle() As Long
    Handle = hWnd
End Property

Public Property Let Handle(ByVal hWndA As Long)
    If IsWindow(hWndA) Then hWnd = hWndA Else hWnd = hNull
End Property
```

I started writing new methods and properties as fast as I could type them, but I gave up after a while because I could see that the class wasn't going to be much use. Feel free to finish the implementation. You can see my first cut in Figure 6-2 on the following page.

The problem with CWindow is that it adds a layer of complication and inefficiency without offering much advantage. For example, imagine that you have some code that retrieves a window handle and then uses it to get some data about the window. Which of the following is easier?

```
With wnd
    f = .CreateFromFind("SciCalc")
    fVisible = .Visible
    sTitle = .Caption
    idProc = .ProcID
End With
```

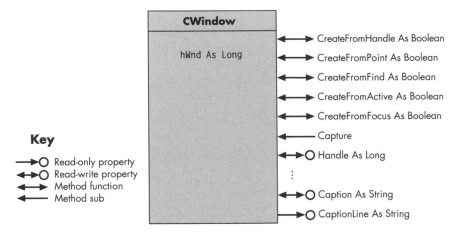

Figure 6-2. *First draft of the CWindow class.*

And here's the alternative:

```
hWnd = FindWindow("SciCalc")
fVisible = IsWindowVisible(hWnd)
sTitle = WindowTextFromWnd(hWnd)
idProc = ProcIDFromWnd(hWnd)
```

Either way, you must write the declarations for the Windows API functions and wrap un-Basic functions in Visual Basic wrappers (as you'll see later). But you're doing the same work—just packaging it differently.

The Windows Way of properties

Windows stores attributes that define every window. For a Visual Basic window, you can usually get at the attributes through properties. For a non–Visual Basic window, you have to use a function. Sometimes access is through an orthogonal pair of Get/Set functions. Sometimes the interface is more obscure.

Table 6-1 compares the Windows Way and the Basic Way of dealing with properties. (Some of the properties that you might expect to see listed here—color, for example—are actually properties of the device context, not the window, and are therefore discussed in Chapter 7.)

The Windows Way of methods

If you can think of something to do to a window, there's probably an API function to do it. Visual Basic provides corresponding methods for many of these operations. In some cases, properties perform operations rather than simply providing access to attributes. Table 6-2 compares the Windows Way and the Basic Way of getting things done.

Attribute	Windows Way	Basic Way
Active window	GetActiveWindow, possibly combined with GetParent	ActiveForm and Active-Control properties
Style bits	GetWindowLong with GWL_STYLE or GWL_EXSTYLE	BorderStyle, Enabled, Visible, WindowState, ControlBox, MaxButton, and MinButton properties
Window title	GetWindowText and SetWindowText	Caption property
Enabled, visible	WS_VISIBLE, WS_DISABLED style bits; IsWindowEnabled, IsWindowVisible, Enable Window, and ShowWindow	Enabled and Visible properties
Tab position	WS_TABSTOP style bit; GetNextDlgTabItem	TabStop and TabIndex properties
Window dimensions	GetWindowRect and SetWindowPos	Left, Top, Width, and Height properties; indirectly, Alignment and AutoSize properties
Client dimensions	GetClientRect	ScaleLeft, ScaleTop, ScaleWidth and ScaleHeight properties
Property list	GetProp, SetProp, and RemoveProp	Tag property (a minimal version)
Device context	GetDC and ReleaseDC	hDC property
Relative windows	GetWindow with GW_ constants, GetNextWindow, and GetParent	Parent property for controls but otherwise no way
Instance handle	GetWindowLong with GWL_HINSTANCE	App.hInstance property
Process ID and handle	GetWindowThreadProcessId and OpenProcess	No way
Class name	GetClassName	No way

Table 6-1. *Window properties.*

As Tables 6-1 and 6-2 (on the following page) show, it's a mixed-up world. You won't always find an obvious comparison between the Basic Way and the Windows Way. But if you are like most hardcore programmers, your eye keeps wandering to those items that show up in the Windows Way column but not in the Basic Way column. That's the challenge the rest of this chapter attempts to meet.

Operation	Windows Way	Basic Way
Show in different states	ShowWindow, OpenIcon, CloseWindow, IsIconic, and IsZoomed	Show and Hide methods; WindowState property
Change position, size, or z-order	SetWindowPos, DeferWindow-Pos, BeginDeferWindowPos, EndDeferWindowPos, BringWindowToTop, and MoveWindow	Move and ZOrder methods; Left, Top, Width, and Height properties
Set active window	SetForegroundWindow, Set-ActiveWindow, and SetFocus	SetFocus method; AppActivate statement
Create	CreateWindow, RegisterClass, and so on	Mostly automatic, but Load statement starts the process
Change window placement	GetWindowPlacement and SetWindowPlacement	Left, Top, Width, and Height properties
Capture mouse	SetCapture, GetCapture, and ReleaseCapture	No way
Destroy	DestroyWindow	Unload statement
Update window	UpdateWindow, Invalidate-Rect, BeginPaint, and a slew of others	Don't worry about it (or turn off AutoRedraw property and handle in Paint event)
Iterate through window hierarchy	EnumChildWindows, Enum-Windows, and GetWindow	No way
Find window	FindWindow, GetActiveWin-dow, and WindowFromPoint	No way
Text output	TextOut, ExtTextOut, GrayString, and others	Print method
Text sizing	GetTextExtentPoint32	TextWidth and TextHeight methods
Text alignment	SetTextAlign, SetText-Justification, and SetText-CharacterExtra functions	No direct comparison

Table 6-2. *Window methods.*

Visual Basic Wrappers for Windows Functions

Although most of the internal Windows data can be read or modified by Windows functions, few of those functions have obvious names and operations. If Windows has widgets, that doesn't mean you'll find GetWidget and SetWidget functions in the Windows API.

The next sections describe the workarounds for performing Windows operations in Visual Basic as well as some of the reasons you might want to take the Windows Way even in Visual Basic.

Getting Windows string data

You're already familiar not only with the Windows Way of getting string data but also with the Basic Way of getting around the Windows Way (explained in "Dealing with Strings," page 72). For example, you can get the class name of a window with GetClassName; to make this look Basic, wrap the access in ClassNameFromWnd:

```
Function ClassNameFromWnd(ByVal hWnd As Long) As String
    Dim sName As String, cName As Integer
    BugAssert hWnd <> hNull
    sName = String$(80, 0)
    cName = GetClassName(hWnd, sName, 80)
    ClassNameFromWnd = Left$(sName, cName)
End Function
```

The window class indicates the kind of window. The main use for the class name is passing it to FindWindow to find other windows of the same class. (The VBFindWindow function was discussed in "Wrapping String Functions," page 78, as an example of how to pass strings to Windows functions.) You can also pass the class name to GetClassInfo to obtain detailed class information that you aren't likely to use in Visual Basic. The following sidebar has more information on classes.

In the section "Wrap It Up" in Chapter 2, you saw an example of the technique for getting strings, using WindowTextFromWnd. Actually, WinWatch uses a slightly different version of this function, named WindowTextLineFromWnd. It's the same function except that it truncates the window text at the first line break. I originally used the WindowTextFromWnd function in WinWatch, but I wasn't counting on windows that use the window text as the content of the window. The WinWatch display needs to truncate multiline window text, but other applications might need to display the entire text, breaks and all.

The window title is useful not only as information but also to pass to the AppActivate statement. This is the Basic Way to set the focus to a particular window. The Windows Way is to pass the window handle to SetForeground-Window.

The Windows Word and the Windows Long

Some of the juiciest chunks of window data are accessed through a somewhat bizarre system of functions and constants. In the original design, if the data you needed was 16 bits in size, you called GetWindowWord with a constant indicating the data you wanted. If the data was 32 bits, you called GetWindowLong with a constant. Similarly, you could use SetWindowWord and SetWindowLong to modify the data.

Thunder Classes

If you are familiar with programming for Windows in C or Pascal, you might notice that this chapter doesn't stress window classes. In fact, window classes—so important to most Windows programmers—are almost irrelevant to Visual Basic programmers.

When programming Windows in C, you first define the classes for your windows by filling in the fields of a WNDCLASS structure and then passing this structure to RegisterClass. Windows provides default classes for control windows (such as the Edit and ComboBox classes), but there is no default class for "normal" windows. You must create and register your own class before you can call CreateWindow to create your windows. As a result, almost every application has a different name for the classes of its windows, even though those classes often contain the same attributes. Program Manager has the Progman class, Notepad has the Notepad class, Calculator has the SciCalc class, and so on.

Visual Basic programmers usually don't need to worry about classes because Visual Basic creates and registers its own and then uses them to create its windows, all behind the scenes. Once you start calling API functions to play with windows, however, you might want to manipulate windows through their class names occasionally.

All the names of the predefined Visual Basic classes start with the word *Thunder*, which was the prerelease code name of Visual Basic 1. (Internally, the Visual Basic folks were distributing a stunning bitmap showing the night sky of Seattle split by lightning and the slogan "The power to crack Windows.") Each Visual Basic program has a main window with class ThunderMain and one or more forms with class ThunderForm. Controls have class names such as ThunderCommandButton, ThunderListBox, and so on. In some cases, Thunder classes are made up of standard Windows control classes. For example, the ThunderComboBox class consists of what Windows calls an Edit control and a ComboBox control.

Although you don't have to worry about classes in your applications, the downside is that you can't use classes to find Visual Basic programs as you can with other programs. Classwise, if you've seen one Visual Basic application, you've seen them all.

This system makes no sense in 32-bit windows. The window word and the window long are both 32 bits. Win32 throws GetWindowWord and SetWindowWord in the trash. You must use GetWindowLong and SetWindowLong for all data. Windows also provides GetClassLong and SetClassLong functions and constants, but they aren't of much use to Visual Basic programmers.

Why aren't these names Word and DWord? Or Short and Long? Why doesn't Windows provide separate functions to get and set each chunk of data? Why have Set functions to modify data (such as the instance handle) that no one in their right mind would modify? What happens if you pass a constant other than the ones provided in WINDOWS.H? Why didn't it occur to the designers of the first version of Windows that the name GetWindowWord would be obsolete if Windows ever became 32-bit? Don't ask.

The required constants are in the Windows API type library, but for reference, I'll show what they would look like in Visual Basic:

```
Public Const GWL_WNDPROC = -4        ' Windows procedure
Public Const GWL_HINSTANCE = -6      ' Instance handle
Public Const GWL_HWNDPARENT = -8     ' Use GetParent instead
Public Const GWL_ID = -12            ' Window ID (whatever that is)
Public Const GWL_STYLE = -16         ' Window style
Public Const GWL_EXSTYLE = -20       ' Extended window style
Public Const GWL_USERDATA = -21      ' Window style
```

In addition, you can use the following constants for dialog boxes:

```
Public Const DWL_MSGRESULT = 0       ' Return value of dialog message
Public Const DWL_DLGPROC = 4         ' Dialog procedure
Public Const DWL_USER = 8            ' User-defined data
```

In previous versions of Visual Basic, there wasn't much you could do with a window or with a dialog procedure address. In this version, the AddressOf operator makes it possible to subclass windows with SetWindowLong and GWL_WNDPROC. We'll experiment later in this chapter

I haven't tried all the options, but I've been told you need to read the fine print twice to figure out the difference between Get/SetParent and Get/SetWindow-Long with GWL_HWNDPARENT. Instance handles aren't nearly as useful in 32-bit Windows as they were in 16-bit Windows, but you can get them. The style bits are the data you're most likely to need, and we'll talk more about them next.

Here is the syntax for getting data with GetWindowLong:

```
Dim afStyle As Long, afExStyle As Long, hInst As Long
hInst = GetWindowLong (hWnd, GWL_HINSTANCE)
afStyle = GetWindowLong(hWnd, GWL_STYLE)
afExStyle = GetWindowLong(hWnd, GWL_EXSTYLE)
```

You can also set window long values with SetWindowLong, and you might want to set the style bits, but that's another story.

Style bits

If you were writing programs for Windows in C, you'd need to specify style bit flags in the CreateWindow function every time you wanted a new window. C doesn't have a form properties window. You'll recognize some of the style bits because many of them correspond directly to form properties.

WinWatch gets the style bits for each window and displays them in the Window information area. GetWndStyle converts the bit flags to a string:

```
Function GetWndStyle(hWnd) As String
    Dim af As Long, s As String
    BugAssert hWnd <> hNull

    ' Get normal style
    af = GetWindowLong(hWnd, GWL_STYLE)
    If af And WS_BORDER Then s = s & "Border "
    If af And WS_CAPTION Then s = s & "Caption "
    If af And WS_CHILD Then s = s & "Child "
    ⋮
```

Windows provides shortcut functions to get style information about the current view state of the window. GetWndView uses these functions to create the View heading:

```
Public Function GetWndView(hWnd) As String
    Dim s As String
    BugAssert hWnd <> hNull
    s = IIf(IsWindowVisible(hWnd), "Visible ", "Invisible ")
    s = s & IIf(IsWindowEnabled(hWnd), "Enabled ", "Disabled ")
    s = s & IIf(IsZoomed(hWnd), "Zoomed ", sEmpty)
    s = s & IIf(IsIconic(hWnd), "Iconic ", sEmpty)
    GetWndView = s
End Function
```

You can learn a lot about how forms really work by studying the WinWatch display. Run a compiled version of WinWatch and a test form with test controls in the Visual Basic environment. Change various properties and see how they affect the Window information display (after you click the Refresh button). You can probably guess most of the effects, but some might surprise you. For example, the ClipChildren style bit corresponds to the form's ClipControls property.

You can also change style bits, but it's not as easy as you might expect. Changing the state of the bits doesn't necessarily change the state of the window; it just knocks the bits and the state out of sync. But there is a way.

The Fun 'n Games project in Chapter 7 has a Clip Controls check box that determines whether the graphics drawn by the program write over or under the controls on the form. In theory you should be able to toggle the ClipControls property, but in reality Visual Basic lets you change the ClipControls property only at design time. It turns out, though, that ClipControls is nothing more than the WS_CLIPCHILDREN style bit. To change the ClipControls functionality (but not the property), you simply call this procedure:

```
Sub ChangeStyleBit(hWnd As Long, f As Boolean, afNew As Long)
    Dim af As Long, hParent As Long
    af = GetWindowLong(hWnd, GWL_STYLE)
    If f Then
        af = af Or afNew
    Else
        af = af And (Not afNew)
    End If
    Call SetWindowLong(hWnd, GWL_STYLE, af)
    ' Reset the parent so that change will "take"
    hParent = GetParent(hWnd)
    SetParent hWnd, hParent
    ' Redraw for added insurance
    Call SetWindowPos(hWnd, HWND_NOTOPMOST, 0, 0, 0, 0, _
                    SWP_NOZORDER Or SWP_NOSIZE Or _
                    SWP_NOMOVE Or SWP_DRAWFRAME)
End Sub
```

The first part of the code is straightforward, but what the heck is that call at the end? The SetWindowPos API function sets the window position and, as a side effect, renews all of the style bits. The trick to this hack is getting the function to perform the side effect without performing the primary effect. The second through sixth parameters of SetWindowPos change the z-order, location, or size of a window, and the final parameter tells how to interpret the earlier parameters. In this case, you pass three NO flags telling the function to ignore it all. By themselves, these flags would simply disable the function, so you must add the SWP_DRAWFRAME flag to ensure that the window gets updated. Pretty slimy, huh? I haven't experimented much with this function, so don't blame me if it doesn't always work for all style bits or for windows without frames.

> **NOTE** I got most of this hack from an article called "Slimy Windows Hacks" in the February 1995 issue of *Visual Basic Programmer's Journal*. The masked author identified himself only as Escher. I can't reveal his identity (although he has given broad hints at speeches at the VBITS conference), but I will note that the Acknowledgments section of this book gives proper credit to all contributors. Later I added the part about resetting the parent to the current parent. I borrowed this insurance technique from similar code in the Microsoft Foundation Classes (MFC) library. I'm not sure whether it makes any difference.

Window position and size

Windows knows everything that you need to know about every window's position—both the rectangle of the window and the rectangle of its client area. A rectangle includes the screen coordinates of the left, right, top, and bottom, thus describing both the size and the position of the window. Various Windows API functions use the rectangle coordinates to control the size and the position of a window.

Of course, you usually won't need these functions in Visual Basic. When you're working on forms and controls, it's easier to read or modify the Left, Top, Width, and Height attributes or to use the Move method. If you're interested only in the client area, you can use the ScaleLeft, ScaleTop, ScaleWidth, and Scale-Height properties.

Occasionally, however, you'll need to perform operations that Visual Basic does not support. When you convert Visual Basic rectangles to Windows rectangles, the following utility functions can make your code shorter:

```
Function xRight(obj As Object) As Single
    xRight = obj.Left + obj.Width
End Function

Function yBottom(obj As Object) As Single
    yBottom = obj.Top + obj.Height
End Function
```

Just be sure that anything you pass to these functions really has Left, Top, Width, and Height properties.

WinWatch has to solve a window coordinate problem. It must find the window located at a given position—specifically, the position the user points to. The cmdPoint_Click event toggles point mode on and off, the Form_MouseMove event displays information for the window to which the user is currently pointing, and the Form_MouseDown event selects the window being pointed to as the current window, forcing an update in various list boxes. Let's look at the code that makes this happen, starting with cmdPoint_Click:

```
Private Sub cmdPoint_Click()
    If cmdPoint.Caption = "&Point" Then
        fCapture = True
        cmdPoint.Caption = "End &Point"
        Call SetCapture(Me.hWnd)
        lblMsg.Caption = "Move mouse for window information"
    Else
        fCapture = False
        cmdPoint.Caption = "&Point"
        ReleaseCapture
        lblMsg.Caption = sMsg
```

```
     End If
End Sub
```

This sub toggles the form-level flag *fCapture*, changes messages and captions, and, most important, sets the form to capture all mouse movements anywhere on the screen. Normally, each window captures only its own mouse events; but with SetCapture on, you get everything.

The Form_MouseMove sub illustrates some of the problems involved in converting Windows screen coordinates to Visual Basic form coordinates:

```
Private Sub Form_MouseMove(Button As Integer, Shift As Integer, _
                          x As Single, y As Single)
    If fCapture Then
        Dim pt As POINTL, hWnd As Long
        Static hWndLast As Long
        ' Set point and convert it to screen coordinates
        pt.x = x / Screen.TwipsPerPixelX
        pt.y = y / Screen.TwipsPerPixelY
        ClientToScreen Me.hWnd, pt
        ' Find window under it
        hWnd = WindowFromPoint(pt.x, pt.y)
        ' Update display only if window has changed
        If hWnd <> hWndLast Then
            lblWin.Caption = GetWndInfo(hWnd)
            hWndLast = hWnd
        End If
    End If
End Sub
```

This code does nothing unless capture mode is on (as indicated by *fCapture*). If it is on, the mouse position that is received by the form is specified in twips, so you must divide by the TwipsPerPixelX or TwipsPerPixelY property of the Screen object to get *x* or *y* in pixels. These adjusted values are put in a POINTL variable (Windows calls it POINT, but that name conflicts with the Visual Basic Point method) and passed to ClientToScreen to make them relative to the screen rather than to WinWatch. The adjusted values can then be passed to the WindowFromPoint function, which will return the window under the mouse pointer.

WindowFromPoint uses one of the ugliest hacks in this book. To understand how it works, look carefully at the C prototypes for both ClientToScreen and WindowFromPoint:

```
BOOL ClientToScreen(HWND hWnd,. LPPOINT lpPoint);
HWND WindowFromPoint(POINT Point);
```

In ClientToScreen, the POINTL variable is passed as a pointer (by reference, in Visual Basic terms). Most functions in the Windows API pass structures this way. WindowFromPoint, its cousin ChildWindowFromPoint, and a few others break the rules by passing POINT parameters by value. You might remember from Chapter 2 that structures (UDTs in Visual Basic) are always passed by reference in order to save stack space. But take a look at the size of a POINTL variable:

```
Public Type POINTL
    x As Long
    y As Long
End Type
```

You have to know a little Windows history to understand the problem. In 16-bit mode, a POINT was two Integers, which equaled one Long. A pointer is also a Long. You would gain nothing if you passed by reference. Apparently, a performance-conscious designer of the first version of Windows decided to save a few clock cycles by passing by value, never anticipating that Windows might someday be ported to 32 bits. Well, it turns out that in 32-bit C you can pass a 64-bit POINTL variable by value. It might not be efficient, but at least it's portable. In Visual Basic, however, you can't pass a UDT variable by value, period—not 16-bit, not 32-bit, not 64-bit. Visual Basic could have supported this for small UDTs, but the Visual Basic designers must have assumed that no one would ever want to do it.

But there is an indirect way of passing a 64-bit structure by value. When you pass any argument, the processor pushes the arguments onto the stack. It turns out that 32-bit Intel processors always push in 32-bit chunks. When you pass a 64-bit chunk, the processor actually pushes two 32-bit values. To make this work in Visual Basic, you make explicit what's actually happening under the surface. The following function is in the Windows API type library, but a Declare statement would look like this:

```
Declare Function WindowFromPoint Lib "USER32" _
    (ByVal xPoint As Long, ByVal yPoint As Long) As Long
```

In your code, you must pass the parts separately rather than in one chunk.

```
hWnd = WindowFromPoint(pt.x, pt.y)
```

If this seems complicated, just be glad that 16-bit Windows is dead. The portable version of this hack described in the last version of my book was twice as complicated.

You might want to examine the Form_MouseDown event procedure to get more details on how a window being clicked is identified and converted into the current window.

Iterating Through Windows

You can learn a lot about Windows by iterating through each window in the system and writing down its attributes. The window hierarchy is usually described as a tree, although it's diagrammed as something more like a root system. I'm told that programmers in many countries draw their trees growing upward, as the name implies. Figure 6-3 shows a tree upside down, the American way. At the top is the desktop window. Below are the top-level windows, the main windows of running programs. Below each top-level window is its own set of child windows—dialog boxes, MDI windows, buttons, and so on.

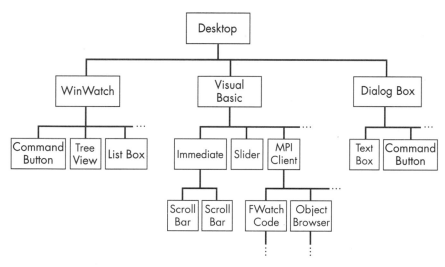

Figure 6-3. *A window tree.*

The approved way to traverse the window tree is to use EnumChildWindows to traverse each window and its children, starting at an arbitrary window. If you want to traverse all windows in the system, you start at the desktop window. You couldn't use EnumChildWindows in previous versions of Visual Basic, but the AddressOf operator makes it easy in version 5. "The Ultimate Hack: Procedure Pointers" in Chapter 2 tells how to do this. The problem with EnumChildWindows is that it provides no easy way to map where you are in the window hierarchy. So just to prove we can do it (and to get a little more flexibility), let's iterate windows the hard way.

Iterating the hard way

The hard way of iterating Windows is to use the GetWindow API function. My IterateChildWindows function will recursively traverse the window tree, doing some project-specific task for each window. In other words, IterateChildWindows will do out in the open what the EnumChildWindows function does behind the scenes. EnumChildWindows takes a procedure variable argument to provide the project-specific task for each window, but IterateChildWindows is written in a wimpy language that doesn't support procedure variables. Instead, we'll have to do the same object hack we did for sorting (see "Sorting, Shuffling, and Searching" in Chapter 5). But let's look at the iterator before we worry about the iterees.

One caveat: the Windows API documentation warns that a window loop like this one risks getting caught in an infinite loop or accessing the handle of a window that no longer exists. EnumChildWindows, on the other hand, is guaranteed to be reliable. I haven't had any problems with IterateChildWindows, but I'm using it as an exploration tool rather than as a way to add functionality to real programs. Use it only when you know that the window hierarchy will not change while it's working.

Recursion makes IterateChildWindows deceptively short, but it's not as simple as it looks:

```
Function IterateChildWindows(ByVal iLevel As Integer, _
                             ByVal hWnd As Long, _
                             helper As IWindowsHelper) As Long
    BugAssert hWnd <> hNull

    ' Handle current window, allowing user to fail

    IterateChildWindows = helper.DoWindow(iLevel, hWnd)
    If IterateChildWindows <> hNull Then Exit Function
    ' Get its child (if any)
    hWnd = GetWindow(hWnd, GW_CHILD)
    ' Iterate through each child window
    Do While hWnd <> hNull
        IterateChildWindows = _
            IterateChildWindows(iLevel + 1, hWnd, helper)
        If IterateChildWindows <> hNull Then Exit Function
        ' Get next child
        hWnd = GetWindow(hWnd, GW_HWNDNEXT)
        ' Give other processes some cycles
        DoEvents
    Loop
    ' Nothing found
    IterateChildWindows = hNull

End Function
```

IterateChildWindows is located in WINITER.BAS. The function has three parameters. The first indicates the window level. It will be incremented each time you recurse to a new level. You can use it to output tabs or indicate indent levels. (The *iLevel* parameter gives IterateChildWindows an advantage over the system EnumChildWindows, which offers no information about the level.) The second parameter is the window handle of the starting window. You must seed each of these values for the first call to IterateChildWindows, but then it automatically figures out the appropriate arguments for subsequent calls to itself. If you want to start at the desktop, use the GetDesktopWindow API function (as WinWatch does). The last parameter is the helper object that we'll discuss in the next section. A call looks like this:

```
Call IterateChildWindows(-1, GetDesktopWindow(), helperFile)
```

WinWatch passes −1 as the starting level to prevent the DoWindow method from putting the desktop window in the treeview control. You could start with some other window handle, such as the handle of the current program:

```
Call IterateChildWindows(0, Me.hWnd, helperFile)
```

Once you have the initial window handle, you can get the handle of its first child window by calling GetWindow with GW_CHILD. The function returns the child window handle, or hNull if the window has no child. You get the next window at the same level (the next sibling) by calling GetWindow with GW_HWNDNEXT. The IterateChildWindows function first gets the child of the current window and then loops through all the sibling windows, calling itself to get the children of each sibling. If that sounds confusing, try stepping through the function. You'll soon feel disoriented, if not completely lost. Computers do recursion better than humans.

Just as you can write IterateChildWindows to emulate the EnumChildWindows API function, you can write IterateWindows to emulate the EnumWindows API function. EnumWindows simply processes top-level windows. (See the Refresh-TopWinList procedure in WINWATCH.FRM.) Realistically, you'd seldom use IterateWindows. EnumWindows is easier and just as powerful.

Doing windows

Let's review polymorphism with Implements and see how it works in WinWatch. The IWindowsHelper interface is the template for any polymorphic class that needs to do something to a window (based on its handle). CWindowToFile is an IWindowsHelper class that writes window information to a file. CWindow-ToForm is an IWindowsHelper class that writes window information to a form—specifically to a label on the form and to a treeview control.

Note that IterateChildWindows and IWindowsHelper are general elements that you might use in any project. They're in the VBCore project. CWindowToFile and CWindowToForm are project specific. They are designed for WinWatch, which is the only project that is likely to need them. Polymorphism turns object-oriented programming upside down. When you write classes for encapsulation, you usually create one class to be used from many programs. When you write classes for polymorphism, you have only one interface, but you create many project-specific classes that implement the interface. You can see how this works in the WinWatch code that uses the IWindowsHelper classes:

```
Private Sub RefreshFullWinList(fLogFile As Boolean)
    Const sLog = "WINLIST.TXT"

    Call LockWindowUpdate(tvwWin.hWnd)
    tvwWin.Nodes.Clear
    HourGlass Me
    If fLogFile Then
        lblMsg.Caption = "Creating log file " & sLog & "..."
        nFileCur = FreeFile
        Open sLog For Output As nFileCur
        Print #nFileCur, sEmpty
        Print #nFileCur, "Window List " & sCrLf
        Dim helperFile As CWindowToFile
        Set helperFile = New CWindowToFile
        helperFile.FileNumber = nFileCur
        ''@B IterateChildWindows
        Call IterateChildWindows(-1, GetDesktopWindow(), helperFile)
        ''@E IterateChildWindows
        Close nFileCur
    Else
        lblMsg.Caption = "Building window list..."
        Dim helperForm As CWindowToForm
        Set helperForm = New CWindowToForm
        Set helperForm.TreeViewControl = tvwWin
        helperForm.ShowInvisible = chkInvisible
        Call IterateChildWindows(-1, GetDesktopWindow(), helperForm)
    End If
    lblMsg.Caption = sMsg
    HourGlass Me
    tvwWin.Refresh
    Call LockWindowUpdate(hNull)
End Sub
```

You create and pass to IterateChildWindows a completely different object, depending on what you're doing. The ISortHelper interface and the CSortHelper class from Chapter 5 at least had object-oriented pretensions. But the IWindows-Helper interface and the CWindowToFile and CWindowToForm classes have no purpose other than to provide a platform for the DoWindow method. In fact, DoWindow is almost all there is to these classes.

Here's the interface the classes are built on:

```
Function DoWindow(ByVal iLevel As Integer, _
                  ByVal hWnd As Long) As Long
End Function
```

That's all there is to it. Here's the CWindowToFile version:

```
Implements IWindowsHelper

Public FileNumber As Integer

Private Function IWindowsHelper_DoWindow(ByVal iLevel As Integer, _
                                         ByVal hWnd As Long) As Long

    BugAssert hWnd <> hNull
    ' Ignore desktop window (level -1)
    If iLevel >= 0 Then
        ' Write data to log file
        Print #FileNumber, GetWndInfo(hWnd, iLevel)
    End If
    ' Always successful
    IWindowsHelper_DoWindow = hNull
End Function
```

Recursion

A good recursive algorithm looks simple and symmetrical but has a magical complexity when you watch it in action. Code your recursive routines carefully to avoid recursing forever. Recursion works best if you have a limited task with clean exits. Also be sure that you don't recurse too deeply and eat up all your stack space. IterateChildWindows recurses once for each level of child windows, but you're not likely to find more than five levels of child windows. In other words, the algorithm recurses frequently but not deeply. Each level releases its stack resources before going on to the next.

If you use algorithms that recurse deeply (recursive sorting algorithms, for example), try to minimize your stack use. Don't use more parameters than necessary, and declare local variables with Static rather than Dim. Static variables save stack space because they aren't stored on the stack. You'll need to watch out for side effects, however. Static variables retain their values across calls, so you should avoid using Static for any variable that you don't specifically initialize on each entrance.

You must also pay attention to how you declare parameters. Notice that the *iLevel* and *hWnd* parameters of IterateChildWindows are passed by value (using ByVal) rather than by reference. Each level keeps its own local arguments on the stack so that changes to the current level don't affect other levels. If you passed by reference, you'd be affecting the *hWnd* of the higher-level calls each time you set *hWnd* in a recursive call. Everything would be fine as long as you were recursing down, but you'd be lost as soon as you started back up.

This class does have one independent property, FileNumber, which must be set by the caller. But the only code is the implementation of DoWindow. It calls the GetWndInfo function to analyze and describe the window. The CWindowTo-Form version is pretty much the same except that it updates a treeview control instead of writing to a file.

Both IterateChildWindows and the DoWindow method are functions. This enables you to search for a window with certain features. For example, you could write your own version of FindWindow to search the window hierarchy for a window with a given class, title, or other feature. Your DoWindow function would return the window handle when it found the appropriate window, but hNull in all other cases. Any found handle would bubble up through the levels of recursion, stopping the iteration process and returning the handle via the top-level call to IterateChildWindows. In the WinWatch versions of DoWindow, we want to continue as long as any windows are left, so we always return hNull to indicate that DoWindow hasn't found the magic window. In WinWatch, the outer call to IterateChildWindows just throws away the returned handle, using the Call syntax.

You can use the log file created by WinWatch to get a snapshot of the window state. Want to know the class name of a button or an icon in a particular program? Run WinWatch and click the Log File button.

More window relationships

IterateChildWindows illustrates how to traverse the window tree with Get-Window. Table 6-3 on the facing page describes some of the other window relationships.

Except for "owner," all these relationships should be obvious. The owner of a window is the window that is notified when something happens to the first window. You can get a better feel for this by browsing the outline in WinWatch's Window Hierarchy box. Most windows in the hierarchy don't have an owner, but a dialog box is owned by the window that launched it. The main Visual Basic window containing the menus and the toolbar is the owner of all the other windows—toolbox, project, properties, and code windows.

If you look at the internal data stored for a window (see "Inside CWindow" page 301), you'll see that only three relatives are stored for each window: the parent, the next sibling, and the first child. (The owner isn't a relative, strictly speaking.) You won't see a first, last, or previous sibling, even though Windows provides the GW_HWNDFIRST, GW_HWNDLAST, and GW_HWNDPREV constants. Each of these relationships can be calculated from the given data. For example, the first sibling is actually the first child of the parent. The last sibling is the first sibling's next sibling's next sibling until the sibling with no next.

Operation	Description
GetWindow with GW_HWNDFIRST	Get the first sibling
GetWindow with GW_HWNDLAST	Get the last sibling
GetWindow with GW_HWNDNEXT	Get the next sibling
GetWindow with GW_HWNDPREV	Get the previous sibling
GetWindow with GW_CHILD	Get the first child
GetWindow with GW_OWNER	Get the owner
GetNextWindow	Get the next or previous sibling
GetTopWindow	Get the top-level window of a specified window
GetDesktopWindow	Get the desktop (the top of the window tree)
GetParent	Get the parent
SetParent	Change the parent of a window
IsChild	Indicate whether two windows are parent and child

Table 6-3. *Window relationships.*

All About Programs

Windows provides a wealth of features for doing everything you could imagine to and about windows. No surprise—that's why they call it Windows. But the features for getting information about the programs that own those windows are not so polished. Getting program information was easy in the 16-bit world using the instance and task handles. It's a whole new world with 32-bit, and the reason is protection.

Passing around too much information about other programs is asking for trouble, which is exactly what a lot of 16-bit programs ran into. It might be convenient to examine the internal data and resources of another program, but it's not safe. Windows 95 and Windows NT are protected-mode operating systems that deliberately limit your program's access to information about other programs. This is good. But sometimes you really do have an innocent need for information about other processes. Some requests can be granted, but Windows NT and Windows 95 have different ways of doling out whatever information they, in their infinite wisdom, will trust you with.

System-Specific API Functions

You might remember the olden days when Windows evangelists claimed that any API function supported in Windows NT should have at least a stub in Windows 95, and vice versa. This was mostly the way things worked in Windows 95 and Windows NT 3.51. But let me warn you that this policy is no longer operable.

I've been informed, by people who know, that many of the new API functions that will be introduced in future versions of Windows might not have stubs in their counterparts. If one version of Windows has API functions another lacks, you must conditionally load the function pointers for the supporting operating system and call the functions dynamically. This is a messy business in C++ and other low-level languages, and I thought it would be impossible in Visual Basic. Not so. It turns out that all API functions defined with Declare statements are called dynamically, and if you need to call one function in one operating system and another in a different system, it's as easy as pie.

That's exactly what you have to do to iterate through processes and modules in Visual Basic. If the host system is Windows 95, you need to call the Tool-Help32 functions located in KERNEL32.DLL. If the host system is Windows NT, you need to call the process functions in PSAPI.DLL. If you call the wrong API function from the wrong operating system, you'll end up with a rude message. Windows NT will inform you that there are no ToolHelp32 functions in KERNEL32.DLL. Windows 95 will tell you that PSAPI.DLL can't be found (even if it's right there). Either way, you won't get what you want.

For the moment, let's ignore the substantial differences between the two different approaches. Just take it on faith that Windows NT starts iterating through processes with a function called EnumProcesses. Windows 95 starts iterating through processes with a function called Process32First. To call these functions from their appropriate operating systems, write Declare statements for each in the same module. I put mine in MODTOOL.BAS.

Notice first that we define both functions. It would be slightly more efficient to use conditional compilation to define the appropriate Declare statement for each operating system, but then we'd end up with two different versions of the program. Instead we'll check at run time and make sure that the wrong function is never called from the right operating system. Notice also that we're using Declare statements, not a type library. A type library won't work in this situation because Visual Basic loads all type library function entries at compile time rather than at run time.

We'll take a closer look at the code shortly, but in summary, you can write a wrapper function that works like this:

```
Function CreateProcessList() As CVector
    If IsNT Then
        f = EnumProcesses(...)
    Else
        f = Process32First(...)
    End If
End Function
```

As long as you call the right function, there's no problem. You can even trap the error that occurs when a function doesn't exist:

```
Function CreateProcessList() As CVector
    On Error Resume Next
    f = EnumProcesses(...)
    If Err Then f = Process32First(...)
End Function
```

How does this work? Well, I don't have access to Visual Basic source code, so I'm not positive. And it doesn't really matter. But it works as if it were coded like the following.

A Declare statement in code creates a UDT variable containing information about the Declare—function pointer address, types, aliases, DLL, etc. The address is the key field here. If the code were written in Visual Basic, the data structure might look like this:

```
Type TDeclare
    proc As Long
    name As String
    dll As String
    hMod As Long
    alias As String
    return As TParam
    params() As TParam
End Type
```

For each Declare statement the compiler would create this variable:

```
Private declGetVersion As TDeclare
```

This happens at compile time. Then at run time, the program might call the declared function:

```
i = GetVersion
```

Behind the scenes Visual Basic checks to see if the DLL is loaded using code that might look like the following.

```
With declGetVersion
    ' Make sure the DLL is loaded
    If .hMod = 0 Then
        .hMod = LoadLibrary(.dll)
        ' Probably set the .hMod for all other Declares with same DLL
    End If
    ' Make sure the procedure variable is set
    If .proc = 0 Then
        If .alias = sEmpty Then .alias = .name
        .proc = GetProcAddress(.hMod, .alias)
    End If
    i = (.proc)() ' Procedure parameter syntax not yet invented
End With
```

Of course you can't really call procedure parameters in Visual Basic, but this gives you some idea of what must be going on behind the scenes. With a type library, the data structure for all function entries are initialized at compile time. If you hit an error such as a missing DLL or a missing function, you'll fail at compile time, not at run time. This is why you have to use Declare statements to iterate through processes.

If you understand how this works, you can use the knowledge to hack around DLL problems such as one encountered by a reader of the first edition of this book. He had a client DLL in a mystery directory that wasn't known until run time. The DLL wasn't in the windows directory, the system directory, or the path, so his Declare statements wouldn't work and he couldn't patch them at run time when he knew the directory. Look back at the pseudocode above to figure out the solution.

The problem is in the LoadLibrary call. But if you look up help on LoadLibrary, you'll see that it looks for the DLL in the current directory among other locations. The solution for this reader was this:

```
sCurDir = CurDir$
ChDir sDllDir
Call FirstFuncInDLL()
ChDir sCurDir
```

LoadLibrary is called only once, so the current directory matters for only the first DLL function.

Processes, Modules, Top Windows, Instances, and Threads

The Top Windows, Processes, and Modules list boxes of WinWatch show three different views of what's going on inside Windows. There is no Instances list box, but instances played a big part in the way the 16-bit version of WinWatch created and synchronized the other list boxes. From their starring role in the 16-

bit world, instances have been reduced to bit parts in 32-bit Windows. The up and coming stars of the 32-bit world are threads—although they haven't yet achieved much notoriety in Visual Basic and don't even merit their own list box in WinWatch.

To understand how all these parts work together, let's start with some definitions:

- A process is a running program, along with all the DLLs it uses. In 16-bit Windows, processes were called tasks, but this temporary aberration has gone the way of the difference between *you* and *thou*. Every process has a process ID that uniquely identifies it. You can pass a process ID to the OpenProcess API function to get a process handle. Most API functions that provide process information require a handle rather than an ID.

- A module is the code, data, and resources of an executable file that has been loaded into memory. Executable file can mean an EXE program or a DLL used by a program. Multiple processes can use the same module.

- A top window is a window providing the visual representation of a process. It's what we normally think of as the program, although processes can actually have multiple top windows or no top window.

- A thread follows a single path of execution through a program and is the fundamental unit scheduled by Windows. Every process has at least one thread, and in some languages you can start additional threads within a process. Visual Basic will start and manage separate threads in some kinds of ActiveX servers, but you as the programmer have little control over it. Put another way, processes don't really exist. They are just holders for threads, which do the real work.

- Instances no longer exist as separate entities with handles. The value we call an instance handle for historical reasons isn't really a handle—it's a pointer. And it probably wouldn't be used at all if compatibility weren't an issue. The term instance handle comes from 16-bit Windows, where an instance handle was tied to the data of a program. Each instance of the program had its own unique data but shared its code with other instances. In 32-bit Windows, each instance of a program has its own separate copy of both the code and the data, and the addresses within that copy are unintelligible to other instances. The function that returned an instance handle in 16-bit Windows (GetWindowLong with GWL_HINSTANCE) now returns the base address of the code, data, and resources of a program (the same thing the module is the handle of). You could do a lot of damage with such a pointer. Windows doesn't care if you do that damage to yourself, but it makes sure you can't use the pointer to trash another program.

The three list boxes help show how the different parts work together. Notice that when you select a different top window or process, the module list is regenerated. This is different from the 16-bit version of WinWatch, which displayed one global list of modules. In 32-bit Windows, each process has its own separate module list. You can't get a global module list (except by merging all the process module lists and eliminating duplicates).

A process usually has one top window, but it can have multiple top windows, no top windows, or invisible top windows. In Visual Basic terms, having one top window means having a startup form; having multiple top windows means starting more than one modal form from Sub Main; having no top windows means doing all processing from Sub Main; having invisible top windows means setting Visible to False on all top-level forms.

The process list—Windows 95 view

You can create a collection of the current processes by calling the CreateProcess-List function, which will return a CVector of CProcess objects. The CVector class is an expandable array in a class wrapper. See "CVector Implementation" in Chapter 4. CreateProcessList works completely different for Windows 95 than for Windows NT, but this wrapper function hides the details so that you don't have to worry about them.

When CreateProcessList is called under Windows 95, it calls ToolHelp32 functions to get a list of all the processes in the system. These functions will look familiar to those who used the 16-bit ToolHelp functions on which they are based. Here's the code for the first half of CreateProcessList:

```
Function CreateProcessList() As CVector
    Dim c As Long, f As Long, sName As String
    Dim vec As CVector, process As CProcess
    Set vec = New CVector

    If MUtility.IsNT = False Then
        ' Windows 95 uses ToolHelp32 functions
        Dim hSnap As Long, proc As PROCESSENTRY32
        ' Take a picture of current process list
        hSnap = CreateToolhelp32Snapshot(TH32CS_SNAPPROCESS, 0)
        If hSnap = hNull Then Exit Function
        proc.dwSize = Len(proc)
        ' Iterate through the processes
        f = Process32First(hSnap, proc)
        Do While f
            ' Put this process in vector and count it
            sName = MUtility.StrZToStr(proc.szExeFile)
            Set process = New CProcess
            process.Create proc.th32ProcessID, MUtility.GetFileBaseExt(sName)
            c = c + 1
```

```
        Set vec(c) = process
        f = Process32Next(hSnap, proc)
    Loop
```

The big difference from the old 16-bit versions is that in 32-bit mode you have to take a snapshot of the system. Because Windows is a multitasking system, a process can disappear at any moment—including the moment you try to examine it. The CreateToolhelp32Snapshot function stores a copy of the system as it exists at the moment. After that, the Process32First and Process32Next can be used to iterate through the stored process list. These functions are equivalent to the TaskFirst and TaskNext functions of the 16-bit TOOLHELP.DLL. The CProcess class simply holds all the process data common to both Windows 95 and Windows NT—not much. The Create method initializes its properties.

This code illustrates an iteration pattern that will soon become familiar:

1. Initialize the loop. In the example above, you create a snapshot and fill in the *dwSize* field to reassure Windows that you really have the right size structure. Details vary, but there's usually some initialization required.

2. Call Process32First (or Module32First or FindFirstFile or some other First function).

3. Test at the top of the loop to handle the unlikely case of no items in the list.

4. Do whatever the loop does. In this case, store the process name in a CVector.

5. Call Process32Next (or some other Next function) until no more items are left.

The Windows NT version gives us an inside view because we'll have to do by hand what the ToolHelp32 functions do automatically behind the scenes.

The process list—Windows NT view

When CreateProcessList is called under Windows NT, it calls the EnumProcesses function to get a list of all the processes in the system. PSAPI.DLL provides EnumProcesses and a variety of other functions for iterating through modules, threads, and more esoteric system data. This DLL isn't part of Windows NT, but it is a standard, redistributable tool provided with the Win32 Software Development Kit. It is also provided on the CD of this book. The DLL works by reading the Windows NT performance database, which is part of the registry. With previous versions of Windows NT, programmers had to read the performance data out of the registry directly. It's a very quirky operation that I wouldn't have attempted in Visual Basic. Enumerating processes with PSAPI.DLL is more complicated than calling the ToolHelp32 functions, but it's a lot easier than reading the weird registry format of the performance database.

Here's the Windows NT half of CreateProcessList:

```
Else
        ' Windows NT uses PSAPI functions
        Dim i As Long, iCur As Long, cRequest As Long, cGot As Long
        Dim aProcesses() As Long, hProcess As Long, hModule As Long
        cRequest = 96        ' Request in bytes for 24 processes
        Do
            ReDim aProcesses(0 To (cRequest / 4) - 1) As Long
            f = EnumProcesses(aProcesses(0), cRequest, cGot)
            If f = 0 Then Exit Function
            If cGot < cRequest Then Exit Do
            cRequest = cRequest * 2
        Loop
        cGot = cGot / 4      ' From bytes to processes
        ReDim Preserve aProcesses(0 To cGot - 1) As Long

        For i = 0 To cGot - 1
            hProcess = OpenProcess(PROCESS_QUERY_INFORMATION Or _
                              PROCESS_VM_READ, 0, _
                              aProcesses(i))
            ' Ignore processes that fail (probably no
            ' security rights)
            If hProcess = 0 Then GoTo NextFor
            ' Get first module only
            f = EnumProcessModules(hProcess, hModule, 4, c)
            If f = 0 Then GoTo NextFor
            sName = String$(cMaxPath, 0)
            c = GetModuleFileNameEx(hProcess, hModule, sName, cMaxPath)
            ' Put this process in vector and count it
            Set process = New CProcess
            process.Create aProcesses(i), Left$(sName, c)
            iCur = iCur + 1
            Set vec(iCur) = process
NextFor:
        Next
    End If
    Set CreateProcessList = vec
End Function
```

This code starts off by reading the process IDs for all the processes into an array. This is equivalent to calling CreateToolhelp32Snapshot under Windows 95. Unfortunately, there's no way to determine the appropriate size of the array except trial and error. I made my initial guess large enough to handle all my processes with one pass through the loop, but you might keep your system even busier than mine.

Once you've got process IDs, the next step is to convert them into handles with OpenProcess. This is a normal Win32 function supported by both versions of Windows. It's in the Windows API type library, so there's no need for a Declare statement. We'll see OpenProcess again in Chapter 11. Once you have a process handle, use it to get a module handle with EnumProcessModules—the function used later to build a module list. In this case, we need only the first module, which in Windows NT is always the main process module.

With the process and module in hand, it's time to get the module name with GetModuleFileNameEx. You might remember GetModuleFileName from 16-bit Windows. It still exists in 32-bit windows, but unlike the 16-bit version, it requires a real module handle rather than an instance handle, and even then it fails for all processes other than the current one. GetModuleFileNameEx works for any process, but it requires both the process and the module handle.

FLAME   The loop in CreateProcessList is a perfect illustration of why Basic programmers need the Continue statement enjoyed by C, C++, and Java programmers. Structured programming fanatics will object to my use of GoTo to skip to the next iteration when a process is discovered to be inaccessible, but two additional levels of nesting would be even more unstructured in my view.

The CreateProcessList function is complicated so that the RefreshProcessList procedure of WinWatch can be simple:

```
Private Sub RefreshProcessList()
    Dim processes As CVector, process As CProcess, i As Long
    Set processes = CreateProcessList
    SetRedraw lstProcess, False
    lstProcess.Clear
    For i = 1 To processes.Last
        lstProcess.AddItem processes(i).EXEName
        lstProcess.ItemData(lstProcess.NewIndex) = processes(i).id
    Next
    SetRedraw lstProcess, True
End Sub
```

The module list

The Modules list box in WinWatch lists each executable file currently running in the system. The main executable (EXE) appears in the list along with all the dynamic link library (DLL), font (FON), and custom control (OCX) files.

WinWatch calls the RefreshModuleList sub, which calls CreateModuleList to create the list of modules. These procedures look a lot like RefreshProcessList and CreateProcessList, so I won't show the code. The biggest difference is that both procedures take a process ID parameter so that they can create the module list for that process.

The top window list

The Top Windows list box in WinWatch lists each top-level window. Top-level windows are what you probably think of as Windows programs. In fact, the top-level window list in WinWatch usually will show the same programs as the taskbar in Windows NT 4 and Windows 95. My bet is that Windows refreshes the taskbar with code very similar to this:

```
Private Sub RefreshTopWinList()
    Dim sTitle As String, hWnd As Long

    SetRedraw lstTopWin, False
    lstTopWin.Clear
    ' Get first top-level window
    hWnd = GetWindow(GetDesktopWindow(), GW_CHILD)
    BugAssert hWnd <> hNull
    ' Iterate through remaining windows
    Do While hWnd <> hNull
        sTitle = WindowTextLineFromWnd(hWnd)
        ' Determine whether to display titled, visible, and unowned
        If IsVisibleTopWnd(hWnd, chkBlank, _
                            chkInvisible, chkOwned) Then
            lstTopWin.AddItem sTitle
            lstTopWin.ItemData(lstTopWin.NewIndex) = hWnd
        End If
        ' Get next child
        hWnd = GetWindow(hWnd, GW_HWNDNEXT)
    Loop
    SetRedraw lstTopWin, True
End Sub
```

The only thing the taskbar has that this code doesn't provide is small icons, and you'll learn how to add them in Chapter 8.

This iteration loop works a lot like the loops for Process32First and Module32-First, except that you pass the constants GW_HWNDCHILD and GW_HWNDNEXT to GetWindow. You could also say that it's like IterateChildWindows (from "Iterating the hard way" earlier in this chapter) without the recursion. You could do the same thing with EnumWindows and your own EnumWindowsProc function, but in this case I think GetWindow is simpler. Either way, GetWindow and EnumWindows are standard Win32 functions, so there's no need to jump through portability hoops as we did with processes and modules.

For each found window, you check to ensure that the window meets certain criteria—that it has a title, is visible, and is not owned by another window. Windows that meet all the criteria (as determined by IsVisibleTopWnd) have their titles and window handles placed in the list box. Here's how the decision is made:

```
Function IsVisibleTopWnd(hWnd As Long, _
              Optional IgnoreEmpty As Boolean = False, _
              Optional IgnoreVisible As Boolean = False, _
              Optional IgnoreOwned As Boolean = False) _
              As Boolean
    If IgnoreEmpty Or WindowTextFromWnd(hWnd) <> sEmpty Then
        If IgnoreVisible Or IsWindowVisible(hWnd) Then
            If IgnoreOwned Or GetWindow(hWnd, GW_OWNER) = hNull Then
            IsVisibleTopWnd = True
            End If
        End If
    End If
End Function
```

The code to fill the top window list uses the values of the Show check boxes to determine which windows to display:

```
If IsVisibleTopWnd(hWnd, chkBlank, _
                  chkInvisible, chkOwned) Then
    lstTopWin.AddItem sTitle
    lstTopWin.ItemData(lstTopWin.NewIndex) = hWnd
End If
```

If you experiment by checking the boxes, one at a time, you'll learn some interesting facts about Windows. For example, if you check the Show Invisible box, you'll learn that Windows maintains a lot of invisible windows behind the scenes. There are also a bunch of windows with blank titles. If you check the Show Owned box, you'll see lots of modeless dialog boxes. For example, if Visual Basic is running, you'll see that all your code windows are actually top-level windows owned by the Visual Basic window.

You might also want to check out RefreshAllLists. This procedure calls Refresh-TopWinList, RefreshProcessList, and RefreshFullWinList (more on that later) to update all the window information on the display. It is called when you load WinWatch, when you click the Refresh button, when you change any of the Show check boxes, or when you select a window that no longer exists.

Now that we've covered top-level windows, modules, and processes, we are ready to talk a little more about handles for windows, modules, and processes.

More About Handles and Process IDs

Almost everything in Windows has a *handle,* an integer value that identifies it. Every window has an HWND, every module has an HMODULE, and every 32-bit process has a process HANDLE. (Don't ask me why it isn't called an HPROCESS.) Each process consists of threads, each of which has a thread HANDLE.

For now, we're interested in three types of handles—window, process, and module. You could also throw in instance handle—except that it's really a pointer, not a handle. In addition, you often need to use process IDs. What you really want before you can do actual work in Visual Basic is the handle to a window, process, or module. Process IDs and instance handles are red herrings thrown in to confuse you. The only thing you can do with them is turn them into usable handles. In fact, turning one thing into another is a common task. Table 6-4 shows a grid of conversion functions:

WE HAVE

	Process ID	Process Handle	Window Handle	Executable Name
Process ID	N/A	Can't go back	ProcIDFromWnd	Can't do it
Process Handle	ProcFromProcID	N/A	ProcFromWnd	Can't do it
Module Handle	ModFromProcID	ModFromProc	ModFromWnd	ModFromExeName
Executable Name	ExeNameFromProcID	Can't do it	ExeNameFromWnd	N/A

(Left margin label: WE WANT)

Table 6-4. *Handle and process ID conversion functions.*

There are a few points worth noting here. There is no row for *window handle* and no column for *module handle.* You can't work back from any of the other handles to get a window handle because any process or module can have multiple windows. You can't start with a module and figure out its process or window because it's at the bottom of the chain.

Some of the conversion procedures are trivial wrappers for API functions. For example, here's how you get a process ID from a window handle:

```
Function ProcIDFromWnd(ByVal hWnd As Long) As Long
    Dim idProc As Long
    Call GetWindowThreadProcessId(hWnd, idProc)
    ProcIDFromWnd = idProc
End Function
```

A process ID isn't much use in itself. Most API functions that control or return information about processes take a process handle. Here's how you get one from a process ID:

```
Function ProcFromProcID(idProc As Long)
    ProcFromProcID = OpenProcess(PROCESS_QUERY_INFORMATION Or _
                                 PROCESS_VM_READ, 0, idProc)
End Function
```

The ProcFromProcID function passes two constant flags to OpenProcess that happen to be the ones that I and others have discovered, through trial and error, to be the most convenient for getting common information about processes. But some applications might want to modify process data or do various other operations that would require different flags. You can call OpenProcess multiple times to get different handles for different purposes from the same process ID. We'll see other uses for process handles in Chapter 11.

Generally, you'll do real work with process handles. There's not much reason to use module handles. A program like WinWatch is the exception. In those rare cases when you need the name of a running program other than your own, the module handle is the only way to get it. The module handle can also be used to access resources (see Chapter 8). The problem is that there's no easy way to get a module handle. The only Win32 function I know of that returns one is GetModuleHandle, but it requires that you know the module name. If you knew that, you wouldn't need the module handle. You must resort to the OS-specific ToolHelp32 and PSAPI functions described earlier.

Here's another example of a translation function that is a simple API wrapper. This one gets an instance handle from a window:

```
Function InstFromWnd(ByVal hWnd As Long) As Long
    BugAssert hWnd <> hNull
    InstFromWnd = GetWindowLong(hWnd, GWL_HINSTANCE)
End Function
```

Very simple, and very useful—in 16-bit Windows. Unfortunately, an instance handle isn't worth much in 32-bit windows because, as noted before, it's not really a handle. It's the base address of the module. In fact, if you trace through the process and module lists, you'll find that the base module address often has exactly the same value as the module handle. Unfortunately, you'll find enough exceptions to make this trend unreliable. Technically, you can get almost anything from an instance handle that you can get from a process handle or ID, but you probably don't want to because the technique is complicated and inefficient. You loop through all the processes in the system. For each one, you compare the base address to your instance handle. When you find a match, you've got the right process and you can use its ID just as if you'd started with that. But you could have gotten the process ID directly from the window and skipped the instance altogether. So that's the last I'll say about instance handles.

Getting the name of an executable file was easy in 16-bit windows. You could get the instance handle from the window and pass it to the GetModuleFileName function. You were supposed to pass a module handle to GetModuleFileName, but an instance handle would do because Windows knew how to find the module from the instance. When Win32 functions say they want a module handle, they mean it. But even with a module handle, there's no portable technique for getting an EXE name. The workaround is on the following page.

```
Function ExePathFromProcID(idProc As Long) As String
    If Not IsNT Then
        Dim process As PROCESSENTRY32, hSnap As Long, f As Long
        hSnap = CreateToolhelp32Snapshot(TH32CS_SNAPPROCESS, 0)
        If hSnap = hNull Then Exit Function
        process.dwSize = Len(process)
        f = Process32First(hSnap, process)
        Do While f
            If process.th32ProcessID = idProc Then
                ExePathFromProcID = StrZToStr(process.szExeFile)
                Exit Function
            End If
            f = Process32Next(hSnap, process)
        Loop
    Else
        Dim s As String, c As Long
        s = String$(cMaxPath, 0)
        c = GetModuleFileNameEx(ProcFromProcID(idProc), _
                            ModFromProcID(idProc), s, cMaxPath)
        If c Then ExePathFromProcID = Left$(s, c)
    End If
End Function
```

The Windows NT version is simple. The PSAPI DLL provides an extended version of the old GetModuleFileName function. You need both the module and process handles, but they're easy enough to get. The Windows 95 section is more difficult. There's no GetModuleFileNameEx as there is in PSAPI, and there's no ModuleFindName as there was in the old 16-bit TOOLHELP DLL. You have to do it the hard way—by looping through all the processes until you find the one with a matching ID.

Unique process IDs

What can you do with a process ID? Two things. You can pass it to OpenProcess to get a process handle, or you can use it for the same thing Windows uses it for—a unique identifier of the process. A process handle can't serve this purpose because there might be multiple handles to the same process. WinWatch stores process IDs in the *ItemData* array of the Processes list box. It stores top window handles in the *ItemData* array of the Top Windows list box. Since it's possible to get a process ID from a top window handle and vice versa, WinWatch can use the *ItemData* information to keep all the list boxes in sync.

Whenever a user clicks on any of the list boxes or takes any other action that could change their contents, the UpdateDisplay procedure is called. This procedure is the heart of WinWatch logic where all exceptions and special cases are worked out. I'm not particularly proud of this procedure, but I can say it's more structured than the baling wire code that held previous versions of Win-Watch together.

I'll let you study UpdateDisplay on your own, but I would like to make one minor point about the event procedures that call it. They use a module-level *fInClick* flag to protect agains circular references. For example, the *lstTopWin-_Click* procedure calls UpdateDisplay, which might set the ListIndex property of *lstTopwin*, which would call *lstTopWin_Click*, which would call UpdateDisplay, which might set the ListIndex property of *lstTopWin*, and so on. You have the potential for an infinite call cycle, or, depending on the program logic, perhaps just one extra call. Instead the *lstTopWin_Click* procedure checks the module-level *fInClick* flag and exits immediately if it is True. If it's False, the procedure sets *fInClick* to True and then calls UpdateDisplay. You might want to use a similar strategy in your programs to guard against recursive Click events.

Handling Multiple Instances

The discussion of Windows so far in this chapter might have enlightened you, but it probably hasn't put much bread on your table. Here's a more practical problem.

What happens if you try to start two copies of the same program? Some programs, such as Calculator, don't mind at all and will keep starting copies until you run out of memory. Others quit after displaying a message box saying that you can run only one copy. Still others, such as Microsoft Exchange, reactivate the current copy every time you try to start a new copy. For every program you write, you need to think about this issue and choose a strategy.

If it's OK to run multiple copies, you don't need to do anything. That's the default. If you want to run only one copy, terminating each additional attempt with an error message, you don't need to do much. Just put the following in Form_Load:

```
If App.PrevInstance Then
    MsgBox "You cannot start more than one copy"
    End
End If
```

This technique has one problem—App.PrevInstance is always False in the Visual Basic environment. You can launch multiple versions of Visual Basic running the same program, but each will think that it's the only one. You'll have difficulty debugging complicated code that uses the PrevInstance property. You can't test it in the environment because it won't behave the same, but you can't easily test it outside the environment because you don't have a debugger.

A bigger problem with putting up an error message in this situation is that it's rarely the right thing to do. It's much better to change the focus to the first copy and terminate the second copy. On the surface, it doesn't seem to be hard to accomplish this in Visual Basic. The technique on the following page (from ALLABOUT.FRM) will work for many programs.

```
If App.PrevInstance Then
    Dim sTitle As String
    ' Save my title
    sTitle = Me.Caption
    ' Change my title bar so I won't activate myself
    Me.Caption = Hex$(Me.hWnd)
    ' Activate other instance
    AppActivate sTitle
    ' Terminate myself
    End
End If
```

Is changing the caption before activating the other instance a neat trick or what? This works great for programs that always have the same title, but what if the other instance has a different title? Notepad's title contains the name of the current file. So does the Visual Basic environment. In fact, the Windows interface standard specifies that any window representing a document should have the document name in the title. But if you don't know the document name, you can't call AppActivate.

WinWatch handles multiple copies the hard way. It calls the GetFirstInstWnd function to find out whether there is another instance. If so, it activates that window by calling the SetForegroundWindow API function. The call looks like this:

```
Dim hWndOther As Long
hWndOther = GetFirstInstWnd(Me.hWnd)
If hWndOther <> hNull Then
    ' Uncomment this line for debugging
    'MsgBox "Activating first instance"
    SetForegroundWindow hWndOther
    End
End If
```

The GetFirstInstWnd function does the actual work. It works by looping through all the top windows until it finds one that has a different process ID, but the same module name. That's the duplicate. The code (in MODTOOL.BAS) looks like this:

```
Function GetFirstInstWnd(hWndMe As Long) As Long
    Dim hWndYou As Long, idMe As Long, sExeMe As String

    ' Get my own process ID and executable name
    idMe = MWinTool.ProcIDFromWnd(hWndMe)
    sExeMe = ExeNameFromWnd(hWndMe)
    ' Get first sibling to start iterating top-level windows
    hWndYou = GetWindow(hWndMe, GW_HWNDFIRST)
    Do While hWndYou <> hNull
        ' Ignore if process ID of target is same
```

```
        If idMe <> MWinTool.ProcIDFromWnd(hWndYou) Then
            ' Ignore if module name is different
            If sExeMe = ExeNameFromWnd(hWndYou) Then
                ' Return first with same module, different process
                GetFirstInstWnd = hWndYou
                Exit Function
            End If
        End If
        ' Get next sibling
        hWndYou = GetWindow(hWndYou, GW_HWNDNEXT)
    Loop
End Function
```

This technique works for most applications, but it's not infallible. Your program might have multiple top-level windows, and the first one returned might not be the one you want to activate. That's why MODTOOL.BAS also contains the GetAllInstWnd function, which returns a Collection of all the window handles of other instances. GetAllInstWnd enables you to follow one of Joe Hacker's favorite design rules: "If in doubt, let the user decide." You could create a dialog box form with a list box of existing instances. Let the user decide whether to cancel the request, launch a new instance, or activate an existing one. This would be an excellent way to handle the new multiple instance model that is becoming popular as an alternative to the Multiple Document Interface—each document is handled by a separate independent instance of a small program rather than by a separate MDI window of a large program.

WARNING Terminating a duplicate instance is one of those rare cases when you should actually use the End statement. Although the name sounds harmless, End is actually more like an Abort statement that means stop by any means even if it can't do normal cleanup. Experienced Visual Basic programmers terminate their programs by unloading all the active forms. Normally, all it takes is an Unload Me statement in the main form. But if you're trying to terminate in the main Form_Load, there is, by definition, nothing to unload. So the rule is simple: Never use End except in Form_Load. In the first edition of this book, I violated this rule by providing a procedure that looked for a duplicate instance and terminated that instance with an End statement inside the procedure. I got a rude surprise when I tried to put that procedure in the VBCore component. Visual Basic won't let you use the End statement in a DLL or a control. The GetFirstInstWnd function can be in a DLL because it returns the other instance rather than trying to take action about it. This is a more flexible structure anyway. The caller of GetFirstInstWnd can decide what it wants to do about the duplicate instance.

Sending and Receiving Messages

Messages make Windows tick, but you wouldn't know it from studying the Visual Basic documentation. Take keyboard events. If you press the B key while a Visual Basic text box has the focus, Windows sends WM_KEYDOWN, WM_CHAR, and WM_KEYUP messages to the text box. But your Visual Basic program sees these messages as the KeyDown, KeyPress, and KeyUp events.

In Visual Basic, most events are caused by Windows messages. Sometimes you'll find a one-to-one mapping, as with the keyboard messages just mentioned. A Form_Load event, however, doesn't correspond directly to a specific message. If you're curious and you happen to have a C or a Pascal compiler, you can use a message filter utility (such as Microsoft's Spy++) to see exactly which messages are being sent to which windows. You'll get bored fast watching these C messages. A Visual Basic event spy might be more interesting. You should be qualified to write one by the time you finish this book.

Hardcore Basic programmers can go beyond the events Visual Basic provides and handle their own messages. Sending messages is relatively easy to do with Windows API calls. Receiving messages, however, is a more difficult problem. It used to require a message capture component (and some programmers might still find this easier), but starting with Visual Basic version 5, you can also receive messages by using the AddressOf operator to redirect them to your own window procedures.

Sending Messages

To understand the point of messages, let's look briefly at how you would write programs for Windows in Visual Basic if you had to write them from scratch the way you do in C. The main routine in every Visual Basic program would look something like this:

```
Dim msg as TMessage
Dim hForm As Long, hControl As Long

hForm = CreateWindow("Form", iFormAttr, ...)
hControl = CreateWindow("Control", iCtrlAttr, ...)

' Get next message from Windows queue
Do While GetMessage(msg)
    ' Send message to appropriate window
    TranslateMessage(msg)
    DispatchMessage(msg)
Loop
End
```

Fortunately, Visual Basic creates all the windows it needs—based on the forms you draw and the attributes you set rather than on the code you write—and then keeps reading messages and sending them out to the windows until it gets a WM_QUIT message. WM_QUIT is the only message that causes GetMessage to return False and terminate the loop (and the program). The messages come from the user interface (the keyboard and the mouse, for instance), from messages sent by the system to the windows, from messages sent by the windows to the system, and from messages sent from one window to another.

Meanwhile, the created windows are gobbling up all the messages sent to them and taking the appropriate actions. Each window has a routine (called a *window procedure*) that processes messages. If window procedures were written in Visual Basic (and now they can be), a typical one might look like this:

```
Function WindowProc(ByVal hWnd As Long, ByVal iMessage As Long, _
                    ByVal wParam As Long, lParam As Long) As Long
    ' Set default return value
    WindowProc = 0
    ' Handle messages
    Select Case iMessage
    Case WM_DOSOMETHING
        DoIt "Whatever it does", wParam, lParam
    Case WM_ASKSOMETHING
        WindowProc = CheckIt("Tell me, please", wParam, lParam)
    Case Else
        ' Call default window procedure
        WindowProc = DefWindowProc(hWnd, iMessage, wParam, lParam)
    End Select
End Function
```

Every form and control in your program (don't confuse me with exceptions) has one of these window procedures. Windows and Visual Basic communicate with them using the SendMessage function, and you can use it, too.

The SendMessage function

The Windows API documentation shows the following syntax:

```
LRESULT SendMessage(
    HWND hWnd,          // Handle of destination window
    UINT Msg,           // Message to send
    WPARAM wParam,      // First message parameter
    LPARAM lParam);     // Second message parameter
```

The *hWnd* parameter is the window to which the message is sent. The *Msg* parameter is the message number—which is usually a constant such as LB_FINDSTRING or WM_COPY. The WPARAM and LPARAM types are actually aliases for 32-bit integers (Long in Visual Basic). The *wParam* and *lParam* parameters differ for each message, as does the return value; you must look up the specific message to see what they mean. Often, *wParam* or the return value is ignored.

The *lParam* parameter is particularly interesting. It is a 32-bit integer, which happens to be the size of a pointer, and this value is often used to pass a pointer to a string or a UDT. In other words, *lParam* is typeless. In Visual Basic, that means that the SendMessage declaration contains the As Any type. Alternatively, you can define several type-safe declarations with different aliases.

You need only one SendMessage Declare statement to cover all your bases:

```
Declare Function SendMessage Lib "USER32" Alias "SendMessageA" ( _
    ByVal hWnd As Long, ByVal Msg As Long, _
    wParam As Any, lParam As Any) As Long
```

Using this Declare you can pass any value by reference. To pass a String or a Long by value, you must give the ByVal keyword in the call. Sometimes you might even have to pack two Integers into a Long and pass the Long by Value. Or you might receive, by reference or in the return value, two Integers packed in a Long. Notice that both *wParam* and *lParam* are passed by reference because either might take a reference argument.

Of course, the Declare only works for ANSI strings, and I try to make all my code portable to Unicode in anticipation of the day when ANSI strings fade to just a bad memory. The Windows API type library has equivalent entries, but for reasons described in "Unicode Versus Basic" in Chapter 2, you can't use the type library equivalent of As Any (void *) to represent strings. Therefore, the type library provides a separate SendMessageStr entry that takes a string *lParam*. It's equivalent to the following Declare statement:

```
Declare Function SendMessageStr Lib "USER32" Alias "SendMessageA"
    (ByVal hWnd As Long, ByVal Msg As Long, _
    ByVal wParam As Long, ByVal lParam As String) As Long
```

Notice that SendMessageStr takes a ByVal Long as its *wParam* parameter despite the theoretical possibility that some message might take a ByRef *wParam* and a string *lParam*. I checked and there is no such message. If you find one, sue me.

I also provide a SendMessageVal that you can use in place of SendMessage with ByVal in the call.

```
Declare Function SendMessageVal Lib "USER32" Alias "SendMessageA"
    (ByVal hWnd As Long, ByVal Msg As Long, _
    ByVal wParam As Long, ByVal lParam As Any) As Long
```

Let's look at an example. Assume you have a multiline text control named *txtEditor*. You can request the selection offset and length with these lines:

```
iPos = txtEditor.SelStart
iLen = txtEditor.SelLength
```

In order to get this information, Visual Basic sends the EM_GETSEL message to the txtEditor window procedure with a call such as the following:

```
Dim iStart As Long, iEnd As Long
Call SendMessage(txtEditor.hWnd, EM_GETSEL, iStart, iEnd)
```

If the window procedure for TextBox controls were written in Visual Basic, it would handle this message in a Select Case block:

```
Case EM_GETSEL
    ' Put offsets of start and end into variables
    wParam = iStartSel
    lParam = iEndSel
```

Visual Basic returns the start of the selection as the SelStart property. It subtracts the start of the selection from the end of the selection and returns the result as the SelLength property. The Visual Basic internal code looks something like this:

```
SelStart = iStart
SelLength = iEnd - SelStart
```

If you have time to burn, you can do this yourself by calling SendMessage instead of using the SelStart and SelLength properties.

What if you want to undo the last editing change? Simple—just call the Undo method. Unfortunately, the TextBox control doesn't have an Undo method. But you've seen it in Notepad; Windows must have an Undo message. Sure enough, if you check the Windows API documentation, you'll find an EM_UNDO message. You can undo the last editing change with this simple statement:

```
Call SendMessage(txtEditor.hWnd, EM_UNDO, ByVal 0&, ByVal 0&)
```

You could also do this with the SendMessageVal alias:

```
Call SendMessageVal(txtEditor.hWnd, EM_UNDO, 0&, 0&)
```

Just to show all the options, you could also use this statement:

```
Call SendMessage(txtEditor.hWnd, EM_UNDO, 0&, 0&)
```

This works, but perhaps not the way you expect. SendMessage takes ByRef parameters, which means it passes the addresses of variables. But a literal constant doesn't have an address. Visual Basic fakes it by creating temporary variables, stuffing constant zeros into them, and passing the addresses of the temporaries. Don't make your programs do this extra work.

This is just the beginning of what you can do with messages. You can check whether there's anything to undo. You can get the number of lines of text, the current line, or the current column. You can set the indent spacing for tab characters. You can do many other editing tasks that Visual Basic doesn't support directly. We'll try many of these editing operations with Edwina the editor, introduced in Chapter 9.

The same principle holds for other controls such as list boxes and combo boxes: Visual Basic supports the most common operations through methods, events, and properties; you must handle others with SendMessage.

Looking up list box items

The Visual Basic ListBox control (and related controls such as ComboBox and FileListBox) provide no direct way to look up the index of an item from its name. There is a workaround using the Text property (see "Collection Methods and Properties," Chapter 11), but it's not as flexible as you might like.

The Windows API provides a way to look up items by name using the LB_FIND-STRING message. It takes only one line of code to send this message and just a few more lines to put the whole thing in a neat little wrapper:

```
#If fComponent Then
Function LookupItem(ctl As Object, sItem As String) As Long
#Else
Function LookupItem(ctl As Control, sItem As String) As Long
#End If
    If TypeName(ctl) = "ComboBox" Then
        LookupItem = SendMessageStr(ctl.hWnd, CB_FINDSTRING, -1&, sItem)
    Else
        LookupItem = SendMessageStr(ctl.hWnd, LB_FINDSTRING, -1&, sItem)
    End If
End Function
```

The key to this code is the LB_FINDSTRING message constant (and the CB_FINDSTRING message for combo boxes). The Windows API documentation tells you that the *wParam* value contains either the index of the item just before the item where the search should start or −1 to search the entire list. The *lParam* value contains a pointer to the case-insensitive string being sought. You can pass a partial string so that "BIG" will find "BigDeal" or "Big Brother", whichever comes first. The return value is the index of the found item (or −1 if none is found). Windows also provides an LB_FINDSTRINGEXACT (and CB_FINDSTRINGEXACT) message for looking up the full case-sensitive string.

Notice that my LookupItem function uses conditional compilation to receive either a Control parameter or an Object parameter, depending on whether the function is located in a component. I want LookupItem to work with any ListBox-like control, so its first parameter can't be more type-specific. I'd also like to avoid the late-binding penalties that come with the Object type but, unfortunately,

Visual Basic won't let you define a Control parameter in a public DLL procedure. Because this function allows you to pass in any control, be sure not to pass one whose underlying Windows control doesn't support the LB_FINDSTRING (or CB_FINDSTRING) message. To be safe, this function should use error trapping to trap message failure, but I compromised. Perhaps you shouldn't.

Before I learned about the LB_FINDSTRING message, I looked up items with a linear search. That's still the way you have to look up items in the ItemData array. Visual Basic implements its ItemData feature using the LB_GETITEMDATA and LB_SETITEMDATA messages, but it doesn't provide an LB_FINDITEMDATA message. You have to do it the hard way:

```
#If fComponent Then
Function LookupItemData(ctl As Object, data As Long) As Integer
#Else
Function LookupItemData(ctl As Control, data As Long) As Integer
#End If
    Dim i As Integer
    LookupItemData = -1
    For i = 0 To ctl.ListCount - 1
        If data = ctl.ItemData(i) Then
            LookupItemData = i
            Exit Function
        End If
    Next
End Function
```

Disabling display during updates

Programs such as WinWatch that update many list items at one time need some way to quiet down the display so that the list box isn't redrawn every time an item is added. I know of three ways to do this:

- Set *Visible = False* while adding items, and then restore *Visible = True* when the additions are complete.

- Call the LockWindowUpdate API function when adding items, and turn off the lock when finished.

- Send the WM_SETREDRAW message with the *wParam* False when adding items; when you've finished, send it again with *wParam* True.

You can experiment with these three solutions by setting different compile-time constants in the RefreshModuleList sub and observing the difference. If you're willing to take my word for it, the code for the winning entry is on the following page.

```
#If fComponent Then
Sub SetRedraw(ctl As Object, f As Boolean)
#Else
Sub SetRedraw(ctl As Control, f As Boolean)
#End If
    Call SendMessageVal(ctl.hWnd, WM_SETREDRAW, -CLng(f), 0&)
End Sub
```

Notice how the flag parameter is a Boolean, but the call converts it to a Long and negates it. This is because the WM_SETREDRAW message is extremely picky. It wants a C style TRUE (1) or FALSE (0). Other values, such as a Visual Basic style True (–1), might not work. The Boolean type converts any weird value you might receive (such as 237) to True or False. The CLng conversion converts the True or False to –1 or 0. The negation converts –1 or 0 to 1 or 0. Ugly. Windows should accept zero and nonzero like everybody else.

Receiving Messages

Visual Basic controls and forms constantly receive messages and translate them into events or attributes according to instructions in the messages. For example, let's say that you used the Menu Editor to define a File menu named mnuFile with items mnuNew, mnuOpen, and so on. When the user of your application chooses Open, the mnuOpen_Click event occurs, and the code in the mnuOpen_Click event procedure executes.

But what really happens behind the scenes? Windows gets a signal from the mouse port that a click has occurred at a certain screen location (or possibly it discovers that the Alt, F, and O keys have been pressed consecutively). Windows checks its internal information to find out which window owns that location and discovers that the click occurred on the Open item of the File menu. It then sends a slew of messages related to this event, culminating in a WM_COMMAND message with the ID number of the Open item.

Meanwhile, the window procedure for the form containing the menu has a Select Case block similar to the one shown here:

```
Select Case iMessage
Case WM_COMMAND
    Select Case wParam
    Case IDM_NEW
        mnuNew_Click
    Case IDM_OPEN
        mnuOpen_Click
    ⋮
    End Select
⋮
End Select
```

This code intercepts the WM_COMMAND message, and the mnuOpen_Click event starts executing. In short, Windows sends messages; Visual Basic turns them into events.

Now consider the system menu. By default, Visual Basic puts the standard system menu on all forms whose ControlBox property is set to True. When a user chooses from a system menu, Windows sends the WM_SYSCOMMAND message to the window (form). The window procedure for a form works this way:

```
' Set default return value
WindowProc = 0&
' Handle messages
Select Case iMessage
Case WM_DOHOPEVENT
    Form.HopEvent_Click
Case WM_GETJUMPDATA
    Form.JumpData = wParam
Case Else
    ' Let default window procedure handle the rest
    WindowProc = DefWindowProc(hWnd, iMessage, wParam, lParam)
End Select
```

Because the WM_SYSCOMMAND message isn't handled by a specific Case statement, it falls through to the Case Else statement to be handled by DefWindowProc. The default window procedure knows how to do the standard operations—move, size, minimize, maximize, close, and switch to—which are the same for any window.

But what if you add an About item to the system menu? Visual Basic won't help you do this, but neither will it stand in your way. It's a simple matter to add an item to the system menu using Windows API calls:

```
Const IDM_ABOUT = 1010
Dim hSysMenu As Long
' Get handle of system menu
hSysMenu = GetSystemMenu(hWnd, 0&)
' Append separator and menu item with ID IDM_ABOUT
Call AppendMenu(hSysMenu, MF_SEPARATOR, 0&, 0&)
Call AppendMenu(hSysMenu, MF_STRING, IDM_ABOUT, "About...")
```

When the user selects this new menu item, Windows sends a WM_SYS-COMMAND message with the IDM_ABOUT value to the window procedure. Having no clue what to do with this message, the window procedure passes it off to DefWindowProc, which also hasn't a clue. Your message rides off into the sunset.

Your own window procedure

Writing your own window procedure and hooking it up to a form or control window is a lot easier than juggling knives, but not much safer. The technique is known as subclassing a window. You simply replace the existing window procedure with your own. Usually your window procedure will identify and handle some specific messages, but defer other messages back to the original window procedure.

So let's start by throwing a few knives. After we've caught them, we'll look at some of the bad things that could have happened had we missed (as I did when writing this code). Here's a window procedure for capturing the About menu item that we put on the system menu in the last section. You can see this code in TSYSMENU.VBP:

```
Public procOld As Long
Public Const IDM_ABOUT As Long = 1010


Public Function SysMenuProc(ByVal hWnd As Long, ByVal iMsg As Long, _
                            ByVal wParam As Long, lParam As Long) As Long
    ' Ignore everything but system commands
    If iMsg = WM_SYSCOMMAND Then
        ' Check for one special menu item
        If wParam = IDM_ABOUT Then
            MsgBox "Callback Test"
            Exit Function
        End If
    End If
    ' Let old window procedure handle other messages
    SysMenuProc = CallWindowProc(procOld, hWnd, iMsg, wParam, lParam)
End Function
```

This code goes in TSYSMENU.BAS. You might prefer to keep everything in the form module, but you can't. Windows procedures, like other callback functions, must be in standard modules so that there will be one and only one copy. Anything that must be accessed by other modules, such as forms, must be public. This issue was summarized in "The Ultimate Hack: Procedure Pointers" in Chapter 2.

The code that attaches the window procedure can be in any module. This code is in the Form_Load procedure of TSYSMENU.FRM:

```
' Install system menu window procedure
procOld = SetWindowLong(hWnd, GWL_WNDPROC, AddressOf SysMenuProc)
```

Here's how you restore the old window procedure in Form_Unload:

```
Call SetWindowLong(hWnd, GWL_WNDPROC, procOld)
```

The first SetWindowLong installs the address of SysMenuProc as the window procedure for the form. Visual Basic has already provided a window procedure for the form, but we're replacing it with our new window procedure. At the same time, we store the address of the old window procedure in *procOld*. Notice that the *procOld* variable is public so that it can be accessed by either the form or the window procedure. The form needs this variable to restore the old window procedure in Form_Unload. The window procedure needs it to pass off most of the work.

As soon as our window procedure, SysMenuProc, is installed, it starts getting messages at a furious pace—perhaps hundreds per second. But we care about only one message—WM_SYSCOMMAND. If you look up WM_SYSCOMMAND, you'll see that it responds not only to system menu commands, but also to other menu commands, to accelerator commands, and to other situations that don't concern us. But we care about only one command—IDM_ABOUT. This is the menu ID that we installed for our new About item in the last section. We could have a Select statement here and handle other menu commands, such as SC_MOVE, SC_SIZE, SC_MAXIMIZE, and SC_MINIMIZE. But we don't want to. The form already knows how to do that stuff. If it's our menu item, we handle it and exit. Otherwise, we pass it on.

The CallWindowProc API function lets us pass control back to the original window procedure, which knows how to do normal form processing. We let that procedure do its thing, and we receive its return value so that we can return it to whoever subclassed us. Keep in mind that you aren't the only programmer in the world who might be subclassing your window. There might be a whole chain of subclassers, and you had better be a polite member of the chain.

Notice that the *lParam* parameter of the window procedure is ByRef, while all the others are ByVal. This is because the CallWindowProc API function is defined in the Windows API type library as taking a void * (equivalent to As Any by reference). So if CallWindowProc is receiving ByRef, then SysMenuProc had better also receive ByRef. You could change SysMenuProc to receive *lParam* ByVal, but if you did, you'd have to change how you pass *lParam* to Call-WindowProc. For example, you could call like this:

```
SysMenuProc = CallWindowProc(procOld, hWnd, iMsg, wParam, ByVal lParam)
```

Either way works for SysMenuProc because the one menu message it handles doesn't use *lParam*. The important thing is that you have to pass on exactly the same bits you receive. If you get your types mixed up, you'll probably crash or hang instantly. You won't be able to step through your code and find the bug. The compiler won't warn you. You won't be able to use Debug.Print. You won't pass Go. You won't collect $200. You won't even go to jail. If you try to pass garbage on the stack several hundred times a second, you won't be forgiven. I didn't learn this from a textbook.

Other subclassing models

The SysMenuProc handles one variation of one message and passes processing of everything else on to the subclassed window procedure. This is a common model, but certainly not the only one. Here are some other scenarios:

- Let the subclassed window procedure handle your messages, and then you do additional processing on them.

- After you process your messages, let the subclassed window procedure do additional processing.

- Take over everything. Handle all messages except generic windows messages that you can pass on to the DefWindowProc API function. You'd better be pretty sure of yourself before you cut lower windows out of the subclassing chain.

- Create your own window. First register a new class with RegisterClass. Write a window procedure for windows of the class. Finally, create a window of that class with CreateWindow. Your window procedure must handle all known messages and pass others on to DefWindowProc. This is how C programmers create Windows programs, and now, thanks to the AddressOf operator, it is possible to make Visual Basic programming just as hard as C programming. It reminds me of how macho assembly language programmers used to write tiny Windows programs in assembler to show how wimpy C programmers were. Generally, I think this is a really bad idea, but there's a time for everything. I know of programmers who create ActiveX controls this way. Rather than delegating to an existing control or using the UserControl surface as the window of their control, they create a control window from scratch. That's a little too hardcore for me, but to each her or his own.

Other messages, other events

The same principle applies to lots of other messages. You can trap any event, whether Visual Basic helps you or not. Here are some ideas:

- Intercept menu messages such as WM_INITMENU and WM_MENU-SELECT so that you can display menu help on a status bar.

- Hit-test with WM_NCHITTEST so that you can display balloon help or perform other operations when the mouse passes certain areas.

- Intercept keyboard or menu events from windows outside your program. You could implement macros this way.

- Intercept setting changes with WM_WININICHANGE, WM_FONT-CHANGE, or similar change messages.

- Check WM_ENTERIDLE to find a good time to do busywork in the background.

Visual Basic already handles most important messages, but you can always find others to experiment with.

Encapsulating Message Traps

Now you know how to subclass windows, but there's something seriously wrong with the model so far. It's missing encapsulation. There are lots of common problems that can be solved by capturing messages, but do you really want to write separate code for every possible message? Of course not. You want to modularize. You want to write classes that make subclassing safe, easy, and preferably invisible. There are two ways to do it.

One way to make subclassing more modular is by writing a generic subclassing control or component. Ed Staffin's Message Blaster control and Matt Curland's callback component are provided on the CD for this book (as they were in the first edition). You can use either of these tools to make subclassing easy and generic, but you do have to ship the extra component with your program. MessageBlaster has one big advantage over the AddressOf technique. It can handle messages between processes. Now that's a hardcore accomplishment for which Ed has my admiration. But I've never subclassed a window outside my current process in a real project.

Personally, I think a generic subclassing control is the wrong way to modularize most projects. Subclassing is difficult, messy, and dangerous—no matter what the tools. This brings me to the second, better method of subclassing, which is wrapping different subclass tasks in classes or controls. For example, assume you want to put new items on the system menu and then handle clicks on them. You can do this at three levels:

- Write specific subclassing code and a window procedure for every program and window that needs to monitor its system menu items. That's what we did a few pages ago.

- Use a subclassing control or other component such as Message Blaster to do the same thing.

- Write a CSysMenu class that can add items to any system menu. Give it events that can be received and implemented by any client.

I prefer the third approach for most subclassing tasks. It concentrates on the solution, not the problem. A programmer who wants to handle system menus wants to worry about item titles and menu events, not about the subclassing chain and window procedures.

There's only one problem with this approach. Subclassing isn't difficult to program; it's just hard to encapsulate. You have to do things that Visual Basic ought to be doing for you. But if it won't, you'll just have to do them yourself.

The SubTimer component provides tools for encapsulating subclasses easily and with relative safety. It also provides two classes that use those tools. The CSys-Menu class encapsulates the system menu code we saw earlier. The CMinMax class encapsulates the WM_GETMINMAXINFO message, which controls the position and size of maximized windows, and the minimum and maximum size of normal windows.

I had to write at least two classes to test my subclassing code because the tricky part of encapsulating subclassed windows is to allow the tools to work for as many messages and as many windows as the user wants. The Test Messages program uses the CSysMenu and CMinMax classes to handle two different messages. It also has a New Form button that clones the form in order to test using both classes with multiple windows. Figure 6-3 shows the test program in action.

Using the CSysMenu Class

The CSysMenu class allows clients to easily add system menus to their forms. The TMESSAGE.FRM form illustrates the technique. You simply declare a CSys-Menu object using the WithEvents syntax. You define the system menu items you want to handle and you write a menu event handler.

Let's look at each part of the code and then review how they fit together. Here are the data declarations:

```
Private WithEvents sysmenu As CSysMenu
Private idAbout As Long
Private idAround As Long
```

You set up the menu items in Form_Load with the following code:

```
' Initialize system menu
Set sysmenu = New CSysMenu
sysmenu.Create hWnd
Call sysmenu.AddItem("-")    ' Separator
idAbout = sysmenu.AddItem("About...")
idAround = sysmenu.AddItem("Around...")
```

The *sysmenu* declaration creates an event, which looks like this in the sample:

```
Private Sub sysmenu_MenuClick(sItem As String, ByVal ID As Long)
    Select Case ID
    Case idAbout
        MsgBox "About time"
    Case idAround
        MsgBox "Around and around"
    End Select
End Sub
```

The WithEvents syntax declares that the *sysmenu* object will handle any events defined by the CSysMenu class (just one in this case). When you use the With-Events clause in a declaration, the object name appears in the Object drop-down list on the code window. The names of all the events created by the class appear in the Procedure drop-down list. Figure 6-3 illustrates how this looks in the Test Messages program. When you choose *sysmenu* from the Object drop-down list and *MenuClick* from the Procedure drop-down list, the IDE automatically creates the necessary event procedure—sysmenu_MenuClick.

The event procedure has ID and string names that uniquely identify the menu item. In Test Messages, the string would be enough to identify the item, but the AddItem method also returns a unique numeric ID that can later be used to identify the menu item even if the menu has duplicate strings.

The first step in initializing a CSysMenu object is to Set it to a New CSysMenu in Form_Load or some other initialization event. You might expect to be able to avoid the Set statement by declaring the object with the following syntax:

```
Private WithEvents sysmenu As New CSysMenu
```

Visual Basic gives a syntax error if you try this shortcut. The second step in initialization is to call the Create method with the handle of the window (usually a form) that will receive the system menu. Once the object is initialized, you define its menu items. The CSysMenu class takes care of the details of adding the items to the system menu, subclassing the window, and raising events when the user selects those menu items. Before I go on to the component side of subclassing, I'll examine one more message capture class from the client side.

Using the CMinMax Class

The CMinMax class handles setting the minimum and maximum size of windows, and setting the position and size of maximized windows. Of course, you don't really need this class to enforce minimum and maximum sizes of forms. You can simply put code in the Resize event to reset invalid sizes to your own minimums and maximums—that is, if you don't mind a little extraneous flashing and repainting.

When you adjust in the Resize event, you're adjusting after the fact and the user sees the result. The preferred way to control minimum and maximum window sizes is to intercept the WM_GETMINMAXINFO message. You set the desired range before the window is repainted with the new size. That way, there's no resizing too large and then adjusting just right. The visual effect is much smoother.

To control the size with subclassing, just declare the object variable:

```
Private minmax As New CMinMax
```

The initialization in Form_Load simply connects the object variable to a window handle and sets properties to control the sizes.

```
' Initialize minimums and maximums
Set minmax = New CMinMax
With minmax
    .Create hWnd
    .MinWidth = fmCapture.Width
    txtMinMax(emmMinWidth) = .MinWidth
    .MinHeight = fmCapture.Height
    txtMinMax(emmMinHeight) = .MinHeight
    .MaxWidth = Screen.Width * 0.5
    txtMinMax(emmMaxWidth) = .MaxWidth
    .MaxHeight = Screen.Height * 0.5
    txtMinMax(emmMaxHeight) = .MaxHeight
    ⋮
```

This class doesn't require an event. You set the sizes you want. I'll let you explore the details of how Test Messages connects the entry text boxes to the properties.

System menu code in the CSysMenu class

Let's get back to the CSysMenu class. It consists of two parts: the class code and the subclass code. The actual class code in SYSMENU.CLS is specific to the system menu problem. The code to subclass a window is generic to any class that needs to capture window messages. It is located in a separate standard module—SUBCLASS.BAS (which is delegated through SUBCLASS.CLS). As you've seen several times already and will see again, the best way to combine generic and specific code in Visual Basic is to use an interface.

The CSysMenu class makes its specific implementation of system menu code available to the generic subclassing code through the ISubclass interface. It makes the results of the window messages it captures available to outside clients through the MenuClick event. The first two lines of SYSMENU.CLS define these two key connections:

```
Implements ISubclass
Public Event MenuClick(sItem As String, ByVal ID As Long)
```

The Implements statement doesn't tell you much until you know what ISubclass does, so here it is:

```
Public Enum EMsgResponse
    emrConsume      ' Process instead of original WindowProc
    emrPostProcess  ' Process after original WindowProc
    emrPreprocess   ' Process before original WindowProc
End Enum
```

```
Public MsgResponse As EMsgResponse

Function WindowProc(ByVal hWnd As Long, _
                    ByVal iMsg As Long, _
                    ByVal wParam As Long, _
                    ByVal lParam As Long) As Long
End Function
```

Any class that intends to subclass a window must start by implementing the WindowProc function and the MsgResponse property. Any CSysMenu object will also be an ISubclass object. In fact, the first thing CSysMenu needs to do in its Create method is pass itself to the generic subclass code in SUBCLASS.BAS:

```
Sub Create(hWndA As Long)
    ' Get handle of system menu
    hSysMenu = GetSystemMenu(hWndA, 0&)
    If hSysMenu = hNull Then ErrRaise eeNoSysWindow
    hWnd = hWndA
    AttachMessage Me, hWndA, WM_SYSCOMMAND
End Sub
```

After getting its system menu handle, the Create method calls the generic Attach-Message procedure, passing a copy of itself (more on that later); the window handle; and the message to be captured. The subclassing mechanism expects only one message per class. CSysMenu handles WM_SYSCOMMAND. CMinMax handles WM_GETMINMAXINFO. You couldn't write several different classes that handle the same message. For example, the WM_SYSCOMMAND messages actually handles various system commands, but if you wanted to handle some of the others, you'd need to add features to CSysMenu rather than write additional classes.

After calling AttachMessage, the client's next step is usually to call the AddItem method to add one or more items to the system menu. You saw the API calls to add system menu items in TSYSMENU.FRM, so I'm going to summarize without showing the code. AddItem will generate an ID number for each item, add the item to the system menu with appropriate API calls, and store that ID along with the item text in an array of TItem UDTs called *aItem*. Later when CSysMenu receives a menu ID number through a message, it can look up the ID in the array to see which menu item was clicked.

After the items are added to the system menu, CSysMenu is ready to receive window messages. When the generic window procedure in SUBCLASS.BAS receives a message, it will check the message and, if appropriate, call the ISub-class_WindowProc function. That's where you handle the system menu aspects of window capture as shown on the next page.

```
Private Function ISubclass_WindowProc(ByVal hWnd As Long, _
                                      ByVal iMsg As Long, _
                                      ByVal wParam As Long, _
                                      ByVal lParam As Long) As Long
    ' Assume original WindowProc will handle
    emr = emrPostProcess
    ' Subclasser should never call unless it's our message
    BugAssert iMsg = WM_SYSCOMMAND
    ' Ignore everything except system commands
    If wParam <= 3000 Then
        ' Check IDs and raise event if found
        Dim i As Long
        For i = 1 To cMaxItem
            If aItem(i).ID = 0 Then Exit For
            If wParam = aItem(i).ID Then
                RaiseEvent MenuClick(aItem(i).sText, aItem(i).ID)
                ' We've finished so original WindowProc not needed
                emr = emrConsume
                Exit Function
            End If
        Next
    End If
End Function
```

The window procedure uses the private *emr* variable (delegated by the ISubclass_MsgResponse property) to indicate whether or not it handled the message. If it's not your message, WindowProc sets the mode to *emrPostProcess*. If it is your message and WindowProc can find a matching ID for it, WindowProc then generates a MenuClick event with the RaiseEvent statement. This calls any event handler the client decides to provide. Raising the event handles the message, so WindowProc sets the mode to *emrConsume* to show that the message has been handled.

Notice that CSysMenu could, theoretically, handle standard system messages such as resize, minimize, close, and so on. I experimented with this long enough to determine that if you do it wrong, you crash. Subclassing is a dangerous, messy business, so don't expect that because you've seen one subclass you've seen them all.

I'll let you examine the cleanup code in the Destroy and RemoveItem methods on your own. The only point I want to make about the Destroy method is that it will call DetachMessage to unhook the message.

System menu code in the CMinMax class

The implementation of CMinMax is similar to that of CSysMenu, so I'm going to summarize quickly. Like any message capture class, it implements ISubclass, and calls AttachMessage and DetachMessage in its Create and Destroy methods.

The unusual thing about CMinMax is that it doesn't raise any events when it detects a captured message. Instead, it can simply set minimum and maximum values based on its properties.

The tricky part about the window procedure is that the WM_GETMINMAXINFO message passes a pointer to a MINMAXINFO structure in the *lParam* of the window procedure. What is Visual Basic going to do with that pointer? You should have this down by now. Pass it on to an API function—in this case CopyMemory. Here's how it works:

```
Private Function ISubclass_WindowProc(ByVal hWnd As Long, _
                                      ByVal iMsg As Long, _
                                      ByVal wParam As Long, _
                                      ByVal lParam As Long) As Long
    Dim mmiT As MINMAXINFO
    ' Copy parameter to local variable for processing
    CopyMemory mmiT, ByVal lParam, LenB(mmiT)
    :
    ' Modify the local variable based on property values
    ' Copy modified results back to parameter
    CopyMemory ByVal lParam, mmiT, LenB(mmiT)
    ' Don't pass back to original WindowProc
    emr = emrConsume
End Function
```

You copy the passed parameter to a local version with CopyMemory, modify the local version as much as you like, and then copy the local version back to the original.

Generic subclassing

The problem with subclassing is that Visual Basic won't allow you to use the AddressOf operator on class methods. You can use only a callback procedure that resides in a standard module. This means that there will be one and only one instance of the window procedure you create.

This won't do for the CSysMenu class (or for any other class that encapsulates a callback). For example, you might have a program with several forms, each of which has system menu items. You need to have multiple CSysMenu objects— one for each form—but you have only one window procedure. How can you make the one window procedure call the appropriate object? Well, you'll just have to keep track of all the objects in a data structure. Then the one and only window procedure can look up the appropriate object and give it the data it needs to handle the message. In other words, you must do manually what Visual Basic should have done automatically.

My first idea was to create a complex data structure in SUBCLASS.BAS. I would have a collection of window objects (indexed by the window handle) for each window that had been subclassed. Since a window might be asked to handle different messages, each window object would have a collection of message objects indexed by message number. The one and only window procedure would know the window handle and the message, and it would use these to find the correct data in the collections. I would have to do these collection lookups several hundred times a second, but since most window messages wouldn't be subclassed, most of the lookups would fail.

I began to have second thoughts. After several hours of pounding my head on the keyboard, and after informal consultation with a blue-ribbon panel of subclassing experts (Glenn Hackney, Ed Staffin, and Matt Curland), I came up with a different strategy.

Windows keeps everything it knows about every window in the system in a small database indexed by the window handle. It even gives you a way to add additional items to the database. What if you could stuff everything the window procedure needs to know into this database when a window is first subclassed? The window procedure could then dig out the items it needs when it needs them. You'd also need a way to clean up the whole mess when the message was unhooked. You wouldn't need to worry about speed when adding or deleting data, but item retrieval would have to be fast enough to handle hundreds of messages per second.

The way you add your own data to the window database is to use the property API functions. SetProp adds a chunk of data (anything that fits in a Long) to the window database, assigning it a string name for later lookup. RemoveProp deletes a chunk of data identified by its string name. GetProp retrieves a chunk of data associated with a string name. In order to use the "prop" functions, you need to assign each chunk of data a unique string that you can regenerate later when you need to look up the data. In other words, the prop database works a lot like string indexing in a collection. There are only two pieces of data that you know both inside the window procedure and outside the procedure when subclassing or unsubclassing; they're the window handle and the message number. So you create the unique lookup keys by converting these two integers to strings.

Attaching and detaching messages

Here's how the data is stored in the AttachMessage procedure:

```
Sub AttachMessage(iwp As ISubclass, ByVal hWnd As Long, _
                  ByVal iMsg As Long)
    Dim procOld As Long, f As Long, c As Long
    ' Validate window
    If IsWindow(hWnd) = False Then ErrRaise eeInvalidWindow
    If MWinTool.IsWindowLocal(hWnd) = False Then ErrRaise eeNoExternalWindow
```

```
    ' Get the message count
    c = GetProp(hWnd, "C" & hWnd)
    If c = 0 Then
        ' Subclass window by installing window procedure
        procOld = SetWindowLong(hWnd, GWL_WNDPROC, AddressOf WindowProc)
        If procOld = 0 Then ErrRaise eeCantSubclass
        ' Associate old procedure with handle
        f = SetProp(hWnd, hWnd, procOld)
        BugAssert f <> 0
        ' Count this message
        c = 1
        f = SetProp(hWnd, "C" & hWnd, c)
    Else
        ' Count this message
        c = c + 1
        f = SetProp(hWnd, "C" & hWnd, c)
    End If
    BugAssert f <> 0
    ' This message had better not be already attached
    If GetProp(hWnd, hWnd & "#" & iMsg) <> pNull Then
        ErrRaise eeAlreadyAttached
    End If
    ' Associate object with message (one per handle)
    f = SetProp(hWnd, hWnd & "#" & iMsg, ObjPtr(iwp))
    BugAssert f <> 0
End Sub
```

The code starts by validating the window handle. Subclassing with AddressOf won't work on windows outside the current process; you use Message Blaster for that. The IsWindowLocal function from (WINTOOL.BAS) is used to guard against this error. It calls the GetWindowThreadProcessId API function to get the process ID of the window and compare it to the ID of the current process.

The rest of the code assigns three kinds of data to the window database. The old procedure and the count of messages are stored on a per-window basis. Each window that passes through our subclassing system is subclassed once. A window that has already been subclassed will already have a count and can be identified by success (return of something other than zero) when you look up the count with GetProp. Windows that haven't yet passed through the system must be subclassed, and the old window procedure that is being replaced must be stored in a property for later retrieval.

The class that is doing the subclassing is associated with the message, not the window handle, and it must be stored in the database whether or not the window has been subclassed. For example, in the Test Messages program the CSysMenu object attaches itself first. The count is zero at this point, so Attach-Message subclasses the form window, stores the old window procedure, sets the count to one, stores the count, and stores the class data (indexed by the message number). Next the CMinMax object attaches itself. The count is now one, so there is no need to subclass the window again; but the count must be incremented and stored, and the class data must be stored. Notice that the object is stored as a pointer, using ObjPtr. Take that on faith for now. I'll get back to ObjPtr later.

Let's ignore what is actually done with the data and take a brief look at how it's cleaned up in DetachMessage:

```
Sub DetachMessage(iwp As ISubclass, ByVal hWnd As Long, _
                  ByVal iMsg As Long)
    Dim procOld As Long, f As Long, c As Long
    ' Get the message count
    c = GetProp(hWnd, "C" & hWnd)
    If c = 1 Then
        ' This is the last message, so unsubclass
        procOld = GetProp(hWnd, hWnd)
        BugAssert procOld <> pNull
        ' Unsubclass by reassigning old window procedure
        Call SetWindowLong(hWnd, GWL_WNDPROC, procOld)
        ' Remove unneeded handle (oldProc)
        RemoveProp hWnd, hWnd
        ' Remove unneeded count
        RemoveProp hWnd, "C" & hWnd
    Else
        ' Uncount this message
        c = GetProp(hWnd, "C" & hWnd)
        c = c - 1
        f = SetProp(hWnd, "C" & hWnd, c)
    End If
    ' Remove unneeded message (subclass object pointer)
    RemoveProp hWnd, hWnd & "#" & iMsg
End Sub
```

First the code looks to see if you are removing the last message handled by the subclassed window. If so, you can unsubclass it, restore the old window procedure, and remove the count and the old window procedure from the window database. If it's not the last message, you decrement and restore the count. Either way, remove the property that stores the class data. The only purpose of the count variable that must be maintained so carefully in AttachMessage is to determine whether to unsubclass the window in DetachMessage. The window procedure has no need for it.

Processing messages

Finally I get to the point of this whole exercise. The one and only window procedure will look up whatever data it needs and call back to the class of any message it recognizes. Here's the code:

```
Private Function WindowProc(ByVal hWnd As Long, ByVal iMsg As Long, _
                           ByVal wParam As Long, ByVal lParam As Long)
                           As Long
    Dim procOld As Long, pSubclass As Long, f As Long
    Dim iwp As ISubclass, iwpT As ISubclass
    ' Get the old procedure from the window
    procOld = GetProp(hWnd, hWnd)
    BugAssert procOld <> pNull
    ' Get the object pointer from the message
    pSubclass = GetProp(hWnd, hWnd & "#" & iMsg)
    If pSubclass = pNull Then
        ' This message not handled, so pass on to old procedure
        WindowProc = CallWindowProc(procOld, hWnd, iMsg, _
                                    wParam, ByVal lParam)
        Exit Function
    End If


    ' Turn the pointer into an illegal, uncounted interface
    CopyMemory iwpT, pSubclass, 4
    ' Do NOT hit the End button here! You will crash!
    BugMessage "Got object"
    ' Assign to legal reference
    Set iwp = iwpT
    ' Still do NOT hit the End button here! You will still crash!
    ' Destroy the illegal reference
    CopyMemory iwpT, 0&, 4
    ' OK, hit the End button if you must--you'll probably still crash,
    ' but it will be because of the subclass, not the uncounted reference

    ' Use the interface to call back to the class
    With iwp
        ' Preprocess
        If .MsgResponse = emrPreprocess Then
            WindowProc = CallWindowProc(procOld, hWnd, iMsg, _
                                        wParam, ByVal lParam)
        End If
        ' Consume
        WindowProc = .WindowProc(hWnd, iMsg, wParam, ByVal lParam)
        ' PostProcess
        If .MsgResponse = emrPostProcess Then
            WindowProc = CallWindowProc(procOld, hWnd, iMsg, _
                                        wParam, ByVal lParam)
        End If
    End With

End Function
```

The first step is to retrieve the previous window procedure by looking it up in the window database with GetProp, using the window handle as an index. You'll need this address regardless of the path taken in the rest of the procedure.

Next I use the value of the window handle combined with the value of the message to look up the object pointer of the associated class. In most cases, the message won't be attached to anything and the lookup will fail. If the return is zero, simply pass the message on to the original window procedure and quit.

If the message is one that you attached, you'll get back a raw object pointer. You have to perform some messy API tricks to turn this object pointer into a Visual Basic object variable. There are two reasons for this hack. First, the data has to be stored and retrieved from the window database as a Long. Second, the object has to bypass normal COM reference counting. Reference counting and how to avoid it will be discussed in detail in Chapter 10. For now, just take it on faith that the variable *iwp* is a legal object variable of type ISubclass.

Once you have an ISubclass variable, it's a simple matter to call back to a window procedure that does the real work in the attaching class (CSysMenu or CMinMax in Test Messages). The window procedure in the attaching class can do the work it knows how to do and then fire an event to pass any additional work up to the client program (as in CSysMenu). The MsgResponse property of the client class controls whether the original window process gets a crack at the message, and if so, when.

FLAME

Subclassing is too hard. It would be so much easier if CSysMenu could simply do the obvious. Instead of calling AttachMessage, the Create method of CSysMenu would subclass the window directly:

```
oldProc = SetWindowLong(hWnd, GWL_WNDPROC, AddressOf WindowProc)
```

The WindowProc would be a method in the CSysMenu class. Since a method has an address unique to the object, the window would automatically be connected to the object without a lot of gyrations with the "prop" functions. So why doesn't Visual Basic just let you use AddressOf on class methods? Because it's hard. It would have taken a lot of development work to make Visual Basic coordinate the objects containing callback methods with the procedures that use the addresses of those methods. Since objects are created and destroyed dynamically at run time, you'd need to define behavior for what happens when an object disappears while a Windows callback function is holding a pointer to its method. I have some idea of how hard this would be in C++ because I had to fake it myself in a much less appropriate language. When Visual Basic program managers point out the difficulties of making complicated things (such as subclassing) easy, my response is: If it's too hot in here, go sit on the porch. Of course it's hard to design a user-friendly high-level language, but if you can't handle it, go work on an assembler or a C compiler. Just don't put half-baked features that require low-level programming in a high-level language.

Debugging subclassed window procedures

Debugging subclassed code can be difficult. If you have any doubt, run the Test System Menu program (TSYSMENU.VBP). Put a breakpoint in the window procedure code. Once your replacement window procedure function is installed, it might be called hundreds of times per second. If you stop at a breakpoint while handling one message, where are all those other messages going to go? Nowhere. You must return from one window message before the IDE can handle the next one. You can't return if you're stopped at a breakpoint, but you can't use the IDE to continue until you return.

At first glance, it appears that the whole IDE is hung. You can't use the Start, Step Into, or Step Over buttons or menu items. Your program might even cover part of the IDE, but you can't move it because it's stopped at a breakpoint. Fortunately, most accelerator keys still work. Unfortunately, F9 (Toggle Breakpoint) usually doesn't work, so you might keep coming back to that breakpoint over and over no matter how many times you hit F5 (Start). It took me a while to figure out that Ctrl+Shift+F9 (Clear All Breakpoints) is the key to escape an endless loop. Even if you figure out how to escape, this isn't an easy way to debug. You can't easily use the Watch or Locals windows, so you'll probably have to put debug messages at key points like they did in the Middle Ages. Even then you have to be careful not to get so many messages that you overflow the Immediate window.

The problem continues at any level as long as the subclassing code is in source code. For example, if you use debug the Test Messages program, you'll encounter the problem if you put a breakpoint in WindowProc in SUBCLASS.BAS. WindowProc calls ISubclass_WindowProc in SYSMENU.CLS, so the same problem follows you there. ISubclass_WindowProc raises the MenuClick event in TMESSAGE.FRM, so you're in trouble again. Fortunately, there is an escape.

The subclassing code is in a separate component called the Subclassing and Timer Assistant (SUBTIMER.DLL). The component also includes the CTimer class (which we'll see in Chapter 7) because it suffers similar debugging problems. If you use the compiled version of SUBTIMER.DLL, most of your problems will go away because the subclassing code is no longer in source code being used by the IDE. You can put breakpoints in the window procedure of the client class or in client events generated by the client class. That doesn't necessarily mean you're out of the soup. Strange things can happen when messages pile up faster than you can debug them. If you set a breakpoint at the start of the CMinMax window procedure and then resize the test form, you'll get dozens of resize messages, but you'll stop in the first. Once you debug through it, the second message will be waiting. You'll find debugging easier if you set breakpoints within conditional blocks that aren't hit continuously. For example, set a breakpoint in the CSysMenu window procedure inside the conditional that identifies potential menu hits rather than outside where all WM_SYSCOMMAND messages come through.

You can debug the TMESSAGE project in three ways. First, you can load the TMESSAGEDEB.VBG file. This gives you all three projects—the sample program in TMESSAGE.VBP, the CMinMax and CSysMenu classes in VBCORE.VBP, and the subclassing code in SUBTIMER.VBP. Avoid this configuration if possible. If there are bugs in my subclassing code, you'll have as much trouble tracking them down as I had putting them in. A better alternative is to load TMESSAGE.VBG, which contains the sample in TMESSAGE.VBP and the client classes in VB-CORE.VBP. The subclassing code is in the compiled SUBTIMER.DLL. This allows you to debug the client classes. Finally, you can load TMESSAGE.VBP to debug the sample source while using VBCORE.DLL and SUBTIMER.DLL. This allows you to debug the MenuClick event raised by CSysMenu, but there's not much you can do with CMinMax because it never runs in client code. If you're confused about the different projects involved, you might want to review the section "Developing for the Real World."

Isolating the subclassing code in a separate DLL solves your debugging problems in two ways. The most dangerous code is isolated in a tested DLL that won't (I hope) suffer from the crashes you experience if you make a mistake when subclassing on a case-by-case basis as we did in "Your own window procedure" earlier in this chapter. Isolating the code also makes it possible to debug the client naturally.

7

Painting Pictures

There's a Visual Basic Way of painting pictures, and there's a Windows Way. The Basic Way is simple and limited. The Windows Way is complicated and powerful. The trick is to make the unlimited Windows Way look like the easy Basic Way. To do this, you have to understand both ways inside and out. And you have to understand a third way that, for lack of a better term, I call the Real Way of painting pictures.

In real life, people create pictures by daubing paint onto canvas, pushing pencil across paper, scraping chalk on blackboard, scribbling crayons in coloring books, molding clay into shapes, even gluing other pictures onto cardboard. Computers can't do any of that. The computer world offers only one way to get a picture onto the screen, and that is pixel by pixel.

Georges Seurat constructed his pictures from tiny bits of paint, but you can be sure that even he wouldn't have tried to paint *Bathers* on a computer screen pixel by pixel. Nevertheless, that's how it would have come out on his screen.

Programming graphics is the art of modeling the different ways of creating real pictures so that they come out on the screen or from the printer in the form of pixels. (Don't confuse the issue with exceptions such as plotters.) This chapter discusses both the Windows Way and the Basic Way of drawing and painting pixels and how to mix the two approaches.

Windows to Basic and Back Again

Whether you program graphics with Visual Basic or with some other language, and whether you use the Windows Way or the Basic Way, you'll work in one of two different modes. The difference is between drawing with a crayon or a pencil and pasting pictures from a magazine. If you're like most of us, you can get nicer results by pasting somebody else's pictures than by creating your own. And you can do it faster.

Vector graphics involves drawing dots, lines, rectangles, ellipses, and other geometric shapes. I call this model *drawing*. Basic was good at drawing long before Visual Basic arrived. The Basic Line and Circle statements (now methods) were more flexible than similar routines in many other languages. Technically, you can take drawing as far as you want—even into three dimensions with shading—if your math is better than mine. But some practical limits will have an effect on how much drawing you'll want to do under Windows, and more limits will affect how much you'll want to do with Visual Basic.

Creating raster graphics involves plunking predefined arrays of pixels onto the screen. I call this model *painting*. Ancient Basics gave a passing nod to the concept with the Get and Put graphics statements, but they got lost in the transition to Visual Basic. Visual Basic painting has always been done with the Picture property. Although painting is central to graphics under Windows, support for it through the Picture property was surprisingly weak until Visual Basic version 4. The PaintPicture method goes a long way toward fixing this limitation, although you might still have to back out to Windows to perform some operations.

Here's the quick tour of Windows drawing and painting features, along with the corresponding Visual Basic features.

Device Contexts and Canvas Objects

In Windows, the surface on which you draw is called a *device context* (*DC*). You access it through a handle called an *HDC*. A device context handle is to graphics what a window handle is to controls and windows.

Once you have the handle to a device context, you can use API calls to put dots, lines, circles, rectangles, text, and existing pictures of various kinds on it. The device context translates your device-independent instructions about what to draw or paint into device-specific instructions for a particular output device. Almost every function in the graphics device interface (GDI) either has an HDC argument or returns an HDC. You simply can't do much graphics work without one.

No official name exists for the corresponding concept in Visual Basic, but some people at Microsoft, who ought to know, refer to objects that have graphics capabilities as *canvas objects*. I'll use that term to describe the various graphics objects. The Form, PictureBox, and Printer objects are the three standard canvas objects; Screen, Image, Shape, and Line objects also have canvaslike properties and methods.

I like to think of a CCanvas class as forming the top of a hierarchy such as the one shown in Figure 7-1. My theory is that Visual Basic objects are implemented internally using inheritance and that in a future version they'll get around to making these classes available to us poor programming peons. I have no inside information on this (and would deny it if I did), but imagining a canvas object hierarchy gives me a useful model of what's going on.

In my theory, the CCanvas class has all the generic properties and methods common to canvas objects, but it's not public so you can't create your own canvas object. It's just something to hang your inheritance on. The CPrinter class is inherited from CCanvas and has all its generic properties and methods: Fore-Color, DrawMode, DrawStyle, ScaleWidth, ScaleHeight, Line, Circle, and so on. It adds its own printer-specific methods such as NewPage and EndDoc, which are implemented internally using API functions such as StartDoc, EndDoc, StartPage, and EndPage.

The CDisplay class is also inherited from CCanvas and is likewise invisible to users. It adds display-oriented properties and methods such as Picture, Image, Cls, and Point. The CForm and CPictureBox classes are inherited from CDisplay, and each one adds its own unique properties and methods—although most of these have nothing to do with graphics.

I tried to throw the Screen, Image, Shape, and Line classes into this hierarchy, but they just muddied my nice, clean diagram.

Now stretch your imagination a bit and imagine that the Visual Basic classes implement interfaces rather than inherit from classes. Let's say that there's an ICanvas interface that provides such members as hDC, Width, Left, Move, ScaleWidth, and ScaleX. Classes that implement this interface include Form, PictureBox, Printer, and UserControl. The IDrawable interface provides drawing members such as Line, Circle, PSet, DrawMode, and CurrentX. It is also implemented by Form, PictureBox, Printer, and UserControl. The IReadable interface provides the Point method. It is implemented by Form, PictureBox, and UserControl, but not by Printer. It doesn't make sense to read the color of a point off a printed page—that's a separate operation that could be provided by an IScanner interface. Figure 7-2 shows how an interface hierarchy might work.

I suspect that the internal Visual Basic approach combines these approaches. I don't think Form and Printer both implement IDrawable separately. They probably inherit a common implementation. As we'll see in this chapter, drawing a line to the printer, a form, or a PictureBox is exactly the same code, except that you use different device contexts.

We can speculate all we want about how Visual Basic is implemented, but if the features aren't made public they might as well be implemented with black magic. If you prefer facts to theories, Table 7-1 shows a matrix of some of the more common properties and methods shared by canvas objects. Note that UserControl, UserDocument, and PropertyPage have the same properties and methods as Form and therefore are not shown separately.

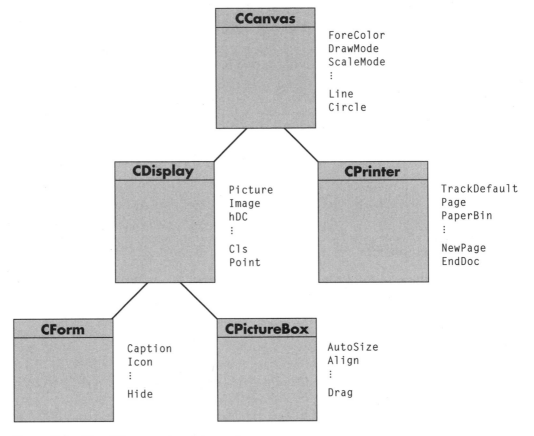

Figure 7-1. *The CCanvas class hierarchy.*

DC attributes, canvas properties

Every device context has attributes such as color, font, pen, and palette. GDI32-.DLL provides access functions for reading and modifying these attributes. In Visual Basic, canvas objects have properties. Table 7-2 shows how to work with these attributes by means of device contexts in Windows and canvas objects in Visual Basic.

For the most part, you can stick with the Basic Way for reading and modifying attributes. Canvas properties don't always match up one to one, but they're usually more convenient. In fact, about the only common task I've found that you can't do with Visual Basic is use a brush (FillStyle) that consists of a bitmap. (After reading "The Windows Way of Painting," page 390, you should be able to figure that out for yourself.)

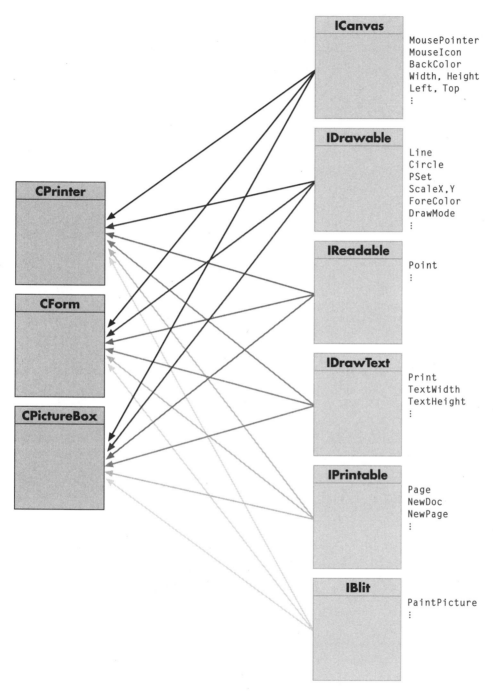

Figure 7-2. *The ICanvas interface hierarchy.*

	Form	Printer	Picture-Box	Image	Shape	Line	Screen
Properties							
hDC	x	x	x				
Picture	x		x	x			
Image	x		x				
MouseIcon, MousePointer	x		x	x			x
Font	x	x	x				
AutoRedraw	x		x				
BackColor	x		x		x		
ForeColor	x	x	x				
FillColor	x	x	x		x		
DrawMode	x	x	x		x	x	
DrawStyle, DrawWidth	x	x	x				
FillStyle	x	x	x		x		
CurrentX, CurrentY	x	x	x				
Width, Height	x	x	x	x	x		x
Left, Top	x		x	x	x		
Scale properties	x	x	x				
TwipsPerPixelX, TwipsPerPixelY		x					x
Methods							
Line, Circle, PSet	x	x	x				
Point	x		x				
Cls	x		x				
Print	x	x	x				
TextWidth, TextHeight	x	x	x				
ScaleX, ScaleY	x	x	x				
PaintPicture	x	x	x				

Table 7-1. *Properties and methods of canvas objects.*

Attribute	Windows Way	Basic Way
Background color	GetBkColor and SetBkColor	BackColor
Background mode	GetBkMode and SetBkMode	FontTransparent
Text color	GetTextColor and SetTextColor	ForeColor
Color palette	CreatePalette, SelectPalette, and other palette functions	Palette and PaletteMode properties
Brush	Brush creation functions and SelectObject	FillColor and FillStyle (but no way to use bitmap brush)
Pen	Pen creation functions and SelectObject	DrawStyle and DrawWidth
Pen color	Pen definition set by Pen creation functions	Color parameter of Line and Circle methods
Pen position	GetCurrentPosition, LineTo, and MoveTo functions	Line method with Step, CurrentX, CurrentY
Drawing mode	SetROP2	DrawMode
Font	Font creation functions and SelectObject	Font object
Mouse pointer	SelectObject, CreateCursor, and other cursor functions	MousePointer and MouseIcon
Clip and redraw state	Various functions related to repainting, managing regions, and clipping	ClipControls, AutoRedraw, and AutoSize
Scale	SetMapMode	ScaleMode
Window extent and origin	GetWindowExtEx, SetWindowExtEx, GetWindowOrgEx, and SetWindowOrgEx	ScaleLeft, ScaleTop, ScaleWidth, and ScaleHeight
Screen capabilities	GetDeviceCaps	Screen object

Table 7-2. *Graphics properties in Windows and in Visual Basic.*

DC functions, canvas methods

The Windows Way of performing graphics operations is to provide every sort of function you can imagine for every operation, no matter how obscure. The Basic Way is to provide the most important graphics operations through a few methods loaded with optional arguments. The Line method, for example, wraps up the functionality of several API functions. Table 7-3 compares device context functions in Windows with canvas methods in Visual Basic.

Operation	Windows Way	Basic Way
Point drawing	SetPixel	PSet
Point reading	GetPixel	Point
Line drawing	LineTo and MoveToEx	Line method or Line control
Circle, pie, and arc drawing	Ellipse, Chord, Arc, and Pie	Circle method or Shape control
Polygon drawing	Polygon, PolyPolygon, and SetPolyFillMode	Draw it line by line
Blitting	BitBlt, StretchBlt, PatBlt, and StretchDIBits	PaintPicture method, Image control with Stretch property
Filling shapes	FloodFill and other Fill functions	Visual Basic can create filled shapes but has no way of filling shapes later
Icon painting	LoadIcon, CreateIcon, DestroyIcon, and DrawIcon	Picture object
Bitmap painting	Various Bitmap functions and SelectObject	Picture object
Metafile recording	CreateMetaFile and CloseMetaFile	No way
Metafile playing	CopyMetaFile, GetMetafile, and DeleteMetaFile functions	Picture object
Scrolling	ScrollDC	No way
Managing regions	Various Rgn and Path functions	No way
Printing	Escape and Doc functions	Methods on Print object
Text output	Many functions including TextOut, ExtTextOut, and GrayString	Print
Text sizing	GetTextExtent	TextWidth and TextHeight
Text alignment	SetTextAlign, SetTextJustification, and SetTextCharacterExtra functions	No way

Table 7-3. *Graphics methods in Windows and in Visual Basic.*

To the hardcore programmer, what Visual Basic doesn't do is more telling than what it does. Some points of interest:

- Visual Basic doesn't provide any way to fill a shape. QuickBasic had the Paint statement, but it didn't survive the transition to Visual Basic. Usually, you don't need to fill shapes as a separate step because you can specify filling when you draw the shape. Nevertheless, "The Windows Way of Drawing," page 377, provides a function for those rare occasions when you need to fill after the fact.

- Visual Basic doesn't draw polygons. You can use the Line method to draw polygons one side at a time, but you might find the Windows Way more convenient.

- Regions are a somewhat obscure part of Windows that you might occasionally need. Visual Basic doesn't do them, and this book doesn't either. But you should be able to apply the general principles described in this chapter to the problem.

- You can draw irregular curves with Bezier curves as described on page 382.

- You can use paths (as described on page 385) to create irregularly shaped regions.

Borrowing Device Context Handles

Visual Basic hides the messy details of maintaining the HDC, but it provides the hDC property with forms, picture boxes, and printer objects for those intrepid souls who like messy details. The hDC property is the bridge between the Windows Way and the Basic Way. You can pass it to any Windows function that takes an HDC parameter.

But you needn't limit yourself to objects that have an hDC property. You can borrow the HDC of anything that has an HWND. *Borrow* is the key word. If an object has an hDC property, it's yours; use it however you want with no concern for what happens when you're done. But if you get the HDC from an HWND, you'd better give it back when you're finished.

The GetDC API function grabs the device context of the client area. If you like to live on the edge, you can use the GetWindowDC function to grab the whole window—border, title bar, minimize and maximize buttons, control box, and all. I'm not going to tell you how to draw pictures of Larry, Curly, and Moe to replace the minimize, restore, and maximize buttons of your forms, but neither Windows nor Visual Basic will try to stop you.

Whether you get the DC of the window or the DC of the client area only, you must return it with ReleaseDC when you're done:

```
' Borrow window DC
hDCCur = GetWindowDC(hWndCur)
' Use the DC to do work
⋮
' Give DC back or die
Call ReleaseDC(hWndCur, hDCCur)
```

We'll talk about other techniques in this code—BitBlt and assigning the Image property to the Picture property—later in this chapter.

Screen Capability

The Screen object provides some information about the current capabilities of the graphics screen, but it's pitifully short of what you might hope for. The GetDeviceCaps API function can tell you anything you need to know about the screen or about any specific device context. This is one of those Swiss-army-knife functions that takes 100 different constants as arguments and returns a different value, depending on which constant you passed.

For example, here's how to determine how many color planes and how many bits per pixel your video supports:

```
cPlanes = GetDeviceCaps(hdcDst, PLANES)
cPixelBits = GetDeviceCaps(hdcDst, BITSPIXEL)
```

You need this information every time you create a bitmap, as you'll see later in this chapter. Although this seems like something the Screen object ought to provide, it doesn't—but the Video object does.

The CVideo class is implemented in VIDEO.CLS in the VBCore component. VBCore also creates a single global instance of this class as the Video object. You can see sample output from it in the AllAbout program (ALLABOUT.VBP) described in Chapter 11. CVideo is a simple class that wraps the GetDeviceCaps function to tell you everything you ever dreamed of knowing about your video device. Here's enough code to show you how it works:

```
Private hdcScreen As Long

Private Sub Class_Initialize()
    hdcScreen = GetDC(hNull)
End Sub

Private Sub Class_Terminate()
    Call ReleaseDC(hNull, hdcScreen)
End Sub

Private Function GetCaps(iCode As Long) As Long
    GetCaps = GetDeviceCaps(hdcScreen, iCode)
End Function

Property Get BitsPerPixel() As Long
    BitsPerPixel = GetCaps(BITSPIXEL)
End Property

Property Get ColorPlanes() As Long
    ColorPlanes = GetCaps(PLANES)
End Property
```

Metafiles 1, Visual Basic 0

Metafiles present several interesting problems to the Visual Basic programmer. It's easy enough to assign a metafile to the Picture property from a resource, a file, the Clipboard, or a picture. You have to jump through some API hoops to send a metafile to the printer, however, because the printer doesn't have a Picture property. (This chapter doesn't cover that task specifically, but it will give some helpful background.)

Visual Basic won't help you create or record metafiles either. Visual Basic drawing methods such as Line and Circle draw to canvas objects, but they don't know anything about metafiles, and you don't have a way to redirect them to the HDC of a metafile.

What Visual Basic needs is a CMetafile class, inherited from the CCanvas class (or perhaps CMetafile should implement the IDrawable interface). CMetafile objects would have all the normal canvas properties and methods plus a Play method to replay the metafile and a Save method to write it to disk. You could call the Clear method to wipe out any previous commands and then draw on the CMetafile object using your favorite drawing and painting methods.

In fact, you could design just such a CMetafile class. The API calls to create a metafile are easy enough. The problem is that you would need to reimplement the whole Visual Basic graphics library to give your CMetafile class the Line, Circle, and other methods it needs. Furthermore, you wouldn't be able to do so completely because the syntax of the Line, Circle, and PSet methods isn't a legal procedure syntax that you can emulate in your own methods.

Nevertheless, you could fake it—if you happen to have several months of spare time. It would be a lot easier for Visual Basic to add this class than for you to do it. Maybe in the next version. In the meantime, it's simpler to create metafiles in a drawing program and then play them through the Picture property.

I've found this class to be overkill in most programs; it's usually easier to just call GetDeviceCaps. But once in a while, CVideo is just what you need.

Two Ways of Drawing

Visual Basic provides excellent support for vector graphics, but drawing lines, circles, and dots isn't necessarily the best way of doing graphics under Windows. If you want complex images, you can usually get them faster by drawing the shape with a bitmap editor or a drawing program and plunking the result onto the screen.

This is particularly true when you get beyond two-dimensional shapes. If you really know your geometry, you can calculate three-dimensional coordinates and rotate them in space. For a shape of any complexity, the calculation takes seconds for wire-frame images. This might impress your engineer friends, but ordinary users will want shaded images instantly. If it can be done in cartoons and movies, why can't you do it in your program? Well, you can, but you might not be willing to wait.

Drawing is one area where p-code can really drag you down. Fortunately, Visual Basic's compiler now gives you a good shot at fast vector graphics comparable to what you could get from a C++ DLL. Nevertheless, my advice on vector graphics is to keep them short and simple. Remember that whatever you draw must be redrawn any time you resize the window, so think twice before making your graphics forms resizable. Setting the AutoRedraw property simply means that Windows will redraw instead of you.

The Basic Way of Drawing

You probably know more about Visual Basic drawing than I do. It's not that I'm ignorant (though I admit to being weak in math); rather, the simple vector graphics I recommend just aren't that difficult.

The fade trick I'm about to show you, however, is fun and isn't what you might expect. You've no doubt seen the fade from black to blue on the setup screens of many Microsoft products. Looking at the output, I would have guessed that it was produced with some sort of palette manipulation. It's not.

The Fade procedure simply draws adjacent lines with increasing color intensity. It uses optional arguments to enable defaults. For example, a simple Fade command with no arguments draws a blue fade from top to bottom of the current form. You can draw the fade on any form or picture box. You can specify red, green, or blue fades or any combination of the three. You can specify a horizontal or vertical fade—or both for a diagonal fade. Here are some examples, using named arguments:

```
' Default black to blue vertical fade on current form
Fade Me
' Make it blue to black
Fade Me, LightToDark:=False
' Red horizontal fade on FBlit
Fade FBlit, Red:=True, Horizontal:=True
' Violet vertical fade on picture box
Fade pbTest(0), Red:=True, Blue:=True
' Black to white diagonal fade on current form
Fade Me, Horizontal:=True, Vertical:=True, _
    Red:=True, Green:=True, Blue:=True
```

Fade draws the background of the Bit Blast program used later in this chapter (BITBLAST.VBP). You'll see it in various figures, starting with Figure 7-6 on page 392, but it's different each time because it is called with random values in the Form_Resize event:

```
Private Sub Form_Resize()
    Fade Me, Red:=Random(0, 1), Green:=Random(0, 1), _
            Blue:=Random(0, 1), Horizontal:=Random(0, 1), _
            Vertical:=Random(0, 1), LightToDark:=Random(0, 1)
End Sub
```

The Fade sub (with other effects in FUN.BAS) is long, but it takes only a few lines to do the real work. Most of the code saves and restores properties and handles defaults based on the optional arguments:

```
Sub Fade(cvsDst As Object, _
        Optional Red As Boolean = False, _
        Optional Green As Boolean = False, _
        Optional Blue As Boolean = True, _
        Optional Vertical As Boolean = True, _
        Optional Horizontal As Boolean = False, _
        Optional LightToDark As Boolean = True)
With cvsDst
    ' Trap errors
    On Error Resume Next

    ' Save properties
    Dim fAutoRedraw As Boolean, ordDrawStyle As Integer
    Dim ordDrawMode As Integer, iDrawWidth As Integer
    Dim ordScaleMode As Integer
    Dim rScaleWidth As Single, rScaleHeight As Single
    fAutoRedraw = .AutoRedraw: iDrawWidth = .DrawWidth
    ordDrawStyle = .DrawStyle: ordDrawMode = .DrawMode
    rScaleWidth = .ScaleWidth: rScaleHeight = .ScaleHeight
    ordScaleMode = .ScaleMode
    ' Err set if object lacks one of previous properties
    If Err Then Exit Sub
    ' If you get here, object is OK (Printer lacks AutoRedraw)
    fAutoRedraw = .AutoRedraw

    ' Set properties required for fade
    .AutoRedraw = True
    .DrawWidth = 3                  ' Must be greater than 1 for dithering
    .DrawStyle = vbInsideSolid  ' vbInvisible gives an interesting effect
    .DrawMode = vbCopyPen           ' Try vbXorPen or vbMaskNotPen
    .ScaleMode = vbPixels
    .ScaleWidth = 256 * 2: .ScaleHeight = 256 * 2
```

(continued)

```
Dim clr As Long, i As Integer, x As Integer, y As Integer
Dim iRed As Integer, iGreen As Integer, iBlue As Integer
For i = 0 To 255
    ' Set line color
    If LightToDark Then
        If Red Then iRed = 255 - i
        If Blue Then iBlue = 255 - i
        If Green Then iGreen = 255 - i
    Else
        If Red Then iRed = i
        If Blue Then iBlue = i
        If Green Then iGreen = i
    End If
    clr = RGB(iRed, iGreen, iBlue)
    ' Draw each line of fade
    If Vertical Then
        cvsDst.Line (0, y)-(.ScaleWidth, y + 2), clr, BF
        y = y + 2
    End If
    If Horizontal Then
        cvsDst.Line (x, 0)-(x + 2, .ScaleHeight), clr, BF
        x = x + 2
    End If
Next
' Put things back the way you found them
.AutoRedraw = fAutoRedraw: .DrawWidth = iDrawWidth
.DrawStyle = ordDrawStyle: .DrawMode = ordDrawMode
.ScaleMode = ordScaleMode
.ScaleWidth = rScaleWidth: .ScaleHeight = rScaleHeight
End With
End Sub
```

The property settings are crucial to making the fade work accurately and efficiently. For example, fading slows to a crawl if you don't set AutoRedraw. The vbInsideSolid draw style is the only one that works properly (although vbInvisible gives an interesting effect). The vbCopyPen draw mode ensures that you overwrite anything on the background rather than interact with it. Setting the scale properties makes it easier to draw in multiples of 256 (the number of color intensities) regardless of the size of the target. All these settings must be saved and restored in case someone else wants to draw on your fade with different settings.

Remember, you're drawing the fade only to the current size of the target object. If you allow the object to be resized, you'll need to put Fade in the Resize event. Since Fade is no speed demon, it might be better to make faded forms a fixed size, as the Bit Blast form is.

WARNING All the statements in the Fade function take advantage of the *With cvsDst* block except the Line statements. Visual Basic's Line, PSet, and Circle statements use a nonstandard format that can't be represented with a normal method syntax. The language parser would have to contain special-case code to handle these statements in a With block. So far, that code has not been written. The request was postponed in Visual Basic version 4 and then postponed again in version 5.

Although we're using a naming convention (*cvsDst*) that implies a canvas type, the actual type is Object—and we're paying the price with late binding. This is where we could use some public access to Visual Basic's internal interfaces. I don't know whether it really exists, and if so, whether they call it ICanvas, IDrawable, or IItsOurSecret, but whatever it's named, Fade could draw a lot faster if it knew the interface of the object it's drawing on. I shouldn't have to write separate FadeForm, FadePictureBox, FadeUserControl, and FadePrinter procedures to get efficient drawing.

Hardcore Drawing

Help is available for all you hardcore programmers who want to draw 3-D shapes in Visual Basic. The OpenGL library is already part of Windows NT, and you can use it on Windows 95 if you get the library through the Win32 Software Developer's Kit. OpenGL supports three-dimensional drawing with shading, lighting, hidden surface removal, texturing, and who knows what else. I was afraid that if I started playing with it, I'd never finish this book so unfortunately you're on your own. I know of several people who have used it successfully from Visual Basic.

The Windows Way of Drawing

When you drop the Visual Basic safety net and start drawing with the Windows API, you'll find yourself dealing with issues that didn't concern you before. Scaling becomes a problem. You must figure out what Visual Basic properties mean to Windows and vice versa. Despite the problems, here are several good reasons why you might want to draw the hard way:

- Some operations you might want to perform are not supported in Visual Basic—drawing polygons, managing regions, and filling, for example.

- Some surfaces on which you might want to draw don't support Visual Basic drawing methods—buttons, menus, list boxes, metafiles, and memory device contexts, for example.

- Windows API functions are often faster than comparable Visual Basic operations. This is because Visual Basic is doing some extra work behind the scenes. If you're willing to do the necessary work yourself, you might get a performance gain. Then again you might not. You have to test the performance on a case-by-case basis.

- You can create generic functions that do some drawing operation on any surface. Instead of providing a canvas parameter (which is actually a late-bound Object), you can provide an hDC parameter and use API functions on it.

Let's look at some examples.

Seeing stars

The Fun 'n Games program (FUNNGAME.VBP) shows you how to draw the hard way. Figure 7-3 shows what might happen when you click the Stars button. The code uses the Polygon API function to draw many random stars and uses the

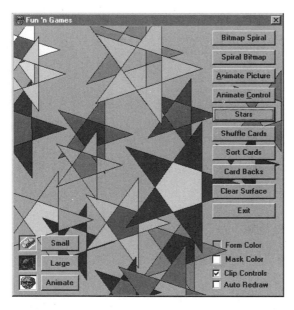

Figure 7-3. *Stars of Windows.*

FloodFill function to fill the centers with various colors. The differences between the Basic Way and the Windows Way are hidden by the VBPolygon and VBFloodFill functions.

Let's start with the Star procedure. Calling it is a simple matter:

```
For i = 1 To Random(5, 20)
    dxyRadius = Random(Height / 8, Height / 4)
    xMid = Random(1, Width): yMid = Random(1, Height)
    ' Black border and two random colors
    Star Me, xMid, yMid, dxyRadius, vbBlack, _
        QBColor(Random(1, 15)), QBColor(Random(1, 15))
    ' Black border and one random color
    'Star Me, xMid, yMid, dxyRadius, vbBlack, QBColor (Random(1, 15))
    ' One filled color
    'Star Me, xMid, yMid, dxyRadius, QBColor(Random(1, 15))
Next
```

You simply pass the canvas object to draw on, the *x* and *y* positions, the radius, the colors of the border, the start points, and the inside area. The comment lines show some alternate calls that will give different star effects.

Here's the code to draw a star:

```
Sub Star(cvsDst As Object, ByVal x As Long, ByVal y As Long, _
        ByVal dxyRadius As Long, clrBorder As Long, _
        Optional clrOut As Long = -1, Optional clrIn As Long = -1)
With cvsDst
    ' Handle optional arguments
    If clrOut = -1 Then clrOut = clrBorder
    If clrIn = -1 Then clrIn = clrOut

    ' Start is 144 degrees (converted to radians)
    Const radStar As Double = 144 * PI / 180

    ' Calculate each point
    Dim ptPoly(1 To 10) As Long, i As Integer
    For i = 1 To 10 Step 2
        ptPoly(i) = x + (Cos((i \ 2 + 1) * radStar) * dxyRadius)
        ptPoly(i + 1) = y + (Sin((i \ 2 + 1) * radStar) * dxyRadius)
    Next

    ' Set colors and style for star
    .ForeColor = clrBorder      ' SetTextColor
    .FillColor = clrOut         ' CreateSolidBrush
    .FillStyle = vbSolid        ' More CreateSolidBrush

    Call MGdiTool.VBPolygon(.hDC, ptPoly)

    ' Set color for center
    .FillColor = clrIn          ' CreateSolidBrush
    Call MGdiTool.VBFloodFill(.hDC, x, y, .ForeColor)
End With
End Sub
```

Star starts with the classic loop for calculating the points of a polygon. You decide how many degrees you want between each point on a circle and then convert degrees to radians. (Multiply degrees by *pi,* and then divide by 180.) Next, loop through each point, using cosine to calculate the *x* points and sine to calculate the *y* points. (Get out your high school geometry book if you want to understand exactly how and why this works.) If you place the points close enough and do enough of them, you'll get a circle, although this isn't a very efficient circle algorithm. If you want a pentagon, use one fifth of a circle (72 degrees). If you want a star, use two fifths of a circle (144 degrees). You end up going around the circle twice (144 × 5 = 720) to return to the starting point.

As you calculate the points, you put them into an array and then pass the array to VBPolygon, a wrapper for the Polygon API function. Putting the points into an array turns out to be messy. Polygon expects an array of POINT UDTs, but VBPolygon will be public and public procedures can't use UDT parameters. Therefore, VBPolygon takes an array of Longs with the *x* and *y* values in every other slot. Another big difference is that VBPolygon takes a Basic-style array while Polygon must take a C-style array (as described in "Arrays" in Chapter 2). The last difference is that VBPolygon receives points measured in twips but must convert them to pixels for Polygon.

The code is messy but not difficult:

```
Function VBPolygon(ByVal hDC As Long, aPoint() As Long) As Boolean
    Dim apt() As POINTL, i As Long, iMin As Long, c As Long
    iMin = LBound(aPoint)
    c = UBound(aPoint) - iMin + 1
    BugAssert 0 = (c Mod 2)      ' Even number of elements
    c = c / 2
    ' Create array of pixel-adjusted points
    ReDim apt(0 To c - 1) As POINTL
    Do While i < c
        apt(i).x = aPoint(iMin) / Screen.TwipsPerPixelX
        iMin = iMin + 1
        apt(i).y = aPoint(iMin) / Screen.TwipsPerPixelY
        iMin = iMin + 1
        i = i + 1
    Loop
    ' Pass first element and count to Polygon
    VBPolygon = Polygon(hDC, apt(0), c)
End Function
```

VBFloodFill works much the same as VBPolygon does, except that it doesn't worry about array conversion. It simply converts its twips arguments to pixel arguments as shown on the top of page 382.

Three Ways of Scaling

One of the most confusing issues in GDI programming is setting the scale. Just try to wade through SetMapMode, SetViewportExtEx, SetViewportOrgEx, and related functions in the Windows API documentation. Visual Basic settles all this nicely for you by doing all calculations in one mode: twips. A twip has an actual size, but it's easier to just think of it as a magical unit. As long as you measure everything with the same units, it doesn't much matter how big the units are.

You can't always use the same kind of units, however. When working with bitmaps, you must usually work in pixel mode (MM_TEXT, in SDK jargon). Visual Basic might convert everything to twips, but when you get down to the API level, you play by API rules, which normally don't use twips. To stir the pot even more, Visual Basic has a lot of COM Automation elements. COM Automation likes to use a mode named MM_HIMETRIC, which you can think of as another kind of magical unit.

A common scenario is that you must work with twips and pixels (and sometimes MM_HIMETRIC units) at the same time. One way to handle mixed modes is to set the ScaleMode property to vbPixels, perform some operations, set the property back to vbTwips, carry out some more operations, and keep changing back and forth as needed. But Visual Basic doesn't recognize MM_HIMETRIC as a ScaleMode value. Besides, changing modes constantly is messy.

You can also use the TwipsPerPixelX and TwipsPerPixelY properties of the Screen object as a means of converting between pixels and the default mode without changing the default. So you might see lines such as these:

```
dx = Width * Screen.TwipsPerPixelX
dy = Height * Screen.TwipsPerPixelY
```

The ScaleX and ScaleY methods provide another way to convert to and from any mode. For example, the following lines are equivalent to the two preceding lines of code:

```
dx = ScaleX(Width, vbPixels, vbTwips)      ' From pixels to twips
dy = ScaleY(Height, vbPixels, vbTwips)
```

The second and third parameters of ScaleX and ScaleY are optional. The default conversion from MM_HIMETRIC betrays the origin of the ScaleX and ScaleY methods, which were intended to make it easy to convert Picture.Width and Picture.Height to twips. The Picture object comes directly from COM Automation, where MM_HIMETRIC is standard; therefore, any property or any argument that expects twips will require the standard conversion shown here:

```
dx = ScaleX(Me.Picture.Width)   ' From MM_HIMETRIC picture to twips
dy = ScaleY(Me.Picture.Height)
```

```
Function VBFloodFill(ByVal hDC As Long, ByVal x As Long, _
                     ByVal y As Long, ByVal clr As Long) As Boolean
    VBFloodFill = FloodFill(hDC, x / Screen.TwipsPerPixelX, _
                            y / Screen.TwipsPerPixelY, clr)
End Function
```

FloodFill works by flooding everything around it until it encounters another color with the specified fill color. This allows some interesting effects in the Fun 'n Games program because you can layer different effects on top of each other. The outside of the star (filled by Polygon) is filled with the current FillColor (Brush, in Windows terminology) regardless of the background, but the center of the star (filled by FloodFill) interacts with its background.

Both VBPolygon and VBFloodFill assume that Visual Basic is operating in twips mode and that Windows is operating in what it calls MM_TEXT (for reasons unknown) but what Visual Basic calls pixel mode. If you change the mode, either in Visual Basic or in Windows, these functions will fail.

Bezier curves

Drawing curves with software is a difficult problem for the math-impaired. You can plot each separate point on a curve defined by a formula, but first you have to figure out the formula. The only variation is what you plot with—points, line segments, arcs, or even bitmaps. The addition of PolyBezier and PolyBezierTo in Win32 makes it easy to draw graceful curves. Making them fit your desired shape is a different matter.

Pierre Bezier invented the technique that bears his name back when the cars he designed were smaller and cost less than the computers he designed with. (Well, maybe cars weren't really smaller than computers in the 1960s, but they did cost less.) Anyway, the simplest Bezier curve is defined by four points. The outside points are the start and the end of the curve. The middle two points control the curve—that is, they pull and push it, they exert a magnetic attraction on it, they whip it into shape, they stretch it…the only way you're going to understand what they do is to try them out.

Figure 7-4 shows the Bezier Curves program (TBEZIER.VBP). You can see the curve here, but you'll have to run the program to see how it works. Drag with the left mouse button to control the top of the curve; drag with the right button to control the bottom of the curve.

The code starts with an array of four points:

```
Private apt(0 To 3) As POINTL
```

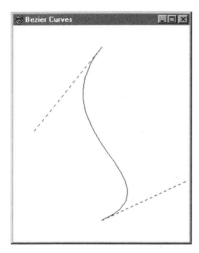

Figure 7-4. *A Bezier curve.*

InitBezier fills these points with initial values:

```
Sub InitBezier(cxClient As Long, cyClient As Long)
    apt(0).x = ScaleX(cxClient / 2, vbTwips, vbPixels)
    apt(0).y = ScaleY(cyClient / 10, vbTwips, vbPixels)
    apt(1).x = ScaleX(cxClient / 4, vbTwips, vbPixels)
    apt(1).y = ScaleY(cyClient / 2, vbTwips, vbPixels)
    apt(2).x = ScaleX(3 * cxClient / 4, vbTwips, vbPixels)
    apt(2).y = ScaleY(cyClient / 2, vbTwips, vbPixels)
    apt(3).x = ScaleX(cxClient / 2, vbTwips, vbPixels)
    apt(3).y = ScaleY(9 * cyClient / 10, vbTwips, vbPixels)
    ForeColor = vbRed
End Sub
```

The points are scaled because PolyBezier, like most GDI functions, expects pixels by default. Points 0 and 3 are the start and the end of the curve. To draw the curve, call DrawBezier:

```
Sub DrawBezier()
    DrawStyle = vbSolid
    PolyBezier hDC, apt(0), 4
    DrawStyle = vbDot
    MoveTo hDC, apt(0).x, apt(0).y
    LineTo hDC, apt(1).x, apt(1).y
    MoveTo hDC, apt(2).x, apt(2).y
    LineTo hDC, apt(3).x, apt(3).y
End Sub
```

MoveTo Comes Full Circle

The Win16 API had a MoveTo function, which returned a DWord containing the packed *x* and *y* coordinates of the previous current position:

```
dw = MoveTo(hDC, x, y)
```

The returned DWord is the equivalent of a 16-bit POINT variable. Some languages (but not Visual Basic) allow you to typecast a DWord to a POINT. Of course, most users don't care about the return value and simply call it like this:

```
MoveTo hDC, x, y
```

Apparently, it never occurred to the designers of MoveTo that Windows might someday have 32 bits. There's no good way to pack two 32-bit variables into a return value. For that reason, MoveTo was marked obsolete several versions ago and replaced with MoveToEx, although MoveTo was still supported for compatibility in 16-bit Windows.

The Win32 API has no MoveTo, only MoveToEx. The new function has a fourth parameter that returns the previous position through a reference variable of type POINT. It also returns a Boolean value to indicate success:

```
f = MoveToEx(hDC, x, y, ptJunk)
```

This is very convenient for the 1 percent of the time when you need to save the last position. The rest of the time, you can pass a null. The MoveToEx in the Windows API type library defines the last parameter with LPVOID (equivalent to As Any) so that you can call it like this:

```
f = MoveToEx(hDC, x, y, ByVal pNull)
```

But optional arguments and aliases enable us to do even better. The type library has an entry equivalent to this Declare statement:

```
Declare Function MoveTo Lib "gdi32" Alias "MoveToEx" ( _
    ByVal hdc As Long, ByVal x As Long, ByVal y As Long, _
    Optional lpPoint As Any = 0) As Long
```

If you ignore the return value (and why not?), you'll end up with this:

```
MoveTo hDC, x, y
```

Look familiar?

The curve is drawn with a solid line style, and lines connecting the control points are drawn with a dotted line style so that you can see how the control points work. In a real-life program, you wouldn't show the control points. Notice that you use the MoveTo and LineTo functions instead of the Visual Basic Line statements. The points are already in pixels, so it's easier to stick with API functions. (Actually, MoveTo isn't an API function; see the sidebar "MoveTo Comes Full Circle," page 384.)

After you run the program for a few minutes, you can probably guess the code for the MouseMove and MouseDown events. They set the foreground color to the background color and call DrawBezier to erase the current curve and control lines. Then they calculate new positions for the control points. Finally they reset the draw color and redraw with DrawBezier.

CHALLENGE   You can draw more than one Bezier curve by adding more elements to the array. Each curve needs three points in the array. The end point of the last curve serves as the starting point of the next curve. The next two points are control points. The last point is the end point of the curve. Your challenge is to enhance the Bezier sample to demonstrate multiple curves. You could also add a Bezier curve drawing tool to the IconWorks sample. Use the Curve tool in Windows Paint as a model.

Paths

Paths are recorded sequences of deferred line drawing commands. The idea is that you can draw an irregular, invisible shape using various commands and then perform an operation on the whole shape at once. Let's try it:

```
' Start recording path
BeginPath hDC
' Do some draw operations
ForeColor = vbYellow
FillColor = vbRed
FillStyle = vbSolid
Line (ScaleWidth * 0.2, ScaleHeight * 0.3)- _
    (ScaleWidth * 0.8, ScaleHeight * 0.7)
Circle (ScaleWidth * 0.5, ScaleHeight * 0.5), _
        ScaleHeight * 0.3
' Stop recording path
EndPath hDC
' Do something to finished path
StrokeAndFillPath hDC
' Update device context
Refresh
```

If you step through this code, nothing happens when you step over the Line and Circle statements. The figures aren't drawn until you reach the StrokeAnd-FillPath procedure, and they usually won't be visible until you call the Refresh method. Both figures are filled (except in the intersection) with the current FillColor and FillStyle, even though the Line statement doesn't have the *F* argument that specifies filling.

We're mixing Visual Basic statements and Windows API statements, but that's OK because the Visual Basic statements are calling API functions under the surface. The Line statement probably calls Rectangle, Circle probably calls Ellipse, and they're both working on the same device context that was passed to the path procedures. The API documentation has a long list of line drawing functions that you can use in paths, but the only Visual Basic statements that work are Line, Circle, and Print.

Print? Since when did Print get to be a line drawing statement? Well, since Windows got TrueType fonts. Try this:

```
' Set a large, TrueType font
With Font
    .Name = "Lucida Console"
    .Bold = True
    .Italic = True
    .Size = 48
End With
ForeColor = vbGreen
FillColor = vbMagenta
FillStyle = vbDiagonalCross
' Make Print statement into a path, and then fill
BeginPath hDC
Print "Hello"
EndPath hDC
StrokeAndFillPath hDC
Refresh
```

This code draws outlined green text filled with magenta cross-hatches. I was going to include a screen shot, but it was just too hideous.

Besides drawing and filling a path, you can also draw it (StrokePath), fill it (FillPath), and turn it into a region (PathToRegion). I don't have much to say about regions, except that paths make them easier to manage. In fact, I'm not going to discuss path-related functions such as FlattenPath, WidenPath, Set-MiterLimit, CloseFigure, or ExtCreatePen. You can explore these on your own.

NOTE   You must set AutoRedraw to True to use paths. I also found that some path features behaved differently under Windows 95 than under Windows NT.

Basic Windows Painting

You can paint, just as you can draw, the Windows Way, the Basic Way, or both ways at once. The Windows Way of painting is to create GDI objects—bitmaps, icons, and metafiles—and then select them into a device context. The Basic Way of painting is to load bitmaps, icons, and metafiles into a Picture property.

Essentially, you're dropping completed pictures onto a canvas. With previous versions of Visual Basic, it was difficult to go beyond that, and, in fact, many fine programs have been written without doing so. But we're going to the second level of painting—blitting—after getting acquainted with the Picture class and GDI objects.

Picture Objects

In early versions of Visual Basic, Picture was a property whose implementation was undefined to all but the most hardcore custom control writers. Today, Picture is a public interface with methods and properties available for inspection in the Object Browser. You can create your own Picture objects with Dim, Private, or Public; assign one Picture object to another with Set; and pass Picture objects as arguments. You can even create a Picture object with code, although Visual Basic won't help you, as you'll see later in Chapter 8. As far as Visual Basic is concerned, you can get Picture objects only indirectly through the LoadPicture function, the LoadResPicture function, or the Load Picture dialog box.

Picture objects are everywhere in Visual Basic, but using them is easier than understanding exactly what they are and why they work. For example, if you search for Picture in the Object Browser, you'll find lots of Picture properties but no Picture type. Instead, you'll find that Picture properties have the type StdPicture and that functions taking Picture arguments (SavePicture) or returning a Picture object (LoadPicture) use an IPictureDisp type. If you right-click in the Object Browser and select Show Hidden Members, you might also see an IPicture type. Picture, StdPicture, IPictureDisp, IPicture—what's the difference?

The Visual Basic help for the misnamed "Picture object" (they mean the Picture class) gives a hint. It states: "You cannot create a Picture object using code like *Dim X As New Picture*. If you want to create a Picture object, you must use the StdPicture object (sic) like this: *Dim X As New StdPicture*." Why not? Well, it turns out that StdPicture is a class, while Picture is an interface. You can never create an interface directly. Figure 7-5 shows a COM's eye view of what's really going on, as seen through the OleView program.

StdPicture (pronounced Stud Picture by some Visual Basic insiders) is what COM calls a coclass and what Visual Basic calls a class. You can always create a new object from a class. StdPicture implements two interfaces: Picture and IPicture. As we learned in "Interfaces," page 150, every Visual Basic class defines an interface with the class name and a leading underscore. This mirror interface is

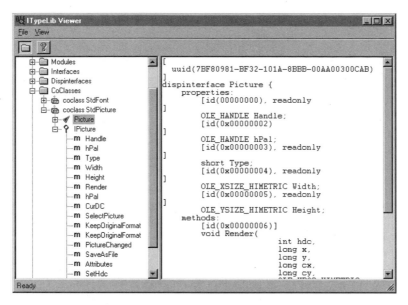

Figure 7-5. *The StdPicture class in OleView.*

called the default interface. For example, the default interface for the CMeToo class is _CMeToo. The StdPicture class wasn't written in Visual Basic, so it need not follow this naming convention. Its default interface is Picture. Through a kind of type library aliasing magic that doesn't concern us here, the Picture interface is the IPictureDisp interface. Don't ask why. Just accept it. Whenever you see IPictureDisp, think Picture (and vice versa). The important point is that you must use the class, not the interface, to create new StdPicture objects.

No matter whether you use the StdPicture class or the Picture interface, the properties and methods are the same. The Handle, hPal, Type, Width, and Height properties will become your friends in the next section and throughout the rest of the book. The Render method should remain forever a stranger, since Visual Basic's PaintPicture method encapsulates it in a friendlier fashion.

In addition to Picture, StdPicture implements the IPicture interface. If StdPicture had been written in Visual Basic, it would have had the following line near the top of the class file:

```
Implements IPicture
```

It would have had to implement properties such as IPicture_KeepOriginalFormat and methods such as IPicture_SaveAsFile. To use the IPicture methods, you would need to create a separate reference object. The code might look like this:

```
Dim pic As New StdPicture, ipic As IPicture
Set pic = pb.Picture
Set ipic = pic
Debug.Print ipic.KeepOriginalFormat
```

The IPicture members are documented in MSDN. Although I imagine that Visual Basic uses these members in its internal implementation of Picture properties and related features, you'll rarely, if ever, use them in your own code.

Picture methods and properties

The Height and Width properties of a picture are different from the Height and Width properties of a form or a picture box. The latter properties have values in the current scale mode (which is twips by default), but the Height and Width properties of a picture always have values in the standard COM mode, vbHimetric (MM_HIMETRIC). Visual Basic wouldn't let you set the scale mode to vbHimetric, even if you had some bizarre reason for doing so. Normally you'll convert all your widths and heights to twips or pixels.

The ScaleX and ScaleY methods are the easiest way to convert from vbHimetric units to twips. For example, the statement *ScaleX(Picture.Width)* converts to twips. Pixels are messier. Sometimes when you're dealing with API functions, you'll need to do a conversion without benefit of an object that has ScaleX and ScaleY methods. In that case, you can use the conversion constants and functions in PICTOOL.BAS. Here are several similar statements:

```
dxBlt = pic.Width * TwipsPerMillimeter / Screen.TwipsPerPixelX / 100
dxBlt = pic.Width * TwipsPerHiMetricUnit / Screen.TwipsPerPixelX
dxBlt = PicXToPixel(pic.Width)
dxBlt = frm.ScaleX(pic.Width, pvHiMetric, vbPixel)
```

I'll let you look up TwipsPerMillimeter, PicXToPixel, and similar conversions in the source code.

The Type property always returns 0 (*vbPicTypeNone*), 1 (*vbPicTypeBitmap*), 2 (*vbPicTypeMetafile*), 3 (*vbPicTypeIcon*), or 4 (*vbPicTypeEMetafile*). You can also load a cursor into a picture; the Type property will show it as *vbPicTypeIcon*.

The Handle and hPal properties are the link between the Basic Way of pictures and the Windows Way of GDI objects. The hPal property is the handle of the palette for bitmaps. (It's meaningless for icons or metafiles because these don't have palettes.)

The Handle property is the handle of the bitmap, icon, or metafile within the picture. You can have lots of fun with these object handles, as you'll see later. The Handle property is the default member. When you assign a value to a Picture property, you're actually assigning it to the handle. For example, the code

```
imgCur.Picture = LoadPicture("Thing.Ico")
```

actually means:

```
imgCur.Picture.Handle = LoadPicture("Thing.Ico")
```

Loading picture objects

Visual Basic provides several ways to load a picture object:

- Use LoadPicture to load from disk. Specifically, you can load a bitmap from a BMP or DIB file. You can load an icon from an ICO file or load a metafile from a WMF file. You can load a cursor from an ICO file or a CUR file.

- Use LoadPicture with no argument to clear a picture file.

- Assign one Picture property from another Picture property, from an Image property, or from any other property with StdPicture or Picture type.

- Use LoadResPicture to load a picture from a resource file attached to your program. (See Chapter 8.)

- Get a GDI object handle from a Windows API function and assign it to the Picture property. There's more to this than meets the eye, however, as you'll see in Chapter 8.

The Windows Way of Painting

The Windows Way of painting is to beg, borrow, steal, or create a GDI object and then select that object into a device context. GDI objects, like almost everything else in Windows, are identified by handle. These handle types include HBITMAP, HPEN, HBRUSH, HFONT, HPALETTE, and HRGN.

I've never found selecting objects into device contexts to be intuitive; I just do it by rote. Let's go through the process with a bitmap. If you can select a bitmap, you can select anything. First you need an HDC to write to, and then you need the handle of a bitmap. How can you get an HBITMAP? Let me count the ways:

- You can create one with CreateBitmap or CreateCompatibleBitmap. We'll do both in a later section, "Inside the Glass," page 408.

- You can use the Handle property of a picture object containing a bitmap. Because the Handle is the default member of the picture object and the picture object is the Picture property, you can think of the Picture property as the handle. But if you already have a picture containing a bitmap, you probably don't need to select it into anything.

- You can get a handle to a bitmap out of a bitmap resource. You can get it into a picture with LoadResPicture (but then you don't need it), or you can get it the hard way, as WinWatch does—by digging it out of an EXE file. See "Finding Resources," Chapter 8.

OK. Assuming that you have an HDC and an HBITMAP, you also need a handle to retain the old bitmap. Even if you created an empty DC and didn't think you put a bitmap there, you'd better be prepared to get one out and put it back when you're done. Your code looks something like this:

```
Private hDC As Long, hBitmap As Long, hBitmapOld As Long
' Get hDC and hBitmap from somewhere
    ⋮
    hBitmapOld = SelectObject(hDC, hBitmap)
```

At this point, if everything goes right, your bitmap appears in the device context. When you're done, you must clean up by selecting the old bitmap (or other object) back into the DC and then deleting your bitmap:

```
Call SelectObject(hDC, hBitmapOld)
Call DeleteObject(hBitmap)
```

I admit that I often ignore the return values. After all, what can you do if your cleanup fails? It's not supposed to. OK, OK; so I should have asserted:

```
f = SelectObject(hDC, hBitmapOld)
BugAssert f
f = DeleteObject(hBitmap)
BugAssert f
```

Is that good enough for you?

Since you don't always know when it's safe to destroy the object, you might find it easier to create a temporary DC, select the bitmap into it, copy your temporary DC to the target DC, and then destroy the temporary:

```
hDCTemp = CreateCompatibleDC(0&)
hBitmapOld = SelectObject(hDCTemp, hBitmap)
' Copy temporary to destination
Call BitBlt(hDCDst, 0, 0, dxDst, dyDst, hDCTemp, 0, 0, vbSrcCopy)
Call SelectObject(hDCTemp, hBitmapOld)
Call DeleteObject(hBitmap)
Call DeleteDC(hDCTemp)
```

Now you're rid of the bitmap and don't need to worry about selecting it out and deleting it later.

The same process applies to pens, brushes, and fonts, although you'll rarely need to use them in Visual Basic. The process is similar for palettes, except that you use the specific SelectPalette function instead of the generic SelectObject. If this seems like Greek to you, follow the instructions explicitly and all will be well.

NOTE Technically, HMETAFILE, HCURSOR, and HICON aren't considered GDI objects because you don't select them as you do the others. But they are in the GDI, they work somewhat like objects, and they are part of the Windows Way. Nevertheless, we'll ignore them here. I'll talk about icon and cursor handles in Chapter 8. Other than the sidebar "Metafiles 1, Visual Basic 0," page 373, you're on your own with metafiles.

A Word About Blitting

Blitting is such a key part of Windows graphics that it's hard to believe Visual Basic got through three major versions without offering any direct support for it. "Blit" is the common pronunciation for BitBlt, which is a contraction of the term *bit block transfer*. (Many books spell this term *blt*, but I couldn't bring myself to write a word with no vowels.) *Blitting* means combining the pixels of one bitmap with the pixels of another—or, at a lower level, combining the bits of one device context with the bits of another.

You can blit the old-fashioned way, using the Windows API BitBlt function (and its cousins StretchBlt and PatBlt). Or you can blit with the newfangled Paint-Picture method. Each way has its strong points. The Bit Blast program (BIT-BLAST.VBP) shown in Figure 7-6 illustrates both approaches. The Use BitBlt

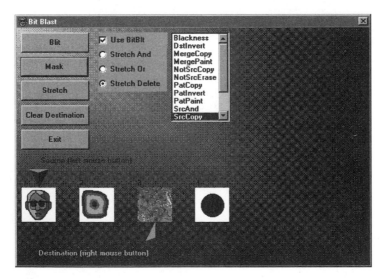

Figure 7-6. *The Bit Blast program.*

check box determines which version is used. Both give similar results, but the code is quite different, as you'll see.

To use Bit Blast, select a source picture with the left mouse button and a destination with the right button. Select one of the blit modes in the list box on the right, and click the Blit button (or double-click the selection in the list box). You can get a variety of effects by combining different pictures with different modes.

BitBlt Versus PaintPicture

To blit, you need a source object to blit from and a destination object to blit to. You must specify the size of both objects as well as the blit mode. Figure 7-7 provides a conceptual view of the operation and examples of how each element fits into the syntax of PaintPicture, BitBlt, and StretchBlt.

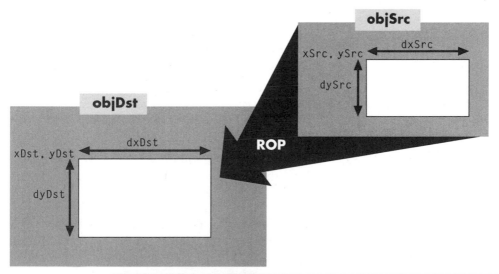

```
objDst.PaintPicture objSrc, xDst, yDst[, dxDst, dyDst, _
                            xSrc, ySrc, dxSrc, dySrc, ROP]
f = BitBlt(objDst.hDC, xDst, yDst, dxDst, dyDst, _
           objSrc.hDC, xSrc, ySrc, ROP)
              ' dxSrc and dySrc understood to be dxDst and dyDst
f = StretchBlt(objDst.hDC, xDst, yDst, dxDst, dyDst, _
               objSrc.hDC, xSrc, ySrc, dxSrc, dySrc, ROP)
```

Figure 7-7. *Three ways to blit.*

The Bit Blast code that combines one picture with another is listed below. A careful study of this code highlights the differences between the Windows Way and the Basic Way:

```
Private Sub cmdBlit_Click()
    Dim rop As Long
    rop = lstROP.ItemData(lstROP.ListIndex)
    If chkBitBlt.Value = vbChecked Then
        Call BitBlt(pbDst.hDC, 0, 0, dxBlt, dyBlt, _
                    pbSrc.hDC, 0, 0, rop)
        pbDst.Refresh
    Else
        pbSrc.Picture = pbSrc.Image
        pbDst.PaintPicture pbSrc.Picture, 0, 0, , , , , , rop
    End If
End Sub
```

The BitBlt function works on the device contexts of source and destination objects. In Visual Basic, you can blit to the hDC property of forms, picture boxes, and the printer. You can also borrow an HDC from any other window (such as the desktop) using the GetDC and ReleaseDC functions (see "Borrowing Device Context Handles," page 371), or you can create a memory device context, as you'll see later. But you can't use BitBlt on Image controls because they don't have an hDC or an hWnd property.

BitBlt, like all API functions, lacks optional arguments. You must provide the starting x and y coordinates (0, 0), the height and width of the blit (*dxBlt, dyBlt*), and the starting coordinates of the source (0, 0). Because the sizes of the source and the destination are always the same, you don't need to provide a source size (although you must do so with StretchBlt). For now, we'll skip the last BitBlt argument, which contains the raster operation (ROP) mode; we'll come back to it in "All About ROPs," page 401.

The *dxBlt* and *dyBlt* values are calculated elsewhere with this statement:

```
With pbTest(3)
    dxBlt = ScaleX(.Width, vbTwips, vbPixels)
    dyBlt = ScaleY(.Height, vbTwips, vbPixels)
```

Since all the images being blitted in Bit Blast are the same size, you can use the size of any one; *pbTest(3)* happens to be convenient. BitBlt and its relatives work in pixels by default, so if you're dealing with twips you must convert. ScaleX and ScaleY usually work best, but the sidebar "Three Ways of Scaling," page 381, explains other methods.

Visual Basic knows nothing about BitBlt and has no idea that you've altered the DC by blitting to it. You must call the Refresh method to make your changes show up on the screen. Refresh is unnecessary when AutoRedraw is set to True on the destination.

If you're familiar with BitBlt (as many Visual Basic programmers are), PaintPicture could take some getting used to. The argument order and the format are very different. The object to be painted is the destination, and the picture painted from is the first parameter. Notice that PaintPicture works on pictures, whereas BitBlt works on device context handles. That means that you can (and often should) use PaintPicture on Image controls.

The PaintPicture method combines the functionality of BitBlt and StretchBlt. (More on StretchBlt later.) In order to emulate both, PaintPicture needs a lot of arguments. Luckily, most PaintPicture arguments (although not enough to suit me) are optional. After the source picture, the arguments are the starting point of the destination, the size of the destination, the starting point of the source, the size of the source, and finally the ROP.

Since Bit Blast does a simple transfer between picture boxes of the same size, default values are OK for all the location and size arguments. You should be able to write this:

```
pbDst.PaintPicture pbSrc.Picture, , , , , , , , ROP
```

It doesn't work that way, however. PaintPicture requires the arguments for the destination starting point instead of defaulting to 0. So, instead, you need the following:

```
pbDst.PaintPicture pbSrc.Picture, 0, 0, , , , , , ROP
```

Maybe the designer was thinking of blitting from a picture box to a form. A value of 0 doesn't make sense in such a case, but it certainly does in my example and in many others.

> **NOTE** The Windows API also provides a PatBlt function to blit a pattern onto a device context. Windows NT goes even further: it provides MaskBlt to create masks and PlgBlt to blit a rectangle onto a parallelogram. Unfortunately, these functions weren't implemented for Windows 95.

StretchBlt Versus PaintPicture

The code for the Stretch button in Bit Blast illuminates more of the differences between the Basic Way and the Windows Way. Figure 7-8 on the following page illustrates what happens when you stretch a bitmap.

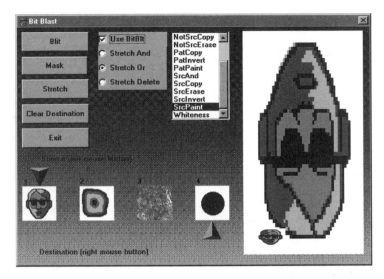

Figure 7-8. *Stretching a bitmap in the Bit Blast program.*

The Stretch button performs two blits: one to stretch the image larger while turning it inside out and one to compress it while turning it backward:

```
Private Sub cmdStretch_Click()
    If chkBitBlt.Value = vbChecked Then
        ' Stretch inside out
        Call StretchBlt(hDC, ScaleX(Width, vbTwips, vbPixels) * 0.97, _
                        ScaleY(Height, vbTwips, vbPixels) * 0.9, _
                        -dxBlt * 3.5, -dyBlt * 6.5, _
                        pbSrc.hDC, 0, 0, dxBlt, dyBlt, vbSrcCopy)
        ' Compress backward
        Call StretchBlt(hDC, ScaleX(Width, vbTwips, vbPixels) * 0.75, _
                        ScaleY(Height, vbTwips, vbPixels) * 0.8, _
                        -dxBlt * 0.9, dyBlt * 0.5, _
                        pbSrc.hDC, 0, 0, dxBlt, dyBlt, vbSrcCopy)
    Else
        With pbSrc
            .Picture = .Image
            ' Stretch inside out
            PaintPicture .Picture, Width * 0.97, Height * 0.9, _
                            -.Width * 3.5, -.Height * 6.5
            ' Compress backward
            PaintPicture .Picture, Width * 0.75, Height * 0.8, _
                            -.Width * 0.9, .Height * 0.5
        End With
    End If
End Sub
```

StretchBlt has the same arguments as BitBlt, except that it adds arguments for the source size. The whole idea of stretching a bitmap is that the source size and the destination size should differ. Despite its name, StretchBlt can also compress. (Think of it as negative stretching.) You can also stretch pictures backward or inside out by changing the signs of the arguments.

Some differences are obvious. StretchBlt requires that you convert to pixels; PaintPicture uses the default mode (twips, in this case). But the subtle differences are more interesting.

Notice the line that assigns the Image property of the source to the Picture property:

```
With pbSrc
    .Picture = .Image
```

This line ensures that the picture being blitted contains a bitmap. For example, the fourth picture box in Bit Blast contains a blank bitmap with a circle drawn over it using the Circle method. The device context of the picture box contains both the circle and the blank bitmap, but its Picture property contains only the bitmap. If you blit with BitBlt, the entire device context is copied. With Paint-Picture, however, you copy only the picture with its blank bitmap. You would have a similar problem if the picture box's picture contained a metafile or an icon, since PaintPicture can't blit these elements with a ROP mode.

The solution is to copy the image to the picture. When you assign the Image property, Visual Basic takes a snapshot of the device context with all its contents—pictures and drawings—and creates a bitmap, which it hands off as the Image property.

If you comment out the image-to-picture assignment, you'll see another difference in the marble pattern shown in the third box. The size of the picture used by PaintPicture is not the same as the HDC used by StretchBlt. The marble bitmap is much larger than the picture box, but it is clipped because AutoSize is False. PaintPicture stretches the entire picture, including the hidden part. StretchBlt stretches the clipped surface. Assigning the image gives the picture the same clipped snapshot you see on the screen.

When you compress a picture, StretchBlt has to merge many rows of pixels into fewer rows. The SetStretchBltMode function sets one of three modes for dealing with the extra lines. You can combine the extra lines with the remaining lines, using either an AND operation or an OR operation, or you can simply delete the extra lines. Using the SetStretchBltMode function on the destination surface has no effect on how PaintPicture compresses images, however. Visual Basic chooses a default mode (apparently the delete mode), and that's that.

The Bottom Line on PaintPicture

PaintPicture lacks the flexibility for the kinds of masking and blitting operations discussed in the rest of this chapter. It is tied to an unchangeable Picture object, whereas BitBlt and StretchBlt are tied to device contexts that you can change however you want. But you shouldn't throw PaintPicture out of your toolbox. It's certainly the easiest and fastest way to draw a thousand copies of a picture or to draw a picture in a thousand pieces. In other words, you can use it to create great visual effects.

If you're going to be copying a picture around, it's best to use an Image control as the picture container because it has lower overhead than a PictureBox. You can make it invisible if you don't want to show the source. Simply pass its Picture property to PaintPicture or to any of your procedures that take Picture parameters. For example, this procedure draws a spiral pattern of bitmaps, just as you might use PSet to draw a spiral pattern of dots (think of the pictures as big dots):

```
Sub BmpSpiral(cvsDst As Object, picSrc As Picture)
With cvsDst
    ' Calculate sizes
    Dim dxSrc As Long, dySrc As Long, dxDst As Long, dyDst As Long
    dxSrc = .ScaleX(picSrc.Width): dySrc = .ScaleY(picSrc.Height)
    dxDst = .ScaleWidth: dyDst = .ScaleHeight
    ' Set defaults (play with these numbers for different effects)
    Dim xInc As Long, yInc As Long, xSize As Long, ySize As Long
    Dim x As Long, y As Long
    xInc = CInt(dxSrc * 0.01): yInc = CInt(dySrc * 0.01)
    xSize = CInt(dxSrc * 0.1): ySize = CInt(dySrc * 0.1)
    Dim radCur As Single, degCur As Integer, angInc As Integer
    degCur = 0: angInc = 55
    ' Start in center
    x = (dxDst \ 2) - (dxSrc \ 2): y = (dyDst \ 2) - (dySrc \ 2)

    ' Spiral until off destination
    Do
        ' Draw at current position
        .PaintPicture picSrc, x, y, , , , , , , vbSrcAnd
        ' Calculate angle in radians
        radCur = (degCur - 90) * (PI / 180)
        ' Calculate next x and y
        x = x + (xSize * Cos(radCur))
        y = y + (ySize * Sin(radCur))
        ' Widen spiral
        xSize = xSize + xInc: ySize = ySize + yInc + 1
        ' Turn angle
        degCur = (degCur + angInc) Mod 360
```

```
    Loop While (x > 0) And (x + dxSrc < dxDst - dxSrc) And _
                (y > 0) And (y + dySrc < dyDst)
End With
End Sub
```

If you have an Image control with a bitmap picture, draw it on the current form with the statement *BmpSpiral Me, imgSmallBmp.Picture.*

Although previous versions of Visual Basic didn't provide a built-in way to blit, they did have a built-in way to stretch. The Stretch property of the Image control provided the moral equivalent of StretchBlt with no ROP mode. If all you want to do with a picture is stretch or compress it, it's hard to beat using the Image control with its Stretch property set to True. So how do you think Visual Basic implements the Stretch and AutoSize properties? Your guess is as good—and probably the same—as mine: StretchBlt.

Once you get the idea, it's not hard to devise ways to change the algorithm for inward spirals and other patterns. You can also experiment with different ROP codes for combining the images. Figure 7-9 shows one effect.

Another PaintPicture trick with many variations is to break a large bitmap into small squares and display the squares in some pattern. For example, you can

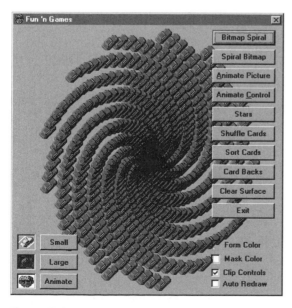

Figure 7-9. *The Bitmap Spiral in Fun 'n Games.*

randomize the position of the squares to form a puzzle and then put them back together. Another variation is to draw the squares in their correct places but create a pattern that makes the picture appear to explode, crush, or spiral onto the surface.

Here's a spiral bitmap effect. To try it, click the Spiral Bitmap button in the Fun 'n Games program. You can load your own digitized pictures or other large bitmaps by clicking the Large button or the picture box adjacent to it.

```
Sub SpiralBmp(cvsDst As Object, picSrc As Picture, _
            ByVal xOff As Long, ByVal yOff As Long)
With cvsDst
    Dim xLeft As Long, xRight As Long, yTop As Long, yBottom As Long
    Dim dxSrc As Long, dySrc As Long, xSrc As Long, ySrc As Long
    Dim xDst As Long, yDst As Long, xInc As Long, yInc As Long
    Dim x As Long, y As Long
    ' Initialize
    dxSrc = .ScaleX(picSrc.Width): dySrc = .ScaleY(picSrc.Height)
    xInc = dxSrc / 20: yInc = dySrc / 20
    xLeft = 0: yTop = 0:
    xRight = dxSrc - xInc: yBottom = dySrc - yInc


    ' Draw each side
    Do While (xLeft <= xRight) And (yTop <= yBottom)
        ' Top
        For x = xLeft To xRight Step xInc
            .PaintPicture picSrc, x + xOff, y + yOff, xInc, yInc, _
                x, y, xInc, yInc, vbSrcCopy
        Next
        x = x - xInc: yTop = yTop + yInc
        ' Right
        For y = yTop To yBottom Step yInc
            .PaintPicture picSrc, x + xOff, y + yOff, xInc, yInc, _
                x, y, xInc, yInc, vbSrcCopy
        Next
        y = y - yInc: xRight = x - xInc
        ' Bottom
        For x = xRight To xLeft Step -xInc
            .PaintPicture picSrc, x + xOff, y + yOff, xInc, yInc, _
                x, y, xInc, yInc, vbSrcCopy
        Next
        x = x + xInc: yBottom = y - yInc
        ' Left
        For y = yBottom To yTop Step -yInc
            .PaintPicture picSrc, x + xOff, y + yOff, xInc, yInc, _
                x, y, xInc, yInc, vbSrcCopy
        Next
        y = y + yInc: xLeft = xLeft + xInc
```

```
     Loop
  End With
  End Sub
```

I can't show you this effect on the page because the movement is the point; you'll have to try it.

All About ROPs

I have postponed discussing what Visual Basic documentation calls *opcodes* and the Windows API documentation calls *ROPs* (raster operations). I don't know the official pronunciation, but I like to think of them as "ropes," for no good reason. Whatever the name, ROPs are binary encodings that indicate how these three elements will be combined: the source picture, the destination background, and any pattern on the destination background.

Pictures are made up of pixels, and pixels are made up of bits. You combine bits with logical operators: AND, OR, XOR, NOT, and COPY. ROPs specify which logical operators will be used to combine (or not combine) the bits of the source, destination, and pattern. There are 15 named combinations, about seven more than you'll ever need. This chapter uses only vbSrcCopy, vbSrcAnd, vbSrcPaint, vbNotSrcErase, vbDstInvert, vbSrcInvert, and vbMergePaint. You can see all of them as RasterOpConstants in the VBRUN library in the Object Browser.

ROP codes are actually hexadecimal numbers, indicating 256 possible combinations of destination, source, and pattern with NOT, AND, OR, XOR, and COPY operators. Most have no practical use. For example, you probably won't need the combination that copies the destination onto itself. You can find the 256 combinations by searching for *Ternary Raster Operations* in MSDN. Incidentally, PaintPicture accepts all 256 combinations, not just the 15 named ones.

Blitting Images onto Backgrounds

The logical meaning of the various operations probably doesn't give you much idea of their practical use. Here are some step-by-step examples of how to put one image onto another. I can't illustrate the color steps on a black-and-white page, so you'll have to start Bit Blast and follow along. Begin by following the steps listed below.

1. Left-click picture 1 (the face) to make it the source, and right-click picture 4 (the circle) to make it the destination. Now click the Mask button to create a mask of the face in picture 4. The mask consists entirely of black pixels (0 bits) and white pixels (1 bits). Later I'll explain how to create a mask with code.

2. Left-click picture 4, and right-click picture 3 (the marble background). Select MergePaint and click the Blit button (or double-click Merge-Paint in the list box) to transfer the mask to the marble. The result is a white

face on the marble background. MergePaint first changed all the black (masked) bits to white, thus reversing the mask. Then it used an OR operation to combine the source bits with the destination bits. The marble bits that were on, combined with the black outside bits, stay on; and the marble bits that were off, combined with masked black bits, stay off. But all the masked white bits stay on, regardless of their status in the marble. MergePaint is a one-step way of doing a DstInvert operation on the mask and then doing a SrcPaint operation from the mask to the marble.

3. Left-click picture 1, and do a SrcAnd from the face to the marble. This puts the face on the marble. That's essentially how we're going to create transparent pictures and animate them.

You might expect that an ROP could do all this in one operation. No such luck. The closest you can get is to SrcAnd the face directly onto the marble. This creates a mixture of the face and the marble, which is an interesting effect but isn't how you write video games.

Click Clear Destination to restore the marble, and then try this exercise:

1. Mask the face over the circle (the picture I usually use as a work area).

2. SrcInvert the face onto the marble.

3. SrcAnd the mask onto the marble.

4. SrcInvert the face onto the marble.

A Short Digression on Patterns

Some ROPs—vbMergeCopy, vbPatCopy, vbPatInvert, and vbPatPaint—work on what SDK documentation calls the *pattern* when it discusses ROPs. When discussing everything else, the document refers to this as the *brush*. Every device context has a brush, and you can change the brush by selecting a new brush into the device context.

In Visual Basic, you change the brush by setting the FillPattern and FillColor properties. Few Visual Basic programmers bother to do this. The default transparent black brush is suitable for most purposes. If you use the default brush, you can ignore all the ROPs that deal with patterns (as I will for the rest of this book).

But first try blitting to and from various boxes with MergeCopy, PatPaint, PatInvert, and PatCopy. You'll see that the leftmost three boxes in Bit Blast have invisible background patterns (set with the FillStyle property) that merge with or overwrite the pictures.

Different process, same result—with some bizarre color combinations along the way. Before you try to figure out why, imagine what your screen would look like if you used this technique to move a transparent picture around the screen: you'd see an ugly color change for every update. We'll follow this path no further because it temporarily changes the whole background.

One more example:

1. Mask the face onto the circle.

2. DstInvert the face. It doesn't matter what the source is because it will be ignored.

3. NotSrcErase the mask onto the face. (You can also do this in two steps: SrcPaint the mask onto the face, and then DstInvert the face.) The face now has an inverted background.

4. SrcAnd the mask onto the marble, which masks out the shape of the image on the background.

5. SrcInvert the face onto the marble. Alternatively, you can SrcPaint the face onto the marble.

This might seem strange, but actually it is the same technique used in the CALL-DLLS sample program provided with Visual Basic—except that the developers cheated. They created the same inverted image you get from steps 1, 2, and 3 in a bitmap editor. They also created a mask like the one you'll create in the next section with a bitmap editor. Then with steps 4 and 5, they combined these two images on the background. The key difference between this third example and the first example you tried is that the first technique uses the original picture (white background) and a reversed (white) mask, whereas this one uses a reversed picture (black background) and a normal (black) mask.

Windows also uses this technique to display icons. In fact, if you dump the data in an icon (using the memory techniques discussed in Chapter 8), you'll see that the icon image displayed on the screen doesn't even exist internally. An icon consists of a monochrome mask (called the XOR mask) with all the opaque bits black and an image with an inverted background (called the AND mask). If you study the source code of the old IconWorks sample, you can see how it's done. (IconWorks isn't provided with Visual Basic, but this book's companion CD provides it.) We'll do this in the rest of the chapter, defining a class that creates the XOR and AND masks only once, when initialized, and then uses them to put a transparent image on the screen as often as you want. In other words, we'll define icons of any size.

But before you can use any of these techniques, you must create masks.

Creating Masks

You can create masks with a bitmap editor. Just use Save As to copy the image, and then fill with black every pixel you want to be opaque and fill with white every pixel you want to be transparent. This works, but it isn't a particularly good idea. First, it's difficult to change the mask every time you change the image. Second, if you have a color image, you'll end up with a color mask consisting of two colors, although you need only a monochrome mask. Depending on your video system, the color mask can take up a lot more memory than a monochrome mask.

It's also possible to create a mask by looping through every pixel in a picture and setting all the colored pixels to black and all the background bits to white, but I don't recommend it. Instead, you can sneak through the back door and create masks on the fly by copying them. Windows will automatically translate a color bitmap into a monochrome bitmap (and vice versa) when you copy it. Therefore, in order to get a monochrome mask, simply copy a color bitmap to a monochrome bitmap of the same size. All the nonwhite pixels will come out black. The trick is getting a monochrome bitmap. As it turns out, you get one by default when you create a memory DC and a bitmap to go into it.

A memory device context is just like any other device context except that it exists only in memory. You can't see it, but you can copy it to the DC of a visible object such as a form, a picture box, or a printer. In other words, it's like a picture box with Visible set to False—except that it takes up fewer resources. Memory DCs are handy because you can use them to mix masks and images out of sight and then, when everything is ready, copy the invisible DC to the visible one. This reduces the number of visible blits and thus reduces the amount of flicker during animation.

Here's how Bit Blast creates a mask:

```
Private Sub cmdMask_Click()
    Dim hdcMono As Long, hbmpMono As Long, hbmpOld As Long

    ' Create memory device context
    hdcMono = CreateCompatibleDC(0)
    ' Create monochrome bitmap and select it into DC
    hbmpMono = CreateCompatibleBitmap(hdcMono, dxBlt, dyBlt)
    hbmpOld = SelectObject(hdcMono, hbmpMono)
    ' Copy color bitmap to DC to create mono mask
    BitBlt hdcMono, 0, 0, dxBlt, dyBlt, pbSrc.hDC, 0, 0, SRCCOPY
    ' Copy mono memory mask to visible picture box
    BitBlt pbDst.hDC, 0, 0, dxBlt, dyBlt, hdcMono, 0, 0, SRCCOPY
    pbDst.Refresh
    ' Clean up
    Call SelectObject(hdcMono, hbmpOld)
```

```
    Call DeleteDC(hdcMono)
    Call DeleteObject(hbmpMono)
End Sub
```

This code creates a mask in a memory DC and then copies that DC to the specified destination. The 0 passed to CreateCompatibleDC tells it to make the new DC compatible with the screen. You could pass it the HDC of something else (a printer, perhaps) to make it compatible with that object. Animation doesn't work too well on printers, so the screen is usually a good choice. CreateCompatibleBitmap creates a bitmap of the given size. At this point, the DC is an imaginary object with no size and no features; you must select something into it with SelectObject to make it real. You might ask (as I did) why a bitmap compatible with a DC compatible with a color screen comes out monochrome. Well, it's just one of those things.

Once you have a monochrome bitmap of the correct size, simply copy and let Windows do the conversion. In Bit Blast, I copy the resulting mask back to a visible picture, but there's usually no need to see the mask so you can leave it in memory. Finally you must clean up the mask when you're done. In Bit Blast, you're done as soon as you copy the mask, but in real life you'll probably need to keep the mask around for the life of the image you're animating. You can clean up in Form_Unload or Class_Terminate. Just be sure to do it. I can assure you from hard experience that the consequences of forgetting are unpleasant.

Animating Pictures

Windows doesn't provide much direct support for animation or transparent images. But it does provide everything you need to create your own, including a model: icons. From the outside, an icon looks like an image on a transparent background. Internally, an icon is simply a bitmap with a corresponding mask. Once you understand how the GDI module uses masks to make icons look transparent, you can make your own transparent images, of any size.

When you create an icon with an editor such as IconWorks, you create only the pixel data. The tool automatically creates an AND mask and an XOR mask and puts both (with a header) into an ICO file. Eventually the icon masks are loaded into memory and become accessible through an icon handle (HICON). Programs can then call DrawIcon, which carves a hole in the background surface in the shape of the mask and puts the image into that hole. You must do essentially the same thing to turn any bitmap into an icon. From there, it takes only a few more steps to make your "icon" into a sprite—that is, a moveable image suitable for animation.

I wrap this functionality up in two ways. First, the CPictureGlass class does it the hard way. We're going to take a long look at the details. Second, XPictureGlass wraps it up the easy way. It takes advantage of the MaskPicture and

MaskColor features of the UserControl object to create a control that works a lot like CPictureGlass with just a few lines of code. CPictureGlass and XPictureGlass each have their advantages. Either way, you get transparent pictures.

> **CHALLENGE** I'm using the term *animate* somewhat loosely. Real animation involves displaying a sequence of transparent images to simulate movement. This chapter does only the simplest form of animation—moving a single image across a background. It's your job to turn the CPictureGlass class into the CMovingPictures collection.

The Glass Picture

The CPictureGlass class does animation the hard way. You pass it the canvas surface you want to draw on and the picture you want to make transparent along with the color you want to be considered the background. Optionally, you can provide x and y coordinates for the point on which you want the picture to be centered.

Behind the scenes, CPictureGlass makes a copy of the background surface that will be covered by the picture, punches a hole in it using a mask, plunks a masked copy of the picture into the hole, and puts the modified background back onto the canvas. So there you have it: transparency. Not only that, but CPictureGlass keeps a copy of the last background used and restores it before moving on to the next position. Now you have moving transparency.

CPictureGlass works kind of like a PictureBox control because the original model in the first edition of this book was that the class would work like a transparent PictureBox. Of course, you couldn't create controls in Visual Basic version 4, so CPictureGlass had to do some hacks by delegating to a real PictureBox. This version abandons the internal PictureBox control but maintains some methods and properties that look suspiciously like those of a PictureBox.

Using CPictureGlass

Let's check out the client code in FUN.FRM (project FUNNGAME.VBP) before we talk about the implementation. The CPictureGlass declaration is at the module level so that it can be accessed from various routines:

```
Private pgPicture As New CPictureGlass
```

Although the *pgPicture* variable is declared at the form level, the New keyword in the declaration means that the object isn't actually created until the first reference. That first reference had better be the Create method, since the object is meaningless without initialization. In the Fun 'n Games program, object creation and initialization occurs in the cmdAnimate_Click sub:

```
Private Sub cmdAnimate_Click()
    If cmdAnimate.Caption = "&Animate Picture" Then
        With pgPicture
            ' Draw picture on center of form with white background
            .Create Me, imgAniBmp.Picture, clrMask, Width / 2, Height / 2
            ' Constant controls pace, sign controls direction
            xInc = .Width * 0.05
            yInc = -.Height * 0.05
        End With
        SetTimer eatPicture
        cmdAnimate.Caption = "Stop &Animate"
    Else
        SetTimer eatNone
        cmdAnimate.Caption = "&Animate Picture"
    End If
End Sub
```

This sub is a toggle that turns animation on or off. After calling the Create method, you can use CPictureGlass properties such as Visible, Left, Top, Width, and Height.

The SetTimer sub tells the Timer control to handle the animation. (The Fun 'n Games program also uses the same Timer control to animate card backs.) We're not interested yet in the details of how SetTimer tells the timer which events to handle. All that matters is that the timer event calls AnimatePicture. The code is listed below:

```
Private Sub AnimatePicture()
    With pgPicture
        If .Left + .Width > ScaleWidth Then xInc = -xInc
        If .Left <= Abs(xInc) Then xInc = -xInc
        If .Top + .Height > ScaleHeight Then yInc = -yInc
        If .Top <= Abs(yInc) Then yInc = -yInc
        .Move .Left + xInc, .Top + yInc
    End With
End Sub
```

This code simply moves the picture around the form, bouncing back in the other direction when it hits a border. Not very difficult. The hard part is inside.

CHALLENGE The Fun 'n Games program takes shortcuts. It sets AutoRedraw to False because otherwise some of the dynamic effects wouldn't work or would be too slow. AutoRedraw works by maintaining a behind-the-scenes bitmap that represents the form surface. When you use PaintPicture with AutoRedraw, you're drawing to this bitmap instead of to the real form surface. That might work for some programs, but it's not fun and games. If you don't let Visual Basic redraw automatically, you're supposed to redraw yourself in the Paint event. That wouldn't be much fun either because you'd have to remember everything you drew and redraw it whenever the window moved or was obscured by another application. Fortunately, we sample programmers can ignore such inconveniences, leaving the toughest parts of animation to real programmers like you.

Inside the Glass

The Create method does most of what CPictureGlass does. This is a long function, so we'll step through it in pieces. But first, here are the private variables used by the Create method and other CPictureGlass methods and properties:

```
Private cvsDst As Object, hdcDst As Long, clrMask As Long
Private hdcImage As Long, hbmpImage As Long, hbmpImageOld As Long
Private hdcMask As Long, hbmpMask As Long, hbmpMaskOld As Long
Private hdcBack As Long, hbmpBack As Long, hbmpBackOld As Long
Private hdcCache As Long, hbmpCache As Long, hbmpCacheOld As Long
Private fExist As Boolean, fVisible As Boolean
Private xOld As Long, yOld As Long
Private dxSrc As Long, dySrc As Long
Private xLeft As Long, yTop As Long
```

This list gives you some idea of the complexity we're going to be dealing with. Notice that the destination canvas *cvsDst* has type Object. That's so you can draw on a form, on a PictureBox, or on a UserControl. But late binding imposes a performance penalty that must be minimized in any animation technique. CPictureGlass does this by saving all the useful properties of the destination canvas in variables. You do this in the Create method, which is called only once and is not speed-critical. You don't want to access late-bound members in the Draw method, which will be called constantly. But this strategy assumes that whatever you save in Create will be unchanged when Draw tries to use it. That's one of the reasons the Fun 'n Games form isn't resizable. Keep this in mind when using CPictureGlass in your own programs. You'll need to call Create again any time important properties of the destination canvas change.

Create starts out by saving data from its arguments and querying the system for additional data:

```
Sub Create(cvsDstA As Object, picSrc As Picture, clrMaskA As Long, _
        Optional x As Variant, Optional y As Variant)

    ' Clean up any old instance before creating a new one
    If fExist Then Destroy
    ' Save at module level for use in properties and methods
```

```
    clrMask = clrMaskA
    Set cvsDst = cvsDstA
    If picSrc.Type <> vbPicTypeBitmap Then ErrRaise eePictureNotBitmap

    ' Catch any errors from canvas that doesn't have needed properties
    On Error GoTo CreateErrorCanvas
    With cvsDst
        hdcDst = .hDC
        ' Get size and position of image in pixels
        dxSrc = .ScaleX(picSrc.Width, vbHimetric, vbPixels)
        dySrc = .ScaleY(picSrc.Height, vbHimetric, vbPixels)
        ' Default is the center
        If IsMissing(x) Then x = .ScaleWidth / 2
        If IsMissing(y) Then y = .ScaleHeight / 2
        xLeft = .ScaleX(x, .ScaleMode, vbPixels)
        yTop = .ScaleY(y, .ScaleMode, vbPixels)
    End With
    Dim cPlanes As Long, cPixelBits As Long
    cPlanes = GetDeviceCaps(hdcDst, PLANES)
    cPixelBits = GetDeviceCaps(hdcDst, BITSPIXEL)
```

The next step is to create a copy of the Picture we're going to make transparent. We can't work on the original because we're going to modify the picture. This is a temporary variable that can be destroyed when we're finished.

```
' Create memory DC compatible with screen for picture copy
Dim hdcSrc As Long, hdcSrcOld As Long, hbmpSrcOld As Long
hdcSrc = CreateCompatibleDC(0&)
' Select bitmap into DC
hbmpSrcOld = SelectObject(hdcSrc, picSrc.Handle)
```

This code first creates a memory DC compatible with the screen. It then selects the bitmap from the picture into the DC. This copy now has the same bits and colors as the picture. But we don't need the same bits for transparency—we need an inverted copy of them. So we create another memory DC:

```
' Create memory DC for image with inverted background (AND mask)
hdcImage = CreateCompatibleDC(0&)
' Create color bitmap same as screen
hbmpImage = CreateBitmap(dxSrc, dySrc, cPlanes, cPixelBits, 0&)
hbmpImageOld = SelectObject(hdcImage, hbmpImage)
' Make copy of picture because we don't want to modify original
Call BitBlt(hdcImage, 0, 0, dxSrc, dySrc, hdcSrc, 0, 0, vbSrcCopy)
```

This is the first of four permanent memory DCs that we'll blit to and from during the animation. In some cases, we could blit directly to the destination, but it's faster to blit to a memory DC than to a screen DC so we'll delay modifying the real destination until the last moment.

Before we can invert the background of the image, we have to create the mask:

```
' Create DC for monochrome mask of image (XOR mask)
hdcMask = CreateCompatibleDC(0&)
' Create bitmap (monochrome by default)
hbmpMask = CreateCompatibleBitmap(hdcMask, dxSrc, dySrc)
' Select it into DC
hbmpMaskOld = SelectObject(hdcMask, hbmpMask)
' Set background of source to the mask color
Call SetBkColor(hdcSrc, clrMask)
' Copy color bitmap to monochrome DC to create mono mask
Call BitBlt(hdcMask, 0, 0, dxSrc, dySrc, hdcSrc, 0, 0, vbSrcCopy)
```

This is the same technique described earlier in "Creating Masks," page 404. The *clrMask* color determines which color will be transparent.

At this point, we're finished with the picture object and the copy we made of it, so we can throw it away:

```
' We've copied and used the source picture, so give it back
Call SelectObject(hdcSrc, hbmpSrcOld)
Call DeleteDC(hdcSrc)
```

The image DC still contains an exact duplicate of the original picture, but we're about to throw away the last vestiges of what we started with. A transparent picture has no use for its background color, and, in fact, that background had better be a known color—black. "Blitting Images onto Backgrounds," page 401, explains why this inversion is necessary.

```
' Invert background of image to create AND Mask
Call SetBkColor(hdcImage, vbBlack)
Call SetTextColor(hdcImage, vbWhite)
Call BitBlt(hdcImage, 0, 0, dxSrc, dySrc, hdcMask, 0, 0, vbSrcAnd)
```

At this point, the CPictureGlass object contains an XOR mask and an AND mask, just as an icon does—and it will use them in the same way.

Finally we create a DC to save the background and one to draw a temporary picture (but don't blit anything to them yet) and wrap up with some error handling:

```
    ' Create memory DCs for old background and cache
    hdcBack = CreateCompatibleDC(0&)
    hbmpBack = CreateBitmap(dxSrc, dySrc, cPlanes, cPixelBits, 0&)
    hbmpBackOld = SelectObject(hdcBack, hbmpBack)
    hdcCache = CreateCompatibleDC(0&)
    hbmpCache = CreateBitmap(dxSrc, dySrc, cPlanes, cPixelBits, 0&)
    hbmpCacheOld = SelectObject(hdcCache, hbmpCache)
```

```
    ' Invalid x and y indicate first move hasn't occurred
    xOld = -1: yOld = -1
    fExist = True: fVisible = True
    Exit Sub
CreateErrorCanvas:
    ErrRaise eeInvalidCanvas
End Sub
```

Cleaning Up Glass

All those bitmaps and device contexts in Create have to be cleaned up. The Destroy method (which is called by the Class_Terminate event procedure) provides a place where you can be sure that cleanup happens. Here's the code:

```
Sub Destroy()
    BugAssert fExist
    ' Select old mask back to DC
    Call SelectObject(hdcMask, hbmpMaskOld)
    ' Now it's safe to delete DC and bitmask
    Call DeleteDC(hdcMask)
    Call DeleteObject(hbmpMask)
    ' Clean up inverted image DC
    Call SelectObject(hdcImage, hbmpImageOld)
    Call DeleteDC(hdcImage)
    Call DeleteObject(hbmpImage)
    ' Clean up cache DC
    Call SelectObject(hdcCache, hbmpCacheOld)
    Call DeleteDC(hdcCache)
    Call DeleteObject(hbmpCache)
    ' Clean up old background DC
    Call SelectObject(hdcBack, hbmpBackOld)
    Call DeleteDC(hdcBack)
    Call DeleteObject(hbmpBack)
    xOld = -1: yOld = -1
    fExist = False
End Sub
```

Moving a Glass Object

Now you have everything necessary to draw a transparent image anywhere. The Draw method does the work. Users can call the Draw method themselves, but generally, they won't. Instead, they'll call the Move method or modify the Left and Top properties, which will, in turn, call the Draw method.

Conceptually, the Draw method works a lot like the GDI DrawIcon function. The code is on the following page.

```
Public Sub Draw()
With cvsDst
    BugAssert fExist
    If fVisible = False Then Exit Sub

    ' Copy old background to its last location
    If xOld <> -1 Then
        Call BitBlt(hdcDst, xOld, yOld, dxSrc, dySrc, _
                    hdcBack, 0, 0, vbSrcCopy)
    End If
    ' Save current background and position for next time
    Call BitBlt(hdcBack, 0, 0, dxSrc, dySrc, _
                hdcDst, xLeft, yTop, vbSrcCopy)
    ' Create cache copy of background to work on
    Call BitBlt(hdcCache, 0, 0, dxSrc, dySrc, _
                hdcDst, xLeft, yTop, vbSrcCopy)
    xOld = xLeft: yOld = yTop
    ' Save color and set to white and black
    Dim clrBack As Long, clrFore As Long
    clrBack = GetBkColor(hdcCache)
    clrFore = GetTextColor(hdcCache)
    Call SetBkColor(hdcCache, vbWhite)
    Call SetTextColor(hdcCache, vbBlack)
    ' Mask the background
    Call BitBlt(hdcCache, 0, 0, dxSrc, dySrc, hdcMask, 0, 0, vbSrcAnd)
    ' Put image in hole created by mask
    Call BitBlt(hdcCache, 0, 0, dxSrc, dySrc, hdcImage, 0, 0, vbSrcPaint)
    ' Restore color
    Call SetBkColor(hdcCache, clrBack)
    Call SetTextColor(hdcCache, clrFore)
    ' Put finished cache on screen
    Call BitBlt(hdcDst, xLeft, yTop, dxSrc, dySrc, _
                hdcCache, 0, 0, vbSrcCopy)
End With
End Sub
```

This method, like every other method and property in CPictureGlass, starts out by asserting that the object exists. This assertion will fail if the user declares a CPictureGlass object but then tries to use it before initializing with the Create method. Draw also terminates without doing anything if *fVisible* (controlled by the Visible property) is False.

Draw next restores the previous background (if there is one) and saves two copies of the current background—one to work on and one to restore next time. Without this step, each drawing would work but wouldn't erase itself; you'd see a trail of image "droppings." Finally you mask out the shape of the image on the background of the temporary copy and plunk the image (with its inverted

Transparent Blits

It has been alleged that some video drivers support transparent blits. I have never come across one, and so, being unable to test the feature, I didn't build it into CPictureGlass. However, the Video tab in the All About program (ALLABOUT-.VBP) will tell you whether your system supports transparent blits. If so, you could do faster, smoother animation with the following code:

```
If GetDeviceCaps(hdcDst, CAPS1) And C1_TRANSPARENT Then
    ordModeOld = GetBkMode(hdcDst, NEWTRANSPARENT)
    clrOld = SetBkColor(hdcDst, clrMask)
    Call BitBlt(hdcDst, xLeft, yTop, dxSrc, dySrc, _
                hdcImage, 0, 0, NEWTRANSPARENT)
    Call SetBkMode(hdcDst, ordModeOld)
    Call SetBkColor(hdcDst, clrOld)
End If
```

This is air code because I had nothing to test it with. This feature has been around long enough that hardware vendors ought to support it, and maybe some do. But not for the hardware I use.

background) into the hole. Only when the whole image and background have been assembled off-screen do you copy the temporary *hdcCache* to the screen. You could do all this blitting and color changing directly on the container, but you'd end up with a whole lot of flicker.

Other Properties and Methods

The Create and Draw methods are the heart of the CPictureGlass class, but the class also needs to supply other properties and methods so that users can move the transparent picture. I chose member names based on the familiar ones used by the PictureBox control. Figure 7-10 on the following page shows a diagram of the CPictureGlass class.

Let's start with the Move method, which is interesting more for how it handles optional arguments than for how it handles the image:

```
Public Sub Move(xLeftA As Long, Optional yTopA As Long = -1)
With cvsDst
    BugAssert fExist
    xLeft = .ScaleX(xLeftA, .ScaleMode, vbPixels)
    If yTopA <> -1 Then yTop = .ScaleY(yTopA, .ScaleMode, vbPixels)
    Draw
End With
End Sub
```

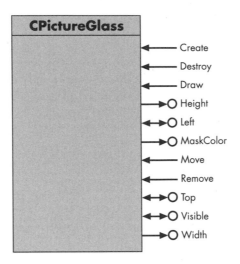

Key

→O Read-only property
←→O Read-write property
←— Method sub

Figure 7-10. *A diagram of CPictureGlass.*

Most Move methods have two additional arguments, Width and Height. But using these arguments changes the size of the object. I suppose I could have made CPictureGlass resizable by using StretchBlt instead of BitBlt, but I'll leave that to you. For now you can't change the size, so these arguments aren't implemented. Because the Move method changes the position of the object, it calls the Draw method to erase the last image and redraw the new one.

The Left and Top Property Let procedures are implemented in the same way as Move. The Width and Height Property Let procedures aren't implemented, for the same reason that Move's Width and Height parameters aren't implemented. The Property Get routines for Left, Top, Width, and Height simply pass back the internal variables representing these properties. Since position and size properties are maintained in pixels, the numbers need to be scaled:

```
Property Get Left() As Single
    BugAssert fExist
    Left = cvsDst.ScaleX(xLeft, vbPixels, cvsDst.ScaleMode)
End Property
```

The Visible property sets or returns the internal *fVisible* variable. The MaskColor property returns the *clrMask* variable. I don't provide a Property Let for Mask-Color, but you could add one. You'd need to create a new mask (*hdcMask*) whenever a user changed the property.

Hardcore Painting

Help is available for all you hardcore programmers who want to do tricks with bitmaps, but I can't even tell you the names of all the APIs, much less how to use them from Visual Basic. Start with DirectX. You might also want to think about Direct3D and ActiveMovie. Those three should provide enough fodder for three books the size of this one. Good luck. You're going to need it because from my preliminary look, these APIs were specifically not designed with Visual Basic programmers in mind. There is at least one commercial control available that attempts to wrap DirectX up in a Basic-friendly wrapper, but I can't say more because I haven't tried it.

The XPictureGlass Control

If you were confused by the code for the CPictureGlass class, you'll like the control version. It requires only four lines of code. Of course, any control requires a lot more than four lines of code, but I'm counting only the ones you have to write yourself. The ActiveX Control Interface Wizard generated the rest.

Although controls are a major feature of Visual Basic version 5, this is the first I've had to say about creating them. I'll have more to say about controls in Chapter 9, but I won't be doing much hand-holding. The documentation on creating controls is good, and I assume you'll use it. I'll only get into a few quirks related to specific tasks I want to accomplish. So here's a brief outline of how I created XPictureGlass.

1. Asked the ActiveX Control Interface Wizard to generate a control that had the same properties, methods, and events as a PictureBox. I didn't delegate to an internal PictureBox; I emulated a new one. I instructed the wizard to delegate all the emulated members to the UserControl. Had I stopped there, I would have had essentially a PictureBox control. If you assign a picture to the Picture property, it appears on the surface of the UserControl just as it would on a normal PictureBox.

2. Gave the control a MaskColor property (but not a MaskPicture property).

3. Changed the BackStyle property of the UserControl to Transparent (0) at design time.

4. Did a few minor fixups that the wizard can't handle such as changing color properties to type OLE_COLOR and using standard enums for properties that need drop-down enumerations. These tasks are documented in manuals and in the wizard's summary report (CTLWIZ.TXT).

415

5. Added the following lines of code:

```
Public Property Set Picture(ByVal New_Picture As Picture)
    Set UserControl.Picture = New_Picture
    ' Begin new code
    Set UserControl.MaskPicture = New_Picture
    If Not New_Picture Is Nothing Then
        UserControl.Width = New_Picture.Width
        UserControl.Height = New_Picture.Height
    End If
    ' End new code
    PropertyChanged "Picture"
End Property
```

That's it.

So why did I go through all that rigamarole with CPictureGlass? Well, XPictureGlass exists at a much higher level than CPictureGlass. The developers of Visual Basic gave UserControl the MaskColor and MaskPicture properties at the last minute (they're documented in the README). You set the MaskColor that you want masked out and the MaskPicture to the picture you want to mask. In this case, the Picture property and the MaskPicture property get the same value. Then behind the scenes—with some sort of magic not entirely different than what you saw in CPictureGlass—they make a mask from the MaskPicture and MaskColor and blit it onto the UserControl surface.

But they do a lot more.... For example, they do events. If you click on a transparent pixel of the control (one that has the MaskColor), you don't get a mouse click event. If you click on an opaque bit, you do. In order to make transparency so easy, the Visual Basic designers had to make high-level decisions about how to work with AutoRedraw and ClipControls properties on the container. The decisions they made will probably work better for you than they did for the Fun 'n Games program.

When you animate the picture, it saves and restores the background, whatever it is. When you animate the control, it respects controls on the form but wipes out anything it interacts with on the form background. The control is designed to be transparent on the bitmap surface that you saved for the form when you set AutoRedraw to True. Furthermore, it doesn't understand the trick (see "Style bits," page 310) used to turn off ClipControls at run time. A partial solution is to set AutoRedraw to True and call the control's Refresh method in the form's Paint event. The problem with that is that none of the other fun effects works as well with AutoRedraw set to True. Never mind. Fun 'n Games is just a demo, and, as noted earlier, real programs will need a more sophisticated painting strategy.

Deal Me In

Every Windows programmer has access to one powerful graphics library: CARDS, the dynamic link library that is used by Solitaire and other Windows-based card games. In one form or another, CARDS comes with all versions of Windows. Figure 7-11 shows the CARDS library in action in the Fun 'n Games program.

The Visual Basic interface is easy for hardcore programmers; it's just a matter of calling the five functions in CARDS32.DLL. Unfortunately, getting the right CARDS32.DLL is not as easy as it should be. Windows NT provides a 32-bit version named CARDS.DLL—the only DLL I have ever encountered that has exactly the same name as a 16-bit DLL. If you install Windows NT over Windows 3.*x,* you'll have 16-bit CARDS.DLL in your Windows directory and 32-bit CARDS-.DLL in your System directory. Windows 95 provides only the 16-bit CARDS.DLL. Apparently, the designers figured that card games were out and action games were in. The Fun 'n Games program needs to find the 32-bit DLL regardless of your operating system. I solved this incompatibility problem by getting permission to provide a 32-bit version of the DLL named CARDS32.DLL, which will be copied to your disk by the companion CD setup regardless of your operating system. You can write and run 32-bit card games even on Windows 95. The Windows NT card games expect a 32-bit CARDS.DLL, so you'll have to keep this duplicate on your Windows NT disk if you want to play the standard games.

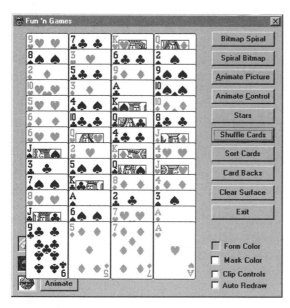

Figure 7-11. *Using CARDS32.DLL in the Fun 'n Games program.*

I'll describe the five functions and a few basic game techniques here; check the Fun 'n Games code for details. The hard part is programming the logic of your favorite card game.

Card Functions

The declarations and enumerations for CARDS are located in CARDS.BAS and duplicated in the Windows API type library.

Here are the four enumerations and five functions of the CARDS DLL in Visual Basic format:

Enum ECardType

This enumeration has three members indicating the three ways that a card can be drawn: ectFaces for the card face, ectBacks for the card back, and ectInvert for the inverted card face.

Enum ECardBack

This enumeration provides constants for the different card backgrounds and for the X and O cards used to represent no card in some games.

Enum ECardSuit

This enumeration provides constants for the four suits: ecsClubs, ecsDiamonds, ecsHearts, and ecsSpades.

Enum ECardFace

This enumeration provides constants for the 13 cards, starting with Ace as the low card and ending with King as high. Often you'll be calculating the card value rather than using its constant.

Function cdtInit

```
Function cdtInit(dx As Long, dy As Long) As Long
```

This procedure initializes the cards and returns the width and height of a card in pixels through the *dx* and *dy* reference variables.

Function cdtDraw

```
Function cdtDraw(hDC As Long, x As Long, y As Long, _
        ecsCard As ECardSuit, ectDraw As ECardType, _
        clr As Long) As Long
```

This procedure draws a card in its normal size at position *x, y* on the device context *hDC*. The *ectDraw* parameter controls whether the front, the back, or the inverted front of the card is drawn. The *ecsCard* parameter controls which card is drawn. If the faces are shown, use the values 0 through 51 to represent each card. You can use the constants *ecsClubs*, *ecsDiamonds*, *ecsHearts*, and *ecsSpades* to represent the first card in each suit, adding multiples of 4 (or the ECardFace constants) to represent cards from ace to king. For example, *ecsDiamonds* + *ecfThree* is the three of diamonds, *ecsHearts* + *ecfAce* is the ace of hearts, and *ecsSpades* + *ecfKing* is the king of spades.

If the backs are drawn, use the following constants for the different backs: *ecbCrossHatch*, *ecbPlaid*, *ecbWeave*, *ecbRobot*, *ecbRoses*, *ecbIvyBlack*, *ecbIvyBlue*, *ecbFishCyan*, *ecbFishBlue*, *ecbShell*, *ecbCastle*, *ecbBeach*, *ecbCardHand*, *ecbX*, and *ecbO*. The *clr* parameter sets the background color for the *ecbCrossHatch* card back, which uses a pattern drawn with lines. All the other backs and fronts are bitmaps, so the color has no effect.

Function cdtDrawExt

```
Function cdtDrawExt(hDC As Long, x As Long, y As Long, _
             dx As Long, dy As Long,
             ecsCard As ECardSuit, ectDraw As ECardType, _
             clr As Long) As Long
```

This procedure is the same as cdtDraw except that you specify the *dx* and *dy* parameters to indicate the size of the card. The card bitmaps are stretched or compressed to the specified size.

Function cdtAnimate

```
Function cdtAnimate(hDC As Long, ecbCardBack As ECardBack, _
             x As Long, y As Long, _
             iState As Long) As Long
```

This function animates the backs of cards by overlaying part of the card back with an alternative bitmap. It creates effects: blinking lights on the robot, the sun donning sunglasses, bats flying across the castle, and a card sliding out of a sleeve. The function works only for cards of normal size drawn with cdtDraw. To draw each state, start with *iState* set to 0 and increment through until cdtAnimate returns 0.

Sub cdtTerm

```
Sub cdtTerm()
```

This procedure cleans up the card resources. You can call cdtTerm in Form_Terminate or Form_Unload.

Timer Loops

Animating the card backs illustrates one of the fundamental problems of Windows programming. Before we get to the specifics of making cards wink and flash, however, let's talk about the problem in general.

Let's say that you want to perform some operation (such as animation) in the background forever. This is easy in MS-DOS:

```
Do
    Draw it, x, y
    If x <= xMax Then x = x + 1 Else x = 0
    If y <= yMax Then y = y + 1 Else y = 0
Loop
```

Even in MS-DOS, however, this often doesn't work very well. Your animation might run too fast, or it might run too fast on some machines and too slowly on others. To even things out, you can insert a Wait statement:

```
Do
    Draw it, x, y
    If x <= xMax Then x = x + 1 Else x = 0
    If y <= yMax Then y = y + 1 Else y = 0
    Wait 100 ' microseconds
Loop
```

This might work fine for a machine running only MS-DOS, but depending on how Wait was implemented, it might be very rude indeed under 16-bit Windows. In the bad old days, Wait functions were often written as busy loops:

```
Sub Wait(msWait As Long)
    Dim msEnd As Long
    msEnd = GetTickCount() + msWait   ' Get microseconds
    Do
    Loop While GetTickCount() < msEnd
End Sub
```

This is the height of bad manners in any non-preemptive multitasking operating system because you are grabbing the processor and throwing away all cycles until you are finished, thus blocking all other programs. A preemptive multitasking operating system such as Windows 95 or Windows NT might be able to jump in and steal control, but you're nevertheless wasting a time slice that could be better used by someone else. Even your MS-DOS programs shouldn't do this because it will cause them to hog the system when running in a Windows MS-DOS session.

One Visual Basic solution is to put DoEvents in the busy loop:

```
Sub DoWaitEvents(msWait As Long)
    Dim msEnd As Long
    msEnd = GetTickCount + msWait
    Do
        DoEvents
    Loop While GetTickCount < msEnd
End Sub
```

This procedure resides in the UTILITY module in VBCore, and is a reasonable way to wait for short periods. I wouldn't use it to wait for more than half a second or so. The DoEvents call releases your time slice to any other processes that are waiting for their turn to run. If DoEvents were written in Visual Basic, it would look something like this:

```
Do While PeekMessage(msg, pNull, 0, 0, PM_REMOVE)
    TranslateMessage msg
    DispatchMessage msg
Loop
Sleep 0
```

In other words, DoEvents handles all pending messages and surrenders its time slice before returning to deal with your next message.

Notice the call to Sleep at the end of the loop. I've heard quite a bit of debate about the relative merits of *Sleep 0* versus *Sleep 1* for giving up your time slice. Here's what the documentation says: "A value of zero causes the thread to relinquish the remainder of its time slice to any other thread of equal priority that is ready to run." This means that if other threads aren't quite ready or aren't of equal priority, they won't run. I've seen tests indicating that *Sleep 1* is often a more effective way of yielding.

So if *Sleep 1* is good way to wait for a very short time, why wouldn't *Sleep 1000* be a good way of waiting for one second? The problem with Sleep is that it really sleeps. Your program gets absolutely no processing time and will not be able to paint or do anything else until the sleep is over. Generally, Sleep is useful for multithreaded applications in which one thread can sleep while another continues working. Sleep is usually a bad idea for a normal Visual Basic program that has only one thread. We'll talk more about threads, processes, and waiting in Chapter 11.

The real problem with using Sleep or DoEvents to wait is that it's not the Windows Way. If other processes use too much time, you'll be way past quitting time when you get control back. In any multitasking system, someone else could want the same time slot you want. Your best chance of getting control at a specific time is to request it politely using a Windows Timer—which, in Visual Basic, means using the Timer control or a timer class.

You're probably not accustomed to thinking of the Timer control as just another looping structure comparable to Do/Loop or For/Next. But why not? Consider the following "bad" loop:

```
Dim x As Integer, y As Integer, secStop As Double
Do
    If x <= xMax Then x = x + 1 Else x = 0
    If y <= yMax Then y = y + 1 Else y = 0
    If Draw(it, x, y) = False Then Exit Do
    secStop = Timer + .1  ' Wait one-tenth second
    Do
        DoEvents
    Loop Until Timer > secStop
Loop
```

Notice the following points:

- This loop is an endless Do Loop.

- The loop has an exit in the middle via Exit Do.

- The loop uses the Timer function in a loop to wait one tenth of a second.

- The loop uses normal local variables, reinitializing them when they exceed a maximum.

Now let's convert to a "good" loop:

```
tmrAnimate.Interval = 100  ' 100 microseconds is one-tenth second
 ⋮
Sub tmrAnimate_Timer()
    Static x As Integer, y As Integer
    If x <= xMax Then x = x + 1 Else x = 0
    If y <= yMax Then y = y + 1 Else y = 0
    If Draw(it, x, y) = False Then tmrAnimate.Enabled = False
End Sub
```

Here's how the code is transformed:

- A Sub statement replaces Do; an End Sub replaces Loop.

- The exit changes from Exit Do to *tmrAnimate.Enabled = False*.

- The time period is set with the Interval property outside the loop.

- The variables must be declared static because you'll leave the loop on every iteration, but you want them to be unchanged when you come back.

We'll see how this technique works in the Fun 'n Games program after a brief look at the CTimer class.

No Timer Control

Visual Basic's Timer control is one of those controls that ought not to be a control. You always have to put it on a form, even if it doesn't belong on one. If you want a Timer on a program or component that has no user interface, tough luck. You'll have to create an invisible Form just to hold the Timer. If you want to encapsulate a timer within another class, you can't do it without weird hacks to communicate between your class and an invisible form.

Yet the Timer has no need for the features offered by controls. It has no visible surface. Its properties are often (if not usually) set at run time rather than design time, so the design-time property list isn't much use. The only reason it's still a control is that a control was the only way to generate events in previous versions of Visual Basic. But no more. Now any class can raise events. Unfortunately, they didn't add a noncontrol Timer to the product—at least not in a completed form. There's actually a timer class named XTimer in one of the sample projects provided with Visual Basic.

I hate to be one of those programmers who can't use anything that's "not invented here." I even thought about throwing my CTimer class away and using the XTimer class provided in the sample. But I like this interface of mine a little better, and it seemed kind of cheap to steal a sample and put it in the VBCore component (although I don't think the XTimer author, Glenn Hackney, would have minded).

Anyway, I'm going to use CTimer, but I'm not going to talk about the implementation except to say that it calls the SetTimer API function to create a timer object, and waits for Windows to call back to TimerProc at the designated interval. This is easier said than done, but it's just a typical callback problem. We handled worse in the subclassing example at the end of Chapter 6. You can study the code in TIMER.CLS and TIMER.BAS.

For now, the only thing of interest is how you create and use a CTimer object. First you have to declare the object at the form level using the WithEvents syntax:

```
Private WithEvents timerAnimate As CTimer
```

Next you must create a CTimer object in an initialization event such as Form_Load:

```
Set timerAnimate = New CTimer
```

A new timer starts out with an interval of zero, so its event won't be called until you set a positive interval. The Fun 'n Games program does this in the SetTimer procedure:

```
Private Sub SetTimer(eatAnimateA As Integer)
    eatAnimate = eatAnimateA
    Select Case eatAnimate
    Case eatNone
        timerAnimate.Interval = 0
        ' Hide XPictureGlass object
        pgControl.Visible = False
        cmdAnimate.Caption = "&Animate Picture"
        cmdAnimateCtl.Caption = "Animate &Control"
        ' Remove active CPictureGlass object from memory
        Set pgPicture = Nothing
    Case eatPicture, eatControl
        timerAnimate.Interval = 10
    Case eatCardBacks
        timerAnimate.Interval = 100
    End Select
End Sub
```

The CTimer class differs from the Timer control in that it doesn't have a separate Enabled property. Setting the CTimer Interval property to 0 is equivalent to setting the Enabled property of Timer to False.

Finally you put your periodic code in the CTimer ThatTime event:

```
Private Sub timerAnimate_ThatTime()
    Select Case eatAnimate
    Case eatNone
        Exit Sub
    Case eatCardBacks
        AnimateBacks
    Case eatPicture
        AnimatePicture
    Case eatControl
        AnimateControl
    End Select
End Sub
```

Debugging the CTimer class in source code can be an adventure. If you don't value your time, try it with FUNNGAMEDEB.VBG. This project group points to SUBTIMER.VBP rather than SUBTIMER.DLL. When debugging source, you can't set breakpoints in the ThatTime event procedure or click the End button while the timer is active. If you try it, you'll see some behavior that will be unpredictable except for its outcome—the lockup and eventual death of Visual Basic. Those timer events just keep coming even when you're stopped in the debugger, and there's no way Visual Basic can break in multiple events at the same time. The CTimer class works fine in the debugger as long as it's compiled. Try it with FUNNGAME.VBG or FUNNGAME.VBP.

Animating Card Backs

In the Fun 'n Games program, clicking the Card Backs button draws 13 card backs plus the X and O cards. The program then turns on the timer and animates cards in the background. Try to find the animated card in Figure 7-12.

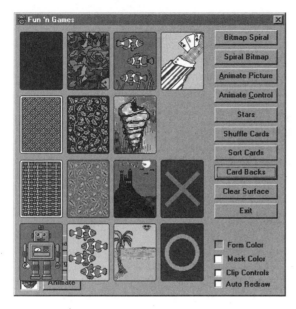

Figure 7-12. *Fun with cards.*

Only 4 of the 13 card backs in CARDS32.DLL are animated, and another changes color. To keep this animation working smoothly, you must manage variables for the *x* position, the *y* position, the card back, and the animation state. It's not a simple loop.

Let's look at the normal loop that draws the cards initially:

```
Private Sub cmdBack_Click()
    Dim ordScale As Integer
    ordScale = ScaleMode: ScaleMode = vbPixels
    SetTimer eatCardBacks
    Cls
    Dim x As Integer, y As Integer, ecbBack As ECardBack
    ecbBack = ecbCrossHatch   ' First card back
    ' Draw cards in 4 by 4 grid
    For x = 0 To 3
        For y = 0 To 3
            cdtDraw Me.hDC, (dxCard * 0.1) + (x * dxCard * 1.1), _
```

(continued)

```
                        (dyCard * 0.1) + (y * dyCard * 1.1), _
                        ecbBack, ectBacks, QBColor(Random(0, 15))
                ecbBack = ecbBack + 1
            Next
        Next
        ScaleMode = ordScale
End Sub
```

The timer loop does essentially the same thing, although its use of static variables makes it look different. Fun 'n Games handles other animation tasks too; AnimateBacks is one of several subs called by the Timer event procedure:

```
Sub AnimateBacks()
    Static x As Integer, y As Integer
    Static ecbBack As ECardBack, iState As Integer

    ' Save scale mode and change to pixels
    Dim ordScale As Integer
    ordScale = ScaleMode: ScaleMode = vbPixels

    ' Adjust variables
    If ecbBack < ecbCrossHatch Or ecbBack > ecbO Then
        ecbBack = ecbCrossHatch
        x = 0: y = 0
    End If
    If x = 4 Then x = 0
    If y = 4 Then y = 0: x = x + 1
    Select Case ecbBack
    Case ecbCrossHatch
        ' Change color of crosshatch
        cdtDraw Me.hDC, (dxCard * 0.1) + (x * dxCard * 1.1), _
                (dyCard * 0.1) + (y * dyCard * 1.1), _
                ecbBack, ectBacks, QBColor(Random(0, 15))
    Case Else 'ecbRobot, ecbCastle, ecbBeach, ecbCardHand
        ' Step through animation states
        If cdtAnimate(Me.hDC, ecbBack, _
                    (dxCard * 0.1) + (x * dxCard * 1.1), _
                    (dyCard * 0.1) + (y * dyCard * 1.1), iState) Then
            iState = iState + 1
            Exit Sub    ' Don't move to next card until final state
        End If
        iState = 0
    ' Case Else
        ' Ignore other cards
    End Select
    ' Move to next card
    ecbBack = ecbBack + 1
```

```
    y = y + 1
    ' Restore
    ScaleMode = ordScale
End Sub
```

Timer loops can be used for a lot more than animation. Think about how to apply them to all your background tasks. Consider doing calculations and file processing while you're handling user input, for instance. In fact, once you become accustomed to thinking in terms of timer loops, you can end up performing tasks in the background that used to be carried out in the foreground.

8

A Handle on Data

Visual Basic is a bit schizophrenic about handling data. It doesn't support the Basic Way of declaring and using data as defined by the developers of early Basics. Instead, it implements its own Visual Basic Way. But the Visual Basic Way proved inadequate, so starting with version 4, Visual Basic began supporting the Windows Way. Unfortunately, it supports the Windows Way only sometimes, sort of, and from the outside rather than as an integrated part of the language.

Confused? OK, let's look at the three ways one by one.

Three Approaches to Data

The Basic Way of handling data is with the Data and Read statements, which fell by the wayside when QuickBASIC became Visual Basic. The Data statement allowed you to define tables of data of mixed types. At design time, you could initialize integers, real numbers, and strings all together in one big table; then, at run time, you could read those statements into variables. It wasn't a great syntax, but it did allow you to initialize simple data types at design time, something that Visual Basic still won't do. In Windows programming, however, what you really need is a way to initialize and read larger, less formatted kinds of data—bitmaps, icons, metafiles, forms, and objects.

The Visual Basic Way of handling data is to allow initialization of properties (including pictures that contain bitmaps, icons, and metafiles) in the Properties window. In early versions of Visual Basic, the actual data was stored directly in the source file and eventually compiled into the executable file. This was easy to do because, historically, Visual Basic source files were encoded and packed. Because the format wasn't documented, Visual Basic could cram data and code together however it liked, as long as it knew how to decode the resulting files.

But binary source files in an undocumented format caused a lot of problems, especially for source-code control programs. Visual Basic version 2 added a text format for source files. All the simple property data was arranged in the hierarchical table format you're familiar with if you've ever looked at a Visual Basic source file with a text editor. The binary data was crammed into FRX files in some undocumented format. This worked so well that starting with version 4, all source files were saved in text format. One curious limitation remains: you can initialize the properties of forms and controls at design time, but you can't initialize variables or objects declared in code.

The Windows Way of storing binary data is very different from the Visual Basic Way. In other programming languages, you maintain binary data for your programs by storing it in resources. Using a visual tool called a *resource editor,* you can create resources such as bitmaps, icons, cursors, menus, and dialog boxes just the way you want them to look in your program. This editor stores the resources in a text file (an RC file) that looks a bit like a simplified Pascal source file. You then use a *resource compiler* to compile RC files into binary RES files, which are in turn inserted directly into executable files so that the resources and the code share the same EXE file. You write code in whatever language you choose to load the resource data at run time.

This seems like a fairly complicated way to do by hand what Visual Basic does automatically. But the Windows Way offers one big advantage over the Visual Basic Way: in Visual Basic, the binary data is tied to the source file. Each FRM file has a matching FRX; if you change the FRM file, you automatically change the FRX. In other words, if you want English, German, and Dutch versions of your program, you must create three versions of each form. In Windows, the resource file is independent of source files. You can create English, German, and Dutch versions of your resource file and combine any one with the executable file without changing a line of source code.

Because many Americans (I'm not without sin) tend to assume that English is the only language worth worrying about, you might not have heard much about this limitation in magazine articles or online forums. But you can bet that Microsoft has heard a lot of complaints about it from foreign programmers as well as from English-language developers who want to sell their software in non-English-speaking countries. As a result, Visual Basic allows you to use resources in Basic programs. The Windows Way, in the form of RES files, and the Visual Basic Way, in the form of FRX files, can exist side by side in the same program.

The Data Initialization Problem

Before we start looking at new kinds of data such as resources, let's look back at one of the problems confronting programmers in any language: initializing variables. What value does a variable have when you first declare it, and what happens if you try to read it before you initialize it? And how do you get an initial value into a variable? And why bother to initialize variables, anyway?

The last question is easy to answer. Take a look at control and form properties. You initialize them at design time in the Properties window. Think of the extra code if you had to initialize every Caption property of every button at run time. Initialization is so important to control and form properties that Visual Basic keeps making property pages more and more sophisticated. For example, you can initialize the strings of a ListBox control at design time, a task you had to perform at run time in early versions. All the good reasons for allowing you to initialize properties are equally good reasons for allowing you to initialize variables in code. You often want not only an initial default value but also the ability to change the default.

In some languages, uninitialized variables have a semirandom value. In C, for example, local variables (but not global or static variables) are undefined. If you want an initial value, you must give it. Fortunately for C programmers, this is easy to do. An undefined variable is a disaster waiting to happen, and careful C coders initialize their variables as close to declarations as possible. In contrast, Visual Basic always initializes all variables whenever they are declared. String variables are initialized to vbNullString, numeric variables are initialized to 0, Variants are initialized to Empty, and object variables are initialized to Nothing.

This difference fits the philosophies of C and Visual Basic. C doesn't initialize variables to a default because local variables must be initialized at run time. This has a cost, and C doesn't do any run-time work unless you ask for it. Undefined variables are dangerous, but that's your problem. Visual Basic is more concerned with safety. If you declare an array of 5000 Integers, Visual Basic will initialize them all to 0 even if it takes extra run-time work to do so.

The problem for Visual Basic programmers is that 0 or Empty might not be the initial value the program needs. In C, you can combine the declaration of a variable with its initialization:

```
int cLastWindow = 20;
```

In Visual Basic, declaration and initialization are different statements:

```
Dim cLastWindow As Integer
cLastWindow = 20
```

This usually works OK for local variables, but it's a problem for module-level (private) or global (public) variables. You must declare these in the Declarations section at the top of the module, where executable statements such as variable assignments aren't allowed.

You need to find some other place to put the initialization statement, and that place must be reached only once—either when the module is loaded or the first time the variable is accessed. No matter how you initialize your variables, the initialization statement will be separated from the declaration in your source file, which makes initialization code difficult to maintain. If you change the declaration, you must go to a completely separate location to change the initialization, even though the two parts are logically related.

What's needed to initialize variables is a combination declaration and initialization such as this:

```
Dim cLastWindow As Integer = 20
Static fFirstTime As Boolean = True
Private sExeFile As String = "VB.EXE"
Public aiCount(1 To 10) As Long = (1, 2, 3, 4, 5, 6, 7, 8, 9, 10)
Public ai3D(1 To 2, 1 To 3) As Long = ((1, 2), (2, 2), (2, 1))
Private perMe As TPerson = ("McKinney", "Bruce", 21, _
                            ("24 First Ave.", "Andula", _
                             "Basic", "Cathistan", 72948 _
                            ) _
                           )
```

As you know, Visual Basic has no such syntax. It's the only major computer language that doesn't.

FLAME I really wanted to delete this whole section from the second edition of my book, but alas, version 5 offers no fixes for the biggest flaw in the Visual Basic language. Instead, it tempts us by offering the exact syntax we need in a less useful context. The new typed optional arguments allow initialization of procedure arguments:

```
Sub GiveMe(Optional rMoney As Double = 1000000)
```

Furthermore, you can also specify a type along with an initial Const value:

```
Const rDoubleOrNothing As Double = 2000000
```

These are both very fine features but little more than fluff compared to what we really need:

```
Private rBigBucks As Double = 8000000
```

Notice that the sample initializations get significantly more complex when you start dealing with arrays, multidimensional arrays, UDTs, and nested UDTs—not to mention initializing collections of arrays of classes. Needless to say, the syntax above is not the only one possible.

Initializing constants is a related problem. Of course, all constants are initialized by definition, but the limited syntax of the Const statement makes it impossible to initialize arrays, UDTs, and strings containing control characters, to mention a few common types. For example, wouldn't it be handy to have the following constants?

```
Const sCrLf = Chr$(13) & Chr$(10)
Const asDays(1 To 7) = ("Sunday", "Monday", "Tuesday", "Wednesday", _
                        "Thursday", "Friday", "Saturday")
```

Neither statement is legal in Visual Basic. You have to get the equivalent by declaring variables and then initializing them later, even though you have no intention of ever modifying them and would prefer that they were constants.

Initializing Local Variables

Although Visual Basic gives you no direct help, it does give you two roundabout ways to initialize variables. The first technique takes advantage of the default initialization to 0, Empty, or Nothing.

If you can rule out the empty string as a valid value for a particular string variable, you can assume that the variable is uninitialized when it has this value. The same goes for 0 and numeric variables. For example:

```
Sub InitializeMe()
    Static sNeverEmpty As String, iNeverZero As Integer
    If sNeverEmpty = sEmpty Then sNeverEmpty = "Default"
    If iNeverZero = 0 Then iNeverZero = -1
    ⋮
End Sub
```

Of course, if *sNeverEmpty* can be changed by some other code, and if *sEmpty* is a valid value, this code won't work because *sNeverEmpty* will be randomly changed to "Default" under certain circumstances. It's easy to imagine lots of string variables that should never be empty, but it's harder to think of integer variables that should never be 0.

Notice that the variables in question are static so that they retain the initialized value across calls. You don't need any special initialization code if the variable is reinitialized every time you enter the procedure:

```
Sub InitializeMe()
    Dim sNeverEmpty As String, iNeverZero As Integer
    sNeverEmpty = "Default": iNeverZero = -1
```

If 0 is valid for your numeric values or *sEmpty* is valid for your strings, you must create a variable specifically for testing:

```
Sub InitializeMe()
    Static fNotFirstTime As Boolean
    Static sAnyValue As String, iAnyValue As Integer
    If Not fNotFirstTime Then
        fNotFirstTime = True
        sAnyValue = "First time": iAnyValue = 1
    End If
    ⋮
```

The double negative makes the code look more complex than it is. Things would be so much clearer if you could initialize the test variable to True:

```
Sub InitializeMe()
    Static fFirstTime As Boolean = True
    Static sAnyValue As String, iAnyValue As Integer
    If fFirstTime Then
        fFirstTime = False
        sAnyValue = "First time": iAnyValue = 1
    End If
    ⋮
```

But if you could initialize *fFirstTime* to True, you wouldn't need it because you could initialize *sAnyValue* and *iAnyValue* the same way.

You can use the same principle on global and module-level variables. The IsMissing function works with optional parameters in the same way. I'll show you some related tricks later.

Initializing Form Variables

The second way to initialize variables is to use an initialization event. Most Visual Basic programmers already know this technique because they've used the Form_Load event to initialize form properties and variables. You should also familiarize yourself with two other initialization events: Form_Activate and Form_Initialize.

When a form is loaded, the sequence of events is the following:

1. A form is a class, and all classes have an Initialize event. Form_Initialize is called (or *fired,* as control developers describe calling events) as soon as you touch any variable or property of a form. Use this event to initialize variables private to the form. Normally, you should not touch any form or control properties here because doing so fires the next event.

2. Form_Load fires after Form_Initialize as the visual elements of the form are being created and default values are being assigned to properties. Normally, you should avoid doing anything that will draw something on the form because that causes an automatic firing of the next event. It might be tempting to call Show in Form_Load and then do further processing with the visible form, but you're usually better off doing this in the next event.

3. Form_Activate fires after you have loaded and shown the form. It's possible to load a form without showing it; in this case, Form_Activate isn't fired until you call the Show method. Form_Activate is also called when you switch from one modeless form to another, or when you switch between MDI forms (but not when you return focus from

another application). If your application has modeless or MDI forms, don't do anything in Form_Activate that you want to happen only once. Or use a static variable (such as *fNotFirst*) to protect against multiple initializations in Form_Activate.

The interactions between the three initialization events can be confusing. Sometimes trial and error is the only way to figure out the right initialization sequence for your application.

Initializing Class Objects and Internal Variables

Class modules have a Class_Initialize event that you can use to initialize private variables. But because Class_Initialize is an event, you can't use it to pass data to the class object from its creator. In other words, you can tell a class how to initialize its own variables, but you can't initialize the class object. Yet many classes are completely undefined and unusable until they are initialized.

What you need is a way to combine declaration and initialization:

```
Dim pgStar As New CPictureGlass = (pbStar)
```

Instead, you must initialize by convention. Give your class a Create method, and tell users that they must always call it before using a class object:

```
Dim pgStar As New CPictureGlass
pgStar.Create pbStar
```

The bottom line is that callers who try to reference an object before initializing it with the Create method get random results. Convention isn't a very good way to enforce good behavior—better to leave users no way but the right way.

Most object-oriented languages allow you to initialize objects in their declarations. Unfortunately, initialization syntax can get very complex, especially with objects consisting of other objects. Inheritance or delegation adds even more complications. It's a difficult problem in language design, which might be why Visual Basic programmers put off dealing with it in version 5. Let's hope they'll bite the bullet and do what needs to be done, however difficult, next time.

Initializing Standard Module Variables

Initializing variables in standard modules is a little trickier. It would be nice to have a Module_Initialize event in which you could initialize internal values, but since there isn't one, you have to do some hacking to initialize variables with the static variable technique described earlier.

You might be laboring under the misconception that Visual Basic doesn't support global initialized variables in standard modules. Not so. Property procedures make it easy, if not obvious. Normally, I think of properties as being attached to forms and classes, but no rule says that a property has to be tied to an object. For example, here's a global variable, *cLastWindow,* initialized to 20:

```
Private fNotFirstTime As Boolean
Private cLastWindowI As Integer
⋮
Public Property Get cLastWindow() As Integer
    If Not fNotFirstTime Then
        fNotFirstTime = True
        cLastWindowI = 20
    End If
    cLastWindow = cLastWindowI
End Property

Property Let cLastWindow(cLastWindowA As Integer)
    fNotFirstTime = True
    cLastWindowI = cLastWindowA
End Property
```

You can use this property from anywhere, just like any other global variable:

```
For i = 1 To cLastWindow
    WipeWindow i
Next
cLastWindow = cLastWindow - 1
```

Users of your standard module needn't be the wiser about how you wrote it, especially if you hide it in a DLL so that no one can see the source.

If your standard module contains several variables that need to be initialized, you can write your own Module_Initialize routine. Call it from every procedure that uses one of the variables:

```
If Not fNotFirstTime Then Module_Initialize
```

This might not be as efficient as you'd like. Testing for *fNotFirstTime* all over the place is no fun, but the test is True only once. Don't forget to initialize *fNotFirstTime* along with the other variables.

A property with a Property Get but no Property Let or Property Set acts like a read-only variable—otherwise known as a constant. Let's take my favorite constant, *sCrLf.* It's simply a string consisting of a carriage return and a linefeed. You can't define it with Const because it has two control characters, which must be tied together with the concatenation operator (& or +). Visual Basic (unlike every other language I've encountered) doesn't allow control characters in constants, even though Chr$(13) and the concatenation operator could easily be evaluated by the compiler at design time.

The following solution isn't really necessary, because Visual Basic provides *vbCrLf* and the Windows API type library provides *sCrLf*. But if you didn't have a type library with the constant, you could define your own in a standard module this way:

```
Public Property Get sCrLf() As String
    Static s As String
    If s = sEmpty Then s = Chr$(13) & Chr$(10)
    sCrLf = s
End Property
```

Using Your Own Resources

Resources are the Windows Way of handling large data chunks in Visual Basic. The Test Resources project (TRES.VBP) illustrates some important points about resources. This is an international program, designed for simultaneous release in the United States of America and the Republic of Swinen. The program was written and will be maintained by American programmers in the United States. Nonprogrammers in the United States and Swinen created separate resource files. Strings were translated to Swinish, and visual elements such as bitmaps, cursors, and icons were modified to meet the cultural expectations of Swinens. The differences are purely cosmetic, however; the program acts exactly the same for American users and for Swinish users.

Figure 8-1 shows the American version of the program; Figure 8-2 shows the Swinish version. To get the full effect, you need to run both versions—sounds and cursors just don't translate to the printed page. I designed the TRES.VBP project file to handle either the American or the Swinish version of the program, but I also provide TRESUS.VBP and TRESSW.VBP, hard-coded to the nationalized versions. You can use these to take an initial look at the program.

Figure 8-1. *The Test Resources program, localized for the United States of America.*

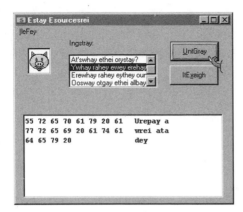

Figure 8-2. *The Test Resources program, localized for the Republic of Swinen.*

Creating a Resource Script

A *resource script* is a text file listing all the data used in a program. It traditionally bears the filename extension RC. After writing your resource script, you compile it into a resource file (RES) and add this file to your Visual Basic project. Visual Basic automatically uses your resources in the environment and compiles them into the EXE file.

The easiest way to understand resource scripts is to look at a sample. Here's the one used by the Test Resources program (TRES.VBP):

```
// TRES.RC - Resource script for Test Resources program

//$ Const ordAppBmp = 101
#if defined(US)
101     BITMAP  "MANHEAD.BMP"
#elif defined(SW)
101     BITMAP  "PIGHEAD.BMP"
#else
#error "No language"
#endif

//$ Const ordAppIcon   = 301
#if defined(US)
301     ICON    "FLGUSA.ICO"
#elif defined(SW)
301     ICON    "FLGSWI.ICO"
#endif

//$ Const ordAppCursor = 401
#if defined(US)
401     CURSOR  "MANHAND.CUR"
```

```
#elif defined(SW)
401     CURSOR  "PIGTAIL.CUR"
#endif

//$ Const ordWavGrunt  = 501
#if defined(US)
501     WAVE    "GRUNT.WAV"
#elif defined(SW)
501     WAVE    "OINK.WAV"
#endif

//$ Const ordTxtData   = 601
601     OURDATA
BEGIN
#if defined(US)
        0x7550, 0x6572, 0x7220, 0x7761
        0x6420, 0x7461, 0x2061
#elif defined(SW)
        0x7255, 0x7065, 0x7961, 0x6120
        0x7277, 0x6965, 0x6120, 0x6174
        0x6564, 0x2079
#endif
END

//$ Const ordFrmTitle  = 1001
//$ Const ordMnuFile   = 1101
//$ Const ordMnuGrunt  = 1102
//$ Const ordMnuExit   = 1103
//$ Const ordLstTitle  = 1201
//$ Const ordLstWhat   = 1301
//$ Const ordLstWhy    = 1302
//$ Const ordLstWhere  = 1303
//$ Const ordLstWho    = 1304
//$ Const ordLstWhen   = 1305
STRINGTABLE
BEGIN
#if defined(US)
    1001    "Test Resources"
    1101    "&File"
    1102    "&Grunt"
    1103    "E&xit"
    1201    "Strings:"
    1301    "What's the story?"
    1302    "Why are we here?"
    1303    "Where are they now?"
    1304    "Who's got the ball?"
    1305    "When do we eat?"
```

(continued)

```
#elif defined(SW)
    1001     "Estay Esourcesrei"
    1101     "&IleFey"
    1102     "&UntGray"
    1103     "ItE&xeigh"
    1201     "Ingstray:"
    1301     "At'swhay ethei orystay?"
    1302     "Ywhay rahey ewey erehay?"
    1303     "Erewhay rahey eythey ouney?"
    1304     "Oosway otgay ethei allbay?"
    1305     "Enwhey oodae eway teeay?"
#endif
END
```

Although this script uses conditional code to create American and Swinish resource files from the same script file, you can just as easily create separate scripts for each language. The conditional statements shown here use the C preprocessor language, which looks a lot like the Visual Basic conditional compilation statements except for lowercase characters and a few other minor differences. Also notice that you must double the backslash character because the backslash is an escape character in C. Of course, your resource compiler might use a different syntax. I expect vendors to create Basic-style resource compilers real soon now.

The resource script contains Visual Basic constants in C-style comments with a unique leading character (//$). This makes it easy to write a wizard program that will search for constant comments and convert them to a Visual Basic module (or a type library). It's easy to maintain the comments next to their data in the resource script, but each time you compile the resource script, you must also update the constant module. You could probably carry this idea further, generating initialization code as well as constants.

Anatomy of a Resource Block

For every resource, you need to supply three pieces of information: the resource type, the resource ID, and the resource data. This gets a little confusing because each can be specified in various ways.

The resource type can be either a predefined type or a type you define. In the sample you just saw, BITMAP, ICON, CURSOR, and STRINGTABLE are predefined resource types. Both Visual Basic and Windows know about these types and include functions and constants to handle them directly. WAVE and OURDATA are custom types for which you must write your own functions.

To access bitmaps, icons, and cursors in Visual Basic, you use the LoadResPicture function. Assume that your resource file has this resource definition:

```
//$ Const ordAppIcon   = 301
#if defined(US)
301     ICON    "FLGUSA.ICO"
#elif defined(SW)
301     ICON    "FLGSWI.ICO"
#endif
```

Your Visual Basic source file should define the following constant (or an equivalent Enum):

```
Public Const ordAppIcon = 301
```

You can then load the resource as shown here:

```
Me.Icon = LoadResPicture(ordAppIcon, vbResIcon)
```

To access string resources, use LoadResString. Assume that your string table in the resource script looks like this:

```
STRINGTABLE
BEGIN
#if defined(US)
    1001    "Test Resources"
    1101    "&File"
    1102    "&Grunt"
    ⋮
```

You can load a string resource as shown here:

```
mnuFile.Caption = LoadResString(ordMnuFile)
```

To access custom data, use LoadResData. Assume that your custom WAVE resource looks like the code shown here.

```
//$ Const ordWavGrunt   = 501
#if defined(US)
501     WAVE    "GRUNT.WAV"
#elif defined(SW)
501     WAVE    "OINK.WAV"
#endif
```

You can load this resource into an array of bytes, as shown here:

```
abWavGrunt = LoadResData(ordWavGrunt, "WAVE")
```

Custom data always comes back as an array of bytes, so you'll need a playwave function that processes bytes. We'll see one in "Using Sounds" later in this chapter.

Cursors Eat Mouse Icons for Lunch

Visual Basic calls them mouse icons. Windows calls them cursors (not to be confused with carets, the pointers in text boxes). Visual Basic programmers complained for years (until version 4) about Visual Basic's inability to set them. Visual Basic now lets you set cursors to your favorite shapes, although this new feature isn't as obvious as it seems.

You can load either cursors or icons into the MouseIcon property, but there's a big difference between them. In fact, their relationship is an artificial one, created by Visual Basic for your convenience. Since icons are so easy to come by and are usually the same size as cursors, Visual Basic provides a shortcut: it automatically converts icons to cursors. But you might not like the price.

Most icons in the Visual Basic icon library (or anywhere else) are in color, but you'll often find that color isn't appropriate for cursors. Furthermore, most icons are designed as—well, as icons, and they don't really fit as cursors. In addition, you have no control over the cursor hot spot when you use an icon. If your cursor is shaped like a pencil, you'll want the hot spot at its point. But if you load a pencil-shaped icon, the hot spot will be in the center. If you click on something small, you might not be selecting what you think you're selecting.

The moral: use cursors instead of icons. Visual Basic provides many of the standard ones if you request them during setup. You can also create your own cursors with ImagEdit, the graphics editor provided in the \Tools\ImagEdit directory. ImagEdit lets you create color or monochrome cursors and set their hot spots. If you really want to use an icon, load it into ImagEdit, copy it, paste the image into a new cursor, and set the hot spot wherever you want it.

There's only one problem with cursors: the Visual Basic IDE doesn't recognize color cursors, even in 32-bit mode. That's the fault of the Picture object, which has been jury-rigged to handle cursors in the MouseIcon property even though it wasn't designed for them. The only way to get a color cursor when running in the environment is to use an icon. You can get color cursors in your 32-bit EXE files, however, if you can live with a little inconvenience during development. Just load your color cursors from resources instead of files. They'll come out in black and white (often with ugly dithering) in the environment, but they'll have the right colors when loaded in the EXE. This isn't so bad, since few customers will ever see your program running in the IDE.

Why do resources work in an EXE but not in the IDE? In an EXE, resources are loaded using the standard Windows resource mechanism that we'll examine later in this chapter. Color cursors work fine. Visual Basic can't use this normal mechanism when running in the environment because you aren't really running your program; you're running Visual Basic. Instead, Visual Basic has to dig the resource data directly out of the RES file. This results in the same limitation that you'll encounter with cursors that are placed directly into the MouseIcon property by using the LoadPicture function or the Load Picture dialog box: the colors get lost.

For each resource, you need to assign an ID string or number. The sample resource script uses ID numbers with a constant defined for each. You can also define ID strings. In the resource script, you could write the following definition:

```
AppBmp          BITMAP  "MANHEAD.BMP"
```

On the Visual Basic side, you can load it this way:

```
imgMascot.Picture = LoadResPicture("AppBmp", vbResBitMap)
```

This technique works for all resources except strings, which can be identified only by ID number. Because ID strings take more data space than ID numbers, you should avoid overusing ID strings for projects that contain many resources.

You can provide the name of a file containing the data on the same line as the ID and the type, or you can provide the actual data in a BEGIN/END block on subsequent lines. Microsoft's resource script language has its share of quirks, but you get the idea. For resource script arcana, see the MSDN CD provided with Visual Basic.

Compiling Resource Scripts

To compile a resource script, you need a stone-age tool called a resource compiler. Historians tell us that Visual Basic compilers used to be invoked from command lines in a manner not unlike that required for the resource compiler, RC.EXE. Now, don't get me wrong. I'm a command-line kind of guy. I use a Windows command-line session the way most people use the Windows Explorer. But resource files are like hot dogs: you don't really want to know where they came from.

Unfortunately, you must handle every step of the resource process by hand, starting with the setup.

Your goal in using the resource compiler is to create a separate RES file for each target language. A batch file such as the one shown here creates them:

```
@echo off
Rem Make US
rc /v /d US /r /fo tresus.res tres.rc
Rem Make Swinish
rc /v /d SW /r /fo tressw.res tres.rc
If "%1"=="" Goto Done
Rem Make version specific if country (US or SW) given on command line
If exist tres%1.res Copy tres%1.res tres.res
:Done
```

If you change from the American version to the Swinish version from the batch file while TRES.VBP is loaded, your program will change its behavior without changing a character of source code. This feature is nice, but the process of using it can only be described as crude. You can probably think of additional parameters to further define the behavior of the batch file, or, if you have a make utility, you can replace the batch file with a make file.

But whatever hacks you use, they shouldn't be necessary. In fact, the whole process is fundamentally flawed. The RC file, not the RES file, should be part of your project. You should be able to edit it in the Visual Basic IDE. Visual Basic should automatically compile it to a RES file whenever the RC file is newer than the RES file. And that's just the trivial implementation. If Visual Basic is going to compete with the new Rapid Application Development tools for Java and Delphi, it's going to need an integrated resource editor. Even user-hostile languages like C++ make resource management easier.

Hmmm. You've seen the simple and consistent format of resource scripts. You've seen the mechanical process of compiling them. You have a computer. You know a computer language. You're hardcore. All the elements are present for solving this problem once and for all.

Imagine the Resource Shop, a resource editor created specifically for Visual Basic. You could create new resources by selecting a resource type in a list box and clicking a New Resource button. You'd have a choice of inserting an existing resource from a file or creating a new one. Each resource type would have its own file editor, which you'd define when you created a new resource type. For example, you could run ImagEdit for icons, cursors, and bitmaps, or you could integrate your own more powerful editor. You'd also need editors for metafiles, wave files, strings, and hexadecimal data. You could scroll through existing resources for a project and edit any you wanted to change. Then you'd click a Save button to invoke an invisible resource compiler to compile your invisible resource script and generate a module containing Visual Basic constants for each ID. You could integrate this wonderful tool into the Visual Basic IDE as an add-in.

Hold that thought while we examine resources more carefully from the inside out.

Using Other People's Resources

The WinWatch program has a feature I discussed only briefly in Chapter 6: for each program or DLL you select, WinWatch shows all the resources of that module in a list box in the lower right corner of the screen. When you select a resource in the list box, WinWatch displays or otherwise handles the item in the Resource Information area (which is actually a picture box). The display varies, depending on the resource type.

It's an adventure to look at resources in the Windows DLLs, Program Manager, and Visual Basic itself. You can learn a lot about resources and how programmers use them in other languages.

Stealing Your Own Resources

To really understand exactly where resources come from, try looking at TRES-.EXE. You already know where those resources came from, but WinWatch gives you a little different view. Figure 8-3 shows WinWatch looking at the resources in TRES.EXE.

The Resources list box shows the same resource ID numbers and types we defined in TRES.RC. If you select one of these, you'll see the resource displayed or described in the Resource Information area. WinWatch displays bitmaps and icons, plays sounds, and loads cursors. It simply dumps data (such as OURDATA) that it doesn't know about. You can enhance WinWatch and your own programs to handle new data types correctly.

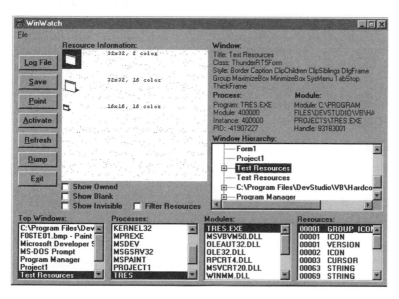

Figure 8-3. *WinWatch looking at TRES.EXE.*

There are some quirks in the display that I can't explain. WinWatch can't display many of the resources it finds, and therefore I've given it a Filter Resources check box. With the check box checked (the default), resources are validated as they are found. If you uncheck this box, you'll see a lot more resources listed, but you won't be able to examine them. Why not? I don't know.

TRES.EXE also has a group icon with ID #1. When you select this resource in WinWatch, you'll recognize it as the standard form icon. If you set the Icon property of the main form in the Test Resources program to a different icon at design time and then recompile, this icon will change. The Test Resources program doesn't bother to set the Icon property at design time because it uses Load-ResPicture to set the country-specific icon at run time. Unfortunately, it's the embedded icon with ID #1 that the operating system displays when you press Alt+Tab to change programs or when you inspect processes with the Windows NT task manager. It would be nice if you could set this resource to a country-specific icon in the resource script, but unfortunately Visual Basic provides no means to do so. Why not? I don't know.

If you browse through the resources in other programs, you'll notice some patterns. Turn off the Filter Resources check box so that you'll see everything, useful or not. Resources with type GROUP_ICON or GROUP_CURSOR are usually listed, but those with type ICON or CURSOR are not. What's the difference? I don't know.

Another interesting quirk is that when you look at the resources of the WinWatch program, you'll get different results depending on whether you're running WINWATCH.EXE or WINWATCH.VBP. WinWatch doesn't really need any resources, but to make this difference more obvious, I've given it the same resource file described earlier for the Test Resources program: TRES.RES. When you run WINWATCH.EXE, you'll be able to see these resources. But if you run WinWatch in the Visual Basic IDE, you'll see a different list of resources. That's because as far as Windows is concerned, you're running VB5.EXE, not WinWatch, and you'll see Visual Basic's resources.

Finding Resources

WinWatch finds resources by using callback functions with the EnumResource-Types and EnumResourceNames functions. Callback techniques were introduced in Chapter 2, but let's go through the specific steps required for enumerating resources.

Loading the module

First we must get the handle of the current module. If the user selects anything that causes a new process to become active, WinWatch will need to get a new module handle and update all the resources. Similarly, if the user selects a DLL or other module in the Modules list box, WinWatch must update the resources. Documentation for many of the Windows API resource functions say that these functions expect an instance handle. Ignore this. What they really want is a module handle (which is usually the same as the instance handle anyway).

Chapter 6 explained how to get a module handle with the ModFromProcID function. Unfortunately, this function only returns a valid module handle for the current program. If you get the module handle this way, you'll only be able to view the resources of programs in your own address space. Under the surface, a module handle is actually a pointer, and a pointer from another program might as well be a pointer from another universe.

If you want to use the resources of a particular module, you'll need to load that module into the current address space. You can do this with either the Load-

Library or the LoadLibraryEx API function (we'll use the Ex version). Normally, LoadLibraryEx is used in other languages to load DLLs dynamically, but usually there's no reason to do this with Visual Basic because DLLs are loaded automatically when you use API functions with the Declare syntax. Visual Basic can't call function pointers retrieved with the GetProcAddress API function anyway. But you can load any EXE, DLL, or FON file into your address space and then use its resources.

That's what the WinWatch UpdateDisplay procedure does in the following code block:

```
sModCur = ExePathFromProcID(idProcCur)
hMod = LoadLibraryEx(sModCur, 0, LOAD_LIBRARY_AS_DATAFILE)
' Save process handle for FreeLibrary
hModFree = hMod
```

Notice that LoadLibraryEx has a flag that specifies that you need to use only resources. This is a little more efficient than loading all the procedure addresses that you couldn't call anyway. When you're done, call FreeLibrary to release the module:

```
' If process changed, update it
If idProc <> idProcCur Then
    idProcCur = idProc
    ' Unload previous process
    If hModFree Then Call FreeLibrary(hModFree)
```

The two preceding fragments are a tiny part of the complex UpdateDisplay procedure, which contains all the logic for figuring out what part of the WinWatch display needs to change and how.

Resource callbacks
Most of the real work of finding resources is done by UpdateResources. It looks like this:

```
Private Sub UpdateResources(ByVal hMod As Long)
    ' Turn on hourglass, turn off redrawing
    HourGlass Me
    Call LockWindowUpdate(lstResource.hWnd)
    lstResource.Clear

    Call EnumResourceTypes(hMod, AddressOf ResTypeProc, Me)

    Call LockWindowUpdate(hNull)
    HourGlass Me
End Sub
```

The EnumResourceTypes API function sets up a callback function named Res-TypeProc. As described in "Limits of Procedure Pointers," page 99, the callback procedure must reside in a BAS module, although it would be a lot handier to put it in WINWATCH.FRM with the UpdateResources procedure. The callback procedure will need access to the form so that it can fill the Resources list box and inspect the Filter Resources check box. How can we make these controls available to the standard module containing the callback? Well, we could always use global variables, but there is a better way. Like most callback functions, EnumResourceTypes has an extra parameter for user-defined data. We can use that parameter to pass the whole form. Here's how it works:

```
Function ResTypeProc(ByVal hModule As Long, ByVal lpszType As Long, _
                   frm As Form) As Long
    ResTypeProc = True       ' Always return True
    If lpszType <= 65535 Then
        ' Enumerate resources by ID
        Call EnumResourceNamesID(hModule, lpszType, _
                               AddressOf ResNameProc, frm)
    Else
        ' Enumerate resources by string name
        Call EnumResourceNamesStr(hModule, PointerToString(lpszType), _
                               AddressOf ResNameProc, frm)
    End If
End Function
```

First look at that ByRef Form parameter. Windows expects that parameter to be a ByVal Long, but Long is the size of a pointer, so we can pass anything we want here as long as we pass it by reference. We couldn't be so fast and loose with types if ResTypeProc were going to be called by Visual Basic, but it's not. Windows is the only caller and as long as it gets 32 bits, it doesn't care what they point to. Notice that the only thing the procedure does with the *frm* parameter is pass it on to EnumResourceNames (which sets up ResNameProc as a callback).

An unusual thing about ResTypeProc is how it handles the string pointer *lpszType*. Actually, this isn't all that unusual. Windows often overloads string pointers to represent integers in some situations. For reasons that need not concern us, pointers always have a non-zero high word. That means that Windows can use a high word of zero to signal that a pointer isn't really a pointer. With resources, Windows uses the low word for standard resource types. There are constants with values of less than 65,536 for common resource types such as icons, bitmaps, and cursors. Unusual and user-defined types have string names. When you're enumerating resource types, you don't know whether you're going to get a real string pointer or one of these constants. The Windows API type library provides EnumResourceNamesID and EnumResourceNamesStr as aliases for the EnumResourceNames API function so you can enumerate the resource names for constants or strings. Here's the callback function:

```
Function ResNameProc(ByVal hModule As Long, ByVal lpszType As Long, _
                     ByVal lpszName As Long, frm As Form) As Long
    Dim sType As String, sName As String
    ResNameProc = True        ' Always return True
    If lpszName <= 65535 Then
        sName = Format$(lpszName, "00000")
    Else
        sName = PointerToString(lpszName)
    End If
    If lpszType <= 65535 Then
        sType = ResourceIdToStr(lpszType)
    Else
        sType = PointerToString(lpszType)
    End If
    If frm.chkFilter = vbChecked Then
        If Not ValidateResource(hModule, sName, sType) Then Exit Function
    End If
    frm.lstResource.AddItem sName & "    " & sType
End Function
```

Once again, you have to check the values of *lpszType* and *lpszName* to see if they are strings or integers. Windows uses integers to represent standard resources such as the stop sign icon or the arrow cursor. In this case, if we get an integer ID for the resource name, we format it as a zero-aligned string so that it will line up correctly in the list box. If we get an integer ID for the type, we look up the type name with the ResourceIdToStr function, which is just a Select Case block that returns string names for the standard type names.

Retrieving the resource

ResProcName finally uses the Form variable, which has been passed down from UpdateResources to EnumResourceTypes to ResTypeProc to EnumResource-Names to ResNameProc. First it looks at the check box and, if appropriate, validates the resource by giving it a trial run. I'm not going to show you the trial run because we're almost ready for the real thing, which is a lot more interesting.

If the resource passes the test, ResNameProc stores it in the list box. Numbered resources come out like this:

```
00002    String
```

Named resources come out like this:

```
CLOCK    Menu
```

When the user clicks an item in the Resources list box, you have to parse the item text for the resource name and type, and then pass them to a procedure that can display the resource as shown on the next page.

```
Private Sub lstResource_Click()
    Dim sType As String, sName As String, i As Integer

    sType = lstResource.Text
    BugAssert sType <> sEmpty
    ' Extract resource ID and type
    If Left$(sType, 1) = "0" Then
        ' Append # so Windows will recognize numbers as strings
        sName = "#" & Left$(sType, 5)
        sType = Trim$(Mid$(sType, 7))
    Else
        i = InStr(sType, " ")
        sName = Trim$(Left$(sType, i - 1))
        sType = Trim$(Mid$(sType, i + 1))
    End If

    ' Clear last resource and handle new one
    ClearResource
    pbResource.AutoRedraw = False
    If UCase$(sType) <> "BITMAP" Then
        BmpTile pbResource, imgCloud.Picture
    End If

    Select Case UCase$(sType)
    Case "CURSOR"
        ShowCursor hModCur, sName
    Case "GROUP_CURSOR", "GROUP CURSOR"
        ShowCursors hModCur, sName
    Case "BITMAP"
        ShowBitmap hModCur, sName
    Case "ICON"
        ShowIcon hModCur, sName
    Case "GROUP_ICON", "GROUP ICON"
        ShowIcons hModCur, sName
    Case "MENU"
        ShowMenu hModCur, sName
    Case "STRING", "STRINGTABLE"
        ShowString hModCur, sName
    Case "WAVE"
        PlayWave hModCur, sName
    Case "AVI"
        PlayAvi hModCur, sName
    Case "FONTDIR", "FONT", "DIALOG", "ACCELERATOR"
        pbResource.Print sType & " selected"
    Case "VERSION"
        pbResource.Print GetVersionData(sModCur, 26)
    Case Else
        ShowData hModCur, sName, sType
```

```
      End Select
      pbResource.AutoRedraw = True
End Sub
```

The first part of this code strips out the type and name, taking advantage of a Windows shortcut that lets you pass numeric ID numbers as strings by prepending the "#" character. This is easier than passing numbers in some cases and strings in others, and the performance cost in WinWatch is negligible.

The second part of the procedure brings us, at last, to the main point of this chapter: what you can do with those resources once you find them.

Using Resources the Windows Way

Digging resources out of other programs is interesting, but from a practical standpoint it's hardly worth the trouble. Visual Basic already provides a better way of getting at most resources, so why even bother with API functions? Well, it turns out that what you get from resource functions is the same thing you get from other API functions: handles to GDI objects or global memory.

No matter what graphics task you attempt, you'll be dealing with handles such as HBITMAPs, HICONs, HCURSORs, and so on. Sometimes you'll be using them indirectly, but you're not going to attain programming freedom until you can change seamlessly back and forth between API handles and equivalent Visual Basic features. We talked a little bit about this in Chapter 7. In this chapter, we're going to look at the most important GDI handle types one by one.

In WinWatch, we'll be using the Show and Play procedures to display the appropriate data on the *pbResource* picture box. Among other things, these procedures save the resource type so that you can call the ClearResource procedure to clean up the current resource before a new resource is loaded. ClearResource removes the representation of the last resource. Sometimes this is as simple as erasing the picture box where the resource was displayed. Other times the procedure must take type-specific cleanup actions, such as restoring the original menu or cursor.

The rest of this chapter looks at the specific Show and Play procedures that use the resources as well as the cleanup code that clears them. In other words, we'll be looking at the mechanics of using Windows handles in Visual Basic code.

We'll also be looking at some resources from the other standpoint—translating Visual Basic data types such as Picture into Windows handles. We'll use the Picture Browser shown in Figure 8-4 to illustrate these techniques. The Picture Browser loads files for bitmaps, icons, cursors, waves, and metafiles. It displays the data graphically and uses API techniques to decipher everything Windows knows about the data.

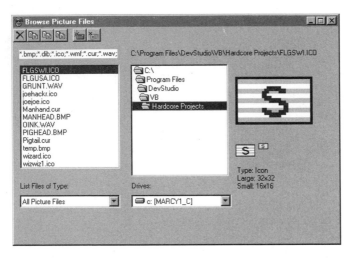

Figure 8-4. *The Picture Browser.*

Using Data Resources

Let's start with raw binary data—if you know how that works, you can figure out what to do with other kinds of data. You can cram any binary data you want into a resource file. Use the predefined RT_RCDATA type, or invent your own resource type name. Of course, WinWatch won't know how to handle unknown data types; the best it can do is dump the binary data in hex format.

The goal is to turn a resource into an array of bytes, which is the approved way for Visual Basic to handle binary data. You can also handle data as strings, but that's politically incorrect, particularly in a chapter such as this, which deals with multiple languages. Here's how ShowData reads and dumps generic data:

```
Sub ShowData(ByVal hMod As Long, sData As String, _
          Optional sDataType As String = "RCDATA")

    Dim hRes As Long, hmemRes As Long, cRes As Long
    Dim pRes As Long, abRes() As Byte
    If sDataType = "RCDATA" Then
        hRes = FindResourceStrId(hMod, sData, RT_RCDATA)
    Else
        hRes = FindResourceStrStr(hMod, sData, sDataType)
    End If
    If hRes = hNull Then
        pbResource.Print "Can't display data: " & sCrLf & sCrLf & _
                    WordWrap(ApiError(Err.LastDllError), 25)
        Exit Sub
    End If
    ' Allocate memory block and get its size
    hmemRes = LoadResource(hMod, hRes)
```

```
    cRes = SizeofResource(hMod, hRes)
    ' Don't dump more than 500 bytes
    If cRes > 500 Then cRes = 500
    ' Lock it to get pointer
    pRes = LockResource(hmemRes)
    ' Allocate byte array of right size
    ReDim abRes(cRes)
    ' Copy memory block to array
    CopyMemory abRes(0), ByVal pRes, cRes
    ' Free resource (no need to unlock)
    Call FreeResource(hmemRes)
    pbResource.Print HexDump(abRes, False)

End Sub
```

First you use FindResourceStrId or FindResourceStrStr (aliases for FindResource) to get a handle to the resource. Then you move through the memory-allocation fire drill described in the sidebar, "The Zen of Windows Memory Management," page 454: allocate, lock, process, unlock, free. You'll learn to recognize this pattern. The *process* step in ShowData copies the resource to a byte array. Refer back to the sidebar, "CopyMemory: A Strange and Terrible Saga," page 90, to find the story of CopyMemory and its aliased friends CopyMemoryToStr and CopyMemoryRef.

You can probably guess what the HexDump function (or its cousins, HexDumpS and HexDumpB) looks like; check it out in UTILITY.BAS. It dumps in either 8-byte rows (if you pass False as the second argument) or the traditional 16-byte format used by most debuggers. I use the 8-byte form in WinWatch so that the dump will fit in the picture box. Your dumps will look a lot better if you set the font of the output object (label, text box, picture box, printer) to a mono-space font.

Using Bitmaps

WinWatch needs to display a selected bitmap in a picture box. There are lots of ways to do this, but we're going to do it the easy way. The reason it's easy is because I've hidden all the ugly details in procedures that we'll look at later. Here's the easy part:

```
Sub ShowBitmap(ByVal hMod As Long, sBitmap As String)
With pbResource

    Dim hPal As Long, hPal2 As Long
    ' Convert resource into bitmap handle
    hResourceCur = LoadBitmapPalette(hMod, sBitmap, hPal)
    If hResourceCur = hNull Then
        pbResource.Print "Can't load bitmap: " & sCrLf & sCrLf & _
                        WordWrap(ApiError(Err.LastDllError), 25)
```

(continued)

```
        Exit Sub
    End If
    ' Convert hBitmap to Picture (clip anything larger than picture box)
    .Picture = BitmapToPicture(hResourceCur, hPal)
    ' Set the form palette to use this picture's palette
    Palette = .Picture
    ' Make sure palette is realized
    Refresh
    DoEvents
    ' Draw the palette
    DrawPalette pbResource, hPal, .Width, .Height * 0.1, 0, .Height * 0.9
    ' Record the type for cleanup
    ordResourceLast = RT_BITMAP
End With
End Sub
```

The first step is to convert the resource into a bitmap handle. Remember, at this point the *sBitmap* string will be either the name of a bitmap resource (MyBitmap)

The Zen of Windows Memory Management

Normally, the Windows Way of managing memory is the least of your worries. Dim, ReDim, Private, Public, and Static do it all for you, and, for the most part, transparently. You don't ordinarily use the Windows memory functions directly because they deal with pointers, and Visual Basic doesn't do pointers. But there are exceptions to every rule, and loading unknown resources is one of them.

Here's a 30-second introduction to the rarely needed art of Windows global memory management:

1. Get a handle to a global memory block. You can create a generic one with GlobalAlloc, or you can create a resource block by calling Load-Resource on the value returned by FindResource. Use resource functions instead of global memory functions on resource blocks. You have several choices for how you want the memory to be allocated, but I'll leave you to the documentation.

2. Measure the memory with GlobalSize (or remember its size if you created it with GlobalAlloc). If it's a resource, use SizeofResource. If you don't know the size of a global memory block, there won't be much you can safely do with it in Visual Basic.

3. Lock the memory handle with GlobalLock (or LockResource if it's a resource handle). This means that you ask the memory manager to let you play with the memory for a while. If your request is granted, you'll be given a pointer to the memory and other users will be locked out of it.

or, more likely, a numeric resource ID converted into a string (#01001). In days of old, we would have read the resource with the simpler LoadBitmap API function, but LoadBitmap only loads device dependent bitmaps. The new LoadImage function loads any bitmap, including device independent bitmaps (DIB), and it can load them from files as well as from resources. It's also more flexible for loading icons and cursors, as we'll see later. Unfortunately, when LoadImage loads a bitmap with a palette, it throws away any accompanying palette. I had to write my own LoadBitmapPalette function to get both. But ignore the palette issue for now.

The *hResourceCur* returned by LoadBitmapPalette is actually a bitmap handle. At this point, I could work directly on the handle. I could select the bitmap into the DC of the picture box. I could create a memory DC, select the bitmap into it, and then blit the memory DC to the DC of the picture box. I demonstrated some of these GDI choices in Chapter 7. But what I really want to do with that Windows-style handle is turn it into a Visual Basic–style picture. Once I have a picture, I can assign it to various Picture properties or blit it with the PaintPicture method.

4. Have your way with the pointer and the stuff it points to. This is the tricky part because, in Visual Basic, a pointer is like a handle—all you can do with it is pass it on to another API function. For example, you can use CopyMemory to copy the memory of a pointer to a Visual Basic string. (You must know the size to do this; see step 2.) If you dare, you can modify the string and copy it back to the pointer (again using CopyMemory). If you change the size of the data, you'll need to call GlobalReAlloc to change the size of the original block before copying. You can find other API functions to pass your memory pointers to (such as sndPlaySound, described later).

5. When you're done with the block, use GlobalUnlock to release the pointer back to the system. Some kinds of global memory don't need to be unlocked, but it does no harm and might save you from a horrible fate if you mix up your fixed and movable memory. I always unlock. The exception to this rule is that you don't need to unlock resources. In fact, the Win32 UnlockResource function is nothing more than a C macro that does nothing. If you like to be consistent, you can call the do-nothing UnlockResource function in the PICTOOL.BAS module.

6. Free the memory if you created it; leave it alone if Windows created it. Use GlobalFree to free memory you created with GlobalAlloc; use FreeResource to free memory loaded with LoadResource.

The BitmapToPicture function does the conversion. Again, I'm ignoring the palette issue until after I check out the COM magic that makes picture conversion possible.

Handle to picture and back

The BitmapToPicture function is one of several Picture conversions I'll be examining. Once you've seen it, IconToPicture, CursorToPicture, and Metafile-ToPicture will be easy. Here's the code:

```
Function BitmapToPicture(ByVal hBmp As Long, _
                        Optional ByVal hPal As Long = hNull) _
                        As IPicture
    ' Fill picture description
    Dim ipic As IPicture, picdes As PICTDESC, iidIPicture As IID
    picdes.cbSizeofstruct = Len(picdes)
    picdes.picType = vbPicTypeBitmap
    picdes.hgdiobj = hBmp
    picdes.hPalOrXYExt = hPal
    ' Fill in magic IPicture GUID {7BF80980-BF32-101A-8BBB-00AA00300CAB}
    iidIPicture.Data1 = &H7BF80980
    iidIPicture.Data2 = &HBF32
    iidIPicture.Data3 = &H101A
    iidIPicture.Data4(0) = &H8B
    iidIPicture.Data4(1) = &HBB
    iidIPicture.Data4(2) = &H0
    iidIPicture.Data4(3) = &HAA
    iidIPicture.Data4(4) = &H0
    iidIPicture.Data4(5) = &H30
    iidIPicture.Data4(6) = &HC
    iidIPicture.Data4(7) = &HAB
    ' Create picture from bitmap handle
    OleCreatePictureIndirect picdes, iidIPicture, True, ipic
    ' Result will be valid Picture or Nothing--either way set it
    Set BitmapToPicture = ipic
End Function
```

First the function fills in the PICTDESC UDT. The Windows version of this structure contains unions so that one structure can contain different fields for bitmaps, icons, and metafiles. The last field of the structure is a Long hPal for bitmaps or two Integer fields (xExt and yExt) for metafiles (it's ignored for icons). Unfortunately, Visual Basic doesn't support writing unions, and it doesn't recognize unions in type libraries. That's OK. Unions are just a cheap trick for assigning different names to the same bits. I fake it by renaming the field hPalOrXYExt.

The next step is to fill a UDT with the magic numbers that uniquely identify the IPicture interface. Finally I call the OleCreatePictureIndirect API function. The last parameter is an IPicture interface which will be set by the function. I haven't seen the source for OleCreatePictureIndirect, but I believe it creates a StdPicture object using the data passed in the *picdes* variable. It then passes back the IPicture interface of the new StdPicture object. As you might recall from Chapter 7, the StdPicture class implements several interfaces, including Picture and IPicture. There's a lot more to the story. In fact, this code probably raises more questions than it answers, but I'll leave the rest to lower level COM books.

So that takes care of the trip from bitmap to picture. The trip from picture to bitmap and palette is shorter and simpler. The StdPicture class and the Picture interface have a Handle property that returns the bitmap (or icon or metafile) handle of the GDI object in the picture. They also have an hPal property containing the palette handle of the bitmap. This property will always be 0 for icons and metafiles and for bitmaps that have no palette. The palette property is all you need to do palette tricks such as the one you'll see in a few pages.

Palette problems

Palettes haven't been much of an issue for Visual Basic programmers. Sure, the last several versions included a few DIB files (rainbow, bright, and pastel) with some obscure instructions about how you can use them to change the palette of your forms. But this was a halfway solution that few programmers took advantage of. This version takes another step toward full palette control. The Palette property lets you assign a custom Palette for a form, and the PaletteMode property gives you some control over which palette will be used. You can learn more about the details from the documentation.

"Wait," you're saying. "What's a palette anyway?" Well, some bitmaps have what's called a logical palette. This is an array containing all the colors that the bitmap would like to use. So if your bitmap has a reddish hue, it will probably have a palette full of reds. Palette colors are a limited resource. There are slots for 256 colors in most contexts on common video adapters. The problem is that all the bitmaps in the system have to get their colors mapped into those same slots. If there are several bitmaps visible on the screen, they will all be fighting for those same slots. There's a constant battle with colors being mapped in and out of the system palette as the focus switches between programs. Your bitmaps will have a better chance of displaying themselves correctly in the foreground and in the background if you supply a list of your desired colors (and only those colors) rather than trying to use whatever the system has available. If you are fortunate enough to have access to a real bitmap editor—the wretched ImagEdit supplied with Visual Basic won't edit bitmaps with palettes—you should use no more than 236 colors so that your choices won't conflict with the 20 reserved system colors.

And that's the short version of a very long story.

To see what WinWatch does with palettes, let's imagine that the ShowBitmap function is looking at bitmap resource 6603 in VB5IDE.DLL. This is one of three

256-color bitmaps of a Visual Basic logo that looks like it must be used in the splash screen. Resources 6600 to 6602 are 16-color versions of the same bitmaps. I'd show you a screen dump, but unfortunately I wasn't able to persuade my publisher to print this book in 256 colors. If I were to convert this bitmap to a picture without the palette, the system wouldn't know how to set the hPal property of the picture. And without the palette, Visual Basic would do its best with the system palette rather than use the palette designed for the bitmap. So I load the real palette with LoadBitmapPalette.

After loading the bitmap and palette handles and applying them with Bitmap-ToPicture, Visual Basic has the information it needs to ask Windows to render the bitmap on the picture box in all its glory. Of course, you needn't take my word for it. WinWatch displays the colors of the palette used at the bottom of the resource picture box. The Browse Picture program shows a similar palette display for bitmaps loaded from files.

The palette display is created by DrawPalette, a procedure that takes a destination canvas (such as the picture box), a palette handle to be drawn, and some optional parameters indicating where and what size to draw. You can see the full code in PALTOOL.BAS, but I'll summarize briefly. First DrawPalette gets the size of the palette using the PalSize function. This is just a wrapper for a variation of the multi-purpose GetObject function, which tells you everything you want to know about any GDI object. DrawPalette then allocates a dynamic array containing the appropriate number of PALETTEENTRY elements. The PALETTE-ENTRY UDT consists of four bytes for the red, green, blue, and flags elements of a color. Next the procedure calls the GetPaletteEntries API function to fill the array with the actual colors of the palette. And finally it loops through the colors, drawing a vertical line for each of them. The width of each line is calculated by dividing the width of the display area by the number of colors.

Loading palettes

Let's go back to the LoadBitmapPalette function. It illustrates two ways of retrieving resources. One is to ask Windows to decode the resource. The other is to decode it yourself. Here's the first part where the data is gathered:

```
Function LoadBitmapPalette(ByVal hMod As Long, vResource As Variant, _
                 hPal As Long) As Long

    ' Make null in case of failure
    Dim hBmp As Long
    hPal = hNull

    Dim hRes As Long, hmemRes As Long, cRes As Long
    Dim pRes As Long, abRes() As Byte
    If VarType(vResource) = vbString Then
        hBmp = LoadImage(hMod, CStr(vResource), IMAGE_BITMAP, _
                    0, 0, LR_CREATEDIBSECTION)
```

```
            hRes = FindResourceStrId(hMod, CStr(vResource), RT_BITMAP)

        Else
            hBmp = LoadImageID(hMod, CLng(vResource), IMAGE_BITMAP, _
                              0, 0, LR_CREATEDIBSECTION)
            hRes = FindResourceIdId(hMod, CLng(vResource), RT_BITMAP)
        End If
        ' If bitmap found, return it
        If hBmp = hNull Then Exit Function
        LoadBitmapPalette = hBmp
        ⋮
```

In the Windows API, resource names and resource IDs are handled with string
pointers that can be numeric or string, as described in "Resource callbacks," page
447. Since this is a Visual Basic function, a Variant parameter can accomplish
the same thing. The hPal parameter is received by reference so that it can return the new palette. You have to initialize it to 0. All you do to get the bitmap
is call LoadImage. Windows does all the work.

The palette is a different matter. You have to get the bitmap data using techniques similar to the ones shown earlier for ShowData. The first step is to call
the appropriate alias for the FindResource API. It returns a handle to a resource,
which you process like this:

```
BugAssert hRes <> hNull      ' Shouldn't fail here
' Allocate memory block, and get its size
hmemRes = LoadResource(hMod, hRes)
cRes = SizeofResource(hMod, hRes)
' Lock it to get pointer
pRes = LockResource(hmemRes)

Dim bmpi As BITMAPINFO256
If cRes > LenB(bmpi) Then cRes = LenB(bmpi)
' Copy memory block to array
CopyMemory bmpi, ByVal pRes, cRes
' Free resource (no need to unlock)
Call FreeResource(hmemRes)

Dim lpal As LOGPALETTE256, cColors As Long, cBits As Long, i As Long
cColors = bmpi.bmiHeader.biClrUsed
cBits = bmpi.bmiHeader.biBitCount
' Like VB, we only return 256-color palettes
If cBits <> 8 Then Exit Function
If cColors = 0 Then cColors = 256

' RGBQUAD in BITMAPINFO has different format from PALETTEENTRY
' in LOGPALETTE, so can't use CopyMemory
```

(continued)

```
For i = 0 To cColors - 1
    ' Copy and translate colors
    lpal.palPalEntry(i).peRed = bmpi.bmiColors(i).rgbRed
    lpal.palPalEntry(i).peGreen = bmpi.bmiColors(i).rgbGreen
    lpal.palPalEntry(i).peBlue = bmpi.bmiColors(i).rgbBlue
    lpal.palPalEntry(i).peFlags = 0
Next
lpal.palNumEntries = cColors
lpal.palVersion = &H300

' Create and return the palette through a reference
hPal = CreatePalette(lpal)

End Function
```

First convert the resource to a pointer, and then copy part of it to a structure called a BITMAPINFO256. If you search Windows documentation, you won't find any such structure. Instead, you'll find a BITMAPINFO and a BITMAP-INFOHEADER. A BITMAPINFO looks like this in C:

```
typedef struct tagBITMAPINFO {
    BITMAPINFOHEADER bmiHeader;
    RGBQUAD          bmiColors[1];
} BITMAPINFO;
```

There's a fixed size BITMAPINFOHEADER member, followed by what looks like an array of one RGBQUAD. In fact, the *bmiColors* field represents a C trick for representing a dynamic array. The array might actually contain 0, 2, 16, or 256 entries. The C language provides a way of typecasting and allocating such arrays at run time, depending on the appropriate size, but Visual Basic provides no such thing and a BITMAPINFO UDT that translated literally would be completely worthless. Instead, I define the BITMAPINFO256 UDT to be the maximum (and in this case the most commonly used) version. It's actually in the Windows API type library, but, written in Visual Basic, it would look like this:

```
Type BITMAPINFO256
    bmiHeader As BITMAPINFOHEADER
    bmiColors(0 To 255) As RGBQUAD
End Type
```

Whenever you use a dynamic array, you have to specify someplace in the call (in a separate parameter or a UDT field) what the actual size is. If I needed to use this structure for a smaller array, I could specify a smaller size. The extra memory would be wasted but would do little harm, especially if it was local data allocated on the stack. In this particular case, the code is written to read only 256-color palettes.

The resource actually contains the bits of the bitmap after the color array, but we don't care about them. We've already got the bitmap handle with LoadImage and don't need to prove that we could get the whole bitmap from raw data (although it wouldn't be much harder).

The *biClrUsed* field of the BITMAPINFOHEADER UDT returns the number of colors used in a bitmap resource, or 0 if the bitmap is rude enough to use the whole palette (256 colors). Either way, we simply loop through all the color entries and convert them to the slightly different format of the LOGPALETTE (logical palette) type. This type follows the same pattern—it is dynamically sized, but my LOGPALETTE256 version has 256 entries. We might not use them all, but the *palNumEntries* field tells how many are used. The CreatePalette function converts the logical palette array into a palette handle.

Now you might wonder (as I did) why there aren't any API calls to just look up the palette handle from the bitmap handle. After all, it is in there. Well, the problem is that a bitmap always stores its palette in the size handled by the current device context. That means that a 44-color logical palette usually gets loaded into a 256-color palette. Most of those colors are black, but there is no trace left of the original size stored in the bitmap file or resource. In fact, if you load a 44-color bitmap with Paint and use the Save As command to save a copy, you'll end up with a 256-color bitmap. Actually, it is possible to algorithmically generate a palette from a bitmap handle by walking through the 256-color palette and eliminating all the black colors. The GetBitmapPalette function does this, and it usually gets close, if not always exact. Check it out in PALTOOL.BAS.

Palette tricks

Palettes can provide some amusing graphics techniques for a very small performance cost. It's much faster to change colors in the hardware palette than to change pixels on the screen, and sometimes the effect can be just as dramatic. For example, you can gradually fade a bitmap on to or off the screen, or you can rotate palette colors to create an illusion of movement.

Visual Basic won't help you with these tricks, and in many cases it will stand in your way as it manages palettes behind the scenes. To get palette management to work seamlessly, you need to push Visual Basic out of the way and take over. Here are some hints about how to do it.

- You can subclass the window where the palette is displayed and intercept the WM_QUERYNEWPALETTE and WM_PALETTECHANGED messages. When you receive WM_QUERYNEWPALETTE, return 1 and exit from the window procedure to indicate that you have handled the message. You're throwing this message away so that Visual Basic won't return zero, preventing you from getting WM_PALETTE-CHANGED. When you receive WM_PALETTECHANGED, check the *wParam* to see if the window that changed the palette is yours and, if not, call the RealizePalette API function to map your palette onto the system palette. This ensures that your palette is handled correctly when it's in the background.

- You might want to turn off Visual Basic palette management. If you're writing a control, you can do this by setting the Palette property to *vbPaletteModeNone*. Unfortunately, this setting works only on User-Control objects. You can get the same effect on Form, UserDocument, or PropertyPage objects by setting the PaletteMode property to *vb-PaletteModeCustom*, and then setting the Palette property to an empty picture.

- When AutoRedraw is True on a form, Visual Basic creates a hidden bitmap containing the representation of the form. You don't know and can't control what Visual Basic is doing with that bitmap or with any palette owned by the bitmap. Therefore, you should turn off Auto-Redraw when manipulating palettes. You might have to do a lot of extra work in the Paint event, but so be it.

There's a lot more to handling palettes at the API level—too much to describe in detail, so here's the executive summary. The first step in manipulating a palette (in the form of a palette handle) is to get its size with the multipurpose GetObject function (or the GetObjectPaletteEntries alias from the Windows API type library). Next you read the palette colors into an array with the GetPaletteEntries API function. Add the flags necessary for palette manipulation and call SetPaletteEntries to put your changes back into the palette. When you're ready to roll, call SelectPalette to select your palette into the device context of the window that will display the palette, and call RealizePalette to map your logical palette onto the system palette. Most palette tricks involve some sort of periodic reordering of the palette colors. For each change, you rearrange the palette colors in the array and call AnimatePalette to update the new colors in the palette. If all goes well, the new colors will appear on the screen in place of the old colors.

The TPALETTE project on the CD illustrates the details of palette management. There's no point in showing a screen dump because the paper pages of this book don't support palettes.

Icons with an Attitude

Before I get to icons in WinWatch, I want to digress to note the big changes that have happened to icons in Windows 95 and in Windows NT version 4. Iconically speaking, the enhanced Windows interface is a whole new metaphor. You'll see icons everywhere—big ones and little ones, in list views, tree views, title bars, and the taskbar. The Picture property has always made standard icons easy to use with Visual Basic, so you might expect that small icons would be a simple extension of an existing feature. Not so. Before we start digging icons out of other people's programs, let's examine icons in our own programs and see how the Picture object handles (or fails to handle) them.

The icons we're most familiar with are 32 by 32 pixels in as many as 16 colors. They consist of a color bitmap of the icon image and a monochrome mask with the outline of the image. They work very much like the CPictureGlass class described in Chapter 7 except that they have a fixed size and built-in API calls to handle them (DrawIcon, CreateIcon, LoadIcon, and so on). Although icons were generally 32 by 32 pixels in previous versions of Windows, the detailed specification allowed any size—a possibility that was rarely tapped. Windows 95 supports four specific icon sizes: small (16 by 16 pixels), large (32 by 32 pixels, with most video adapters), huge (48 by 48 pixels), and shell size (determined by the user on the Appearance tab of the Display Properties dialog box). In addition, you can define icons of arbitrary sizes, although Windows leaves you on your own to manage them.

The ICO file format supports multiple images. You can and should put small icons and large icons in the same file. Unfortunately, the icon tool of choice, IconWorks, doesn't know a small icon from smallpox. You have to use the ImagEdit tool provided in the \Tools directory on the Visual Basic CD to create icons with multiple images. (Or better yet, purchase one of the excellent shareware icon editors.) Technically, you could put images of any size in ICO files, but ImagEdit supports only 32 by 32 pixels, 16 by 16 pixels, and—for that one last CGA monitor left on earth—32 by 16 pixels. The icons supplied with Visual Basic version 5 contain large and small images, although most parts of Visual Basic can't do much with the small image, at least not without a little help.

Visual Basic has always supported the concept of a Picture object that can contain an icon, a metafile, or a bitmap. The Picture object (like the Font object) is one of the features COM Automation took from Visual Basic. See "Picture Objects" in Chapter 7 for a more detailed discussion of the Picture object. Unfortunately, when Windows changed the way it uses icons, COM Automation didn't change the Picture object to match. A Picture can still contain only one icon image. So— if you call LoadPicture on an icon file that contains multiple images, which image is loaded? The same question applies to LoadResPicture and the Load Picture dialog box. You could handle this problem in several ways, but all of them require redesigning the Picture architecture, a redesign that didn't take place for this version of Visual Basic.

Let's compare the new Windows way of icons to the Basic way of icons and try to figure out some hacks to bring Visual Basic around to the Windows point of view.

The problem of single icons in the Picture object was well known in the Visual Basic version 4 time frame. Since the Picture object isn't owned by Visual Basic, there's nothing Visual Basic could do to fix it, but the owners of the Picture object could have fixed it. Unfortunately, ownership changed sometime after Visual Basic version 4 shipped and promises to redesign the Picture object were "forgotten." As a result, the Picture object remains a feature designed for 16-bit Windows and completely ignores innovations added by 32-bit Windows. Fortunately, Visual Basic controls such as Image and PictureBox have fixed some of their bugs related to how they display icons.

The new Windows icons versus Visual Basic icons

In the Windows interface, the size of shell icons is determined by the user. Try it. Right-click on the desktop and choose Properties to bring up the Display Properties dialog box. Select the Appearance tab, click the Item combo box, and select Icon. Chances are you'll see the default icon size, 32. Change it to 37 or 24, and click Apply. All the icons on your desktop will change to the new size. If you move to Windows Explorer and set Large Icons mode, you'll see the same size. This feature is part of the new philosophy of allowing users to customize more parts of the desktop. Users with visual disabilities can make their icons as large as they want. Those who want to cram as much stuff as they can onto their screens, visibility be damned, can have small icons everywhere.

So what happens when you perform similar operations in Visual Basic? The Test Icons program (TICON.VBP) shown in Figure 8-5 illustrates. The sample program displays icons on a background of clouds so that you can tell that they're really icons and not just bitmaps drawn on a solid background. Of course, this doesn't do any good on the PictureBox control because it doesn't have a transparent mode. In real life, you probably won't put icons in the PictureBox Picture property (although you could draw them transparently on the Picture with DrawIconEx).

In order to make image differences more visual, I used a modified dual-image icon (I.ICO) that has a blue *L* in the large icon image and a pink *S* in the small image. (Don't try this at home.) When I captured the screen shot, my desktop icon size was 24 by 24 pixels, the size that showed up in a shortcut to the Test Icons program (also shown in Figure 8-5 for comparison). In this example, the Image controls have Stretch set to False and the PictureBox controls have Auto-Size set to True. The Basic icon is loaded with Visual Basic's LoadPicture. The rest are loaded with my LoadAnyPicture.

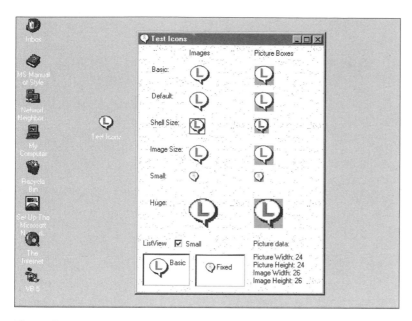

Figure 8-5. *Icons for every occasion.*

- The large (Default) icon comes out at 32 by 32 pixels whether you get it from Visual Basic's LoadPicture function or from my LoadAnyPicture function. This is, alas, the system icon size (from GetSystemMetrics) of my monitor. My boss turned down my request for a 48-inch monitor with a 4096 by 4096 pixel display and 48 by 48 pixel icons. In fact, I've never seen a display adapter with a system icon size other than 32, so I'm not sure what Visual Basic would do with one.

- The Shell Size icon comes out the right size in both the Image and the PictureBox controls. If you look closely, you'll see some jaggies on the icon edge, indicating that this image has been compressed from its real image size (32 by 32 pixels).

- The Image Size icon comes out to the actual size of the large icon. But since the icon file contains both a 32 by 32 pixel and a 16 by 16 pixel image, how did the program know which one to use? I'll get to that.

- The small and huge icons display correctly in both controls. The small icon gets the small image. The huge icon uses the large image, but stretches it out to a 48 by 48 frame. Notice the jaggies from stretching the icon image.

You have to do some extra work to get the appropriate image, but at least the controls do the right thing if you give them the right stuff. This is a marked improvement over Visual Basic version 4, which did a particularly poor job of displaying non-standard icons in PictureBox controls.

Visual Basic and the Picture object just don't have a Windows state of mind about icons. Windows programs are supposed to display large icons with code like this:

```
cx = GetSystemMetrics(CX_ICON)
cy = GetSystemMetrics(CY_ICON)
f = DrawIconEx(hdc, x, y, hIcon, cx, cy, 0, NULL, DI_NORMAL)
```

I imagine that under the surface, DrawIconEx calls StretchBlt to stretch the image and mask bitmaps of the icon from their actual size to the desired icon size. Small icons work the same way except that they must stretch the actual icon bitmaps down to the hard-coded size of 16 by 16 pixels. Shell size icons get the user-selected size using a technique similar to that found in my GetShellIconSize function. You can see the code in PICTOOL.BAS.

Often, when Windows uses multiple-image icon files or resources, it doesn't need to do any stretching. It can simply blast a 16 by 16 pixel image onto a small icon or a 32 by 32 pixel image onto a large icon with the default size. If the target icon size doesn't match any of the images in the file or resource, Windows probably has an algorithm for deciding which image will best stretch into the target size.

This works out pretty well for C programmers because they load icons from resources or files, which can contain multiple images. Visual Basic programmers load icons from Picture objects, which can contain only a single image. Worse yet, none of the ways to load an icon into a Picture object gives you any choice about which image to load. For example, the Visual Basic LoadPicture function and the Load Picture dialog box always load the system metrics size. If the user keeps the default icon size (usually 32 by 32 pixels), LoadPicture always loads a 32 by 32 pixel icon. If the icon file being loaded contains a single 16 by 16 pixel image, LoadPicture stretches it to 32 by 32 pixels before storing it in the Picture object. A small icon puffed into a large icon container looks just as bad as a large icon crammed into a small icon container.

The only thing Visual Basic does right with dual-image icons is display them correctly in the Icon property. Small icons appear correctly in the Taskbar and in the left corner of the application's title bar. Large icons are displayed correctly if they are placed on the desktop. This is the most pervasive use of large and small icons, so it's fortunate that it works. But you can do lots of other things with icons—things that hardcore programmers won't give up on easily just because Visual Basic doesn't help them.

A better LoadPicture

You can load any icon into a picture if you have a handle for the icon. The IconToPicture function (PICTOOL.BAS) turns an icon handle into a Picture object in the same way BitmapToPicture turns a bitmap into a picture. (For more information, see "Using Bitmaps," page 453). Therefore, if you could get the handle of a small icon image out of a multi-image icon file, you could load it into a picture.

It so happens that the Win32 API has a new LoadImage function that delivers icons, cursors, and bitmaps. I don't need it for bitmaps, and I haven't figured out a good way to use it for cursors, but it works fine for icons. You tell it what size icon you want, and it gives you a handle to that icon. As an added benefit, LoadImage can load from either an ICO file or from an icon resource. In other words, it does most of the work of the Visual Basic LoadPicture and LoadRes-Picture functions. I use LoadImage to create a better LoadAnyPicture that takes an additional optional argument that specifies what kind of icon to load. Here's how the Test Icons program calls my new LoadPicture:

```
' Load icon with Basic's LoadPicture (system metrics size)
Set img(eipBasic).Picture = LoadPicture("i.ico")
Set pb(eipBasic).Picture = LoadPicture("i.ico")
' Load icon with Basic's LoadPicture (system metrics size)
Set img(eipDefault).Picture = LoadAnyPicture("i.ico", eisDefault)
Set pb(eipDefault).Picture = LoadAnyPicture("i.ico", eisDefault)
' Load icon stretched to system metrics size
Set img(eipShell).Picture = LoadAnyPicture("i.ico", eisShell)
Set pb(eipShell).Picture = LoadAnyPicture("i.ico", eisShell)
' Load first icon image in file with its real size
Set img(eipImage).Picture = LoadAnyPicture("i.ico", eisImage)
Set pb(eipImage).Picture = LoadAnyPicture("i.ico", eisImage)
' Load small (16 by 16) icon, squashing if necessary
Set img(eipSmall).Picture = LoadAnyPicture("i.ico", eisSmall)
Set pb(eipSmall).Picture = LoadAnyPicture("i.ico", eisSmall)
' Load huge (48 by 48) icon
Set img(eipHuge).Picture = LoadAnyPicture("i.ico", eisHuge)
Set pb(eipHuge).Picture = LoadAnyPicture("i.ico", eisHuge)
```

Notice the fourth set of commands (the ones with the *eisImage* parameter). This is how you load small icons and other icons of unusual size from single-image icon files. Normally, Visual Basic stretches these icons to the system metrics size, but if you give the *eisImage* constant, you should get the real size of the image. In most cases, you should let Windows decide which image to use and when. But if you had an icon editor that let you define icons of any size, you could use LoadAnyPicture with *eisImage* to get transparent images for animation.

Here's the code for the better LoadPicture from PICTOOL.BAS:

```
Function LoadAnyPicture(Optional sPicture As String, _
                        Optional eis As EIconSize = eisDefault _
                        ) As Picture
    Dim hIcon As Long, sExt As String, xy As Long, af As Long
    ' If no picture, return Nothing (clears picture)
    If sPicture = sEmpty Then Exit Function
    ' Use default LoadPicture for all except icons with argument
    sExt = MUtility.GetFileExt(sPicture)
    If UCase$(sExt) <> ".ICO" Or eis = -1 Then
        Set LoadAnyPicture = VB.LoadPicture(sPicture)
        Exit Function
    End If

    Select Case eis
    Case eisSmall
        xy = 16: af = LR_LOADFROMFILE
    Case eisHuge
        xy = 48: af = LR_LOADFROMFILE
    Case eisImage
        xy = 0: af = LR_LOADFROMFILE Or LR_LOADREALSIZE
    Case eisShell ' Get icon size from system
        xy = GetShellIconSize(): af = LR_LOADFROMFILE
    Case Is > 0   ' Use arbitrary specified size--72 by 72 or whatever
        xy = eis: af = LR_LOADFROMFILE
    Case Else       ' Includes eisDefault
        xy = 0: af = LR_LOADFROMFILE Or LR_DEFAULTSIZE
    End Select
    hIcon = LoadImage(0&, sPicture, IMAGE_ICON, xy, xy, af)
    ' If this fails, use original load
    If hIcon <> hNull Then
        Set LoadAnyPicture = IconToPicture(hIcon)
    Else
        Set LoadAnyPicture = VB.LoadPicture(sPicture)
    End If
End Function
```

This function deals only with icons. The first section of code checks for other types or for a command line without an optional argument, and then calls the normal LoadPicture to do the work. If an optional argument is provided, the code sets up the appropriate size and flags and calls LoadImage. Finally it checks to see whether LoadImage worked, and, if not, it again falls back on the original LoadPicture. The LoadImage function is implemented as a stub under Windows NT 3.51, so you'll always fall through to the old LoadPicture. That's OK because all icons are the same size in that environment.

A little better LoadResPicture

Since LoadImage can load from resources as well as from files, it's relatively easy to enhance LoadResPicture in the same way you enhanced LoadPicture. It's a little more complicated because you have to deal with resources specified by string name or by integer index, but most of the code is the same.

There is one big difference, however. LoadImage can read icons from resources in an EXE file, but it hasn't a clue about how to read them in the Visual Basic environment. When you run in the environment, you're not really running your own program; you're running VB5.EXE. If you try to load icon resource 25 using the Windows API, you'll get Visual Basic's resource 25 or, more likely, you'll get an error. LoadResPicture knows how to dig your resource out of some internal format known only to Madame Basic's crystal ball. The best LoadAnyResPicture can do is detect the environment with a function called IsExe and then call the real LoadResPicture.

You might think that having icons be one size in the environment and another in an EXE would be unworkable. Actually, it's not so bad. For example, assume that you put multi-image icons in a resource file and then load them into an ImageList control as small icons at run time. You'll end up with large icons squished to small icons in the environment, but your small icons will come out as small icons in the EXE. You can do the same thing for Image controls by playing with the image size and the Stretch property. It's an annoying problem for you, but your customers will never be the wiser.

Back to icons in WinWatch

Since WinWatch is getting its icons from the resources of another program, it has to do things the hard way. It handles single icons (resource RT_ICON) differently than it handles icon groups (RT_GROUP_ICON). An icon group is comparable to an icon file containing multiple images.

It's a simple matter to show a single icon: just load the icon handle with Load-Icon, and then call DrawIcon to display it. When you're done, call DestroyIcon to release the resource. That's how I handled icons in early versions of Win-Watch, but eventually I found a better way. Here's the ShowIcon code:

```
Sub ShowIcon(ByVal hMod As Long, sIcon As String)
    BugAssert (hMod <> hNull) And (sIcon <> sEmpty)

    ' Load icon resource
    hResourceCur = LoadImage(hMod, sIcon, IMAGE_ICON, 0, 0, 0)
    With pbResource
        If hResourceCur <> hNull Then
            ' Convert icon handle to Picture
            Dim pic As New StdPicture
```

(continued)

469

```
        Set pic = IconToPicture(hResourceCur)
        pbResource.PaintPicture pic, 0, 0
        ordResourceLast = RT_ICON
    Else
        pbResource.Print "Can't display icon: " & sCrLf & sCrLf & _
                        WordWrap(ApiError(Err.LastDllError), 25)
    End If
End With

End Sub
```

The code starts by calling the LoadImage function with arguments that indicate that the icon should be displayed at its actual image size. All the single icon resources I've encountered in WinWatch have been 32 pixels square. Once the icon resource is converted to an icon handle, we call IconToPicture (which looks a lot like BitmapToPicture) to convert it to a picture. From there we can draw the icon with PaintPicture. The PaintPicture method knows the difference between an icon and a bitmap, and draws the icon transparently.

Icon groups usually contain several different icons of different sizes and possibly different resolutions. The system is supposed to go through the list of images and pick the image that best matches the current display adapter and context. The StdPicture class doesn't know anything about multiple images in the same icon file, so I'll have to use raw GDI functions to process multiple icons. Worse, there's no good API function to iterate through the images in an icon resource. You have to do it the hard way by reading semi-random bytes from semi-random offsets in the resource memory.

NOTE You can use icons to create animation. The technique works much like the CPictureGlass class described in Chapter 7 except that Windows does all the dirty work. Just create an icon of the desired size and draw it wherever you want. The problem is that you'll seldom want to do animation based on the standard icon sizes, but it's difficult to get icons of arbitrary size. Many icon tools know how to create only standard sizes. The icon editor in Visual C++ 5.0 can create an icon of arbitrary size, but you must make sure that your 56 by 45 pixel icon image is the only one in the resulting icon file. The icon editor will try to give you a second icon image of standard size, but you should delete it. You can't load your arbitrary-sized icon into a Picture with Visual Basic's LoadPicture or with my IconToPicture, but you can load it and get an icon handle with LoadImage. Once you've got the handle, you can draw the transparent image with DrawIconEx.

Reading the resource data works the same as the ShowData function discussed in "Using Data Resources," page 452. Once you get the memory, there are two possible ways to process it. One way is to use the structures described in obscure parts of the Windows documentation. Unfortunately, these structures are connected dynamically. There's a header structure containing information about the icon file, including how many entries there are. This is followed by a separate structure for each entry, but you don't know how many entries there are until run time. You could theoretically write a UDT to represent the maximum size (like LOGPALETTE256 and BITMAPINFO256 described earlier), but the maximum size is unknown. Processing dynamic structures is not Visual Basic's strong point, but you do it by processing the data as a blob of bytes. Study the structures to find the offsets of the data you need, and then read the data with the blob functions introduced in "Reading and Writing Blobs" in Chapter 5.

It's an ugly business, so instead of showing the whole thing, I'll just show pseudocode up to the interesting point. You can read the rest of it in WINWATCH.FRM.

```
Sub ShowIcons(ByVal hMod As Long, sIcon As String)
    ' Find the resource
    ⋮
    ' Allocate memory block, get size, get pointer, and allocate array
    ⋮
    ' Get image count and set up first entry
    ⋮
    For i = 0 To cImage - 1
        ' Get size and colors of current icon in write to string s
        ⋮
        ' Find, load, size, allocate, and copy entry
        ⋮
        ' Real code begins here

        ' Create an icon from resource data
        hIcon = CreateIconFromResource(abEntry(0), cRes, True, &H30000)
        ' Draw icon and print description
        Call DrawIconEx(pbResource.hDC, 0, pbResource.CurrentY, hIcon, _
                        dxIcon, dyIcon, 0, hNull, DI_NORMAL)
        pbResource.Print s
        ' Move to next entry
        pbResource.CurrentY = pbResource.CurrentY + dyIcon
        pbResource.CurrentX = 75
        iImage = iImage + cEntrySize
    Next
    pbResource.ScaleMode = vbTwips
    hResourceCur = hIcon
    ordResourceLast = RT_ICON

End Sub
```

At the point where we pick up the story, the call to the CreateIconFromResource API function, you have a blob named *abEntry* containing one icon block of length *cRes*. The True parameter means this is an icon (False means cursor) and &H30000 is a random version number. Once you have the icon handle, the most accurate way to draw it is with DrawIconEx, which knows how to draw an icon of any size at any location. (The DrawIcon function assumes that all icons are the same size.) After drawing the icon and printing information about its size and the number of colors it supports, you move to the next icon image. When the last icon is drawn, you restore the ScaleMode property to twips. Often, when working in GDI mode, it's easiest to change the ScaleMode to pixels to perform your calculations. Just be sure to change it back when you're done.

ExtractIcon

All that fancy code to extract resources from executable files is wasted on icons. Windows provides the ExtractIcon and ExtractIconEx API functions to do it all for you (although it lacks corresponding ExtractBitmap and ExtractCursor functions). If you simply need icons, do it the easy way. The following code loops through all the icons in a program:

```
c = ExtractIcon(App.hInstance, sExe, -1)
For i = 0 To c - 1
    hIcon = ExtractIcon(App.hInstance, sExe, i)
    ' Do something with icon here
Loop
```

ExtractIconEx is similar, but it can read all the large and small icons into an array.

Using Cursors

Early versions of Visual Basic lacked any means of assigning a custom mouse pointer, although this is a common technique in Windows-based programs. Many programmers who tried to get around this limitation turned to the Windows API, but even then solutions proved unexpectedly difficult.

Visual Basic now provides a simple and intuitive solution (see the sidebar "Cursors Eat Mouse Icons for Lunch," page 442). But WinWatch can't use the Visual Basic Way because it gets cursors from resources. If you check out the Windows API Help, the solution looks simple: just call SetCursor. When you try this, however, the new cursor flickers on and then disappears. Every time you move the cursor, Visual Basic's original cursor is restored.

Here's how WinWatch works around this limitation:

```
Sub ShowCursor(ByVal hMod As Long, sCursor As String)
    ' Get cursor handle
    hResourceCur = LoadImage(hMod, sCursor, IMAGE_CURSOR, 0, 0, 0)
    If hResourceCur <> hNull Then
        ordPointerLast = MousePointer
        MousePointer = vbCustom
        MouseIcon = CursorToPicture(hResourceCur)
        ordResourceLast = RT_CURSOR
        Call DrawIconEx(pbResource.hDC, 0, 0, hResourceCur, _
                        0, 0, 0, hNull, DI_NORMAL)
    Else
        pbResource.Print "Can't display cursor: " & sCrLf & sCrLf & _
                        WordWrap(ApiError(Err.LastDllError), 25)
    End If
End Sub
```

It simply calls the CursorToPicture function and sets the resulting picture to the form's MouseIcon property. That's half the operation. You must also restore the cursor when you change resources. Here's the part of the Select Case block in ClearResource that restores the previous cursor.

```
Case RT_GROUP_CURSOR, RT_CURSOR
    MousePointer = ordPointerLast
```

You saw the BitmapToPicture function, and I told you that IconToPicture looked the same. You can probably guess what CursorToPicture looks like. But you guessed wrong:

```
Function CursorToPicture(ByVal hIcon As Long) As IPicture
    ' It's just an alias
    Set CursorToPicture = IconToPicture(hIcon)
End Function
```

The StdPicture class is notoriously ignorant about cursors. It accepts them but doesn't distinguish them from icons. The MouseIcon property, however, knows the difference, and that's all that matters.

ShowCursor also uses the DrawIconEx function (which also doesn't distinguish between icons and cursors) to draw a static picture of the cursor. The Draw-Cursors procedure uses code similar to that in ShowIcons to draw each of the cursors in a cursor group. Then it uses the same code as ShowCursor to load the one that best fits the current environment.

Using String Resources

It's unlikely that you'll need to use string resources from a DLL or a program that you didn't write, but it was so easy in 16-bit programs that WinWatch implemented it. Just pass the ID number of the string to the LoadString API function, along with a string buffer and a maximum length. The code looked something like this:

```
Dim c As Integer, s As String, id As Long
c = 256
s = Space$(c)
c = LoadString(hMod, Val(Mid$(sString, 2)), s, c)
If c <> 0 Then pbResource.Print WordWrap(Left$(s, c), 25)
```

Unfortunately, that didn't work in 32-bit, and for a long time I couldn't figure out why. Well, it turns out that many 32-bit resource strings are Unicode strings. I'm not sure how C programs are supposed to load Unicode string resources. It didn't seem like something a Visual Basic programmer would want to spend time researching, so I just dumped them in hex format. It doesn't do much good, but neither does it do any harm. The code for ShowString is almost exactly like the ShowData code we saw earlier.

Using Sounds

WinWatch is just a demo, and showing a hex dump of unknown data formats is good enough. But you'll have to do better than that in real life. WinWatch does know about one nonstandard resource: sounds in the WAVE format.

Nonstandard formats can be a problem unless everyone who uses the format agrees on the type name. Someone might put a wave file in a program as an RCDATA resource type. If that someone was you, you'd know what to do. But to WinWatch, it's just data. You could turn the data into a string and search the string for some identifying data instead of producing a hex dump. A hex dump of wave data, for example, looks like this:

```
52 49 46 46 B2 87 00 00   RIFF....
57 41 56 45 66 6D 74 20   WAVEfmt
```

WinWatch could test data blocks to see whether they contain such recognizable formats, but that's up to you. My version recognizes only wave data that has the type name WAVE. This works for TRES. If you see a resource with type WAVE in another program, there's a good chance you'll be able to play it, although you have no guarantee that a particular wave resource won't contain waves for a surfing program.

Assuming that you do have a wave sound resource, here's the code to play it:

```
Sub PlayWave(ByVal hMod As Long, sWave As String)
    ' Convert wave resource to memory
    Dim hWave As Long, hmemWave As Long, pWave As Long
    hWave = FindResourceStrStr(hMod, sWave, "WAVE")
    hmemWave = LoadResource(hMod, hWave)
    pWave = LockResource(hmemWave)
```

```
        Call FreeResource(hmemWave)
        ' Play it
        If sndPlaySoundAsLp(pWave, SND_MEMORY Or SND_NODEFAULT) Then
            pbResource.Print "Sound played"
        Else
            pbResource.Print "Can't play sound: " & sCrLf & sCrLf & _
                             WordWrap(ApiError(Err.LastDllError), 25)
        End If
    End Sub
```

If this isn't clear, you might refer to "The Zen of Windows Memory Management" on pages 454–455. The sndPlaySoundAsLp function is a type-safe alias to the multimedia sndPlaySound function. The Windows API type library provides two other aliases. You can use the raw version to play sound files or system alerts. For example, use this statement to play a wave file:

```
f = sndPlaySound("c:\windows\wave\helpme.wav", SND_SYNC)
```

Use this statement to play the sound associated with SystemExclamation in the registry:

```
f = sndPlaySound("SystemExclamation", SND_SYNC)
```

When you load a sound with LoadResData, you get back an array of bytes. The Test Resources program uses the sndPlaySoundAsBytes alias to play a wave string. It's wrapped in the following function in UTILITY.BAS.

```
Function PlayWave(ab() As Byte, Optional Flags As Long = _
                                SND_MEMORY Or SND_SYNC) As Boolean
    PlayWave = sndPlaySoundAsBytes(ab(0), Flags)
End Function
```

You can play sounds with the Multimedia MCI control, which is appropriate in the context of other multimedia features, but it's overkill if you're simply playing sounds. Adding a control takes up a good chunk of memory resources, whereas using the sndPlaySound function takes up very little.

A bit of advice: if you're tempted to start putting sound resources in your programs left and right, think again. Ask the guy across the hall from me how much he enjoyed those amusing sounds in the Test Resources program the 500th time he heard them during my debugging phase. He'll suggest that you use the sounds associated with existing events in the registry. You can find the standard events in the \HKEY_CURRENT_USER\AppEvents\EventLabels key. The sounds associated with the events are in \HKEY_CURRENT_USER\AppEvents\Schemes-\Apps. By using the registry, you give users the opportunity to override your choice of sounds (or perhaps remove them) with the Sounds applet in the Control Panel. I'll examine the registry in more detail in Chapter 10, but this should give you some idea of how to let users have the final say about potentially annoying noises.

Using Version Data

I was once foolish enough to write what must have been the most complicated batch file ever to ship with a commercial product. I speak of the disastrous MASM 5.0 SETUP.BAT, powered by the infamous batch utility WHAT.EXE. I won't lead you through that sad history (except to note that writing polite batch files is harder than programming in assembler). But I would like to mention the batch file versioning problems I experienced with early versions of MS-DOS, since they relate to version problems we still suffer with Visual Basic.

In those days, a new MS-DOS version (and operating systems that emulated it) seemed to come out every few months, each with a different undocumented trick for displaying a blank line in a batch file. In some versions, two spaces following the ECHO command did the job. In others, you had to use a text editor that let you insert the ASCII character 0 or 255 after ECHO. The current method (ECHO followed immediately by a dot) didn't work in early versions.

You might have hoped to escape such problems in Windows and Visual Basic, but version differences remain the bane of all those who program for Windows. You'll still find controls and DLLs that change their interface in a fashion that seems as random as the MS-DOS batch language. If your system seems to crash in unexpected ways, chances are good that somehow you're running an outdated version of a DLL or a control you didn't even know you had.

Fortunately, Windows 3.1 added resources for embedding version data in your programs and an API for finding version information in other programs. The same system is used in 32-bit Windows. That's why you'll see a version resource in every polite 32-bit executable file (EXE or DLL). Although version data are stored as resources, you don't use the normal resource system to access them. Instead, you pass the filename of the file to be examined and then use a series of complicated API calls to extract the data. The whole process is so Byzantine that it really needs to be wrapped in a user-friendly package—such as my CVersion class.

Using the CVersion class

When you click on a version resource in the Resources list box of WinWatch, the name of the current module (*sModCur*, saved from when the module changed) is passed to the GetVersionData function. Notice that the module handle isn't involved. GetVersionData simply creates a CVersion object and reads its properties, formatting them into a given maximum width. Here's the first part of the code:

```
Function GetVersionData(sExe As String, _
                    Optional ByVal cMaxChar As Long = 40) As String
```

```
    Dim version As New CVersion, s As String
    On Error GoTo NoVersionData
With version
    ' Initialize version object
    version = sExe
    ' Read and return properties
    s = s & WordWrap(.ProductName, cMaxChar) & sCrLf
    s = s & "Exe type: " & .ExeType & sCrLf
    s = s & "Internal name: " & .InternalName & sCrLf
    ⋮
```

WinWatch works great for displaying the version data of running executables, but you might prefer to find version data by filename. If so, use the Version tab of the All About program. Clicking the New button brings up an Open dialog box in which you can select a program, a DLL, a control, a font file, or another executable file. You can learn a lot about resources by experimenting on various programs and DLLs, including compiled Visual Basic programs. Compare programs created with versions 3 and 4 of Visual Basic. Compare system DLLs to programs, or compare programs created with other languages to Visual Basic programs.

Normally, version data comes from a resource script (an RC file). Version data has a special format similar to (but more complicated than) the resource formats described in the sidebar "Anatomy of a Resource Block," page 440. It's possible to enter version data in a resource script and compile it into your Visual Basic program as described in Chapter 7, but Visual Basic provides an easier way: you can use the Make tab of the Project Properties dialog box, accessed by clicking the Options button in the Make Project dialog box. Figure 8-6 shows the Project Properties dialog box entries for the All About program. Figure 8-7 (on the following page) shows how these entries are displayed in the All About program.

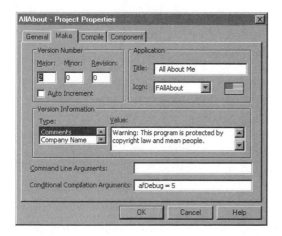

Figure 8-6. *The Project Properties dialog box.*

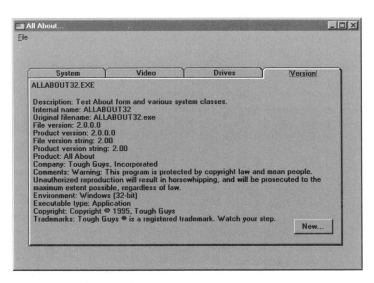

Figure 8-7. *The version resources of the All About program.*

Testing version numbers

You can use the Windows API version functions to display version information of EXEs (as WinWatch and All About do), but more likely you'll want to read the version numbers of DLLs (or controls) used by your program. Then, if the DLL version is incompatible with your program, you can terminate with a polite request to update the DLL rather than with a rude command to boot the system.

For example, imagine you had a DLL written in C++ named VBUTIL32.DLL (similar to the one provided with the first edition of this book). Let's say you wanted to make sure you hadn't accidentally overwritten the Visual Basic Utilities DLL with the Vermont Business University Tools for Industrial Liquidity DLL:

```
Sub ValidateVBUtil()
    Dim verUtil As New CVersion, f As Boolean
    Const sUtil = "C Utility Functions for Visual Basic"
    verUtil = "VBUTIL32.DLL"
    If verUtil.FileVersionString <> "1.00" Or _
        verUtil.Company <> "MS-PRESS" Or _
        verUtil.Description <> sUtil Then
        MsgBox "Invalid DLL"
        End
    End If
End Sub
```

Why not use this technique on VBCore? Because VBCore is a COM component, and components have a more sophisticated and flexible version system. Normally, you use version validation only on DLLs that aren't COM components.

What's in a Name?

How do you name a program? Let me count the ways:

- You can assign a name as the caption of your main form. The main form name in WinWatch is WinWatch, and you can see from its display that its class name is ThunderForm. You can expand it to see all the separate windows for its controls. Its owner is the window described in the next item.

- You can assign a name to the Title property of the App object by assigning a string to the property at run time. You can assign App.Title at design time by filling in the Title field of the Make tab of the Project Properties dialog box. In WinWatch, the title is Windows Watcher. The WinWatch display shows this as a separate window with class ThunderMain. You can't see this window on the screen. Perhaps it's hiding behind the main form. The App.Title name, not the caption of the main form, appears in the Top Windows list box (and in the Windows task list).

- You can enter a Product Name value in the Type field of the Project Properties dialog box. In WinWatch, this name is WindowsWatcher (no space in order to distinguish it from the Title). This name is embedded in the EXE file as a version resource. You can see it when you view VERSION resources for WINWATCH.EXE. This name is also the App.ProductName property.

- You can enter a name in the Project Name field on the General tab of the Project Properties dialog box. For WinWatch, this name is the last unique name I could think of: WinWatcher. The Project Name is used in the Visual Basic title bar and in the Object Browser. It will be used as the OLE server name if you make your project a server.

- And, of course, you have the project filename (WINWATCH.VBP) and the program filename (WINWATCH.EXE).

CVersion class implementation

Once somebody (me, in this case) writes a version class, the rest of us (you, in this case) can simply use it without understanding how it works. The code of CVersion is somewhat complex, but it doesn't introduce any new programming techniques, so I'll just give a "Cliff notes" summary here and encourage you to look up the details in VERSION.CLS.

Version data comes in two parts. The first part is a block of numeric data in a UDT. This comes out the same in any language: version 1.0 in Japanese or Urdu is still version 1.0. The second part consists of language-specific string data. One block of strings—the only one currently recognized by CVersion—is in a translated form meant to be usable from any version of the program.

The Create method starts by calling GetFileVersionInfoSize. You pass this function the name of the executable file, and it returns the size of the version data and a handle to the data. You then pass the size, the handle, the executable name, and a buffer (of the given size) to GetFileVersionInfo, which fills the buffer.

You now have a block of version data in an unreadable format. You must call VerQueryValue to read it. You pass some semirandom strings to VerQueryValue to first get the fixed UDT portion of the data and later get a hexadecimal key (case-sensitive and with leading zeros) that identifies the translated version of the data. You could then call VerLanguageName to get language-specific data, but I don't. The Create method of CVersion saves the key, the UDT for fixed data, and the data block (as a string) in private variables of the class.

Class properties based on fixed data simply return fields of the internal UDT variable. Class properties based on the language-specific string data call VerQueryValue, passing the saved key and data string to it.

Got all that? There will be a quiz. Actually, the Windows API documentation on this subject is not very clear, and programming the class was not easy. It's much easier to follow my completed code.

CHALLENGE CVersion implements only the most common part of version resources, so there's plenty of room to enhance it. For example, you can embed language-specific version information in a file and then use version resource functions to extract different version data for different languages.

Using Other Resources

WinWatch recognizes several other types of resources that you probably won't need to use in Visual Basic.

For example, most programs written in C and other languages have dialog resources. You can load these with the CreateDialog (modeless) or DialogBox (modal) function. You can see the dialog boxes on screen, but you would still need a window procedure to handle all the dialog events. You could probably attach a window procedure using the AddressOf operator, but if you didn't create the dialog resource, you wouldn't know how to write the window procedure. Of course, you could design your own dialog boxes with a resource editor, embed the resource in your Visual Basic program, and write a window procedure to handle the dialog events. But what's the point? Forms are better. If you have a good reason to try this, you're on your own.

The same with accelerators and menus. You probably won't know how to use somebody else's, and you won't need to use your own. Despite the obvious foolishness of loading the menus of another program, it's so easy that I couldn't resist doing it in WinWatch. I'm not going to show you how to install a menu resource with LoadMenu, GetMenu, and SetMenu, but you can see the code in the ShowMenu procedure in WINWATCH.FRM. The effect of seeing the normal WinWatch File menu replaced with the menus of some foreign program is disconcerting but amusing.

WinWatch could probably handle fonts using techniques similar to those shown for icons and bitmaps. There is an OleCreateFontIndirect API function that promises to work a lot like OleCreatePictureIndirect. I didn't try it, partly because I've never encountered a 32-bit executable file that has a font embedded as a resource. Generally, I've found the Visual Basic font mechanism adequate, but I'm sure you could find some use for API functions to deal with fonts.

The situation is similar for metafiles. Nothing prevents you from embedding them as resources, although I've never found a metafile resource in any of the programs I've looked at with WinWatch. If you ever did find such a resource, you could load it with LoadImage and convert it to a picture with my MetafileToPicture function (PICTOOL.BAS).

If you use WinWatch to compare programs written in Visual Basic with those written in C and other languages, you'll notice an important difference. Visual Basic programs have menus, dialogs, and accelerators, but they don't store the data in resources. This is a change. If you used the old 16-bit version of WinWatch to examine Visual Basic version 3 programs, forms appeared to be some type of dialog resource. The current Visual Basic apparently implements menus, dialogs, and accelerators by creating them at run time rather than using resources.

Creating Your Own Resources

It should be obvious from the way sounds are handled that you can put any kind of data into resources. In concept, the steps for creating your own resource types are simple. Let's go through them with the new, previously undocumented TimeTravel resource type, which enables users with appropriate TimeTravel expansion cards and device drivers to experience anything, anyplace, anytime.

1. Define a binary format for your resource. You'll probably want to create an editor that translates user-friendly commands into a tightly compressed binary format. The TimeTravel Editor allows you to select the time, place, and conditions of your appearance in easy-to-use dialog boxes. It then compiles these into a TTV file.

2. Put the data into a resource file. The TimeTravel Editor can automatically insert TTV files in an RC file. The line might look like this:

```
1492      TimeTravel   "c:\\ttv\\columbus.ttv"
```

481

3. Compile the resource script into a RES file, and add the RES file to your Visual Basic project.

4. Write procedures that will process the data. You can write them in Visual Basic provided the data is simple enough. Because LoadResData returns an array of bytes, you just need to write code that processes the bytes, converting them to a UDT or another data type if necessary. The TimeTravel resource, however, requires some low-level, high-speed communication between software and device driver. Therefore, the TimeTravel Development Kit (TDK) comes with an OLE server (TTAPI.DLL). Simply register the type library (TTAPI.TLB) in the References dialog box, and you're ready to load the Destination property and call the TravelThruTime method. Here's an example:

```
Dim someday As New CWhenever
someday.Destination = LoadResData(1492, "TimeTravel")
someday.TravelThruTime
```

While it's easy to use TimeTravel resources once you get your hands on them, I didn't have room to put the software on the companion CD. Furthermore, the hardware required to use time travel data is difficult to find and prohibitively expensive on this planet. For now, you'll have to play with wave and metafile resources.

9

Writing Code for the Ages

Shortly after I started working at Microsoft, many years ago, I found myself at a party listening to an old-timer reminisce about days past when real programmers wrote programs on punch cards. Well, maybe it wasn't that far back, but the stories were fascinating to a programmer wanna-be. The most startling story went something like this. (I never saw the guy again, so if he reads this, I hope he won't hold me to the quotes or the details.)

"It was my first programming job. I was this green kid working for an old-timer who used to toggle his programs in with switches or something. Still, I thought I was hot stuff. I was smart, I worked long hours, and, most amazing, the things I wrote worked. My boss was short-tempered and generally obnoxious, but I figured that's just the way programmers were. So one day I was coding away, far gone in some hack, when suddenly I felt this really hard blow on the side of the head. I turned around, and there was my boss. He'd been watching me code for who knows how long.

"Dammit! Don't ever write the same code twice when you're working for me."

This event had made a strong impression on the narrator, and his story made a strong impression on me. I would never walk into your office and slap you on the side of the head, but as an author I can get away with outrageous metaphors. So take this chapter as the literary equivalent of a slap upside the head.

"Dammit! Don't ever write the same code twice when you're reading my book."

Of course, everyone gives lip service to modular code, but writing it in Visual Basic isn't as easy as you might hope. Have you ever found yourself reusing code with the cut-and-paste-and-modify method rather than writing a single module and including it in various projects? The temptation is hard to resist.

The message-based Windows architecture makes it difficult to write truly modular code. Visual Basic simplifies the architecture with forms and events, but you still need to share a lot of data among different parts of your code. Making all the parts into independent code entities that you can plug into any project isn't always simple. Versions 4 and 5 added a lot of features that make modular code easier to write. This chapter will examine some of the ways you can write code that works for everybody, anytime, everywhere.

Edwina and the XEditor Control

Meet Edwina, a text editor with more features than Notepad or WordPad. Your mission in this chapter is to create Edwina with as few lines of code as possible. After you create this text editor, you might want to go a step further and clone Edwina and then turn the clone into Edwina II (EdII for short), a Multiple Document Interface (MDI) editor with the same features as Edwina. For EdII, the challenge is to change as few lines of Edwina code as possible—in fact, all the changes should relate to MDI, not to editing. The ultimate mission would be to put either an editor or a file viewer with any or all of Edwina's features into any application you want with as much flexibility and as little code as possible.

You might point out that there are already many fine editor controls on the market, and many of them have features far beyond anything we could add in one chapter, even if it is a hardcore chapter. We're not going to attempt redefinition of editing keys, extended editing commands, multiple levels of undo, or many of the other sophisticated features available. But these features are probably overkill if your applications need only simple text editing or viewing features. If the features of Notepad, WordPad, or the Visual Basic editor look adequate, you probably don't need the extra expense and overhead of a third-party editor control. You can write your own in Visual Basic.

> **NOTE** I regret to announce the death of Edwina's older brother, Edward. Some of you might remember Edward from the previous edition of this book. The poor devil was based on a TextBox and wore a fake toolbar and status bar made of (don't laugh) 3D panel controls. He was a tough little guy who preferred camping out in the 16-bit wilderness. Although he sometimes visited Windows 95 and Windows NT, he never felt at home there and died of a broken heart when the last 64K segment rolled off the assembly line.

The XEditor Control

The Visual Basic TextBox control doesn't directly support a lot of the features you need. The RichTextBox control is better, but it's still a text box, not an editor. If you want to find and replace text or load a file using the common dialog, you'll need to write your own code. You can find some sample editing code in the MDINote program that is supplied as an example with Visual Basic. The problem with this sample editing code is that it's designed to illustrate MDI programming, not editing. You could reuse parts of the program by cutting, pasting, and modifying, but you'd soon find yourself doing more modifying than pasting.

What you want is the TextBox control, but with more methods and properties. Wouldn't it be nice, for instance, if the TextBox control had an Undo method? Wouldn't it be nice to simply specify a filename and see the TextBox control instantly fill with the file text? It would also be handy to have a FileOpen method that uses the Open common dialog to load a file into the text box and a FileSave method to save the modified contents to a file.

Let's see now… while you have the menu open, you might as well order a few more features. How about SearchFind, SearchFindNext, and SearchReplace methods? Let's use OptionFont and OptionColor methods to set the font and the color of text, using the appropriate common dialogs. Why not have a FilePrint method? Many editors have a status bar that displays information about file size and current positions, so you'll want Line, Column, and Character. And, of course, you'll want an OverWrite property to control insert and overwrite modes.

Vendors, Users, and Clients

To avoid confusion when discussing who uses your code, let's define some terms. You, the designer and programmer of the Editor control, are the *vendor*. The programmers who use the control are your *clients*. The people who use programs created with the control are *users*. Users are the customers of your clients. Your responsibility to clients is direct; your responsibility to users is indirect.

Forget for the moment that, in many cases, the vendor, the client, and the user will be the same person—you. You'll write better code if you pretend that thousands of clients will buy your control from computer magazines, software stores, and the World Wide Web, and that hundreds of thousands of users will buy programs built with the control. If the users don't like the programs, they won't call you; they'll call your clients. Then the clients will call you.

You have two goals: making it easy for clients to satisfy users and making clients happy. You make it easy for clients to satisfy users by providing the features users want in their editors and viewers. You make clients happy if they can install these editing features easily. For example, clients will be very happy if they can get standard editing features by simply adding one statement to every edit-related menu, key, or button event. They'll be happier still if they can add unusual or customized editing features with a little more work.

If you had all these features, creating an editor would be a matter of creating the menus, toolbars, buttons, and keystrokes necessary for the editor's user interface and then tying each of these to the appropriate methods and properties. That's what the XEditor control presented in this chapter does. It packs into one interface just about all the functionality a TextBox or RichTextBox control could possibly have.

The XEditor control is a handy tool that you could use in your projects either as is or with enhancements. More important, however, I will use it in the following sections to explain and illustrate techniques for writing truly reusable components.

Edwina's Interface

Like many editors, Edwina has a dual interface. Figure 9-1 shows Edwina in raw-meat mode—that is, nothing but editing space and status bars. (Ignore the menu bar and toolbar for now.) This editor might have commands, but only for those who memorize them from a book (not supplied). Furthermore, clicking various locations on the status bars produces various actions, but you'll have to figure this out for yourself.

The only thing wimpy about this editor is the menu bar and toolbar. Those menus and toolbar buttons are your entry to quiche mode, where friendly dialog boxes hold your hand as they guide you through easy versions of the commands and let you customize colors and fonts. Figure 9-2 provides a menu map.

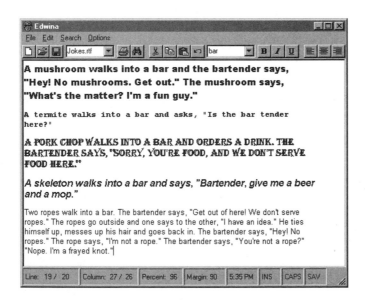

Figure 9-1. *Edwina the editor.*

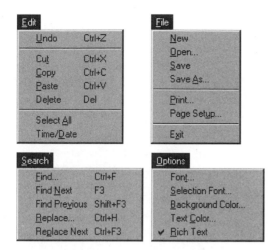

Figure 9-2. *Edwina's menu map.*

The quiche interface needs no introduction; we all know how menus and dialog boxes work. The raw-meat interface is a little trickier. For example, look at the Line, Column, and Percent items on the bottom status bar—items you would expect to find in any editor. But if you click one of these items, it becomes an entry box in which you can enter a new line, column, or percent value. When you enter a value, the editor moves to the new location.

There's more. When you click the time display, it toggles to a date. When you click the INS item, it grays and switches you to overwrite mode. Click the CAP item, and you toggle the Caps Lock status.

The status bar is simply a StatusBar control, and Line, Column, Percent, and Margin items are Panel objects. But unknown to the casual viewer, an invisible text box hides behind the XEditor control on Edwina's form. When you click a modifiable panel, Edwina moves the hidden text box over the correct panel, fills it with the current entry as a default, makes it visible, and gives it the focus. When you finish editing (by pressing Enter or changing the focus), the text box disappears, and the panel displays the result. More important, the new value is assigned to the Line property of the XEditor control, and the cursor—uh, make that the caret—moves to the new location. You can check this code out in EDWINA.FRM.

The XEditor control is designed throughout to work with both the raw-meat and the quiche interfaces (or with any other interface you dream up). A direct interface contains lots of options and alternatives that you can hook up whatever way you choose. And there's a simple interface that hooks to the typical menu items. The simple interface is less flexible for clients but friendlier for users.

The XEditor Control

Controls are supposedly one of the hottest features in Visual Basic version 5, but here we are in Chapter 9 with very little sign of them. Well, the time has come. But first a little history.

The previous edition of this book presented a CEditor class. It had a Create method that took a TextBox or RichTextBox control as an argument (we'll assume RichTextBox control in this discussion). Once it had a reference to an internal RichTextBox control, it hid the members it didn't need to expose, changed many of the members it did expose, and added new members not available in rich text boxes. I called this class a "control" because I was trying to emulate the behavior of a real control, but using it as a control required a certain suspension of disbelief. The user had to set some of the properties of the delegated rich text box at design time, but some rich text box properties were illegal for delegated controls. Once the rich text box was handed off to the CEditor class at run time, the user wasn't supposed to touch the original rich text box again. All interaction was supposed to be through CEditor, but there were exceptions because CEditor couldn't do events.

In short, the whole scheme relied on conventions, and that's a pretty weak basis for any design. Your working assumption should be that if there's any possible way to do something wrong, some user will find that way. Your job is to define your component so that the component users can't do anything wrong. It's not a matter of catching mistakes after they're made—don't even give them a syntax for making mistakes. The new UserControl gives you a flexible way of at least approaching this goal. The XEditor control uses delegation in a manner very similar to the original CEditor, but now you have the tools to make it be a control, not just act like one.

If you look closely at a TextBox control, you will see that it's actually two controls in one: an entry-field control and an editor control, depending on whether you set the MultiLine property. In entry-field mode, a text box doesn't need properties like ScrollBars and Locked. Similarly, in editor mode, it doesn't need properties like PasswordChar and MaxLength. Other TextBox properties are shared (although some are more useful in one mode than in the other). The RichTextBox control is clearly better suited for editing than for data entry, but it inherits a lot of characteristics from TextBox for compatibility.

Coding the XEditor control consists of first creating the control and then passing on all the standard editing features of a text box. After that, you can start adding goodies.

Initialize It

A control created with Visual Basic is normally made up of a UserControl and any constituent controls placed on the UserControl. The Visual Basic documentation spends hundreds of pages explaining what this means and I'm not going to try to duplicate it. Instead, I will describe a common pattern that many controls follow—delegating all of the outer behavior of the control to a single internal control.

The XEditor control is, at heart, a RichTextBox control. XEditor has a UserControl that acts as the surface of the control, but after some initialization, it is mostly ignored. The internal RichTextBox control does all the work. When I created XEditor, the first step was to place a RichTextBox control on the UserControl. I gave this internal control the name *txt*. You'll be seeing a lot more of the *txt* variable. I sized the internal control to about the size of the UserControl and wrote code to make sure the user sees the rich text box as being the control. I also enforced a minimum size on the control. In theory, this code should simply go in UserControl_Resize. Unfortunately, a bug in UserControl resizing prevents the obvious from working. If you simply put your resizing logic in the Resize event, your minimum size logic will be ignored every other time you try to resize by dragging from the top or left. To work around this limitation, put a Timer control on the UserControl and add code like the following:

```
Private Sub hack_Timer()
    hack.Enabled = False
    ' Enforce minimum size
    If Width < xMin Or Height < yMin Then Size xMin, yMin
    ' Adjust internal RichTextBox to be the size of the UserControl
    txt.Move 0, 0, UserControl.ScaleWidth, UserControl.ScaleHeight
End Sub

Private Sub UserControl_Resize()
    ' Bug in resizing code forces us to move resizing to Timer event
    hack.Enabled = True
End Sub
```

I can't imagine why this hack is necessary. I don't think it's the delay that does the trick, since the *hack.Interval* property is set to 1. You should also be wary of recursion in the Resize event. In some cases, resizing in the UserControl_Resize event can cause the event to be called a second time. These aren't the only gotchas you're likely to encounter when coding standard UserControl events such as Initialize, InitProperties, ReadProperties, WriteProperties, Show, Ambient-Changed, and others. There are rules for using these properties (and exceptions to those rules), but you'll have to figure most of them out from the documentation or from trial and error.

But before we abandon UserControl and move on to the delegated *txt* control, I want to identify a new UserControl "event" that isn't in the documentation. This one is called UserControl_Load, and it works kind of like Form_Load except that you have to create and raise it yourself. Often you need to do some initialization task after a control's properties have been initialized, no matter how the control was created. But there's no built-in event that always occurs. Instead, there are two alternate paths where you need to create by convention the UserControl_Load event that Visual Basic doesn't give you.

If you create a new control by clicking on the Toolbox, the control will get a UserControl_Initialize event where you are supposed to initialize properties. At the end of this event, raise the UserControl_Load event like this:

```
Private Sub UserControl_InitProperties()
    ' Initialize properties
    ⋮
    UserControl_Load
End Sub
```

If you load an existing control by loading its form, the control will get a UserControl_ReadProperties event where properties will be initialized from disk (through a PropertyBag object). At the end of this event, raise the UserControl_Load event like this:

```
Private Sub UserControl_ReadProperties(PropBag As PropertyBag)
    ' Read properties from disk
    ⋮
    UserControl_Load
End Sub
```

You have to write UserControl_Load from scratch because Visual Basic won't show it as a standard event in the Procedure drop-down list. For example:

```
Private Sub UserControl_Load()
    ' Initialize standard properties
    ⋮
End Sub
```

The XEditor control uses this event to initialize some internal variables that won't be persisted in the property bag. For example, some properties might be initialized from the registry with GetSetting rather than persisted on the form. I'll talk later about some of the things XEditor sets here, including variables for the dirty bit and overwrite mode. In my first attempt, I put this initialization code in the UserControl_Show event. It always happens at the right time (just after my UserControl_Load), but it can also happen at the wrong time—such as when the Visible property changes from False to True.

In the CEditor class provided with the previous edition, I used conditional compilation to allow clients to choose, at design time, whether they wanted to delegate to a TextBox or to a RichTextBox control. Those who wanted minimal functionality and minimal resource use could choose a TextBox control. This version could have supported a similar feature, but not at design time because there's no way to use conditional compilation to indicate embedding different controls in a Form or UserControl.

To provide the same functionality here, I could have created two separate controls—one delegating TextBox and one delegating RichTextBox. These could have, in turn, delegated most of their shared functionality to a separate standard module. Alternatively, I could have put both a TextBox and a RichTextBox control on the same UserControl and provided a property to determine which one to delegate. Instead, I chose a different strategy. XEditor just delegates the RichTextBox control but provides a TextMode in which the RichTextBox is dumbed down to act more like a TextBox.

In the original CEditor class I had to check that the user hadn't passed an invalid RichTextBox. For example, the MultiLine property had to be True and the ScrollBars property had to be rtfBoth to create a real editor. I checked these in the Create method and threw out clients who dared to violate my rules. XEditor doesn't have these problems. I set the properties exactly the way I wanted them on the internal RichTextBox control at design time. I can make sure that the internal control has the normal settings of an editor or viewer rather than those of a data entry field.

The client view of XEditor is also completely changed from CEditor. Rather than creating a CEditor object and passing it a RichTextBox control at run time, the client simply adds an XEditor control from the Toolbox.

If I had my choice, XEditor would be part of VBCore. Unfortunately, Visual Basic doesn't allow you to put public controls in a public class component or to put public classes in a controls component. This is kind of an artificial distinction, but we have to live with it. As a result, Editor and VBCore are separate but not completely independent. The XEditor control depends on procedures or classes in VBCore, so you must ship VBCore with any projects that use XEditor. VBCore, however, has no dependency on Editor.

Name It Right

I flamed about the hated XEditor1 convention in Chapter 1. Well, the buck stops here. The only way I'm ever going to succeed in my campaign against evil is to stop making it so damn easy. If you want to name an instance of my control XEditor1, you're going to have to type it in yourself. I define the preferred prefix name as *edit*. For the first XEditor control you place on a form, I give you the name *edit*. Normally, you'll need only one XEditor per project, but if you're going to have more than one, you'll probably want to rename it to *editRight*, *editTop*, or something similar. In the unlikely case that you fail to rename your first XEditor and then request a second, its name will come out as *edit1*.

The code that makes this work starts when the control is created in the User-Control_InitProperties event:

```
Extender.Name = UniqueControlName("edit", Extender)
```

The UniqueControlName function creates a unique name for the current instance, based on the given prefix. The code resides in CTLTOOL.BAS, a module for tools that are related to creating controls:

```
Function UniqueControlName(sPrefix As String, Ext As Object) As String
    Dim v As Variant, s As String, c As Long, fFound As Boolean
    On Error GoTo UniqueControlNameFail
    s = sPrefix
    Do
        fFound = False
        ' Search for a control with the proposed prefix name
        For Each v In Ext.Container.Controls
            If v.Name = s Then
                ' Nope, try another name
                fFound = True
                c = c + 1
                s = sPrefix & c
                Exit For
            End If
        Next
    Loop Until fFound = False
    ' Use this name
    UniqueControlName = s
    Exit Function

UniqueControlNameFail:
    ' Failure probably means no Extender.Container.Controls
    UniqueControlName = sPrefix
End Function
```

Visual Basic designers would probably be horrified at the use I've put to the Extender object. This isn't what it was designed for. But I could have done worse.

You can get around my naming convention enforcement by copying an existing XEditor control and pasting it onto the form. Visual Basic will ask if you want a control array, and if you say no, it will give you the hated name XEditor1. I tried to intercept and rename the control in this situation and, after much experimenting, I found a way. But my fix had a side effect. If a user deliberately typed *XEditor1* as the instance name, I would change the name to *edit1* the next time the form was loaded. Even I am not rude enough to leave code like that in my control.

Pass It On

Most of the XEditor properties and methods are simply the methods and properties of the internal *txt* control. It's a simple (but tedious) matter to initialize and write all these properties. Let's look at a simple one:

```
Property Get BackColor() As OLE_COLOR
    BackColor = txt.BackColor
End Property

Property Let BackColor(ByVal clrBackColor As OLE_COLOR)
    txt.BackColor = clrBackColor
    PropertyChanged "BackColor"
End Property
```

This in itself isn't enough to make the BackColor property work properly. You have to save the property value in the UserControl_WriteProperties event so that it will be saved as part of its containing form:

```
PropBag.WriteProperty "BackColor", .BackColor, vbWindowBackground
```

You also have to read the property from its saved state on the form in the UserControl_ReadProperties event:

```
.BackColor = PropBag.ReadProperty("BackColor", vbWindowBackground)
```

That's easy. Now you just have to pass through all the other standard properties and methods of the RichTextBox control. This isn't my idea of fun, but fortunately you have a wizard to handle the details. The sidebar "Wizard or Secretary?" on the following page details my philosophy and practice with regard to wizards.

Wizard or Secretary?

Wizard. The name raises certain expectations. In fact, you'll find that most wizards work more like secretaries. They'll do your repetitive typing for you, but only if you give them very explicit instructions. If you give them bad instructions, they can type a lot of bad code fast and it will take you many hours to undo the damage. Programmers who have used the Wizards in Visual C++ or the Experts in Borland C++ know what I'm talking about. Visual Basic programmers didn't have to worry about wizards in previous versions because the language made it easy to design forms and dialog boxes that would have been created by wizards in less friendly languages. But Visual Basic version 5 has lots of wizards for creating all sorts of things—including controls.

I don't want to say that wizards are a bad idea. I'm in the wizard business myself (see Bug Wizard, Global Wizard, and Collection Wizard) and I'm sympathetic to many of the problems that wizard designers encounter. But I prefer language features to wizards. My wizards, for example, work around problems that the language ought to handle, such as assertions, global classes, and collections. I'd like to see a language statement that could simply reuse an existing control. (I don't care if it works through inheritance or delegation.) You would write only the code to modify or extend the internal control—no wizard needed. I haven't seen a language that can do this. Perhaps I'm asking too much.

In the meantime, there's the ActiveX Control Interface Wizard. All I can say about this wizard is that I don't trust it (or any other wizard, including the ones I write). It can help you create bad controls very quickly and very easily. It can help you create good controls less quickly and less easily.

In my experience, the most important part of using a wizard is to get all your members in a row before you start. If you don't know exactly what properties and methods you're going to delegate, you'll probably find the wizard's suggestions incomplete. The Object Browser is a useful way to get the complete list of members that you might want to delegate from the internal control as well as from UserControl.

The second thing about wizards is that you should always check their work. Very few wizards are polite enough to let you choose the coding conventions. That's because it takes twice as much work to write configurable wizards. It's much easier to force users to accept your preferences. I plead guilty here for my own wizards, but at least you get the source code to mine. It's also not unknown for wizards to generate code that is inefficient or just plain wrong. If you're as picky about your code as I am about mine, you'll want to have the last word. I had the last word on my control code, and in most cases, you can't tell whether I used a wizard or not.

Passing properties through appears to be simple, but there are as many exceptions as there are rules. Here are a few of the special cases:

- Read-only properties need a Property Get procedure, but not a Property Let or Set procedure. Some people prefer to define the Property Let and have it raise its own error, but I'm satisfied with the default error. The hWnd property is an example.

- Properties that are objects require a Property Set rather than Property Let procedure. Font and MouseIcon are examples.

- Design-time read-only properties such as Appearance and ScrollBars can't be passed through. Although your XEditor control has a design time and a run time, the RichTextBox control to which you are delegating never has a design time that can be addressed with code. You can set the ScrollBars property of the internal *txt* control on the UserControl designer, but when you try to change the setting in UserControl_ReadProperties, it's too late—the delegated control is in run time. You're hosed—unless you want to do tricks with the window style bits. The technique is similar to the one discussed in Chapter 6. You can check out the details in the ScrollBars property on EDITOR.CTL.

- Some properties make sense only at run time. You select these in the Procedure Attributes dialog box and check *Don't show in Property Browser*. No code required.

- Extender properties such as Left and Top are provided by the host. You don't know where your control is unless the host (through the Extender object) tells you. Fortunately, you don't have to do anything to get these properties.

- The UserControl provides properties such as Width and Height. You have to adjust the delegated RichTextBox control to be the same size as the UserControl in the UserControl_Resize event.

Delegating properties can get messy, but methods are easy. Most are one-liners:

```
Public Sub Refresh()
    txt.Refresh
End Sub
```

Passing properties through is an annoyance to get past. The interesting part is enhancing and extending properties.

Replace It

Some of the RichTextBox properties just don't make sense for XEditor. Others don't work with a simple pass-through strategy. And still others can be improved. As an example, consider the FileName property.

The RichTextBox control has two ways to load the contents of a file into the control. You can set the FileName property or you can call the LoadFile method. The LoadFile method has a parameter that specifies whether to load the file in text or in RTF format, but design-time properties can't have parameters. This leads to some confusion. You can't control how a file is loaded if you use the FileName property, but you can't load at design time with the LoadFile method.

My solution is that XEditor has both a design-time-only FileName property and a run-time-only LoadFile method, and that the FileName property actually uses the LoadFile method. I maintain my own internal variable for the complete file path and never use the FileName property of the delegated RichTextBox control. In addition, I provide a read-only FilePath property that returns the full path of the file. (FileName returns only the base and extension.) In other words, I provide most of the same functionality, but with a different architecture. Let's take a look.

I start with a private *sFilePath* variable. It contains either an empty string, if the contents of the control did not come from a file, or the full path of the current file. Any code that can load a new file must ensure that this variable is always valid. Here's how the FileName and FilePath properties deal with *sFilePath*:

```
' Read-only, run-time only
Property Get FilePath() As String
    FileName = sFilePath
End Property


' Run time or design time
Property Get FileName() As String
    If sFilePath <> sEmpty Then FileName = GetFileBaseExt(sFilePath)
End Property


' Design-time only (use LoadFile at run time)
Property Let FileName(sFileNameA As String)
    If Ambient.UserMode Then ErrRaise eeSetNotSupportedAtRuntime
    ' Can't pass through design-time errors
    On Error GoTo FailFileName
    If sFileNameA = sEmpty Then
        ' Empty text only if it comes from a file
        If sFilePath <> sEmpty Then Text = sEmpty
        sFilePath = sEmpty
    Else
        sFileNameA = GetFullPath(sFileNameA)
```

```
        LoadFile sFileNameA
        sFilePath = sFileNameA
    End If
    PropertyChanged "FileName"
    Exit Property
FailFileName:
    ' Could empty FileName and Text, but I choose to ignore them
End Property
```

The Property Get procedures simply return the variable in the appropriate format. First, the Property Let uses the Ambient.UserMode property to prevent runtime changes. Then it deals with the three possibilities: an empty string, a valid filename, and an invalid filename. Notice that actual loading of files is deferred to the LoadFile method shown below:

```
' Run-time only (use FileName at design time)
Sub LoadFile(sFileNameA As String, _
             Optional ordTextModeA As ELoadSave = elsDefault)
    If sFileNameA = sEmpty Then Exit Sub
    BugAssert ordTextModeA >= elsDefault And ordTextModeA <= elstext
    If ordTextModeA = elsDefault Then
        ordTextModeA = IIf(TextMode, elstext, elsrtf)
    End If
    If TextMode Then Set Font = fontDefault
    ' Don't reload clean file
    sFileNameA = GetFullPath(sFileNameA)
    If sFileNameA = sFilePath And DirtyBit = False Then Exit Sub
    ' Use RichTextBox method (raise unhandled errors to caller)
    txt.LoadFile sFileNameA, ordTextModeA
    sFilePath = sFileNameA
    DirtyBit = False
End Sub
```

This method uses the LoadFile property of the delegated RichTextBox control. The code uses the TextMode and DirtyBit properties, which I'll discuss shortly. Unlike the FileName property, this function lets unhandled errors pass through to the caller (which might be the FileName property). Methods are always run-time-only, but this one can be called by a design-time-only property. The SaveFile method works much the same as LoadFile. XEditor has other properties that can change the filename, but they all work by calling LoadFile or SaveFile.

XEditor Extends RichTextBox

The RichTextBox control is a fine control, but it isn't an editor. To make it into an editor, you're going to have to throw away the parts that don't fit the editor model and add new parts that give the editor enhanced editing features.

There are several ways to extend an editor that is based on a TextBox or RichTextBox control. One is to massage the text; you can search the text, parse it, or whatever. You can tack on features that make it easier to manipulate RichTextBox properties. You can also disable RichTextBox properties that are inappropriate for an editor. And finally, you can use features of the Windows RichEdit control that aren't supported by the ActiveX RichTextBox control. What's the difference?

The Windows control is the underlying window that handles messages that control the appearance and features of the window. The ActiveX control is the COM wrapper that turns those messages into properties and methods. The RichEdit Windows control is a superset of the Edit Windows control from which the TextBox ActiveX control is created. RichEdit understands the Edit messages and adds its own. You can recognize the Edit and RichEdit message constants in the Win32 help files because they have *EM_* as a prefix.

The ActiveX RichTextBox control passes most of these messages on as properties. For example, EM_LIMITTEXT corresponds to the MaxLength property. But you might also notice some interesting messages that don't correspond to RichTextBox properties. Why not?

ActiveX controls provide methods and properties for the most popular features or, to be more specific, for the favorite features of the Visual Basic designers. The designers seem to like a few more features in each new version. For example, the TextBox and RichTextBox controls now have a Locked property. In older versions of Visual Basic you had to fake it with the EM_SETREADONLY message. But there are plenty of other obscure and not so obscure features that haven't yet made it into the ActiveX control.

The Dirty Bit

When you try to quit a file, any civilized editor will warn you if your file has changed and will ask whether you want to save it. To do this, the editor saves the dirty or clean status in a flag (often called a bit, even when it isn't). The first time the user alters the file, the editor sets the dirty bit. When the user saves the file, the editor clears the dirty bit. If the user wants to change files or quit, the editor checks the dirty bit and, if it is set, posts a warning.

In the TextBox control, the DataChanged property controls the dirty bit. You won't discover this in any Visual Basic documentation. All references to the DataChanged property claim that DataChanged is for bound controls. Nevertheless, it also works fine for unbound text boxes. Unfortunately, this "bug" has been fixed in the RichTextBox control. No matter. The dirty bit of a RichEdit or Edit control is actually controlled by the EM_GETMODIFY and the EM_SETMODIFY messages. It's easy to implement a DirtyBit property by using SendMessage. This design separates testing for unbound data changes from testing for bound changes. Here's the code for DirtyBit:

```
Property Get DirtyBit() As Boolean
    DirtyBit = SendMessage(txt.hWnd, EM_GETMODIFY, ByVal 0&, ByVal 0&)
End Property

Property Let DirtyBit(ByVal fDirtyBitA As Boolean)
    Call SendMessage(txt.hWnd, EM_SETMODIFY, _
                      ByVal -CLng(fDirtyBitA), ByVal 0&)
    StatusEvent
End Property
```

Edwina uses the DirtyBit property to identify when a file needs to be saved before the user quits or changes files. Edwina also displays the current save state in a panel on the status bar. The bar is updated whenever a PositionChange event occurs. That's part of why the DirtyBit Property Let calls the StatusEvent procedure, but I'll get to the details later.

You can also change the status by clicking the status bar. For example, to throw away your latest changes, click the SAV item before you exit; Edwina won't prompt you to resave. The Click event procedure (in *statEdit_PanelClick*) toggles the DirtyBit property and then changes the panel to match the state as shown here:

```
edit.DirtyBit = Not edit.DirtyBit
.Enabled = edit.DirtyBit
```

The dirty bit is managed at several different levels by different players. Edwina (and any other editors you create with XEditor) will maintain the correct status for the DirtyBit property as long as you load and save files through the Load, Open, Save, and Save As commands that I'll discuss later. Of course, nothing prevents you from grabbing the contents out of the Text or TextRTF property and saving it in your own way. If you do this, make sure you manage the DirtyBit property yourself.

When a client editor such as Edwina terminates, opens a new file, or takes some other action that might destroy a dirty file, it has two choices. It can test the DirtyBit property itself and take appropriate action; or it can call the DirtyDialog method to test DirtyBit and, if necessary, query the user about the appropriate action to take. DirtyDialog is so named because it tests the dirty bit and also because it is a quick-and-dirty hack based on the MsgBox function. You might want to call a form-based dialog box in a more sophisticated editor, but DirtyDialog gives you an easy model of how such a form might work:

```
Public Function DirtyDialog() As Boolean
    Dim s As String
    DirtyDialog = True ' Assume success
    ' Done if no dirty file to save
```

(continued)

```
        If Not DirtyBit Then Exit Function
        ' Prompt for action if dirty file
        s = "File not saved: " & FileName & sCrLf & Save now?"
        Select Case MsgBox(s, vbYesNoCancel)
        Case vbYes
            ' Save old file
            FileSave
        Case vbCancel
            ' User wants to terminate file change
            DirtyDialog = False
        Case vbNo
            ' Do nothing if user wants to throw away changes
        End Select
End Function
```

Edwina calls the DirtyDialog method from the mnuFileNew_Click, mnuFile-Open_Click, and Form_QueryUnload event procedures. It doesn't need to call DirtyDialog from mnuFileExit_Click because QueryUnload will catch that case. Here are two examples, a positive test and a negative test:

```
Private Sub mnuFileNew_Click()
    If edit.DirtyDialog Then edit.FileNew
    dropFile.Text = edit.filename
End Sub
```

```
Private Sub Form_QueryUnload(Cancel As Integer, UnloadMode As Integer)
    If Not edit.DirtyDialog Then Cancel = True
End Sub
```

Text and Rich Text Modes

The RichTextBox control is chock full of cool features that often get in your way and cause headaches. Sometimes multiple fonts and formatted text are overkill. Sometimes you just want a souped-up Notepad.

Fortunately, the RichEdit Windows control has EM_GETTEXTMODE and EM-_SETTEXTMODE messages. Unfortunately, these messages are undocumented and appear to have absolutely no effect on any of the syntax variations I could think of. Well, that's how it goes with undocumented features. I'll have to hack out my own version by maintaining an internal *fTextMode* variable and disabling all the rich text features when it is True.

The implementation of the TextMode property is the classic Get/Let pair that simply returns or modifies the *fTextMode* variable.

```
Property Get Textmode() As Boolean
    TextMode = fTextMode
End Property
```

```
Property Let TextMode(ByVal fTextModeA As Boolean)
    ' Change to TextMode dirties the file, but not vice versa
    If Not fTextMode and fTextMode <> fTextModeA Then DirtyBit = True
    fTextMode = fTextModeA
    PropertyChanged "TextMode"
End Property
```

The interesting part is what you do with the TextMode properties in XEditor properties and methods. For example, here's what happens in the SaveFile method:

```
Sub SaveFile(sFileNameA As String, _
            Optional ordTextModeA As ELoadSave = elsDefault)
    If sFileNameA = sEmpty Then Exit Sub
    BugAssert ordTextModeA >= elseDefault And ordTextModeA <= elstext
    If ordTextModeA = elsDefault Then
        ordTextModeA = IIf(TextMode, elsText, elsRTF)
    End If
    ' Use RichTextBox method (raise unhandled errors to caller)
    sFileNameA = GetFullPath(sFileNameA)
    txt.SaveFile sFileNameA, ordTextModeA
    sFilePath = sFileNameA
    DirtyBit = False
End Sub
```

The LoadFile method shown earlier works much the same. In both cases, the work is delegated to the appropriate method (LoadFile or SaveFile) of the internal RichTextBox control. This method takes an argument that specifies whether to save the Text property or the TextRTF property. Most of the code in SaveFile and LoadFile deals with figuring out the appropriate mode to save in.

When I started working with the RichTextBox, I had some preconceptions about how LoadFile and SaveFile should work. This might be obvious to everyone else, but bear with me while I explain a little text mode history.

The text file format

A text file contains ASCII characters and control characters. The traditional text format for text files was to separate each line with a carriage return/line feed sequence (a CR/LF for short). If you download Unix or Macintosh text files, your lines might only be separated by a carriage return—or maybe a line feed. I can never remember, and I wish MS-DOS had followed this better, more efficient system. The CR/LF convention apparently comes from some old teletype standard where a carriage return would return to the start of the line without advancing to the next and a line feed would advance to the next line without returning to the beginning. You needed both to start the next line. In other words, this convention has little relevance to computer text files, and the Rich-TextBox control appears to ignore it. The control seems to display lines exactly the same whether they are separated by a carriage return, a line feed, or both.

The GUI age has brought us another definition of a text file. Rather than hard-coding line breaks with control characters, word processors generally string all the text of a paragraph together, leaving the application to set the margin and determine where to wrap lines. The simplest form of this syntax is to have each paragraph separated by a CR/LF. Notepad, for example, has a WordWrap setting on its Edit menu that toggles whether you want lines to wrap at Notepad's margin or at the end of each line marked by a CR/LF. The RichTexBox control doesn't have a direct way of turning off word wrap, but if you set a large enough right margin, it won't be a problem. I provide a constant that does this for you:

```
edit.RightMargin = NoWordWrap
```

This works by setting the largest possible margin: 65,535. I also provide a Save-WordWrap property that uses the EM_FMTLINES message to tell the RichTextBox property to save what it calls "soft linebreaks" for text that is wrapped at the margin rather than at a CR/LF. A soft linebreak is two carriage returns and a line break. (Call it a CR/CR/LF.) I can't imagine why you'd want such a thing, but RichEdit provides it, although RichTextBox, perhaps wisely, doesn't pass it through.

The rich text file format

A rich text file is a standard format that is supposed to provide a way for word processors with different formats to exchange files. It uses escape characters to specify formatting. For example, an RTF file consisting of an unformatted letter *A* looks like this when displayed as text:

```
{\rtf1\ansi\deff0\deftab720{\fonttbl{\f0\fBunch more font junk...}}
{\colortbl\red0\green0\blue0;}
\deflang1033\pard\plain\f2\fs14\b A
\par }
```

A real formatted file looks the same, except worse. For our purposes, the important thing is that you can't convert an RTF file to a text file by loading it as a text file, although loading text files as RTF files is often just what you want to do when converting text files to formatted documents. The file extension doesn't have anything to do with the format; it's that escape \rtf1 embedded at the start of the file that indicates it's an RTF file. The solution is to load the file as text, switch to rich text mode, modify it, and then save it as rich text. There are many ways this logic could work so that the XEditor control doesn't guess. A client program, such as Edwina, can handle the details with error trapping or other techniques.

Loading an RTF file as a text file works, but it's not necessarily something you want to do. The Text property will get the RTF text, and the TextRTF property will get a strange mishmash of RTF surrounded by RTF. There are other gotchas. For example, once a file has been loaded, there's no easy way to tell whether it's an RTF file or not. The TextRTF property will always have the magic RTF codes regardless of whether it's an RTF file. The only way to tell is before you load. The IsRTF function in UTILITY.BAS opens a file and checks the first five characters. Of course, a randomly generated binary file just might happen to contain the magic characters, but I wouldn't worry about it.

The FileOpen method uses IsRTF to see what kind of file you've really loaded. If you want to translate a file to rich text, you can change the TextMode property before saving it. It's a good idea to use the proper extensions—TXT for text and RTF for rich text—but XEditor leaves that to you.

Turning off rich text

If you set TextMode to True, XEditor goes to a lot of trouble to disable rich text features. All the selection formatting features are turned off with code like this:

```
Property Get SelBold() As Variant
    If TextMode Then
        SelBold = Null
    Else
        SelBold = txt.SelBold
    End If
End Property

Property Let SelBold(ByVal vSelBold As Variant)
    If TextMode Then Exit Property
    txt.SelBold() = vSelBold
End Property
```

But there's more to it than that. What does the TextColor property mean in rich text mode? The RichTextBox control doesn't have a ForeColor or TextColor property for setting the color of the entire text. How would such a property work? Would it wipe out all existing color formatting? RichTextBox finesses the question. It provides a SelColor property for coloring the current selection but leaves it to you to use the select everything option before you use SelColor if you want to change all the color text. The situation is reversed in a TextBox control. It doesn't make sense to color a selection, but there's no problem with changing the text color.

XEditor disables TextColor in rich text mode, but in TextMode it uses the SelColor property of the delegated control to set the color of all the text. To do this, it hides the selection with the SelVisible method, saves the current selection position and length, saves a copy of the DirtyBit, selects all the text, changes the selection color, and then restores the selection and the visibility. Notice that you have to save and restore the DirtyBit because changing the selection color automatically dirties the file by changing the formatting. That makes perfect sense in rich text mode because the color is part of the file, but in text mode color is just a display feature that won't be saved.

Similar logic applies to fonts. The RichTextBox control has both a Font property and a SelFont property, but the Font property changes the font from the beginning of the text only until it reaches a selection with a different color. My choices were to copy this broken behavior, try to fix it with advanced logic for changing text past the first font change, or disable the limited Font feature completely. In this case, I left the incomplete behavior. Changing the Font property works fine when you convert a text file to a rich text file, but it might not work the way you expect at other times. SelFont is disabled in text mode.

If you study the rest of the XEditor source, you'll find a few other surprises related to the TextMode property.

Undo Methods and Properties

The editing area in WordPad is a Windows RichEdit control, and WordPad has an Undo command. The ActiveX RichTextBox control is also based on the RichEdit control, but it doesn't have an Undo method. If WordPad can have one, why can't we?

Well, we can. We just have to roll our own by sending the appropriate messages. Windows maintains an undo buffer for Edit and RichEdit controls and provides three edit messages to control the buffer: EM_UNDO, EM_CANUNDO, and EM_EMPTYUNDOBUFFER. It's easy enough to wrap these up as features of the XEditor control:

```
Sub EditUndo()
    Call SendMessage(txt.hWnd, EM_UNDO, ByVal 0&, ByVal 0&)
End Sub

Sub ClearUndo()
    Call SendMessage(txt.hWnd, EM_EMPTYUNDOBUFFER, ByVal 0&, ByVal 0&)
End Sub

Property Get CanUndo() As Boolean
    CanUndo = SendMessage(txt.hWnd, EM_CANUNDO, ByVal 0&, ByVal 0&)
End Property
```

This is about as simple as SendMessage gets. You pass the handle, the message constant, and zeros for the *wParam* and *lParam* parameters.

Edwina has an Edit menu with an Undo item. Here's the menu event:

```
Private Sub mnuEditUndo_Click()
    edit.EditUndo
End Sub
```

Edwina doesn't use the ClearUndo method, but she does use the CanUndo property to disable the Undo menu item when there's nothing to undo. The main Edit menu event procedure handles the update:

```
Private Sub mnuEdit_Click()
    mnuEditUndo.Enabled = edit.CanUndo
End Sub
```

Usually, you don't attach code to the event procedure for the top menu items, but it's handy for updating either the disabled or checked state of items that might be changed by events outside the menu. This wouldn't work for the Undo toolbar button, but few programs disable toolbar buttons. I could disable it nevertheless in the PositionChange event, which I'll get to soon.

Edwina's undo feature isn't as sophisticated as the undo feature in more powerful editors. It has only one level of undo, and it might not undo some commands the way you think it should. But it's easy to implement and better than nothing.

Notice the naming convention in the menu code. Where appropriate, I create method names from the name of the menu (Edit) and the item (Undo) where you would normally put the method names. Of course, nothing prevents you from tying this method to a button or a keystroke or even from putting it on some other menu with some other name. I copy the Notepad interface here because most developers are familiar with Notepad even if they (like me) prefer something (anything) different.

Status Methods and Properties

Whoever heard of an editor that doesn't display status such as the current line and column? I'm happy to say that the example of such an editor mentioned in the first edition of this book no longer applies, but longtime Visual Basic programmers can probably guess which one I'm talking about.

Edwina displays its line and column status, getting the information from the XEditor control, which, in turn, gets it by sending messages to the internal RichEdit control of the RichTextBox control. RichEdit knows a lot about its current status, but the way to get at the status is far from straightforward.

The XEditor control can supply status information through properties. The Lines, Columns, and Characters properties provide the total number of lines, columns, and characters. Similarly, the Line, Column, and Character properties provide the current line, column, and character. The Percent property supplies the current position as a percentage of the total text length.

The client could check these properties repeatedly to update its display, possibly with a Timer event, or by checking events that might change the position such as KeyUp or MouseDown. The second technique is how I handled it with the old CEditor class. But XEditor can raise events. It knows everything that might cause a position change, and it can give the client one event with all the required information any time something happens. The client doesn't have to worry about what caused the event.

The StatusEvent procedure takes care of getting everything the client might need to know and passing it on to the client. Here's the code:

```
Private Sub StatusEvent()
    Dim iLine As Long, cLine As Long, iCol As Long, i As Long
    Dim cCol As Long, iChar As Long, cChar As Long

    ' Count of lines
    cLine = SendMessage(txt.hWnd, EM_GETLINECOUNT, ByVal 0&, ByVal 0&)
    ' Current line (zero adjusted)
    iLine = 1 + txt.GetLineFromChar(txt.SelStart)
    ' Current character
    iChar = txt.SelStart + 1
    ' Length is position of last line plus length of last line
    cChar = SendMessage(txt.hWnd, EM_LINEINDEX, ByVal cLine - 1, ByVal 0&)
    i = SendMessage(txt.hWnd, EM_LINELENGTH, ByVal cChar - 1, ByVal 0&)
    cChar = cChar + i
    ' Column count is current line length
    cCol = SendMessage(txt.hWnd, EM_LINELENGTH, ByVal iChar - 1, ByVal 0&)
    ' Column is current position minus position of line start
    i = SendMessage(txt.hWnd, EM_LINEINDEX, ByVal iLine - 1, ByVal 0&)
    iCol = iChar - i
    RaiseEvent StatusChange(iLine, cLine, iCol, cCol, iChar, cChar, DirtyBit)
End Sub
```

What Windows has isn't exactly what you need, but it is what you need to get what you need. Most of the information comes from SendMessage calls, but the current line comes from the RichTextBox GetLineFromChar method and the current character position is simply the zero-adjusted SelStart property. Notice that I chose to define Columns as the length of the current line; you could make a case for defining it as the width of the longest line in the text box or as the current screen width of the text box, based on the average character width of the current font.

This code could look cleaner if I had used the existing Line, Lines, Column, Columns, Character, and Characters properties, all of which contain essentially the same code. It would have saved file space in EDITOR.CTL and on this page, but it would have wasted code. That's because several pieces of the information depend on others. You'd end up sending more Windows messages, as you can confirm by studying the properties. Of course, there might be other cases in which the client needs only part of the position information, which is why XEditor also provides each piece as a separate property.

I started out by calling StatusEvent from every event procedure that might cause a position change—MouseDown, KeyUp, and so on. But after some experimentation, I discovered that these events all triggered the SelChange event. That's the only movement event where I needed to raise the StatusChange event. I also called StatusEvent from the Property Let of the DirtyBit property. The DirtyBit property is set in several other places such as LoadFile and UserControl_Load because these events indirectly cause the status to change.

Edwina handles the StatusChange event with the following code:

```
Private Sub edit_StatusChange(LineCur As Long, LineCount As Long, _
                    ColumnCur As Long, ColumnCount As Long, _
                    CharacterCur As Long, _
                    CharacterCount As Long, DirtyBit As Boolean)
With statEdit
    .Panels(epLine).Text = "Line: " & FmtInt(LineCur, 4) & _
                    " / " & FmtInt(LineCount, 4, True)
    .Panels(epCol).Text = "Column: " & FmtInt(ColumnCur, 3) & _
                    " / " & FmtInt(ColumnCount, 3, True)
    Dim iPercent As Integer
    iPercent = (CharacterCur / (CharacterCount + 1)) * 100
    .Panels(epPercent).Text = "Percent: " & FmtInt(iPercent, 3)
    .Panels(epSav).Enabled = DirtyBit
    .Panels(epIns).Enabled = Not edit.OverWrite
End With
With barEdit
    .Buttons(sBold).Value = _
        IIf(edit.SelBold, tbrPressed, tbrUnpressed)
    .Buttons(sItalic).Value = _
        IIf(edit.SelItalic, tbrPressed, tbrUnpressed)
    .Buttons(sUnderline).Value = _
        IIf(edit.SelUnderline, tbrPressed, tbrUnpressed)
End With
End Sub
```

The XEditor control also has LineText, LinePosition, and LineLength methods that return the text, the character position, and the length of either the current line or a selected line. Here's the code for LineLength:

```
Property Get LineLength(Optional iLine As Long = -1) As Long
    If iLine = -1 Then iLine = Line
    LineLength = SendMessage(txt.hWnd, EM_LINELENGTH, _
                        ByVal LinePosition(iLine), ByVal 0&)
End Property
```

Basic must be the only computer language ever invented whose formatting features don't allow you to right-justify integers—that is, to generate a simple list of numbers that looks like this:

```
 345
  62
   9
1053
```

Just try doing that with the Format function or the Print statement. A Basic program manager once told me that the ability to right-justify numbers wasn't worth adding because spaces don't have the same width as digits in proportional fonts. Well, yes, but.... Fortunately, this quirk is more an annoyance than a limitation. The FmtInt function (UTILITY.BAS) allows you to left-justify or right-justify an integer in a field of a given width. The heart of this function consists of the following expression:

```
Right$(Space$(iWidth) & iVal, iWidth)
```

You prepend the maximum number of spaces and trim off the extra. Not difficult, but it shouldn't be necessary.

Notice that the LineLength property can access the Line property without qualification. For example, you could call it with either of these lines:

```
c = LineLength        ' Get length of current line
c = LineLength(5)      ' Get length of line 5
```

Many of the other status properties allow indexing. For example, you can call the Line or Column property with an index that is the current character position in the file.

Common Dialog Extensions

XEditor obviously needs some way to open and save programs. It should also be able to change the printer setup, the font, and the color of the background or text. Luckily, the CommonDialog control provides all this functionality in a neat package. But there are a few minor problems.

First, the CommonDialog control is actually a control; however, you don't need a control. In fact, the control can really get in the way. A control has to reside on a surface such as a form, but I frequently use common dialogs in programs that don't have forms. That's not a problem for XEditor because I could put the CommonDialog control on the UserControl, although that would mean adding overhead and forcing clients to ship an extra control. But my real objection to the CommonDialog control is that its design is...well, it doesn't really have a design. It was created back in the old days when controls were the only way to provide packaged functionality, and a whole bunch of properties were sort of thrown together in an ugly mishmash. Nowadays, components that have no visual interface and no events can be provided in a much more convenient format as public classes.

Fortunately, Visual Basic version 5 comes with a non-control component called the Microsoft Dialog Automation Objects (DLGOBJS.DLL). Forget the control. You can create a dialog object and call its methods and properties without any form. I got pretty excited when I discovered this component in the \Tools-\Unsupprt directory of the Visual Basic CD. It's much easier to use than the CommonDialog control. Unfortunately, when they say unsupported they mean unsupported. I found one serious limitation that I couldn't work around, and a few other minor problems that I didn't want to work around. I hope that, eventually, the dialog objects will become a supported part of Visual Basic and will be integrated into the language library.

In the meantime...control! What control? We don't need no stinkin' CommonDialog control!

I implement common dialogs the old-fashioned way—as a library of procedures. I get rid of the overhead of the control and eliminate the need to ship a separate component file (although the module is also built into VBCore). You end up with a lean and mean layer of Windows and Visual Basic code that uses named and optional arguments to give your code the look and feel (but not the cost) of object-oriented programming.

The Windows/Basic Way of Implementing Common Dialogs

Let's compare several different approaches to common dialogs. I'll start with one of the simpler dialogs, color selection, and show you several different ways to display it.

First, here's the traditional technique using the CommonDialog control. This assumes that the control is embedded somewhere in a Form, UserControl, or PropertyPage:

```
Function OptionColor(Optional ByVal clr As Long = vbBlack) As Long
With dlgColor
    ' No VB constant for CC_SOLIDCOLOR, but it works
    .Flags = cdlCCRGBInit Or CC_SOLIDCOLOR
    ' Make sure it's an RGB color
    .Color = TranslateColor(clr)
    .hWnd = hWnd
    ' Can only recognize cancel with error trapping
    .CancelError = True
```

(continued)

509

```
    On Error Resume Next
    .ShowColor
    ' Return color, whether successful or not
    If Err Then
        OptionColor = clr
    Else
        OptionColor = .Color
    End If
End With
End Function
```

This is a little bit messy. You have to put constants into a Flags property to control the behavior of the dialog, and Visual Basic doesn't supply all the possible constants. Fortunately, the control is a very thin wrapper for Windows API functions and it recognizes any constant you can find in the API documentation. Handling the Cancel button is atrocious, but it used to be even worse. Those of you who used the first version of the CommonDialog control know what I'm talking about, and those of you who didn't use it don't want to know.

The Dialog Automation Objects version is much better:

```
Function OptionColor(Optional ByVal clr As Long = vbBlack) As Long
Dim choose As New ChooseColor
With choose
    ' Make sure it's an RGB color
    .Color = TranslateColor(clr)
    .hWnd = hWnd
    ' No property to specify solid colors.
    ' Return color, whether successful or not.
    If .Show Then
        OptionColor = choose.Color
    Else
        OptionColor = clr
    End If
End With
End Function
```

Properties are used to define the characteristics of the dialog. You set them before. You read them afterward. But the designer didn't give me the one property I wanted—displaying only solid colors, as opposed to displaying both solid and dithered colors. The RichTextBox editor won't accept dithered colors for the text background or foreground, so why display them? Because the designer was trying to make things easy for most users, and if his or her choices don't match yours or mine, we're out of luck.

Finally, here's my API wrapper version:

```
Function OptionColor(Optional ByVal clr As Long = vbBlack) As Long
    ' Make sure it's an RGB color
    clr = TranslateColor(clr)
    ' Choose a solid color
    Call VBChooseColor(Color:=clr, AnyColor:=False, Owner:=hWnd)
    ' Return color, whether successful or not
    OptionColor = clr
End Function
```

Instead of properties, I use named arguments. I'm the designer, so of course I give myself the parameters I need, but perhaps you want different parameters— ones that I didn't think anyone would ever want. In this example, my code is shorter, but that's not always the case, and anyway, I prefer the more structured interface of the dialog objects. I'd drop my version in a minute if the dialog objects did everything I need.

There's one other option for displaying common dialogs—create your own versions. I'll do that later with the Find and Replace dialog boxes. I'll also build a Picture display dialog box that looks sort of like the File Open dialog box later in this chapter.

Using Common Dialogs

XEditor uses all the common dialogs except Find and Replace (for reasons I'll get to later). Let's look at the ones implemented in the COMDLG module and called by XEditor in EDITOR.CLS:

- The FileOpen method calls VBGetOpenFileName, which calls Windows GetOpenFileName.

- The FileSaveAs method calls VBGetSaveFileName, which calls Windows GetSaveFileName.

- The FilePrint method calls VBPrintDlg, which calls Windows PrintDlg.

- The FilePageSetup method calls VBPageSetupDlg, which calls Windows PageSetupDlg.

- The OptionFont method calls VBChooseFont, which calls Windows ChooseFont.

- The OptionColor method calls VBChooseColor, which calls Windows ChooseColor.

If you've seen one common dialog function, you've seen them all, so let's go through the process for the most common and most complicated function—the Open dialog box. The Save As dialog box is almost identical, and the Font and

Color dialog boxes are simple by comparison. The Print and Page Setup dialog boxes are a little different, but I won't get into the details.

It all starts with the mnuFileOpen_Click event:

```
Private Sub mnuFileOpen_Click()
    If edit.DirtyDialog Then edit.FileOpen
    dropFile.Text = edit.filename
    SetTextMode edit.TextMode
End Sub
```

After checking that the current file is saved, call the FileOpen method of the XEditor object. FileOpen in turn calls VBGetOpenFileName:

```
Function FileOpen() As Boolean
    Dim f As Boolean, sFile As String, fReadOnly As Boolean
    f = VBGetOpenFileName( _
            FileName:=sFile, _
            ReadOnly:=fReadOnly, _
            Filter:=FilterString, _
            Owner:=hWnd)
    If f And sFile <> sEmpty Then
        TextMode = Not IsRTF(sFile)
        LoadFile sFile
        If fReadOnly Then Locked = True
        FileOpen = True
    End If
End Function
```

In any case, pass whatever you get to the LoadFile method.

Implementing VBGetOpenFileName

Finally we get to the hard part—implementing a wrapper for GetOpenFileName. The trick is to use the UDT that's expected by the Windows GetOpenFileName function, but to hide it behind named arguments. From the call example, VBGet-OpenFileName might look object-oriented, but it's really a function in a Visual Basic module. The COMDLG module contains all the private types and declarations used by the public functions VBGetOpenFileName, VBGetSaveFileName, VBChooseColor, VBChooseFont, VBPrintDlg, and VBPageSetupDlg.

The OPENFILENAME UDT

In "Variable-Length Strings in UDTs" in Chapter 2, I discussed part of the OPEN-FILENAME structure. Let's take a look at the whole works:

```
Private Type OPENFILENAME
    lStructSize As Long         ' Filled with UDT size
    hwndOwner As Long           ' Tied to Owner
```

```
    hInstance As Long            ' Ignored (used only by templates)
    lpstrFilter As String        ' Tied to Filter
    lpstrCustomFilter As String  ' Ignored (exercise for reader)
    nMaxCustFilter As Long       ' Ignored (exercise for reader)
    nFilterIndex As Long         ' Tied to FilterIndex
    lpstrFile As String          ' Tied to FileName
    nMaxFile As Long             ' Handled internally
    lpstrFileTitle As String     ' Tied to FileTitle
    nMaxFileTitle As Long        ' Handled internally
    lpstrInitialDir As String    ' Tied to InitDir
    lpstrTitle As String         ' Tied to DlgTitle
    Flags As Long                ' Tied to Flags
    nFileOffset As Integer       ' Ignored (exercise for reader)
    nFileExtension As Integer    ' Ignored (exercise for reader)
    lpstrDefExt As String        ' Tied to DefaultExt
    lCustData As Long            ' Ignored (needed for hooks)
    lpfnHook As Long             ' Ignored (good luck with hooks)
    lpTemplateName As Long       ' Ignored (good luck with templates)
End Type
```

That's a big, ugly UDT, but you don't need all the fields. I ignored some parts because they're frills. For example, you don't need to return the positions of the filename and the extension in the resulting full pathname because, if you really need them, you can parse them out yourself or call GetFullPathName. The fields I do handle are adequate to provide the required features 98 percent of the time.

CHALLENGE   In previous versions of Visual Basic, using hooks and templates to customize the standard dialog boxes would have been a challenge for the gods. But the addition of the AddressOf operator brings this challenge into the realm of hardcore mortals. Good luck.

Fields of the UDT are used for both input and output. You put data in before the call; you get other data out afterward. Some fields (*Flags*, for instance) work for both. Our function can receive output information through variables that are passed by reference. Of course, you don't have to pass variables because all except one of the arguments are optional. For example, you could ignore the *Flags* parameter or pass it as a constant. If you ignore or pass a constant, the function won't know the difference and will write the results back to the temporary variable created by Visual Basic. No harm done, but you won't see any results.

Handling optional parameters

The first part of the VBGetOpenFileName function handles optional arguments, giving defaults for any missing values:

```
Function VBGetOpenFileName(FileName As String, _
                           Optional FileTitle As String, _
                           Optional FileMustExist As Boolean = True, _
                           Optional MultiSelect As Boolean = False, _
                           Optional ReadOnly As Boolean = False, _
                           Optional HideReadOnly As Boolean = False, _
                           Optional Filter As String = "All (*.*)| *.*", _
                           Optional FilterIndex As Long = 1, _
                           Optional InitDir As String, _
                           Optional DlgTitle As String, _
                           Optional DefaultExt As String, _
                           Optional Owner As Long = -1, _
                           Optional Flags As Long = 0) As Boolean

    Dim opfile As OPENFILENAME, s As String, afFlags As Long
With opfile
    .lStructSize = Len(opfile)

    ' Add in specific flags and strip out non-VB flags
    .Flags = (-FileMustExist * OFN_FILEMUSTEXIST) Or _
             (-MultiSelect * OFN_ALLOWMULTISELECT) Or _
             (-ReadOnly * OFN_READONLY) Or _
             (-HideReadOnly * OFN_HIDEREADONLY) Or _
             (Flags And &H1FF1F)
    ' Owner can take handle of owning window
    If Owner <> -1 Then .hwndOwner = Owner
    ' InitDir can take initial directory string
    .lpstrInitialDir = InitDir
    ' DefaultExt can take default extension
    .lpstrDefExt = DefaultExt
    ' DlgTitle can take dialog box title
    .lpstrTitle = DlgTitle
    ⋮
```

That's a whole lot of parameters, but the only one that isn't optional is *FileName*, since it's the whole point of the function.

The other parameters specify input and, in a few cases, output. For example, the *HideReadOnly* parameter specifies whether to put the Open As Read-Only check box on the display. The *ReadOnly* parameter sets the initial value of the check box on input. When the function returns, the variable you passed to the *ReadOnly* parameter will indicate whether the user checked the Open As Read-Only check box. Again, you must pass a variable. If you pass a constant, you won't have any place to receive the result.

The *FileMustExit, MultiSelect, ReadOnly,* and *HideReadOnly* parameters represent the most common known flags. There are more than a dozen flags, and more might be added in future versions of Windows. The *Flags* parameter lets you handle any other flags that interest you. In other words, you're not locked into my implementation.

Handling filters, filenames, and flags

VBGetOpenFileName expects filter strings to be separated by a pipe character (|) or a colon. The CommonDialog control only recognizes the pipe character, but I follow the lead of the Dialog Automation Objects component, which permits you to separate the description from the extension with a colon:

```
Rich text files (*.rtf): *.rtf|...
```

The CommonDialog format also works. Neither of these formats satisfies Windows, which expects to find a null character separating each string, and a double null at the end. You must do the conversion and put the modified string in the field. Here's the code:

```
' To make Windows-style filter, replace | and : with nulls
Dim ch As String, i As Integer
For i = 1 To Len(Filter)
    ch = Mid$(Filter, i, 1)
    If ch = "|" Or ch = ":" Then
        s = s & vbNullChar
    Else
        s = s & ch
    End If
Next
' Put double null at end
s = s & vbNullChar & vbNullChar
.lpstrFilter = s
.nFilterIndex = FilterIndex
```

After the new filter string is created, you simply assign it to the pointer field in the UDT variable. See "Variable-Length Strings in UDTs" in Chapter 2 for an explanation of why this works.

The *lpstrFile* and *lpstrFileTitle* fields must point to string buffers that are long enough to hold any potential value. That maximum length is given in the *nMaxFile* and *nMaxFileTitle* fields. You set this length with the constants *cMaxPath* and *cMaxFile* (from the Windows API type library) and pad each string out to this maximum. That way you can ensure that you won't fail because of a small buffer. I'll convert the resulting strings back to a Visual Basic format later:

```
' Pad file and file title buffers to maximum path
s = FileName & String$(cMaxPath - Len(FileName), 0)
.lpstrFile = s
.nMaxFile = cMaxPath
s = FileTitle & String$(cMaxFile - Len(FileTitle), 0)
.lpstrFileTitle = s
.nMaxFileTitle = cMaxFile
' All other fields set to zero
```

Let Windows do the rest

At this point, you've provided all the necessary input data in the UDT variable, which is ready to pass to the Windows GetOpenFileName function. The data that is provided by the dialog box comes back in the Windows format as null-terminated strings. You must do a little translation to get it back to the Visual Basic caller in a suitable format:

```
If GetOpenFileName(opfile) Then
    VBGetOpenFileName = True
    FileName = MUtility.StrZToStr(.lpstrFile)
    FileTitle = MUtility.StrZToStr(.lpstrFileTitle)
    Flags = .Flags
    ' Return the filter index
    FilterIndex = .nFilterIndex
    ' Look up the filter the user selected and return that
    Filter = FilterLookup(.lpstrFilter, FilterIndex)
    If (.Flags And OFN_READONLY) Then ReadOnly = True
Else
    VBGetOpenFileName = False
    FileName = sEmpty
    FileTitle = sEmpty
    Flags = 0
    FilterIndex = -1
    Filter = sEmpty
End If
```

The strings in the UDT variable are actually buffers padded to the maximum length. Windows will write the output string into the variable, but it will not change the padding. You must strip the padding yourself and pass it back to the reference variable that the user passed in to receive it. If the user didn't pass in a variable for an output parameter, Visual Basic creates a temporary variable for it.

The *Filter* and *FilterIndex* parameters were input-only parameters in the first edition of my book. Thanks to Hardcore programmer Silvio Lupo (a reader of the German version of the first edition) for pointing out that you couldn't use my function to see which filter the user selected. Note that the *Filter* parameter will be modified to return the one selected filter, so you'd better make sure you pass a copy of the complete filter string rather than the original.

VBOpenFileName serves as a model for other Visual Basic common dialog functions. Check them out in COMDLG.BAS. The XEditor control provides methods that access the dialog functions; however, these methods don't really take advantage of all their features.

Find and Replace Extensions

If you look in the Windows API documentation, you'll find that the common dialog DLL (COMDLG32.DLL) contains Find and Replace dialog boxes, which are called with the FindText and ReplaceText functions. These dialog boxes look a lot like those in Notepad and Write. But you won't see hide nor hair of these functions in the CommonDialog control or in the Dialog Automation Objects.

Is this a conspiracy to make you write your own dialog forms instead of using the ones Windows provides? As a hardcore programmer, you don't have to take this lying down. What's to stop you from implementing VBFindText and VB-ReplaceText functions that wrap the internal API functions? Well, I wasted three or four days trying to prove that nothing could stop me, and I'm not one to give up easily. But eventually I did stop. Here's why.

The Find and Replace dialog boxes are different from all the other common dialogs in one important way: they're modeless. Once you pop them up on the screen, you can go back to your editor and keep working. The dialog box sticks around until you specifically close it. For a modeless dialog box to communicate with the editor window, the application must handle keyboard messages in its main window loop. In "Sending and Receiving Messages" in Chapter 6, I talked about message loops and why Visual Basic programmers don't usually have to worry about them. But in the case of the Find and Replace dialog boxes, you do want to get into the main message loop and handle certain keyboard events, such as those involving the Tab and Enter keys.

You don't need to hear the details of how I wasted time trying to capture keyboard events in a DLL hook procedure or with a message control. Suffice it to say that I pulled out every trick in this book, and none of them worked. I could display the dialog boxes on the screen. I could read text and settings from them. The mouse worked fine. But I couldn't get the Tab and Enter keys to work.

If you want to try this yourself, you'll probably suffer some of the same frustrations I encountered, and possibly some new ones. Or maybe you'll find the solution. But before you start down that road, consider the alternatives.

If you try 20 different editors and word processors, you're likely to encounter 20 different kinds of Find and Replace dialog boxes. The standard Find and Replace dialog boxes aren't very popular with Windows programmers; everyone seems to have a different idea about how to find strings. Some applications have modal dialog boxes (Visual Basic version 3); others have modeless dialog boxes (Visual Basic versions 4 and 5). There's something to be said for both approaches. You'll also see a lot of variations in button names, available features, and the way certain features work. If you roll your own, you choose the features; if you use the standard dialog boxes, Windows chooses.

Remember that, in this chapter, you're writing a library module for others. Your goal is to make it easy for your clients to offer their users whatever the clients think is most appropriate. But, of course, you must also try to judge the needs of the end users. In designing a library, as in designing an application, you have to make compromises. Ideally, you'd like to offer clients the ability to pass arguments that would specify whatever kind of Find and Replace dialog boxes they want to use. Realistically, if you try to offer every variation ever seen in a text editor, you'll never finish.

A reasonable compromise is to design Find and Replace dialog boxes that you like, but also to provide low-level search functions so that clients can design their own dialog boxes or other user interfaces, but use XEditor properties and methods to do the actual searching.

Designing Find and Replace Dialog Boxes

Because I like the design of Visual Basic's Find and Replace dialog boxes, I used them as the model for XEditor's dialog boxes (although I sometimes wish that the Find dialog box was modal instead of modeless).

The obvious design solution is to create both a Find form and a Replace form, on the premise that these are separate operations. But if you carefully study Figure 9-3 on the facing page, you'll notice a lot of shared features. In fact, the Find dialog box morphs into the Replace dialog box with a simple mouse click. I'd argue that the most efficient way to implement them in Visual Basic is to create one form that can appear in Find or Replace format, depending on how you set the properties.

The trade-off here is code versus data. If you create two dialog boxes, you get two forms plus doubles of all the controls that appear in both. You also duplicate the code that handles common features. If you create one dialog box, you get only one form, one copy of each control, and one copy of all the code that handles the controls—although you need to add morphing code to hide unnecessary controls in the Find dialog box, to move controls around, to change button names, and so on.

As you can see in Figure 9-4, XEditor's Find and Replace dialog boxes differ a little from those in Visual Basic. The framed Search options in the Visual Basic dialog boxes—which allow you to choose the current procedure, module, project, or selected text—don't apply to a general text editor, so you can use that area for messages instead.

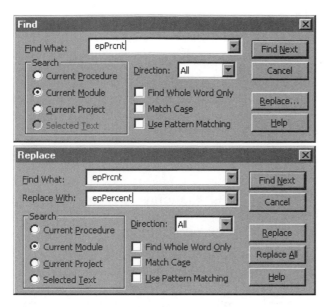

Figure 9-3. *Visual Basic's Find and Replace dialog boxes.*

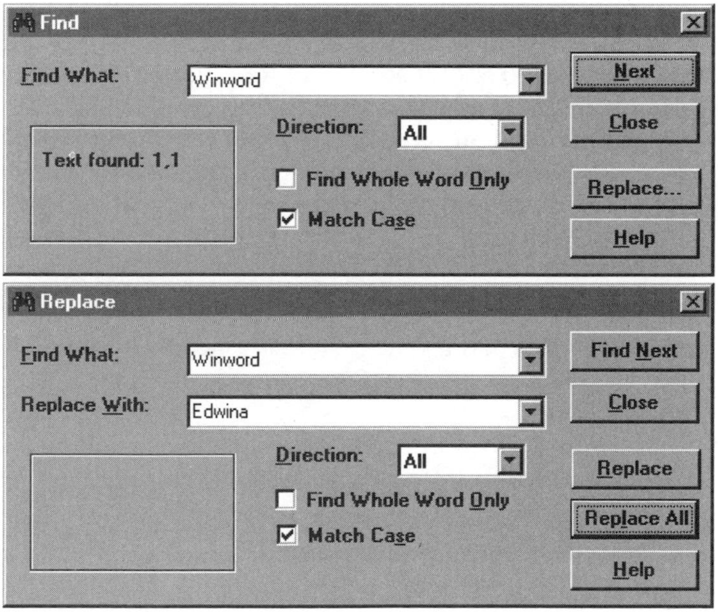

Figure 9-4. *XEditor's Find and Replace dialog boxes.*

The Use Pattern Matching check box is also missing. Although the Visual Basic library has the power to help you provide pattern matching, it doesn't make that power easily available. The Visual Basic Like operator supplies a powerful pattern-matching language for comparing strings, but you need an InStrLike for finding them. I've seen code that does clever hacks with the Like operator for kludge pattern searching, but I don't have an extra chapter to explain something that works only part of the time. Maybe we'll see the equivalent of InStrLike someday. Recognizing whole words is a much simpler problem.

Implementing the FSearch Form

The XEditor control uses a private FSearch form that resides in the control project. Clients of XEditor don't need to use the form. They might prefer a toolbar, menu, or keyboard interface for search operations. Since the FSearch form is never loaded into memory unless you call the form procedures, it can be ignored without much cost.

For maximum flexibility, all the raw power of finding and replacing is built into XEditor. The FSearch form doesn't know a thing about how to find or modify text within an editor; it only knows how to handle the buttons and other controls on the form.

Loading the FSearch form

Let's take a high-speed look at how XEditor loads the FSearch form for finding text. (We'll slow down in Chapter 10 and look more closely at the relationship between XEditor and FSearch.) In the normal sequence (followed by Edwina), the client program provides a Find item on a Search menu. The menu event procedure calls the SearchFind method of the XEditor control. XEditor implements SearchFind by creating a new search form and initializing key properties of the form, particularly an Editor property. The Editor property enables the form to call XEditor methods, such as FindNext, that actually do the work of finding text.

Now let's examine this process a little more slowly. Here is Edwina's menu event procedure:

```
Private Sub mnuSearchFind_Click()
    edit.SearchFind
End Sub
```

And here's how SearchFind loads the FSearch form, which is declared As New at the module level:

```
Sub SearchFind()
    ' Set properties on form
```

```
      Set finddlg.Editor = Me
      finddlg.ReplaceMode = False
      ' Load, but don't show yet
      Load finddlg
End Sub
```

SearchFind sets two key properties (ReplaceMode and Editor) and then loads the form.

Search and Edit in Different Universes

The FSearch form is intimately tied to the XEditor control. It's a private form that resides in the same control project with XEditor and has intimate knowledge of XEditor methods and properties—including ones completely unrelated to searching. This design is one of the many compromises I accepted to publish this book before Visual Basic version 6. In a world with infinite time and infinite resources, I would have made the search form and the editor control completely independent.

The search form should be a public class CSearch in VBCore rather than a private form FSearch in HardControl. Clients of the XEditor control can get the CSearch dialog boxes by default, or they can install their own dialog boxes or no dialog boxes. Other clients can use CSearch directly for their own programs or editor controls.

This kind of independence won't come automatically. To make CSearch and XEditor know about each other without depending on each other, you're going to have to give them interfaces. CSearch will require that its clients implement the ISearchee interface. ISearchee has methods such as FindNext and properties such as SearchOptionDirection. But it doesn't have (or need) all the other editor methods and properties unrelated to searching. CSearch will use these methods and properties in response to user interaction with its buttons and other controls. Any client that wishes to use CSearch must implement ISearchee and pass an ISearchee interface as a parameter of the CSearch Load method.

But there's more. The Load method isn't really a method of CSearch. It's a method of the ISearcher interface. CSearch implements ISearcher. Other search dialog classes could do the same. So any class that implements ISearchee can work with any class that implements ISearcher, and vice versa. This is a much cleaner and safer design. The cooperating classes know only what they need to know about each other.

ReplaceMode determines whether in a particular instance, the form will be used as a Find form or as a Replace form. In fact, if you look at the SearchReplace method, you'll find that it looks the same as SearchFind except that it sets the ReplaceMode property to True. The ReplaceMode property in FSearch is implemented with a private variable controlled by standard Property Get and Let procedures.

The Editor property provides nothing less than the whole XEditor control, including events. Notice that SearchFind sets this property to Me, thereby giving the form access to the control—including features unrelated to searching. This puts a lot of trust in the FSearch form. It works because FSearch is a private form in the same project as XEditor. I wrote both modules and I made them cooperate. But this isn't a particularly robust system. The preceding sidebar "Search and Edit in Different Universes" suggests a better way.

The Editor property works as if it were defined as a simple Public property in FSearch. For this chapter, you should assume that it's implemented with the following line:

```
Public Editor As XEditor
```

Its real implementation is complex, so we're going to defer discussion of it to Chapter 10 where we'll explore some of the mysteries of COM reference counting and circular references.

The FSearch form is a temporary object that disappears into the ozone as soon as a user clicks Close. Notice that the form is loaded but not shown. The Load statement turns over control to the Form_Load procedure of the form, which will show itself when it's good and ready.

WARNING If the HideSelection property of the XEditor control is True, the strings found by the FSearch form won't be highlighted on the screen. This is because the focus will be on the modal FSearch form, not on the client's display. Normally, you should avoid setting HideSelection in client programs that will use the FSearch form. That's why the default XEditor setting of HideSelection is False rather than True as it is in the RichTextBox and TextBox controls. The SearchActive property of XEditor tells you whether a search form is active. You could check it if you wanted to turn HideSelection on when the selection display isn't needed.

Resizing forms and moving controls

The FSearch form first resizes and redraws itself based on the information passed to it in the ReplaceMode property. The drawing code is isolated in a private sub named DrawForm. Form_Load calls this sub and so does the Replace button-click event, which morphs the Find dialog box into the Replace dialog box.

You might expect that moving controls around would be easy and that resizing the form to fit the new control positions would be even easier. But you might be wrong. To make everything come out right, you have to pay close attention to the difference between the Top and Height properties on the one hand and the closely related ScaleTop and ScaleHeight properties on the other. (The FSearch form moves vertically only, so you can ignore similar potential problems with Left and Width.)

Part of the confusion results from the dual purpose of the Scale properties of forms. You set the ScaleTop and ScaleHeight properties to change the form's coordinate system and you read ScaleTop and ScaleHeight to get the size of the form's client area, perhaps when you're doing graphics work or when you're resizing. There's not much relationship between reading and setting these properties, and I'd argue that Visual Basic should have provided separate properties for each purpose. In any case, I find it helpful to think of the Scale properties as read-only when moving and resizing. If you start modifying the coordinate system by changing the ScaleTop and ScaleLeft settings, you will have made the coordinate system for Height and Width completely different from the system for ScaleHeight and ScaleWidth, and all bets are off for moving and resizing.

When you move controls around on the form, their positions are in the client area, which is determined by the ScaleTop and ScaleHeight properties. When you resize the form, you are working with the entire form, whose area is determined by the Top and Height properties. This makes for messy calculations. To resize, for example, you calculate the desired height of the client area and then add the height of the title bar and any form border, which can be calculated as Height minus ScaleHeight. Figure 9-5 on the following page illustrates this.

I avoid complex calculations of control positions by saving the original positions of the controls (set at design time) and then moving controls into relative positions. This approach assumes that all controls have the same height, which they do on the FSearch form. You might not have this luxury on your own forms. Here's the code that saves the original control and button positions:

```
' Get initial button and control positions for later placement
If fNotFirst = False Then
    fNotFirst = True
    yControl2 = dropWith.Top
    yControl3 = cboDirection.Top
    yControl4 = chkWord.Top
    yControl5 = chkCase.Top
    yButton5 = cmdHelp.Top
End If
```

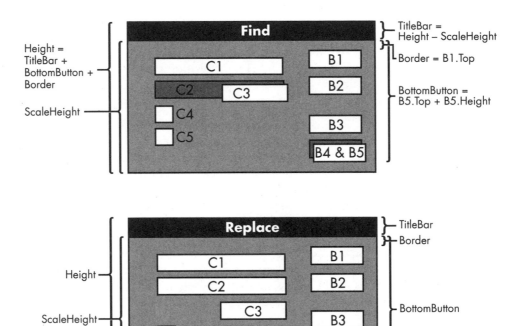

Figure 9-5. *Calculations for redrawing the FSearch form.*

Once you have the positions, you can place the controls properly. Here's the Find portion of the code; you can see the Replace section in SEARCH.FRM:

```
' Modify buttons and controls for current mode
If fReplaceMode = False Then
    cmdFindNext.Caption = "&Next"
    cmdFindNext.Default = True
    cmdCancel.Caption = "&Close"
    cmdReplace.Caption = "&Replace..."
    Caption = "Find"
    cmdAll.Visible = False
    lblWith.Visible = False
    dropWith.Visible = False
    cmdHelp.Top = cmdAll.Top
    frmMessage.Top = yControl2
    cboDirection.Top = yControl2
    lblDirection.Top = yControl2
    chkWord.Top = yControl3
    chkCase.Top = yControl4
Else ' Replace
```

When the controls are in the correct position, you must calculate the new form height, as shown here:

```
Dim dyTitleBar As Double, dyBtnLow As Double, dyBorder As Double
' Calculate height of title bar
dyTitleBar = Height - ScaleHeight
' Add height of lowest element (help button moves up and down)
dyBtnLow = cmdHelp.Top + cmdHelp.Height
' Add border around closest element (top button)
dyBorder = cmdFindNext.Top
' Set height
Height = dyTitleBar + dyBtnLow + dyBorder
```

Initializing controls on the FSearch form

The FSearch form must initialize all the properties of its controls based on the information passed in the Editor property. It does this in the Form_Load procedure (SEARCH.FRM). The information must be reloaded every time the form is loaded because, like all polite forms, this one goes away when not in use. It is possible to hide a form instead of unloading it, and this might seem like an attractive way to retain form data. But a form retained in memory when not in use steals memory from other programs. The form data might not be very expensive, but the form representation is.

For that reason, the settings of all the FSearch controls are stored in the form's copy of the XEditor object and accessed through properties. You need to load all these properties into the form at load time and then update them in the XEditor object whenever a user changes them in the FSearch form controls. Incidentally, this makes it possible for any client program to control the same settings from an interface that doesn't use an FSearch form. You'll see an example later. Here's the first part of the code that initializes the FSearch controls:

```
With Editor
    BugLocalMessage "FSearch Load"
    ' Initialize all control values from editor
    DrawForm
    .SearchActive = True
    chkWord.Value = -.SearchOptionWord
    chkCase.Value = -.SearchOptionCase
    cboDirection.ListIndex = .SearchOptionDirection
```

Consider the case-sensitivity setting. SearchOptionCase is a Boolean property of the XEditor control that stores the setting. The chkCase control is a check box that has the same setting. This code initializes the check box to the values of the XEditor object. Notice the negation sign that changes the Boolean property setting (0 or −1) to the format expected by a CheckBox control (0 or 1). Of course, when the user changes the setting on the form, the XEditor setting must also change. Here's the event procedure that does it:

```
Private Sub chkCase_Click()
    Editor.SearchOptionCase = Not Editor.SearchOptionCase
End Sub
```

> **WARNING** There's a small hole in the mechanism that keeps XEditor properties in sync with form controls. If a user changes a property from a client program while a modeless form is active, the search form property will be out of sync with the editor property. You could solve the problem with a timer on the form to update the controls periodically, just in case. But this seems unlikely (and is, in fact, impossible in Edwina).

It's easy to load and keep in sync the settings for case, whole word, and direction, but managing the Find and Replace string lists is more difficult. The drop-down lists of the most recently used search strings look like combo boxes, but they're actually a little more complicated. If you wanted to use combo boxes to create these lists, you'd need to add additional code to manage the lists. Since this additional code is always boilerplate, why not abstract it? In fact, what we need is not a function that works on combo boxes, but a new control that does exactly what we need for search lists—no more, no less.

The XDropStack Control

The primary purpose of the XEditor control is to expand the RichTextBox control. The primary purpose of the XDropStack control is to limit the ComboBox control. It's a different emphasis, but there are similarities. In fact, almost any control that delegates to a constituent control will do some extending and some limiting.

XDropStack extends ComboBox by keeping items in a specific order just as XEditor extends RichTextBox by adding lots of new editing features. XDropStack limits ComboBox by setting properties such as Style, Locked, and IntegralHeight to desired settings and disabling them in the control interface. XEditor does the same thing with the MultiLine and MaxLength properties of RichTextBox. The controls supplied with Visual Basic are general purpose controls. One of the main reasons to delegate to them in your own controls is to focus on and simplify one specific use of the general control.

The XDropStack control focuses on a feature that you've probably seen in other applications. Microsoft Internet Explorer, for example, has a drop-down list of the most recently requested URLs. Visual Basic's Find dialog box has a drop-down list of the most recently used search strings. That's the functionality we'll be duplicating in the FSearch form and in Edwina's toolbar.

An XDropStack has these features:

- The combo box contains a stack of all the search strings in the order they were added. You can specify a maximum number with the MaxItem property so that the oldest strings will be aged off the list. The default value of 0 means no limit.

- If the user types in a string in the text input field of the combo box, the resulting string will be added to the top of the list. If the string already exists later in the list, the second instance will be deleted. There are never duplicate entries in a drop stack.

- If the user clicks an entry in the drop-down list, it moves to the top of the stack.

- The client can enter a string at the top of the stack programmatically by assigning a string to the Text property. There's no way to add items to the middle of the stack.

Any combo box features that don't match this specification are eliminated. If you think about how these features compare to a stack as a data structure, you can see that the name drop stack, while evocative, isn't quite accurate. Adding a new item is like pushing a string on a stack, but there's no comparable pop operation. The way items age off the bottom is more like a queue. And the operation of moving a clicked item to the top isn't like a stack or a queue. If you have a better name for this control, let me know.

Using a Drop Stack

Edwina uses two drop stacks—one for the current file and another for the find text. XEditor's FSearch form also uses two drop stacks—one for the find text and another for the replace text. To make matters even more interesting, the find stack on Edwina's toolbar needs to be synchronized with the find stack on the FSearch form. And both find stacks are intimately tied to the lower-level FindWhat and ReplaceWith properties of the XEditor control. We're not going to cover every detail, but we'll hit the high points.

Let's start on the FSearch form with the dropWhat control that specifies what to find. By the time the XEditor control gets a command to load the FSearch form, it might already have a list of search strings. In Edwina, those search strings could have been entered with the drop stack on the toolbar. Your client program might create the drop stack in some other way. In any case, the FSearch form has to initialize the list with the following code (inside a *With Editor* block) in Form_Load:

```
Dim i As Long
dropWhat.MaxCount = .FindWhatMax
For i = .FindWhatCount To 1 Step -1
    dropWhat.Text = .FindWhat(i)
Next
```

There are two sides to this operation. On the right side are the FindWhatMax, FindWhatCount, and FindWhat properties of the XEditor control. They manage the real search list that will be used by the FindNext method. The MaxCount and Text properties of the XDropStack control manage the display list.

I'll get back to the related XEditor properties shortly, but first let's look at the only XDropStack event that really matters:

```
Private Sub dropWhat_Completed(Text As String)
    If fInCompleted Then Exit Sub
    fInCompleted = True
    lblMessage.Caption = sEmpty
    Editor.FindWhat = Text
    fInCompleted = False
End Sub
```

In a combo box, several events can create a new entry. First, there's clicking an item in the drop-down list. Second, there's typing in an entry in the text field. And third, there's losing focus. When you handle a combo box, you usually need to handle all of these events separately to recognize new entries. Well, the XDropStack takes care of all three, combining them into a Completed event that signals a new entry without telling you where it came from. You can use the result as you see fit. Here, the FSearch form just assigns the result back to the XEditor control and clears the status message.

The only other place the FSearch form uses the dropWhat control is in the Click event procedure of the Find Next button:

```
Private Sub cmdFindNext_Click()
With Editor
    Dim i As Integer
    ' Must be something to find
    If dropWhat.Text = sEmpty Then
        dropWhat.SetFocus
        Exit Sub
    End If
    ' When Replace user selects Next once, make it default
    cmdFindNext.Default = True
    ' Find next item
    i = .FindNext(dropWhat)
    ' Deal with failed search
    If i = 0 Then
        lblMessage.Caption = "Text not found"
```

```
            .SelLength = 0
        Else
            lblMessage.Caption = "Text found: " & .Line & "," & .Column
        End If
        dropWhat.SetFocus
    End With
End Sub
```

This code doesn't even need to read the Text property because the text was already assigned in the Completed event. The only thing it needs the dropWhat control for is to manage the focus.

XDropStack Calling XEditor

Now let's take a closer look at the XEditor search properties and methods used by the XDropStack control. The FindWhat property and its cousin ReplaceWith are the keys.

The FindWhat property represents the top of the stack (or front of the list) and is normally used without an index. You read from it to find the current find string:

```
sFind = edit.FindWhat
```

You write to it to add an item to the list:

```
edit.FindWhat = sFind
```

But it is also possible to index the FindWhat property to read all the items out of the list. Let's look at the FindWhat property and its relatives to see how this works:

```
Property Get FindWhat(Optional iIndex As Long = 1) As String
With nFindWhat
    If .Count = 0 Or iIndex > .Count Then Exit Property
    FindWhat = .Item(iIndex)
End With
End Property

Property Let FindWhat(Optional iIndex As Long = 1, sWhatA As String)
With nFindWhat
    ' Don't use optional parameter on Let
    BugAssert iIndex = 1
    Dim v As Variant, i As Long
    For i = 1 To .Count
        ' If item is in list, move to start of list
        If .Item(i) = sWhatA Then
            .Add sWhatA, , 1
```

(continued)

```
                .Remove i + 1
                NotifySearchChange eseFindWhat
                Exit Property
            End If
        Next
        ' If item isn't in list, add it
        If .Count Then
            .Add sWhatA, , 1
        Else
            .Add sWhatA
        End If
        NotifySearchChange eseFindWhat
    End With
End Property

Property Get FindWhatCount() As Long
    FindWhatCount = nFindWhat.Count
End Property

Property Get FindWhatMax() As Long
    FindWhatMax = cFindWhatMax
End Property

Property Let FindWhatMax(cFindWhatMaxA As Long)
    cFindWhatMax = cFindWhatMaxA
    Dim v As Variant, i As Integer
    For i = nFindWhat.Count To cFindWhatMax + 1 Step -1
        ' If item is in list beyond maximum, remove it
        nFindWhat.Remove i
    Next
    NotifySearchChange eseFindWhat
End Property
```

The most important point about the FindWhat property is that it hides an internal Collection of strings. The default argument makes FindWhat look like a simple string property, and some simple clients might prefer to use the current string as if there were no others. But clients (such as the FSearch form) who wish to initialize a list can do so. What they can't do is modify any item other than the top item because that would contradict the definition of a drop stack. The definitions of Property Get, Set, and Let procedures with the same name must all match—if one has an optional parameter, all must have the same optional parameter. You can't prevent clients from writing code that uses the index, but you can assert that what they are doing is illegal, and if they do it anyway, ignore their foolish request.

The Property Let is what really makes the list work. It adds each new string to the list and ensures that the list isn't too long and that the list doesn't have duplicates. Finally, it calls NotifySearchChange, which raises a SearchChange event so that if the FSearch form modifies the search list through its drop stack, any other client using the list can recognize the change and update its list. The remaining search option properties also call NotifySearchChange in case a client represents them in some other way. Edwina monitors only FindWhat property changes, but your clients might want to monitor other options such as case sensitivity or direction. The FSearch form also monitors the SearchChange event so that any changes from the client made while the modal search form is active will be recognized as they happen.

The XDropStack implementation looks a lot like the implementation of the FindWhat list. Of course, combo boxes work a little differently than collections, so there are some differences in design. Figure 9-6 shows a picture of how the data is organized in both formats. You can check out the code details in DROPSTACK.CTL.

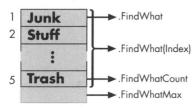

XEditor's FindWhat list

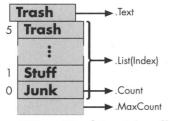

XDropStack's string list

Figure 9-6. *A find list in XEditor and XDropStack.*

Your next assignment is to save the Find and Replace lists with the SaveSetting function when Edwina terminates and to restore them with GetSetting at startup. You might notice that the XEditor control doesn't allow you to enter items in the FindWhat list at design time. It would certainly be possible to do this in much the same way that you can enter list or combo box items in the List property at design time, but this isn't the way search lists are normally maintained. My copy of Edwina has a different search list than your copy. While it's saving the search list, Edwina should probably save the user's favorite font and colors. And, of course, any respectable editor should provide a list of the most recently edited files and reopen the last one with the cursor position restored.

Finding and replacing text

Once you have set up the form in the proper format, managed all the controls, and coordinated communications with XEditor, only one minor detail is left—finding and replacing the text. You must provide both general functions that you can call from any interface and a specific form implementation to find and replace in response to clicking buttons on the FSearch form.

The task of finding and replacing text is especially susceptible to bugs because it is so boring. Handling all the options and variations can deaden the mind and give you an unjustified sense of confidence. Most of us write this kind of code every day, but we don't want to pay for pages and pages of it in a programming book, so I'll leave you to explore the details. But I will offer you a small map for your self-guided tour.

Your first tour stop should be FindNext, the workhorse of XEditor. Even the ReplaceNext method leans heavily on FindNext. Most of the work in FindNext consists of handling the case and direction options.

Next, look at ReplaceNext. Again, most of the code deals with finding the next match, handling options, and ensuring that the matching text is selected. Once that's done, replacing is as simple as assigning the SearchWith text to the SelText property.

Also, you will probably want to stop at some of the places in EDWINA.FRM where user interface code calls FindNext and ReplaceNext. For example, the mnuSearchFindNext_Click event calls edit.SearchFindNext. If the FindWhat property has text, SearchFindNext calls FindNext. Otherwise, SearchFindNext calls SearchFind to get something to search for. You can also see FindNext called from the dropWhat_Completed event of the toolbar XDropStack control.

Finally, look at the way FindNext and ReplaceNext are called from the cmdFindNext_Click and cmdReplace_Click events of the FSearch form. The code is more complex than you might expect, but most of it deals with coordinating buttons and other controls, not with the actual searching. Unlike the Visual Basic Find and Replace dialog boxes, the FSearch form doesn't signal when you wrap back to the beginning of the file; it just keeps wrapping forever. That's the way I like it, but you could easily add code to signal a complete wrap.

Of course, at some point, you have to actually search. FindNext passes this task off to FindString, a function in UTILITY.BAS that knows about searching backwards and forwards, for text or whole words, with or without case sensitivity. But FindString still isn't doing the actual searching. It passes that task off to InStr for forward searches, and to InStrR for backward searches. Visual Basic doesn't provide a reverse search function, so I had to write my own InStrR. Check it out in UTILITY.BAS.

NOTE   I didn't expect to have to use InStr and InStrR to find text. After all, the RichTextBox control has a Find method that duplicates most of the functionality of the XEditor FindNext method. It even has a flag to search for whole words. The only problem is that the Find method won't search backward. You might expect that if you passed a starting position greater than the ending position, Find would search backward. But a backward search always fails. My first thought was that this was a brain-dead implementation by RichTextBox. Not so. The Find method is apparently implemented using the EM_FINDTEXT or EM_FINDTEXTEX message of the RichEdit Windows control. I tried both of these with SendMessage, but got the same result. The RichEdit control got some new features and fixes since the first edition of this book, but backward searching wasn't among them.

The Keyboard Object

Visual Basic used to come with a handy Key State control for displaying or changing the state of control keys such as Caps Lock, Num Lock, and Insert. For compatibility, KEYSTA32.OCX is still shipped in the \Tools\Controls directory of the Visual Basic CD. My advice is to leave it there and to delete any stray copies you might have on your disk. Why pay a heavy cost in disk space and Windows resources when you can roll your own in Visual Basic for almost nothing? Besides, the fonts and colors in the predefined buttons are a little garish for my taste.

Edwina achieves a more subtle look (similar to that of the status bar in Word for Windows) by displaying the key state in gray or black in status bar panels. You could use an invisible Key State control to achieve this effect, but the code required to do the same thing in Windows is so simple that the control isn't worth the trouble. Instead, I'll wrap up everything in the CKeyboard class, and then create a single Keyboard object that represents the one and only system keyboard.

NOTE   When I say KEYSTA32.OCX has a heavy cost, I'm not just talking about its 116 KB size. The real problem is that it requires MFC42.DLL (988 KB) and MSVCRT40.DLL (319 KB), which the intrinsic Visual Basic controls no longer require. You don't know if your customers already have those DLLs on their disk, so you have to ship them with any application that uses Key State. The same limitation applies to the other controls that are provided, but not installed, by Visual Basic—Animated Button, Gauge, Graph, Grid, Outline, Spin, and Three D. One of the important behind-the-scenes achievements of Visual Basic version 5 was to eliminate the MFC dependency from the language library and the primary controls. A few controls didn't make the grade for conversion because they duplicated other controls or had functionality that could be achieved without controls. If at all possible, you should change to one of the new controls. This is going to bite a few users the way it bit me. The original Win-Watch displayed the window hierarchy using the Outline control. It worked fine, and I didn't want to do the extra work to change to TreeView. But I also didn't want to ship 1.4 megabytes of MFC DLLs with my book. So I changed. If you have MFC DLLs on your disk, don't blame me.

Using the Keyboard Object

From a user's perspective, the Keyboard object represents the entire keyboard. Just as the System object is the only instance of the CSystem class, the Keyboard object is the only instance of the CKeyboard class. PublicNotCreatable instancing ensures that you can't create a false model of your computer with an array of 20 keyboards.

The CKeyboard class, shown in Figure 9-7, has properties that allow you to read or modify the state of any key. Of course, most users are interested only in the state of the toggle keys Caps Lock, Insert, Num Lock, and Scroll Lock. Therefore, CKeyboard provides properties that offer easy access to these keys: CapsState, InsState, NumState, and ScrollState.

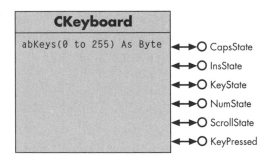

Key

←→O Read-write property

Figure 9-7. *The CKeyboard class.*

Let's look at how Edwina handles the Caps Lock key with the CapsState property. There are two parts of this problem: the Caps display and the actual Caps state. The status bar handles the display automatically. You just assign a status panel of type Caps by assigning *sbrCaps* to the Style property. The panel will automatically display the text *CAPS* in black (if the CAPS state is on), or in disabled gray (if the CAPS state is off). Unfortunately, it works only one way. You can't change the CAPS state by changing the Enabled property of the panel as you could with the Key State control. But you can turn off the CAPS state with the Keyboard object. Here's how it's done in the Select Case block that handles the status bar panels:

```
keyboard.CapsState = Not keyboard.CapsState
```

You don't need to do anything to make the panel display update to show the correct state. I imagine there must be a timer in the StatusBar control that periodically checks the current state.

You could add ScrollLock, NumLock, and Insert panels that work the same way. Unfortunately, such an Insert panel would show the global insert state correctly, but it wouldn't show Edwina's true insert state.

Controlling the RichTextBox Insert State

Every RichTextBox control has its own insert state that is independent of the global insert state as well as the insert state of all other RichTextBox controls. That would be fine if you had some way to read and change the state. But you don't. The RichTextBox control has no property to check the state, and the underlying RichEdit control has no message to check the state.

This might seem like pretty dumb behavior, but it's consistently dumb. The control always starts with insert mode on and then toggles every time the user presses the Insert key. Since we control creation of XEditor's internal RichTextBox control, we can read the initial state (always insert on) and keep track of it. We can change it whenever we want by sending a fake insert keystroke.

The OverWrite property controls the insert state, and it, in turn, is controlled by the *fOverWrite* member variable. When the control is created, the OverWrite value set by the user at design time will be read into *fOverwrite* by UserControl-_ReadProperties. There are two possibilities, depending on whether the *fOverWrite* variable is False or True. If the *fOverWrite* variable is False (meaning insert mode is on), the RichEditBox insert mode is always on when the control is created, so the variable matches the real insert state. But if the OverWrite mode is True, the real state does not match the flag and must be changed.

The change happens in the UserControl_Load event, which occurs just once after all the properties have been read from the form.

```
If fOverWrite Then
    ' Make overwrite state match fOverWrite variable
    SendMessage txt.hWnd, WM_KEYDOWN, ByVal VK_INSERT, ByVal &H510001
    SendMessage txt.hWnd, WM_KEYUP, ByVal VK_INSERT, ByVal &HC0510001
End If
```

The WM_KEYDOWN and WM_KEYUP messages send an insert key to the internal control, changing its state. After you get the insert state in sync, you have to keep it that way. There are two ways that the state can change. One is if someone changes the OverWrite property. Here's the code that makes that happen:

```
Property Get OverWrite() As Boolean
    OverWrite = fOverWrite
End Property

Property Let OverWrite(ByVal fOverWriteA As Boolean)
    ' Only change if value changed
    If fOverWriteA <> fOverWrite Then
        fOverWrite = fOverWriteA
        ' Change the keystate to match
        SendMessage txt.hWnd, WM_KEYDOWN, ByVal VK_INSERT, ByVal &H510001
        SendMessage txt.hWnd, WM_KEYUP, ByVal VK_INSERT, ByVal &HC0510001
        StatusEvent
        PropertyChanged "OverWrite"
    End If
End Property
```

Again you have to change the key state the hard way. Notice that you call StatusEvent to generate a StatusChanged event so that clients (such as Edwina) can update any insert state display.

The only other way the insert state can change is if a user presses the insert key, but you can monitor key presses in the KeyUp event of the XEditor control:

```
Sub txt_KeyUp(KeyCode As Integer, Shift As Integer)
    If KeyCode = vbKeyInsert Then
        ' Insert state changed, so change the variable to match
        fOverWrite = Not fOverWrite
        StatusEvent
    End If
    RaiseEvent KeyUp(KeyCode, Shift)
End Sub
```

The OverWrite property sent a keystroke to change the internal state. The KeyUp event changes the variable to match the state. Think for a minute about what would happen if sending an insert key message in the OverWrite property caused the KeyUp event to fire. This code wouldn't work because the *fOverWrite* variable would be toggled one too many times. Fortunately, faking the key with SendMessage doesn't fire the KeyUp event.

Handling the insert state is messy business, but fortunately XEditor handles the details so that Edwina and other clients can simply read or write the OverWrite property. Instead of using a real Insert panel in the status bar, Edwina uses a normal text panel with the letters *INS* on it. Edwina can update the insert display in the StatusChange event and toggle the OverWrite property when the user clicks on the insert panel.

CHALLENGE The KeyUp event in XEditor is the perfect place to add new command keys or to change the editing behavior of the class in other ways. In your own enhanced version of XEditor you might want to add macro handling or key reassignment.

The CKeyboard Class Implementation

CKeyboard is a simple wrapper for the Windows functions GetKeyboardState and SetKeyboardState. These two functions work on an array of 256 bytes that represent the 256 keys on the keyboard. What? Your keyboard doesn't have 256 keys? Well, if it did, you could put them in this array. Windows is just leaving room for expansion.

The Byte type in Visual Basic makes key handling easy. The CKeyboard property procedures share the following private array:

```
Private abKeys(0 To 255) As Byte
```

To read the state of a key, you get all the key states and then read the one you want, using the virtual key code as an index into the key array:

```
Property Get CapsState() As Boolean
    ' Get toggled and pressed state of all keys
    GetKeyboardState abKeys(0)
    ' Check low bit for state
    CapsState = abKeys(VK_CAPITAL) And 1
End Property
```

The low bit of each toggle key indicates whether the toggle is on or off. Notice how we pass the array to GetKeyboardState by passing the first element. "Arrays" in Chapter 2 explains how this works.

Virtual key codes in the Visual Basic format (such as vbKeyInsert) are in the VBRUN type library under KeyCodeConstants. You can also find them with Windows-style names (VK_DELETE) in the Windows API type library under UserConst.

To change the state of a key, you must read in the current key states, modify the key in the array, and write the result back with SetKeyboardState:

```
Property Let CapsState(fCapsStateA As Boolean)
    ' Get toggled and pressed state of all keys
    GetKeyboardState abKeys(0)
    ' Set low bit to new pressed state
    If fCapsStateA Then
        abKeys(VK_CAPITAL) = abKeys(VK_CAPITAL) Or 1
    Else
        abKeys(VK_CAPITAL) = abKeys(VK_CAPITAL) And &HFE
    End If
    ' Store changed array
    SetKeyboardState abKeys(0)
End Property
```

The KeyPressed property works the same way, except that it will check any key. The pressed state of a key is stored in the high bit, and you must provide the virtual key code of the key. Here's the Property Get procedure:

```
Property Get KeyPressed(iKey As Integer) As Boolean
    ' Get toggled and pressed state of all keys
    GetKeyboardState abKeys(0)
    ' Check high bit for state
    KeyPressed = abKeys(iKey) And &H80
End Property
```

A Property Get procedure with an argument makes the property look like an array element, as described in the sidebar "Property Arrays" in Chapter 4. Check out the KeyPressed Property Let in KEYBOARD.CLS.

Here's how you can use KeyPressed to read keys:

```
fShift = Keyboard.KeyPressed(VK_CONTROL) ' Is Ctrl key down?
```

You can also press a key programmatically:

```
Keyboard.KeyPressed(VK_F1) = True    ' Press F1
DoEvents
Keyboard.KeyPressed(VK_F1) = False   ' Release F1
```

So why didn't I use the KeyPressed property to press the insert key in the XEditor control? Because KeyPressed puts the key into the system keyboard queue, and the system determines what window to route the key to. I wanted to send the key to a specific window.

10

COM Behind the Curtain

When Visual Basic version 5 hit the streets, Biff Bummer, vice president of software development at Tough Guys, Incorporated, laid down the law:

"Don't write the same code twice while you're working for me. I want every line of code coming out of this shop from here on out to be a COM component. Drawing forms isn't real programming, and we're not going to pay real programmers to do it. You need a square root? Don't let me catch you calling the Sqr function in some event procedure on a form. No, you had better call the Square method of a CCalc object. Or better yet, write an XCalc control. We're not paying ten different people to calculate the same thing ten different places. We write one public calculator class for everybody, and everybody better use it."

Some wise guy pointed out that Tough Guys sold products to end users, not to developers. End users weren't likely to buy classes or forms. But Biff had that covered.

"We've hired some high school students to come in after school and string your components together into applications."

This ultimatum was met with skepticism at first. But the policy was not without its supporters and its successes. The official calculator component was indeed written, and it was indeed used by all, despite some quiet grumbling about the pointlessness of using the Subtract method instead of the subtraction operator. Young Joe Hacker Jr. won praise for his complex XWidgit control with its ten-level object hierarchy, starting with CDooDad as the base class and working its way up to the NWonkers collection. And, indeed, a bright high school student was found to create—with a little coaching from Joe—a Wigician application from the component, although it turned out to be a pretty thin wrapper. Still, no one denied that the Wigician was far superior to the old Widgiterium program with its 50 command-line options.

But many programmers felt the component thing was getting a little out of hand. There just might be some code somewhere that didn't need to be shared with the whole world. Sally Clockstein was leader of the opposition, and everyone knew she was a dangerous opponent. No one was surprised when Biff came to work one morning and found his empty office locked and his personal effects in boxes in the hall. Sally moved in the next day, and Biff's protégés started shopping their résumés. A week later, Sally laid down the law:

"Interfaces are the wave of the future. I want every class you write from here on out to implement interfaces. Everybody prints; everybody implements IPrint. Everybody walks; everybody implements IVariantWalker. Everybody loves me; everybody implements ILoveYou.

This edict was met with the wild enthusiasm reserved for all such cultural revolutions. But gradually, hard disks began to fill up with COM components implementing such interfaces as IPlus, IMinus, and IEnthusiasm.

Every parable has its limit, and this one passed its limit some time ago. So let's cut to the moral: use COM, but don't let it use you. Alas, I'm going to ignore my own advice throughout most of this chapter. I'll be doing some fairly obscure tasks and looking behind some out-of-the-way curtains (whether or not I have permission). Who knows? You might even run across one or two practical techniques that you can use in real programming projects.

The COM Vision

COM represents Microsoft's vision of the future. I use the word *vision* in its religious sense, which is how Microsoft's public relations department thinks of it. Even the titles of the practitioners are religious. Go to any conference where programmers gather, and you just might find a seminar taught by a person whose official title is COM Evangelist.

COM Terminology

COM. ActiveX. Automation. OLE. If you're not confused, you must be dead. Here's a personal and somewhat irreverent look at COM terminology.

- **Component Object Model (COM).** The center of the universe. The purpose of existence. The wave of the future. Technically, anything that has an IUnknown and implements QueryInterface, AddRef, and Release (which I'll examine later). Practically, COM is a technology for transparently transferring encapsulated data across boundaries. Whether the boundaries are separate modules, threads, processes, or machines isn't supposed to matter. COM is the Microsoft way of doing this.

- **ActiveX.** The cool part of COM. Honestly, I don't know why some parts of COM are considered ActiveX and other parts aren't. See "Automation" on the facing page.

- **OLE.** An acronym for Object Linking and Embedding. This includes various forms of compound document technology—nothing more, nothing less.

- **Automation.** Anything that makes something else work automatically. The official Microsoft terminology uses Automation (with a capital *A*) to mean the part of COM that makes one application programmable from another. But that's like saying if you capitalize the term air, you can make it the official Air of your company. I always use the term COM Automation to distinguish it from puppet automation or vehicle automation. So why isn't COM Automation part of ActiveX? Beats me. Originally, COM Automation was implemented through the IDispatch interface and was used to program applications such as Excel. Today, the term usually includes implementing dual interfaces and programming DLL and OCX components in contexts that hardly fit the normal meaning of automation.

- **Server and Component.** In the Visual Basic department, the term server is out and component is in. What used to be called an OLE server is now an ActiveX component. If you need to be more specific, call them ActiveX Controls, ActiveX Documents, ActiveX DLLs, and ActiveX EXE components. But if I sometimes talk about EXE servers and DLL servers, I hope you'll know what I mean.

In summary, things are a little mixed up and what you think you know now might not be the same thing you know later. Although the terms have changed, the technology behind them hasn't changed that much, except that more of it is available to Visual Basic programmers.

COM From All Angles

It's a little-known fact that Visual Basic is the leader of an insidious conspiracy to take over the world for COM. Here are some of the ways Visual Basic preaches and practices the COM doctrine.

- **Controls.** Visual Basic changed the world by popularizing the concept of a visual interface object encapsulated in an independent executable file known as a control. We've come a long way since then. Controls came before COM, but now ActiveX controls are a part of COM. Although there are differences under the surface, they're still as easy to use and as revolutionary as they were in Visual Basic version 1.0.

- **ActiveX Controls.** Now you can write your own ActiveX controls in Visual Basic. This is a dangerous new capability. It's very easy to write bad controls. It's moderately difficult to write good ones. But a lot of

Visual Basic programmers will meet the challenge. This is going to change the world again.

- **ActiveX DLLs.** The Visual Basic run-time library is an ActiveX DLL. My VBCore component is an ActiveX DLL. You can enhance the language by adding your own ActiveX DLLs. They can have global functions and public classes, just like the Visual Basic library.

- **Type Libraries.** Visual Basic supports type libraries (which you install with the References dialog box and view in the Object Browser). Most well-behaved COM components, including the Visual Basic libraries and controls and any components you create with Visual Basic, have type libraries. Another kind of type library makes a non-COM DLL (such as the Windows system DLLs) look like a COM object. The Windows API type library supplied with this book is such a library. See Chapter 2 for details about how to load it in the References dialog box and how to use the functions in it.

- **Interfaces.** You create them and use them behind the scenes all the time. Now you can write your own and implement them. You can also implement standard interfaces supplied by COM or Windows, although this isn't as easy as it ought to be. Nevertheless, you'll do it in this chapter.

- **Object Linking and Embedding (OLE).** OLE is now a tiny subset of COM. If you took seriously the title of this chapter in the first edition ("The OLE Gospel"), repeat with me: "Won't get fooled again." Anyway, Visual Basic supports linking and embedding through the OLE control. Using this control is too easy for a hardcore book, so this is the last time you'll see the insignificant term OLE.

- **COM Automation.** Visual Basic allows you to program applications that expose themselves through COM Automation. I see a lot of requests for assistance with this, but most are concerned with the application side of the problem. I'm not going to talk about programming the object models of applications such as Microsoft Word for Windows, Microsoft Excel, and Visio because I don't know which ones you have. Besides, other books cover this topic. Microsoft Press publishes two good ones: *Developing Applications with Microsoft Office for Windows 95,* by Christine Solomon (1996); and *Microsoft Guide to Object Programming with Visual Basic 4 and Microsoft Office for Windows 95,* by Joel P. Dehlin and Matthew J. Curland (1996).

- **Add-Ins.** The Visual Basic environment is itself a COM Automation server. You can customize it by creating your own components in a specific format known as an *add-in*. Add-ins must program the environment's VBIDE object and must provide objects that the VBIDE object knows how to talk to. I described and enhanced the add-in model in the first edition of this book, but the whole thing changed for Visual Basic version 5. The version 4 model was notoriously wimpy, so the new model has to be better. But I didn't have time to figure out how much better. Add-ins aren't covered in this edition.

■ **ActiveX Documents?** Yes, but not in this book.

The Prime Number Server

If you skipped Chapter 3 in order to go directly to the COM chapter, do not pass Go, do not collect $200. Under Visual Basic, components must be object-oriented. You can't implement them without implementing classes. You can look at this as a hoop to jump through and simply turn your functions into methods of a global class (as described in Chapter 5). Or you can take it as an opportunity to rethink your application. As a sample, let's implement the sieve of Eratosthenes ActiveX component.

The sieve of Eratosthenes algorithm has traditionally been used as a benchmark for measuring the performance of different machines, operating systems, programming languages, and compilers and interpreters. Here I'll expand it to measure the difference between different kinds of ActiveX components. In the process, I'll examine servers and clients in "slow motion." You don't really need to know every detail in order to create or use components, but since you're hardcore, you might as well know the inside story.

I'll show you both client and server written in Visual Basic because COM communication is easier to understand if you control both parts. But keep in mind that COM doesn't know or care what language is used. Often, when you purchase a component, you won't know what language it was written in. Similarly, if you create a component in Visual Basic, your clients need not know what language you used.

FLAME

In real life, you'll always need to create a test client to make sure that your component works. Visual Basic is the ideal language in which to write your test client, even if you choose to write the component in C++ or some other language. In fact, Visual Basic is an informal standard of what component containers should do. If your component behaves badly in Visual Basic, it will probably behave badly in other containers that emulate Visual Basic. On the other hand, if you do write your component in Visual Basic, that doesn't give you an excuse to assume your clients will do the same. Curses on all those arrogant developers who write public components specifically for their favorite language. The market will punish you.

The Sieve Client

The sieve of Eratosthenes Client program in Figure 10-1 counts prime numbers. The obvious purpose of this application is to tell you how many prime numbers there are up to a given maximum, and to list them. If you check the Display box, the program will do exactly that. But in reality, this is the least important purpose of the sieve.

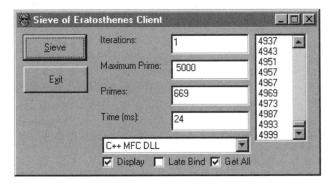

Figure 10-1. *The sieve of Eratosthenes Client.*

The real purpose is to compare the performance of the same algorithm in as many formats as possible. That's why the client program has functional versus object-oriented, early-bound versus late-bound, Basic versus C++, and getting all the primes at once versus getting one at a time. We don't really care about the prime numbers, only about how long it takes to calculate them in different environments.

You'll usually want to calculate all primes up to a given number several times to get useful values. If you're simply testing speed, you can throw away the results but you do need a display mode to prove that the numbers you're calculating are really primes. The timing is useless with the display on, however, because you're timing more display than calculation.

Simply writing the fastest possible algorithm would be an unrealistic test of ActiveX components. A server has to serve something, so you should at least pretend that the user of your class really needs the data. So let's say that prime numbers are very useful in calculating proportional radial intensity vectors of the newly discovered subatomic particles called quinks. To properly serve the powerful programs searching the universe for quinks, you need an ActiveX component that hands over prime numbers.

A Functional Way of Prime Numbers

The first task in converting existing code to a component is to change the model from functional to object-oriented. Of course, if you're starting from scratch, you can start out object-oriented but you still need to put yourself in an object state of mind. Most of us still program in functional mode. Here's how I changed my way of thinking about the sieve of Eratosthenes.

First look at the sieve in functional form. The algorithm shown here is pretty much the same as the one presented in *Byte* magazine in 1983 and used by hundreds of reviewers in many languages ever since. Variable names have been changed to protect the guilty. The function interface has been changed to accept an array that will be filled with the prime numbers the algorithm finds. The only logical change in the algorithm is that nonprime numbers are marked with True rather than False to take advantage of Visual Basic's automatic initialization to 0.

```
Function Sieve(ai() As Integer) As Integer
    Dim iLast As Integer, cPrime As Integer, iCur As Integer, i As Integer
    Dim af() As Boolean
    ' Parameter should have dynamic array for maximum number of primes
    If LBound(ai) <> 0 Then Exit Function
    iLast = UBound(ai)
    ' Create array large enough for maximum prime (initializing to zero)
    ReDim af(0 To iLast + 1) As Boolean
    For iCur = 2 To iLast
        ' Anything still zero is a prime
        If Not af(iCur) Then
            ' Cancel its multiples because they can't be prime
            For i = iCur + iCur To iLast Step iCur
                af(i) = True
            Next
            ' Count this prime
            ai(cPrime) = iCur
            cPrime = cPrime + 1
        End If
    Next
    ' Resize array to the number of primes found
    ReDim Preserve ai(0 To cPrime) As Integer
    Sieve = cPrime
End Function
```

The Select Case block of the client program where the function version is called looks like this:

```
Case estBasicLocalFunction
    ' Get all at once
    ms = timeGetTime()
    For i = 1 To cIter
        ReDim ai(0 To cPrimeMax)
```

(continued)

```
        cPrime = Sieve(ai())
        If fDisplay Then
            lstOutput.Clear
            For iPrime = 0 To cPrime - 1
                lstOutput.AddItem ai(iPrime)
                lstOutput.TopIndex = lstOutput.ListCount - 1
                lstOutput.Refresh
            Next
        End If
    Next
    txtTime.Text = timeGetTime() - ms
    txtPrimes.Text = cPrime
```

Our job is to convert the local sieve function into a local CSieve class. After that, we can worry about converting to other kinds of COM components.

An Object-Oriented Way of Prime Numbers

One way to make the program object-oriented is to turn the sieve function into a method that fills an array of prime numbers passed by reference. The CSieve class does this through the AllPrimes method. The code is very similar to the local sieve function. The problem with this kind of method is that you must calculate all the prime numbers before you can get the first one. But some clients can't wait. Those quink scientists I mentioned earlier, for example, want a steady stream of numbers fed to them one at a time.

This is the classic trade-off you'll come to know in COM design. The purpose of any server is to transfer data across boundaries. Often, setting up the transfer is the most expensive part. You can be more efficient by passing larger chunks of data. But the larger the chunk, the longer the client has to wait. In this exercise, you'll be testing the extremes—all at once versus one at a time. In real programs, you might want to compromise by transferring medium-sized chunks.

The trick in getting numbers one at a time is to break the sieve function—which seems like an integrated whole—into its parts. Here's what sieve really does:

- Keeps its state (number of primes, current number) in local variables

- Initializes an array to False by redimensioning it

- Loops through each potential prime number

- Marks out all multiples of primes

- Counts the primes as it finds them

You can break these tasks into the following members, methods, and properties:

- The state is kept in private variables shared by all the methods and properties rather than in local variables. This includes the array of flags for each potential prime (*af*), the number currently being tested (*iCur*), the maximum prime (*iMaxPrime*), and the count of primes (*cPrime*).

- A ReInitialize method resets all the internal variables and starts counting again from 0.

- A MaxPrime property sets the upper bound on the search for primes. From a user's viewpoint, it would be better not to have a maximum and instead to simply calculate whether each number is a prime without reference to later primes. But you'd have to turn to someone other than Eratosthenes for an algorithm. So let's stick with the sieve. When you change MaxPrime, you break the algorithm. Therefore, the Max-Prime Property Let procedure must call ReInitialize to start counting from 0.

- A NextPrime property calculates and returns the next prime.

- A Primes property (read-only) tells you how many prime numbers have been counted so far.

Here's the code to implement these methods and properties:

```
Private af() As Boolean, iCur As Integer
Private iMaxPrime As Integer, cPrime As Integer

Private Sub Class_Initialize()
    ' Default size is largest integer
    iMaxPrime = 32766
    ReInitialize
End Sub

Sub ReInitialize()
    ReDim af(0 To iMaxPrime)
    iCur = 1: cPrime = 0
End Sub

Property Get NextPrime() As Integer
    ' Loop until you find a prime or overflow array
    iCur = iCur + 1
    On Error GoTo OverMaxPrime
    Do While af(iCur)
        iCur = iCur + 1
```

(continued)

```
    Loop
    ' Cancel multiples of this prime
    Dim i As Long
    For i = iCur + iCur To iMaxPrime Step iCur
        af(i) = True
    Next
    ' Count and return it
    cPrime = cPrime + 1
    NextPrime = iCur
OverMaxPrime:         ' Array overflow comes here
End Property

Property Get MaxPrime() As Integer
    MaxPrime = iMaxPrime
End Property

Property Let MaxPrime(iMaxPrimeA As Integer)
    iMaxPrime = iMaxPrimeA
    ReInitialize
End Property

Property Get Primes() As Integer
    Primes = cPrime
End Property
```

As you can see, the NextPrime property does most of the work. It looks quite different from the Sieve function, but it does essentially the same thing. You might need to study both the Sieve function and the NextPrime property for a minute to see the connection.

The code that calls the class methods looks a little different from the code that calls the function.

```
Case estBasicLocalClass
    ' Basic local class
    Dim sieveLocal As New CSieve
    sieveLocal.MaxPrime = txtMaxPrime.Text
    If chkAll = vbUnchecked Then
        ' Get one at a time
        ms = timeGetTime()
        For i = 1 To cIter
            sieveLocal.ReInitialize
            Do
                iPrime = sieveLocal.NextPrime
                If fDisplay And iPrime Then
                    lstOutput.AddItem iPrime
                    lstOutput.TopIndex = lstOutput.ListCount - 1
                    lstOutput.Refresh
```

```
            End If
        Loop Until iPrime = 0
    Next
    txtTime.Text = timeGetTime() - ms
    txtPrimes.Text = sieveLocal.Primes
Else
    ' Get all at once
    ⋮
```

The code calling the AllPrimes method to get all the primes at once looks a lot like the functional version, so there's no need to show it here.

The ActiveX DLL Way of Prime Numbers

Once you have an object-oriented solution, you're just a few clicks away from an ActiveX DLL server. Here's all you have to do to turn the CSieve class into a Sieve component. None of the steps require writing code:

1. Select New from the File menu, and choose ActiveX DLL in the project type list. Name the project SieveBasDllN. This will be a native code DLL component written in Visual Basic.

2. Remove the dummy class the IDE automatically puts in a new project, and insert the file SIEVE.CLS (the local CSieve class from the last section).

3. Change the name property from CSieve to CSieveBasDllN. Use Save As commands to name the class file SieveBasDllN.CLS and the project file SieveBasDllN.VBP.

4. Change the instancing property from private to MultiUse (5). This is the generic way to make a class public. If this class were to be part of an object hierarchy and it were created by the top-level class of the hierarchy, you might want to set it to PublicNotCreatable (2) so that clients couldn't create it directly. We discussed the reasons for setting GlobalMultiUse back in Chapter 5. Figure 10-2 on the following page shows the settings so far.

5. Open the Project Properties dialog box, and fill out blank fields starting with Project Description. The description is optional, but you'll have a rude server indeed if you fail to provide it. Any client that wanted to register and use your services would have to guess your purpose from the project name. When you write a server, you don't know who will use it. It might be called from Excel, from Word, or from a program you've never heard of. Visual Basic itself is a typical client. It offers a References dialog box for loading and registering servers, and it has an Object Browser for displaying public classes. Both use the description to identify the server.

6. Write a help file for your server, and provide the filename and context ID of the server help topic in the Help File Name and Project Help ContextID fields. Why doesn't my server have a help file? Well, uh... it has a virtual help file.

7. Leave the Startup Object as None. In version 4 you had to specify a startup module—even if it did nothing. Now if your startup doesn't need to do anything, Visual Basic won't specify it for you automatically. Keep in mind that any startup done in a Sub Main specified by this dialog box occurs once for the whole component and all the classes in it. It's not the same as the object-specific startup that occurs in Class_Initialize events.

8. Ignore the Upgrade ActiveX Controls checkbox. The server has no controls to upgrade.

9. The SieveBasDllN component has no user interaction, so you mark it as having Unattended Execution. This makes it suitable for running with multithreaded clients. I discuss the implications of Unattended Execution in "Threads and Synchronization" in Chapter 11.

10. On the Component tab, I accept the default setting of Project Compatibility. If I were creating a new implementation of an existing component (such as one of the Sieve components from the first edition of this book), I might want to set Binary Compatibility. I'll talk more about this issue later.

11. Compile the DLL to native code. The client program also uses a p-code version of the DLL. It's created in exactly the same way except that the name and the compile options are different. When the server is compiled in the IDE, it is automatically registered. I'll look at component registration in more detail in "Registering components" later in this chapter.

Figure 10-2. *Settings for ActiveX DLL server.*

PERFORMANCE

Problem: Compare calculating prime numbers functionally, locally, externally, with objects, and with early or late binding.

Problem	P-Code	Native Code
Local Basic function	.1270 sec	.0380 sec
Early-bound Local Basic class, one at a time	.1750 sec	.0400 sec
Late-bound Local Basic class, one at a time	.7550 sec	.6120 sec
Early-bound Local Basic class, all at once	.1460 sec	.0330 sec
Late-bound Local Basic class, all at once	.1540 sec	.0330 sec
Basic global function in DLL	.1210 sec	.0350 sec
Early-bound Basic class in DLL, one at a time	.1710 sec	.0390 sec
Late-bound Basic class in DLL, one at a time	.8380 sec	.6040 sec
Early-bound Basic class in DLL, all at once	.1450 sec	.0330 sec
Late-bound Basic class in DLL, all at once	.1510 sec	.0330 sec
Early-bound Basic class in EXE, one at a time	9.8660 sec	9.2240 sec
Late-bound Basic class in EXE, one at a time	20.5320 sec	18.9650 sec
Early-bound Basic class in EXE, all at once	.2040 sec	.0810 sec
Late-bound Basic class in EXE, all at once	.2210 sec	.1040 sec
Basic class in control, one at a time	.5930 sec	.3660 sec
Basic class in control, all at once	.1470 sec	.0340 sec
Early-bound C++ class in ATL DLL, one at a time	NA	.0150 sec
Late-bound C++ class in ATL DLL, one at a time	NA	.2900 sec
Early-bound C++ class in ATL DLL, all at once	NA	.0150 sec
Late-bound C++ class in ATL DLL, all at once	NA	.0160 sec
Early-bound C++ class in MFC DLL, one at a time	NA	.0830 sec
Late-bound C++ class in MFC DLL, one at a time	NA	.1660 sec
Early-bound C++ class in MFC DLL, all at once	NA	.0230 sec
Late-bound C++ class in MFC DLL, all at once	NA	.0240 sec

Conclusion: Switching from a functional approach to an object-oriented approach doesn't have a significant cost, but you do need to worry about late binding. Passing data across process boundaries has a significant cost, but you can reduce it by using early binding and transferring data in large chunks. Of course, total performance might not be an important goal; some clients could prefer an even flow of data instead of big chunks that take a long time to process. Visual Basic native code isn't too far behind C++ native code, and when you compare to MFC, Visual Basic is actually faster. That's because MFC doesn't have dual interfaces as do Visual Basic and ATL. But notice that MFC is faster for late-bound operations (because it implements a fast, custom version of the IDispatch interface). In most cases, which kind of late-bound server is faster matters about as much as which breed of cart horse is faster.

The client code to access a public class in an ActiveX DLL server is pretty much the same as the code to access a private class in the current application. Only the class and the object variable names change. So instead of looking at this boilerplate, let's take a quick look at the dark side—late binding. The only reason the Sieve Client program does late binding is to prove how slow it is. The reason I'm showing it here is to demonstrate that it can sometimes be more flexible than early binding.

```
            ' Set variable at run time
            Dim sieveLate As Object
            Select Case cboServer.ListIndex
            Case estBasicLocalClass
                Set sieveLate = New CSieve
#Const fUseTypeLib = 1
#If fUseTypeLib Then
            Case estBasicDllPCode
                Set sieveLate = New CSieveBasDllP
            Case estBasicDllNative
                Set sieveLate = New CSieveBasDllN
                ⋮
#Else
            Case estBasicEXE
                Set sieveLate = CreateObject("SieveBasDllP.CSieveBasDllP")
            Case estBasicDllNative
                Set sieveLate = CreateObject("SieveBasDllN.CSieveBasDllN")
                ⋮
#End If
            End Select
            sieveLate.MaxPrime = txtMaxPrime.Text
            If chkAll = vbUnchecked Then
                ' Get one at a time
                ms = timeGetTime()
                For i = 1 To cIter
                    sieveLate.ReInitialize
                    Do
                        iPrime = sieveLate.NextPrime
                        ' More of the same...
```

An interesting point is that the same variable can be used for all the different kinds of servers. In the early binding branch of this code, every server uses a different class and must have a different object variable. Therefore, the code to calculate the prime numbers must be duplicated for each class, with no difference other than the variable name. In the late binding branch, the same variable can work for any class because the class isn't selected until run time. As a result, the code needs to be written only once. We could get the same behavior for early binding by writing an ISieve interface and making all the sieve classes implement it. But that's not the point of this exercise.

Notice that there are two ways of creating a new late-bound object—one using the New statement and the other using CreateObject. In this case, there's a type library, so New is slightly more efficient. But in most cases where you have a type library, you can use early binding. Use CreateObject for those cases (rare in my experience) where you don't have a type library or don't know the name of the class until run time.

NOTE You shouldn't think of your DLL or OCX components as complete until you select the DLL base address. You do this on the Compile tab of the Project Properties dialog box. Visual Basic gives you a default base address, but if you accept it, your component will have a very good chance of being bumped by one of the other dummies who accepted the default address instead of selecting their own. If two components in the system have the same base address, the operating system will have to relocate one or the other. You don't want it to be yours. The operating system expects base addresses to be on 64-KB boundaries, so there are 32,512 64-KB chunks in the available address range. You have a very good chance of avoiding everybody else's range if you select your range randomly. The Address-o-matic program (as seen on TV) doesn't aspire to being a wizard, but it will assign you a base address that isn't in my range or in the Visual Basic range. You could enhance it to keep a database of known addresses to avoid, including the ranges for your company, your clients, and major component vendors. By the way, my range is one megabyte starting at &H2E8B0000. Keep out!

The ActiveX EXE Way of Prime Numbers

The Sieve Client program also uses ActiveX EXE components. When you look at the "Performance" sidebar on page 551, it's easy to get the impression that I created the EXE versions of the component for no other reason than to persuade you never to use them. Well, not exactly. I do want to stress the toll for using EXE components, but there are situations in which the toll is worth paying.

Sending data from a DLL to a program is fast because the program and the DLL are in the same address space. System DLLs like USER32.DLL and GDI32.DLL are very efficient. COM adds some overhead for ActiveX DLLs, but it's still fast. An EXE server, on the other hand, is a completely different program, and COM has to set up a rather complex communication system called marshaling to make data transfers work. The overhead of sending data across process boundaries is high, and, of course, the overhead for machine boundaries is even higher.

That doesn't mean you always want DLL components. Microsoft Excel isn't a DLL, although clearly its Automation clients would run faster if it were. If your server does nothing but serve, build the DLL server. If your server is primarily a program and secondarily a server, build the EXE server. If your server must communicate with clients on other machines (possibly running different operating systems), you have only one choice: EXE server. If your server must create multiple threads, build the EXE server. The server described in "The server side of file notification" in Chapter 11, for example, is an EXE server so that its operation won't affect the performance of its clients.

The Sieve Client program creates an artificial situation. It uses six different sieve components and a local class—all of them containing the same code. Normally, you choose the most appropriate format for all clients rather than forcing one client to accommodate all possible servers. Let's just say that the Sieve Client has exotic tastes.

The steps for creating an EXE server are almost the same as those for creating a DLL server. To make the comparison a little more realistic, let's assume that the SieveBasExeN component is actually a program whose main purpose is to calculate prime numbers and hand them over directly to users through a user interface. But as a sideline, the program can also provide the same numbers to any outside clients that need them. In other words, SieveBasExeN works a lot like Microsoft Excel.

To create the server, I started with the same steps you saw earlier. I created a new ActiveX EXE project containing CSieve and renamed the project Sieve-BasExeN. This project also needs a form for its user interface, so I inserted the FSieveClient form and renamed it FSieveBasExeN. This form doesn't need to get prime numbers from 11 different sources, so I removed the combo box and all the code that references it, leaving only the code to access one sieve class, CSieveBasExeN.

In an ordinary program, I would set FSieveBasExeN to be my startup form, but you can't have a form as the startup object in an ActiveX EXE server. I had to add a standard module with a Sub Main and have Sub Main load the form:

```
Sub Main()
    If App.StartMode = vbSModeStandalone Then
        Dim frmSieve As New FSieveBasExeN
        frmSieve.Show
    End If
End Sub
```

The form won't be loaded if the EXE is started by an ActiveX client such as the Sieve Client program. Following are a few other settings differences (as shown in Figure 10-3):

■ On the General tab, the Startup Object must be set to Sub Main.

- The Unattended Execution settings are disabled because a form can't be unattended. But if this server (like the DLL version) didn't have a user interface, you could set it for unattended execution and set options to control how it uses threads for its multiple objects. None of this applies to the sieve server because there is only one class in the component and you're not likely to create multiple instances of it. These settings aren't the only way you can create multiple threads in Visual Basic—I'll explore these interesting possibilities in "Threads and Synchronization" in Chapter 11.

- On the Component tab, set Standalone as the Start Mode when testing the component as a stand-alone application. Set ActiveX Component when testing the component as a server. When you create the compiled server, the client will always do the right thing by itself—connect to the visible server if it is running, or start the server without a user interface if it is not running. These settings enable you to test both scenarios in the IDE. They have no effect on the finished server.

- The Instancing property for the class could be set to either SingleUse or MultiUse. I could have created separate p-code and native code versions with each of these settings and timed the differences in their performance, but the sieve classes will usually have only one instance, so this setting doesn't matter much. I randomly chose MultiUse. You need to study the implications when creating real EXE servers.

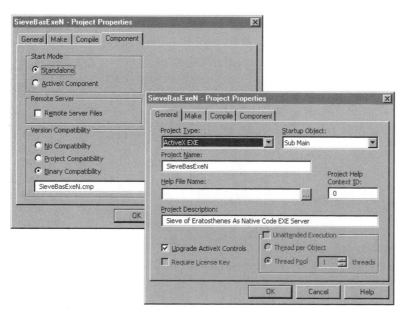

Figure 10-3. *Project settings for the SieveBasExeN server.*

C++ Sieve Servers

Any server that you can write in Visual Basic you can also write in C++. But is it worth the trouble? Well, you're asking the right person. I've written the Sieve server four different ways in C++, and it was a struggle every time.

The first edition of this book came with a raw C++ version. I borrowed some boilerplate code, but I had to put everything together myself into a dense, unintelligible mass of code. Never again. The Microsoft Foundation Classes (MFC) version was a lot easier to write and understand, but its performance was unsatisfactory. Next I converted to the ActiveX BaseCtl framework—the same code base used to create the controls provided with Visual Basic 5. And finally I rewrote it with the ActiveX Template Library (ATL). I described this version in the August, 1996, issue of *Visual Basic Programmer's Journal*.

I believe MFC and ATL will be the tools of choice for writing ActiveX components, so those versions are provided on the disk. The performance of the raw and BaseCtl versions was about the same as the ATL version anyway. The MFC version is a different matter. As the "Performance" sidebar on page 551 shows, it is actually considerably slower than the native code Visual Basic DLL. This is an object lesson in the value of dual interfaces, as described in Chapter 3. The only thing MFC has to recommend it for COM development is that it's easier than ATL. But what's the point when Visual Basic is so much easier than C++?

It's difficult and not very meaningful to compare Visual Basic and C++ code, but let's do it anyway. The SIEVE.CLS file contains 77 lines of code. The SIEVE.CPP and SIEVE.H files from the ATL version provide the same functionality in about 191 lines. The Visual Basic code is definitely more compact and readable. The C++ version has to do some COM setup that isn't directly related to prime numbers. If you count only the executable lines that calculate prime numbers, the two versions are roughly the same. In either case, the code you see is the tip of the iceberg. A lot more C++ code hides in the COM DLLs. With the Visual Basic version, you see even less of the iceberg but mostly it's the same iceberg. The Visual Basic library code that connects Visual Basic servers to the COM DLLs is written in C++, and it must perform essentially the same tasks as the ATL framework code surrounding the C++ class.

You can see that the extra work put into the ATL version pays off in better performance, but it's not an overwhelming advantage and I'd still choose Visual Basic if that were the only factor. But the ATL version wins big in one other way. The component is about 16 KB in size with no dependencies. The Visual Basic native code version is about 11 KB, but it requires a run-time DLL of about 1.3 megabytes. If your clients are Visual Basic programs, you have to have that DLL anyway. But if you're writing for other clients, the ATL version has a certain appeal.

You don't have to worry about debugging the CSieveBasExeN class because its code is the same as the CSieve class and that's already debugged. But in real life, you will need to debug EXE servers, and the technique is significantly different than for DLL components. Instead of putting the project in a VBG, you start one instance of Visual Basic containing the component and then start another instance containing the client. Set breakpoints in each project, and switch back and forth between the appropriate IDE. This is easier said than done, and there will be times when you wish for a simple little DLL component.

CHALLENGE If you have Visual Basic Enterprise Edition, you can make the ActiveX EXE version work across machines by using DCOM. I didn't try this, but in theory the server should work without any code changes. You could then add DCOM performance statistics to the numbers presented in the "Performance" sidebar on page 551. I don't think this would be particularly informative. Your results would depend more on the speed of your network connection than on any code in the server or client.

The XSieve Control

Turning the sieve of Eratosthenes into an ActiveX control is a really bad idea. The only reason I did it was to show how bad an idea it is. You pay a performance penalty. You get no particular convenience benefit. Don't pay more for less.

I've already complained about controls that shouldn't be controls (Timer and CommonDialog). Don't add yours to the list. In fact, I advise you to skip the rest of this section and go back to the "Performance" sidebar on page 551 to see for yourself how much slower a control is than an ActiveX DLL with exactly the same code.

I had to use a slightly different technique to create the ActiveX control versions of the sieve server. You start by creating a new ActiveX control project, but you can't just rename the CSieve class as a UserControl. Instead, you copy the text out of the CLS file and copy it into a new CTL file. That's really all you need to create a working control, but of course, there's a little more to it if you want your control to at least pretend it's a real control.

First, your control should have a visual representation at design time so that you can find it and delete it after you're done proving that a nonvisual control is a bad idea. I created a simple sieve bitmap for the Toolbox and put the same bitmap on the control surface. I also added a label with the word *Sieve* in a nice bold font. But there's no reason to show this junk on the client's surface at run time, so you turn it off by setting the InvisibleAtRuntime property of the UserControl to True.

In controls, you should do initialization tasks both in the UserControl_Read-Properties and UserControl_InitProperties events by raising the UserControl-_Load "event" described in Chapter 9, page 483. These are the same kinds of tasks that you would do in Class_Initialize or Form_Load for classes or forms, respectively. The ReInitialize method is called by Class_Initialize in the CSieve class, but UserControl_Initialize happens too early in the XSieve controls. Re-Initialize needs to use the MaxPrime property, but properties aren't initialized until after UserControl_ReadProperties reads them from the PropertyBag. Initialization should be done at this point. UserControl_ReadProperties doesn't happen when the control is created, so the same initialization code needs to be called in UserControl_InitProperties.

The sieve server has several properties, but only one of them—MaxPrime—is appropriate for setting at design time in the Properties window. The Sieve Client program doesn't use it even then. Instead, it gets the appropriate value from the user at run time. Other properties, such as NextPrime and Primes, are read-only properties that can be calculated only at run time, so they're disabled in the Properties window.

None of these minor differences adds any advantage for the client. Most controls with no user interface are nothing more than an annoyance.

Behind the Scenes at the COM Factory

In order to fully understand what COM does behind the scenes, let's create an imaginary language called B--. This language looks a lot like Visual Basic, with one minor difference. It doesn't know COM from calm. In other words, it's a lot like C or C++. We're still going to create and use COM objects, but we'll have to manage them ourselves.

To make this exercise work, we're going to have to take some poetic license. Some steps will be skipped. Some impossible leaps will be taken. Some white lies will be told. If you've programmed COM objects in C++, you might be amused, or perhaps outraged. Never mind. There's no B-- compiler, so you can't prove me wrong when I say that the following interface is behind all the other things in COM:

```
' IUnknown interface
Function QueryInterface(iid As GUID) As Object
End Sub

Sub AddRef()
End Sub

Sub Release()
End Sub
```

Those of you who know COM in a language other than B-- might laugh to see that I've changed QueryInterface into a Function and changed AddRef and Release into Subs. Bear with me. It will all work out in the end.

The Name of the Class

When I showed you the sieve of Eratosthenes class, I claimed that the name of the class was CSieve. That was a lie. The real name of the class is 0F590920-F220-11CE-8D2E-00AA004A5C59. How convenient. Wouldn't it be fun to program like the code shown below:

```
Dim sieve As New 0F590920-F220-11CE-8D2E-00AA004A5C59
```

That's essentially what C++ and B-- programmers have to do. Every class and every interface has its 128-bit identifier that is normally shown as a hexadecimal number with dashes at seemingly random dividing points. This is obviously too confusing, even for C++ masochists. Instead of using the full name, C++ programmers use constants such as CLSID_SIEVE for classes and IID_SIEVE for interfaces. The B-- language supports the same feature with a special GUID type, which can be initialized with a constant like this:

```
Const CLSID_SIEVE = 0F590920-F220-11CE-8D2E-00AA004A5C59
```

Keep in mind that the hexadecimal representation of the class identifier (class ID) is just a crutch for weak human memories. The real name is 128 bits of memory arranged in a UDT that looks like this:

```
Type GUID
    Data1 As Long
    Data2 As Integer
    Data3 As Integer
    Data4(0 To 7) As Byte
End Type
```

You might remember that we actually filled one of these GUIDs with a magic number back in Chapter 8.

Why can't we just call our class CSieve? Well, one reason is that someone else might want to use the name CSieve. Maybe they're wrapping the sieve of Pythagoras, or perhaps their sieve class sifts flour and baking soda. We want our class names to be simple and obvious, but the more simple and obvious they are, the more likely it is that they will duplicate someone else's simple and obvious name. So behind every simple class name there's a GUID, which brings us to the first principle of GUIDs.

NOTE	Let me indulge readers from my part of the world by describing the pronunciation of GUID as geoduck without the "uck." Those of you who don't know a geoduck from a mallard can just say "Goo-Id."

GUIDs are unique

A properly generated GUID distinguishes your class from all other COM classes that ever have been or will be created. I admit I was a little skeptical about this claim the first time I heard it. True, 128 is a whole lot of bits, but forever is a long, long time. Fortunately, these aren't just any 128 bits.

GUIDs should be generated with the CoCreateGuid API function, which uses a complex algorithm to calculate a new number that is based partly on the instant when the function was called and partly on the unique network number of your machine (or on other unique characteristics of your machine if you aren't networked). Since no else can have your machine at the exact instant you generate the GUID, it can't be duplicated. Or at least not without cheating.

Visual Basic calls CoCreateGuid when it creates a class, an interface, or a type library. You can also create GUIDs manually using GUIDGEN (a GUI program that puts GUIDs on the clipboard) or UUIDGEN (a command line program that writes GUIDs to standard output). If worst comes to worst, you can call CoCreate-Guid yourself from code. Normally, you don't have to worry about GUIDs (in fact you don't get to) because Visual Basic generates them for you. Which brings us to the second principle of GUIDs.

GUIDs are eternal

A published GUID is carved in stone. The GUID for the original SIEVE DLL component was generated on a machine I don't use anymore, and part of the number came from the network adapter on that machine. I could never generate that GUID on my current development machine no matter how many billions of times I ran GUIDGEN. Yet I'm bound by the immutable laws of COM to keep using that GUID for every version of the component until the mountains crumble to the sea.

The first edition of this book provided EXE and DLL versions of the Sieve component. When I created the components for this version, I had to decide whether to make them compatible with the old versions. The methods and properties of this version are exactly the same, so compatibility would have been possible. Of course, in those days you couldn't write controls or global libraries in Visual Basic, and you couldn't compile to native code, so the only candidates for compatibility were the p-code DLL and EXE versions.

Realistically, buyers of the second edition don't need to run my new servers from the old Sieve client program. But I could do it if I wanted to prove a point. Nothing but common sense keeps me from creating a compatible native code version of my DLL component that would scream with the old version 4 Sieve client. Of course, I'd have to keep both version 4 and version 5 run-time libraries available, but...I didn't actually try this. If there's a problem, I don't want to know.

If I had wanted a compatible version, I would have had to set binary compatibility and point the compatible file field to the appropriate DLL and EXE components. To avoid overwriting the old versions and getting sharing violations, I would have renamed the old versions to a new extension. CMP is becoming a semi-standard extension for compare versions. I wouldn't have been able to rename the classes or make any other changes, no matter how small. My new component would have had a different implementation, but for all COM purposes it would have been the same component. The GUIDs for all its interfaces, classes, and type libraries would have been identical, and it would have looked the same (except for a higher version number) in the registry. But of course I ignored all that crap and created completely new components that just happened to have the same methods and properties.

It's a different situation for the Notify server that will be discussed in Chapter 11. The old version of this server would be just as useful to Visual Basic version 5 applications as it was for version 4 applications (or for C++ applications, for that matter). The only reason to update it is to take advantage of better performance features, but as you'll learn when you read the details, performance isn't critical for this particular application. The old version is fast enough.

What You Don't Know

Let's go back to the root of everything in COM—IUnknown. Every COM interface is derived from it. Every COM class must implement it. In Visual Basic, you don't need to know anything about this. Everything about IUnknown happens behind the scenes. You don't need to know, for example, what it means to be "derived" from IUnknown. But in B--, it's a different story.

Using IUnknown

First you must use IUnknown every time you connect to a class. There is no Set statement in B--. There is an assignment operator, but assigning any object isn't enough. Let's say that you had the following code in Visual Basic:

```
Dim toughluck As CHardway, toobad As CHardway
Set toughluck = New CHardway
Set toobad = toughluck
```

Here's how you might do the same thing:

```
'' Dim toughluck As CHardway, toobad As CHardway
Dim toughluck As CLSID_CHardway = 0, toobad As CLSID_CHardway = 0
'' Set toughluck = New CHardway
toughluck = CreateInstance(CLSID_CHardway, IID_IHardway)
If toughluck = 0 Then GoTo ErrorHandler
'' Set toobad = toughluck
toobad = IUnknown(toughluck).QueryInterface(IID_IHardway)
If toobad = 0 Then Goto ErrorHandler
```

It doesn't look like much fun, does it?

(If the casting syntax *IUnknown(object).Method* looks unintelligible, just take it on faith for now. We'll see how Visual Basic can get a similar syntax in "Interface casting" on page 585.

You don't have to do any of this crap in Visual Basic. You don't have to call the imaginary CreateInstance function to create a new instance. You don't have to call QueryInterface to make sure your object variable actually supports the appropriate interface. You don't have to call Release and AddRef to do reference counting.

Notice that although classes have class IDs, QueryInterface doesn't care about them. Class IDs are a mechanism for creating objects, but once the object is created, the interface is all that counts. You can see a little more about how this works by looking at the implementation of a class in B--.

Implementing IUnknown

Visual Basic does a lot of work behind the scenes to make classes work. If you want a class to work properly in B--, you have to manage everything yourself. Here's one possible version of the CHardway class:

```
' CHardway (CLSID_CHardway)
Implements IID_IHardway   ' Every class implements default interface
Implements IID_IUnknown   ' Every interface implements IUnknown
                          ' Any class can implement additional interfaces
⋮

' Private variables
⋮

Function IUnknown_QueryInterface(iid As GUID) As Variant
    Select Case iid
    Case IID_IUnknown
        IUnknown_QueryInterface = IUnknown(Me)
    Case IID_IHardway
        IUnknown_QueryInterface = IHardway(Me)
    ' Case IID_IAnyOtherInterface
        ' IUnknown_QueryInterface = IAnyOtherInterface(Me)
    Case Else
        IUnknown_QueryInterface = 0
        Exit Function
    End Select
    IUnknown_AddRef
End Function

' AddRef and Release discussed later
Sub IUnknown_AddRef()
⋮
```

```
' IHardway delegates to IUnknown
Function IHardway_QueryInterface(iid As GUID) As Variant
    IHardway_QueryInterface = IUnknown_QueryInterface(iid)
End Function

' The rest of the class
Property Get IHardway_Name(sNameA As String)
    ⋮
```

Visual Basic classes also implement the IDispatch interface to support late binding through a complicated mechanism that I don't even want to think about, much less describe. Fortunately, this example supports only early binding.

In the QueryInterface implementation, requests for unrecognized interfaces fall through to the Else clause and fail. If the interface is recognized, an AddRef is done on the newly referenced object. We'll see what that means shortly.

Don't worry if this doesn't make sense. The main point Visual Basic programmers need to know about QueryInterface is that it's not free. Things you normally don't know or care about are going on in the background all the time.

Creating objects

So far, our fantasy implementation of B-- has been able to keep kind of close to earth. C++ COM programmers might actually recognize part of our implementation of IUnknown. But creating new instances of objects presents some problems that we can't easily get around when we're inventing a language that handles COM but doesn't support pointers.

I'm going to cop out by saying that the CreateInstance function resides in the B-- run-time library (so that I don't have to show code for it). It calls the COM library function CoCreateInstance to create objects. I used CreateInstance rather than CoCreateInstance in my B-- examples because the real CoCreateInstance takes extra arguments that are beyond the scope of this discussion. Visual Basic does the same thing with its CreateObject function, which is simply a wrapper for COM object creation functions. This is the signature for CreateInstance:

```
Function CreateInstance(clsid As GUID, iid As GUID) As Object
```

The implementation creates the object by allocating memory for it, setting up the vtable for its method pointers, reference counting it, and raising the Class_Initialize event. If the object is successfully created, it will have a reference count of 1 and a nonzero value (*obj* Is Nothing = False). A created object owns memory that was allocated with ReDim and that should be deallocated with Erase when the object is destroyed.

Reference Counting and Not Reference Counting

The QueryInterface method might be mildly interesting, but for the most part, it's transparent in Visual Basic and there's not much you can do about it. That's not always the case with reference counting.

COM didn't invent the concept of reference counting. It's been around for a long time, and you might even find it handy in your own classes. We'll use a form of it in the file notification server in Chapter 11.

The idea is that any object that might be referenced by multiple users keeps a count of how many users it has. Whenever a new user connects to the object, the count is incremented. When a user disconnects from the object, the count is decremented. When the count reaches zero, no one is using the object and it can call its Terminate event and deallocate its data. In simple reference counting schemes such as COM's, it doesn't matter what the count is, just whether it's zero. The scheme works if all the participants faithfully do their part to keep the reference count accurate.

COM objects are responsible for keeping a reference count, and Visual Basic, as a good implementor of COM, keeps reference counts religiously—sometimes too religiously. This all happens behind the scenes: you can't see how it works and you can't change its behavior through legal means. Of course, hardcore programmers can do anything they want, but let's take a closer look at the automatic system before attempting to modify it.

COM programmers in C, C++, and B-- don't have the luxury of ignoring reference counts. In these COM-ignorant languages, any reference counting that gets done must be done by you, the class implementor.

Counting references

Let's take another look at the B-- implementation of CHardway. Our first look concentrated on QueryInterface. This time we'll focus on AddRef and Release:

```
' CHardway (CLSID_CHardway)
Implements IID_IHardway    ' Every class implements default interface
Implements IID_IUnknown    ' Every interface implements IUnknown
                           ' Any class can implement additional interfaces
  ⋮

' Private variables
Private c As Long          ' Internal reference count

Function IUnknown_QueryInterface(iid As GUID) As Object
  ⋮

Sub IUnknown_AddRef()
    c = c + 1
End Sub
```

```
Sub IUnknown_Release()
    c = c - 1
    If c = 0 Then
        RaiseEvent Me.Class_Terminate
        Erase Me
    End If
End Sub

' The rest of the class
⋮
```

This code is speculative because there isn't really a B-- to write it with. In particular, the *Erase Me* statement in Release is based on the speculation that the object was originally allocated with *ReDim*.

Reference counting in clients

Now let's look at some client code. Assume the following real Visual Basic fragment:

```
Dim toughluck As CHardway, toobad As CHardway, forgetit As CHardway
Set toughluck = New CHardway
Set toobad = toughluck
Set forgetit = toobad
Set toobad = Nothing
Set toughluck = forgetit
```

Notice that the last assignment is redundant because *toughluck* already has a CHardWay object, but we're going to do it anyway to illustrate a point. Let's work through the reference counting using the B-- dialect:

```
'' Dim toughluck As CHardway, toobad As CHardway, forgetit As CHardway
Dim toughluck As CLSID_CHardway = 0, toobad As CLSID_CHardway = 0
Dim forgetit As CLSID_CHardway = 0
'' Set toughluck = New CHardway
toughluck = CreateInstance(CLSID_CHardway, IID_IHardway)      ' c = 1
if toughluck = 0 Then Goto ErrorHandler
'' Set toobad = toughluck
' Includes automatic AddRef by QueryInterface
toobad = IUnknown(toughluck).QueryInterface(IID_IHardway)      ' c = 2
if toobad = 0 Then Goto ErrorHandler
'' Set forgetit = toobad
' Includes automatic AddRef
forgetit = IUnknown(toobad).QueryInterface(IID_IHardway)      ' c = 3
if forgetit = 0 Then Goto ErrorHandler
'' Set toobad = Nothing
IUnknown(toobad).Release                                      ' c = 2
```

(continued)

```
toobad = 0
'' Set toughluck = forgetit
IUnknown(toughluck).Release                              ' c = 1
' Includes automatic AddRef
toughluck = IUnknown(forgetit).QueryInterface(IID_IHardway) ' c = 2
if toughluck = 0 Then Goto ErrorHandler
```

An assignment statement in Visual Basic translates into two statements in B--. The first B-- statement calls Release on the object variable being assigned to (the left side) to unreference whatever that variable referenced before. The second B-- statement calls QueryInterface on the object being assigned (the right side) and passes the type of the object being assigned to (the left side). If the types are compatible, the assignment succeeds and AddRef will be called on the assigned object variable to count the new reference.

Make sure you never call QueryInterface, Release, or AddRef on an object variable that is Nothing (0). Nothing has no methods, and calling them will get you in big trouble.

If you think this doesn't look all that bad, well, you're not seeing how many times I had to rewrite the code to get it past the human compilers, Glenn Hackney and Marc Young. Of course, we still don't know whether this code would compile on a real B-- compiler.

When reference counting goes wrong

Visual Basic always does reference counting behind the scenes whether you need it or not. For example, consider this code:

```
Dim toughluck As CHardway, toobad As CHardway
Set toughluck = New CHardway      ' c = 1
Set toobad = toughluck            ' c = 2
' Use toobad...
Set toobad = Nothing              ' c = 1
' Use toughluck...
```

When *toobad* is set, the reference count is incremented. When *toobad* is destroyed, the reference count is decremented. But you can see that, in this case, the use of *toobad* is nested within the lifetime of *toughluck*. There's really no need to mess with the reference count if you know the second reference is nested within the first. In C++ or B--, you can optimize this code by not doing the nested reference count. In Visual Basic, the reference count always happens behind the scenes whether you need it or not. This is no big deal because reference counting is cheap and situations in which you can determine at compile time that a reference is always nested are rare. Skipping this optimization in exchange for having the language take care of all the reference counting for you is a good trade-off.

In real Visual Basic code, references are rarely destroyed explicitly by setting an object variable to Nothing. Instead, they are created and destroyed automatically when you pass objects to procedures, return them from functions, set or get them with properties, or destroy other objects that hold references to them. Think of your program as a display panel in a science fiction movie where mysterious lights blink on and off in unintelligible patterns. You're supposed to follow the plot of the movie, not try to figure out exactly what makes each light go on or off.

But there is one situation in which you have to understand and override the default reference counting behavior. That situation involves circular references. Let's say you create object A. Object A creates object B. B and A have to communicate with each other, so A passes a reference of itself to B. B has a reference to A. A has a reference to B. Now you, the creator of A, have a reference to A, but you don't have a direct reference to B.

Now suppose you're done with A, so you attempt to terminate it, releasing your reference to A. You might wish that terminating A would cause A to release its reference to B, but A has no way to do this. B still has a reference to A, so A's reference count isn't zero and it can't terminate. B can't terminate because A still has a reference to B. And now you, the creator of A, no longer have a reference to A. Both A and B live on as independent objects and you have no way to destroy either of them.

If you're running in the Visual Basic environment, your program won't terminate normally when you unload its forms. You have to hit the End button to kill it. The independent objects will continue to eat up resources even though you're finished with them and don't want them in memory. This can cause lots of problems—in extreme cases you might even have to use the Task Manager to terminate rogue EXE servers.

A rogue reference count example

Let's look at the EdII program proposed early in Chapter 9. The example used throughout the chapter was a text editor called Edwina. EdII (Edwina II) was a proposed multiple document interface (MDI) enhancement to Edwina. EdII would have an XEditor control on each child form. When a child form was closed, its XEditor control would be destroyed, but EdII would keep running. The situation I'm about to describe applies to EdII because it happens only when the component goes away but the program continues.

Imagine that a user of EdII opens a child window. That window creates an instance of XEditor with a reference count of 1. Next the user selects Find from the Search menu and an FSearch form appears. The FSearch form needs a reference to the same XEditor instance so that it can pass search requests back to the editor. The XEditor instance now has a reference count of two. The XEditor instance created the FSearch form and keeps the only reference to it, but since the FSearch form is modal, it operates independently of its creator, the XEditor instance.

Now assume the user clicks the Close button on the FSearch form and the form unloads itself. The XEditor's reference is decremented and, since the form now has a reference count of zero, COM destroys it. Everything is fine.

But what if the user closes the MDI child window instead of the FSearch form? COM calls the Release method to destroy the child window's XEditor instance, but since the FSearch form still has an outstanding reference to the XEditor control, the reference count will not reach 0, the control will not be destroyed, and the Terminate event will not be called. The FSearch form and its XEditor instance will live on, using resources even though the form that was supposed to control it has disappeared. The FSearch form is like Frankenstein's monster— independent and out of control. The user sees the form, but not the editor being searched. Technically, this problem also occurs in Edwina, but because Edwina terminates at the same time that the XEditor instance is destroyed, Visual Basic automatically kills the rogue search form.

Since the XEditor instance creates the search form, we'd like XEditor to own FSearch and be able to terminate it. The lifetime of the search form should be bounded by the lifetime of XEditor. But there's no way for XEditor to know when it's being destroyed because the FSearch reference to XEditor keeps the Terminate event from being fired.

If we were writing XEditor and FSearch in C++ or B--, this would be a simple problem. Don't call AddRef and Release on the FSearch reference to XEditor. The XEditor on FSearch is actually owned by the creating XEditor, so there's no need for it to have a separate reference count. XEditor will destroy this form when it's ready. With this fix, the reference count of XEditor will be 1, not 2, and when the child window tries to destroy XEditor, the count will go to 0, the control will be destroyed, and XEditor's Terminate event can unload FSearch and set its reference variable to Nothing. Everything comes out right. Of course, we don't really want to manage all reference counting just to avoid this problem. We want a way to handle the problem in Visual Basic.

Not reference counting

Unfortunately, Visual Basic doesn't have a syntax for creating an uncounted reference. Any reference you create will be counted automatically. Fortunately, there's a way to immediately decrement that reference as if it never happened. Let's look at the code for how this is done in the FSearch form. We'll do this with a very unusual Property Get/Set pair. First let's look at the internal variable shared by the Get and Set procedures:

```
' Pointer for XEditor reference
Private pEditor As Long
```

Behind all the fancy talk, a COM object is nothing more than a pointer, and we'll have to treat it as a pointer if we want to avoid the normal behavior that is so convenient in most situations but so much in the way for owned objects.

We talked about how the XEditor control creates and initializes an FSearch form in Chapter 9. The key point is that XEditor passes a reference to itself to FSearch with the following line:

```
Set finddlg.Editor = Me
```

This calls the Editor Property Set procedure on FSearch. Let's see how it works:

```
Friend Property Set Editor(ByVal editorA As XEditor)
    ' Store an Editor pointer rather than an Editor object
    ' No AddRef for storing the pointer
    pEditor = ObjPtr(editorA)
End Property
```

The undocumented ObjPtr function (introduced with its cousins StrPtr and VarPtr in Chapter 2) returns a dumb pointer rather than a smart object. Dumb is the idea here. The Property Set procedure will be called just once—when FSearch is created. It stores the pointer and every time FSearch needs to use the XEditor instance, it calls the Property Get. That's where the real magic happens:

```
Friend Property Get Editor() As XEditor
    Dim editorI As XEditor
    ' Turn editorI into an illegal, uncounted interface pointer
    CopyMemory editorI, pEditor, 4
    ' Do NOT hit the End button here! You will crash!
    ' Assign to legal reference (VB AddRefs it)
    Set Editor = editorI
    ' Still do NOT hit the End button! You will still crash!
    ' Destroy the illegal reference
    CopyMemory editorI, 0&, 4
    ' OK, hit the End button if you must
    ' Internal XEditor reference goes out of scope (VB Releases it)
End Property
```

This looks dangerous—and it is. The whole point is to access XEditor without permanently incrementing its reference count. The local copy *editorI* will hold the unreferenced copy. The CopyMemory API procedure is used to copy the object pointer to the object, thus bypassing the normal object reference scheme. The *editorI* object will not have its reference count incremented. If you terminate your program early (by clicking End where I told you not to), Visual Basic will try to destroy the XEditor instance twice—once for the original reference and once for this uncounted reference. The first time it will call Release, which will decrement the reference and, finding a count of 0, destroy the object. The second time it will call Release on an object that no longer exists. Crash!

As long as you don't try to release it, the illegal reference works fine. You can assign it to a legal reference, such as the return value of the Property Get. What you can't do is let this illegal reference go out of scope. If you do, Visual Basic will release it, which will destroy the XEditor object, and the next time anyone tries to access XEditor from FSearch or anywhere else—crash! The purpose of the second CopyMemory is to set the illegal reference to Nothing (which happens to be a null pointer) without decreasing its reference count. Visual Basic won't call Release on Nothing, and *editorI* won't cause a crash when it goes out of scope.

COM RAQs

These are the answers to some Rarely Asked Questions that ought to be asked more often.

How can I make a copy of an object?

You can't.

As you should know by now, setting an object variable to another object variable makes another reference to the same object. It doesn't create a new object. But there might be times when you really do want multiple copies of an object. Surely there must be some language feature that allows you to make a copy if you really want one. Or failing that, there must be a way to hack it with CopyMemory.

Nope.

This problem isn't unique to Visual Basic. Every object-oriented language has it. The trouble is, the only thing that knows how to copy an object is the object itself. The language can't do it and the operating system can't do it. To understand why, let's look at what it would take to copy some classes.

The CSieve class described earlier in this chapter has four internal variables that keep track of the state of the sieve algorithm. If you could somehow copy those four internal variables from a *sieve* object to a *sieveNew* object of the same type, you'd have an exact duplicate. Even if you made the copy just after you discovered that 1427 is the prime number after 1423, you could keep calculating with *sieveNew* and it would tell you the same thing as *sieve*—that 1429 is the next prime number in line.

So why doesn't Visual Basic provide a CopyObject procedure that would do just that? Because it's more easily said than done. One of the private members of CSieve is a dynamic array whose size is determined at run time by the value of one of the other members. The language can't determine how you arrived at the size of the array, but in this case it could theoretically check the UBound and LBound to determine the size of the array. Some classes could be duplicated with a simple CopyMemory, but others would involve more complex calculations. It is possible to imagine a CopyObject procedure that could successfully duplicate CSieve objects.

But what about the CPictureGlass class described in Chapter 7? You might very well want to copy a transparent bitmap object and move the copy to another area of the screen. The CPictureGlass class has several private *hdc* variables. If you copied those variables to another object, you wouldn't really have a copy. The *hdc* variables of both objects would be referring to the same device contexts. If you changed the position of one copy, the other would move with it. To successfully copy the object, you'd need to create new device contexts for the copy, but give them the same state as the old ones. I'm not even going to think about what kind of Windows API calls that might require, but I can tell you there's no way the language could provide a CopyObject procedure to do it for you.

Copywise, every class is different. Classes that refer to files or registry entries or other complex state data must define for themselves what it means to copy that data. The only thing a language can do to help is to provide some standard mechanism for defining your own copy mechanism.

C++, for example, provides copy constructors and redefinition of the equality operator as standard means of defining copy semantics. While Visual Basic might someday get constructors, let's hope it never gets operator overloading. Java provides a more likely scenario. It provides (through a mechanism that need not concern us) a standard Clone method. Any class that wants to be cloneable can implement a Clone method that defines what copying means. A client of the class can call the standard Clone method to create a copy.

Visual Basic doesn't provide any standard mechanism for copying, but you could easily define your own standard. For example, for every class you think should be copyable, provide a method with the following signature:

```
Function Clone() As <Type>
```

Here's some air code showing how the Clone method might be implemented for the CSieve class:

```
Function Clone() As CSieve
    Dim sieveNew As New CSieve
    With sieveNew
        .MaxPrime = iMaxPrime
        .Primes = cPrime
        .Current = iCur
        .CopyArray af
    End With
    Set Clone = sieveNew
End Function
```

You can't actually write this method for the CSieve because MaxPrime is the only member used that currently exists. CSieve has a Primes property, but it's read only. To implement the Clone method, you need to add a Primes Property Let procedure, a Current Property Let Procedure, a Current Property Get procedure, and a CopyArray method. Since no one other than you will need these members, you can make them Friends. Without these Friend members, you have no means to create a duplicate object.

The Clone standard could even work in situations where you don't know whether the objects can be cloned. For example, you could use code like this:

```
On Error Resume Next
For Each obj In oldobjects
    ' Copies cloneable objects, ignores the rest
    newobjects.Add obj.Clone
Next
```

In real life this isn't as much of a problem as you might expect. Most objects don't need to be copied, and when they do, you can provide a method that copies them.

What's the difference between ByVal and ByRef object parameters?
You can use ByVal and ByRef on object parameters just as you can with intrinsic types. They look the same. You use them for the same reasons. But they work very differently. And their performance is different, depending on the type of COM marshaling being done.

Let's review how ByVal and ByRef work for intrinsic types. Assume the following test procedure:

```
Sub TestIntParam(ByRef iRefp As Integer, ByVal iValp As Integer)
    iRefp = 5: iValp = 5
End Sub
```

You call it with the following code:

```
    Dim iRef As Integer, iVal As Integer
    iRef = 4: iVal = 4
    TestIntParam iRef, iVal
    Debug.Print "ByRef integer: " & iRef
    Debug.Print "ByVal integer: " & iVal
```

The results are:

```
ByRef integer: 5
ByVal integer: 4
```

Changes made internally to the ByVal parameter have no effect on the outside integer because it's a different copy.

The same thing happens with strings, although, internally, they work quite differently. If you pass a string by value, Visual Basic has to allocate a new string and copy each character. When you write this:

```
Sub DoString(ByVal s As String)
    ⋮
```

Visual Basic does this:

```
Sub RealDoString(ByRef sParam As String)
    Dim s As String
    s = sParam
        ⋮
```

This extra work is more expensive (see the "Performance" sidebar on page 551) so normally, Visual Basic programmers pass strings by reference and take extra care not to modify arguments intended for input only. But if you really need a temporary string and you don't want changes to it to affect the original, you might as well let Visual Basic create that string through a ByVal parameter rather than declaring and creating it yourself.

This leads back to our original topic—passing objects by value. In the following example, assume that the CParam class has a string property called Name.

```
Sub TestObjParam(ByRef refP As CParam, ByVal valP As CParam, _
                 ByRef refNewP As CParam, ByVal valNewP As CParam)
    Dim refNew As New CParam, valNew As New CParam
    ' Change properties
    refNew.Name = "Changed": valNew.Name = "Changed"
    ' Change objects
    Set refNewP = refNew: Set valNewP = valNew
    refP.Name = "Changed": valP.Name = "Changed"
End Sub
```

You call the test procedure like this:

```
    Dim ref As New CParam, val As New CParam
    Dim refNew As New CParam, valNew As New CParam
    ref.Name = "Unchanged": val.Name = "Unchanged"
    refNew.Name = "Unchanged": valNew.Name = "Unchanged"
    TestObjParam ref, val, refNew, valNew
    Debug.Print "ByRef object: " & ref.Name
    Debug.Print "ByVal object: " & val.Name
    Debug.Print "ByRef new object: " & refNew.Name
    Debug.Print "ByVal new object: " & valNew.Name
```

The results are:

```
ByRef object: Changed
ByVal object: Changed
ByRef new object: Changed
ByVal new object: Unchanged
```

At first you might think that passing an object variable by value would cause the compiler to make a copy of the object just like it makes a copy of a string. Changing properties of the ByVal object wouldn't affect the outside object. However, as I pointed out in the last section, Visual Basic doesn't know how to make a copy of the object and couldn't do so even if it wanted to. But it doesn't want to because you didn't pass an object by value—you passed an object variable by value. Visual Basic copies the object variable, not the object. The copied object variable still references the same object, and any changes to the object still can be seen from the outside.

| NOTE | All bets are off when you pass objects of type Object. Late-bound objects work by different rules because it's not a simple matter for Visual Basic to decide what you really want when you change the object variable. I'm not going to get into the details because I've been trying to persuade you not to pass late-bound objects around anyway. If you really need to do this, just be aware that you'll need to do further research to figure out the different rules. |

The second part of the test demonstrates that changing the object variable inside the procedure affects the outside variable passed by reference, but has no effect on the outside variable passed by value. That might not be the obvious behavior, but you can see that it's right if you think it through.

Now for the performance issues. When you pass an object variable by value, a new copy of that variable is created and set to the same object. You write this:

```
Sub DoObject(ByVal obj As CParam)
    ⋮
```

Visual Basic does this behind the scenes:

```
Sub RealDoObject(ByRef objParam As CParam)
    Dim obj As New CParam
    Set obj = objParam
    ⋮
```

The hidden Set statement causes an AddRef to increment the reference count. A Release is done when the object variable goes out of scope. There's a cost for the hidden AddRef and Release. As long as you're dealing with local or in-process classes, it's more efficient to pass objects by reference. If you're changing only the object, not the object variable, you might as well pass by reference. This is the normal case.

Things are a little different when you pass objects between processes, threads, or machines. In this case, the cost of AddRef and Release is dwarfed by the cost of marshaling the data across the boundary. If you pass a parameter ByVal, you're saying that the parameter has to be marshaled across the boundary, but it doesn't need to come back. If you pass by reference, you're saying that the transfer has to go both ways. If the procedure won't modify the object variable, it's much more efficient to pass it by value.

Can I get the current reference count?

No.

The reference count is none of your business. You're not supposed to know its value. The only thing that matters is whether it's zero, and that only matters to Visual Basic, not to you. Every class decides how it wants to store and maintain the reference count. A COM object can be written in any number of languages, and different languages can arrange private class data differently. Even if the class made the obvious decision to store the reference count in a member variable, you couldn't know for sure where the variable was in relation to the start of the class.

Yes, but can I get the reference count?

What do you want with the damn reference count anyway?

Well, I'm debugging a Visual Basic object that is supposed to go away, but it doesn't. If I could check the reference count at various points in the program, maybe I could tell what's going wrong.

OK, but don't call me if you have trouble:

```
Public Function VB5GetRefCount(ByVal pUnk As IUnknown) As Long
    If pUnk Is Nothing Then Exit Function
    ' Get count from magic offset in object
    CopyMemory VB5GetRefCount, ByVal ObjPtr(pUnk) + 4, 4
    ' Adjust to account for references to parameter
    VB5GetRefCount = VB5GetRefCount - 3
End Function
```

It's not in VBCore or anywhere else on the CD. You have to type it in yourself. If it fails, it might be because your hair color is different from mine. I'm not even going to try to explain why it works. It won't work for out-of-process objects. It probably won't work for objects written in languages other than Visual Basic. And it might not work for Visual Basic objects in future versions. All I can say is that it worked for me on at least one occasion for at least one class written in Visual Basic version 5.

Why can't I pass structures as public method parameters or properties?

Shut up and eat your mush.

Wait a minute! C++ programmers can pass structures to COM objects. Why can't Visual Basic programmers do the same?

Because C++ programmers write their own type libraries. The complete type library syntax lets you marshall many kinds of language-specific data. Visual Basic creates type libraries for you automatically behind the scenes, but it knows only how to use the standard COM Automation types, which just happen to be exactly the same as the Visual Basic types.

While it's true that C++ programmers can pass structures, arrays of various sorts, unsigned integers, and simple null-terminated strings (LPSTR type) through COM servers, it's also true that such servers can be recognized only by clients developed in C++ or other low-level languages. Making a component language-specific defeats one of the main purposes of COM. There might be a few cases where a C++ to C++ connection is exactly what is needed, but generally controls and other general-purpose components should follow the COM Automation standards so that they can be used by any client.

But why doesn't COM Automation recognize structures?

Well, it could, and I've heard rumors that it will in some future version. But what will it allow you to put in those structures? Different languages handle data types differently—especially strings and arrays. The Windows API already uses some C-specific data structures that are very difficult to use from Visual Basic. We don't need more of that confusion. Even if COM Automation allows structures in the future, those structures will probably be limited to a subset of data types that any COM Automation client can recognize.

OK, but that doesn't help me with my code. I need to pass some structured data in parameters and properties. How am I going to do it?

Well, there are several workarounds. First, if your objects are local, you can pass UDTs around anywhere you like as long as you make your methods and properties Friends. The Friend keyword bypasses the normal COM marshalling system. A Friend parameter or property can have any type—just like a private procedure or a procedure in a standard module.

That's handy to know, and I'll keep it in mind for future projects. But right now I need to pass structured data to an ActiveX component. How am I going to do it?

There's a hack, and there's a solution, but you probably won't like either one. The hack is to pass your data in byte arrays. Let's say your client has a UDT with some structured data that you want to pass around. You ReDim an array of bytes with the same size as the structure, then CopyMemory the UDT to the array and pass the array to the server as a property or method parameter. The server knows that the array actually represents a UDT, so it declares a UDT variable of the right type and CopyMemorys the array to the UDT. Alternatively, both sides can treat the data as a blob, using the byte access techniques described in "Reading and Writing Blobs" on page 277, to get or put data at the appropriate offsets. This hack isn't much fun, but there are times when it's worth the trouble.

Usually it's better to change your mind rather than try to fit your code into old mindsets. If you've got a design that uses lots of UDTs, chances are you're trying to fit an old structured programming design into an object-oriented mold without much work. Think again, then do the right thing. Redesign your structures as classes. Turn the fields of your UDTs into properties. Convert procedures that take UDT parameters into methods. In most cases, you'll end up with a better design anyway, and you might even save coding time in the long run.

Interfaces Everywhere

Interfaces are the latest fad in operating system design. You access system features (or let the system access your features) through interfaces rather than through API functions. Since interfaces are what make Visual Basic classes tick, you'd think that system interfaces and Visual Basic would be a good match.

Unfortunately, most system interface designers seem to work in C or C++ and assume that everyone else does the same. Of course, designers of API functions often have the same short-sighted view, but Visual Basic provides the Declare, Type, and Const statements as a means of bridging the API gap. There's no such bridge between system interfaces and Visual Basic. The only way to make system interfaces available to Visual Basic programs is through type libraries—and even then you have to lie about the types.

IShellLink—Shortcuts the Long Way

As an example, let's consider two system interfaces—IShellLink and IPersistFile. IShellLink is provided by Windows as a means of managing shortcuts—the icons on your desktop that represent programs, directories, printers, and other system resources. IPersistFile is provided by COM as a means for classes to make themselves persistent, that is, to store themselves on disk. The only reason we're interested in IPersistFile is that the standard implementation of IShellLink uses it to save shell links (shortcuts).

Creating shortcuts is such a useful task that you might expect Windows to provide a simple API function to do it. Since Windows doesn't, you might expect that the designers of Visual Basic would fill the gap. But they don't either, or at least not directly. They do it themselves, but they don't give you a legal means to do it.

There's a function called fCreateShellLink in the VB5STKIT.DLL provided with the setup kit. If you're willing to make sure all your customers keep this file even after setup, and if you aren't worried about changing the Declare for every version, and if you can figure out the undocumented parameters, there it is. But why don't they just put it in the language and document it? I guess then I wouldn't have this excuse to tell how to wrap the Visual Basic-hostile IShellLink interface in a nice, friendly CShortcut class.

I did this once before. In the December, 1996, issue of *Visual Basic Programmer's Journal,* I described how to create a CShortCut class in C++ using the ActiveX Template Library. At the time, I believed it was impossible to use interfaces from Visual Basic. I was half right. You need to write a Visual Basic–friendly type library for the interface, and you have to write it in a foreign language that doesn't look much like Visual Basic. But once you figure out how to write the type library (or get one off the CD of this book), you can use it in Visual Basic.

By the way, I didn't discover this technique on my own. Brian Harris worked it out with a little help from Matt Curland, and the results are in sample programs in the following directories of your Visual Basic CD:

>   \Tools\Unsupprt\ShellLnk

>   \Tools\Unsupprt\IHandler

There's no documentation for these unsupported samples, but hardcore programmers could probably figure out the techniques from the program comments even if I weren't about to describe them.

Interface Type Libraries

Interface type libraries can be written either in Object Description Language (ODL) or in Interface Description Language (IDL). ODL is the language preferred by the Visual Basic group and they provide the MKTYPLIB compiler on the Visual Basic CD. IDL is the language preferred by the C++ group and they provide the MIDL compiler with their product. Both of these compilers are poorly documented and bedeviled by bugs, but I prefer the new bugs in MIDL to the old bugs in MKTYPLIB. Since this is a Visual Basic book, I won't go very far into the details of IDL or ODL. If you have a little C background, you can learn a lot from examples and comments in the source to the Windows API type library, which is provided with this book. The CD also has an article about writing type libraries with ODL, but the emphasis is on API functions rather than interfaces.

To give you some idea of what I'm talking about, I'll have to show part of the IDL source for IShellLink. You can see the whole thing in the SHLOBJ.IDL file on the CD:

```
[   odl,
    helpstring("Visual Basic version of IShellLink interface"),
#ifdef UNICODE
    uuid(000214F9-0000-0000-C000-000000000046)
#else
    uuid(000214EE-0000-0000-C000-000000000046)
#endif
]
interface IVBShellLink : IUnknown {

    [ helpstring("Retrieves the path and filename … ") ]
    HRESULT GetPath([in, out] LPTSTR pszFile,
                    [in] int cchMaxPath,
                    [in, out] LPVOID pfd,
                    [in] ESLGP fFlags);

    [ helpstring("Retrieves the list of … identifiers") ]
    HRESULT GetIDList([out, retval] LPITEMIDLIST * ppidl);
    [ helpstring("Sets the list of shell link item identifiers") ]
    HRESULT SetIDList([in] LPCITEMIDLIST pidl);

    [ helpstring("Retrieves the … description string") ]
    HRESULT GetDescription([in, out] LPTSTR pszName,
                           [in] int cchMaxName);
    [ helpstring("Sets the shell link description string") ]
    HRESULT SetDescription([in] LPCTSTR pszName);

    [ helpstring("Retrieves the … working directory") ]
    HRESULT GetWorkingDirectory([in, out] LPTSTR pszDir,
                                [in] int cchMaxPath);
    [ helpstring("Sets the … working directory") ]
    HRESULT SetWorkingDirectory([in] LPCTSTR pszDir);

    [ helpstring("Retrieves the … command-line arguments") ]
    HRESULT GetArguments(LPTSTR pszArgs, int cchMaxPath);
    [ helpstring("Sets the … command-line arguments") ]
    HRESULT SetArguments([in] LPCTSTR pszArgs);

    [ propget, helpstring("Retrieves or sets the … hot key") ]
    HRESULT Hotkey([out, retval] WORD *pwHotkey);
    [ propput ]
    HRESULT Hotkey([in] WORD wHotkey);
    ⋮
    [ helpstring("Resolves a shell link … ") ]
    HRESULT Resolve([in] HWND hwnd,
                    [in] ESLR fFlags);
```

(continued)

```
    [ helpstring("Sets the … path and filename") ]
    HRESULT SetPath([in] LPCTSTR pszFile);
};
```

This shows a few key parts of the interface. In real life, there's no such thing as part of an interface. Every method and property must be present with parameters of exactly the right size in exactly the right order. You must use the *uuid* attribute to provide the correct GUID, and you must derive the interface from either IUnknown or from an interface that derives from IUnknown. Don't worry about what derive means; just use the syntax shown above. Once you meet those requirements, the rest can be lies.

My version of the interface lies about the method names and parameters. Just as we can lie with aliases in Declare statements, we can lie to improve interfaces. If you can get your hands on the original C header file SHLOBJ.H from which I created SHLOBJ.IDL, you can see what kind of whoppers I'm telling. For example, the official names of the Hotkey property Get and Let procedures are GetHotkey and SetHotkey, and normally they don't have the propget and propset attributes because C and C++ don't support properties. I'd like to turn GetDescription and SetDescription into properties, too, but because they use LPTSTR parameters for strings, the Get and Set must be different and can't be converted to properties.

I'm also lying about some of the types. The WORD type used by the Hotkey property and the DWORD type used by the Resolve method are unsigned integers in the original interface, but I make them signed integers compatible with Visual Basic's Integer and Long types by using alias features that you don't really want to know about.

The IVBShellLink interface provides a template for defining the methods and properties of an imaginary class. A shell link file is just a binary file, and, theoretically, we could figure out its format and write the code to create and read such files. Also, we could use this code to implement the methods and properties of IVBShellLink. But Windows already implements this interface. We don't need to reinvent the wheel; we just need some way to hook up the Windows implementation to our template. Here's the type library syntax:

```
[    uuid(00021401-0000-0000-C000-000000000046),
     helpstring("Visual Basic CShellLink class")
]
coclass CShellLink {
    [default]
    interface IVBShellLink;
};
```

COM uses the term *coclass* to describe what Visual Basic calls a class. The Windows developers who created the system implementation of IShellLink gave it a magic GUID number starting with 00021401, and we can reuse their implementation by declaring a coclass with the magic number.

There's one more piece to the puzzle. The Windows implementation of IShellLink depends on an interface called IPersistFile. You can look this one up in OAOBJ.IDL on the CD. We'll only be dealing with its Load and Save methods.

This should give you another piece of the COM language puzzle. When you create the CJumpStart class, Visual Basic creates a default interface named _CJumpStart with all the methods and properties you give your class. It creates a co-class named CJumpStart that implements the default interface. It generates hidden GUIDs for both the interface and the coclass and puts them in a hidden type library. Now you're ready to write your own COM language that competes with Visual Basic.

From CShellLink to CShortcut

Using the CShellLink coclass is halfway between using Visual Basic objects and using API functions. The syntax looks right, but the methods seem to be written by a child who hasn't learned how to speak proper Visual Basic yet. So rather than forcing our users to decipher the illiterate scrawls of CShellLink, we'll filter them through a more intelligible CShortcut wrapper class.

Figure 10-4 on the following page shows a sample program that uses CShortcut. I'm not going to get into this much except to say that the GUI doodads on the form represent CShortcut properties. To create a shortcut, you set some properties on the form and click the Save button. A shortcut with those properties will be written to the specified location. Normally, you'll save shortcuts to the desktop, but you might also write them to the Programs submenu on the Start menu, or to any other place you choose.

The controls in the Target File frame normally allow you to specify the program or other file that the shortcut will point to, but when you select an LNK file, everything works backwards. The Resolve method is automatically called on LNK files to get the shortcut object. Once the object is updated, the form is filled out with the resulting properties.

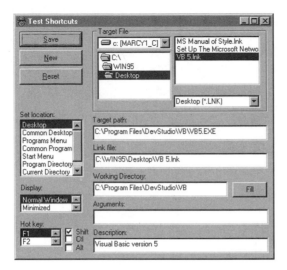

Figure 10-4. *The Test Shortcuts program.*

Since the example is a little bit messy, I'll show you some simpler code that creates a new shortcut:

```
With shortcut
    .Path = "C:\HelpMe\HelpMe.Exe"
    .Arguments = "Right now"
    .DisplayMode = edmMaximized
    sLink = .Save(edstDesktop)
End With
```

This illustrates how to create a shortcut—set all the desired properties and then save them. It takes only a few more lines of code to open a link file, change the display setting, and then execute the target program:

```
With shortcut
    .Resolve GetDesktop & "HelpMe.LNK"
    .DisplayMode = edmMinimized      ' Change to minimize
    sPath = .Save(edstDesktop)       ' Save the changes
    Shell sPath                      ' Run the shortcut program
End With
```

You might well argue that this object-oriented interface isn't really any easier than a couple of procedures with optional arguments. OK. The GShort module (SHORT.CLS) has the procedures you want: CreateShortcut and UpdateShortcut.

CreateShortcut is simpler in the functional format:

```
CreateShortcut edstDesktop, "C:\HelpMe\HelpMe.Exe", edmMinimized
```

Use the named arguments if you want to give lots of arguments in any order. You can probably guess the simple implementation:

```
Sub CreateShortcut(LinkFile As Variant, _
                   Path As String, _
                   Optional DisplayMode As Long = edmNormal, _
                   Optional WorkingDirectory As String, _
                   Optional Arguments As String, _
                   Optional Description As String, _
                   Optional IconIndex As Long = 0)
    Dim shortcut As New CShortcut
    With shortcut
        .Path = Path
        .WorkingDirectory = WorkingDirectory
        .DisplayMode = DisplayMode
        .Arguments = Arguments
        .Description = Description
        .Icon = IconIndex
        .Save LinkFile
    End With
End Sub
```

UpdateShortcut is messier because it must return all its data through reference parameters. I prefer the object-oriented format. The implementation looks like a backward version of CreateShortcut. Check it out in SHORT.CLS.

CHALLENGE My shortcut example has a HotKey list box and check boxes for Shift, Control, and Alt keys, but this interface looks crude when compared to the user interface on the shortcut properties dialog box. The Shortcut Key field looks like an ordinary text box, but when you press keys, it automatically enters the text for the corresponding keys and shift masks. It wouldn't take much to give your applications the same feature. An XHotkey control would let you easily add hot key functionality to any program. The shortcut properties dialog box also has a Change Icon button that displays all the icons embedded in the current EXE and allows you to browse for icon files that you might want to attach to the shortcut. You could write a CIconPicker class that provides the same behavior. Use the ExtractIcon API function (see Chapter 8) to create the list of embedded icons.

The CShortcut Class

Earlier I mentioned a CShortCut server written in C++. Notice that the name of the Visual Basic version has a different case. Of course, the real difference between these components is their GUIDs. Their interfaces are actually very similar, and their implementations aren't much different either. Aside from petty language differences such as curly braces, the difference is that dealing with Variants and Strings is a whole lot easier in Visual Basic. The C++ version is on the CD if you want to compare them.

The IShellLink interface seems to be designed specifically to cause trouble for Visual Basic programmers. On the one hand it ignores interface capabilities, such as properties, that would make access easy. Furthermore, it uses types, such as unsigned integers, that Visual Basic doesn't understand. Like many API functions, it's designed to enable every possible feature, not to be convenient or easy to use. In other words, it needs a Visual Basic–friendly wrapper:

```
Private link As New CShellLink
```

CShellLink wraps the IShellLink interface and *link* represents a particular shell link. The main purpose of the CShortcut class is to transfer the properties of the *link* object to and from a corresponding LNK file.

The Save method

CShortcut saves its link object to a file using the Save method:

```
' Link file parameter is Variant to accept any of these:
'       edstDesktop            - Put on desktop
'       edstCommonDesktop      - Put on shared desktop
'       edstPrograms           - Put on programs menu
'       edstCommonPrograms     - Put on shared programs menu
'       edstStartMenu          - Put on start menu
'       edstCurrent            - Put in current directory
'       edstPath               - Put in same directory as target file
'       [directory]            - Put in hardcoded path
'       [file.LNK]             - Put in hardcoded file
Function Save(vLinkFile As Variant) As String
    Dim sLink As String
    ' Convert constant or directory to full path
    sLink = FixLocation(vLinkFile)
    If sLink = sEmpty Then ErrRaise eeFileNotFound

    ' Save the object to disk
    MCasts.IVBPersistFile(link).Save sLink, APITRUE
    Save = sLink
End Function
```

Since the link file might be passed in as a constant representing a standard location, the method returns the real path in case the caller needs to locate the link file.

Interface casting

The Windows implementation of the IShellLink interface also implements the IPersistFile interface. You need to call the Save method of IPersistFile to save your changes to the link file. The Visual Basic way of doing this is to create a separate object variable for the persistent object:

```
Dim persist As IVBPersistFile
Set persist = link
persist.Save sLink, APITRUE
```

This technique is a little messy because it leaves unnecessary object variables lying around. Most object-oriented languages support a casting syntax so that you can typecast one object to another type with which it is polymorphic. The syntax varies depending on the language and on whether inheritance is used, but a compatible Visual Basic syntax might look like this:

```
IVBPersistFile(link).Save sLink, APITRUE
```

Or perhaps Visual Basic could have provided an operator and made the syntax look like this:

```
link@IVBPersistFile.Save sLink, APITRUE
```

Unfortunately, Visual Basic doesn't support either of these syntaxes, but you can fake it by writing a typecasting function. The global module GCasts contains casting functions for all the interfaces provided by VBCore and by the Windows API type library. Here's an example:

```
Function IVBPersistFile(obj As IVBPersistFile) As IVBPersistFile
    Set IVBPersistFile = obj
End Function
```

All the other casting functions look exactly like this one except for the function name, which is also the name of the interface type being typecast. Since the CShortcut class resides in the same component as the casting functions, you must further qualify the casting function with the name of the MCasts object as explained in Chapter 5.

```
MCasts.IVBPersistFile(link).Save sLink, APITRUE
```

Your own references to casting functions won't need this qualification.

By the way, APITRUE is a C-style True with a value of 1, indicating something that matters for certain uses of IPersistFile. It has no effect in the architecture of CShortcut.

The Resolve method

Resolve is the opposite of Save. You pass it the name of the LNK file you want to open. You can also pass optional parameters that control what happens if the LNK file you specify doesn't contain a valid shortcut:

```
' Flags control behavior if LNK file reference can't be resolved:
'    SLR_ANY_MATCH - Display a dialog (with hWnd parameter as parent
'                    window) asking user whether to search for reference
'    SLR_NO_UI     - Search the disk for the time period specified by
'                    TimeOut parameter
Sub Resolve(sFileA As String, _
            Optional Flags As ESLR = SLR_ANY_MATCH, _
            Optional hWnd As Long = hNull, _
            Optional TimeOut As Integer = 0)
    ' Load from LNK file and resolve
    MCasts.IVBPersistFile(link).Load sFileA, STGM_DIRECT
    If Flags = SLR_NO_UI And TimeOut > 0 Then
        Flags = Flags Or MBytes.LShiftDWord(TimeOut, 16)
    End If
    link.Resolve hWnd, Flags
End Sub
```

Sometimes LNK files get out of date when a user moves the executable file that the shortcut references. The default flag, SLR_ANY_MATCH, specifies that a dialog box will ask the user what to do for unresolved shortcuts. The SLR_NO_UI specifies that an appropriate (we hope) action will be taken without user interaction.

CShortcut properties

The CShortcut properties work as you would expect, except that the underlying CShellLink uses API-style strings while the friendly versions have to use Visual Basic strings. The Arguments property is typical:

```
Property Get Arguments() As String
    Dim s As String
    s = String$(cMaxPath, 0)
    link.GetArguments s, cMaxPath
    Arguments = MUtility.StrZToStr(s)
End Property

Property Let Arguments(sArgumentsA As String)
    link.SetArguments sArgumentsA
End Property
```

The Property Get works like any API string access function. You pass the underlying *link* object a string buffer and a maximum length. It fills the buffer with a null-terminated string, which you convert to a Visual Basic string. The other properties are similar. Some of them have a little more code to set defaults or validate input.

What's next

If you can figure out how to use the IShellLink interface, you should be able to use other interfaces, starting with the new ones introduced by Windows 95 and now available in Unicode variations for Windows NT 4.0.

The most important interface behind what you see on your screen and in Windows Explorer is IShellFolder. It's the manager behind the new object hierarchy starting on your desktop with My Computer and moving up to the directories and files on your system. Ideally, this new paradigm would be everywhere by now. All sorts of programs, not just Windows Explorer, would be organizing objects in similar hierarchies. You do see that in a few programs, but it certainly hasn't become pervasive. My theory of why starts with the semi-random name assigned to this hierarchy—the shell namespace. Nobody understands what it is, much less how to program it. How can you take something seriously when its main data structures are named PIDL and SHITEMID. Furthermore, the samples for it are written in tortured C, not C++. As for Visual Basic, well, this is probably the most Visual Basic–hostile interface you'll ever encounter, and frankly I don't think it's all that great for C++ either. Nevertheless, we'll do a few things with IShellFolder in Chapter 11.

IShellFolder is intimately related to other new interfaces that let you create helpers for any new document types your programs create. For example, IContextMenu lets you access the context menus for registered file types. IShellPropSheetExt lets you write property sheet extensions that display information about the file type when users right click on a file and select Properties from the context menu. Context menu handlers, drag-and-drop handlers, property sheet handlers, and file viewers are not the same as similar features in your application because they affect your documents, not your program. In fact, your program might not be running when the shell extension goes into action. The idea was that everybody who creates a new document type would automatically provide all the appropriate handlers. Unfortunately, they forgot to make it easy. I was hoping to get around to that for this book, but I guess I'll leave it to you. Of course, by the time you're ready to start, new interfaces associated with Internet Explorer and future versions of Windows might lure you away from the task. Let's hope they make these new interfaces easier to program.

Next on my list is IStorage. The Visual Basic file I/O system is nothing to brag about. It carries a lot of compatibility baggage and lacks some fundamental features, such as the ability to commit changes without closing an open file. COM provides the IStorage interface and some related API functions as an enhanced I/O system that does everything normal file systems do plus a few other tricks you've never seen before. Even if it didn't do that extra stuff, it would still be a better, more object-oriented system than the one built into Visual Basic. Alas, you'll have to fight with COM to get it to work with Visual Basic. Too bad. But don't let that stop you. You might even want to combine IStorage and IShell-Folder to create a complete object hierarcy representing all the system objects and all of their contents.

Something else you might think about is implementing ITypeInfo in order to create object browsing tools. Don't bother. Visual Basic comes with the TypeLib Information component (TLBINF32.DLL), which already provides everything you need and more. This is the same component that provides all the information used by Visual Basic's Object Browser and other browsing features. The only problem is figuring out how to use it. There's no documentation. There's no support. But all you have to do is load the DLL in the References dialog box. Then look at the members with the Object Browser. You'll have to figure the object hierarchy from the names only. It's not a project for the faint of heart, but I'd rather try to decipher this DLL than try to implement ITypeInfo from scratch.

Visual Basic comes with an ActiveX Control Interface Wizard that fakes inheritance of controls with delegation, but it doesn't do anything about faking inheritance of classes. All you need to do is use the TypeLib Information component to read in all the properties, methods, and enums of the public class you want to enhance. Use this information to create the delegated members of classes in the same way that the wizard does it for controls. It's one more project I wanted to do for this book, but never got around to.

NOTE At this point you may be feeling annoyed. If I really know how to do this stuff, why don't I tell you the details? Why don't I do it myself? I have to plead guilty. In fact, I'm downright embarrassed. My feeble excuse is that half of the problem involves type libraries, and since this book is about Visual Basic, I don't have to explain the foreign IDL and ODL languages in detail. Besides, I give you hints (if you study them long and hard enough) in the CShortcut example. But the real reason is that I ran out of time. Sorry.

Registry Blues

Mastery of the registry is one of the skills necessary to join the elite group of Hardcore COM programmers. Technically, the registry isn't directly related to COM, and it can be used in many contexts unrelated to COM. But the reverse isn't true. You won't get far understanding COM without being able to at least examine, and often modify, registry entries.

The registry has been around for quite a while, but usually you could ignore it under 16-bit Windows. The fatal flaw of the 16-bit registry was its 64-KB capacity.

Certain programs filled up a good chunk of that all by themselves, leaving you with little idea of how much registry space was left or what would happen if it overflowed. For all practical purposes, the 16-bit registry was left for OLE applications, which used it transparently.

It's a different story in Win32. You now have all the space you need. Microsoft strongly recommends that you stop using INI files and similar techniques and instead make the registry your one-stop data storage mechanism. This is more easily said than done. There are two problems. First, the registry functions are among the most quirky and difficult to use in the Windows API. Second, even if you figure out how to use them, you still have to figure out what's where in the registry.

Registry Tools

The names and behavior of the registry functions have little relation to my mental picture of the registry. One glance at the Registry Editor tells you that it contains a tree data structure, but unfortunately, the Windows designers chose to call the registry elements keys and values instead of branches and leaves, nodes and items, or some other evocative names. I'm sure this terminology is a metaphor for some real life object that has keys of keys or keys of values, but so far I haven't run into one of those objects.

The way I imagine it, the registry is a tree of *node* objects. Each node can contain more nested node objects, and it can contain one or more *item* objects. Every node is named, but often you can access a node more efficiently through its handle.

The first item of any node (the default) is unnamed, and it might or might not have a value. In 16-bit Windows, that was the end of the story. In 32-bit Windows, a node can contain multiple named items in addition to the first unnamed one. Generally, you'll only find multiple items on the final nodes (those without nested nodes), but there's no rule to that effect, and if you choose to put lists of items on your middle level nodes, you won't be alone.

Items are where the registry data is actually stored. The most common formats are strings, integers, and binary data—String, Long, and Byte array in Visual Basic terms. The 16-bit registry supported only string items, and you'll see compatibility remnants such as integers stored as strings rather than as integers.

This structure might seem inconsistent, but that's the idea. You're supposed to be able to put anything you want anywhere in the registry. And you can. But the price is that when inspecting the registry, you have to be ready to extract anything from anywhere.

The functions required to do anything from any language are necessarily complex, but I've simplified them at two levels. First, the MRegTool module (REG-TOOL.BAS) makes some of the messier API functions more consistent and less

Visual Basic–hostile, but still leaves the look and feel of a functional API. The CRegNodes and CRegItems collections provide an easier object-oriented interface.

NOTE Some of the API functions are inherited from 16-bit Windows but have enhanced 32-bit versions with Ex on the end (RegCreateKeyEx rather than RegCreateKey). Don't even think about using the old versions. Assuming any relationship between the 16-bit and 32-bit registries leads to madness. If you think you see functions called RegCreateKey, RegOpenKey, RegEnumKey, RegQueryValue, and RegSetValue in the Win32 documentation, it's an illusion. Only the Ex versions really exist. I made this myth a reality in the Windows API type library. If you really want to use the old compatibility versions, you'll have to write the Declare statements yourself.

Opening and reading keys

There's a standard pattern to reading registry values, but it's not as obvious as reading from a more typical tree structure such as the file directory tree. You can't simply pass a string indicating the point at which you want to enter the tree. You have to worry about handles to root keys, handles to subkeys, and value types. Let's look at the simplest useful example.

GetRegStr gets the most common type of registry data—a string. Usually, if you want a registry string, you know exactly what you're looking for and where to find it. You don't want to mess with key handles or data types. So if you want some Control Panel data, just ask for it:

```
Debug.Print GetRegStr("Control Panel\Desktop", "IconTitleFaceName")
```

Here's the function that makes this possible:

```
Function GetRegStr(sKey As String, sItem As String, _
                   Optional ByVal hRoot As EROOTKEY _
                     = HKEY_CURRENT_USER) As String
    Dim e As Long, hKey As Long, s As String
    ' Open a subkey
    e = RegOpenKeyEx(hRoot, sKey, 0, KEY_QUERY_VALUE, hKey)
    ApiRaiseIf e
    Dim ert As EREGTYPE, c As Long
    ' Get the length and make sure it's a string
    e = RegQueryValueEx(hKey, sItem, 0&, ert, 0&, c)
    ApiRaiseIf e
    BugAssert ert = REG_SZ
    If c <> 0 Then
        s = String$(c - 1, 0)
```

```
        ' Read the string
        e = RegQueryValueExStr(hKey, sItem, 0&, ert, s, c)
        ApiRaiseIf e
    End If
    RegCloseKey hKey
    GetRegStr = s
End Function
```

First you call RegOpenKeyEx to open a subkey of one of the root keys. There are six root keys, of which you'll generally use HKEY_CLASSES_ROOT for COM data and HKEY_CURRENT_USER or HKEY_LOCAL_MACHINE for general data. Most of the juiciest string data is in HKEY_CURRENT_USER, so GetRegStr makes it a default argument.

One unusual thing about registry functions is that they always return a Win32 error code rather than returning useful data and letting you check errors with GetLastError (Err.LastDllError in Visual Basic). My registry wrappers use the ApiRaiseIf procedure (see "Turning API Errors into Basic Errors" on page 251) to turn any non-zero error codes into raised Visual Basic errors.

Next you call RegQueryValueEx to get the size and type of the item. This is where the messy part usually begins because you have to take different actions depending on what type you come up with. But this function assumes the caller wants a string and asserts for anyone foolish enough to pass an invalid request. A second call to a string-specific RegQueryValueEx alias gets the data. Having got what we came for, we close the subkey handle and leave.

Reading values

If the registry portion of the Windows API had been written in Visual Basic, everyone (including C++ programmers) would have an easier time. The problem is that a registry value can be any of several types, but C++ doesn't have a type that can contain any of several types. Visual Basic has Variant. We can make the registry API functions much simpler by mapping the messy parts of getting typeless types into Variant wrappers.

When using raw API functions, you can get values by name with RegQuery-ValueEx or by index number with RegEnumValue. Normally, you use RegEnum-Value to enumerate through all the items in a node. I wrap these functions in the more Visual Basic–friendly GetRegValue and GetRegValueNext functions. These functions look pretty much the same, so I'll show only GetRegValueNext:

```
Function GetRegValueNext(ByVal hKey As Long, _
                    i As Long, _
                    sName As String, _
                    vValue As Variant) As Long
    Dim cName As Long, cData As Long, sData As String
```

(continued)

```
Dim ordType As Long, cJunk As Long, ft As FILETIME
Static hKeyPrev As Long, cNameMax As Long
' When enumerating, cache required data the first time
If hKeyPrev <> hKey Or cNameMax = 0 Then
    hKeyPrev = hKey
    GetRegValueNext = _
        RegQueryInfoKey(hKey, sNullStr, cJunk, pNull, _
                        cJunk, cJunk, cJunk, cJunk, _
                        cNameMax, cJunk, cJunk, ft)
    If GetRegValueNext Then Exit Function
End If

' Get the value name and type in the first call
vValue = Empty
cName = cNameMax + 1
sName = String$(cName, 0)
GetRegValueNext = _
    RegEnumValue(hKey, i, sName, cName, _
                 pNull, ordType, pNull, cData)
If GetRegValueNext Then
    If GetRegValueNext <> ERROR_MORE_DATA Then
        Exit Function
    End If
End If
sName = Left$(sName, cName)

' Handle each type separately
Select Case ordType
Case REG_DWORD, REG_DWORD_LITTLE_ENDIAN
    Dim iData As Long
    GetRegValueNext = _
        RegEnumValueInt(hKey, i, sName, cName + 1, _
                        pNull, ordType, iData, cData)
    vValue = iData

Case REG_DWORD_BIG_ENDIAN  ' Unlikely, but you never know
    Dim dwData As Long
    GetRegValueNext = _
        RegEnumValueInt(hKey, i, sName, cName + 1, _
                        pNull, ordType, dwData, cData)
    vValue = MBytes.SwapEndian(dwData)

Case REG_SZ, REG_MULTI_SZ ' Same thing to Visual Basic
    sData = String$(cData - 1, 0)
    GetRegValueNext = _
        RegEnumValueStr(hKey, i, sName, cName + 1, _
                        pNull, ordType, sData, cData)
```

```
            vValue = sData

    Case REG_EXPAND_SZ          ' Expand environment variables
        sData = String$(cData - 1, 0)
        GetRegValueNext = _
            RegEnumValueStr(hKey, i, sName, cName + 1, _
                            pNull, ordType, sData, cData)
        vValue = MUtility.ExpandEnvStr(sData)

    Case Else        ' Catch REG_BINARY and anything else
        Dim abData() As Byte
        ReDim abData(cData)
        GetRegValueNext = _
            RegEnumValueByte(hKey, i, sName, cName + 1, _
                             pNull, ordType, _
                             abData(0), cData)
        vValue = abData

    End Select

End Function
```

The function starts by calling RegQueryInfoKey to get all possible information about the current key. Most of it is junk in this context, but the length of the longest value will be needed later and is therefore cached for subsequent calls. Afterward, we pretend to get the data but provide a too small buffer. All we want here is the name and the type. Notice that the first call uses a generic RegEnumValue. After we have acquired the type, we use API aliases such as RegEnumValueInt, RegEnumValueStr, and RegEnumValueByte to get the appropriate type-specific data.

Registry Nodes and Items

CRegNode and CRegItem are a pair of cooperating classes that enable you to manipulate registry items with a collection-like syntax. A registry node is simultaneously a collection of items and a collection of nested nodes. Let's look at some of the common registry operations you might want to do. The samples are taken from the Test Registry sample (TREG.VBG).

Accessing the registry

The first step in accessing the registry collections is to declare a node object variable and connect it to a registry node:

```
Dim nodesTop As New CRegNode
' Connect to first-level node by name
nodesTop.Create "Software\VB and VBA Program Settings"
```

The Create method can be used in several ways. Its signature looks like this:

```
Sub Create(vIndex As Variant, _
           Optional RootKey As Long = HKEY_CURRENT_USER, _
           Optional AccessRights As Long = KEY_ALL_ACCESS)
```

You'll need to provide a *RootKey* parameter to connect to anything other than HKEY_CURRENT_USER. The *vIndex* parameter is a Variant so that it can take either a string or numeric argument. It can be a key name (as shown above), a remote computer name, or the handle of a previously opened key.

You can also connect a registry node by using the default Key property. Here are some examples:

```
' Connect HKEY_CLASSES_ROOT node
nodesTop.Key = HKEY_CLASSES_ROOT
' Connect VBCore.CAbout node in current node (HKEY_CLASSES_ROOT)
nodesTop.Key = "VBCore.CAbout"
' Connect Software node in specified root HKEY_LOCAL_MACHINE
nodesTop.Key(HKEY_LOCAL_MACHINE) = "Software"
' Open first node of current node
nodesTop.Key(nodesTop.Key) = 1
```

Once you've connected to a node, you can read its item values by name:

```
v = node.Items("Bytes")
```

Or you can get an item's value by the item's position number:

```
v = node.Items(1)
```

Either way you get back a Variant that could contain a Long, a String, or an array of Bytes. You have to check the type with VarType to decide what to do with it. The sample simply converts any type to a string, but real programs might have to do something more sophisticated—especially with binary data stored in Byte arrays.

You can also set item values of any registry type. Here's how to add binary data named *Bytes*:

```
Dim ab() As Byte
' Add bytes item
ab = "The bytes"
node.AddItem ab, "Bytes"
```

You can also add strings containing environment variables such as this string named *ExpandString*:

```
node.AddItem "A %TEMP% string", "ExpandString"
```

The string will be saved in the registry as is, with the percent signs intact, but it will be extracted with the TEMP environment variable expanded. Here are a few more examples showing how item values can be added to named nodes:

```
node("SecondLevel1").AddItem "DefaultString"
node("SecondLevel1").AddItem "Stuff", "Value1"
node("SecondLevel2").AddItem 689, "Value1"
```

The first argument is the value of the item, the second is its name. If you don't give a name, the value will become the default value, which will always be stored as a string even if it isn't one.

You can remove items by name or by position:

```
node.RemoveItem 1
node.RemoveItem "String"
```

You can also remove nodes by name or position, but whether you succeed will depend on whether the node has children. Here's an attempt to remove a child-less node:

```
f = nodesTop.RemoveNode("FirstLevel", AllChild:=False)
```

This call will fail if the specified node has children. You might want to specify the optional argument as False to avoid accidentally deleting large branches from the registry. The default is to remove the node and all its children. Note that a node can't remove itself.

Iterating through the registry

You can iterate through the registry items and nodes the way you expect to iterate through any collection. Iterate through items by index like this:

```
For i = 0 To node.ItemCount - 1
    With node.Items(i)
        s = s & .Name & "(" & i & ") = " & VarToStr(.Value) & sCrLf
    End With
Next
```

The VarToStr function in this loop is local to the test program. It converts numeric, integer, or binary data to a string in the following format:

```
(0) = Default
Bytes(1) = 54 00 68 00 65 00 20 00  ...
String(2) = A String
Number(3) = &H00000005 (5)
ExpandString(4) = A C:\temp string
```

Normally, it's easier to iterate with For Each. The CRegItemWalker and CReg-NodeWalker classes do the hard work (as explained in Chapter 4) so that you can iterate easily:

```
For Each nodesSub In node
    s = s & nodesSub.Name & sCrLf
    ' Iterate items with For Each
    For Each item In nodesSub.Items
        s = s & item.Name & " = " & VarToStr(item.Value) & sCrLf
    Next
Next
```

The outer loop walks through nodes, and the inner loop walks through the items of each node.

You can use these techniques to iterate yourself, but there's an even easier way. CRegNode knows how to walk using the WalkNodes, WalkItems, and WalkAll-Nodes methods. Let's look at WalkAllNodes, which walks recursively through all the nested nodes at and below the current node. WalkAllNodes keeps walking through nodes with For Each, calling itself on each node it finds until there are no nodes left to walk. There's only one problem. How does WalkAllNodes know what to do with what it walks? It doesn't. Only the client can say what needs to be done, and the way to ask the client is through an interface.

The IUseRegItems interface provides the template for registry operations on items or nodes:

```
Function UseNode(node As CRegNode, ByVal iLevel As Long) As Boolean

End Function

Function UseItem(item As CRegItem, ByVal iLevel As Long) As Boolean

End Function
```

The client of the CRegNode class implements the IUseRegItems interface and passes an IUseRegItems object to CRegNode. In the Test Registry program, the main form does the implementing. It provides IUseRegItems_UseItem and IUse-RegItems_UseNode functions that append formatted text for each node or item to a module-level string, which is written to a textbox when the walk is finished. In real life, you'd probably want to do something more interesting—such as put the nodes in a TreeView and the items in a ListView.

The WalkAllNodes method calls back to the IUseRegItems object you pass it so that your code can handle the real work. The client code is easy:

```
node.WalkAllNodes Me, node, 0
```

The first parameter of WalkAllNodes is the IUseRegItems object that tells what to do with each node and item. Since the client form implements IUseRegItems, it can simply pass itself. The second parameter is the starting node. The third parameter is the indent level. Each nested call to WalkAllNodes increments the indent level, which is passed back to the client in the UseNode and UseItem procedures. The client can use the level to produce formatted output. For example, here's how the Test Registry form implements the UseNode procedure:

```
Private Function IUseRegItems_UseNode(node As CRegNode, _
                                    ByVal iLevel As Long) As Boolean
With node
    sOut = sOut & Space$((iLevel) * 4) & .Name & " : " & sCrLf
    .WalkItems Me, iLevel
    DoEvents
End With
End Function
```

After writing the formatted node information, the code calls WalkItems to handle the item information. For each note item, WalkItems calls UseItem, which Test Registry implements like this:

```
Private Function IUseRegItems_UseItem(item As CRegItem, _
                                    ByVal iLevel As Long) As Boolean
With item
    sOut = sOut & Space$((iLevel - 1) * 4) & " > " & _
                .Name & " : " & VarToStr(.Value) & sCrLf
End With
End Function
```

The last piece of this puzzle is the implementation of WalkAllNodes in the CRegNode class. First it calls the UseNode method of the IUseRegItems object to display the current node. Then it calls WalkAllNodes recursively to do the same thing again on each node in the current node.

```
Function WalkAllNodes(use As IUseRegItems, nodeStart As CRegNode, _
                    ByVal iLevel As Long) As CRegNode
    If use.UseNode(nodeStart, iLevel) Then
        Set WalkAllNodes = nodeStart
        Exit Function
    End If
    Dim i As Long, nodeT As CRegNode
    ' Iterate by index for greater speed
    For i = 0 To nodeStart.NodeCount - 1
        Set WalkAllNodes = WalkAllNodes(use, nodeStart.Nodes(i), _
                                    iLevel + 1)
    Next
End Function
```

Notice that WalkAllNodes and UseNode are functions (as are WalkNodes, Walk-Items, and UseItem). This enables you to write registry search procedures. Your implementation of UseNode could check for items that meet a certain condition and return True when it is found. WalkAllNodes would recognize the return as a signal to stop walking and return the current node up through the recursion chain. The Test Registry sample program doesn't use this feature. It always returns False so that the walk continues until there are no more nodes.

Let me make one more point about node and item walking. Under Windows NT there are many things in the registry that your programs might not have the right to access. I'm not going to get into the security issues now. The point is that if you walk through a place you have no right to walk, you'll encounter an access denied error (5). If you're not careful, this will terminate your walk, leaving additional walkable objects unwalked. The CRegNode and CRegItem classes have to trap errors and skip unwalkable objects rather than failing on them. This requires some messy code, particularly in the More method of the CRegNodeWalker class.

What to Write Where

Knowing how to read and write registry data is only half the battle. The real trouble comes in figuring out what to write where. Let's look at the registry from the viewpoint of an ActiveX component and then from the viewpoint of a typical Windows program.

COM and the Registry

COM uses the registry to make connections between interface and class ID GUIDs and the components they represent. The HKEY_CLASSES_ROOT key has all the class data. This key is actually an alias for HKEY_LOCAL_MACHINE-\SOFTWARE\Classes, but COM needs the data so often that it's easier to keep a more specific root key for it. To get some idea of how it all fits together, let's look at the registry entries for a familiar component, SieveBasExeN.

A Sieve in the Registry

One way or another, the Sieve client program is going to need all the information it can get about its Sieve components. The client needs the settings and the information from Figure 10-5.

How can the server share the information and how can the client find it? Part of the information is shared through the system registry. Figure 10-5 shows all the data in the registry related to the SieveBasExeN program. This is the god's-eye view; you can't really see all these entries at one time in the Registry Editor.

If you haven't used the Registry Editor, you'd better load it up and follow along. I find the Windows 95 version (REGEDIT.EXE) to be more user-friendly than the Windows NT version (REGEDT32.EXE), and it works under Windows NT.

```
HKEY_CLASSES_ROOT
├── CLSID
│    ├── {00020424-0000-0000-C000-000000000046}          PSOAInterface
│    │    ├── InprocServer                                ole2disp.dll
│    │    └── InprocServer32                              oleaut32.dll
│    │                                                    ThreadingModel=Both
│    │
│    └── {B4A64DA0-D292-11D0-B253-00AA005754FD}           Sieve of Eratosthenes
│         ├── Implemented Categories
│         │    └── {40FC6ED5-2438-11CF-A3DB-080036F12502}
│         ├── LocalServer32                               C:\HARDCORE2\sievebasexen.exe
│         ├── ProgID                                      SieveBasExeN.CSieveBasExeN
│         ├── TypeLib                                     {B4A64DA1-D292-11D0-B253-00AA005754FD}
│         ├── Version                                     1.0
│         └── Programmable
│
├── Interface
│    └── {B4A64DA9F-D292-11D0-B253-00AA005754FD}          CSieveBasExeN
│         ├── ProxyStubClsid                              {00020424-0000-0000-C000-000000000046}
│         ├── ProxyStubClsid32                            {00020424-0000-0000-C000-000000000046}
│         └── TypeLib                                     {B4A64DA1-D292-11D0-B253-00AA005754FD}
│                                                         Version=1.0
│
├── SieveBasExeN.CSieveBasExeN                            Sieve of Eratosthenes
│    └── Clsid                                            {B4A64DA0-D292-11D0-B253-00AA005754FD}
│
└── TypeLib
     └── {B4A64DA1-D292-11D0-B253-00AA005754FD}
          ├── 1.0                                         Sieve of Eratosthenes As Native Code EXE Server"
          │    └── 0
          │         └── win32                             C:\HARDCORE2\sievebasexen.exe
          ├── FLAGS                                       0
          └── HELPDIR                                     C:\HARDCORE2
```

Figure 10-5. *An ActiveX component in the system Registery.*

If you have access to both operating systems, try copying REGEDIT.EXE to your Windows NT system directory. The Windows NT version has one advantage: it monitors and automatically updates registry entries made from the outside. With the Windows 95 version you have to use the Refresh command to get recently changed values.

If you check all the cross-links in Figure 10-5, you'll start to get an idea of what's going on. Some of the registry entries are named, and some are GUIDs. Named entries have GUID subentries, and GUID entries contain data such as the title and location of the server. If, at run time, Visual Basic knows only the name of the component it needs to use, it goes to the registry and looks up the name. Visual Basic retrieves the GUID item and then looks up the GUID entry. It uses data under the GUID to load the correct DLL or EXE server. This is what happens when you call CreateObject to connect to a public class. If you load a type library, Visual Basic already knows the GUID. It can skip the name lookup and go directly to the data from the GUID. Furthermore, it can read the COM data it needs out of the registry at design time rather than at run time.

There's a lot more to this process than I care to get into here. COM has functions that take care of the details of registering servers, handling class IDs, and looking up data in the registry. Visual Basic has functions that take care of calling those COM functions. You simply fill in dialog boxes, declare objects, and call properties and methods. In theory, you should never have to worry about registering and unregistering components and type libraries, but if you ever deal with beta software, you should get used to the idea of sometimes examining or removing COM registry entries by hand.

In theory, you could even register components by hand by adding all the appropriate registry entries yourself in the Registry Editor. No thanks. It's not out of the question, however, to write Visual Basic code that automatically handles examination, modification, and cleanup of COM registry items. But you need to understand normal registration before you try to mess with it.

Registering components

You register an EXE server by running it. You can check this out with the SieveBasExeN program. Open the Registry Editor, and then find the SieveBasExeN.CSieveBasExeN class using the Find menu item (on the Search, View, or Edit menu, depending on your registry editor). Delete the entry. The Sieve is gone. Now run the SieveServerEXE program. Restart or refresh the Registry Editor. The Sieve is back.

By using the command-line options */regserver* and */unregserver,* you can register or unregister any COM EXE server without invoking the program's normal user interface. If you want to register SieveBasExeN.EXE without taking over the user's screen, you can do it from your setup program with this statement:

```
Shell "SieveBasExeN.EXE /regserver"
```

It seems a little strange that all your ActiveX EXE components are able to recognize command-line options without any programming by you, but it's part of the COM library code that is added to a program when you specify that a program should be an ActiveX component.

Setup programs created with the Setup Toolkit will automatically register your components. As a practical matter, this issue affects you, not your customers. Chances are you'll run your EXE server program from the IDE sometime during development of the program. It will be registered automatically, and you'll have no trouble. Then you'll put the client and server programs on a disk for a fellow programmer who also runs Visual Basic (thus bypassing setup). Your client program will fail rudely because the server isn't registered on your colleague's disk. The workaround is easy; just tell your colleague to run the server program once before running the client.

Now try running a DLL server with the */regserver* command-line option:

```
SieveBasDllN.DLL /regserver
```

Ha! You know better than to run a DLL. Never mind. Hidden away in the \Tools-\RegUtils directory on your Visual Basic distribution CD (not copied to your disk during setup) are several registration programs, including REGSVR32.EXE. Here's the real command line to register your DLL:

```
regsvr32 SieveBasDllN.DLL
```

REGSVR32 has a */u* option to unregister a server and a */s* (silent) option to register a server without displaying a success dialog box. The setup programs created by the Setup Toolkit can handle this registration for your customers. When you choose the Make DLL File menu item, Visual Basic automatically registers the DLL. In other words, you usually won't need to call REGSVR32, but it's there if you really need it.

The Windows Programs in the Registry

Let's take a look at one fine, upstanding citizen, and see whether you can learn anything about registry duties. If any program ought to be well-behaved under Windows 95, it's WordPad. Figure 10-6 on page 603 shows an abbreviated version of WordPad's registry entries on my machine, and the following list provides some explanation.

■ The DOC extension is registered as the official extension for several document types, including Microsoft Word for Windows and WordPad. DOC is a popular extension, and your machine might have other document entries.

■ WordPad is OLE-enabled so that you can embed or link WordPad documents. This is the purpose of the entry in the CLSID branch. We're not particularly interested in this capability right now, but you can see the general idea.

■ The DOC extension is registered under QuickView so that WordPad files can be browsed when you select Quick View from a document's context menu. It would be nice if you could enable a QuickView viewer for document types that your programs create. I'll talk about that briefly later.

■ The document type Wordpad.Document.1 has several entries. Notice that the CLSID entry has a GUID pointing to the OLE CLSID entries. (See the second item in this list.) The DefaultIcon entry provides the location of the WordPad document icon, which is embedded as resource 1 in WORDPAD.EXE. The command entries for *open*, *print*, and *printto* give the command line that is invoked if you choose Open or Print from the document context menu or if you drag the document to a Printer object. If you thought command lines were out of fashion under the enhanced Windows interface, think again. It's a good idea to add similar command-line options and command entries to any program that creates and manages documents.

■ All the permanent WordPad settings from dialog boxes and toolbars are saved in the registry rather than in INI files. If you use the new Settings functions, all your 32-bit settings are saved in the same place.

■ WordPad stores its location in the App Paths branch of HKEY_LOCAL-_MACHINE. This allows Windows to find and run WordPad even if it isn't in the PATH environment variable. For example, you can type *WordPad* from the Run item of the Start menu or use the Start command in a command-line session. Under MS-DOS first and later under Windows, it seemed that every setup program tried to insinuate its startup directory into the PATH environment, resulting in endless paths of long-forgotten directories. The App Paths entry allows programs to stop this rudeness, although I wouldn't bet much that they will. By default, setup programs created with the Setup Wizard or the Setup Toolkit will register the App Paths for you.

You have two types of registry settings: document and application. None of the sample programs in this book create their own document types, but most programs in real life do. About document types, I'll say only that you should study the Windows interface guidelines and do the right thing. If you can write one item to the registry, you can write anything. Let's concentrate on the application settings. The most common ones—those holding permanent program settings—are handled for you by GetSetting, GetAllSettings, SaveSetting, and DeleteSetting.

You'll find a small difference between the recommended settings location (followed by WordPad) and the location that is used by Visual Basic programs. The Windows interface guidelines recommend that the settings be placed under a CompanyName branch in the Software branch of HKEY_CURRENT_USER. Visual Basic settings are placed in a branch called VB and VBA Program Settings. So if your application name is the same as someone else's Visual Basic program name, your settings could conflict with theirs. Another possibility is that multiple users might log on to the same machine. If you want settings to apply to all users of a machine rather than to the current user only, you should save the settings in HKEY_LOCAL_MACHINE. If you have any doubts about Visual Basic's default location for settings, you should write your own registry functions to put program settings where you want them.

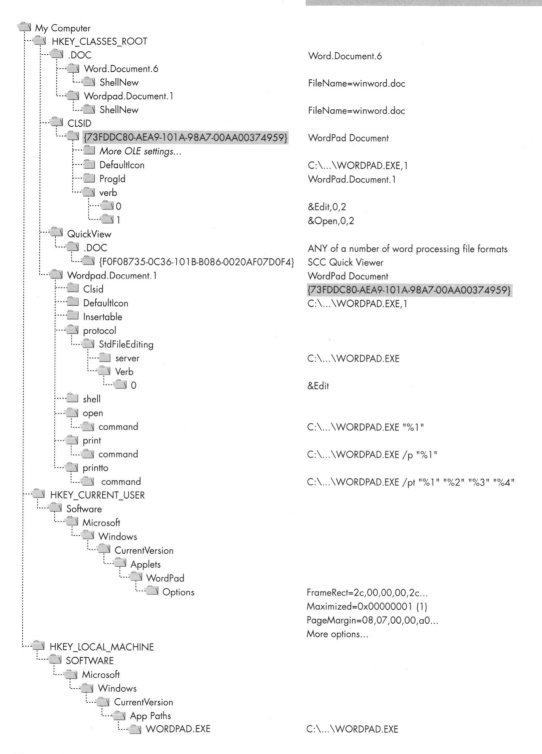

Figure 10-6. *WordPad registry entries.*

For some reason, registry editors tend to be crude and ugly. The Windows 95 editor is a step in the right direction, but it still has a long way to go to meet my user interface standards. It should be as easy to use as the Windows Explorer, and it should provide a good way to switch between related entries. So what's the problem? All you need is a tree view on the left, a list view on the right, a toolbar, a status bar, and a few menu items. No problem.

11

Stir-Fry

"What's for dinner?"

"Stir-fry."

"Oh, no."

"I thought you liked my stir-fry."

"Well, sometimes. But...Hey, what is that? You're not going to put rhubarb in there, are you?"

"I'll have you know that rhubarb is the definitive ingredient in the matchless stir-fries of the Basic tribe of northeastern Cathistan."

"Oh, sure. Now you're a master of authentic ethnic cooking. But tell me—do those folks use picante sauce in their stir-fries?"

"Who said anything about picante sauce?"

"I tasted it in one of your concoctions, just last week."

"Yeah, and you went back for seconds. It was good, wasn't it?"

"Well, not as bad as I expected. But it wasn't really stir-fry. Not with corn and avocados. Hey! Put that Worcestershire back where you got it."

"Who's doing the cooking here?"

"I don't get it. You've got three brands of Chinese stir-fry sauce and one of Korean, two kinds of soy sauce, three kinds of teriyaki, Thai peanut and fish sauces, God knows what else from the Philippines and Malaysia, and that's not even mentioning your Indian spices. You've got enough without visiting other continents."

"I just don't want my cooking to get predictable."

"I wouldn't worry about that."

You shouldn't worry about this chapter being predictable, either. It's just your Basic, everyday stir-fry. I've thrown in all the vegetables, sauces, and algorithms that don't fit anywhere else. It's not as bad as you think; quite tasty, actually.

Everything You Always Wanted to Know About...

These days, almost every application you see puts system information in its About dialog box. There's no official ABAPI standard, but everyone seems to be doing it. In early Windows-based programs, the About dialog box simply named the application, but over the years About boxes have come to serve serious (and not so serious) roles.

Some About dialog boxes contain secret commands that activate an animation or a list of developers. Others provide system information such as available memory and other resources. You'll also find stern copyright warnings, serial numbers, jokes, and copy protection schemes.

The latest addition to About dialog boxes in Microsoft applications (including Visual Basic) is a System Info button that brings up Microsoft's information application, MSINFO32.EXE. Microsoft provides this program with many of its applications so that you can display, print, or write to a disk every piece of information about your system that an internal or external support person might need. Any of your customers who have recent Microsoft applications (Visual Basic included) will have the information program.

You can add the About dialog box presented here to your applications with very little work—just set any application-specific CAbout property and load the CAbout class. The dialog box displays some general system information and provides a button to activate an information application. Of course, like any self-respecting About dialog box, this one has an undocumented command that starts an animation sequence.

The All About program (ALLABOUT.VBP) demonstrates the About dialog box, along with tabs containing other information. Figure 11-1 on the following page shows the All About program in action. I'll discuss the Version and System tabs in this chapter. The Video tab exercises the CVideo class, which was discussed in Chapter 7. The Drives tab exercises the CDrive class and the CDrives collection covered in Chapters 3 and 4.

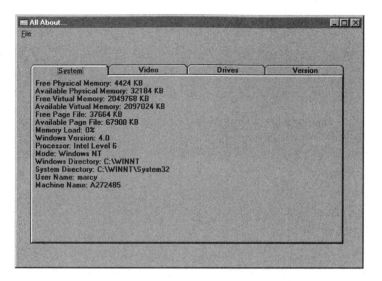

Figure 11-1. *The All About program.*

Using the CAbout Class

All you need to create your own About dialog box is to write some code in the event procedure from the About menu of the All About program, as shown in the following sample:

```
Private Sub mnuAbout_Click()
    Dim about As New CAbout
    With about
        On Error GoTo FailAbout
        ' Set properties
        Set .Client = App
        Set .Icon = Forms(0).Icon
        .UserInfo(2) = "Don't even think " & _
                       "about stealing this program"
        ' Load after all properties are set
        .Load
        ' Modal form will return here when finished
        Exit Sub
    End With
FailAbout:
        MsgBox "I don't know nuttin'"
End Sub
```

Figure 11-2 shows the results.

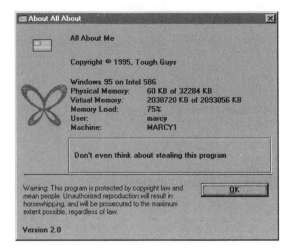

Figure 11-2. *About All About.*

You create and load a CAbout object, but what you see is the FAbout form. Forms can't be public in a component (such as VBCore), so you have to wrap the internal form in a public class. Actually, I think of this as a benefit, not a burden. If you could expose a form without a wrapper, clients would get access to all the properties and events of the form. It wouldn't be an About form if the user could modify anything through the standard form methods and properties.

The CAbout class gets its information from several sources. You pass an App object through the Client property to provide the title and other information about the program. You can pass an icon through the Icon property. The UserInfo array property lets you enter three lines of general text information. The example provides only one line, but puts it in position 2 of the array so that it will be centered. The InfoProg, Copyright, and Comments properties (not used in the sample) allow you to override information that the form ordinarily figures out from the Client property. Additional system information comes from the System object described in "The CSystem Class and the System Object" later in this chapter. The form gets its undocumented animation command from...well, if I told you, it wouldn't be undocumented.

After you set the properties you want displayed, call the Load method to make the form appear. Unlike the wrapping forms of most classes, the CAbout class doesn't return any information from the user, so there's no need to check properties after the form terminates.

Unlike most of the classes in this book, CAbout and its FAbout form aren't in VBCore. They're in a separate component called VisualCore, along with all the other classes that wrap forms and thus have a user interface. That's so that VBCore can be marked for Unattended Execution, a subject I'll discuss in the "Threads and Synchronization" section later in this chapter. The other visual classes in VisualCore include CColorPicker (discussed later in this chapter) and COpenPictureFile (used by the Fun 'n Games program).

A Class Wrapping a Form

The class wrapper for a form doesn't do much of anything. It creates a form object and passes through a few properties. But its most important job is to shield the user from all the form's unnecessary methods, properties, and events. Here are the properties the form passes through:

```
' Private form variable
Private about As New FAbout

' Could be App object, or anything with the same version properties
Public Client As Object
' Normally the icon of the client application
Public Icon As Picture
' Miscellaneous properties
Public InfoProg As String
Public Copyright As String
Public Comments As String
Public SecretButton As Integer
Public SecretKey As Integer
Public SecretShift As Integer
Public Animator As IAnimation
```

None of these properties needs validation, so they can be public variables. The UserInfo property works the same, but requires Get and Let procedures (not shown) because it's an array. Technically, I could just implement all these properties with Let procedures so that I could have the first class in history with write-only properties exclusively.

The Load method passes the properties on to exact duplicate properties on the form variable. The form is a private form in the VisualCore component. Outside applications have no way to get to it except by setting CAbout properties and calling the Load method:

```
Sub Load()
With about
    ' We need version properties to display on About form
    If Client Is Nothing Then ErrRaise eeAppNotInit
```

(continued)

```
' Pass other optional properties through to form
Set .Client = Client
Set .ClientIcon = Icon
.InfoProg = InfoProg
.Copyright = Copyright
.Comments = Comments
.SecretButton = SecretButton
.SecretKey = SecretKey
.SecretShift = SecretShift
.UserInfo(1) = UserInfo(1)
.UserInfo(2) = UserInfo(2)
.UserInfo(3) = UserInfo(3)
' Show the form
.Show vbModal
End With
End Sub
```

The most interesting feature is the required Client property. From Visual Basic, you'll usually set this to the App object of your program, but note that it is declared with Object type, not with App type. The App type is private to the Visual Basic library. Technically, Visual Basic ought to display an error if you try to pass the private App object, but it doesn't. Nevertheless, it's not a good idea for two reasons. First, the documentation forbids it and says that bad things might happen if you modify and return private objects. That's not a problem in this case because the Client property will be read but not modified. The second reason is that ActiveX is supposed to be a language-independent standard, and it wouldn't be very polite to require a C++ client to pass a Visual Basic App object. Therefore, CAbout doesn't require an App object. It does require that any late-bound object have some of the same properties as the App object—specifically those containing version information. It would be easy for a C++, Delphi, or Java client to create and pass such an object if they knew exactly which properties the About form uses. I'm planning to put the full requirements in the CAbout help file "real soon now" for the benefit of all those thousands of C++ clients who desperately want to use the VBCore component.

A Form Wrapped by a Class

When the CAbout Load method is called, it calls the Show method of the FAbout form, which calls Form_Load. That's where the real work finally gets done:

```
Sub Form_Load()
With Client
    BugMessage "Loading About"
    If anim Is Nothing Then Set anim = New CButterFly
    Set anim.Canvas = pbAnimate
    Me.Caption = "About " & .ProductName
    lblApp.Caption = .Title
```

```
    Const sInfo = "\msapps\msinfo\msinfo32.exe"
    ' Allow override because some customers might not have MSINFO
    If InfoProg = sEmpty Then
        InfoProg = System.WindowsDir & sInfo
    End If
    If ExistFile(InfoProg) = False Then cmdInfo.Visible = False


    ' Icon from first form is application icon
    If Not ClientIcon Is Nothing Then
        If ClientIcon.Type = vbPicTypeIcon Then
            Set Me.Icon = ClientIcon
        End If
        Set imgIcon.Picture = ClientIcon
    End If
    lblMode.Caption = System.Mode & " on " & System.Processor
    lblPhysicalMemory.Caption = System.FreePhysicalMemory & _
        " KB of " & System.TotalPhysicalMemory & " KB"
    lblVirtualMemory.Caption = System.FreeVirtualMemory & _
        " KB of " & System.TotalVirtualMemory & " KB"
    lblMemoryLoad.Caption = System.MemoryLoad & "%"
    lblUser.Caption = System.User
    lblMachine.Caption = System.Machine
    If UserInfo(1) = sEmpty And UserInfo(2) = sEmpty And _
                            UserInfo(3) = sEmpty Then
        fmUserInfo.Visible = False
    Else
        fmUserInfo.Visible = True
        lblUserInfo(0).Caption = UserInfo(1)
        lblUserInfo(1).Caption = UserInfo(2)
        lblUserInfo(2).Caption = UserInfo(3)
    End If
    If Copyright = sEmpty Then Copyright = .LegalCopyright
    lblRights.Caption = Copyright
    If Comments = sEmpty Then Comments = .Comments
    lblComment.Caption = Comments
    lblVersion.Caption = "Version " & .Major & "." & .Minor
End With
End Sub
```

The rest of FAbout continues in the same vein. It gets a little bit of information here, and a little bit there. I'll let you figure out the rest.

Animating

I can't tell you much about the secret animation features of the About form because they're secret. You'll just have to click every possible location and press every possible key combination to figure them out. Or you could look at the source code.

All I'm going to say is that you can replace my crude butterfly object with your own sophisticated animation object. Just write your own class that implements the IAnimate interface using CButterFly (BUTTERFLY.CLS) as a model. Create an object of your animation type in the client and pass it in the Animator property.

The CSystem Class and the System Object

Visual Basic provides some useful global objects—App, Printer, and Screen—but, until now, it lacked a System object to tell you everything you need to know about your environment. In Chapter 5, I explained what makes the System object the one and only instance of the CSystem class in VBCore. Now I'll discuss what the System object does.

The System tab of the All About program in Figure 11-1 shows the information you can get from the System object. These properties fall into one of two categories. Some pieces of information—such as the operating system version and the processor—never change, at least not while a program is running. For this kind of information, CSystem gets all the data it needs in Class_Initialize and stores it in private variables.

```
Private Sub Class_Initialize()
    Dim dw As Long, c As Integer
    dw = GetVersion()
    iWinMajor = dw And &HFF&
    iWinMinor = (dw And &HFF00&) / &H100&
    sMode = IIf(dw And &H80000000, "Windows 95", "Windows NT")
    GetSystemInfo sys
End Sub
```

You can then access this data through Property Get procedures such as the following:

```
Property Get WinMajor() As Integer
    WinMajor = iWinMajor
End Property
```

Other pieces of information—the amount of memory available, for instance—change all the time and must be calculated on request in Property Get procedures.

```
Property Get MemoryLoad() As Long
    Dim mem As MEMORYSTATUS
    mem.dwLength = Len(mem)
    GlobalMemoryStatus mem
    MemoryLoad = mem.dwMemoryLoad
End Property
```

Rather than explain the memory information returned by the System object, I'm going to explain what it doesn't return—system resources. Under 16-bit systems, information about remaining resources could predict your success in launching an additional application or tell you why an application that usually works is going haywire today. Fortunately, that's generally not a problem for today's 32-bit systems. Between real and virtual memory, there's usually enough memory, and if there isn't, interpreting what the GlobalMemoryStatus API function returns about physical memory, virtual memory, and the size of the swap file is a black art.

The System object returns all the information, but the numbers are a moving target. What you really want to know is whether your next big memory allocation is going to slow your machine to a thrashing, grinding crawl. The MemoryLoad property of the System object purports to give you a general idea of your memory use as a percentage of total memory, but I've found this number to be completely unreliable under Windows 95. I don't trust its magic formula based on undocumented algorithms.

The number most users think they want is Free Resources. Windows 3.1 displayed it. Windows 95 shows it on a System Properties sheet. It must be of some use. Well, maybe. Free Resources affects only 16-bit programs. Under 16-bit Windows, memory could be allocated only in 64-KB segments. Windows used one of these segments to store all the miscellaneous data needed by the User DLL (controlling windows) and used another for data needed by the GDI DLL (controlling display graphics). When either segment got filled up, things started going wrong, and not always in very polite ways. It happened even when you had megabytes of system memory left. Fortunately, it never happens with 32-bit programs because both User and GDI get their memory out of the same big pool. It never happens to 16-bit programs under Windows NT. But Windows 95 contains a lot of old 16-bit code and some experts claim that there might be some connection between Free Resources and the performance of your 16-bit programs.

No matter what arguments I give, some of you will still ask, "Windows 95 gets them. Why can't I?" Because you can't thunk in Visual Basic. The Win32 API doesn't provide any way to get Free Resources because all resources are free, but Windows 95 gets them anyway by using a complicated process called thunking to call 16-bit Windows API functions from 32-bit code. Thunking is documented with assembly language examples in the Win32 Software Development Kit. I've never seen it done in C, much less in Visual Basic. But if you have a copy of Visual Basic version 4 hanging around, thunking is easy. Just create a 16-bit ActiveX EXE component that calls the Windows 3.1 GetFreeSystemResources function and returns the value as a property. You can then load this server from your 32-bit program and use the properties. I don't recommend this, and I don't support it in my System object. But if your client insists, that's how you can deliver.

Sorting List Boxes

The ListBox control has been good enough for many years. Why fix it if it isn't broken? Well, that's a matter of opinion. The ListBox control isn't exactly broken, but it hasn't reached its full potential. Most limitations of list boxes also apply to combo boxes. Here are a few things both of them could do better:

- You can't replace a list box item with a simple assignment. Instead, you must remove the old item and put another in its place.

- The Sorted property is Boolean. If sorting is good, then it would be even better to sort in ascending or descending order, case sensitive or case insensitive, or in a custom defined sort mode.

- If a list box is sorted, it should be able to do command completion so that it would move immediately to the first entry that matches the characters you've typed so far.

- List boxes look and work a lot like collections. They should work even more like collections with For Each support, key lookups, and collection-like names for methods and properties.

Those are some of the new features of the XListBoxPlus control. XListBoxPlus is another delegation control. You should have delegation mastered by now, based on the XPictureGlass, XEditor, and XDropStack controls. In this case, the control delegates to an internal ListBox control. The internal list box is what the user sees on the screen, but XListBoxPlus is what the user interacts with. All properties, methods, and events are intercepted so that the list box items can be kept in the proper order.

I discussed sorting and searching in "Sorting, Shuffling, and Searching," in Chapter 5; now it's time to put those algorithms to work. The Test Sort program (TSORT.VBP) also appeared in Chapter 5, but at that time, I was interested in sorting arrays. Now I'm interested in the list box part of the program. Check it out in Figure 11-3 on the following page.

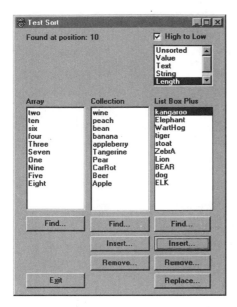

Figure 11-3. *Sorting arrays, collections, and list boxes.*

Collection Methods and Properties

My biggest beef with list boxes is that although they look and act like collections, they're not quite collections. For one thing, they're zero-based instead of one-based. For another, they have the wrong property and method names—ListCount, List, AddItem, and RemoveItem instead of Count, Item, Add, and Remove. Furthermore, they don't work with For Each.

You can curse the darkness or you can light a candle. I did both. The XListBox-Plus control has one-based collection methods and properties. It looks and works like a collection.

The design of XListBoxPlus is more interesting than its code. This class tries to combine the best features of list boxes and collections, keeping in mind that list boxes can't work quite the same way as collections work. The biggest difference is that list boxes have a selected item, and collections don't. Other differences are simply limitations of list boxes—limitations that XListBoxPlus attempts to eliminate. Table 11-1 compares what you can do with a list box, a collection, and a sorted list box (represented by *lst*, *n*, and *srt*, respectively).

Operation	ListBox	Collection	XListBoxPlus
Get item 3	s = lst.List(2)	s = n.Item(3)	s = srt.Item(3)
Get "Pig" index	Can't do it	Can't do it	i = srt("Pig")
Select "Pig"	lst.Text = "Pig"	Undefined	srt.Text = "Pig" srt.Current = "Pig"
Change item 3	lst.List(2) = "Dog"	Can't do it	srt.Item(3) = "Dog"
Change "Dog"	Can't do it	Can't do it	srt("Dog") = "Cat"
Select item 3	lst.ListIndex = 2	Undefined	srt.Current = 3
Get index	i = lst.ListIndex	Can't do it	i = srt.Current
Get selected	s = lst.Text	Undefined	s = srt.Text
Add "Cat"	lst.AddItem "Cat"	n.Add "Cat"	srt.Add "Cat"
Remove item 3	lst.RemoveItem 2	n.Remove 3	srt.Remove 3
Remove "Pig"	Can't do it	n.Remove "Pig"	srt.Remove "Pig"
Iterate by item	Can't do it	For Each v in n	For Each v in srt
Iterate by index	For i = 0 To _ lst.ListCount −1	For i = 1 To _ n.Count	For i = 1 To _ srt.Count

Table 11-1. *List box and collection operations.*

Most of these operations are clear once you understand list boxes and collections, but a few bear further study. I programmed with list boxes for years before I understood two of their more useful, but obscure, features. I knew that the Text property was important for combo boxes, but I didn't know it even existed for list boxes. I always wrote this redundant code to access the selected item:

```
s = lst.List(lst.ListIndex)
```

Every time I wrote it I cursed the authors of the ListBox control for requiring such an ugly syntax, and I took a little jab at them in the first edition of this book. Well, I like my crow with catsup. Here's what you can do instead:

```
s = lst.Text
```

The Text property can also be used to look up an item. (Yum! Feathers and all.) You can select the *Crow* item with this syntax:

```
lst.Text = "Crow"
```

If there is no *Crow* item, you'll deselect whatever is currently selected (ListIndex = −1). The lookup is case insensitive (*crow* finds *Crow*), but complete (*Cro* doesn't find *Crow*).

This is cool, but the XListBoxPlus is even more so. You can index by number or by string value. It works kind of like collections, but

```
i = n("Pig")
```

and

```
i = srt("Pig")
```

don't mean exactly the same thing. Indexed collections return objects, as explained later in this chapter in "Sorted Collections," but sorted list boxes contain strings, not objects. Indexing has to mean something different.

I made the default Item property return a numeric index if you pass a string, or a string if you pass an index. Purists might object to a property returning different types for different arguments, but it works in this case.

Here are few other points for users of the XListBoxPlus class:

- Properties that are read-only at design time are the bane of the control delegator. I couldn't figure out a way to delegate the cool new Check-Box style, the MultiSelect property, or the IntegralHeight property.

- There's no way to duplicate the neat little drop-down editing box that you get for the List and ItemData properties. XListBoxPlus uses a property page instead.

- In sorted mode, you can have only one copy of each item. I could have designed the class to allow duplicate entries, but that doesn't make much sense for sorted items.

- When no item is selected, the Index property is 0 rather than –1. This makes for easier conditional testing. You can also set Index to 0 to select nothing.

CHALLENGE   I'd like to have a sorted version of the FileListBox control, but couldn't create one by delegating because the original control doesn't allow addition or removal of items. Technically, you don't need to add or remove items to sort a list box, but you do need to exchange items, and that can't be done with a FileListBox control because nothing can be assigned to List items. You could, however, design a class to make an internal list box look and act like a FileListBox control, except that it could be sorted by date, name, extension, or attributes. To do this, you would use the Dir function to reload the list box in the current sort order at appropriate times. I've always wanted a file list box like that, and the only reason I didn't create one for this book is that I can do most of what I want with the ListView control. But the ListView has its problems, so you might want to use XListBoxPlus as a model for your own XFileListPlus control.

Finding Items

Rather than examining all of the code, let's just look at a few interesting properties. The Item property illustrates indexing by number or by string, and its Property Get procedure has a quirky return value that changes depending on the argument.

Remember that the Item property is the default. It can be used for reading items:

```
Debug.Print srt(3)
Debug.Print srt("Lion")
```

Numeric indexing of XListBoxPlus works like using the List property of ListBox, except that it is one-based. String indexing does a lookup on the data:

```
Property Get Item(ByVal vIndex As Variant) As String
    If VarType(vIndex) <> vbString Then
        ' For numeric index, return string value
        Item = lst.List(vIndex - 1)
    Else
        ' For string index, return matching index or 0 for none
        Item = Match(vIndex)
        If Item = 0 Then ErrRaise eseItemNotFound
    End If
End Property
```

The Match function is used here and in many other parts of the implementation to do string lookups. How do you suppose it works? If you remember Chapter 6, you might want to use LookupItem, which is a wrapper for the SendMessage API function with the LB_FINDSTRING message. But this message is case insensitive, and that's not what you need for searching some kinds of sorted data. Furthermore, Windows doesn't know that the internal list box is sorted; the only way it can find an item is with a linear search. But you know that it's sorted. The most efficient way to find a sorted item is with a binary search—the same one we talked about in Chapter 5. Here's the code for Match:

```
Private Function Match(ByVal sItem As String) As Integer
    Dim iPos As Integer
    Select Case esmlMode
    Case esmlUnsorted, esmlShuffle
        Match = LookupItem(lst, sItem) + 1
```

```
    Case Else    ' Some kind of sorting
        If BSearch(sItem, iPos) Then Match = iPos + 1 Else Match = 0
    End Select
End Function
```

Either way, Match will come up with an index to the item, if it exists. Match is also used in the Item Property Let, which enables you to assign items:

```
.Item(3) = "Deer"
.Item("Lion") = "Big Cat"
```

It works this way:

```
Property Let Item(ByVal vIndex As Variant, sItemA As String)
    ' For string index, look up matching index
    If VarType(vIndex) = vbString Then
        vIndex = Match(vIndex)
        ' Fail if old item isn't found or if new item is found
        If vIndex = 0 Then ErrRaise eseItemNotFound
        If Match(sItemA) Then ErrRaise eseDuplicateNotAllowed
    End If
    ' Assign value by removing old and inserting new
    Remove vIndex
    Add sItemA
End Property
```

This code converts a string index to a numeric index and then uses the Remove and Add methods to assign it in the proper sort order. I could go on to show how Remove finds and deletes items, but the code is the same as the Item Property Get. The Add method is more interesting:

```
Sub Add(sItem As String, Optional iPos As Integer = 1)
With lst
    ' Adding differs depending on the mode
    Select Case esmlMode
    Case esmlUnsorted
        ' Add where directed (start is default)
        .AddItem sItem, iPos - 1
    Case esmlShuffle
        ' Add at random position
        iPos = GetRandom(0, .ListCount - 1)
        If .ListCount Then
            .AddItem sItem, iPos
        Else
            .AddItem sItem
        End If
```

(continued)

```
        Case Else   ' Some kind of sorting
            ' Binary search for the item
            If BSearch(sItem, iPos) Then
                ErrRaise eseDuplicateNotAllowed
            Else
                ' Insert at sorted position
                If .ListCount Then
                    .AddItem sItem, iPos
                Else
                    .AddItem sItem
                End If
            End If
        End Select
    End With
End Sub
```

Add recognizes the optional position argument in unsorted modes, but ignores it if the data is sorted. The data is always inserted at the correct position so that the list remains sorted. The only time you actually have to sort the data is if you change the sort mode. Notice that the code raises an error if you try to insert an item that already exists into a sorted list. Duplicate items could have been permitted, but I made a design judgment that most applications that want sorted lists would not want duplicates.

There's a lot more to XListBoxPlus, but I'll leave you to explore the rest.

Sorted Collections

A list box is just a collection with a different syntax. If you have a sorted list box class, you're not very far from having a sorted collection class. So have at it. Clone XListBoxPlus. Delete the properties and methods unique to list boxes (those dealing with selected items and the list box interface). Change some names here and there, and you've got it.

Whoa! Not so fast. Collections can be either indexed or unindexed. Collections contain objects, not strings. You'll need to deal with those differences. You could create a CSortedStrings class by cloning because a collection of strings is unindexed by definition. But a collection of objects sorted by a specified field is a different matter.

I've supplied you with code to sort collections in a procedural style. Check out SortCollection and BSearchCollection in SORT.BAS, and then look at how they are used to sort a collection of strings in TSORT.VBG. This should help you get started writing your own CSortedCollection class. But keep in mind that making your CSortedCollection class a wrapper for the Collection class probably will not be nearly as fast as writing the class from scratch. See the Challenge on page 179 for more opinions on this topic.

Other People's Programs

One of the best ways to leverage your application's power is to get other people's programs to do part of the work. The Shell command makes this easy at the first level, but hardcore programmers must do more than simply call Shell. They have to hack around problems such as these:

- Shell assumes that you are sending a child program off to perform some independent task and that you no longer care what it does. If your program depends on results from the child program, you'll need to do extra work to determine when the program has finished.

- Programs can return a value called an exit code, indicating their results to their parent. Shell ignores this value. You need to do extra work to get it.

- Shell assumes that you are running a Windows-based program. If you are running either an MS-DOS or a 32-bit console application, you might want to take extra steps to run it politely.

- Shell assumes that you are willing to let Windows decide where and how your Windows-based program will appear on the desktop. You'll have more work to do if you don't like the default behavior.

- Shell assumes that you know which program you want to run, but it's also possible to specify a document file and let Windows decide which program should work on the document.

The Test Execute program shown in Figure 11-4 on the following page illustrates some of the more interesting ways you can launch other people's programs. You can use this program to experiment with different arguments to the various shell functions. When you've determined what works best for your situation, hard-code the appropriate settings.

Using Shell

The first thing you have to decide when running someone else's program is whether to run synchronously or asynchronously. Generally, programs written for Windows want to run asynchronously. You send your children off to the video parlor and forget about them. Or you keep in touch by phone—COM, DDE, or the Clipboard, in Windows' terms. Character-based programs (at least those that have survived the Windows onslaught) will usually prefer to operate synchronously. You send your children to the store to get some flour and eggs, but you can't finish baking until they get back with the goods—usually a modified file. Of course, nothing prevents character-based programs from working independently or Windows-based programs from modifying data for their parents.

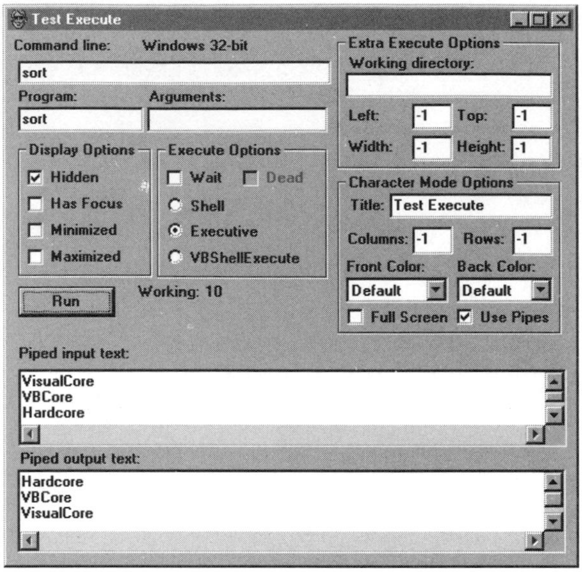

Figure 11-4. *The Test Execute program.*

The Shell function assumes that you want to run programs asynchronously. Running programs synchronously requires an extra effort. In olden times, hardcore 16-bit Visual Basic programmers used the GetModuleUsage API function to wait for programs to terminate. The 32-bit version works much differently.

The Shell function returns a process ID. Process IDs and handles were introduced in "The process list—Windows NT view" in Chapter 6. To summarize, every process has an ID number that uniquely identifies it, but most operations on processes require handles. You can get a handle from an ID with the Win32 OpenProcess function, which requires you to specify what you would like permission to do with the handle. You can open multiple handles with different permissions. The WaitOnProgram procedure hides some of the details. If you want to wait for a program to finish, you can call it like this:

```
Dim idProg As Long, iExit As Long
idProg = Shell("mktyplib shelllnk.odl", vbHide)
iExit = WaitOnProgram(idProg)
If iExit Then MsgBox "Compile failed"
```

WaitOnProgram returns the exit code of the shelled program. This assumes that the program chooses to return a meaningful exit code and isn't written in Visual Basic. Most character-mode programs set exit codes out of habit, but many Windows programs don't bother. Visual Basic itself returns an exit code when launched from the command line, but it doesn't provide any means for you to set an exit code in your own programs. (If you're thinking you could call the ExitProcess API yourself, forget it. I tried that, but the exit code you set doesn't show up on the outside.)

The WaitOnProgram function takes an optional *WaitDead* parameter that determines which of two strategies will be used. The default (False in the example above) polls for termination in a DoEvents loop. If the *WaitDead* argument is True, the calling program is stopped dead in its tracks. Here's the code:

```
Function WaitOnProgram(ByVal idProg As Long, _
                       Optional ByVal WaitDead As Boolean) As Long
    Dim cRead As Long, iExit As Long, hProg As Long
    ' Get process handle
    hProg = OpenProcess(PROCESS_ALL_ACCESS, False, idProg)
    If WaitDead Then
        ' Stop dead until process terminates
        Dim iResult As Long
        iResult = WaitForSingleObject(hProg, INFINITE)
        If iResult = WAIT_FAILED Then ErrRaise Err.LastDllError
        ' Get the return value
        GetExitCodeProcess hProg, iExit
    Else
        ' Get the return value
        GetExitCodeProcess hProg, iExit
        ' Wait, but allow painting and other processing
        Do While iExit = STILL_ACTIVE
            DoEvents
            GetExitCodeProcess hProg, iExit
        Loop
    End If
    CloseHandle hProg
    WaitOnProgram = iExit
End Function
```

If you take the dead wait route, the WaitForSingleObject API function puts the Test Execute program into hibernation. You can click away as much as you want, but nothing fazes the Test Execute program until the child terminates. This is very efficient for other programs in the system because you're not using any resources while you wait. But it's a pretty rude way to behave if the calling program has a user interface. The program won't even be repainted. In fact, if you do this in the IDE, Visual Basic itself will hibernate because it's the real program waiting for the shelled program to finish. Generally you'll only want to use the dead wait option from programs that have no user interface.

Executive Privilege

The Shell function is fine for normal use, but you can get better control of your programs with a CExecutive object. CExecutive does directly what the Shell function does behind the scenes, but instead of hard-coding defaults whether or not you want them, it puts you in control by letting you set lots of optional properties.

The base functionality of CExecutive is similar to Shell. The simplest command line looks like this:

```
Dim exec As New CExecutive
exec.Run "Notepad"
```

At first glance, CExecutive doesn't seem to be bringing much to the party. But it starts to make a little more sense when you set the WaitMode and Show properties:

```
With exec
    .WaitMode = ewmWaitIdle
    .Show = vbHide
    .Run "mktyplib shelllnk.odl"
    If .ExitCode Then MsgBox "Compile failed"
End With
```

You don't have to save the process ID and exit code in variables or call a separate WaitOnProgram because all that is built into the class. And there's more. For Windows programs, you can request a position for the new window as in this example (which assumes you've set a With block):

```
' Notepad half the screen size 20 percent in from left and top
.Left = Screen.Width / Screen.TwipsPerPixelX * 0.2
.Top = Screen.Height / Screen.TwipsPerPixelY * 0.2
.Width = Screen.Width / Screen.TwipsPerPixelX * 0.5
.Height = Screen.Height / Screen.TwipsPerPixelY * 0.5
.Show = vbNormalFocus
.InitDir = "C:\"
.WaitMode = ewmNoWait
.Run "Notepad colors.txt"
```

Of course, a requested window position and size is just a request. The program itself can override anything the caller asks for. Calculator, for example, determines its own size and will ignore your requests to the contrary.

Character-Mode Sentenced to Execution

CExecutive also knows a lot about how to handle primitive character-mode programs. There are two types of character-mode programs: MS-DOS programs and Win32 console programs. Although they often look and work the same, 32-bit Windows does a much better job of handling its native console programs. Unfortunately, you won't find many of them under Windows 95. Even the command processor, COMMAND.COM, is an MS-DOS program. Things are much better under Windows NT. Its command processor, CMD.EXE, is a 32-bit console application, and so are most of its command-line tools such as FIND, SORT, and XCOPY.

If you're stuck with a lot of old MS-DOS programs, there's a limit to how much Win32 can do. You'll often get better control if you define program information files (PIFs) and execute them instead of the programs.

When dealing with command-line oriented programs such as filters and other utilities, it's important to understand what parts of the command line are handled by the operating system and what parts by the command processor. Redirection and command-line piping are done by the command processor. It won't do you any good to provide the redirection and piping characters on a command line that is passed directly to the CExecutive Run method or to the Shell function. You need to ask the command processor to execute your program indirectly. Furthermore, if you go through the command processor, you can give built-in commands such as Dir and Type. Since the command processor differs depending on the operating system and potentially on settings made by the user, you should always use the COMSPEC environment variable rather than a hard-coded name. For example, this Shell statement redirects the output of the Dir command to a file:

```
Shell Environ$("COMSPEC") & " /c dir > dir.out"
```

The Run method of CExecutive has a shortcut. It recognizes and expands environment variables enclosed in percent signs:

```
exec.Run "%COMSPEC% /c dir > dir.out"
```

If you're curious how this works, check the ExpandEnvStr function in UTILITY.BAS. It's a Visual Basic wrapper for the ExpandEnvironmentStrings API function.

Many CExecutive properties have no effect on Windows-based programs, but instead control Win32 console applications. Keep in mind that they'll have limited effect on MS-DOS programs. You can specify the title, the number of rows and columns, and the color:

```
.Title = "The Meaning of Life"
.Left = Screen.Width / Screen.TwipsPerPixelX * 0.1
.Top = Screen.Height / Screen.TwipsPerPixelY * 0.1
' Start a red on cyan command session 70 columns by 64 rows
```

(continued)

```
.Columns = 70
.Rows = 64
.BackColor = qbGreen
.ForeColor = qbLightYellow
.Run "%COMSPEC%"
```

The color argument puts yellow text on a hideous green background. Does that take you back or what? Some of us remember when we had only 16 colors and specified them in the high and low nibbles of a byte. Those are the 16 colors that are still supported through the QBColor function. I added constants for them in the Windows API type library. Even those of us who remember the old colors don't remember being able to make our screens 70 columns by 64 rows. Back in those days, you could have 80 or 40 columns and 25, 43, or 50 rows—take it or leave it.

The final trick in CExecutive's bag is piping input and output. This is different than piping input and output between programs on a command line. You can give a string as the standard input of a program and then read its standard output back into another string:

```
.PipedInText = sUnsortedText
.Show = vbHide
.WaitMode = ewmWaitDead
.Run "sort"
sSortedText = .PipedOutText
```

This technique links the oldest style of programming with the newest. You can send the output of a command like Dir directly onto a web page and leverage your old programs rather than writing procedures that do the same thing. The technique works for MS-DOS programs, Win32 console programs, and for the few Windows programs that take advantage of standard input and output handles.

The Executive's Mom

The Run method of CExecutive calls one of the top ten most complicated Win32 functions, CreateProcess. Actually, CreateProcess isn't quite as bad as it looks—once you figure out that most of its argument variations don't apply to you. In the CExecutive class, it's the properties that do the work. Most of them set up the STARTUPINFO structure containing input, and a few of them read the process and thread handles returned in the PROCESS_INFORMATION structure. I'm not going to get into the messy details of using these structures. Let's just say that after your ducks are lined up, knocking them over with the Run method is no big deal.

```
Sub Run(sCmd As String)

    ' Process any environment variables
    Dim sCmdLine As String, sPipeOut As String, sPipeErr As String
    sCmdLine = MUtility.ExpandEnvStr(sCmd)
    sProg = MParse.GetQToken(sCmdLine, " ")

    ' Create standard input, output, and error pipes
    CreatePipes

    ' Create process and run it
    If CreateProcess(sNullStr, sCmdLine, ByVal pNull, ByVal pNull, _
                     APITRUE, 0&, pNull, sInitDir, start, proc) Then

        ' Must close write end of out and err handles before you can read
        CloseHandleNull hWriteStdOut
        CloseHandleNull hWriteStdErr

        Select Case ewm
        Case ewmWaitIdle
            ' Wait, but allow painting and other processing
            Do
                GetExitCodeProcess proc.hProcess, iExit
                DoEvents
            Loop Until ReadPipeChunk And ReadPipeErrChunk And Completed
        Case ewmWaitDead
            ' Stop dead until process terminates
            Dim iResult As Long
            iResult = WaitForSingleObject(proc.hProcess, INFINITE)
            If iResult = WAIT_FAILED Then ErrRaise Err.LastDllError
            ' Get the return value
            GetExitCodeProcess proc.hProcess, iExit
            Do
            Loop Until ReadPipeChunk And ReadPipeErrChunk And Completed
        Case Else
            ' Caller must call use ExitCode and pipe chunks directly
        End Select
        CloseHandleNull proc.hProcess
        CloseHandleNull proc.hThread
    Else
        ApiRaise Err.LastDllError
    End If
End Sub
```

Most of the work here is handling the WaitMode property (represented by the *emw* variable). It's very similar to what you already saw in WaitOnProgram.

The code to handle standard input and output pipes is the most difficult part. The standard input, standard output, and error pipes are set up in the CreatePipes procedure. The output can be read all at once from the PipedOutText property when Run is finished. If *WaitMode* is *ewmNoWait*, you can read the pipe in chunks the way you see it done in the Run method. Windows is not very forgiving in its handling of pipes. If you get anything wrong, you'll crash, as I learned the hard way over and over again. But I think I've finally got the kinks worked out so that you can pipe safely with CExecutive.

NOTE   The Shell function takes the same constants known to Create-Process, ShellExecute, and their obsolete API ancestor WinExec. These are the same constants used by ShowWindow to modify the appearance of an existing window, and, frankly, many of them don't make sense in the context of starting a new program. The Display Options settings in the Test Execute program—Hidden, Has Focus, Minimized, and Maximized—work better for me. Take a look at the logic in the check box event procedures and the GetDisplay function (TEXECUTE.FRM), which translates these sensible settings into the arbitrary constants required by Windows.

Using ShellExecute

Use Shell or CExecutive to run other people's programs when you know what you're doing. But when only the user knows what you're doing you might find ShellExecute more convenient. For example, if you want to let Windows decide how to process a document, you can pass the document name to ShellExecute. In the Test Execute program, you can try this by setting the mode to VBShell-Execute, typing a document filename in the Arguments field, and leaving the Program field blank.

ShellExecute has a lot of arguments, most of which have defaults. This sounds like a case for optional arguments; check out VBShellExecute in PROCTOOL-.BAS. You pay a performance price for the extra convenience of ShellExecute, so don't call it when you don't need it.

Unlike Shell and CExecutive, ShellExecute doesn't search the PATH environment variable for your program. If you're passing it an executable file, you need to search the path yourself by calling SearchForExe (in UTILITY.BAS). It calls the SearchDirs function described in "SearchPath" in Chapter 5. ShellExecute returns what the documentation claims is an instance handle, but isn't. Whatever it is, you can't use it to tell when a process has terminated. Never mind. You usually call ShellExecute in response to a user selecting a document. If you don't even know which program will process the document, you're probably not going to depend on the results. Therefore, the Wait option is disabled in the Test Execute program when the VBShellExecute mode is active.

When All Else Fails, Hit It with a Hammer

If the techniques described in this section seem too complex, try this low-tech batch file solution. Your calling program can create a batch file. The batch file creates a temporary file, calls the target program, and then deletes the temporary file. You write the batch file to disk, run it, and then periodically check to see whether the temporary file still exists. When the temporary file disappears, your program is finished and you can delete the batch file.

Interprocess Communication

Windows has always had a variety of ways for programs to communicate with each other. Fashions change. Here's what's in and what's out in Visual Basic interprocess communications:

- ActiveX components are hot. They are the most convenient way to share data and code inside your own process, across processes, and even across machines.

- DDE (Dynamic Data Exchange) is out of fashion. It is still supported for compatibility, and Visual Basic still supports it as fully as in previous versions. But this technology has reached a dead end and will never be enhanced.

- A Remote Procedure Call API exists for calling procedures on different machines. I've never used this API, and I can't think of a good reason to do the hard way what DCOM makes easy.

- Drag and Drop is cool. In fact, the new form of it, using the OLEDrag-Mode and OLEDropMode properties, is such an easy way to allow a user to transfer data between programs that it's not Hardcore and thus didn't make it into this book.

- ActiveX hasn't done anything to invalidate the Clipboard, which is still an effective way to make data from your program available to other programs and to use data made public by other programs. If you're supplying the data, the problem is letting other programs know it's there. If you're receiving the data, the problem is knowing when useful information is available.

- AppActivate and SendKeys provide a convenient way to activate another program and send it keystrokes. For example, you can send keystrokes to the other program to make it paste from the Clipboard. SendKeys is a Visual Basic implementation of the more general technique mentioned in the following item.

- You can easily send Windows messages to another program with SendMessage or PostMessage. You might expect to be able to receive messages using callbacks accessed through the AddressOf operator. Good luck. The messages you capture will return foreign pointers from another address space. There's a lot more work involved in cross-process messages. Fortunately, the MessageBlaster control supplied with this book does it for you. On the other hand, there's a good reason why 32-bit Windows keeps pointers in separate address spaces. You might want to think twice before trying to get around those limitations.

- Win32 adds an important new message, WM_COPYDATA, that allows you to send chunks of data from one program to another. Copying data is more complicated than you might expect. All data resides at addresses in memory, but each program has a different address space and can't understand anything about data in another program's address space. The WM_COPYDATA message hides the details of getting data from your address space to the address space of another process. Internally, the WM_COPYDATA message uses memory-mapped files.

- You can share data between processes with memory-mapped files. I'll show you an example shortly.

- The Win32 file notification APIs allow you to monitor file events in other processes (or in your own process). I'll show you this one, also.

Let's take a look at two of the more interesting techniques for interprocess communications.

Shared Memory Through Memory-Mapped Files

Memory-mapped files provide a way to look at a file as a chunk of memory. This feature is very useful in languages that support examining memory at arbitrary addresses. You map the file and get back a pointer to the mapped memory. You can simply read or write to memory from any location in the file mapping, just as you would from an array. When you've processed the file and closed the file mapping, the file is automatically updated. In other words, the operating system takes care of all the details of file I/O.

The API calls to create a file mapping are relatively simple, and you could easily call them from Visual Basic. There's only one problem. See if you can spot it:

```
' Open file
hFile = CreateFile(sFileName, GENERIC_READ Or GENERIC_WRITE, 0, _
                   pNull, OPEN_ALWAYS, FILE_ATTRIBUTE_NORMAL, _
                   pNull)
' Open file mapping called MySharedMapping
```

```
hFileMap = CreateFileMapping(hFile, pNull, PAGE_READWRITE, 0, 0, _
                            "MySharedMapping")
' Get pointer to memory representing file
pFileMap = MapViewOfFile(hFileMap, FILE_MAP_WRITE, 0, 0, 0)
```

At this point, *pFileMap* is the address of a block of memory containing the file contents. Now, what can you do in Visual Basic with a pointer you receive from an API function? Repeat after me: "Pass it to another API function." In other words, you're stuck.

In C, you can treat a pointer like an array:

```
pFileMap[0] = 'A'
bTest = pFileMap[1]
```

But Visual Basic provides no similar capability. You can use CopyMemory to copy the file mapping to some other location in memory, but that usually defeats the purpose. The idea is to be able to use it in place. The fact is, memory-mapped files won't be much use to Visual Basic programmers until they're integrated into the language. Imagine this code:

```
Dim abFileMap() As Integer
hFileMap = FreeFile
Open sFileName For FileMap With abFileMap As #hFileMap
For i = 0 to UBound(abFileMap)
    abFileMap(i) = CalculateMagicNumber(abFileMap(i))
Next
Close hFileMap
```

This might not be the best syntax. In fact, the next version of Visual Basic might implement file mapping behind the scenes with the existing syntax.

Although Visual Basic doesn't support using memory-mapped files for file I/O, it doesn't stand in your way if you want to use them for shared memory. You can create a file mapping that isn't mapped to a file by passing a magic number (−1) instead of a handle to the CreateFileMapping function. This gives you a pointer to a named chunk of memory. Any program that knows the name can also get a pointer to the memory. You still can't access the memory at that location directly in Visual Basic, but any program can use CopyMemory to read or write to the memory.

The process is a little complicated, so I encapsulated it in the CSharedString class. You'll need to run more than one instance of the test program shown in Figure 11-5 (TSHARE.VBP) to see the point. Change the text in one copy, and click the Set String button. Go to another instance of the program, and click the Get String button to read the current value.

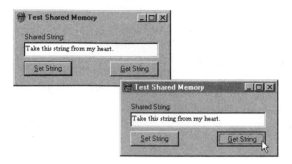

Figure 11-5. *Sharing strings.*

Here's the code to use a shared object:

```
Private ss As New CSharedString

Private Sub Form_Load()
    ss.Create "MyShare"
    If ss = sEmpty Then
        ss = "Hello from the Creator"
    End If
    txtShare = ss
End Sub

Private Sub cmdSet_Click()
    ss = txtShare
End Sub

Private Sub cmdGet_Click()
    txtShare = ss
End Sub
```

Default members make using a shared string look a lot like using an ordinary string. Of course with normal strings you don't have to call a Create method to assign a string name, which is different from the string value and different from the variable name. And you don't have to remember that name any time you want to access that string from another program. But then you can't access normal strings from another program anyway.

When the first test program creates a CSharedString object, the value is an empty string, so the program initializes to a string of its choice. When subsequent programs create objects, the value is whatever the previous program set. You can specifically destroy a shared string object by setting it to Nothing, but that's usually unnecessary. The object is destroyed automatically when it goes out of scope during program destruction.

Most of the implementation work is done in the Create method, where the internal variables (*h* for handle and *p* for pointer) are initialized. The Class_Terminate method undoes what Create did:

```
Private h As Long, p As Long

Sub Create(sName As String)
    Dim e As Long
    If sName = sEmpty Then ApiRaise ERROR_BAD_ARGUMENTS
    ' Try to create file mapping of 65535 (only used pages matter)
    h = CreateFileMapping(-1, pNull, PAGE_READWRITE, 0, 65535, sName)
    ' Save "error" value which may not be an error value
    e = Err.LastDllError
    If h = hNull Then ApiRaise e

    ' Get pointer to mapping
    p = MapViewOfFile(h, FILE_MAP_WRITE, 0, 0, 0)
    If p = pNull Then
        CloseHandle h    ' Undo what we did
        ApiRaise Err.LastDllError
    End If
    ' Check cached value to see if new value
    If e <> ERROR_ALREADY_EXISTS Then
        ' Set size of new file mapping by copying 0 to first 4 bytes
        CopyMemory ByVal p, 0, 4
    ' Else
        ' Existing file mapping already initialized
    End If
End Sub

Private Sub Class_Terminate()
    UnmapViewOfFile p
    CloseHandle h
End Sub
```

First the code calls CreateFileMapping to create a read-write memory mapping that is 65,535 bytes in length, with the name passed in the Create method. Wait a minute! You don't want 65,535 bytes of memory just to share a 20-byte string. Don't worry. Through the wonders of memory paging, you'll use only the pages you touch. In other words, you'll use one page of memory (4 KB) for that 20-byte string. That's enough to make you a little careful about how many shared memory objects you create, but it's not the same as throwing away 64 KB. Still, you'll probably want to use CSharedString for large strings and create some other shared memory class (perhaps a CSharedStrings array) for sharing lots of little strings.

After you create a file mapping (memory mapping would be more accurate in this context), you need to call MapViewOfFile to get a pointer to it. You'll get the same return (a pointer) whether you're opening an existing mapping or creating a new one. You need to distinguish these two cases, and the only way to do so is to check the error value for ERROR_ALREADY_EXISTS, which isn't really an error. If it's a new mapping, you need to initialize the data. Here is my code to read and write the data:

```
' Default property
Property Get Item() As String
    If h = hNull Then ErrRaise ERROR_INVALID_DATA
    BugAssert p <> pNull
    ' Copy length out of first 4 bytes of data
    Dim c As Long
    CopyMemory c, ByVal p, 4
    If c Then
        ' Copy the data
        Item = String$(c, 0)
        CopyMemoryToStr Item, ByVal (p + 4), c * 2
    End If
End Property

Property Let Item(s As String)
    If h = hNull Then ErrRaise ERROR_INVALID_DATA
    BugAssert p <> pNull
    Dim c As Long
    c = Len(s)
    ' Copy length to first 4 bytes and string to remainder
    CopyMemory ByVal p, c, 4
    CopyMemoryStr ByVal (p + 4), s, c * 2
End Property
```

In your own shared memory classes, you can initialize and organize the data anyway you like as long as everyone who uses the data knows the convention. I save a shared string as a Long containing the string length, followed by the bytes of the string. I thought about various schemes for allowing multiple chunks of data and perhaps multiple data types—such as arrays. But I decided to leave you to design the CSharedCollection class.

WARNING When you test shared string objects, don't terminate by using the End toolbar button, the End item on the Run menu, or the End statement. Instead, unload your forms. This is good practice in general, but it's particularly important with the shared string class. Ending a program short-circuits the normal destruction mechanism, and you'll "End" up with dangling copies of the shared memory. A shared memory mapping is destroyed only when all of its clients have unmapped it. If a program dies without unmapping, its mapping handle dies with it. The only way to get rid of the shared data is to log off.

Threads and Synchronization

Perhaps the most interesting new capability of Win32 is its ability to create new threads of execution and to synchronize operations among them. In the long run, this will be the way to make operations run independently and interact smoothly. But don't expect multithreading to solve all your problems in this version.

Visual Basic itself doesn't use threads in critical areas. For example, the next time you print a Visual Basic project, notice how the Print dialog box works. You specify what you want to print, click on OK, and then watch a print message box until the print job is finished. You can't edit or do anything else in the IDE until your document has been shipped off to the printer. In a multithreaded print implementation, you wouldn't have to wait. The print thread would be launched independently, and you could do other chores while it worked in the background.

Of course, background operations can be implemented in other ways. Many 16-bit programs have had background printing for years, but it wasn't always smooth and clean. I haven't tried it, but I imagine that you could implement background printing by launching a modeless form that handles the printing. The form would have a timer that periodically calls timer events to do chunks of the print job. But this technique depends on your ability to break the background task into chunks. A multithreaded implementation lets the operating system break the job into chunks.

Visual Basic provides an automatic form of multithreading, but it only works in limited situations. You can create a multithreaded ActiveX EXE component by specifying Unattended Execution on the General tab of the Project Properties dialog box. That means it can't have a user interface. The Visual Basic documentation describes in detail the multithreading arrangement used for such servers. The File Notification Server described in the next section will be this kind of component, but I won't have much to say about the multithreading part because it works automatically.

Visual Basic ActiveX DLL components can cooperate with multithreaded clients as long as they are marked for Unattended Execution. There are two kinds of multithreaded programs that might call such a DLL: the ActiveX EXE components mentioned above, and programs written in other languages. In particular, two new Microsoft technologies, Internet Information Server (IIS) and the

Microsoft Transaction Server (MTS), expect any components they work with to be multithread-capable. That's why, late in the development of this book, I had to rip all the classes with user interfaces out of VBCore and put them in a separate VisualCore component. VBCore is marked for Unattended Execution; VisualCore is not. That means that VBCore has no forms and no calls to MsgBox or InputBox. When a thread from a multithreaded client calls, VBCore is guaranteed not to block calls from the client's other threads. If one thread calls SortArray with 100,000 items, the next thread won't have to wait for the sort to finish.

I'll leave you to explore the full implications of multithreaded EXE servers and thread-safe DLLs. The important thing for this discussion is that the Visual Basic library has to be at least partially thread-safe to support these technologies. And if the library can work with Visual Basic's automatic multithreading, what's to stop it from working with not so automatic multithreading?

As a hardcore programmer, you're undoubtedly saying, "If there's an API to launch threads, I'm sure I could call it." Indeed, there is a CreateThread function, and with the AddressOf operator, it's easy to use it to send threads off to do their appointed tasks. Whether they'll ever come back is another matter. But what the heck. Crashing only hurts for an instant.

Where Angels Fear to Thread

The Test Thread program shown in Figure 11-6 starts a thread and lives to tell the tale—or at least it does if you can keep your hands off the debugging commands. That's the first rule of thread debugging in the IDE. Don't. Debug.Print seems to work for displaying status messages, but that's about it.

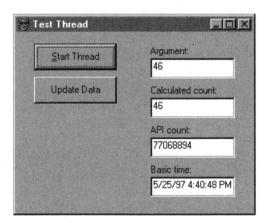

Figure 11-6. *The Test Thread program.*

The program consists of two buttons that update four text boxes with data maintained by the thread. The main button toggles between starting the thread while passing it a parameter, and stopping the thread while receiving a return value:

```
Private Sub cmdStartStop_Click()
    If cmdStartStop.Caption = "&Start Thread" Then
        StartThread txtStartStop
        cmdStartStop.Caption = "&Stop Thread"
        lblStartStop.Caption = "Return value:"
        cmdUpdate_Click
    Else
        txtStartStop = StopThread
        cmdStartStop.Caption = "&Start Thread"
        lblStartStop.Caption = "Argument:"
        cmdUpdate_Click
    End If
End Sub

Private Sub cmdUpdate_Click()
    txtCalc = CalcCount
    txtAPI = APICount
    txtBasic = BasicTime
End Sub
```

The CalcCount, APICount, and BasicTime functions are just public functions that return private variables modified by the thread procedure in THREAD.BAS. The thread procedure, like any procedure used with the AddressOf operator, must be in a standard module. You're used to that from earlier experience with callbacks in Chapters 2 and 6. Here's the code to start the thread procedure:

```
Sub StartThread(ByVal i As Long)
    ' Signal that thread is starting
    fRunning = True
    ' Create new thread
    hThread = CreateThread(ByVal pNull, 0, AddressOf ThreadProc, _
                           ByVal i, 0, idThread)
    If hThread = 0 Then MsgBox "Can't start thread"
End Sub
```

First we signal that the thread is starting by using the most primitive and inflexible method of thread synchronization—a global variable. Bear with me. Then we call CreateThread to start a thread in the procedure ThreadProc. The first argument is the security attribute, which we ignore. The second is the stack size, which we pass as zero to let the operating system decide. The third argument is the address of the procedure that will run the thread. The fourth is a 32-bit parameter passed to the thread. This could be a pointer to something useful (such as a string or a UDT), but in this case, it's just numeric data. The fifth argument is for options flags, but we don't have any. The last argument is a reference to a variable that will receive the thread ID, a unique identifier which the sample program stores in the global variable *idThread* and then ignores. The function returns a thread handle, which is also stored in a global variable.

The thread procedures you start have some leeway in what they do, but some parts are invariant, as this example shows:

```
Sub ThreadProc(ByVal i As Long)
    ' Use parameter
    cCalc = i
    Do While fRunning
        ' Calculate something
        cCalc = cCalc + 1
        ' Use an API call
        cAPI = GetTickCount
        ' Use a Basic function
        datBasic = Now
        ' Switch immediately to another thread
        Sleep 1
    Loop
    ' Return a value
    ExitThread cCalc
End Sub
```

The main purpose of this thread is to prove that we can indeed run a thread and do calculations, make API calls, and use Visual Basic statements inside it. After updating several global variables, the thread sleeps so that other threads can continue working immediately. When the main thread (the calling process) signals to stop by changing the *fRunning* variable, the thread exits by calling ExitThread, passing whatever it wishes to return to the process that started it.

The documentation for CreateThread says that the thread procedure can be a function that returns a Long value and that ExitThread will be called automatically. Well, that might be true in C or C++, but I crashed when I made ThreadProc a function and returned without explicitly calling ExitThread. I changed to a sub to make absolutely clear that the return value must go through ExitThread.

My StopThread procedure is what causes the thread loop to terminate so that ExitThread will be called:

```
Function StopThread() As Long
    ' Signal thread to stop
    fRunning = False
    ' Make sure thread is dead before returning exit code
```

```
    Do
         Call GetExitCodeThread(hThread, StopThread)
    Loop While StopThread = STILL_ACTIVE
    CloseHandle hThread
    hThread = 0
End Function
```

It might take a while after the global variable is changed before the thread procedure checks the signal variable and terminates the thread, so StopThread has to loop until GetExitCodeThread comes up with a valid exit code.

The Next Thread

That doesn't look so bad now, does it? Of course there's a lot more to multithreading. The first step in enhancing my sample would be to get rid of that *fRunning* global variable and use a real synchronization technique such as semaphores, events, mutexes, or critical sections. You might also want to send data between threads using handle sharing, pipes, mailslots, or other communication techniques or define some data for your thread using the Thread Local Storage (TLS) API functions. At some point, you would probably want to encapsulate common thread behavior in public classes, although the actual thread procedures must remain in standard modules. In fact, someone with more thread experience than me could probably write a book as long as this one called *Hardcore Visual Basic Threads*.

The first question a person determined to become a Visual Basic thread expert would have to ask is this: What can you safely do in a Visual Basic thread? In other words, what parts of the language are thread-safe? *Thread-safe* means that the code has been written so that it can be safely reentered at any time by any thread. When multiple threads are running, the operating system automatically switches between them. One thread might be in the middle of the Hobgoblin function when it loses control. Another independent thread gets control and calls the Hobgoblin function. But the first thread has modified a global variable used by Hobgoblin. The second thread comes in and modifies the same variable. The first thread gets control back, but the variable it was depending on to have the same value it had just a few microseconds ago has been mysteriously modified. If the modified variable contained a pointer to something (such as a string), you'll probably crash. If it contained numeric data, you might be lucky enough to get random results.

Thread-safe libraries must be written very carefully to ensure that each thread has independent data or, if data is shared, that different threads cooperate in accessing it. Part of the Visual Basic library has been rewritten to be thread-safe. If this weren't true, the automatic threading in ActiveX EXE components marked for unattended execution wouldn't work. But you're on your own figuring out exactly which parts. You're usually safe using any Visual Basic procedure that

639

has no connection with a user interface, but anything related to forms, controls, or message boxes is suspect. You can guess, but the only way to know for sure is to try it. The official Visual Basic position is that multithreading isn't supported, and if you go whining to the support people about crashes in your thread procedures, you'll probably hear muffled laughter on the other end of the phone.

That leaves you in a tough position. If something goes wrong (and it will), you don't know whether to blame the Visual Basic library or your code. There are definitely some parts of the Visual Basic language that are not thread-safe, but nobody's going to tell you what those parts are. On the other hand, coding for multiple threads is such a different way of thinking for most Visual Basic programmers that you also have to suspect your own code. And debugging code for multiple threads ranges from difficult to impossible in the Visual Basic IDE. It's actually easier to debug by compiling to native code and debugging in the thread-aware Visual C++ environment rather than in the Visual Basic environment.

All these problems remind me of a Mark Twain story that lampooned a certain type of ridiculous adventure story common in his day. After taking his heroes through a series of increasingly harrowing situations, he ended the story with the comment that he had created an impossible predicament and had no idea how to resolve it. That's where I'm going to leave you with the multithreading adventure. Have fun and good luck.

In the long run, I think Visual Basic multithreading will only be safe and reliable when it is added to the language. Not only will the library have to be modified to be completely thread-safe, but statements and attributes will have to be added so that you could specify that a procedure is a thread. High level features would also be needed to make the most common types of synchronization easy. And, of course, the debugger must be enhanced to handle threads. Maybe we'll see that in the next version. (That's what I said last time.)

File Notification

Try this experiment. Run Windows Explorer in one window, go to a command-line session or another instance of Windows Explorer, and delete a file in the directory shown by the original Explorer. Watch what happens to the Explorer window. How does Windows Explorer know that a file has changed? The same way your programs can know: by using FindFirstChangeNotification, FindNextChangeNotification, and FindCloseChangeNotification.

The Client Side of File Notification

The File Notification Server (NOTIFY.VBP) encapsulates the file change notification in an ActiveX application that you can use from any program. You can see how it works in the Browse Picture Files program (BROWSE.VBP), which acts as a client of the File Notification Server. The program allows you to browse through picture files, seeing and hearing each of them. You can see the program at work in Figure 11-7. It not only displays icons, cursors, bitmaps, metafiles, wave files, and AVI clips, but it also copies, deletes, renames, and moves them. And it updates its display when other processes remove, create, or modify picture files or directories.

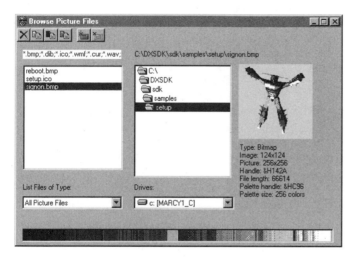

Figure 11-7. *Browsing pictures.*

The Browse Picture Files program receives file notifications from a CFileNotify object by way of an IFileNotifier interface. The key declarations for this connection are at the top of the main client form:

```
' Create an object that notifies client of file changes
Private notify As CFileNotify

' Implement an interface that connects to CFileNotify
Implements IFileNotifier
```

The *notify* object is the EXE server that will use Win32 file notification API functions to watch for any changes to files or directories. But the client has to tell the server object which directories to watch by calling its Connect and Disconnect methods. Whenever the user changes a directory in the browser, it uses the following code to disconnect the old directory and connect the new one:

```
Private Sub dirPic_Change()
With notify
    ' Synchronize the file control and select the first file
    filPic.Path = dirPic.Path
```

(continued)

```
        If filPic.ListCount > 0 Then filPic.ListIndex = 0

        ' Watch whole drive for directory changes
        If hNotifyDir <> -1 Then .Disconnect hNotifyDir
        hNotifyDir = .Connect(Me, dirPic.Path, _
                            FILE_NOTIFY_CHANGE_DIR_NAME, False)
        ' Watch current directory for name changes (delete, rename, create)
        If hNotifyFile <> -1 Then .Disconnect hNotifyFile
        hNotifyFile = .Connect(Me, dirPic.Path, _
                            FILE_NOTIFY_CHANGE_FILE_NAME, False)
        ' Watch current directory for modifications of file contents
        If hNotifyChange <> -1 Then notify.Disconnect hNotifyChange
        hNotifyChange = .Connect(Me, dirPic.Path, _
                            FILE_NOTIFY_CHANGE_LAST_WRITE, False)
    End With
End Sub
```

Skip the first few lines that handle normal directory changes, and concentrate on the code that connects the FBrowsePictures form to the server. First you disconnect any previous connection, and then you connect the server to the new directory. The first connection tells the server to report any changes to the current directory. The last Boolean parameter indicates whether to check child directories. Windows 95 doesn't support True, so you should supply False if you want the client to work on all platforms. Changes include any directories that have been created, removed, or renamed. The next connection looks for any files whose names have changed in the current directory. Deleting a file or creating a new file obviously changes the filename. The third connection looks for files that have been modified. If you change the current image file with ImagEdit or some other tool, the change appears in the Browse Picture Files program as soon as you save the file.

Notice that each call to Connect passes the form object in the first parameter. The Connect method actually takes an IFileNotifier type for this parameter, but since the form implements IFileNotifier, it is an IFileNotifier and can be early-bound to the server. In the previous edition of this book, the form was passed through an Object parameter. The server had to trust that the client would implement an object with the correct methods. The IFileNotifier interface makes the connection fast and type-safe. The interface consists of a single method:

```
' Interface for CFileNotify to communicate with its clients
Sub Change(sDir As String, efn As EFILE_NOTIFY, fSubTree As Boolean)

End Sub
```

Here's how the FBrowsePictures form implements IFileNotifier:

```
Private Sub IFileNotifier_Change(sDir As String, _
                                 efn As FileNotify.EFILE_NOTIFY, _
                                 fSubTree As Boolean)
    BugMessage "Directory: " & sDir & _
               " (" & efn & ":" & fSubTree & ")" & sCrLf
    Select Case efn
    Case FILE_NOTIFY_CHANGE_DIR_NAME, FILE_NOTIFY_CHANGE_FILE_NAME
        Dim i As Integer
        ' Refresh drive, directory, and file lists
        i = filPic.ListIndex
        filPic.Refresh
        filPic.ListIndex = IIf(i, i - 1, i)
        dirPic.Refresh
        drvPic.Refresh
    Case FILE_NOTIFY_CHANGE_LAST_WRITE
        ' Refresh current picture in case it changed
        filPic_Click
    End Select
End Sub
```

This code is a little sloppy, although there's no harm done in this case. It refreshes everything in sight rather than trying to figure out exactly what changed. You might be able to be more exact in your code. Now let's look at where those notification calls come from.

The Server Side of File Notification

The File Notification Server is a slow EXE server, not a fast DLL server. Why? Because a DLL server would be too efficient. You want the server code to run in a separate thread, and, in Visual Basic, putting it in a separate EXE is the best way to do that. Performance isn't really an issue with file notification. The more important issue is making sure notifications don't slow down normal operation of the client.

The Connect method is what launches each file notification thread, but before we examine it, let's look at some of the data it uses. The server maintains an array of notification handles. In addition, it must keep a parallel array of the data associated with each handle. Later you'll see why the handles need to be in a separate array. For each notification, the server maintains four pieces of information: the directory to be watched, the type of event, a flag indicating whether to check subdirectories, and the IFileNotifier object to be called when a file event occurs. The data looks like this:

```
Public Type TConnection
    sDir As String
    efn As EFILE_NOTIFY
```

(continued)

```
        fSubTree As Boolean
        notifier As IFileNotifier
End Type

' Actually cLastNotify + 1 allowed
Public Const cLastNotify = 28
' One extra blank item in each array for easy compacting
Public ahNotify(0 To cLastNotify + 1) As Long
Public aconNotify(0 To cLastNotify + 1) As TConnection
Public aerr(errFirst To errLast) As String
' Count of connected objects managed by class
Public cObject As Long
```

I use arrays with a fixed size because it's easier than dealing with dynamic structures. In a single-threaded server, you'd have one handle and one connection
block for each client, but the Notify server is marked for unattended execution
with a thread pool of four. Each of those threads will have its own array of
handles, so potentially you could have more than 100 clients. Realistically it's
pretty unlikely that the server would have more than four simultaneous clients.
Regardless of threads and clients, the notification handles must be arranged in
an array because, as you'll see shortly, that's the way WaitForMultipleHandles
expects them. That's why handles and object data are kept in parallel arrays.
Notice that the array is public data residing in NOTIFY.BAS, not in NOTIFY.CLS.
Every client (within the same thread) shares the same arrays of handles and
notifications.

Here's how the Connect method initializes this data for each notification request:

```
Function Connect(notifier As IFileNotifier, sDir As String, _
                 efn As EFILE_NOTIFY, fSubTree As Boolean) As Long
    Connect = hInvalid ' Assume fail
    Dim i As Long, h As Long
    ' Find blank handle space
    For i = 0 To cLastNotify
        If ahNotify(i) = hInvalid Then
            ' Set up notification
            h = FindFirstChangeNotification(sDir, fSubTree, efn)
            Connect = h
            If h = hInvalid Then
                ' Change notification unsupported on remote disks
                If Err.LastDllError <> ERROR_NOT_SUPPORTED Then
                    RaiseError errInvalidArgument
                End If
                Exit Function
            End If
            ' Store information
            ahNotify(i) = h
```

```
            With aconNotify(i)
                Set .notifier = notifier
                .sDir = sDir
                .efn = efn
                .fSubTree = fSubTree
            End With
            Exit Function
        End If
    Next
    RaiseError errTooManyNotifications
End Function
```

Connect looks for a blank slot in the array. When it finds one, it initializes the slot with a file notification handle obtained by calling the FindFirst-ChangeNotification API function. You can see what happens to the parameters passed by the client. If everything goes well, Connect stores the handle and other data in the appropriate arrays. You can look through the code to see the details of how RaiseError handles errors and Disconnect undoes the work done by Connect.

The important point about this code is that FindFirstChangeNotification requests that the kernel send off a thread to watch for file events. All you need to do is wait for the event to happen. But wait where? Who will the kernel notify when it gets a file event? It can't wait in the Connect event (which must return to the client), but where else can it go?

The only other place is in the server's standard module. You need a loop that checks periodically for changes. Theoretically, you could put the loop in Sub Main (as I did in the previous version of this book). But changes in the way Visual Basic handles server startup forced me to change. I use the Main procedure to initialize server data, but at some point I have to return control to the client. So instead of looping in Main, I use a Windows timer to start a separate loop procedure. Here's the initialization code:

```
Sub Main()

    Dim i As Integer
    For i = 0 To cLastNotify
        ahNotify(i) = hInvalid
    Next
    aerr(errInvalidDirectory) = "Invalid directory"
    aerr(errInvalidType) = "Invalid notification type"
    aerr(errInvalidArgument) = "Invalid argument"
    aerr(errTooManyNotifications) = "Too many notifications"
    aerr(errNotificationNotFound) = "Notification not found"
    BugMessage "Initialized static data"
```

(continued)

```
' Start the wait loop and return to the caller
Call SetTimer(hNull, 0, 200, AddressOf WaitForNotify)
BugMessage "Started Timer"

End Sub
```

The SetTimer function specifies that a callback called WaitForNotify will be started every 200 milliseconds. You can see a better example of a Windows timer in the CTimer class (TIMER.BAS and TIMER.CLS), which I mentioned in Chapter 7. The callback procedure must satisfy the very specific format shown below. The first part of this code simply kills the timer (we only want it to execute once). After that, it starts the real notification loop:

```
Sub WaitForNotify(ByVal hWnd As Long, ByVal iMsg As Long, _
                  ByVal idTimer As Long, ByVal cCount As Long)
    ' Ignore all parameters except idTimer

    ' This one-time callback is used only to start the loop
    KillTimer hNull, idTimer
    BugMessage "Killed Timer"

    Dim iStatus As Long, f As Boolean
    ' Keep waiting for file change events until no more objects
    Do
        '   Wait 100 milliseconds for notification
        iStatus = WaitForMultipleObjects(Count, ahNotify(0), _
                                                 False, 100)
        Select Case iStatus
        Case WAIT_TIMEOUT
            ' Nothing happened
            BugMessage "Waited for timeout"
            DoEvents
        Case 0 To Count
            BugMessage "Got a notification"
            ' Ignore errors from client; that's their problem
            On Error Resume Next
            ' Call client object with information
            With aconNotify(iStatus)
                .notifier.Change .sDir, .efn, .fSubTree
            End With
            ' Wait for next notification
            f = FindNextChangeNotification(ahNotify(iStatus))
            BugAssert f
        Case WAIT_FAILED
            ' Indicates no notification requests
            ' BugMessage "No notification requests"
            DoEvents
        Case Else
```

```
        BugMessage "Can't happen"
      End Select
    ' Class Initialize and Terminate events keep reference count
    Loop Until cObject = -1
End Sub
```

The WaitForMultipleObjects function waits for what Windows calls an object. A Win32 object can be a process, a thread, a mutex, an event, a semaphore, console input, or a change notification. I'm not even going to define these things, much less explain why or how you would want to wait on one. The point is that you must put the handles of those objects in a contiguous array and pass the number of objects, followed by the address of the first object. You must also indicate whether you want to wait until all objects have returned or wait only for the first one. In this case, you pass False to wait for the first file notification object. Finally you pass the timeout period, 100 milliseconds.

When I say that WaitForMultipleObjects waits, I mean that literally. As soon as the thread executing this Visual Basic server code hits WaitForMultipleObjects, it stops dead. The server is no longer running. All the other programs in the system get all the cycles, and you get nothing. That's what you asked for. If you doubt it, change the timeout period to the constant INFINITE (–1). The server locks tight, and absolutely nothing happens in it except responses to file events. The client keeps running and responding to file change notifications, but when the client tries to call the server's Disconnect method, no one's home. A timeout period is desperately needed in the WAIT_TIMEOUT case so that the server can get control and respond to other Connect and Disconnect requests.

When a file notification object does come through, WaitForMultipleObjects returns its index into the handle array. The *Case 0 to Count* block handles the notifications by using the stored client object to call the client's FileChange event procedure. It must then call FindNextChangeNotification to wait for the next event. Incidentally, Count is simply a Property Get procedure that counts the handles in the array.

The New Look and Feel

The biggest challenge you face in adapting applications to 32-bit mode is handling the enhanced Windows interface. Visual Basic gives you some of these features free, but others require additional work. A few demand serious hacking with the Windows API.

Before you can figure out what you have to do, you need to know the results you want. That's where the *Windows Interface Guidelines for Software Design* (Microsoft Press, 1995) comes in. If you want to get the true Windows spirit, you should get to know this book. It's like a tourist brochure that tells you what Windows looks like and why you should go there. The following sections are a preliminary Visual Basic street map that tells you how to get to some of the more interesting places in Windows.

The 3-D Feel

Windows 95 and Windows NT version 4 have a 3-D feel throughout. Buttons and windows with squared corners give a more sharply defined effect than the rounded corners of previous versions.

The three-dimensional effect is easy to achieve by setting the Appearance property to 3D (the default). You can provide the same feel at a lower level using Win32 draw functions. We'll talk briefly about two of these, DrawEdge and DrawFrameControl.

DrawEdge creates the low-level 3-D effects that the system uses to draw 3-D buttons and other controls. You can also use it to draw your own controls. Imagine writing your own Button control that does everything CommandButton does, and more. The Test Edges program (in TEDGE.VBP) demonstrates the techniques you might use in such a control. You can play with the check boxes to see which flags give different effects. Some combinations aren't meaningful, but you can experiment until you find the ones you like. Figure 11-8 shows some of the more common effects. For a surprising effect, click the Adjust check box repeatedly.

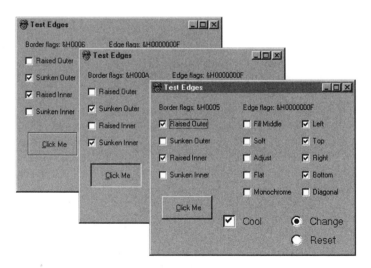

Figure 11-8. *Drawing edges and controls.*

The fake CommandButton in the example is actually the following RECT variable:

```
Private cmd As RECT
```

Here's the code that initializes and draws the button:

```
With lblButton
    cmd.Left = .Left
    cmd.Top = .Top
    cmd.Right = .Left + .Width
    cmd.bottom = .Top + .Height
End With
InitButton
```

The RECT variable is used to draw the button edges over a transparent label containing the button text. This makes it easy to size the rectangle and to respond to clicks on the label as if they were on the button. In this sample, the ScaleMode of the form is set to vbPixel so that RECT values can be assigned directly. If your programs need to use a different ScaleMode (such as the default twips), you'll need to convert control coordinates to pixel values for RECT variables.

The InitButton procedure sets up the initial check box states and calls Update-Button. UpdateButton initializes flags based on the check box settings and then draws the button using the following statement:

```
DrawEdge hDC, cmd, afBorder, afStyle
```

The *afBorder* and *afStyle* variables are bit flags corresponding to the check boxes on the sample form.

The DrawFrameControl function works at a higher level than DrawEdge. This function can draw different kinds of predefined buttons and other controls such as the Cool CheckBox control and the Change and Reset OptionButton controls shown in Figure 11-8. You pass flags that describe the type and the state of the control. Like the button control shown earlier, the fake button is drawn on top of a transparent label so that the label can respond to mouse events. Here's how the Click event of the label calls DrawFrameControl to toggle the check box:

```
Private Sub lblBigCheck_Click()
    If afChk <> (DFCS_BUTTONCHECK Or DFCS_CHECKED) Then
        afChk = DFCS_BUTTONCHECK Or DFCS_CHECKED
    Else
        afChk = DFCS_BUTTONCHECK
    End If
    DrawFrameControl hDC, chk, DFC_BUTTON, afChk
End Sub
```

The checkbox and the option buttons shown in the example are just two of the many common elements you can draw with DrawFrameControl. See the Win32 documentation for more details. If you like DrawEdge and DrawFrameControl, check out the other new draw functions: DrawAnimatedRects, DrawCaption, DrawState, DrawStatusText, and DrawTextEx.

The built-in controls make DrawEdge and DrawFrameControl unnecessary in most cases, but I can think of a few situations where they might be useful. First you could make a set of ActiveX controls that encapsulate check boxes and option buttons with user-defined sizes. Before you spend a lot of time on this, try exploring the new DisabledPicture, DownPicture, Picture, Mask-Color, UseMaskColor, and Style properties of the CheckBox and OptionButton controls. You might be able to get the effect you want (or an even better effect you never considered) without DrawFrameControl. The DrawEdge function can be used to get around an annoying limitation when delegating ActiveX controls. You'll find that you can't delegate the Appearance property because it is (for no good reason) read-only at run time. You could, however, implement your own Appearance property with Draw-Edge. In fact, you could give your better Appearance property more settings. Instead of limiting users to Flat and 3D, you could offer Flat, Raised, Sunken, and Etched.

System Colors and Sizes

What was the first difference that jumped out at you the first time you loaded Visual Basic under Windows 95 (assuming for the moment that you were experienced with Visual Basic version 3)? Chances are you said something like, "Holy Hypotenuse, Batman! They've changed the default color of forms. Windows has adopted bat colors—yellow with a black title bar." Or perhaps not. Actually, most people saw gray forms with a blue title bar. But whatever color you saw, you didn't really see it, because, by default, forms don't have a color.

The default BackColor property of forms is *vb3DFace*, a constant that evaluates to &H8000000F. (Look it up on the System tab of any color property.) Color values are made up of red, green, and blue elements in the first 3 bytes of a Long, but this number has &H80 in the fourth byte. In other words, it's not a valid RGB color; it's a constant that represents a system color. In cruder languages such as C++, you must call an API function:

```
BackColor = GetSysColor(COLOR_3DFACE)
```

Visual Basic does this for you when you write this:

```
BackColor = vb3DFace
```

It's your responsibility to use the system constants faithfully rather than hard-coding specific colors. If your user creates a Batman color scheme with the Display Properties dialog box, who are you to argue? Obviously, there are exceptions. If you're writing a hospital application and decide that it's important to make your forms a sickly green color, you might decide to consciously override a user's color choices with your own.

It's important to understand the difference between the system colors you assign to Visual Basic properties and the RGB colors you pass to most GDI functions. For reasons known only to historians, system colors have the type OLE_COLOR. If you give a property this type in a UserControl, it will display the standard color picker in the Properties window. If you make the property type Long, it will be just another integer property. On the other hand, if you pass a system color to an API function that expects an RGB color, you probably won't like the result. To complicate things further, there's a third kind of color—an index into the current color palette. You probably won't find much use for these colors unless you go far beyond the meager palette techniques discussed in "Using Bitmaps" in Chapter 8.

If you have a system color but want an RGB color, you can use the OleTranslate-Color function to find the real color behind the color. This is one of the most hideously complicated simple functions in the API. My TranslateColor wrapper function makes it easy to do common operations like this:

```
rgbButtonFace = TranslateColor(vbButtonFace)
```

Here's the code that makes it work:

```
Function TranslateColor(ByVal clr As OLE_COLOR, _
                        Optional hPal As Long = 0) As Long
    If OleTranslateColor(clr, hPal, TranslateColor) Then
        TranslateColor = CLR_INVALID
    End If
End Function
```

If you're wondering what the *hPal* parameter is or what OleTranslateColor returns, check it out in the API documentation.

Under the new Windows interface, the user can change a lot besides colors. On the Appearance tab of the Display Properties dialog box, for instance, you can change not only colors but also sizes for many elements. So if you're a hard-core programmer whose programs use the size of window elements, such as the height of the title bar or the width of a scroll bar, make sure that you get the true size of these elements. The same goes for fonts. The user can change almost any font used in menus, windows, or other standard elements. Information about your system is available from one of two places. You can get system colors and many other system parameters by using GetSystemMetrics. Values specific to the user interface are located in the registry, specifically in the \Control Panel\Desktop\WindowMetrics key of HKEY_CURRENT_USER. It's better not to read them directly if you can find an alternative, however, because the registry isn't guaranteed to always be in sync with the Windows desktop.

More Interface Stuff

Here are some other enhanced interface issues you might be interested in:

- Wouldn't it be nice to have a drop-down list for selecting drives and directories, like the one in Windows Explorer and the Open common dialog? Well, tough luck. Windows provides no way to reuse the standard control. Not in Visual Basic or in any other language. You can, however, produce a similar but cruder effect with the Browse For Folder dialog box. I wrap the SHBrowseForFolder API function in the Visual Basic function BrowseForFolder (in FOLDTOOL.BAS). You pass in arguments to set the initial state of the dialog box, and then get the results from the return value. To see it in action, click on the button next to the Destination field in the Windows Interface Tricks application shown in Figure 11-10 on page 666. Fortunately, someone wasn't ready to take this crude tool for granted. Take a look at the control supplied by hardcore programmer Andrea Wyss. You'll see an example of this on the companion CD.

- You can add files to the Documents list on the Start menu by calling the AddToRecentDocs procedure (in FOLDTOOL.BAS), which in turn calls SHAddToRecentDocs. You can clear the list with ClearRecent-Docs. The Windows Interface Tricks application has buttons that demonstrate these functions.

- If your application needs to put a status icon on the Taskbar, you can call Shell_NotifyIcon to install or remove the icon. I wrap the Shell_NotifyIcon function in the CTrayIcon class; you can see it in action in the Windows Interface Tricks application. The class uses the subclassing system described at the end of Chapter 6 to handle mouse messages from the installed tray object. To create a new CTrayIcon object, declare it using the WithEvents syntax, then call the Create method to pass in a window handle, an icon, and a tip string. CTray-Icon uses this information to install your icon and generate events whenever the user interacts with it. (Be careful when debugging the application. If you interrupt the program with the End button, you'll never hit the Unload event where tray objects are destroyed. You'll end up with orphaned icons on your Taskbar.) CTrayIcon is very easy to install and use even if you don't care how it works, but hardcore programmers might also want to study the implementation in TRAYICON.CLS.

- You can make good use of new help features such as the What's This? help button. There's a programming element to this, but most of the work lies in creating the help files. (I confess to not writing a single help file for the samples provided with this book. You're on your own.)

- To support Plug and Play, you can install the System Information control, through which you can monitor various events, particularly those that change the screen size. Unfortunately, this is another control that shouldn't be a control. I wanted to attach the same events to the System object described on page 612, but I didn't get around to it.

- Use property sheets everywhere you can. Create a property sheet form for your document types, using either the TabStrip or the Tabbed Dialog control. Put a Properties item on your toolbars and your context menus whenever appropriate.

Grid Boxes

Visual Basic's Properties window offers a convenient color dialog box that pops up when you click on the down arrow for BackColor, ForeColor, or any other color property. Wouldn't it be nice to include a similar dialog box in your own programs?

In fact, you might have noticed one when testing the Fun 'n Games program (FUNNGAME.VBP) discussed in Chapter 7. I skipped the Color dialog box in that chapter, but now I'm ready to talk about it and about how you could expand on the idea. You can also see this dialog box in the Test Color Pickers program (TCOLORPICK.VBP) shown in Figure 11-9.

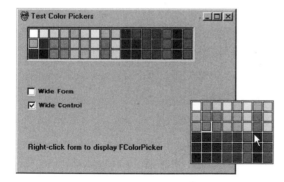

Figure 11-9. *The Test Color Pickers program.*

The CColorPicker Class

The public CColorPicker class is a simple wrapper for the private FColorPicker form. As you saw with AllAbout earlier in this chapter, forms can't be public and that's just as well. The CColorPicker class hides all the form details that you don't want users to see.

In the sample, a color picker dialog box pops up whenever you click the right mouse button. The MouseUp event procedure illustrates how CColorPicker changes the color:

```
Private Sub Form_MouseUp(Button As Integer, Shift As Integer, _
                         X As Single, Y As Single)
    If Button = 2 Then
        Dim getclr As New CColorPicker
        Static clrLast As Long
        ' Load last color used
        If clrLast <> 0& Then getclr.Color = clrLast
        ' Load dialog at given position and shape
        getclr.Load Left + X, Top + Y, -chkWideForm
        ' Save chosen color for next time
        clrLast = getclr.Color
        ' Change color of form and check boxes
        AllColors clrLast
    End If
End Sub
```

This color picker form can come in two shapes—the 16 by 3 cell shape familiar from Visual Basic version 4, and the 8 by 6 cell shape used in the current version. The Wide property controls the shape; the Color property sets the initial color and gets the selected color when the dialog box is finished. The Load command loads the dialog box and the dialog box doesn't go away until the user selects a color or presses the escape key.

The implementation comes in two parts—CColorPicker and FColorPicker. CColorPicker just passes the work on to FColorPicker. The Load method gives you an idea of how simple this is:

```
Private frm As New FColorPicker

Sub Load(Optional ByVal Left As Single = -1#, _
         Optional ByVal Top As Single = -1#, _
         Optional ByVal Wide As Boolean = True)
    frm.Wide = Wide
    If Left <> -1# Then frm.Left = Left
    If Top <> -1# Then frm.Top = Top
    frm.Show vbModal
End Sub
```

The real work is done on the form. A quick summary of the implementation follows:

■ The form has its MinButton, MaxButton, and ControlBox properties set to False and its Caption property left empty so that the form won't have a title bar. The BorderStyle property is set to Fixed Single to prevent the user from resizing it. The ScaleMode property is set to Pixel so that everything can be measured exactly in pixels. AutoRedraw is set to False, which means that the form must handle its Paint event.

- The InitArray procedure redimensions and initializes the color array in either a 16 by 3 or 8 by 6 format, depending on the Wide property.

- Form_Resize sets the exact width and height so that you don't need to size the form at design time.

- Form_Paint draws the color boxes and fills them with the colors from the array.

- Form_MouseDown calculates which color box is under the mouse pointer and draws a selection box around the color.

- Form_MouseUp sets an internal variable with the selected color and unloads the form.

- The Color Property Get procedure returns the selected color from its internal variable. The Color Property Let procedure searches for the color array entry that matches a given color and makes it the default. This allows you to initialize the form with the color that was selected the last time you loaded the form.

I won't explain the code in detail, but the Form_Paint sub will give you the flavor:

```
Private Sub Form_Paint()
    Dim ix As Long, iy As Long
    ' Draw colors in their boxes
    FillStyle = vbSolid
    For ix = 1 To ixMax
        For iy = 1 To iyMax
            FillColor = aColor(ix, iy)
            Line (((ix - 1) * 17) + 1, _
                ((iy - 1) * 17) + 1)-Step(15, 15), , B
        Next
    Next
    DrawSelection ixCur, iyCur, True
End Sub
```

The only other point I want to make about the FColorPicker form is that its properties are Friends. Instead of this:

```
Public Property Get Color() As Long
```

you define this:

```
Friend Property Get Color() As Long
```

This is a global optimization that you can add to any form that shares information by providing properties or methods. Think about it. Forms are always private. When you declare a "public" property on a form, it's not really public in the same way that a class method can be public. Nobody outside your application or component can see it—which happens to be the definition of Friend. So from a user standpoint, Public and Friend have exactly the same effect in forms. But internally they work differently.

A form is actually a kind of class, and like all classes, it uses COM to make its methods and properties available to other modules. A standard module, on the other hand, doesn't work through COM and can therefore make its procedures available more directly. The Friend keyword makes classes work more like standard modules. I don't know the technical details, but you can see the results in the TimeIt application. In native code, a Friend property on a form works about five times faster than an equivalent Public property.

Generally, properties on forms are just about the last place you'd voluntarily spend time optimizing. The better performance certainly isn't going to make any visible difference when loading an FColorPicker form, but as Joe Hacker says: "If you can get better performance for free, take it—whether you need it or not."

You can see more of the code in COLORPICKER.FRM, which as noted in "Using the CAbout class," resides in VisualCore rather than VBCore.

The XColorPicker Control

The CColorPicker class is great as far as it goes, but in some applications you might want to have a color palette always available on the form instead of one that pops up in response to your clicking a button. In that case, you want a control. The XColorPicker control looks like the FColorPicker form except that it is on a UserControl. Instead of returning the selected color through a property, it generates a Picked event when a color is selected. You can set the initial color in the Properties window at design time.

Of course, there are significant code differences between a form and a control. The control has a design-time life as well as a run-time life. Those differences caused me quite a bit of trouble, but they aren't interesting enough to show here. You can see the details in COLORPICKER.CTL.

CHALLENGE Unlike the color picker in the Properties window, CColorPicker and XColorPicker do not include rows for custom colors, nor do they provide a separate tab for picking a system color. That's your job.

Bit Editors

The CColorPicker class and the XColorPicker control are handy, but the real point of this section is to talk about one of the many projects I didn't get around to when I wrote the first edition of this book and still haven't got around to. I'd planned to show you a complete bit editor that would create or edit bitmaps (any size), icons (large or small), cursors (hot spot included), toolbar buttons (showing up and down states), or any other kind of bit picture. It would have done automatic conversions—bitmap to icon, large icon to small icon, icon to cursor, color to mono—and would have had all kinds of cool drawing tools. For now, however, this program exists only in my imagination. I'll have to describe it in a very high-level pseudocode—English.

First let's look at CColorPicker. What is it? It's a grid of cells that knows when you click on it and then takes an action based on the chosen cell. What is a bit editor? It's a grid of cells that knows when you click on it and then takes an action based on the chosen cell. The only difference is the action. Most bit editors have a big-bits mode in which bits are shown larger than life—much like the color cells in CColorPicker. But even in actual size, it's still just a grid of one-pixel cells.

CColorPicker is hard-coded to either a 16 by 3 grid or an 8 by 6 grid. The CBitEdit class must be dynamic, to accommodate any size grid. It should also have bit-picture modes. In icon mode, the grid has submodes for the common sizes—16 by 16 and 32 by 32—but it can create icons of any size for hardcore Windows programmers. Icon mode must also know about masks and transparency. Cursor mode creates a 32 by 32 grid and handles transparency as well as hot spots. Bitmaps are always a custom size; in fact, you should be able to resize the grid by dragging it. The CBitEdit class needs properties to set the mode and resize the grid, subject to conversion rules. It also needs both big-bit and life-size modes, and it should be able to display both modes at once on separate canvases.

CColorPicker is hard-coded to give each cell a specific color. CBitEdit must be able to read different colors into its grid from a file. It must also be able to save its grid to a file with the appropriate extension—BMP, ICO, CUR, and so on. The file format to save is determined by the bit-picture mode.

CColorPicker is hard-coded to set its Color property to the color of the cell you click. CBitEdit needs various methods to determine what happens for each click and drag. A Draw method sets the cell to the current color, and a Spray method colors the surrounding cells in a diminishing pattern. A Fill method starts at the current cell and fills all the surrounding cells up to the closest border. A Line method starts a stretch operation that determines the end points of a line. And so on.

What Is a File?

The concept of a file used to be simple, but no more. Under 32-bit Windows, files are complicated and getting more so. COM introduces the concept of structured files that look more like directory trees than the simple files we're used to. But that's getting ahead of the story. This version of Visual Basic doesn't handle structured storage (although you could implement it by using the IStorage interface). Ordinary files have enough new features anyway. Here are some of them:

- Filenames are long—up to 256 characters. Filenames are case-sensitive (sort of) and can have *"Embedded Spaces and.multiple.extensions"* as this one does.

- Files have new dates and times. Under MS-DOS and Windows 3.*x*, the date of the last file modification was stored with the file. Under Win32, three dates are stored with each file: creation, last modification, and last access. These dates can differ depending on the file system. I'll have more to say on this later.

- Files have new attributes—compressed and temporary. You won't have much reason to deliberately manipulate these attributes under Visual Basic, but you should be aware that documentation for the Visual Basic GetAttr function and SetAttr statement isn't exactly telling the truth when it lists six file attributes instead of eight.

- Full file paths can be specified in the UNC format (*server**share*). This isn't new, but it has become more pervasive. You can always use UNC directory names to access network resources without saving a connection to them.

- Each file has a document type that controls how it is handled by Windows Explorer and Open dialog boxes. Some of the information that can be associated with a document type includes large and small icons, an OLE verb, a file viewer, and commands for printing and performing drag-and-drop operations. The most common way to define a document type is to associate it with a filename extension.

- You can perform new operations on files: delete, copy, move, and re-name. You don't consider those operations new? We'll see.

File Dates and Times

The official Visual Basic FileDateTime function still believes that the last file modification time is the only time available. The new and improved FileAny-DateTime function knows not only about the last modification time but also about the creation time and the last access time. What it doesn't know is which file system you have. Some file systems save only part of the file times, and you can't get more than the system provides.

Windows 95 supports one file system on each local drive. It will be either VFAT or FAT32, depending on when the operating system was purchased and other factors that don't concern us because you use the same code to program either system. VFAT and FAT32 are enhancements of the FAT (file allocation table) system, known and despised by MS-DOS and Windows 3.*x* programmers. Windows NT supports FAT32 or any other installable file system you choose. The default is the Windows NT file system (NTFS). Windows 95 can access NTFS files through networks.

Under MS-DOS, file times were accurate to the nearest two seconds since 1980. Under Win32, they're accurate to the nearest micromillisecond (or some such) back to sometime just after Columbus logged onto America with his Z80 computer (or whatever they had back then). Or, to be explicit, they're supposed to be accurate to the number of 100-nanosecond intervals since January 1, 1601, and, under NTFS, they are. But in an effort to be compatible with the old FAT system, VFAT and FAT32 had to compromise. The file creation date is indeed fully accurate to the precision mentioned. The last modification time is accurate to two seconds (the same as on FAT). The last access time is accurate to one day—in other words, you only get the date, not the time.

My better FileAnyDateTime function works like FileDateTime except that it takes additional optional arguments for the last access and creation times. The function returns the modification time directly and the other two times by reference:

```
Dim datModified As Date, datCreated As Date, datAccessed As Date
datModified = FileAnyDateTime(sFile, datCreated, datAccessed)
Debug.Print "Last modified: " & datModified
Debug.Print "Last accessed: " & datAccessed
Debug.Print "Created: " & datCreated
```

Under NTFS, the output looks like this:

```
Last modified: 7/12/96 12:48:52 PM
Last accessed: 7/12/96 1:31:35 PM
Created: 7/6/96 3:49:24 PM
```

Under VFAT or FAT32, the output looks like this:

```
Last modified: 7/12/96 12:48:52 PM
Last accessed: 7/12/96
Created: 7/6/96 3:49:24 PM
```

Here's the code that returns all those dates:

```
Function FileAnyDateTime(sPath As String, _
                    Optional datCreation As Date = datMin, _
                    Optional datAccess As Date = datMin) As Date
```

(continued)

```
    ' Take the easy way if no optional arguments
    If datCreation = datMin And datAccess = datMin Then
        FileAnyDateTime = VBA.FileDateTime(sPath)
        Exit Function
    End If

    Dim fnd As WIN32_FIND_DATA
    Dim ftCreate As FILETIME, ftAccess As FILETIME, ftModify As FILETIME
    Dim hFind As Long, f As Boolean, stime As SYSTEMTIME
    ' Get all three times in UDT
    hFind = FindFirstFile(sPath, fnd)
    If hFind = hInvalid Then ApiRaise Err.LastDllError
    FindClose hFind
    ' Convert them to Visual Basic format
    datCreation = Win32ToVbTime(fnd.ftCreationTime)
    datAccess = Win32ToVbTime(fnd.ftLastAccessTime)
    FileAnyDateTime = Win32ToVbTime(fnd.ftLastWriteTime)
End Function
```

The key function called from this code is Win32ToVbTime. In earlier versions, I did time conversion the hard way—from FindFirstFile to Win32ToVbTime, which then went from FileTimeToLocalFileTime to FileTimeToSystemTime to DateSerial plus TimeSerial. It was a long, slow conversion involving two API functions and two Visual Basic functions. Here's how I do it now:

```
' Difference between day zero for VB dates and Win32 dates
' (or #12-30-1899# - #01-01-1601#)
Const rDayZeroBias As Double = 109205#    ' Abs(CDbl(#01-01-1601#))

' 10000000 nanoseconds * 60 seconds * 60 minutes * 24 hours / 10000
' comes to 86400000 (the 10000 adjusts for fixed point in Currency)
Const rMillisecondPerDay As Double = 10000000# * 60# * 60# * 24# / 10000#

Function Win32ToVbTime(ft As Currency) As Date
    Dim ftl As Currency
    ' Call API to convert from UTC time to local time
    If FileTimeToLocalFileTime(ft, ftl) Then
        ' Local time is nanoseconds since 01-01-1601
        ' In Currency that comes out as milliseconds
        ' Divide by milliseconds per day to get days since 1601
        ' Subtract days from 1601 to 1899 to get VB Date equivalent
        Win32ToVbTime = CDate((ftl / rMillisecondPerDay) - rDayZeroBias)
    Else
        ApiRaise Err.LastDllError
    End If
End Function
```

Math is a lot faster than function calls, and this technique avoids one API call and two Visual Basic calls that, behind the scenes, did what you see here out in the open. I wish I had thought of it, but the code actually comes from an article by Jim Mack in *Windows Developer's Journal* (May, 1997). Notice that Win32ToVbTime takes a Currency parameter. Now what in the world could Currency have to do with dates? Nothing really. This is just a continuation of the concept introduced in "Large Integers and Currency" in Chapter 2. The Windows API passes dates around in FILETIME structure variables. A FILETIME is a crude way of representing a 64-bit integer in two 32-bit integer fields called *dwLowDateTime* and *dwHighDateTime*. You never mess with these fields individually. FILETIME is just a package for passing a variable of undefined format from one API function to another. In Visual Basic, it's a lot easier to pass those packages in a Currency type. The advantage is that Currency, unlike FILETIME, is a legal COM Automation type that can be passed in public properties or parameters.

Many Windows API functions pass time parameters as pointers to FILETIME structures, but the Windows API type library redefines these as LPVOID, the type library equivalent of As Any. You can pass a real FILETIME structure to them if you prefer. Unfortunately, there's no way to be ambiguous about UDT fields. The type library uses the Currency type for structures such as WIN32_FIND-_DATA that would normally have FILETIME fields. For those who don't like shortcuts, I provide an equivalent WIN32_FIND_DATAO structure with the FILETIME fields. API functions that use these structures take As Any parameters so that you can pass the one you prefer.

Politically Correct File Operations

Deleting, copying, renaming, and moving files should be simple, right? Visual Basic provides the Kill, FileCopy, and Name statements for the first three operations and, contrary to the documentation, you can also use Name to move files across disks. Who could be offended by such simple features?

Well, you might be offended if the FileCopy statement overwrote an important file without asking for confirmation. I might be ticked off if your Kill statement accidentally killed all the files in the DeleteMe.Not folder, with no way to recover them. Our customers might be frustrated and confused if our FileCopy brought the whole system to a halt while copying a 1-MB file from a remote drive to a floppy disk with no visual clue to why the keyboard and the mouse weren't responding.

The SHFileOperation function provides the means to delete, rename, copy, and move files with all the protections, warnings, and status reports you could ever imagine—and some that you never dreamed of. I use SHFileOperation in my CopyAnyFile, DeleteAnyFile, RenameAnyFile, and MoveAnyFile functions.

For the SHFileOperation function, I use both Visual Basic UDT and Declare statements because they work better than the type library for strings in structures. There's something very unusual about the C structure, so let's have a look:

```
Private Declare Function SHFileOperation Lib "shell32.dll" _
    Alias "SHFileOperationA" (lpFileOp As SHFILEOPSTRUCT) As Long

Private Type SHFILEOPSTRUCT
    hWnd As Long            ' Window owner of any dialogs
    wFunc As Long           ' Copy, move, rename, or delete code
    pFrom As String         ' Source file
    pTo As String           ' Destination file or directory
    fFlags As Integer       ' Options to control the operations
```

Busted

Many old programs (including the previous version of a well-known programming environment which I won't name because it has been fixed) provide an example of how not to program files under 32-bit Windows. When these programs modify a file, the creation time and the modification time are always the same. In other words, they don't really modify the files when you save them. Instead, they re-create the file, probably in the same way most 16-bit programs modify a file. They copy to a temporary file, make the changes on the copy, and, if all goes well, close the temporary, delete the old version, and rename the temporary to the old name.

Uh-oh. What's that flashing red light in the mirror?

"OK, buddy. You know what you did wrong?"

"I didn't do anything, officer. I've been saving files that way for years, and nobody ever complained before."

"Yeah, that's because you were driving on 16-bit roads. We couldn't recognize you guys there, but I can spot an old MS-DOS programmer a mile off on this new 32-bit superhighway."

"Hey, how did you know?"

"Look at that file creation time. When I see one that's the same as the write time, 95 times out of 100 it's one of you old programmers replacing a file without copying the time and attributes."

"What's wrong with that?"

```
        fAnyOperationsAbortedLo As Integer ' Indicates partial failure
        fAnyOperationsAbortedHi As Integer
        hNameMappingsLo As Long      ' Array indicating each success
        hNameMappingsHi As Long
        lpszProgressTitleLo As Long ' Title for progress dialog
        lpszProgressTitleHi As Long
End Type
```

The first few fields indicating the operation and the files to work on are easy.
But there's something wrong with the *fFlags* field. It's an Integer instead of a
Long, and in the C include files the designer took special steps to declare that
the structure members shouldn't be aligned on DWORD boundaries. Visual Basic
(and some other languages) always align structure fields on DWORD boundaries because it makes access more efficient. The only way to fake the original
alignment is to split the fields into separate high and low words. Fortunately,

"I'll bet this file is actually three months, maybe a year old. You're falsifying data.
It might be an innocent mistake, but you're hurting yourself. The file taxes are
higher on newer files. And it also screws up our maintenance equipment. Tell
you what—I'll give you a break. Just take this warning ticket into the station
within three days and pick up our ReplaceFile function from FILETOOL.BAS.
Use it from now on, and we'll cancel the 4-MB disk fine."

```
Sub ReplaceFile(sOld As String, sTmp As String)
    Dim fnd As WIN32_FIND_DATA, hFind As Long, hOld As Long, f As Boolean
    ' Get file time and attributes of old file

    hFind = FindFirstFile(sOld, fnd)
    If hFind = hInvalid Then ApiRaise Err.LastDllError
    ' Replace by deleting old and renaming new to old
    Kill sOld
    Name sTmp As sOld
    ' Assign old attributes and time to new file
    hOld = lopen(sOld, OF_WRITE Or OF_SHARE_DENY_WRITE)
    If hOld = hInvalid Then ApiRaise Err.LastDllError
    f = SetFileTime(hOld, fnd.ftCreationTime, _
                    fnd.ftLastAccessTime, fnd.ftLastWriteTime)
    If f Then ApiRaise Err.LastDllError
    lclose hOld
    f = SetFileAttributes(sOld, fnd.dwFileAttributes)
    If f Then ApiRaise Err.LastDllError
End Sub
```

"Now why didn't I think of that? Hey, thanks."

"No problem, buddy. But if I catch you overwriting file times again, I'm going
to throw the disk at you."

these fields aren't as important as the other fields, and in fact, my code doesn't use them. But if you want to, you're in for a struggle.

| FLAME | Why the packing? Normally, the only reason to pack structures is so that you can store more of them on disk, but nobody's going to be using a big array of these structures. If the designers had some good reason (that I can't imagine) to pack the structure and make the *fFlags* field (with its bad Hungarian name) an Integer rather than a Long, why not put it at the end so it doesn't throw all the others out of alignment? This is typical of the SH functions, all of which seem half-baked, unfinished, and inconsistent with the rest of the Windows API. For example, why is the structure given the redundant name SHFILEOPSTRUCT instead of SHFILEOP or just FILEOP? If you like hopeless arguments about API design, the shell functions leave plenty of room for debate. |

The CopyAnyFile function illustrates the general form of my wrapper functions. You can find the others in FILETOOL.BAS.

```
Function CopyAnyFile(sSrc As String, sDst As String, _
                     Optional Options As Long = 0, _
                     Optional Owner As Long = hNull) As Boolean
    If MUtility.HasShell Then
        Dim fo As SHFILEOPSTRUCT, f As Long
        fo.wFunc = FO_COPY
        Debug.Print TypeName(fo.wFunc)
        fo.pFrom = sSrc
        fo.pTo = sDst
        fo.fFlags = Options
        fo.hWnd = Owner
        ' Mask out invalid flags
        fo.fFlags = fo.fFlags And FOF_COPYFLAGS
        f = SHFileOperation(fo)
        CopyAnyFile = (f = 0)
    Else
        ' For Windows NT 3.51
        On Error Resume Next
        ' FileCopy expects full name of destination file
        FileCopy sSrc, sDst
        If Err Then
            Err = 0
            ' CopyAnyFile can handle destination directory
            sDst = MUtility.NormalizePath(sDst) & _
                    MUtility.GetFileBaseExt(sSrc)
            FileCopy sSrc, sDst
        End If
```

```
        ' Enhance further to emulate SHFileOperation options
        ' such as validation and wild cards
        CopyAnyFile = (Err = 0)
    End If
End Function
```

The trick in calling FileCopy, FileMove, FileRename, and FileDelete is to pass the correct flags. Table 11-2 offers a brief summary of the flags. The default behavior is to produce a confirmation dialog box if anything is to be deleted or overwritten and to put up a progress dialog box if the operation lasts long enough to make a user wonder what's going on. You can test other operations with the Windows Interface Tricks application, shown in Figure 11-10 on the following page.

Flag	Purpose
FOF_NOCONFIRMATION	Overwrite or delete files without confirmation
FOF_ALLOWUNDO	Put deleted files (except those from floppy disks) in Recycle Bin
FOF_SILENT	Prevent display of a progress dialog box for slow operations
FOF_SIMPLEPROGRESS	Simplify the progress dialog box by not showing filenames
FOF_RENAMEONCOLLISION	Create new numbered files (*Copy #1 of...*) if copied or moved files conflict with existing files
FOF_MULTIDESTFILES	Copy or move a wildcard source to multiple target files rather than to a single destination directory
FOF_FILESONLY	Interpret a wildcard source to mean files only, not directories
FOF_NOCONFIRMMKDIR	Create any needed destination directories without confirmation

Table 11-2. *Option flags for file operation functions.*

Getting File Interface Information

Open up Windows Explorer, and set the display mode to *Details*. You'll see some information that we all know how to get as well as some you probably haven't seen before and don't know how to deal with in Visual Basic.

Notice that Windows Explorer lists some filenames with extensions and some without. Actually, Windows Explorer isn't showing filenames at all. You are seeing display names, which you can get by calling the SHGetFileInfo API function. Windows creates a display name based on information registered for the file document type. If a file doesn't have a registered document type, the shell will report the full filename, including the extension, as the display name. Generally, Windows uses the extension to determine the document type. In some cases, the system can use a binary pattern in the first part of the file to distinguish documents that have the same extension. COM structured storage files have a file type unrelated to any extension.

When you get the display name, you can also get other information from SHGet-FileInfo, including the file type string, the file attributes, the executable type, and various forms of large and small icons. All this comes from the registry entry for the document type. (Windows has defaults for files that have no document file type.) SHGetFileInfo will also work on directories, disk drives, and special folder locations such as My Computer, Network Neighborhood, Desktop, and Recycle Bin.

Using the file information wrapper class

The SHGetFileInfo function is complicated, in the typical API style. In other words, it's un-Basic and needs some wrappers. I wrote my wrappers as a class named CFileInfo. As usual, let's watch this class in action before we start to examine how it works.

The Windows Interface Tricks application (TWHIZ.VBP) demonstrates the information you can get and the operations you can perform on files. Figure 11-10 shows a frozen screen shot of the program, but to really get a feel for what you can do, you'll have to run it. There's a lot going on in this application; you'll need to study the Win32 API Help to fully understand the functions.

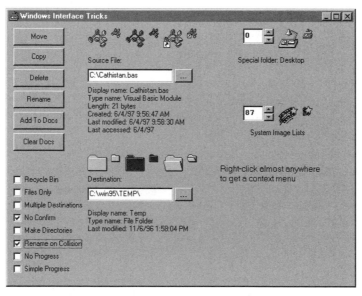

Figure 11-10. *File information and operations.*

The following code from the program shows how to get the information displayed for the source file, including large and small icons in Image controls:

```
Private Sub NewSource()
With fiSrc
    Dim s As String, sOld As String
    On Error GoTo FailNewSource
    sOld = fiSrc
    ' Assign a file name to a file information object
    fiSrc = txtSrc.Text
    ' Get back all the information about the file
    s = s & "Display name: " & .DisplayName & sCrLf
    s = s & "Type name: " & .TypeName & sCrLf
    s = s & "Length: " & .Length & " bytes" & sCrLf
    s = s & "Created: " & .Created & sCrLf
    s = s & "Last modified: " & .Modified & sCrLf
    s = s & "Last accessed: " & .Accessed & sCrLf
    lblSrc.Caption = s
    Set imgLIcon.Picture = .ShellIcon()
    Set imgSIcon.Picture = .SmallIcon()
    Set imgLIconSel.Picture = .ShellIcon(SHGFI_SELECTED)
    Set imgSIconSel.Picture = .SmallIcon(SHGFI_SELECTED)
    Set imgLIconLink.Picture = .ShellIcon(SHGFI_LINKOVERLAY)
    Set imgSIconLink.Picture = .SmallIcon(SHGFI_LINKOVERLAY)
    ⋮
```

That example shows one side of the CFileInfo class, but the default Item property is actually a Variant. You can pass it a string file name as shown above, or you can pass it an integer representing an item in the shell name space. The shell name space is the organization of icons you see in the Explorer under Windows 95 and Windows NT. The idea is to represent everything used by your computer, not just files, in a hierarchical structure. I'll take a closer look at this new way of organizing data shortly.

For now, notice the UpDown control (upper right corner of the screen in Figure 11-10) that lets you select a special folder location. You can cycle through constants representing special folder locations. The most interesting are CSIDL-_BITBUCKET (Recycle Bin), CSIDL_DESKTOP (Desktop), and CSIDL_DRIVES (My Computer). The following code gets the information for a special folder location:

```
Private Sub NewSpecialFolder(ByVal iInc As Long)
    Do
        On Error Resume Next
        fiFolder = udSpecLoc                  ' Folder to CFileInfo object
        If Err = 0 Then Exit Do
```

(continued)

```
            udSpecLoc.Value = udSpecLoc + iInc  ' Skip missing numbers
            ' Wrap property doesn't work on assignment
            If udSpecLoc = udSpecLoc.Min Then udSpecLoc = udSpecLoc.Max
            If udSpecLoc = udSpecLoc.Max Then udSpecLoc = udSpecLoc.Min
        Loop
        lblSpecLoc.Caption = "Special folder: " & fiFolder.DisplayName
        imgLSpecLoc = fiFolder.ShellIcon
        imgSSpecLoc = fiFolder.SmallIcon
End Sub
```

Some values in the range of special folder constants are invalid, so the code has to cycle through until it finds an acceptable constant.

You can also get information from a CFileInfo object by assigning it a data structure called a PIDL, which you receive from the shell name space. A PIDL is actually a pointer stored in a Long. But that's another story—unfortunately, a horror story.

Wrapping up file information

Most of the work of creating a CFileInfo object (FILEINFO.CLS) is done in the Item property Let procedure of the class. Item is the default property so that you can create a new object by assigning a file name, a special folder, or a PIDL to the object. The code in this procedure is a wrapper for the FindFirstFile and SHGetFileInfo API functions. It will get all the information it can about the file and store it in the following private variables:

```
Private Enum EItemState
    eisNotCreated
    eisFile                   ' File or directory
    eisDrive                  ' Drive
    eisID                     ' PIDL passed to us
    eisFolder                 ' PIDL created by us from special folder
End Enum
Private eis As EItemState     ' How object was created
Private vItem As Variant      ' File name or PIDL
Private shfi As SHFILEINFO    ' Info from SHGetFileInfo
Private fd As WIN32_FIND_DATA ' Info from FindFirstFile
Private afAttr As Long        ' File attributes
Private afOption As Long      ' Options for SHGetFileInfo
```

SHGetFileInfo is one of those multipurpose functions that tries to do too many things at once, but ends up not doing enough. You pass it a structure and any combination of 15 different flags. It looks at all the flags to determine what to return in the structure. Even with all of that, it doesn't return all the information you might need and you have to call FindFirstFile to get additional information.

Here's the code to analyze what kind of item is being created and to set up all the necessary options and make the appropriate API calls:

```
Property Let Item(vItemA As Variant)
    Dim h As Long, f As Long, af As Long
    Destroy      ' Clear any previous assignment
    If VarType(vItemA) = vbString Then
        ' String item is a file, directory, or drive
        If Len(vItemA) <= 3 And Mid$(vItemA, 2, 1) = ":" Then
            ' Must be drive, get attributes
            afAttr = 0: afOption = 0
        Else
            ' No terminating backslashes
            MUtility.DenormalizePath vItemA
            ' For file, get information in advance
            h = FindFirstFile(vItemA, fd)
            If h = hInvalid Then ApiRaise Err.LastDllError
            FindClose h
            afAttr = fd.dwFileAttributes
            afOption = SHGFI_USEFILEATTRIBUTES
        End If
        eis = eisFile
        af = afOption And (Not SHGFI_PIDL) Or _
            SHGFI_DISPLAYNAME Or SHGFI_TYPENAME
        f = SHGetFileInfo(vItemA, afAttr, shfi, LenB(shfi), af)
    Else
        ' Integer item is a special folder constant or pidl
        If vItemA < 50 Then
            ' Turn special folder location into a pidl
            Dim pidl As Long
            SHGetSpecialFolderLocation 0, CLng(vItemA), pidl
            vItemA = pidl
            eis = eisFolder
        Else
            eis = eisID
            pidl = vItemA
        End If
        ' For special folders or other PIDLs, everything comes from system
        afAttr = 0: afOption = 0
        ' Get item ID pointer, but don't use attributes
        af = SHGFI_PIDL Or SHGFI_DISPLAYNAME Or _
            SHGFI_TYPENAME
        f = SHGetItemInfo(pidl, afAttr, shfi, Len(shfi), af)
    End If
    If f Then
        vItem = vItemA
    Else
        eis = eisNotCreated
    End If
End Property
```

This code follows several different paths, but ultimately it comes down to either calling SHGetFileInfo for a file object or calling SHGetItemInfo for a PIDL object. These are both aliases for the SHGetFileInfo function, but the Windows API type library offers versions that take a different type for the first parameter. In C++, a string is a pointer and a PIDL is a pointer, so with the appropriate type-casting, you can pass either one in the same parameter. That's not such a good idea in Visual Basic (and I don't think much of it in C++ either).

The GetFileItemInfo function takes a Variant parameter and determines from the Variant type which API alias to call. Most of the CFileInfo methods call GetFile-ItemInfo to get additional information about a file. For example, here's the SmallIcon method:

```
Function SmallIcon(Optional afOverlay As Long = 0) As Picture
    Dim shfiT As SHFILEINFO
    If eis = eisNotCreated Then Exit Function
    ' Filter out any invalid flags -- only overlays allowed
    afOverlay = afOverlay And (SHGFI_LINKOVERLAY Or SHGFI_SELECTED _
                        Or SHGFI_OPENICON)
    ' Add in standard and small icon flags
    afOverlay = afOverlay Or afOption Or SHGFI_ICON Or SHGFI_SMALLICON
    GetFileItemInfo vItem, shfiT, afOverlay, afAttr
    Set SmallIcon = MPicTool.IconToPicture(shfiT.hIcon)
End Function
```

The *afOverlay* parameter allows you the option of specifying whether the standard icon will appear selected, as a shortcut, or open. The open overlay isn't really an overlay; it's a completely different icon indicating that a folder is open. The open flag is ignored for files, which don't have a separate icon for the open state.

You can probably guess the implementation of the Length, Created, Modified, and Accessed methods, which use data received from the call to FindFirstFile. There's a lot more detail to the CFileInfo class. For example, it also handles drives and supplies appropriate drive data in properties—but I'll leave you to struggle through that yourself.

NOTE SHGetFileInfo retrieves additional data not used in the CFileInfo class. For example, large and small icons used by the system are maintained in two internal ImageLists. Unfortunately, the Visual Basic ImageList control doesn't give you a way to use them. It's possible to iterate through the system ImageList control directly by using ImageList API functions with SHGetFileInfo. This technique is illustrated in the Windows Interface Tricks application. It turned out to be a dead end, however; I couldn't find anything useful to do with system ImageLists in Visual Basic that couldn't be done more easily without them.

Walking Through Files

Sometime during your programming career, you've probably known the frustration of working with the Dir$ function. For simple operations, it's very easy to use but it runs out of power quickly.

The worst limitation of Dir$ is documented right up front; you can't call it recursively. This is a severe limitation for a function that ought to be able to iterate through your entire hard disk, finding files that match a given description or displaying directory trees. Workarounds exist, but the performance is unacceptable as shown in the "Performance" sidebar below. The other problem with Dir$ is that it returns only the filename. If you're building a file display with attributes, file length, and file time, you have to hit the disk once for each item for each file.

But nothing prevents you from calling the Win32 FindFirstFile, FindNextFile, and FindClose functions to iterate through files yourself. You can recurse as much as you like and grab all the file data you need in one fell swoop. That's what Dir$ is doing under the surface, anyway—but it's throwing away all the information it finds except the filename.

The following WalkAllFiles function walks recursively through all the files and directories from a given starting directory. It calls the UseFile method of the

PERFORMANCE

Problem: Compare the speed of finding files with the Dir$ function to equivalent techniques, such as using FindFileFirst and using the operating system's Find dialog box.

Problem	Native code	P-code
Use the Visual Basic Dir$ function	39 seconds	39 seconds
Use the Win32 FindFirstFile function	9 seconds	9 seconds
Use the Windows Explorer Find dialog	6 seconds	

Conclusion: The Dir$ function is clearly a loser, whereas FindFirstFile performs quite well. Your results will vary, depending on the host operating system, the size of the disk, and how many levels of nested directories it has. The times above were recorded under Windows 95 on a machine with a 1 GB hard disk. Try it for yourself with the Time It program. You might find a use for the function being tested (FindFiles in FILETOOL.BAS) in your own programs. It finds all occurences of a given file and returns the locations in a collection.

IUseFile interface to pass all the file data it finds back to the client. Here's IUseFile:

```
Function UseFile(UserData As Variant, FilePath As String, _
                 FileInfo As CFileInfo) As Boolean

End Function
```

The first parameter is any user-defined integer that the caller wants to pass to the client. Since UserData is passed by reference, the client can modify the data and pass it back. The *FilePath* parameter might be useful to clients, especially during a recursive walk. The *FileInfo* parameter contains everything the client might want to know about the file.

Here's the WalkAllFiles function that uses IUseFile:

```
Function WalkAllFiles(fileit As IUseFile, _
                      Optional ByVal ewmf As EWalkModeFile = ewmfBoth, _
                      Optional ByVal Start As String) As Boolean

    ' Statics for less memory use in recursive procedure
    Static sName As String, fd As WIN32_FIND_DATA, iLevel As Long
    Static fi As New CFileInfo
    Dim hFiles As Long, f As Boolean
    If Start = sEmpty Then Start = CurDir$
    ' Maintain level to ensure collection is cleared first time
    If iLevel = 0 Then Start = MUtility.NormalizePath(Start)
    iLevel = iLevel + 1

    ' Find first file (get handle to find)
    hFiles = FindFirstFile(Start & "*.*", fd)
    f = (hFiles <> INVALID_HANDLE_VALUE)
    Do While f
        sName = MBytes.ByteZToStr(fd.cFileName)
        ' Skip . and ..
        If Left$(sName, 1) <> "." Then
            ' Create a file info object from file data
            fi.CreateFromFile Start & sName, fd.dwFileAttributes, _
                        fd.nFileSizeLow, fd.ftLastWriteTime, _
                        fd.ftLastAccessTime, fd.ftCreationTime
            If fd.dwFileAttributes And vbDirectory Then
                If ewmf And ewmfDirs Then
                    ' Let client use directory data
                    WalkAllFiles = fileit.UseFile(iLevel, Start, fi)
                    ' If client returns True, walk terminates
                    If WalkAllFiles Then Exit Function
                End If
                ' Call recursively on each directory
```

```
                WalkAllFiles = WalkAllFiles(fileit, ewmf, _
                                            Start & sName & "\")
            Else
                If ewmf And ewmfFiles Then
                    ' Let client use file data
                    WalkAllFiles = fileit.UseFile(iLevel, Start, fi)
                    ' If client returns True, walk terminates
                    If WalkAllFiles Then Exit Function
                End If
            End If
        End If
        ' Keep looping until no more files
        f = FindNextFile(hFiles, fd)
    Loop
    f = FindClose(hFiles)
    ' Return the matching files in collection
    iLevel = iLevel - 1
End Function
```

The client can use all or part of the data it receives in any way it wants. The WalkAllFiles function passes the recursion level in the *UserData* parameter to allow the client to format data according to its nesting level. A client that wants to use WalkAllFiles as a search engine can stop the walk by returning True from the UseFile method when it finds a file that meets its search criteria. In the Test Shell Folders application in Figure 11-11, the walk can be stopped by clicking the Stop button, which sets a flag telling the client to return True on the next iteration. You'll soon get a chance to compare WalkAllFiles to the similar Walk-AllFolders function, which walks through the shell name space.

I provide a similar WalkFiles function that iterates through a single directory. I'm not going to show the code, but here's the signature:

```
Function WalkFiles(fileit As IUseFile, _
               Optional ByVal ewmf As EWalkModeFile = ewmfBoth, _
               Optional ByVal Start As String, _
               Optional UserData As Variant) As Boolean
```

WalkFiles also calls the IUseFile interface to pass data to the client, but the *UseFile* parameters have a different purpose for a single-directory walk. The path doesn't have much value in this case and will usually be ignored. The level wouldn't be of much use either, so instead WalkFiles takes an optional *UserData* parameter that will be passed on to the client in the UserData parameter of UseFile. The client implementation can pass back modified data. For example, the Test Shell Folders program passes a count variable with an initial value of zero. The UseFile implementation increments this count for each file and then displays the count of files at the end of the walk.

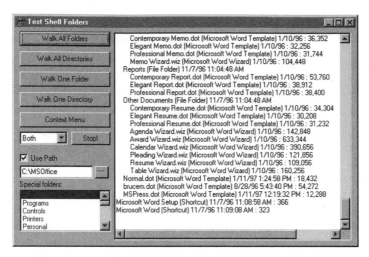

Figure 11-11. *The Test Shell Folders application.*

Walking Through Folders

Iterating through files is the old-fashioned way. Modern programs are supposed to iterate through the shell name space using IShellFolder. Unfortunately, IShell-Folder seems specifically designed to test the limits of Hardcore programming. I spent many hours with the inadequate documentation and C-oriented design and finally got the Visual Basic code working a few days before this book shipped.

I could probably do another chapter this long on IShellFolder, but you'll have to be satisfied with the Cliff's Notes version. So let's start at the beginning—with a question: What is a folder? It's a container in the shell namespace that contains some sort of items. The most common kind of folder is a file system directory filled with file items, but any group of objects can be defined as a folder. The Printers folder, for example, contains printers rather than files. The Desktop folder on my system contains My Computer, the Recycle Bin, and My Briefcase. Theoretically, you can define your own folders. Some applications define ZIP or CAB files as folders containing their compressed contents as items. But we'll have enough trouble walking through the shell namespace without worrying about extending it.

Folders and items

You can compare folders and items to the registry. In fact, I probably should have written CShellNode and CShellItem classes that work the same as the CRegNode and CRegItem classes described in Chapter 10. Go ahead. I dare you. It would be considerably more difficult because the shell name space is even more anarchical than the registry.

Shell items, for example, have a binary format that can be defined and known only by their designer. You aren't supposed to know anything about an item except that its first two bytes contain the number of bytes in the item. Items are arranged in lists which are terminated with a null item consisting of nothing more than two bytes containing a count of zero. This is the kind of data structure that would normally be managed through a handle and some functions that operate on the handle. But there are no handles for items. All you get is a pointer to a list of items. This is the infamous PIDL—which as far as I can tell stands for Pointer to ID List. The official name of an item is an Item ID, and the C data structure that represents it is called a SHITEMID. I think the SH stands for shell. In any case, programmers are supposed to write their own functions to manage PIDLs, but you don't have to because I did it for you. Generally, you can just think of a PIDL as a kind of handle and use the following functions from FOLDTOOL.BAS to manipulate them:

Function	Purpose
ItemIDSize(ByVal pidl As Long) As Integer	Gets the byte size of an ID list
PidlCount(ByVal pidl As Long) As Long	Counts the item IDs in an item ID list
NextItemID(ByVal pidl As Long) As Long	Gets the next item ID in an item ID list
DuplicateItemID(pidl As Long) As Long	Duplicates an item ID (creator must free)
DuplicateItemIDs(ByVal pidl1 As Long, _ ByVal pidl2 As Long) As Long	Concatenates two item IDs
PathFromPidl(ByVal pidl As Long) As String	Converts a PIDL to a file system path
PidlFromPath(sPath As String) As Long	Converts a file system path to a PIDL
ToPidl(ByVal i As Long) As Long	Converts an integer representing a special folder location constant to a PIDL. This function also accepts a PIDL and passes it through unchanged

Table 11-2. *Shell folder functions.*

I'm not going to say much more about these functions, but they will be used (directly or indirectly) in the next few sections. There's one other unusual thing about the PIDLs; you must free them with the system allocator. The creator of an item ID (Windows or the designer of a shell extension) uses the system allocator to allocate memory for the item. It's your responsibility to track that item and free it when you're finished with it. This is worse than un-Basic; it's anti-Basic. Our language is supposed to clean up memory for us behind the scenes. Ideally, someone would come up with a way of encapsulating PIDLs so that they would always be cleaned up automatically. In the meantime, we must free the memory ourselves, just as C programmers do for almost all their data structures. I did manage to encapsulate the system allocator in VBCore. Just use the global Allocator object to free your PIDLs:

```
Allocator.Free pidl
```

Moving on raPIDLy, we also need a few tools to manage folders. The most important folder is the one at the top of the hierarchy—the Desktop folder. You can get it with the GetDeskTopFolder function (from VBCore):

```
Set folder = GetDeskTopFolder
```

You can also turn a file system directory into a folder, using a procedure so bizarre that you'll have to look it up to figure it out. The FolderFromItem function turns what I call an item into a folder, using many of the utility functions shown earlier. It can also return a PIDL representing an item in the folder. Often you'll need both a folder and a PIDL within the folder to do anything useful. (I'll get to the useful part soon.) An item in this context is actually a Variant that can take a file system path string, a PIDL, or a constant representing a special folder location. Special folder locations include the Desktop, Printers, My Computer, and so on. We saw special folders in the TWHIZ project described earlier in this chapter. Anyway, to convert an item, you call FolderFromItem like this:

```
Dim pidlOut As Long
Set folder = FolderFromItem("C:\Hard\Core", pidlOut)
' Use the folder
⋮
' Free the PIDL when done
Allocator.Free pidl
```

That's the path version. The PIDL and special folder versions are similar:

```
Set folder = FolderFromItem(pidlIn, pidlOut)
Set folder = FolderFromItem(CSIDL_BITBUCKET, pidlOut)
```

And now for one last utility function. Once you've got a folder and a PIDL, you might want an intelligible name for the item. You can get the name from the GetDisplayNameOf method of the IShellFolder interface. Unfortunately, this method returns one of the most bizarre data types ever devised—what windows calls STRRET and what I call the type from hell. It represents the returned string in one of three different formats, each of which presents a new challenge for the hardcore Visual Basic programmer. Fortunately, you don't have to worry about it because I already did your crashing for you. Just call the GetFolderName function like this:

```
sName = GetFolderName(folder, pidl, SHGDN_FORPARSING)
```

The last parameter is an Enum that will give you either a full path or a more attractive format (SHGDN_FORPARSING or SHGDN_NORMAL, respectively). There are a couple of other values that give minor variants in display format.

Doing something with folders

After all those preliminaries, we're ready to actually do something. Let's start with the Test Shell Folders program (TFOLDER.VBG) shown in Figure 11-11. It can walk through files or folders, one at a time or all at once. You can start with either a path or one of the locations shown in the Special Folders list box. You can click the Context Menu button to bring up a context menu on the current path or special folder, and then you can click the button with three dots to browse for a starting folder. And as a bonus, you can stop a walk. You'll see what this button is for if you try to walk the whole desktop.

Let's start with the Walk All Folders button:

```
Private Sub cmdWalkFolders_Click()
    Dim folder As IVBShellFolder
    txtOut = "Walk folders recursively: " & sCrLfCrLf
    fStop = False
    fWalkAll = True
    If chkPath Then
        Set folder = FolderFromItem(txtPath)
    Else
        With lstSpecial
            Set folder = FolderFromItem(.ItemData(.ListIndex))
        End With
    End If
    WalkAllFolders folder, Me, 0, WalkType(cboWalk.ListIndex)
End Sub
```

The event procedure uses FolderFromItem to turn a special folder constant or a path into a folder. Once you have a folder, you can start walking. The form implements the IUseFolder interface, which WalkAllFolders will call back in the same way that WalkAllFiles calls IUseFile. The *Me* argument represents the form's IUseFolder object. And finally, after several pages of preliminaries, we're ready to do some actual work. I don't think WalkAllFolders will be an anticlimax:

```
Function WalkAllFolders(folder As IVBShellFolder, foldit As IUseFolder, _
                        Optional ByVal Level As Long = 0, _
                        Optional ByVal ewm As EWalkMode = ewmBoth, _
                        Optional ByVal hWnd As Long = hNull) As Long
    InitIf  ' Initialize if in standard module

    Dim idenum As IVBEnumIDList, folderNew As IVBShellFolder
```

(continued)

```
        Dim pidl As Long, cFetched As Long, afAttrib As Long

        ' Get the IEnumIDList object for the given folder
        On Error GoTo WalkAllFoldersFail
        folder.EnumObjects hWnd, ewm, idenum

        ' Enumerate through the list of folder and nonfolder objects
        On Error GoTo WalkAllFoldersFail2
        Dim hRes As Long
        Do
            hRes = idenum.Next(1, pidl, cFetched)
            ' 0 means got another, 1 means no more, anything else is error
            ' but there had better not be any errors because we'll ignore them
            If hRes Then Exit Do

            ' Pass to user-implemented interface to do something with folder
            ' (True in return means user requested termination)
            WalkAllFolders = foldit.UseFolder(Level, folder, pidl)
            If WalkAllFolders Then
                Allocator.Free pidl
                Exit Function
            End If

            ' It's not in the docs, but you pass in the attributes you want
            ' to check and GetAttributes passes back whether those attributes
            ' are set, ignoring all others
            afAttrib = SFGAO_HASSUBFOLDER Or SFGAO_FOLDER
            folder.GetAttributesOf 1, pidl, afAttrib

            ' If there are subfolders, process them recursively
            If afAttrib And (SFGAO_HASSUBFOLDER Or SFGAO_FOLDER) Then
                folder.BindToObject pidl, 0, iidShellFolder, folderNew
                WalkAllFolders = WalkAllFolders(folderNew, foldit, Level + 1, ewm)
            End If
WalkAllFoldersFail2:
            ' Free the pidl from Next
            Allocator.Free pidl
        Loop
WalkAllFoldersFail:

End Function
```

The walk is accomplished through a call to the EnumObjects method of IShell-Folder. It returns an IEnumIDList object, which looks and works a lot like the IEnumVARIANT interface described in Chapter 4. Of course, as we've noted several times (especially in Chapters 3, 4, and 10), most system interfaces are Basic-hostile, forcing us to use Basic-friendly binary-compatible versions called IVBShellFolder and IVBEnumIDList.

Once we've created an ID enumerator, we can call its Next method to walk through all the items in the folder. For each item, we call the UseFolder method of IUseFolder to let the client do whatever they want with the folder. The Use-Folder method takes a CFileInfo parameter, providing the client with all the information they could possibly want. You can check out my FileInfoFromFolder function to see how a folder and a PIDL become a CFileInfo object. If the user doesn't tell us to stop (by returning True), we call the GetAttributesOf method to see whether this folder has subfolders. If it does, we call the BindToObject method to bind the current folder object to a new subfolder object. Finally we call ourselves recursively to handle the new folder.

Whew!

And that's just the start. You might also want to check out ContextPopMenu. It starts out similar to WalkAllFolders, but instead of binding to a nested folder, it calls the GetUIObjectOf method to get an IVBContextMenu object and then uses that object to display the standard context menu for the item. ContextPopMenu is based on a C version in a *PC Magazine* article by Jeff Prosise.

Ideally, I'd provide other functions or classes that integrate other shell features such as property sheet handlers, icon extractors, and drag and drop handlers. Another time.

Famous Explorers and Common Controls

I remember my amazement, back in the dark ages of Windows 1 and 2, when I learned that every programmer who wanted an Open dialog box had to write the code to fill the list box by reading the files out of the directory. The common dialog functions introduced in Windows 3 solved the problem for dialog boxes, but everyone still had to write their own toolbars, outlines, status bars, and what have you.

Somewhere during the time frame of Windows for Workgroups, the common controls DLL was created and used to implement the toolbars of File Manager. The source code for this DLL appeared as a sample in the Software Development Kit, and it later became available on the Microsoft Developer Network. COMMCTRL.DLL became a kind of standard, though not official. It was one of three toolbar implementations used by different groups at Microsoft. (You can see the differences if you study old Microsoft applications carefully.)

Microsoft didn't necessarily start the industry trend toward toolbars, status bars, and property sheets, but it jumped on the bandwagon and eventually standardized most common controls by expanding the 16-bit COMMCTRL.DLL into COMCTL32.DLL. Visual Basic wrapped this C-specific DLL into the Microsoft Windows Common Controls—a single OCX file containing TreeView, ListView, ImageList, Toolbar, StatusBar, TabStrip, ProgressBar, and Slider. This version of

Visual Basic introduces Microsoft Windows Common Controls 2 with Animation and UpDown controls. Perhaps we'll soon see new controls providing the interface doodads introduced in Microsoft Internet Explorer.

Of course, rather than hold your breath, you could turn to other hardcore programmers for assistance. Ramon Guerrero and Andrea Wyss wrote components that wrap some of the coolest new interface gadgets. I'm not going to have a chance to explain these controls in the book, but they're provided on the companion CD with samples and READMEs.

On the surface, the common controls, especially TreeView and ListView, seem to offer an easy way to create applications that look like Windows Explorer. Personally, I like the idea of Windows Explorer more than its implementation. I was looking forward to creating my own better explorer. My plan was to clone the real Explorer and then start adding features. I planned to name this application after one of my favorite explorers, Meriwether Lewis. Unfortunately, the attempt met with dismal failure in the first edition of this book and I ended up naming my pitiful explorer after Columbus, the man who never did reach the East by sailing west.

Well, I'm happy to say that Meriwether has been resurrected. It took some help from new Visual Basic features such native code and better access to interfaces. Also, I've learned a lot and spent more time on the problem. Figure 11-12 shows Meriwether at publication time. I might be able to get a better version on the companion CD. The current version isn't full-featured, and the performance doesn't quite match the Windows Explorer. But it's a reasonably efficient program that you can enhance to create your own better explorer.

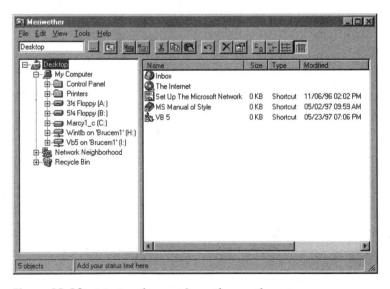

Figure 11-12. *Meriwether explores the northwest.*

Writing a real explorer program is a major task that I didn't have time to finish or explain completely, but I will use Meriwether (and some other samples) to briefly examine common controls. The Visual Basic documentation explains normal use, so I'll focus on some problems and workarounds you won't find in the manual.

The ImageList Control

ImageList controls work behind the scenes in the Toolbar, ListView, TreeView, StatusBar, and TabStrip controls. The Visual Basic control that implements the ImageList concept is specifically designed to work with its partner controls. But if you look closely at ImageLists, you'll see that they also have a wider potential. Unfortunately, the control doesn't provide built-in features for some of the things you might like to do with it. Fortunately, it does provide a handle to the underlying control, and a Hardcore programmer with a handle knows no limits.

An ImageList is a collection of images of the same size and type, but they're more than just images. When you insert an image into the list, the control gives it a mask. If the image is an icon, its internal mask is reused. If it is a bitmap or a metafile, a mask is created, probably using a technique similar to the one used for CPictureGlass (see "Animating Pictures," in Chapter 7). The end result is a collection of icons of the same size. When you attach an ImageList to another control, you don't need to worry about what gets drawn and how, but you'll understand the process better if you experiment with the methods of an unattached ImageList.

The Test ImageList program (TIMAGE.VBP), shown in Figure 11-13, illustrates operations you can perform directly with ImageList controls. The images on the

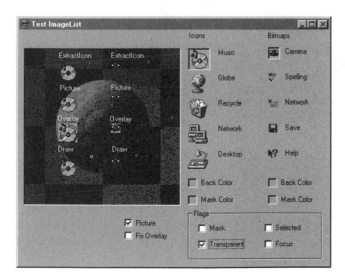

Figure 11-13. *Drawing with ImageLists.*

right side of the form represent the images in lists of icons and bitmaps, respectively. The bitmap on the left provides a background to demonstrate how images can be drawn in different ways. To see how the different operations work on a solid background, use the Picture check box to turn the picture off. You can experiment with this program to understand the fundamental difference between icons and bitmaps and how you can handle each correctly in ImageLists.

CHALLENGE Check out the splitter bars on the Meriwether program. Hardcore readers Vadim Katsman and Elliot Witticar took up my challenge and suggested several enhancements to the original horizontal and vertical splitter classes provided with the first edition. I'm not going to say any more about splitters except that you'll see enhanced splitter classes on the companion CD. You can find lots of ways to use splitters. You might start by giving Edwina two resizable editing windows (like those in the Visual Basic editor).

Figure 11-14 shows a map of ImageList methods and properties. ImageLists provide four ways of placing images on a surface: the Picture property, the ExtractIcon method, the Overlay method, and the Draw method. Two properties, BackColor and MaskColor, affect the operations of the four drawing mechanisms.

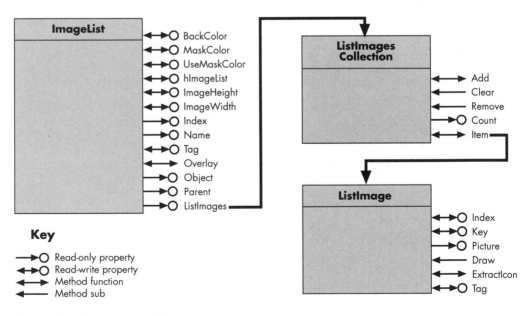

Figure 11-14. *An ImageList map.*

The Picture property and the ExtractIcon method

The Picture property of the ListImage object simply returns the picture you put into the ImageList. If you put in an icon, you get back an icon; if you put in a bitmap, you get back a bitmap. This works for icons no matter where you place the picture, but bitmaps don't look good unless they contain a solid image or unless the background of the image is the same as the background of the target picture. This makes the Picture property somewhat inflexible for general use, but of course you can use PaintPicture to do anything you want with it.

The ExtractIcon method converts an image to an icon. If the image already is an icon, ExtractIcon is the equivalent of the Picture property. With a bitmap, ExtractIcon stretches or compresses it to the standard icon size, as determined by GetSystemMetrics, and uses the MaskColor property of the ImageList to make the image transparent. You can save the result to a file with SavePicture; just make sure that you set the MaskColor property to the color of the bitmap background. To see how this works in Test ImageList, use the Mask Color check box to set different colors that appear in the bitmap. This is a roundabout way to convert a bitmap to an icon. It's much easier to use ImagEdit, although most bitmaps look terrible when converted to icons. The mechanism would be a lot more flexible if you could convert to an icon of any size (the size of the bitmap, for example). What you really want from ExtractIcon is its transparency, not a standard icon size. More on that later.

The Overlay method

You can use the Overlay method to combine any two ListImage objects in an ImageList. This works fine on a solid background, but, as Figure 11-13 illustrates, icons don't come out right. The top image is placed transparently on the bottom image, but the bottom image is placed opaquely on the background. In other words, the Overlay method converts an icon to a bitmap. You can get around this bug (still not fixed from version 4) by inserting the overlaid image back into the ImageList and then using ExtractIcon to remove it as an icon. Here's the code to use Overlay normally and the code to fix the problem:

```
With imlstIcons
    If chkOverlay.Value <> vbChecked Then
        ' Overlay without bug fix
        imgIconOverlay.Picture = .Overlay(iIconsLast, iIcons)
    Else
        ' Save old background and mask color
        Dim clrBack As Long, clrMask As Long
        clrBack = .BackColor: clrMask = .MaskColor
        ' Set color that does not occur in image
        .BackColor = vbMagenta: .MaskColor = vbMagenta
        ' Insert overlay, extract as icon, remove, and restore color
        .ListImages.Add 1, , .Overlay(iIconsLast, iIcons)
```

(continued)

```
        imgIconOverlay.Picture = .ListImages(1).ExtractIcon
        .ListImages.Remove 1
        .BackColor = clrBack: .MaskColor = clrMask
    End If
End With
```

This technique works in the sample because I found a temporary background and mask color, *vbMagenta*, that didn't occur in any of the sample icons. But what if you were loading the icons at run time? I suppose you could check every pixel in the icon with the Point method, but it's easier to simply draw the images on top of each other using the techniques shown in the next section.

The Draw method and the DrawImage function

The Draw method allows you to draw an image from an ImageList directly onto a form, a picture box, or anything else that has an hDC property. This method does, however, illustrate a flaw in the ImageList design, one that belies the purpose of the underlying ImageList API functions.

You call the Draw method as shown here:

```
imlstBmps.ListImages(iBmps).Draw pb.hDC, x, y, imlNormal
```

The final parameter is an Enum of type ImageDrawConstants containing the constants *imlNormal*, *imlTransparent*, *imlSelected*, or *imlFocus*. The latter two specify that an image should be dithered to different degrees to give a shaded effect. The values of these constants are 0 through 3. You select one and only one. But what if you want to draw a transparent selected image? In fact, transparent is the only way I'd ever want to draw an image as selected or with focus.

Let's look at the API functions behind the Draw method. An image list is created with the ImageList_ family of API functions. The Draw method uses either the ImageList_Draw function or its enhanced cousin, ImageList_DrawEx. To keep things simple, I'll use ImageList_Draw, which is called this way:

```
f = ImageList_Draw(hImageList, i, hdc, x, y, _
                ILD_TRANSPARENT Or ILD_SELECTED)
```

Notice the final style argument. It's obviously a bitfield, not an enumeration. The values of the ILD_ constants confirm this; they're &H0, &H1, &H2, &H4, &H10— not 0, 1, 2, 3. Furthermore, there are five of them, not four. ILD_MASK draws a monochrome mask of the image, but you won't find a parallel *imlMask* constant. Perhaps the designer of the ImageList control didn't know why a Visual Basic programmer would want a mask. But you do (if you read Chapter 7). The constant ILD_NORMAL has the value 0, which indicates the absence of any modifying bits rather than a separate kind of image.

Hardcore programmers have to forget the ImageList Draw method and go down to the API to get what they need. When using the hImageList property, keep in mind that the default scale mode of the API is pixels, not twips, and that API indexes are zero-based, not one-based. Here's a DrawImage function that replaces the Draw method:

```
Sub DrawImage(imlst As Control, vIndex As Variant, ByVal hDC As Long, _
            ByVal x As Long, ByVal y As Long, _
            Optional ByVal afDraw As EILD = ILD_TRANSPARENT)
#End If
    ImageList_Draw imlst.hImageList, _
                imlst.ListImages(vIndex).Index - 1, hDC, _
                x / Screen.TwipsPerPixelX, _
                y / Screen.TwipsPerPixelY, afDraw
End Sub
```

This version is hard-coded to assume twips. Notice that it adjusts the one-based ImageList index. By default, it draws transparent images.

ImageList Challenge

The ImageList API functions have other features that aren't passed through in the ImageList control. Here are some ideas you might try, using the declarations, constants, and functions in COMCTL.BAS and the Windows API type library. Look at the extra arguments of ImageList_DrawEx. You can stretch an image to any size and control its background and foreground colors. Unfortunately, you can't use ROP arguments to blit images as you can with the PaintPicture method or the BitBlt function. The ImageList_ExtractIcon and ImageList_GetIcon functions give you a handle to an icon. If you carefully study the earlier section on icons, you can come up with a way to get the transparency of an icon without stretching it to the standard icon size (even if you have inserted a bitmap). Use the handle to draw directly with the DrawIconEx API function.

It wouldn't be difficult to create a new ActiveX control that fixes many of the ImageList control's limitations. For that matter, you could totally replace the ImageList with your own implementation using the API. Since ImageList doesn't have events, there's a good case for making it an ActiveX DLL component rather than a control anyway. Of course, you wouldn't be able to initialize the images of an ImageList server at design time, but many programs could live with that limitation. Unfortunately, other controls that require ImageList controls probably wouldn't be able to use your enhanced component.

Normally, you use an ImageList like a roll of snapshots that you can access by name or by number. But if you arrange these snapshots in sequential order, like movie frames, you could generate a moving picture just by playing them in sequence. It wouldn't be too difficult to build an animation class based on an ImageList control.

I would rather have designed this function to take a ListImage object instead of an ImageList control and an index, calling it like this:

```
DrawImage imlstIcons.ListImage(iIcons), hDC, x, y
```

But the hImageList property is on ImageList, and ListImage has no Parent property to refer back to the ImageList. I must supply an extra argument:

```
DrawImage imlstIcons, iIcons, hDC, x, y
```

You can use similar techniques to get around limitations of other common controls. ImageList is invisible and has its own special handle and API functions. Other controls have an hWnd property that you can use to send messages to their windows.

The Toolbar and StatusBar Controls

Check out the toolbar and the status bar in Edwina. I won't get into the code but will simply say that I had to implement these features the same way everyone else does—with blood, sweat, and profanity. Figure 11-15 shows a map that will perhaps lessen your frustration.

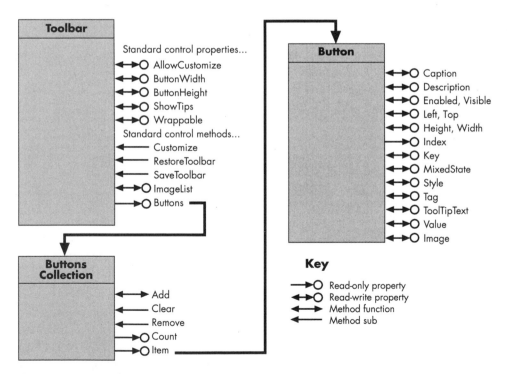

Figure 11-15. *A Toolbar map.*

To use a Toolbar control efficiently, you must understand ImageLists and collections inside and out. Plan the buttons in detail, and get your ImageList right the first time because every time you change a button image, you're in trouble. You must unhook the ImageList from the Toolbar control to modify, insert, or delete an image, even though unhooking means that all your button indexes are destroyed and that you must reinitialize them one by one. You might even consider attaching the ImageList with code at run time rather than trying to manage it at design time.

Most of the work involved in creating a toolbar is directed toward managing the Buttons collection and coordinating it with the ListImages collection of the ListImage. The Panels collection of the StatusBar control is a little easier because you don't have to worry about ImageLists.

FLAME

I don't mind that toolbars are based on the ImageList control, but I shouldn't have to worry about it. When I set up toolbar buttons, I want to just click a button that brings up the Picture dialog box and lets me install the button image. If the dialog box adds the image to an ImageList behind the scenes and ties the image index to a button index, that's OK with me. But as a user, I don't care about this implementation detail. I just want to put images on buttons. Any add-in vendor who gives me a tool that hides the connection between toolbars and ImageLists will get my business. It should be a simple matter now that you can create delegated controls. In fact, there isn't much wrong with a Toolbar control that couldn't be fixed by giving it a more sophisticated and user-friendly property page. It's kind of a disgrace that toolbars are still treated as some extra feature that you can add if you have the patience. But toolbars aren't an extra feature—they're the standard. Every program should have one. They should have a toolbar editor that is as integrated and easy to use as the Menu editor. But enough of this ranting. At least now I can put a Flame button on my toolbars.

The TreeView Control

The TreeView control (which is mapped in Figure 11-16 on the following page) could more accurately be called OutlineView because it certainly isn't designed to handle what programmers commonly call a tree. The control works fine if you know how many levels of data you'll have, but it's difficult to use for recursive data such as directory, registry, or windows trees. I've been able to use several different strategies to get around inherent limitations of the control.

The first problem you'll encounter is initializing your outline data. The design of the TreeView control lends itself to completely filling out the data during

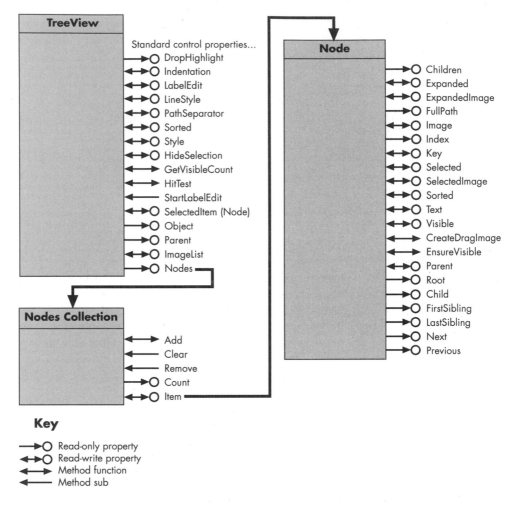

TreeView

Standard control properties...
- ➙O DropHighlight
- ⬌O Indentation
- ⬌O LabelEdit
- ⬌O LineStyle
- ⬌O PathSeparator
- ⬌O Sorted
- ⬌O Style
- ⬌O HideSelection
- ⬌ GetVisibleCount
- ⬌ HitTest
- ⬅ StartLabelEdit
- ⬌O SelectedItem (Node)
- ➙O Object
- ➙O Parent
- ⬌O ImageList
- ➙O Nodes

Node

- ➙O Children
- ⬌O Expanded
- ⬌O ExpandedImage
- ➙O FullPath
- ⬌O Image
- ➙O Index
- ⬌O Key
- ⬌O Selected
- ⬌O SelectedImage
- ⬌O Sorted
- ⬌O Text
- ⬌O Visible
- ⬌ CreateDragImage
- ⬌ EnsureVisible
- ⬌O Parent
- ➙O Root
- ➙O Child
- ➙O FirstSibling
- ➙O LastSibling
- ➙O Next
- ➙O Previous

Nodes Collection

- ⬌ Add
- ⬅ Clear
- ⬅ Remove
- ➙O Count
- ⬌O Item

Key

- ➙O Read-only property
- ⬌O Read-write property
- ⬌ Method function
- ⬅ Method sub

Figure 11-16. *A TreeView map.*

initialization, but of course that's not generally what you want to do with a recursive tree. It would take a very long time to fill an Explorer-style program with all the files on a large network disk. Furthermore, the levels could get out of sync if other programs deleted or created files after the control was initialized. You'd also have serious memory problems. A better strategy is to fill each level as it is expanded. The problem is that if you don't fill in the next branch of a TreeView, that branch won't have a plus button, and the user won't have any way to expand it.

This isn't really a problem with the underlying Windows TreeView in COMCTL32.DLL. It's a problem introduced by an incomplete implementation in the ActiveX control. The problem occurs at two levels. First, the control fails to support one of the most common TreeView operations—one that TreeViews in common programs, such as Windows Explorer and the registry editor, do all the time. Second, the control doesn't provide the handles you need to work around the problem with the API. The TreeView control has a handle property that returns the handle of the underlying TreeView window, but the nodes of a TreeView are also controlled through handles. The TreeView control has these node handles (it couldn't work without them), but it won't share them with you. ListView and several other common controls containing collections have the same limitation.

Meriwether has to hack to get expandable nodes. First you determine whether the data you're adding to the TreeView node has children. If it does, you fill the node with a single fake child so that the TreeView will display the node as expandable. When the user expands the node, you delete the fake child and fill in the real children (filling any of the child nodes that have children with fakes). The whole process has to be done in reverse when a node collapses. Fake children have to have a name that is easily recognizable, but illegal for real children. I used ":" as the fake name.

The WinWatch program, which stores the window tree in a TreeView, had a different initialization problem. It initializes the entire tree at once, but it does so in a recursive function that doesn't know its complete context. You can review the background for this problem in "Doing windows" in Chapter 6. The function IterateChildWindows walks through the windows tree, calling the Do-Window method of the IWindowsHelper interface to handle each window. Chapter 6 showed the simple implementation of IWindowsHelper (CWindow-ToFile in WFILEHLP.CLS) that writes window information to a log file. The more complicated implementation (CWindowToForm in WFORMHLP.CLS) writes window data to the nodes of a TreeView. The DoWindow method has level and window handle parameters, but when the method is called, you don't know whether the current window should be added as a sibling of the last node or as a child of some other higher level node. The class maintains a stack of the last node and key used at each level. Check out the implementation of CWindow-ToForm to get the details of how it efficiently finds the correct tree position for each new node.

If you want data stored in a TreeView to be keyed for easy lookup, you're in for more trouble. Every key must be unique, but what are your chances of finding a disk with no duplicate directory names? In fact, what are the chances of finding any tree-structured data without duplicates? One of the main reasons to use a tree is so that each node can be independent. A TreeView control would be much easier to manage if it were organized as a collection of collections instead of as one big collection (like CRegNode in Chapter 10). That's not to say you can't use keys with TreeViews, but you might need to come up with a complicated scheme to avoid duplicate keys without using too much memory.

Creating unique keys might not be a problem if every item in the tree happens to have a numeric ID. WinWatch, for example, uses the handle of each window as the key. Handles are guaranteed to be unique, but unfortunately, TreeView won't accept keys with a digit as the first character. Probably this has something to do with how it distinguishes string keys from numeric indexes when doing node lookups. In any case, you have to prefix your numeric keys with a non-digit prefix (such as *H*).

Images in the ImageList for a TreeView (or a ListView) should be keyed, but you must be careful how you insert the keys. For example, in Meriwether, each file type must have one and only one image with the file type name as the key. For every file, I use error trapping to identify whether the image for the current file type is already in the ImageList. If the key doesn't exist, I insert it. This can't be doing much for performance, but I couldn't figure out another way.

The ListView Control

ListView (which is mapped in Figure 11-17) doesn't have as many problems as TreeView, but you might need a few tricks to make it do everything you want.

For starters, you might want to store data that isn't visible in a ListView, which doesn't have the *ItemData* array common to ListBox-type controls. This was a serious limitation for some applications in Visual Basic version 4. Fortunately, in version 5, the Tag property of ListItems has changed from String to Variant type. This allows you to cram any data you want—Double, Currency, Date, Object—into each ListView item. Don't confuse the Tag property of the ListView control with the Tag property of each ListItem. The one and only Tag property of ListView still has String type, but the Tag property of each ListItem is Variant. The same applies to all the other collections in the Common Controls OCX—ListImages in ImageList, Nodes in TreeView, Panels in StatusBar, Tabs in TabStrip, and Buttons in Toolbar.

Another problem with ListViews is that they don't have an ItemDblClick event, but you need to identify double-clicks on ListView items to know when to open them. ListViews do have a DblClick event, but it won't tell you which item was clicked. You can work around this limitation by using the SelectedItem property in the DblClick event.

```
Private Sub lvwFiles_DblClick()
    Dim item As ListItem
    Set item = lvwFiles.SelectedItem
    If item Is Nothing Then
        Debug.Print "Double-clicked column: ?"
    Else
        Debug.Print "Double-clicked item: " & item.Text
    End If
End Sub
```

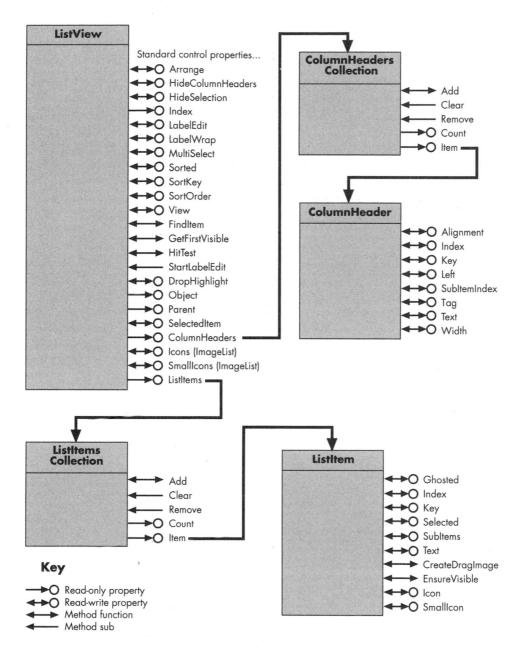

Figure 11-17. *A ListView map.*

This only works if you double-click on the item, which points out one of the most annoying limitation of ListViews. You can't identify clicks or double-clicks on any column other than the first one. This fits the normal designed use of a

ListView, but, in fact, I'd like to use a ListView as a kind of Grid and recognize clicks on any cell. I'd like to create a simple XGrid control by delegating to a ListView control, but the ListView doesn't provide the column information I need.

The solution involves translating the x and y coordinates of a click into the corresponding row and column. Once you have the row, you can figure out the item. Let's start with that. Thanks to hardcore programmers Jim Collins and Larry Marshall for the following API code. To identify clicks, you use MouseUp rather than Click because this event has coordinates. The DblClick event doesn't have coordinates, but you can save them in module-level variables in MouseDown and then read the variables in DblClick. Once you have the coordinates, you can get the item from the following function:

```
Function ListItemFromLinePosition(lvw As ListView, _
                ByVal y As Single) As ListItem
    Dim rc As RECT, i As Integer, c As Long, dy As Long
    c = lvw.ListItems.Count
    If c = 0 Then Exit Function
    ' Get the height of a single item
    rc.Left = LVIR_BOUNDS
    SendMessage lvw.hWnd, LVM_GETITEMRECT, ByVal 0&, rc
    dy = rc.bottom - rc.Top
    ' Calculate the index of the item under the mouse pointer
    i = lvw.GetFirstVisible.Index - 1 + _
        ((y \ Screen.TwipsPerPixelY) - (dy / 2)) / dy
    ' Return the item (if any)
    If i > 0 And i <= c Then
        Set ListItemFromLinePosition = lvwFiles.ListItems(i)
    End If
End Function
```

Here's how you could call this code from the DblClick event of a ListView:

```
Private Sub lvwFiles_DblClick()
    ' Use module-level yList saved from MouseDown event
    Dim item As ListItem
    ' Determine if user double clicked anywhere on the line
    Set item = ListItemFromLinePosition(lvwFiles, yList)
    If Not item Is Nothing Then
        Debug.Print "You double-clicked on the line of item: " & item.Text
    End If
    ' Make any click on the line select the item
    Set lvwFiles.SelectedItem = item
End Sub
```

I find it very annoying when a ListView application ignores or takes random actions when I click on a column. The last line of the sample above selects the item when you click on a column. This might not be the right action for every program, but users click columns for a reason. Don't just ignore them.

Unfortunately, figuring out the column in the SubItems collection when a user clicks a column is more difficult than figuring out the line. I don't know the solution. My first idea was to add up the widths of the ColumnHeaders collection to figure out what column the x position is on. That would probably work when the ListView is scrolled all the way left, but when you scroll right you're lost. The ListView window has a notification message called LVN_COLUMN-CLICK. Maybe you can subclass that message to analyze column clicks. That's where I'd start my experiments.

One Last Challenge

All the tools are now in place to create the Hardcore Hacker's Object Chop Shop. Let's take a little tour through this not-so-Basic development factory. It's a set of add-ins that teach the Visual Basic IDE some new tricks.

For example, the Chop Shop knows resources. It can build RES files from RC files. It can build RC files from dialogs that allow you to select existing resources or create new ones, which leads to a second point.

The Chop Shop knows pictures. It can create or edit picture files containing bitmaps, icons, cursors, and metafiles. Iconically speaking, it knows small icons, large icons, and icons of any other size you want. It also knows about standard-sized bitmaps such as toolbar buttons. It can put these pictures in resource files, or it can load them into picture properties at design time.

The Chop Shop also knows projects. It can switch easily between modes where components are compiled or in source code.

The Chop Shop knows debugging. It handles asserts and log messages transparently.

And finally the Chop Shop knows source code. It can automatically call out to a real programmer's editor, or it can intercept keystrokes in the code windows and translate them into macros. Either way, you can remap your keyboard and can get the code templates and other advanced editing features that hardcore programmers expect.

Sound good? Well, don't expect to find support for all of these features in the VBIDE add-in model. You're going to have to subclass a few windows and do other low-level API hacking to get what you want. But of course, that's no problem. In fact, there's nothing between you and that dream environment but a few weekends—OK, some weeknights too—of Hardcore Visual Basic.

INDEX

H

T

W

Bruce McKinney recently ended his career in Microsoft soccer after arguments with coaches who ordered him to abandon outside activities and concentrate on his game. Known for his pinpoint passes and unexpected moves (but not for defense or shooting), McKinney was recruited 12 years ago by the languages team. Because of his lack of formal computer training, reporters have speculated he was originally hired as a "ringer" with no expectation that he would actually try to program computers. But to everyone's surprise, McKinney built a successful programming career on the side. At first he wrote manuals for assembler, Basic, and C, later became a developer on C and FOR-TRAN products, and finally wrote programming books for Microsoft Press.

In the end, however, this dual career took its toll. Long-time observers agree that he has slowed down considerably in the last year. Fans attributed the problem to time wasted on nonsoccer activities. One angry teammate was more specific: "I blame it on Visual Basic. That language is driving him crazy." The source said that McKinney hadn't been to practice in weeks. "He's gained 20 pounds, and there are rings under his eyes. We're just not getting the goals and assists we expect from him." When confronted, McKinney decided to start a new career on his own rather than change his habits.

In an interview after the sudden split, McKinney said he still thinks "futbol" is the most important thing but insisted it's not the only thing. He plans to spend more time on soccer in his new life outside Microsoft but will continue to write programs and perhaps even articles. When asked whether programming and writing had damaged his game, he admitted that perhaps a vacation from Visual Basic and book writing wouldn't do any harm.

You can send him mail about soccer or other topics at brucem@pobox.com, or visit his web site at pobox.com/HardcoreVB.

The manuscript for this book was submitted to Microsoft Press in electronic form. Galleys were prepared using Microsoft Word 97. Pages were composed using Adobe PageMaker 6.5 for Windows, with text type in Garamond and display type in Futura Medium. Composed pages were delivered to the printer as electronic prepress files.

Cover Graphic Designer
Greg Erickson

Cover Illustrator
Glenn Mitsui

Interior Graphic Designer
Kim Eggleston

Principal Artist
Michael Victor

Principal Compositor
Peggy Herman

Indexer
Shane-Armstrong Information Systems

The **hottest** guide ever
to data access with
Microsoft® Visual Basic® 5.0
and Microsoft SQL Server™ 6.5.

This indispensable bestseller is known as the missing link in information about client/server programming. And the newest edition is better than ever. Greatly expanded and updated, it gives you a ton of "how it works" and "how to work it" information for using Visual Basic to design, code, debug, and tune front-end applications for SQL Server. Plus, you get thorough coverage of the new possibilities that Microsoft Visual Basic 5.0 offers through powerful RDO enhancements. There's also full coverage of ODBCDirect, the new programming model that lets you use DAO to bypass Jet. Finally, the companion CD-ROM is packed with new and fully updated software tools. Encyclopedic in breadth and filled with deep practical insight, this is industrial-strength information—all in Bill Vaughn's reader-friendly style.

U.S.A.	**$49.99**
U.K.	£46.99 [V.A.T. included]
Canada	$69.99
ISBN 1-57231-567-9	

Microsoft®Press

Get active!

ACTIVE VISUAL BASIC® 5.0 introduces the features and capabilities of Visual Basic that allow for the creation of Internet-enabled applications and interactive Web content. After a technical overview of the Internet and the Internet-related capabilities of Visual Basic, the book covers the Internet Control Pack, ActiveX™ control creation, and creating Doc Objects. Advanced topics in the final section include overviews of developing Internet servers and accessing the Windows® Internet API. If you're entering this exciting growth area for Visual Basic development, you'll want this book.

U.S.A.	**$39.99**
U.K.	£37.49 [V.A.T. included]
Canada	$54.99
ISBN 1-57231-512-1	

Microsoft®*Press*

The most *popular*

office suite*—and the*

top

development platform.

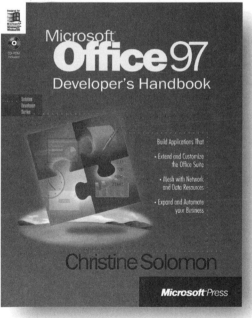

In this thoroughly revised edition, well-known author and experienced consultant Christine Solomon shows systems professionals and developers how to automate and re-engineer a wide assortment of businesses on the powerful Microsoft® Office 97 platform. You'll find plenty of information on new features and technologies. And everything is clarified with detailed explanations, sample applications, anecdotes, examples, and case studies. Plus, the enclosed CD-ROM contains source code and files for sample applications. Get MICROSOFT OFFICE 97 DEVELOPER'S HANDBOOK. And find out why Microsoft Office 97 is a whole new development.

U.S.A. **$39.99**
U.K. £37.49 [V.A.T. included]
Canada $53.99
ISBN 1-57231-440-0

Microsoft®*Press*

IMPORTANT—READ CAREFULLY BEFORE OPENING SOFTWARE PACKET(S). By opening the sealed packet(s) containing the software, you indicate your acceptance of the following Microsoft License Agreement.

MICROSOFT LICENSE AGREEMENT
(Book Companion CD)

This is a legal agreement between you (either an individual or an entity) and Microsoft Corporation. By opening the sealed software packet(s) you are agreeing to be bound by the terms of this agreement. If you do not agree to the terms of this agreement, promptly return the unopened software packet(s) and any accompanying written materials to the place you obtained them for a full refund.

MICROSOFT SOFTWARE LICENSE

1. GRANT OF LICENSE. Microsoft grants to you the right to use one copy of the Microsoft software program included with this book (the "SOFTWARE") on a single terminal connected to a single computer. The SOFTWARE is in "use" on a computer when it is loaded into the temporary memory (i.e., RAM) or installed into the permanent memory (e.g., hard disk, CD-ROM, or other storage device) of that computer. You may not network the SOFTWARE or otherwise use it on more than one computer or computer terminal at the same time.

2. COPYRIGHT. The SOFTWARE is owned by Microsoft or its suppliers and is protected by United States copyright laws and international treaty provisions. Therefore, you must treat the SOFTWARE like any other copyrighted material (e.g., a book or musical recording) except that you may either (a) make one copy of the SOFTWARE solely for backup or archival purposes, or (b) transfer the SOFTWARE to a single hard disk provided you keep the original solely for backup or archival purposes. You may not copy the written materials accompanying the SOFTWARE.

3. OTHER RESTRICTIONS. You may not rent or lease the SOFTWARE, but you may transfer the SOFTWARE and accompanying written materials on a permanent basis provided you retain no copies and the recipient agrees to the terms of this Agreement. You may not reverse engineer, decompile, or disassemble the SOFTWARE. If the SOFTWARE is an update or has been updated, any transfer must include the most recent update and all prior versions.

4. DUAL MEDIA SOFTWARE. If the SOFTWARE package contains more than one kind of disk (3.5", 5.25", and CD-ROM), then you may use only the disks appropriate for your single-user computer. You may not use the other disks on another computer or loan, rent, lease, or transfer them to another user except as part of the permanent transfer (as provided above) of all SOFTWARE and written materials.

5. SAMPLE CODE. If the SOFTWARE includes Sample Code, then Microsoft grants you a royalty-free right to reproduce and distribute the sample code of the SOFTWARE provided that you: (a) distribute the sample code only in conjunction with and as a part of your software product; (b) do not use Microsoft's or its authors' names, logos, or trademarks to market your software product; (c) include the copyright notice that appears on the SOFTWARE on your product label and as a part of the sign-on message for your software product; and (d) agree to indemnify, hold harmless, and defend Microsoft and its authors from and against any claims or lawsuits, including attorneys' fees, that arise or result from the use or distribution of your software product.

DISCLAIMER OF WARRANTY

The SOFTWARE (including instructions for its use) is provided "AS IS" WITHOUT WARRANTY OF ANY KIND. MICROSOFT FURTHER DISCLAIMS ALL IMPLIED WARRANTIES INCLUDING WITHOUT LIMITATION ANY IMPLIED WARRANTIES OF MERCHANTABILITY OR OF FITNESS FOR A PARTICULAR PURPOSE. THE ENTIRE RISK ARISING OUT OF THE USE OR PERFORMANCE OF THE SOFTWARE AND DOCUMENTATION REMAINS WITH YOU.

IN NO EVENT SHALL MICROSOFT, ITS AUTHORS, OR ANYONE ELSE INVOLVED IN THE CREATION, PRODUCTION, OR DELIVERY OF THE SOFTWARE BE LIABLE FOR ANY DAMAGES WHATSOEVER (INCLUDING, WITHOUT LIMITATION, DAMAGES FOR LOSS OF BUSINESS PROFITS, BUSINESS INTERRUPTION, LOSS OF BUSINESS INFORMATION, OR OTHER PECUNIARY LOSS) ARISING OUT OF THE USE OF OR INABILITY TO USE THE SOFTWARE OR DOCUMENTATION, EVEN IF MICROSOFT HAS BEEN ADVISED OF THE POSSIBILITY OF SUCH DAMAGES. BECAUSE SOME STATES/COUNTRIES DO NOT ALLOW THE EXCLUSION OR LIMITATION OF LIABILITY FOR CONSEQUENTIAL OR INCIDENTAL DAMAGES, THE ABOVE LIMITATION MAY NOT APPLY TO YOU.

U.S. GOVERNMENT RESTRICTED RIGHTS

The SOFTWARE and documentation are provided with RESTRICTED RIGHTS. Use, duplication, or disclosure by the Government is subject to restrictions as set forth in subparagraph (c)(1)(ii) of The Rights in Technical Data and Computer Software clause at DFARS 252.227-7013 or subparagraphs (c)(1) and (2) of the Commercial Computer Software — Restricted Rights 48 CFR 52.227-19, as applicable. Manufacturer is Microsoft Corporation, One Microsoft Way, Redmond, WA 98052-6399.

If you acquired this product in the United States, this Agreement is governed by the laws of the State of Washington.

Should you have any questions concerning this Agreement, or if you desire to contact Microsoft Press for any reason, please write: Microsoft Press, One Microsoft Way, Redmond, WA 98052-6399.

Register Today!

Return this
HARDCORE VISUAL BASIC, *Second Edition*
registration card for
a Microsoft Press® catalog

U.S. and Canada addresses only. Fill in information below and mail postage-free. Please mail only the bottom half of this page.

1-57231-422-2A *HARDCORE VISUAL BASIC®, Second Edition* *Owner Registration Card*

_____
NAME

_____
INSTITUTION OR COMPANY NAME

_____
ADDRESS

_____

_____
CITY   STATE   ZIP

Microsoft®*Press*
Quality Computer Books

For a free catalog of
Microsoft Press® products, call
1-800-MSPRESS

BUSINESS REPLY MAIL
FIRST-CLASS MAIL   PERMIT NO. 53   BOTHELL, WA

POSTAGE WILL BE PAID BY ADDRESSEE

MICROSOFT PRESS REGISTRATION
HARDCORE VISUAL BASIC®, Second Edition
PO BOX 3019
BOTHELL WA   98041-9946